AQA Science Physics

Teacher's Book

New GCSE

Darren Forbes

Pauline Anning

Bev Cox

Gavin Reeder

Series Editor
Lawrie Ryan

Nelson Thornes

Published in 2011 by:
Nelson Thornes Ltd
Delta Place
27 Bath Road
CHELTENHAM
GL53 7TH
United Kingdom

11 12 13 14 15 / 10 9 8 7 6 5 4 3 2 1

A catalogue record for this book is available from the British Library

ISBN 978 1 4085 0833 6

Cover photograph: iStockphoto (background); David Deas/Getty Images (boy)

Page make-up by Tech-Set Ltd, Gateshead

Printed and bound in Spain by GraphyCems

GCSE Physics   Contents

Welcome to AQA Physics!

New AQA GCSE Science remains the only series to be endorsed and approved by AQA. This Physics Teacher's Book is written and reviewed by experienced teachers who have worked closely with AQA on their specifications. This book is structured around the Student Book and offers guidance, advice, support for differentiation and lots of practical teaching ideas to give you what you need to teach the AQA specifications.

Learning objectives

These tell you what your students should know by the end of the lessons and relate to the learning objectives in the corresponding Student Book topic, although extra detail is provided for teachers.

Learning outcomes

These tell you what your students should be able to do to demonstrate that they have achieved against the learning objectives. These are differentiated where appropriate to provide suitable expectations for all your students. Higher Tier outcomes are labelled.

AQA Specification link-up: Physics P1.1

These open every spread so you can see the AQA specification references covered in your lessons, at a glance.

Lesson structure

This provides you with guidance and ideas for tackling topics in your lessons. There are short and long starter and plenary activities so you can decide how you structure your lesson. Explicit **support** and **extension** guidance is given for some starters and plenaries.

Support

These help you to give extra support to students who need it during the main part of your lesson.

Extend

These provide ideas for how to extend the learning for students aiming for higher grades.

Further teaching suggestions

These provide you with ideas for how you might extend the lesson or offer alternative activities. These may also include extra activities or suggestions for homework.

Summary answers

All answers to questions within the Student Book are found in the Teacher's Book.

Practical support

For every practical in the Student Book you will find this corresponding feature which gives you a list of the equipment you will need to provide, safety references and additional teaching notes. There are also additional practicals given that are not found in the Student Book.

The following features are found in the Student Book, but you may find additional guidance to support them in the Teacher's Book:

 Did you know ... ?

 How Science Works

 Maths skills

Activity

How Science Works

There is a chapter dedicated to 'How Science Works' in the Student Book as well as embedded throughout topics and end of chapter questions. The teacher notes within this book give you detailed guidance on how to integrate 'How Science Works' into your teaching.

End of chapter pages

And at the end of each chapter you will find Summary answers and AQA Examination-style answers. You will also find:

Kerboodle resources

Kerboodle is our online service that holds all of the electronic resources for the series. All of the resources that support the chapter that are provided on Kerboodle are listed in these boxes.

Where you see **k** in the Student Book, you will know that there is an electronic resource on Kerboodle to support that aspect.

Just log on to www.kerboodle.com to find out more.

AQA Practical suggestions

These list the suggested practicals from AQA that you need to be aware of. Support for these practicals can be found on Kerboodle, or are covered within the practical support section of the Teacher Book. The **k** indicates that there is a practical in

Kerboodle. The indicates that there is a 'How Science Works' worksheet in Kerboodle. The 📖 indicates that the practical is covered in this Teacher's Book.

Bump up your grades

These are written by AQA examiners giving advice on how students can pick up additional marks to improve their grades.

AQA Examiner's tip

These are written by AQA examiners giving advice on what students should remember for their exams and highlighting common errors.

How does science work?

Learning objectives

Students should learn:

- that observations are often the starting point for an investigation
- that a hypothesis is a proposal intended to explain certain facts or observations
- that a prediction is an intelligent guess, based on some knowledge
- that an experiment is a way of testing your prediction
- that a conclusion is when you decide whether or not your prediction was correct.

Learning outcomes

Students should be able to:

- make first-hand observations
- distinguish between a hypothesis and a prediction
- explain the purpose of an experiment
- show how results can help to decide whether a prediction was correct.

Support

- When carrying out the 'bouncing ball' activity, students could be given the headings for the method in the form of a flow chart, with an 'either/or' option at each stage.

Extend

- Students could be allowed to use the internet to find out more about how the different squash balls are graded and colour-coded according to their bounciness.

AQA Specification link-up: How Science Works

'How Science Works' is treated here as a separate chapter. It offers the opportunity to teach the 'thinking behind the doing' as a discrete set of procedural skills. However, it is of course an integral part of the way students will learn about science, and those skills should be nurtured throughout the course.

It is anticipated that sections of this chapter will be taught as the opportunity presents itself during the teaching programme. The chapter should also be referred back to at appropriate times when these skills are required and in preparation for the Controlled Assessment ISAs.

The thinking behind the doing

Science attempts to explain the world in which we live. It provides technologies that have had a great impact on our society and the environment. Scientists try to explain phenomena and solve problems using evidence. The data to be used as evidence must be repeatable, reproducible and valid, as only then can appropriate conclusions be made.

A scientifically literate citizen should, amongst other things, be equipped to question, and engage in debate on, the evidence used in decision-making.

The repeatability and the reproducibility of evidence refers to how much we trust the data. The validity of evidence depends on these as well as whether the research answers the question. If the data is not repeatable or reproducible the research cannot be valid.

To ensure repeatability, reproducibility and validity in evidence, scientists consider a range of ideas which relate to:
- how we observe the world
- designing investigations so that patterns and relationships between variables may be identified
- making measurements by selecting and using instruments effectively
- presenting and representing data
- identifying patterns, relationships and making suitable conclusions.

These ideas inform decisions and are central to science education. They constitute the 'thinking behind the doing' that is a necessary complement to the subject content of biology, chemistry and physics.

Lesson structure

Starters

Key words – Create a quiz looking at the meaning of key words used in this lesson: knowledge, observation, prediction and experiment. Support students by making this activity into a card sort. Extend students by asking them to put the key words into a context, i.e. the television remote control idea. *(5 minutes)*

Good science – Collect newspaper articles and news items from the television to illustrate good and poor uses of science. *(10 minutes)*

Main

- Students should begin to appreciate the 'thinking behind the doing' developed during KS3. It would be useful to illustrate this by a simple demonstration of a torsion pendulum. A simple torsion pendulum can be made by taking an empty can, putting some sand in it, and hanging it from a bar.

  If you wind the can round ten times and then let go, it will unwind, wind itself up the other way, unwind again and so on. This can continue many times until the system loses all its energy. The time that it takes to completely unwind and then wind itself up in the other direction could be thought of as the time period.

  Students could be asked, e.g., 'What could I alter that might affect the time period?' (e.g. length of strings, number of support strings, mass of sand inside the can, the number of turns it is given to start with).

- It is expected that students will be familiar with:
  - the need to work safely
  - making a prediction
  - controls
  - the need for repetition of some results
  - tabulating and analysing results
  - arriving at appropriate conclusions
  - suggesting how they might improve methods.

- Revealing to the students that they use scientific thinking to solve problems during their everyday life can make their work in science more relevant. Use everyday situations to illustrate this and discuss in groups or as a class.

  For example: 'How can I clear the car windscreen when it "mists" up in the winter? It only seems to happen when we get into the car [observation]. The windscreen is probably cold, and I know we breathe out moist air [knowledge].'

  'I can use observations and knowledge to make a prediction that switching on the hot air fan next to the windscreen will clear the "mist". I can test my prediction and see what the results are. I can check again the next day to see whether I get the same results [repeatability].'

- Students should now be asked to investigate the 'Bouncing balls' activity.

Plenaries

Misconceptions – Produce a list of statements about practical work, some of which are true and others false. Support students by getting them to simply write 'true' or 'false' by each statement. Extend students by asking them to write down why the false statements are untrue. *(5 minutes)*

Poor science – Using the internet, organise a competition for who can bring in the poorest example of science used to sell products – shampoo adverts are very good examples! *(10 minutes)*

How Science Works

H1 How does science work? (k)

Learning objectives
- What is meant by 'How Science Works'?
- What is a hypothesis?
- What is a prediction and why should you make one?
- How can you investigate a problem scientifically?

links
You can find out more about your ISA by looking at H10 The ISA at the end of this chapter.

This first chapter looks at 'How Science Works'. It is an important part of your GCSE because the ideas introduced here will crop up throughout your course. You will be expected to collect scientific **evidence** and to understand how we use evidence. These concepts will be assessed as the major part of your internal school assessment.

You will take one or more 45-minute tests. These tests are based on **data** you have collected previously plus data supplied for you in the test. They are called **Investigative Skills Assignments (ISA)**. The ideas in 'How Science Works' will also be assessed in your examinations.

How science works for us

Science works for us all day, every day. You do not need to know how a mobile phone works to enjoy sending text messages. But, think about how you started to use your mobile phone or your television remote control. Did you work through pages of instructions? Probably not!

You knew that pressing the buttons would change something on the screen (**knowledge**). You played around with the buttons, to see what would happen (**observation**). You had a guess based on your knowledge and observations at what you thought might be happening (**prediction**) and then tested your idea (**experiment**).

Perhaps 'How Science Works' should really be called 'How Scientists Work'.

Science moves forward by slow, steady steps. When a genius such as Einstein comes along, it takes a giant leap. Those small steps build on knowledge and experience that we already have.

The steps don't always lead in a straight line, starting with an observation and ending with a conclusion. More often than not you find yourself going round in circles, but each time you go around the loop you gain more knowledge and so can make better predictions.

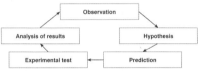

Each small step is important in its own way. It builds on the body of knowledge that we have, but observation is usually the starting point. In 1581 Galileo, during a long service at Pisa Cathedral, observed a lamp swinging from a long chain attached to the ceiling. This started him thinking about what factors affect the time period of a pendulum. After many tests on pendulums, he was able to come up with a **hypothesis** that would enable him to predict what the time period would be for any given length of pendulum.

Figure 1 Albert Einstein was a genius, but he worked through scientific problems in the same way as you will in your GCSE

Activity

Bouncing balls

No matter how good a basketball player you are, if the ball is not properly inflated, you cannot play well. As the balls get used during the game it is possible that some of them will get soft. They should all bounce the same.

How high the ball bounces will depend on lots of variables. It will depend on:
- what the ball is made of
- how much air has been pumped in
- what the temperature of the ball is
- what the floor surface is made of, and
- how hard you throw it.

It is impossible to test all of these during a match. The simple way is to drop a ball from a certain height and see how high it bounces. Can you work out a way to see how changing the height from which a ball is dropped can affect how high it bounces? This could then be used as a simple test during the match to see whether the balls are good enough.

You can use the following headings to discuss your ideas. One person should be writing your thoughts down, so that you can discuss them with the rest of your class.
- What prediction can you make about the height the ball is dropped from and the height it will bounce to?
- What would you vary in each test? This is called the independent variable.
- What would you measure to judge the effect of varying the independent variable? This is called the dependent variable.
- What would you need to keep unchanged to make this a fair test?
- Write a plan for your investigation.
- These are called control variables.

Figure 2 Playing basketball

Summary questions

1 Copy and complete the paragraph using the words below:

experiment knowledge conclusion prediction observation

You have learned before that a cup of tea loses energy if it is left standing. This is a piece of .... You make an .... that dark-coloured cups will cool faster. So you make a .... that if you have a black cup, this will cool fastest of all. You carry out an .... to get some results, and from these you make a ....

Further teaching suggestions

Common misconceptions

Some common misconceptions that can be dealt with here and throughout the course are about:
- the purpose of controls – some students believe that it is about making accurate measurements of the independent variable.
- the purpose of preliminary work – some believe that it is the first set of results.

Some students also think that:
- the table of results is constructed after the practical work – students should be encouraged to produce the table before carrying out their work and to complete it during their work
- anomalies are identified after the analysis – they should preferably be identified during the practical work or at the latest before any calculation of a mean
- they should automatically extrapolate the graph to its origin
- lines of best fit must be straight lines
- you repeat readings to make sure your investigation is a fair test.

Fundamental ideas about how science works

Learning objectives

Students should learn:

- to distinguish between opinions based on scientific evidence and non-scientific ideas
- the importance of continuous and categoric variables
- what is meant by valid evidence
- the difference between repeatability and reproducibility
- to look for links between the independent and dependent variables.

Learning outcomes

Students should be able to:

- identify when an opinion does not have the support of valid and reproducible science
- recognise measurements as continuous, or categoric
- suggest how an investigation might demonstrate its validity
- distinguish between repeatability and reproducibility
- state whether variables are linked, and if so, in what way.

Support

- When looking at materials that conduct electricity, simply use the brightness of a lamp to judge conductivity.

Extend

- When looking at materials that conduct electricity, use an ammeter to record the current. Extend the discussion to other variables that may be affecting the outcome, e.g. length of wire, thickness of wire, applied potential difference.

AQA Specification link-up: Controlled Assessment P4.3

Demonstrate an understanding of the need to acquire high quality data, by:

- appreciating that, unless certain variables are controlled, the results may not be valid [P4.3.2 a)]
- identifying when repeats are needed in order to improve reproducibility. [P4.3.2 b)]

Lesson structure

Starters

Crazy science – Show a video clip of one of the science shows that are aimed at entertainment rather than education or an advert that proclaims a scientific opinion. This should lead into a discussion of how important it is to form opinions based on sound scientific evidence. *(5 minutes)*

Types of variable – Produce a list of observable or measurable variables, e.g. colour, temperature, time, type of material. Ask students to sort them into two types: these can then be revealed as being either categoric or continuous. Support students by giving them a full definition of categoric and continuous variables. Extend students by asking them to add other examples of their own to the lists. *(10 minutes)*

Main

- Discuss some examples of adverts that make 'scientific' claims about products.
- From a light-hearted look at entertainment science, bring the thalidomide example into contrast and discuss how tragic situations can be created by forming opinions that are not supported by valid science. Search for video clips about thalidomide at www.britishpathe.com.
- Show how some metals conduct electricity better than others. Review some of the terminology from KS3. Discuss, in small groups, the different ways in which the independent and dependent variables could be measured, identifying these in terms of continuous or categoric measurements.
- Discuss the usefulness in terms of forming opinions of each of the proposed measurements.
- Consider that this might be a commercial proposition and the students might be advising an investor on which metal to use in a product.
- Discuss how they could organise the investigation to demonstrate its validity and reproducibility to a potential investor.
- Discuss whether the relationship shows a causal link.

Plenaries

Evidence for opinions – Bring together the main features of scientific evidence that would allow sound scientific opinions to be formed from an investigation. *(5 minutes)*

Analyse conclusions – Use an example of a poorly structured investigation and allow the students to critically analyse any conclusions drawn, e.g. data from an investigation into different forms of insulation, using calorimeters and cooling curves. Support students by telling them the mistakes that had been made in the design and ask them to say why this would make the conclusion invalid. Extend students by allowing them to first identify the mistakes in the design. *(10 minutes)*

Practical support

The resistance of a wire

Equipment and materials required

A range of different wires (e.g. 36 s.w.g. constantan, 36 s.w.g. copper and 24 s.w.g. copper), low-voltage supply (e.g. 1.5 V cell or power supply, connecting wires, 1.5 V bulb and an ammeter), ruler and wire cutters.

Details

Students use the same length of each type of wire in turn and note the brightness of the bulb and/or the current shown by the ammeter.

Safety: Take care when handling the wires as they may get hot when a current is passed through them.

How Science Works

H2

Fundamental ideas about how science works

Learning objectives

- How do you spot when an opinion is not based on good science?
- What is the importance of continuous and categoric variables?
- What does it mean to say that evidence is valid?
- What is the difference between a result being repeatable and a result being reproducible?
- How can two sets of data be linked?

Examiner's tip

Read a newspaper article or watch the news on TV. Ask yourself whether any research presented is valid. Ask yourself whether you can trust that person's opinion and why.

Figure 1 Road sign that uses solar cells

Science is too important for us to get it wrong

Sometimes it is easy to spot when people try to use science poorly. Sometimes it can be funny. You might have seen adverts claiming to give your hair 'body' or sprays that give your feet 'lift'!

On the other hand, poor scientific practice can cost lives.

Some years ago a company sold the drug thalidomide to people as a sleeping pill. Research was carried out on animals to see whether it was safe. The research did not include work on pregnant animals. The **opinion** of the people in charge was that the animal research showed the drug could be used safely with humans.

Then the drug was also found to help ease morning sickness in pregnant women. Unfortunately, doctors prescribed it to many women, resulting in thousands of babies being born with deformed limbs. It was far from safe.

These are very difficult decisions to make. You need to be absolutely certain of what the science is telling you.

a Why was the opinion of the people in charge of developing thalidomide based on poor science?

Deciding on what to measure: variables

Variables are physical, chemical or biological quantities or characteristics.

In an investigation, you normally choose one thing to change or vary. This is called the **independent variable**.

When you change the independent variable, it may cause something else to change. This is called the **dependent variable**.

A **control variable** is one that is kept the same and is not changed during the investigation.

You need to know about two different types of these variables:

- A **categoric variable** is one that is best described by a label (usually a word). The 'colour of eyes' is a categoric variable, e.g. blue or brown eyes.
- A **continuous variable** is one that we measure, so its value could be any number. Temperature (as measured by a thermometer or temperature sensor) is a continuous variable, e.g. 37.6 °C, 45.2 °C. Continuous variables can have values (called quantities) that can be found by making measurements (e.g. light intensity, flow rate, etc.).

b Imagine you were testing a solar cell, what would be better: putting a light bulb into the circuit to see how bright it was, or using a voltmeter to measure the potential difference?

Making your evidence repeatable, reproducible and valid

When you are designing an investigation you must make sure that other people can get the same results as you. This makes the evidence you collect **reproducible**.

A measurement is **repeatable** if the original experimenter repeats the investigation using the same method and equipment and obtains the same results.

A measurement is reproducible if the investigation is repeated by another person, or by using different equipment or techniques, and the same results are obtained.

You must also make sure you are measuring the actual thing you want to measure. If you don't, your data can't be used to answer your original question. This seems very obvious but it is not always quite so easy. You need to make sure that you have controlled as many other variables as you can, so that no one can say that your investigation is not **valid**. A measurement is valid if it measures what it is supposed to be measuring with an appropriate level of performance.

Figure 2 Student recording a range of temperatures – an example of a continuous variable

c State one way in which you can show that your results are valid.

How might an independent variable be linked to a dependent variable?

Looking for a link between your independent and dependent variables is very important. The pattern of your graph or bar chart can often help you to see whether there is a link.

But beware! There may not be a link! If your results seem to show that there is no link, don't be afraid to say so. Look at Figure 3.

The points on the top graph show a clear pattern, but the bottom graph shows random scatter.

Examiner's tip

When designing your investigation you should always try to measure continuous data whenever you can. This is not always possible, so then you have to use a label (categoric variable). You might still be able to put the variables in an order so that you can spot a pattern. For example, you could describe flow rate as 'fast flowing', 'steady flow' or 'slow flowing'.

Figure 3 Which graph shows that there might be a link between x and y?

Did you know ...?

Aristotle, a brilliant Greek scientist, once proclaimed that men had more teeth than women! Do you think that his data collection was reproducible?

Summary questions

1 Copy and complete the paragraph using the words below:

continuous   independent   categoric   dependent

Stefan wanted to find out which was the strongest supermarket plastic carrier bag. He tested five different bags by adding weight to them until they broke. The type of bag he used was the .... variable and the weight that it took to break it was the .... variable. The 'type of bag' is called a .... variable and the 'weight needed to break' it was a .... variable.

2 A researcher claimed that the metal tungsten 'alters the growth of leukaemia cells' in laboratory tests. A newspaper wrote that they would 'wait until other scientists had reviewed the research before giving their opinion.' Why is this a good idea?

Key points

- Be on the lookout for non-scientific opinions.
- Continuous data give more information than other types of data.
- Check that evidence is reproducible and valid.

Answers to in-text questions

a The original animal investigation did not include pregnant animals and was not carried out on human tissue. Therefore, it was not valid when the opinion was formed that it could be given to pregnant women.

b ii Using a voltmeter; continuous measurements (variables) are more powerful.

c Control all (or as many as possible) of the other variables.

Summary answers

1 independent, dependent, categoric, continuous

2 The investigation can be shown to be reliable if other scientists can repeat their investigations and get the same findings. Because it is reproducible, opinions formed from it are more useful.

H3

Starting an investigation

AQA Specification link-up: Controlled Assessment P4.2 & P4.3

Develop hypotheses and plan practical ways to test them, by:
- being able to develop a hypothesis [P4.1.1 a)]
- being able to test hypotheses. [P4.1.1 b)]

Make observations, by:
- carrying out practical work and research, and using the data collected to develop hypotheses. [P4.3.1]

Learning objectives

Students should learn:
- how scientific knowledge can be used to observe the world around them
- how good observations can be used to make hypotheses
- how hypotheses can generate predictions that can be tested.

Learning outcomes

Students should be able to:
- state that observation can be the starting point for an investigation
- state that observation can generate hypotheses
- describe how hypotheses can generate predictions and investigations.

Lesson structure

Starters

Demo observation – Begin the lesson with a demonstration – as simple as lighting a match or more involved such as a bell ringing in a bell jar, with air gradually being withdrawn. Students should be asked, in silence, and without further prompting, to write down their observations. These should be collated and questions should be derived from those observations. *(5 minutes)*

Linking observation to knowledge – Discuss with students any unusual events they saw on the way to school. If possible, take them into the school grounds to look and listen to events. Try to link their observations to their scientific knowledge. They are more likely to notice events that they can offer some scientific explanation for. Support students by prompting with some directed questions. Extend students by getting them to start to ask questions about those observations. *(10 minutes)*

Main

- If in the laboratory, allow students to participate in a 'scientific happening' of your choice, e.g. by dropping paper cups with different masses in. Preferably use something that they have not met before, but which they will have some knowledge of. As an alternative, if possible, take students onto the school field where there will be many opportunities to observe the roof structure of buildings, or size of wires on electricity pylons compared to telephone wires, or siting of phone masts.

- If students need some help at this point, they should read through the section on observation in the Student Book. Then answer in-text questions **a** and **b**.

- In groups they should discuss possible explanations for one agreed observation. Encourage a degree of lateral thinking.

- Ask the group to select which of their explanations is the most likely, based on their own knowledge of science.

- Work these explanations into a hypothesis.

- Individually, each student should try in-text question **c**. Gather in ideas and hypotheses. Use a hypothesis that suggests that the bridge started to oscillate at a certain wind speed.

- Students, working in groups, can now turn this into a prediction.

- They could suggest ways in which their prediction could be tested using a model and wind tunnel. Identify independent, dependent and control variables and the need to make sure that they are measuring what they intend to measure.

- Go over in-text question **c** as a class.

Support

- Assist students in the 'dropping paper cup' activity by giving them a list of possible explanations and asking them to choose which is the most likely.

Extend

- Extend students in the dropping paper cup activity by getting them to vary the number of cups stacked together and to make predictions regarding the effect this would have.

Plenaries

Poster – Ask students to design, but not make, a poster that links 'Observation + knowledge → hypothesis → prediction → investigation'. *(5 minutes)*

Discussion – Ask students to give examples of ideas of the past that have been later disproved. An idea might be to focus on the shape and position of the Earth in our galaxy. Support students by saying that at one time people believed that the Earth was flat. Discuss the observations that have led to the modern idea that the Earth is spherical (e.g. ships disappearing below the horizon, the shadow of the Earth on the Moon). Extend students by discussing the development of knowledge that the planets revolve around the Sun – it could be useful here to illustrate how scientists struggled with these ideas in the past. The story could be used at many points in this chapter but is particularly useful here.

Briefly use secondary sources to look up the following scientists' work. Aristarchus (third century BCE) proclaimed that the Earth revolved around the Sun. Copernicus (sixteenth century CE) reasserted the idea that all objects fall towards Earth. Tycho Brahe (late in the sixteenth century CE) was given immense sums of money to investigate the theory that the Earth orbits the Sun. Johannes Kepler (Tycho's assistant) predicted the position of the planets.

It is thought that these ideas about the Earth revolving around the Sun gave rise to the modern use of the term 'revolutionary'. *(10 minutes)*

Practical support

Dropping paper cups
Equipment and materials required
Paper cups or baking cases, small masses or sticky-tac, balance, stopwatch.

Details
Students drop a baking case from a fixed height and measure how long it takes to reach the ground. They then repeat this with two, three, four, etc. baking cases stacked inside each other. Extend this experiment by adding small masses or sticky-tac to the inside of the baking cases. Encourage the students to think about how they control the variables in this experiment.

Safety: Protect feet, bench and floor from falling masses.

How Science Works

H3 — Starting an investigation

Learning objectives
- How can you use your scientific knowledge to observe the world around you?
- How can you use your observations to make a hypothesis?
- How can you make predictions and start to design an investigation?

Figure 1 A wind turbine

Observation

As humans we are sensitive to the world around us. We can use our senses to detect what is happening. As scientists we use observations to ask questions. We can only ask useful questions if we know something about the observed event. We will not have all of the answers, but we know enough to start asking relevant questions.

If we observe that the weather has been hot today, we would not ask whether it was due to global warming. If the weather was hotter than normal for several years, we could ask that question. We know that global warming takes many years to show its effect.

When you are designing an investigation you have to observe carefully which variables are likely to have an effect.

a Would it be reasonable to ask whether the wind turbine in Figure 1 generates less electricity in the rain? Explain your answer.

Amjid was waiting to cross at a zebra crossing. A car stopped to let him cross when a second car drove into the first car, without braking. Being a scientist, Amjid tried to work out why this had happened . . . while the two drivers argued! He came up with the following ideas:
- The second driver was tired.
- The second car had faulty brakes.
- The first car stopped too quickly.
- The second car was driving too fast.
- The second car was travelling too close.
- The second car had worn tyres.
- The first car had no brake lights.

b Discuss each of these ideas and use your knowledge of science to decide which three are the most likely to have caused the crash.

Observations, backed up by really creative thinking and good scientific knowledge can lead to a hypothesis.

Testing scientific ideas

Scientists always try to think of ways to explain how things work or why they behave in the way that they do.

After their observations, they use their understanding of science to come up with an idea that could explain what is going on. This idea is sometimes called a **hypothesis**. They use this idea to make a prediction. A prediction is like a guess, but it is not just a wild guess – it is based on previous understanding.

A scientist will say, 'If it works the way I think it does, I should be able to change **this** (the independent variable) and **that** will happen (the dependent variable).'

Predictions are what make science so powerful. They mean that we can work out rules that tell us what will happen in the future. For example, electricians can predict how much current will flow through a wire when an electric cooker is connected. Knowing this, they can choose the right thickness of cable to use.

When a steady wind blows against a structure like a bridge or tall chimney, it can cause 'vortex shedding.' This exerts an oscillating force on the structure, a force that can be predicted.

c Look at the photograph in Figure 2, Note down anything that you find interesting. Use your knowledge and some creative thought to suggest a hypothesis based on your observations.

Not all predictions are correct. If scientists find that the prediction doesn't work, it's back to the drawing board! They either amend their original idea or think of a completely new one.

Figure 2 The Tacoma Narrows Bridge in the USA twisting just before it collapsed

Starting to design a valid investigation

observation + knowledge → hypothesis → prediction → investigation

We can test a prediction by carrying out an **investigation**. You, as the scientist, predict that there is a relationship between two variables.

The independent variable is one that is selected and changed by you, the investigator. The dependent variable is measured for each change in your independent variable. Then all other variables become control variables, kept constant so that your investigation is a fair test.

If your measurements are going to be accepted by other people, they must be **valid**. Part of this is making sure that you are really measuring the effect of changing your chosen variable. For example, if other variables aren't controlled properly, they might be affecting the data collected.

d Look at Figure 3. Darren was investigating the light given out by a 12 V bulb. He used a light meter in the laboratory that was set at 10 cm from the bulb. What might be wrong here?

Figure 3 Testing a light bulb

Summary questions

1 Copy and complete the paragraph using the words below:
controlled dependent independent knowledge prediction hypothesis
An observation linked with scientific .... can be used to make a .... A .... links an .... variable to a .... variable. All other variables need to be ....

2 What is the difference between a prediction and a guess?

3 Imagine you were testing whether the length of a wire affected its resistance. The current through the wire might cause it to get hot.
a How could you monitor the temperature?
b What other control variables can you think of that might affect the results?

Key points
- Observation is often the starting point for an investigation.
- Testing predictions can lead to new scientific understanding.
- You must design investigations that produce valid results if you are to be believed.

Answers to in-text questions

a Yes/no depending on response and how much detail of physics you want to go into at this stage!

b The second driver was tired.
The second car was travelling too fast.
The second car was travelling too close.
The first car had no brake lights.
Any three of the above would be appropriate.

c E.g. Observation: bridge is twisting. Hypothesis: high wind velocity caused it to twist.

d He did not use a blackout, light was coming from other sources. The results are not valid.

Summary answers

1 knowledge, hypothesis, prediction, independent, dependent, controlled

2 A prediction is based on knowledge or observation, a guess is not.

3 **a** By using a temperature sensor or probe fixed to the wire.

   b Examples include cross-sectional area of the wire, which might vary along its length.

H4

Planning an investigation

Learning objectives

Students should learn:

- how to design a fair test
- how to set up a survey
- how to set up a control group or control experiment
- how to reduce risks in hazardous situations.

Learning outcomes

Students should be able to:

- identify variables that need to be controlled in an investigation
- design a survey
- design a fair test and understand the use of control variables and control groups
- identify potential hazards and take action to minimise risk.

Support

- Show students the 'energy testing' experiment and ask them to write down as many hazards as they can think of. If necessary, give them a list of about 10 different hazards, some of which are relevant and some not, and ask them to tick the ones that they think apply here.

Extend

- Get students to rank the hazards in order of the amount of risk, and then think of a control measure for each one.

AQA Specification link-up: Controlled Assessment P4.2 & P4.3

Assess and manage risks when carrying out practical work, by:
- identifying some possible hazards in practical situations [P4.2.1 b]]
- suggesting ways of managing risks. [P4.2.1 b]]

Demonstrate an understanding of the need to acquire high quality data, by:
- appreciating that, unless certain variables are controlled, the results may not be valid. [P4.3.2 a]]

Lesson structure

Starters

Risk assessment – Give students a picture sheet illustrating a situation showing a number of hazards. Ask the students to spot the hazard and write down what could be done to minimise the risk. The situation illustrated could be one in the school laboratory, or it could be outside the school environment, e.g. in the road, in a factory or on a farm. *(5 minutes)*

Head start – Start, for example, with a video clip of a 100 m race. (Search for 'marathon' or 'race' at www.video.google.com or www.bbc.co.uk). This has to be a fair test. How is this achieved? Then show the mass start of the London marathon and ask if this is a fair test. Support students by asking why there is no official world record for a marathon. (Instead they have world best times.) This could lead to a discussion of how difficult it is to control all of the variables in the field. Extend students by going on to discuss why athletes can break the 100 m world record and this may not be recognised because of a helping wind. *(10 minutes)*

Main

- Start with a group discussion about fair testing. Highlight any misconceptions about fair testing and stress that repeat readings do not make a test fair. Effectively controlling variables is what makes a test fair.

- Challenge students with a test you set up in an 'unfair' way. You can differentiate by making some errors obvious and some more subtle. Students can observe then generate lists of mistakes in small groups. Ask each group to give one error from their list and record what should have been done to ensure fair testing until all suggestions have been considered.

- Start group discussions on how and why we need to produce survey data. Use a topical issue here. It might be appropriate to see how it should *not* be done by using a vox pop clip from a news programme.

- Students will be familiar with the idea of a placebo, but possibly not with how it is used to set up a control group. This might need explanation.

- Consider the case of whether it is possible to tell the difference in taste if the milk is put in before or after the tea. R. A. Fisher tested this using a double-blind taste test, and went on to devise 'Statistical Methods for Research Workers'.

- Use the school or college laboratory rules to review safety procedures.

- Ask students to carry out a risk assessment on the 'energy testing' experiment.

Plenaries

Key words – Using a card sort, ask students to match the definitions to the five key words introduced in this lesson. *(5 minutes)*

Survey – Ask students to imagine they have been asked to conduct a survey to find out whether or not people prefer a particular brand of toothpaste. They should produce a questionnaire that lists the questions that you could ask people on the street. Support students by supplying them with a list of questions, some of which would be relevant, others irrelevant. Ask students to tick which questions would be the most appropriate. Extend students by asking them to suggest how many people should be chosen and on what basis they should be selected. *(10 minutes)*

Practical support

Risk assessment on energy testing

Equipment and materials required
Beaker, thermometer, low-voltage electric immersion heater, low-voltage power supply.

Details
Students could use an electric immersion heater to heat a small quantity of water in a beaker and measure the temperature rise.

Before doing so, they should identify any possible hazards and then write down ways in which they would minimise any risk. After carrying out the experiment, they should discuss whether or not their plans for risk reduction were sufficient.

Safety: Take care with hot water and use mains electricity carefully.

H4   Planning an investigation

Learning objectives
- How do you design a fair test?
- How do you set up a survey?
- How do you set up a control group or control experiment?
- How do you reduce risks in hazardous situations?

Fair testing
A **fair test** is one in which only the independent variable affects the dependent variable. All other variables (called control variables) should be kept the same. If the test is not fair, the results of your investigation will not be valid.

Sometimes it is very difficult to keep control variables the same. However, at least you can **monitor** them, so that you know whether they have changed or not.

a How would you set up an investigation to see how the wing setting on the rear of a car affected its top speed down the straight?

Figure 1 How do wing settings on the rear wing of a sports car affect its top speed?

Surveys
Not all scientific investigations involve deliberately changing the independent variable.

If you were investigating the effect that using a mobile phone may have on health you wouldn't put a group of people in a room and make them use their mobile phones to see whether they developed brain cancer!

Instead, you might conduct a **survey**. You might study the health of a large number of people who regularly use a mobile phone and compare their health with those who never use a mobile phone.

You would have to choose people of the same age and same family history to test. The larger the sample size you test, the better your results will be.

Control group
Control groups are used in investigations to try to make sure that you are measuring the variable that you intend to measure. When investigating the effects of a new drug, the control group will be given a **placebo**. This is a 'pretend' drug that actually has no effect on the patient at all. The control group think they are taking a drug but the placebo does not contain the drug. This way you can control the variable of 'thinking that the drug is working' and separate out the effect of the actual drug.

Usually neither the patient nor the doctor knows until after the trials have been completed which of the patients were given the placebo. This is known as a **double-blind trial**.

AQA Examiner's tip

If you are asked about why it is important to keep control variables constant, you need to give a detailed explanation. Don't just answer, 'To make it a fair test'.

When you are asked to write a plan for your investigation, make sure that you give all the details. Ask yourself, 'Would someone else be able to follow my written plan and use it to do the investigation?'

Risks and hazards
One of the first things you must do is to think about any potential **hazards** and then assess the **risk**.

Everything you do in life presents a hazard. What you have to do is to identify the hazard and then decide the degree of risk that it gives. If the risk is very high, you must do something to reduce it.

For example, if you decide to go out in the pouring rain, lightning is a possible hazard. However, you decide that the risk is so small that you will ignore it and go out anyway.

If you decide to cross a busy road, the cars travelling along it at high speed represent a hazard. You decide to reduce the risk by crossing at a pedestrian crossing.

How Science Works
Energy testing

Imagine you were using an electric immersion heater to see how much energy it supplied to a beaker of water when switched on.

Electric immersion heater

Water

- What are the **hazards** that are present?
- What control measures could you take to reduce the **risk** from these hazards?

Figure 2 The hazard is the busy road; we reduce the risk by using a pedestrian crossing

AQA Examiner's tip

Before you start your practical work you must make sure that it is safe. What are the likely hazards? How could you reduce the risk caused by these hazards? This is known as a **risk assessment**. You may well be asked questions like this on your ISA paper.

Key points
- Care must be taken to ensure fair testing – as far as is possible.
- Control variables must be kept the same during an investigation.
- Surveys are often used when it is impossible to carry out an experiment in which the independent variable is changed.
- Control groups allow you to make a comparison.
- A risk assessment must be made when planning a practical investigation.

Summary questions
1. Copy and complete the paragraph using the words below:

   investigation   hazards   assessment   risks

   Before you carry out any practical ...., you need to carry out a risk .... You can do this by looking for any potential .... and making sure that the .... are as small as possible.
2. Explain the difference between a control group and a control variable.
3. Briefly describe how you would go about setting up a fair test in a laboratory investigation. Give your answer as general advice.

Further teaching suggestions

Which?
Look at some recent *Which?* reports on consumer goods. Discuss issues such as:
- Was the size of the sample surveyed sufficient?
- Could the people who were surveyed have been biased?
- Could the people conducting the survey have been biased?

Answers to in-text questions

a Suggestions: measure final speed of car for set distance/time (dependent); change wing settings (independent); control variables include same starting speed, same wind direction, wind strength, same amount of fuel, same weight of car, same driver.

Summary answers

1. investigation, assessment, hazards, risks
2. In an experiment to determine the effect of changing a single variable, a **control** is often set up in which the independent variable is not changed, thus enabling a comparison to be made. If the investigation is of the survey type (q.v.), a control group is usually established to serve the same purpose.
3. Control all the variables that might affect the dependent variable, apart from the independent variable whose values you select.

H5

Designing an investigation

Learning objectives

Students should learn:

- how to choose the best values for the variables
- how to decide on a suitable range
- how to decide on a suitable interval
- how to ensure accuracy and precision.

Learning outcomes

Students should be able to:

- use trial runs to establish the best values for the variables
- use trial runs to establish a suitable range for the independent variable
- use trial runs to establish a suitable interval for the independent variable
- design a fair test that will yield valid and repeatable results.

AQA Specification link-up: Controlled Assessment P4.1 & P4.3

Develop hypotheses and plan practical ways to test them, by:

- using appropriate technology [P4.1.1 c)]

Demonstrate an understanding of the need to acquire high quality data, by:

- appreciating that, unless certain variables are controlled, the results may not be valid [P4.3.2 a)]
- identifying when repeats are needed in order to improve reproducibility [P4.3.2 b)]
- recognising the value of further readings to establish repeatability and accuracy [P4.3.2 c)]
- considering the resolution of the measuring device [P4.3.2 d)]
- considering the precision of the measured data where precision is indicated by the degree of scatter from the mean [P4.3.2 e)]
- identifying the range of the measured data. [P4.3.2 f)]

Lesson structure

Starters

Interval – Give students a graph of extension against force for a spring. The spring should have reached its elastic limit so that the graph line becomes non-linear. However, because of the large interval chosen, it is impossible to see at which point this change occurred. Ask students to suggest what other values should be tested in order to ascertain the elastic limit more accurately. *(5 minutes)*

Preliminary work – Give students an expendable steel spring that reaches its elastic limit at about 10 newton. Tell them that the main experiment would be to collect data to show how the extension of the spring varies with the force applied. Support students by giving them a number of 1.0 N weights and asking them to carry out a quick test to suggest a suitable range for the weights to be added. Extend students by giving them a selection of different weights (e.g. 0.1 N, 1.0 N, 10 N) and asking them to suggest a suitable interval for the weights to be added. *(10 minutes)*

Main

- Discuss the results of the preliminary work on springs.
- Carry out the main investigation on springs. Allow students to compare the results of different groups. Compile a table of pooled results and discuss the possible reasons for any differences
- Discuss the benefits of repeating results.
- It is important that students appreciate the difference between accuracy and precision. Get students to plot their results on a large class graph, and then draw a line of best fit. Discuss the amount of scatter, and how far away the points are from the best-fit line (this is an indication of the **precision** of the individual measurements). Then discuss how far away from the 'true value' (the teacher's result?) the graph shows the extension to be for a weight somewhere in the middle of the range. Accurate readings will be taken by those who use their equipment most carefully.

Plenaries

Prize giving! – Award a prize to the group achieving (a) the most accurate result; (b) the most precise results. Let the groups try to explain their success. *(5 minutes)*

Out of range – Ask students to predict from the class graph what the extension would be for a weight of double the maximum tested. Support students by asking them what the value would be if the pattern showed by the graph continued in the same way, and then ask them why this might not happen. Extend students by asking them to discuss whether the precision is greater at the start of the range, greater near the end of the range or the same throughout the range. *(10 minutes)*

Support

- In the spring experiment, students may find it easier to measure the total length of the spring rather than the extension.

Extend

- The 'springs' practical can be extended to investigate what happens beyond the elastic limit, and include a discussion as to why such data would not be valid.

Practical support

Springs

Equipment and materials required

Expendable steel springs, stand, G-clamp, selection of slotted weights, ruler, plasticine or sticky-tac.

Details

Use a G-clamp to secure the stand. Hang weights from the spring using a weight hanger and measure the extension. Fix ruler vertically behind weight hanger and measure extension from the same point on the hanger. Run some preliminary tests using a range of weights. Suggest a suitable range of weights to test and a suitable interval for the weights.

Safety

Wear eye protection.

How Science Works

H5 Designing an investigation

Learning objectives

- How do you make sure that you choose the best values for your variables?
- How do you decide on a suitable range?
- How do you decide on a suitable interval?
- How do you ensure accuracy and precision?

Figure 1 Measuring the output voltage from a solar cell

Choosing values of a variable

Trial runs will tell you a lot about how your early thoughts are going to work out.

Do you have the correct conditions?

An experiment to measure the output voltage from a solar cell might not give an output at all. Perhaps the light isn't bright enough, perhaps the surface area of the cell is too small, or maybe the voltmeter that you are using cannot measure such a small voltage.

Have you chosen a sensible range?

Range means the maximum and minimum values of the independent or dependent variables. It is important to choose a suitable range for the independent variable, otherwise you may not be able to see any change in the dependent variable.

For example, if the results are all very similar, you might not have chosen a wide enough range of light intensities.

Have you got enough readings that are close together?

The gap between the readings is known as the **interval**.

For example, you might alter the light intensity by moving a lamp to different distances from the solar cell. A set of 11 readings equally spaced over a distance of 1 metre would give an interval of 10 centimetres.

If the results are very different from each other, you might not see a pattern if you have large gaps between readings over the important part of the range.

Accuracy

Accurate measurements are very close to the **true value**.

Your investigation should provide data that is accurate enough to answer your original question.

However, it is not always possible to know what that true value is.

How do you get accurate data?

- You can repeat your measurements and your mean is more likely to be accurate.
- Try repeating your measurements with a different instrument and see whether you get the same readings.
- Use high-quality instruments that measure accurately.
- The more carefully you use the measuring instruments, the more accuracy you will get.

Precision, resolution, repeatability and reproducibility

A **precise** measurement is one in which there is very little spread about the mean value.

If your repeated measurements are closely grouped together, you have precision. Your measurements must be made with an instrument that has a suitable **resolution**. Resolution of a measuring instrument is the smallest change in the quantity being measured (input) that gives a perceptible change in the reading.

It's no use measuring the time for a fast reaction to finish using the seconds hand on a clock! If there are big differences within sets of repeat readings, you will not be able to make a valid conclusion. You won't be able to trust your data!

How do you get precise data?

- You have to use measuring instruments with sufficiently small scale divisions.
- You have to repeat your tests as often as necessary.
- You have to repeat your tests in exactly the same way each time.

If you repeat your investigation using the same method and equipment and obtain the same results, your results are said to be **repeatable**.

If someone else repeats your investigation in the same way, or if you repeat it by using different equipment or techniques, and the same results are obtained, it is said to be **reproducible**.

You may be asked to compare your results with those of others in your group, or with data from other scientists. Research like this is a good way of seeing whether your results are reproducible.

A word of caution!

Precision depends only on the extent of random errors – it gives no indication of how close results are to the true value. Just because your results show precision does not mean they are accurate.

- **a** Draw a thermometer scale reading 49.5 °C, showing four results that are both accurate and precise.

AQA Examiner's tip

You must know the difference between accurate and precise results.

Imagine measuring the temperature after a set time when a fuel is used to heat a fixed volume of water. Two students repeated this experiment, four times each. Their results are marked on the thermometer scales below:

- A **precise** set of repeat readings will be grouped closely together.
- An **accurate** set of repeat readings will have a mean (average) close to the true value.

| Precise | Accurate |
| (but not accurate) | (but not precise) |

Key points

- You can use a trial run to make sure that you choose the best values for your variables.
- The range states the maximum and minimum values of a variable.
- The interval is the gap between the values of a variable.
- Careful use of the correct equipment can improve accuracy and precision.
- You should try to reproduce your results carefully.

Summary questions

1 Copy and complete the paragraph using the words below:

range   repeat   conditions   readings

Trial runs give you a good idea of whether you have the correct .... to collect any data; whether you have chosen the correct .... for the independent variable; whether you have enough ....; and if you need to do .... readings.

2 Use an example to explain how a set of repeat measurements could be accurate, but not precise.

3 Explain the difference between a set of results that are reproducible and a set of results that are repeatable.

Further teaching suggestions

Repeatability

- Using the data from the experiment, consider the range of their repeat measurements and judge repeatability. Find the maximum range for the whole class – who got the highest reading and who got the lowest? Can we explain why?

Graphs and charts

- The spring experiment can be expanded – discuss whether the results should be plotted on a line graph or a bar chart.

Answers to in-text questions

a Diagram of thermometer showing the true value with four readings tightly grouped around 49.5 °C.

Summary answers

1 conditions, range, readings, repeat

2 Any example that demonstrates understanding of the two terms, e.g. I measured the resistance of the wire as 3.5 Ω, 4.8 Ω, 2.2 Ω, 3.8 Ω, 3.2 Ω. There was a lot of scatter around the mean, so the individual results were not very precise. However, the mean of my results is 3.5 Ω and the manufacturer's results are 3.5 Ω. So my mean result was accurate.

3 **Repeatable:** a measurement is repeatable if the original experimenter repeats the investigation using the same method and equipment and obtains the same results.

Reproducible: a measurement is reproducible if the investigation is repeated by another person, or by using different equipment or techniques, and the same results are obtained.

H6

Making measurements

Learning objectives

Students should learn:

- that they can expect results to vary
- that instruments vary in their accuracy
- that instruments vary in their resolution
- the difference between systematic errors and random errors
- that human error can affect results, and what to do with anomalies.

Learning outcomes

Students should be able to:

- distinguish between results that vary and anomalies
- explain that instruments vary in their accuracy and resolution
- explain that anomalies should be discarded or repeated before calculating a mean.

Support

- Students will need support when interpreting data and identifying evidence for systematic and random errors. For systematic errors, they should look to see whether the measured values are always larger or smaller than the calculated values. For random errors, they should look to see whether there is any scatter around the mean.

Extend

- Demonstrate a different experiment in which there is a built-in systematic error, e.g. measuring the effect of temperature on the rate of an exothermic reaction.

AQA Specification link-up: Controlled Assessment P4.5

Review methodology to assess fitness for purpose, by:

- identifying causes of variation in data *[P4.5.2 a)]*
- recognising and identifying the cause of random errors. When a data set contains random errors, repeating the readings and calculating a new mean can reduce their effect *[P4.5.2 b)]*
- recognising and identifying the cause of anomalous results *[P4.5.2 c)]*
- recognising and identifying the cause of systematic errors. *[P4.5.2 d)]*

Lesson structure

Starters

Demonstration – Demonstrate different ways of measuring the width of the laboratory. Use a 30 cm rule, a metre rule, a tape and a laser/sonic measure. Discuss the relative merits of using each of these devices for different purposes. Discuss the details of the measuring instrument – its percentage accuracy, its useful range and its resolution. *(5 minutes)*

Human reaction time – Allow students to test their reaction times using a computer program (e.g. www.bbc.co.uk. Search for 'Sheep Dash'.) and then by dropping and catching a ruler, using a stopwatch. Discuss the advantages and disadvantages of each method. Support students by explaining that human reaction time is normally about 0.2 s. Extend students on the 'dropping the ruler' method by getting them to explain whether it would be better for the same person to drop the ruler and operate the watch, or whether it would be better to use two different people. *(10 minutes)*

Main

- In small groups, plan the most accurate way to measure a person's height. Students can have any equipment they need. They will need to think about what a person's height includes, e.g. hair flat or not, shoes on or off. They might suggest a board placed horizontally on the head, using a spirit level, removing the person being measured and then using the laser/sonic measure placed on the ground.

- Stress that we do not have a true answer. We do not know the person's true height. We trust the instrument and the technique that is most likely to give us the most accurate result – the one nearest the true value.

- Demonstrate an experiment in which there is a built-in systematic error, e.g. weighing some chemicals using a filter paper without using the tare, or measuring radioactivity without taking background radiation into account.

- Point out the difference between this type of systematic error and random errors. Also, how you might tell from results which type of error it is. You can still have a high degree of precision with systematic errors.

- Complete questions **a** and **b** individually.

- Encourage students to identify anomalies while carrying out the investigation, so that they have an opportunity to check and replace them.

Plenaries

Human v. computer – Class discussion of data logging compared to humans when collecting data. Stress the importance of data logging in gathering data over extended or very short periods of time. *(5 minutes)*

Checklist – Ask students to draw up a checklist for an investigation so that every possible source of error is considered. Support students by giving them a list of possible sources of error that includes a mixture of relevant and irrelevant suggestions. Ask them to tick the ones that they think are relevant. Extend students by asking them to suggest what they could do to minimise the effect of any errors. *(10 minutes)*

Further teaching suggestions

Data logging

- Data logging provides a good opportunity to exemplify changes in dependent variables.

  Use data logging to illustrate how detailed measurements taken frequently can show variation in results that would not have been seen by other methods.

  Data logging can increase the accuracy of readings that can be taken where it might not otherwise be possible to take readings accurately.

For example:

- Compare two students taking their hand temperatures – one with a thermometer, one with a logger.
- Set the logger to record room temperatures until the next lesson.
- Compare measurements using a tape measure with those of a distance sensor linked to a computer. Draw attention to the ability to measure distances as you move the sensor.

How Science Works

Making measurements

H6 | Making measurements

Learning objectives

- Why do results always vary?
- How do you choose instruments that will give you accurate results?
- What do we mean by the resolution of an instrument?
- What is the difference between a systematic error and a random error?
- How does human error affect results and what do you do with anomalies?

Figure 1 Matt testing how fast a trolley goes down a ramp

AQA *Examiner's tip*

If you are asked what may have caused an error, never answer simply 'human error' – you won't get any marks for this.

You need to say what the experimenter may have done to cause the error, or give more detail, e.g. 'Human reaction time might have caused an error in the timing when using a stopwatch.'

Using instruments

Try measuring the temperature of a beaker of water using a digital thermometer. Do you always get the same result? Probably not! So can we say that any measurement is absolutely correct?

In any experiment there will be doubts about actual measurements.

a Look at Figure 1. Suppose, like this student, you tested the time it takes for one type of trolley to run down a ramp. It is unlikely that you would get two readings exactly the same. Discuss all the possible reasons why.

When you choose an instrument you need to know that it will give you the accuracy that you want. You need to be confident that it is giving a true reading.

Perhaps you have used a simple force meter in school for measuring force. How confident were you that you had measured the true force? You could use a very expensive force meter to calibrate yours. The expensive force meter is more likely to show the true reading that is accurate – but are you really sure?

You also need to be able to use an instrument properly.

Instruments that measure the same thing can have different sensitivities. The **resolution** of an instrument refers to the smallest change in a value that can be detected. This is one factor that determines the precision of your measurements.

Choosing the wrong scale can cause you to miss important data or make silly conclusions. We would not measure the distance to Jupiter in centimetres – we would use kilometres.

b Match the following timers to their best use:

Used to measure	Resolution of timer
Time taken to sail around the world	milliseconds
Timing a car rolling down a slope	seconds
Time taken for a bullet to travel to its target	minutes
Timing a pizza to cook	hours

Errors

Even when an instrument is used correctly, the results can still show differences.

Results may differ because of **random error**. This is most likely to be due to a poor measurement being made. It could be due to not carrying out the method consistently.

If you repeat your measurements several times and then calculate a mean, you will reduce the effect of random errors.

The **error** might be a **systematic error**. This means that the method was carried out consistently but an error was being repeated. A systematic error will make your readings be spread about some value other than the true value. This is because your results will differ from the true value by a consistent amount each time a measurement is made.

No number of repeats can do anything about systematic errors. If you think that you have a systematic error, you need to repeat using a different set of equipment or a different technique. Then compare your results and spot the difference!

A **zero error** is one kind of systematic error. Suppose that you were trying to measure the length of your desk with a metre rule, but you hadn't noticed that someone had sawn off half a centimetre from the end of the ruler. It wouldn't matter how many times you repeated the measurement, you would never get any nearer to the true value.

Look at the table. It shows the two sets of data that were taken from the investigation that Matt did. He tested five different trolleys. The bottom row is the time that was expected from calculations:

Type of trolley used	A	B	C	D	E
Time taken for trolley to run down ramp (seconds)	12.6	23.1	24.8	31.3	38.2
	12.1	15.2	24.3	32.1	37.6
Calculated time (seconds)	10.1	13.1	22.1	30.1	35.3

c Discuss whether there is any evidence of random error in these results.
d Discuss whether there is any evidence of systematic error in these results.

Anomalies

Anomalous results are clearly out of line. They are not those that are due to the natural variation you get from any measurement. These should be looked at carefully. There might be a very interesting reason why they are so different. You should always look for anomalous results and discard them before you calculate a mean, if necessary.

- If anomalies can be identified while you are doing an investigation, it is best to repeat that part of the investigation.
- If you find anomalies after you have finished collecting data for an investigation, they must be discarded.

Summary questions

1 Copy and complete the paragraph using the words below:

accurate discarded random resolution systematic use variation

There will always be some .... in results. You should always choose the best instruments that you can in order to get the most .... results. You must know how to .... the instrument properly. The .... of an instrument refers to the smallest change that can be detected. There are two types of error: .... and .... Anomalies due to random error should be ....

2 What kind of error will most likely occur in the following situations?
   a Asking everyone in the class to measure the length of the bench.
   b Using a ruler that has a piece missing from the zero end.

Key points

- Results will nearly always vary.
- Better quality instruments give more accurate results.
- The resolution of an instrument refers to the smallest change that it can detect.
- Human error can produce random and/or systematic errors.
- We examine anomalies as they might give us some interesting ideas. If they are due to a random error, we repeat the measurements. If there is no time to repeat them, we discard them.

Answers to in-text questions

a Generally a failure to control variables, e.g. trolley not taking the same route; not recording the time as it crosses the line. Student might not react as quickly when stopping the watch.

b

Used to measure	Resolution of timer
Time taken to sail around the world	1 hour
Timing a car rolling down a slope	0.1 seconds
Time taken for a bullet to travel to its target	1.0 seconds
Timing a pizza to cook	1 minute

c First attempt for **B** is the random error.

d Average results are close to individual results, which are consistently different to the calculated time.

Summary answers

1 variation, accurate, use, resolution, random, systematic, discarded

2 a Random.
   b Systematic.

H7

Presenting data

AQA Specification link-up: Controlled Assessment P4.4

Learning objectives

Students should learn:

- what is meant by the range and the mean of a set of data
- how to use tables of data
- how to display data.

Learning outcomes

Students should be able to:

- express accurately the range and mean of a set of data
- distinguish between the uses of bar charts and line graphs
- draw line graphs accurately.

Show an understanding of the value of means, by:

- appreciating when it is appropriate to calculate a mean *[P4.4.1 a)]*
- calculating the mean of a set of at least three results. *[P4.4.1 b)]*

Demonstrate an understanding of how data may be displayed, by:

- drawing tables *[P4.4.2 a)]*
- drawing charts and graphs *[P4.4.2 b)]*
- choosing the most appropriate form of presentation. *[P4.4.2 c)]*

Lesson structure

Starters

Newspapers – Choose data from the press – particularly useful are market trends where they do not use the origin (0,0). This exaggerates changes. This could relate to the use of data logging, which can exaggerate normal variation into major trends. *(5 minutes)*

Spreadsheet – Prepare some data from a typical investigation that the students may have recently completed. Use all of the many ways of presenting the data in a spreadsheet program to display it. Allow students to discuss and reach conclusions as to which is the best method. Support students by presenting data as either a line graph or a simple bar chart, so that they can make the link between continuous data and line graphs and between categoric data and bar charts. Extend students by showing graphs and charts that have non-linear scales or false origins. *(10 minutes)*

Main

- Choose an appropriate topic to either demonstrate or allow small groups to gather data, e.g. cooling of water against time; using food labels to determine saturated fat content of different foods; force applied and degree of bending in rules; investigate the period of a pendulum. Choose any topic that will allow rapid gathering of data. Be aware that some data will lead to a bar chart; this might be more appropriate to groups struggling to draw line graphs.

- Students should be told what their task is and should therefore know how to construct an appropriate table. This should be done individually prior to collecting the data. Refer to the first paragraph under 'Tables' in the Student Book.

- Start a group discussion on the best form of table.

- Carry out data gathering, putting data directly into the table. Refer to the second paragraph under 'Tables' in the Student Book.

- Individuals produce their own graphs. Refer to the section 'Displaying your results' in the Student Book.

- Graphs could be exchanged and marked by others in the group, using the criteria in the section mentioned above.

Support

- Some students struggle with plotting graphs. They should start with bar charts and move on to line graphs.

Extend

- Students could be asked to handle two dependent variables in the table and graph, e.g. cooling and weight loss of a beaker of water with time, with repeat readings included.

- They could also be given more difficult contexts that are more likely to produce anomalies. They could, for example, be given a context that produces both random and systematic errors.

Plenaries

Which type of graph? – Give students different headings from a variety of tables and ask them how best to show the results graphically. This could be done as a whole class, with individuals showing answers as the teacher reveals each table heading. Each student can draw a large letter 'L' (for line graph) on one side of a sheet of paper and 'B' (for bar chart) on the other, ready to show their answers. *(5 minutes)*

Key words – Students should be given key words to prepare posters for the laboratory. Key words should be taken from the summary questions in the first six sections. Support students by giving them a poster in two sections – one containing the key word, the other the definition. Students should then match the pairs together correctly. Extend students by getting them to write their own definitions. *(10 minutes)*

Further teaching suggestions

ICT link-up

- Students could use a set of data within spreadsheet software to present the data as pie charts, line graphs, bar charts, etc. Allow them to decide on the most appropriate form. Care needs to be given to 'smoothing', which does not always produce a line of best fit.

H7 Presenting data

Learning objectives

- How do you calculate the mean from a set of data?
- How do you use tables of results?
- What is the range of the data?
- How do you display your data?

Figure 1 Student using an LDR with a light bulb

For this section you will be working with data from this investigation:

Mel shone a bulb on to a light-dependent resistor (LDR). She recorded how quickly energy was transferred to the bulb and the resistance of the LDR. Then she changed the rate of energy transferred to the bulb by altering the setting on the power supply and repeated the experiment.

The room was kept as dark as possible while she made the readings.

Tables

Tables are really good for getting your results down quickly and clearly. You should design your table **before** you start your investigation.

Your table should be constructed to fit in all the data to be collected. It should be fully labelled, including units.

You may have to have extra columns for repeats, calculations of means or calculated values.

Checking for anomalies

While filling in your table of results you should be constantly looking for anomalies.

- Check to see whether any reading in a set of repeat readings is significantly different from the others.
- Check to see whether the pattern you are getting as you change the independent variable is what you expected.

Remember, a result that looks anomalous should be checked out to see whether it really is a poor reading.

Planning your table

Mel had decided on the values for her independent variable. We always put these in the first column of a table. The dependent variable goes in the second column. Mel will find its values as she carries out the investigation.

So she could plan a table like this:

Rate of energy transferred to the bulb (W)	Resistance of LDR (Ω)
0.5	
1.4	
2.6	
4.8	
8.4	

Or like this:

Rate of energy transferred to the bulb (W)	0.5	1.4	2.6	4.8	8.4
Resistance of LDR (Ω)					

All she had to do in the investigation was to write the correct numbers in the second column to complete the top table.

Mel's results are shown in the alternative format in the table below.

Rate of energy transferred to the bulb (W)	0.5	1.4	2.6	4.8	8.4
Resistance of LDR (Ω)	4000	3000	1000	350	150

The range of the data

Pick out the maximum and the minimum values and you have the range of a variable. You should always quote these two numbers when asked for a range. For example, the range of the dependent variable is between 150 Ω (the lowest value) and 4000 Ω (the highest value) – and don't forget to include the units!

a What is the range for the independent variable and for the dependent variable in Mel's set of data?

Maths skills

The mean of the data

Often you have to find the **mean** of each repeated set of measurements.

The first thing you should do is to look for any anomalous results. If you find any, miss these out of the calculation. Then add together the remaining measurements and divide by how many there are.

For example:

- Mel takes four readings, 350 Ω, 355 Ω, 420 Ω and 345 Ω.
- 420 Ω is an anomalous result and so is missed out. So 350 + 355 + 345 = 1050.
- 1050 ÷ 3 (the number of valid results) = 350 Ω.

The repeat values and mean can be recorded as shown below:

Rate of energy transferred to the bulb (W)	Resistance of LDR (Ω)			
	1st test	2nd test	3rd test	Mean

Displaying your results

If one of your variables is categoric, you should use a **bar chart**. If you have a continuous independent and a continuous dependent variable, a **line graph** should be used. Plot the points as small 'plus' signs (+).

Summary questions

1 Copy and complete the paragraph using the words below:

categoric   continuous   mean   range

The maximum and minimum values show the .... of the data. The sum of all the values in a set of repeat readings divided by the total number of these repeat values gives the .... Bar charts are used when you have a .... independent variable and a continuous dependent variable. Line graphs are used when you have .... independent and dependent variables.

2 Draw a graph of Mel's results from the top of this page.

Key points

- The range states the maximum and the minimum values.
- The mean is the sum of the values divided by how many values there are.
- Tables are best used during an investigation to record results.
- Bar charts are used when you have a categoric variable.
- Line graphs are used to display data that are continuous.

Answers to in-text questions

a Independent variable −0.5 to 8.4 W; dependent variable – 150 Ω to 4000 Ω.

Summary answers

1 range, mean, categoric, continuous

2 Graph should be a line graph, with resistance on the *x*-axis and rate of energy transferred on the *y*-axis.

H8 Using data to draw conclusions

Learning objectives

Students should learn:

- how to use charts and graphs to identify patterns
- how to identify relationships within data
- how to draw valid conclusions from relationships
- how to evaluate the repeatability of an investigation.

Learning outcomes

Students should be able to:

- draw a line of best fit when appropriate
- identify different relationships between variables from graphs
- draw conclusions from data
- evaluate the repeatability and validity of an investigation.

Support

- Provide students with a flow diagram of the procedure used to draw conclusions so that they can see the process as they are going through it.

Extend

- Students could take the original investigation and then design out some of the flaws, producing an investigation with improved validity and repeatability.
- Summary question 2 could be examined in some detail and the work researched on the internet.

AQA **Specification link-up: Controlled Assessment P4.5 & P4.6**

Identify patterns in data, by:
- describing the relationship between two variables and deciding whether the relationship is causal or by association. *[P4.5.3 a)]*

Draw conclusions using scientific ideas and evidence, by:
- writing a conclusion, based on evidence that relates correctly to known facts *[P4.5.4 a)]*
- using secondary sources *[P4.5.4 b)]*
- identifying extra evidence that is required for a conclusion to be made *[P4.5.4 c)]*
- evaluating methods of data collection. *[P4.5.4 d)]*

Review hypotheses in the light of outcomes, by:
- considering whether or not any hypothesis made is supported by the evidence. *[P4.6.1a)]*

Lesson structure

Starters

Conclusions – Prepare a number of tables of results, some of which show that as *x* increases *y* increases, some that show that as *x* increases *y* decreases, and some where there is no relationship between *x* and *y*. Ask students what conclusion they can draw from each set of results. *(5 minutes)*

Starter graphs – Prepare a series of graphs that illustrate the various types of relationship in the specification. Each graph should have fully labelled axes. Students, in groups, should agree to statements that describe the patterns in the graphs. Support students by giving them graphs that illustrate simple linear relationships. Extend students by giving them more complex graphs with curved lines, and encourage them to use terms such as 'directly proportional' and 'inversely proportional'. Gather feedback from groups and discuss. *(10 minutes)*

Main

- Using the graphs from the previous lesson, students should be taught how to produce lines of best fit. Students could work individually with help from Figures 1 and 2 in the Student Book.
- They should identify the pattern in their graph.
- They now need to consider the repeatability and validity of their results. They may need their understanding of reliability and validity reinforced. Questions can be posed to reinforce their understanding of both terms. If the investigation was not carefully controlled, it is likely to be invalid, thus posing many opportunities for discussion. There is also an opportunity to reinforce other ideas such as random and systematic errors.
- A brief demonstration of a test, e.g. finding the energy transfer when burning crisps of different mass, could be used. Students should observe the teacher and make notes as the tests are carried out. They should be as critical as they can be, and in small groups discuss their individual findings. One or two students could be recording the results and two more plotting the graph, as the teacher does the tests. A spreadsheet could be used to immediately turn the results into graphs.
- Return to the original prediction. Look at the graph of the results. Ask how much confidence the group has in the results.
- Review the links that are possible between two sets of data. Ask them to decide which one their tests might support.
- Now the word 'conclusion' should be introduced and a conclusion made... if possible! It is sometimes useful to make a conclusion that is 'subject to ... e.g. the repeatability being demonstrated'.

Plenaries

Flow diagram – When pulling the lesson together, it will be important to emphasise the process involved – graph → line of best fit → pattern → question the repeatability and validity → consider the links that are possible → make a conclusion → summarise evaluation. This could be illustrated with a flow diagram generated by a directed class discussion. *(5 minutes)*

Evaluating – Students could review the method used in the demonstration experiment of heating water. Support students by asking them to identify where errors could have been made. Extend students by asking them to suggest improvements that could be made to minimise these errors. *(10 minutes)*

Further teaching suggestions

Case studies
- Students should be able to transfer these skills to examine the work of scientists and to become critical of the work of others. Collecting scientific findings from the press and subjecting them to the same critical appraisal is an important exercise. They could be encouraged to collect these or could be given photocopies of topical issues suitable for such appraisal.

H8 — Using data to draw conclusions

Learning objectives
- How do we best use charts and graphs to identify patterns?
- What are the possible relationships we can identify from charts and graphs?
- How do we draw conclusions from relationships?
- How can we decide if our results are good and our conclusions are valid?

Identifying patterns and relationships

Now that you have a bar chart or a line graph of your results you can begin to look for patterns. You must have an open mind at this point.

First, there could still be some anomalous results. You might not have picked these out earlier. How do you spot an anomaly? It must be a significant distance away from the pattern, not just within normal variation. If you do have any anomalous results plotted on your graph, circle these and ignore them when drawing the **line of best fit**.

Now look at your graph. Is there a pattern that you can see? When you have decided, draw a line of best fit that shows this pattern.

A line of best fit is a kind of visual averaging process. You should draw the line so that it leaves as many points slightly above the line as there are points below. In other words it is a line that steers a middle course through the field of points.

The vast majority of results that you get from continuous data require a line of best fit.

Remember, a line of best fit can be a straight line or it can be a curve – you have to decide from your results.

You need to consider whether your graph shows a linear **relationship**. This simply means, can you be confident about drawing a straight line of best fit on your graph? If the answer is yes – is this line positive or negative?

a Say whether graphs **i** and **ii** in Figure 1 show a positive or a negative linear relationship.

Look at the graph in Figure 2. It shows a positive linear relationship. It also goes through the origin (0, 0). We call this a **directly proportional** relationship.

Your results might also show a curved line of best fit. These can be predictable, complex or very complex! Look at Figure 3 below.

Figure 1 Graphs showing linear relationships

Figure 2 Graph showing a directly proportional relationship

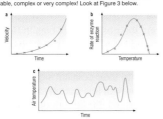

Figure 3 a Graph showing predictable results **b** Graph showing complex results **c** Graph showing very complex results

Drawing conclusions

If there is a pattern to be seen (for example as one variable gets bigger the other also gets bigger), it may be that:
- changing one has caused the other to change
- the two are related, but one is not necessarily the cause of the other.

Your conclusion must go no further than the evidence that you have.

Activity

Looking at relationships

Some people think that watching too much television can cause an increase in violence.

The table shows the number of television sets in the UK for four different years, and the number of murders committed in those years.

Year	Number of televisions (millions)	Number of murders
1970	15	310
1980	25	500
1990	42	550
2000	60	750

Plot a graph to show the relationship.

- Do you think this proves that watching television causes violence? Explain your answer.

Poor science can often happen if a wrong decision is made here. Newspapers have said that living near electricity substations can cause cancer. All that scientists would say is that there is possibly an association.

Evaluation

You will often be asked to evaluate either the method of the investigation or the conclusion that has been reached. Ask yourself: Could the method have been improved? Is the conclusion that has been made a valid one?

Summary questions

1 Copy and complete the paragraph using the words below:

anomalous complex directly negative positive

Lines of best fit can be used to identify .... results. Linear relationships can be .... or .... If a straight line goes through the origin of a graph, the relationship is .... proportional. Often a line of best fit is a curve which can be predictable or ....

2 Nasma knew about the possible link between cancer and living near to electricity substations. She found a quote from a National Grid Company survey of substations:

'Measurements of the magnetic field were taken at 0.5 metre above ground level within 1 metre of fences and revealed 1.9 microteslas. After 5 metres this dropped to the normal levels measured in any house.'

Discuss the type of experiment and the data you would expect to see to support a conclusion that it is safe to build houses over 5 metres from an electricity substation.

AQA Examiner's tip

When you read scientific claims, think carefully about the evidence that should be there to back up the claim.

Did you know ... ?

Pythagoras of Samos declared that 'Everything is number'. He believed that everything in the universe can be explained by simple mathematical relationships. He went on to discover the relationship between the length of a string and the sound it produces when it vibrates.

He developed this idea into a theory that the Sun, the Moon and the planets produced a sort of music that kept them in their orbits!

Key points
- Drawing lines of best fit helps us to study the relationship between variables.
- The possible relationships are linear, positive and negative; directly proportional; predictable and complex curves.
- Conclusions must go no further than the data available.
- The reproducibility and repeatability of data can be checked by looking at other similar work done by others, perhaps on the internet. It can also be checked by using a different method or by others checking your method.

Answers to in-text questions

a Graph **i** – positive linear.

Graph **ii** – negative linear.

Summary answers

1 anomalous, positive, negative, directly, complex

2 Survey of substations; measure magnetic field drop; measure 'microteslas' at different distances from substation; also in houses well away from substations; repeat all readings several time; fieldwork; check accuracy of measuring instruments.

H9

Scientific evidence and society

Learning objectives

Students should learn:

- that science must be presented in a way that takes into account the reproducibility and the validity of the evidence
- that science should be presented without bias from the experimenter
- that evidence must be checked to appreciate whether there is any political influence
- that the status of the experimenter can influence the weight attached to a scientific report.

Learning outcomes

Students should be able to:

- make judgements about the reproducibility and the validity of scientific evidence
- identify when scientific evidence might have been influenced by bias or political influence
- judge scientific evidence on its merits, taking into account the weight given to it by the status of the experimenter.

Support

- Groups could prepare posters that use scientific data to present their case for or against any of the developments discussed.

Extend

- Arrange a class debate and nominate individuals to speak for or against any of the developments discussed.

AQA Specification link-up: Controlled Assessment P4.5

Distinguish between a fact and an opinion, by:

- recognising that an opinion might be influenced by factors other than scientific fact [P4.5.1 a)]
- identifying scientific evidence that supports an opinion. [P4.5.1 b)]

Lesson structure

Starters

Ask a scientist – It is necessary at this point to make a seamless join between work that has mostly been derived from student investigations and work generated by scientists. Students must be able to use their critical skills derived in familiar contexts and apply them to second-hand data. One way to achieve this would be to bring in newspaper cuttings on a topic of current scientific interest. They should be aware that some newspaper reporters will 'cherry-pick' sections of reports to support sensational claims that will make good headlines. Students could be supported by highlighting key words in the article. To extend students, ask them to produce a 'wish-list' of questions they would like to put to the scientists who conducted the research and to the newspaper reporter. *(5 minutes)*

Researching scientific evidence – With access to the internet, students could be given a topic to research. They should use a search engine and identify the sources of information from, say, the first six webpages. They could then discuss the relative merits of these sources in terms of potential for bias. *(10 minutes)*

Main

- The following points are best made using topics that are of immediate importance to your students. The examples used are only illustrative. Some forward planning is required to ensure that there is a plentiful supply of newspaper articles, both local and national, to support the lesson. These could be displayed and/or retained in a portfolio for reference.

- Working in pairs, students should answer in-text question **a**. They should write a few sentences about the headline and what it means to them.

- It might be possible to expand on this discussion using secondary sources to find out what is unsafe about X-rays. It should lead to a balanced discussion of the possible benefits and hazards of having an X-ray.

- Use the next section to illustrate the possibility of bias in reporting science. Again use small group discussions, followed by whole class Plenary.

- If you have access to the internet for the whole class, it is worth pursuing the issue of mobile phone masts in relation to their political significance. Pose the question: 'What would happen to the economy of this country if it was discovered that mobile phone masts were dangerous?' Would different people come together to suppress that information? Should they be allowed to suppress scientific evidence? Stress that there is no such evidence, yet people have that fear. Why do they have that fear? Should scientists have the task of reducing that fear to proper proportions? There is much to discuss.

- Small groups can imagine that they are preparing a case against the siting of a nuclear power station close to their village. They could be given data that relates to pollution levels from similar power stations. Up-to-date data can be obtained from many websites. Students could be given the data as if it were information provided at a public enquiry for the nuclear power station. They should be asked to prepare a case that questions, e.g., the reproducibility and the validity of the data.

Plenaries

Contentious issues – Make a list of contentious issues on which scientists might be able to make a contribution to the debate. Examples might include the siting of wind farms or sewage works, the building of new motorways, the introduction of new drugs, etc. *(5 minutes)*

Group report – Groups should report their findings on the nuclear power station case to the class. Support students by allowing them to present their findings by posters. Extend students by asking individuals to give a one-minute talk to the rest of the class. *(10 minutes)*

Further teaching suggestions

Role play

● Students could role-play a public enquiry. They could be given roles and asked to prepare a case for homework. The data should be available to them so that they all know the arguments before preparing their case. Possible link here with the English department. This activity could be allocated as a homework exercise.

Local visit

● Students might be able to attend a local public enquiry or even the local town council as it discusses local issues with a scientific context or considers the report of a local issue.

The limitations of science

Examples could be given of the following issues:

● We are still finding out about things and developing our scientific knowledge (e.g. the use of the hadron collider).
● There are some questions that we cannot yet answer, maybe because we do not have enough valid evidence (e.g. are mobile phones completely safe to use?).
● There are some questions that science cannot answer at all (e.g. Why was the universe created?).

H9 — Scientific evidence and society

Learning objectives

● How can science encourage people to trust its research?
● How might bias affect people's judgement of science?
● Can politics influence judgements about science?
● Do you have to be a professor to be believed?

Did you know ...?

A scientist who rejected the idea of a causal link between smoking and lung cancer was later found to be being paid by a tobacco company.

AQA Examiner's tip

If you are asked about bias in scientific evidence, there are two types:

● The measuring instruments may have introduced a bias because they were not calibrated correctly.
● The scientists themselves may have a biased opinion (e.g. if they are paid by a company to promote their product).

Now you have reached a conclusion about a piece of scientific research. So what is next? If it is pure research, your fellow scientists will want to look at it very carefully. If it affects the lives of ordinary people, society will also want to examine it closely.

You can help your cause by giving a balanced account of what you have found out. It is much the same as any argument you might have. If you make ridiculous claims, nobody will believe anything you have to say.

Be open and honest. If you only tell part of the story, someone will want to know why! Equally, if somebody is only telling you part of the truth, you cannot be confident about anything they say.

a 'X-rays are safe, but should be limited' is the headline in an American newspaper. What information is missing? Is it important?

You must be on the lookout for people who might be biased when representing scientific evidence. Some scientists are paid by companies to do research. When you are told that a certain product is harmless, just check out who is telling you.

b Suppose you wanted to know about safe levels of noise at work. Would you ask the scientist who helped to develop the machinery or a scientist working in the local university? What questions would you ask, so that you could make a valid judgement?

We also have to be very careful in reaching judgements according to who is presenting scientific evidence to us. For example, if the evidence might provoke public or political problems, it might be played down.

Equally, others might want to exaggerate the findings. They might make more of the results than the evidence suggests. Take as an example the siting of mobile phone masts. Local people may well present the same data in a totally different way from those with a wider view of the need for mobile phones.

c Check out some websites on mobile phone masts. Get the opinions of people who think they are dangerous and those who believe they are safe. Try to identify any political bias there might be in their opinions.

Science can often lead to the development of new materials or techniques. Sometimes these cause a problem for society where hard choices have to be made.

Scientists can give us the answers to many questions, but not to every question. Scientists have a contribution to make to a debate, but so do others such as environmentalists, economists and politicians.

The limitations of science

Science can help us in many ways but it cannot supply all the answers. We are still finding out about things and developing our scientific knowledge. For example, the Hubble telescope has helped us to revise our ideas about the beginnings of the universe.

There are some questions that we cannot answer, maybe because we do not have enough reproducible, repeatable and valid evidence. For example, research into the causes of cancer still needs much work to be done to provide data.

There are some questions that science cannot answer at all. These tend to be questions where beliefs, opinions and ethics are important. For example, science can suggest what the universe was like when it was first formed, but cannot answer the question of why it was formed.

Figure 1 The Hubble space telescope can look deep into space and tell us things about the universe's beginning from the formations of early galaxies

VILLAGERS PROTEST AGAINST WIND FARM

There was considerable local opposition from local villagers to building a wind farm near the A14 road in Cambridgeshire. Planners turned down the application after seven months of protests by local residents. Some described it as being like 16 football pitches rotating in the sky. Others were concerned at the effect on the value of their houses. Friends of the Earth were, in principle, in favour. The wind farm company said that it would provide energy for 20,000 homes.

Summary questions

1 Copy and complete the paragraph using the words below:
status   balanced   bias   political
Evidence from scientific investigations should be given in a .... way. It must be checked for any .... from the experimenter. Evidence can be given too little or too much weight if it is of .... significance. The .... of the experimenter is likely to influence people in their judgement of the evidence.

2 Collect some newspaper articles to show how scientific evidence is used. Discuss in groups whether these articles are honest and fair representations of the science. Consider whether they carry any bias.

3 Extract from a newspaper report about Sizewell nuclear power station:
A radioactive leak can have devastating results but one small pill could protect you. Our reporter reveals how for the first time these life-saving pills will be available to families living close to the Sizewell nuclear power station.
Suppose you were living near Sizewell power station. Who would you trust to tell you whether these pills would protect you from radiation?

Key points

● Scientific evidence must be presented in a balanced way that points out clearly how valid the evidence is.
● The evidence must not contain any bias from the experimenter.
● The evidence must be checked to appreciate whether there has been any political influence.
● The status of the experimenter can influence the weight placed on the evidence.

Answers to in-text questions

a E.g. what level of X-rays is safe?; if they are safe, why should they be limited?; what is meant by limited?; who did the research?

b Scientists in the local university; e.g. did she repeat her tests?; did she get someone else to repeat them?; what instruments were used?; what was the resolution of the instruments?; how were the readings of noise level taken?

c Identification of any political bias; this could be from companies and individuals as well as governments.

Summary answers

1 balanced, bias, political, status

2 Identification of any bias in the reports.

3 The person should be independent, have the necessary skills as a scientist and not be capable of being influenced politically.

H10

The ISA

AQA Specification link-up: Controlled Assessment P4.5 & P4.6

Learning objectives

Students should learn:
- how to write a plan
- how to make a risk assessment
- how to make a hypothesis
- how to make a conclusion.

Learning outcomes

Students should be able to:
- structure a plan for an investigation so as to include key points such as the range and interval of the independent variable
- identify potential hazards in practical work
- show how the results of an experiment can confirm or refute a hypothesis
- reach a valid conclusion from the results of an investigation.

Distinguish between a fact and an opinion, by:
- recognising that an opinion might be influenced by factors other than scientific fact [P4.5.1 a)]
- identifying scientific evidence that supports an opinion. [P4.5.1 b)]

Review hypotheses in the light of outcomes, by:
- considering whether or not any hypothesis made is supported by the evidence [P4.6.1a)]
- developing scientific ideas as a result of observations and measurements. [P4.6.1b)]

Lesson structure

Starters

Structure of an investigation – Use an interactive whiteboard or sticky labels that show the different stages of an investigation and ask students to arrange them in the correct order. *(5 minutes)*

Predictions and hypotheses – Make a table containing one column of hypotheses and another column of predictions. Students should match the prediction to the correct hypothesis. *(10 minutes)*

Main

These activities may be spread over more than one lesson:
- Use a specimen ISA to guide students through the different stages that will be required.
- Start by outlining the problem that is to be investigated. Set a context for the investigation. Ask the students to develop a hypothesis and discuss.
- Research one or two (depending on the investigation) possible methods that can be used to carry out an experiment to test the hypothesis. Get them to practise making brief notes, similar to the notes they will be able to make for the real ISA.
- Review any possible hazards. Discuss how any risk associated with these hazards could be reduced.
- Discuss the control variables that should be kept constant in order to make it a fair test.
- Students should decide the range and interval of the values of the independent variable, and whether or not repeats will be needed.
- Allow the students to carry out a rough trial with the equipment in order to establish suitable values for these.
- Students should now be able to write a structured plan for the investigation.
- Ask students to design a blank table ready for the results. This should contain space to record all the measurements that will be taken during the experiment. Stress the need to include proper headings and units.
- Students carry out the investigation, recording their results.
- Draw a chart or graph of the results.
- Analyse the results and discuss any conclusion that could be reached. Make sure the students refer back to the hypothesis when making their conclusion.

Support

- Groups could prepare posters that show a flow diagram for the different stages of an ISA investigation.
- Students can be provided with a plan if their plan is unworkable, unsafe or unmanageable. An example plan will be provided by the AQA. Students should not lose any marks if their plan is unworkable for a good reason (i.e. lack of equipment). However, if their plan is dangerous or unworkable this must be reflected in their mark.

Extend

- Give students a hypothesis and ask them to make a prediction based on it.

Plenaries

Graph or bar chart – Give students a list of titles of different investigations and ask them to decide whether the results should be plotted on a bar chart or on a line graph. *(5 minutes)*

Comparing results – Groups should report their findings to others and compare results. Support students by making a table of pooled results. Extend students by asking individuals to give a one-minute talk to the rest of the class explaining why they think their results are or are not repeatable and reproducible. *(10 minutes)*

Further teaching suggestions

Writing a plan
- Give students a plan of an investigation that contains a number of errors, e.g. control variables not kept constant, or unsuitable range or interval of the independent variable, and ask them to spot and explain the mistakes.

How Science Works

The ISA

H10 The ISA

Learning objectives
- How do you write a plan?
- How do you make a risk assessment?
- What is a hypothesis?
- How do you make a conclusion?

There are several different stages to the ISA.

Stage 1

Your teacher will tell you the problem that you are going to investigate, and you will have to develop your own hypothesis. They will also set the problem in a context – in other words, where in real life your investigation could be useful. You should have a discussion about it, and talk about different ways in which you might solve the problem. Your teacher should show you the equipment that you can use, and you should research one or two possible methods for carrying out an experiment to test the hypothesis. You should also research the context and do a risk assessment for your practical work. You will be allowed to make one side of notes on this research, which you can take into the written part of the ISA.

You should be allowed to handle the equipment and you may be allowed to carry out a preliminary experiment.

Make sure that you understand what you have to do – now is the time to ask questions if you are not sure.

AQA Examiner's tip

When you are making a blank table or drawing a graph or bar chart, make sure that you use full headings, e.g.
- the length of the leaf', **not** just 'length'
- the time taken for the reaction', **not** just 'time'
- the height from which the ball was dropped', **not** just 'height'
and don't forget to include any units.

Figure 1 Doing practical work allows you to develop the skills needed to do well in the ISA

How Science Works

Section 1 of the ISA

At the end of this stage, you will answer Section 1 of the ISA. You will need to:
- develop a hypothesis
- identify one or more variables that you need to control
- describe how you would carry out the main experiment
- identify possible hazards and say what you would do to reduce any risk
- make a blank table ready for your results.

a What features should you include in your written plan?
b What should you include in your blank table?

Stage 2

This is where you carry out the experiment and get some results. Don't worry too much about spending a long time getting fantastically accurate results – it is more important to get some results that you can analyse.

After you have got results, you will have to compare your results with those of others. You will also have to draw a graph or a bar chart.

c How do you decide whether you should draw a bar chart or a line graph?

Stage 3

This is where you answer Section 2 of the ISA. Section 2 of the ISA is all about your own results, so make sure that you look at your table and graph when you are answering this section. To get the best marks you will need to quote some data from your results.

How Science Works

Section 2 of the ISA

In this section you will need to:
- say what you were trying to find out
- compare your results with those of others, saying whether you think they are similar or different
- analyse data that is given in the paper. This data will be in the same topic area as your investigation
- use ideas from your own investigation to answer questions about this data
- write a conclusion
- compare your conclusion with the hypothesis you have tested.

You may need to change or even reject your hypothesis in response to your findings.

AQA Examiner's tip

When you are comparing your conclusion with the hypothesis, make sure that you also talk about the **extent** to which your results support the hypothesis. Which of these answers do you think would score the most marks?
- My results support the hypothesis.
- In my results, as *x* got bigger, *y* got bigger, as stated in the hypothesis.
- In my results, as *x* got bigger, *y* got bigger, as stated in the hypothesis, but unlike the hypothesis, *y* stopped increasing after a while.

Key points
- When you are writing the plan make sure that you include details about:
  - the range and interval of the independent variable
  - the control variables
  - the number of repeats.
- Try to put down at least two possible hazards, and say how you are going to minimise the risk from them.
- Look carefully at the hypothesis that you are given – this should give you a good clue about how to do the experiment.
- Always refer back to the hypothesis when you are writing your conclusion.

Summary questions

1 Copy and complete the paragraph using the words below:
control independent dependent
When writing a plan, you need to state the variable that you are deliberately going to change, called the .... variable. You also need to say what you expect will change because of this; this is called the .... variable. You must also say what .... variables you will keep constant in order to make it a fair test.

Answers to in-text questions

a Control variables, interval and range of the independent variable. Identify possible hazards and how to reduce any risk.

b Columns for quantities that are going to be measured, including complete headings and units.

c A bar chart if one of the variables is categoric, a line graph if both variables are continuous.

Summary answers

1 independent, dependent, control

Summary answers

1 There could be some differences, which would be fine, e.g.: hypothesis; prediction; design; safety; controls; method; table; results; repeat; graph; conclusion; improve.

2 a Scientific opinion is based on repeatable, reproducible and valid evidence. An opinion might not be.

b Continuous variable because it is more powerful than an ordered or categoric variable.

3 a A hypothesis is an idea that fits an observation and the scientific knowledge that is available.

b As the diameter of the wire increases, the resistance decreases
or
as the diameter of the wire increases, the resistance increases.

c The hypothesis could be supported or refuted or it might cause you to change your hypothesis.

d The theory on which you based the hypothesis might have to be changed.

4 a When all variables but the one being used as the independent variable are kept constant.

b Do you have the correct conditions? Have you chosen a sensible range? Have you got enough readings that are close together? Will you need to repeat the readings?

c If repeat results are close enough together.

d See how close the actual results are to the predicted results.

5 E.g. was the electromagnet wiped clean after each test? Was the current/voltage kept constant? Was the weighing machine tared?

6 a Take the highest and the lowest.

b the sum of all the readings divided by the number of readings

c when you have an ordered or categoric independent variable and a continuous dependent variable

d when you have a continuous independent variable and a continuous dependent variable

7 a Examine to see whether it is an error; if so, repeat it. If identified from the graph, it should be ignored. Be aware that it could lead to something really interesting and to a new hypothesis.

b Identify a pattern.

c That it does not go further than the data and the repeatability, reproducibility and validity allow.

d by repeating results, by getting others to repeat your results and by checking other equivalent data

8 a The science is more likely to be accepted.

b They might be biased because of who is funding the research or because they are employed by a biased organisation. There might be political influences; the public might be too alarmed by the conclusions.

9 a For many scientific developments, there is a practical outcome that can be used – a technological development. Many technological developments allow further progress in science.

b Society.

10 a Increasing the height of the turbine blades would increase the power output.

Summary questions

1 Put these words into order. They should be in the order that you might use them in an investigation.
design; prediction; conclusion; method; repeat; controls; graph; results; table; improve; safety; hypothesis

2 a How would you tell the difference between an opinion that was scientific and a prejudiced opinion?

b Suppose you were investigating the loss of energy from a beaker of hot water. Would you choose to investigate a categoric or a continuous variable? Explain why.

3 a You might have noticed that different items of electrical equipment in the house use different diameters of wire. You want to find out why. You use some accepted theory to try to answer the question.
Explain what you understand by a hypothesis.

Figure 1 Different diameters of wire in a household

b The diameter of the wire can affect the resistance of the wire. This is a hypothesis. Use this to make a prediction.

c Suppose you have tested your prediction and have some data. What might this do for your hypothesis?

d Suppose the data does not support the hypothesis. What should you do to the theory that gave you the hypothesis?

4 a What do you understand by a fair test?

b Suppose you were carrying out an investigation into how changing the current in an electromagnet affects the magnetic field. You would need to carry out a trial. Describe what a trial would tell you about how to plan your method.

c How could you decide if your results showed precision?

d It is possible to calculate the theoretical magnetic field around a coil. How could you use this to check on the accuracy of your results?

5 Suppose you were watching a friend carry out an investigation using the equipment shown in Figure 2. You have to mark your friend on how accurately he is making his measurements. Make a list of points that you would be looking for.

Figure 2 Student using an electromagnet to pick up iron filings

6 a How do you decide on the range of a set of data?

b How do you calculate the mean?

c When should you use a bar chart?

d When should you use a line graph?

7 a What should happen to anomalous results?

b What does a line of best fit allow you to do?

c When making a conclusion, what must you take into consideration?

d How can you check on the repeatability and reproducibility of your results?

8 a Why is it important when reporting science to 'tell the truth, the whole truth and nothing but the truth'?

b Why might some people be tempted not to be completely fair when reporting their opinions on scientific data?

9 a 'Science can advance technology and technology can advance science.' What do you think is meant by this statement?

b Who answers the questions that start with 'Should we … '?

---

b height of the turbine blades

c power output

d 32–85 m.

e Use the same turbine in the same location or same weather condition.

f It is not easy to control all variables, e.g. wind speed. To obtain more accurate results, the tests should have been repeated several times and a mean calculated.

g 139 kW is significantly lower than 162 kW and so could be considered an anomaly produced by random error.

h Resolution is probably 1 kW. The data in the table show the results to the nearest whole kilowatt.

i correct labelling; correct units; correct plotting; reasonable axes; height on *x*-axis, power output on *y*-axis

j line of best fit that ignores the anomaly

k Positive linear relationship between the height of the wind turbine and the power generated. (Note: if they think it is a curve they have probably plotted the 85 m reading as 90 m.)

l Increasing the height has increased the power output. However, this was only in the weather conditions at that time and there was some doubt over the 32 m reading, which should have been repeated.

m It might help them to show that the turbine would need to be placed at a height that would be unacceptable to people living in the neighbourhood.

n independent expert

0 Wind turbines are an increasingly popular way of generating electricity. It is very important that they are sited in the best place to maximise energy output. Clearly they need to be where there is plenty of wind. Energy companies have to be confident that they get value for money. Therefore they must consider the most economic height at which to build them. Put them too high and they might not get enough extra energy to justify the extra cost of the turbine. Before deciding finally on a site they will carry out an investigation to decide the best height.

The prediction is that increasing the height will increase the power output of the wind turbine. A test platform was erected and the turbine placed on it. The lowest height that would allow the turbines to move was 32 metres. The correct weather conditions were waited for, and the turbine began turning and the power output was measured in kilowatts.

The results are in the table.

Height of turbine (m)	Power output Test 1 (kW)	Power output Test 2 (kW)
32	162	139
40	192	195
50	223	219
60	248	245
70	278	270
80	302	304
85	315	312

Figure 3 Wind turbines

a What was the prediction for this test?

b What was the independent variable?

c What was the dependent variable?

d What is the range of the heights for the turbine?

e Suggest a control variable that should have been used.

f This is a fieldwork investigation. Is it possible to control all of the variables? If not, say what you think the scientist should have done to produce more accurate results.

g Is there any evidence for an anomalous result in this investigation? Explain your answer.

h What was the resolution of the power output measurement? Provide some evidence for your answer from the data in the table.

i Draw a graph of the results for the second test.

j Draw a line of best fit.

k Describe the pattern in these results.

l What conclusion can you reach?

m How might this data be of use to people who want to stop a wind farm being built?

n Who should carry out these tests for those who might object?

AQA Examiner's comments

Changes to How Science Works

Although HSW has remained largely unchanged, there have been some additions in this specification, particularly with regard to the Controlled Assessment Unit (ISA).

These include a requirement for candidates to:

- identify potential hazards and devise a plan to minimise risk
- understand the term 'hypothesis'
- test and/or make a prediction
- write a plan for an investigation, having been shown the basic technique to be used. Candidates should be able to decide upon issues such as the range and interval of the independent variable, the control variables and the number of repeats.

P1 1.1

Infrared radiation

Learning objectives

Students should learn:

- that infrared radiation is the transfer of energy by electromagnetic waves
- that all objects emit and absorb infrared radiation
- that the amount of infrared radiation emitted in a given time increases with the temperature of the object.

Learning outcomes

Most students should be able to:

- describe infrared radiation as electromagnetic waves
- state that there is radiation, similar to light but invisible; that it is emitted by all objects
- explain that the hotter an object is, the more infrared radiation it emits in a given time.

Support

- Concentrate on sharing the key ideas, the transfer of energy by radiation (point out the similarities to light) and look for correct drawings of rays of 'energy'. Link this to a change in temperature when this energy is emitted (cooling) or absorbed (heating).

Extend

- Students could explore infrared satellite imagery. This is used in weather forecasting and analysis of land use. Students could investigate how infrared satellites are used to monitor the weather and to analyse how land is used in different countries. They could find out how different types of vegetation or habitation show up in infrared imagery or even other parts of the electromagnetic spectrum. There are many excellent images available to explore on the internet: students could start with the various 'landsat' or weather forecasting websites.

Specification link-up: Physics P1.1

- All objects emit and absorb infrared radiation. *[P1.1.1 a)]*
- The hotter an object is the more infrared radiation it radiates in a given time. *[P1.1.1 b)]*

Controlled Assessment: P4.1 Plan practical ways to develop and test candidates' own scientific ideas. *[P4.1.1 a) b) c)]*; P4.3 Collect primary and secondary data. *[P4.3.2 a) f)]*

Lesson structure

Starters

Seeing at night – To support students, you could search the internet for infrared images, show them and ask students to identify the objects. Can students identify the hotter parts of the objects from the colder ones? Many pictures come with scales to help. *(5 minutes)*

Hand warming – Ask students to draw a diagram explaining why holding your hands *in front* of a fire warms them up. Students should use a ray diagram to show the radiation leaving the fire and being absorbed by the hands. *(10 minutes)*

Main

- Why is it that being in sunlight makes you feel warm while the shade can feel cool? Start the main part of the lesson by discussing this idea; try to draw out the scientific language, absorb and transmit.
- Discuss infrared images and how all objects are giving off invisible infrared radiation due to the energy in them. Link the temperature of the object to the amount of energy emitted in a given time.
- Demonstrating the rise in temperature mentioned in the text requires a bright white light source. A sensitive thermometer or sensor should also be used.
- Discuss the meaning of the words 'radiate' (to spread out from a source) and 'radiation' (the energy that is spread) to make sure students have a full understanding.
- Emphasise that there is empty space (a vacuum) between the Earth and the Sun and that infrared radiation passes through this vacuum easily, otherwise we would receive no energy from the Sun. Check that students can understand or draw a ray diagram showing this information.
- You could use a diagram to show how all of the energy is focused in a solar oven, pointing out that the rays travel in straight lines – just like visible light. A concave mirror could be used to focus rays on a blackened thermometer bulb to show the effect. As a simple alternative, use a magnifying glass to ignite a piece of paper to show how high temperatures can be reached by bringing rays together.
- A discussion of the greenhouse effect is best presented using a diagram to point out what you mean by wavelength. Show two waves and discuss the energy the waves carry; the shorter the wavelength, the more energy the wave carries. Another two diagrams could be used to link the greenhouse effect with a real greenhouse. To support students, you could provide incomplete diagrams of the greenhouse effect for them to annotate with important information.
- Students could plan the investigation 'A huddle test' to practise 'How Science Works' skills (see Student Book).

Plenaries

- **Temperature order** – Show a list of objects or materials (e.g. the Sun's surface, boiling water, etc.) and ask students to put them in temperature order. You could provide students with some cards showing the actual temperatures to match up with the objects after they have been placed in order. For example, solid carbon dioxide: −78 °C, melting ice: 0 °C, boiling ethanol: 78 °C, boiling water: 100 °C, melting iron 1538 °C , surface of sun 6000 °C. *(5 minutes)*
- **By stealth** – If you have a passive infrared detector in your room, you could test its sensitivity. It responds to changes in energy and, if you move slowly enough, it will not trigger. Some students could have a competition to see how far they can travel (very slowly) without being detected. *(10 minutes)*

Practical support

Detecting infrared radiation

You may prefer to do this as a demonstration if you don't want to coat a lot of thermometers with paint.

Equipment and materials required

For each group: bright white light source (power supply and ray box), sensitive thermometer (to 0.5 °C) with bulb painted matt black, clean prism.

Details

Shine the light through the prism and produce the spectrum. (This could be projected on the wall if you are just demonstrating.) Position the thermometer just beyond the red part of the spectrum and the temperature reading will rise.

Demonstrating a solar oven

Small solar ovens are available and could be used to boil small quantities of water. As an alternative, an old parabolic car headlight could be used. If a match is mounted at the focus of the parabola (this takes some practice) and the headlight is pointed towards a bright light source (such as the Sun or another headlight), the match will ignite.

Energy transfer by heating

Infrared radiation

P1 1.1   Infrared radiation

Learning objectives

- What is infrared radiation?
- Do all objects give off infrared radiation?
- How does infrared radiation depend on the temperature of an object?

Figure 1 Keeping watch in darkness

📖 links

For more information on infrared heaters, see P1 1.9 Heating and insulating buildings.

❓❓ Did you know … ?

A **passive infrared (PIR) detector** in a burglar alarm circuit will 'trigger' the alarm if someone moves in front of the detector. The detector contains sensors that detect infrared radiation from different directions.

📖 links

For more information on electromagnetic waves, see P1 6.1 The electromagnetic spectrum.

Seeing in the dark

We can use special cameras to 'see' animals and people in the dark. These cameras detect **infrared radiation**. Every object gives out (**emits**) infrared radiation.

The hotter an object is, the more infrared radiation it emits in a given time.

Look at the photo in Figure 1. The rhinos are hotter than the ground.

a Why is the ground darker than the rhinos?
b Which part of each rhino is coldest?

Practical

Detecting infrared radiation

You can use a thermometer with a blackened bulb to detect infrared radiation. Figure 2 shows how to do this.

- The glass prism splits a narrow beam of white light into the colours of the spectrum.
- The thermometer reading rises when it is placed just beyond the red part of the spectrum. Some of the infrared radiation in the beam goes there. Our eyes cannot detect it but the thermometer can.
- Infrared radiation is beyond the red part of the visible spectrum.

What would happen to the thermometer reading if the thermometer were moved away from the screen?

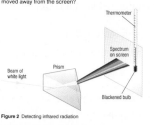

Figure 2 Detecting infrared radiation

The electromagnetic spectrum

Radio waves, **microwaves**, infrared radiation and **visible light** are parts of the electromagnetic spectrum. So too are ultraviolet rays and X-rays. Electromagnetic waves are electric and magnetic waves that travel through space.

Energy from the Sun

The Sun emits all types of electromagnetic radiation. Fortunately for us, the Earth's atmosphere blocks most of the radiation that would harm us. But it doesn't block infrared radiation from the Sun.

Figure 3 shows a solar furnace. This uses a giant reflector that focuses sunlight.

The temperature at the focus can reach thousands of degrees. That's almost as hot as the surface of the Sun, which is 5500 °C.

The greenhouse effect

The Earth's atmosphere acts like a greenhouse made of glass. In a greenhouse:

- short wavelength infrared radiation (and light) from the Sun can pass through the glass to warm the objects inside the greenhouse
- infrared radiation from these warm objects is trapped inside by the glass because the objects emit infrared radiation of longer wavelengths that can't pass through the glass.

So the greenhouse stays warm.

Gases in the atmosphere, such as water vapour, methane and carbon dioxide, trap infrared radiation from the Earth. This makes the Earth warmer than it would be if it had no atmosphere.

But the Earth is becoming too warm. If the polar ice caps melt, it will cause sea levels to rise. Reducing our use of fossil fuels will help to reduce the production of 'greenhouse gases'.

Figure 3 A solar furnace in the Eastern Pyrenees, France

⚙️ How Science Works

A huddle test

Design an investigation to model the effect of penguins huddling together. You could use beakers of hot water to represent the penguins.

Figure 4 Penguins keeping warm

Summary questions

1 Copy and complete a and b using the words below. Each word can be used more than once.

temperature   radiation   waves

a Infrared .... is energy transfer by electromagnetic ....
b The higher the .... of an object is, the more .... it emits each second.

2 a Copy and complete the table to show if the object emits infrared radiation or light or both.

Object	Infrared	Light
A hot iron		
A light bulb		
A TV screen		
The Sun		

b How can you tell if an electric iron is hot without touching it?

3 Explain why penguins huddle together to keep warm.

Key points

- Infrared radiation is energy transfer by electromagnetic waves.
- All objects emit infrared radiation.
- The hotter an object is, the more infrared radiation it emits in a given time.

Further teaching suggestions

A coffee conundrum

Equipment and materials required

Two identical cups, coffee powder, milk, kettle and data loggers. No tasting in laboratory.

- A cup of coffee is left for 10 minutes to cool down. Would the coffee be cooler if the milk was poured in immediately after it was made, after 5 minutes, or immediately before drinking it? Extend students by asking them to plan and carry out an experiment that would test their theories. Analysis of the results of an experiment like this will allow discussion about the rate of energy transfer and lead to the conclusion that the rate of energy transfer is proportional to the temperature difference between an object and the surroundings.

Temperature measurement

- There are a number of methods of measuring temperature, so students could be assigned the task of investigating one or another. You could assign different students different techniques such as: thermal imaging, infrared, thermocouples, thermistors, resistance temperature detectors, bimetallic strips, Galilean thermometers. Some of these are more complex than others, so select which to assign to individual students allowing for clear differentiation by task.

Answers to in-text questions

a The ground is cooler than the body surface of each rhino.

b The feet are the coldest parts of each rhino.

Summary answers

1 a radiation, waves
   b temperature, radiation

2 a

Object	Infrared	Light
A hot iron	✓	✗
A light bulb	✓	✓
A TV screen	✗	✓
The Sun	✓	✓

   b Put your hand near it and see if it gets warm due to radiation from the iron.

3 They lose less heat through radiation when they huddle together because they radiate energy to each other.

P1 1.2

Surfaces and radiation

Learning objectives

Students should learn:

- that matt black surfaces are the best emitters and best absorbers of infrared radiation
- that shiny surfaces are the worst emitters, worst absorbers and best reflectors of infrared radiation.

Learning outcomes

Most students should be able to:

- describe which surfaces are the best emitters of infrared radiation
- describe which surfaces are the best absorbers and reflectors of infrared radiation.

Some students should also be able to:

- explain how the choice of a surface colour can affect the rate of temperature change of an object.

Answers to in-text questions

a Sand makes the ice surface dark and matt so it absorbs radiation from the Sun better. The sand grains become warm and melt the ice.

b A dark matt surface absorbs more radiation from the Sun.

Support

- As in the last lesson, look for the clear idea of energy being transferred leading to heating and cooling. You could provide support worksheets for either of the practical tasks, so that students can focus on collecting evidence.

Extend

- Students could analyse the shape of cooling curves to determine that the rate of cooling depends on the temperature difference between objects. They should be able to link this to the change in gradient of the cooling graphs; the graphs are flatter towards the end of the experiments. Students will return to this idea later.

AQA Specification link-up: Physics P1.1

- Dark, matt surfaces are good absorbers and good emitters of infrared radiation. *[P1.1.1 c)]*
- Light, shiny surfaces are poor absorbers and poor emitters of infrared radiation. *[P1.1.1 d)]*
- Light, shiny surfaces are good reflectors of infrared radiation. *[P1.1.1 e)]*

  Controlled Assessment: P4.1 Plan practical ways to develop and test candidates' own scientific ideas. *[P4.1.1 a) b)]*

Lesson structure

Starters

Definitions – Show students the key words for this spread (absorb, reflect, emit). Ask students to match up descriptions of these processes and diagrams showing them taking place. Check that these diagrams are using the idea of rays demonstrating the transfer of energy. *(5 minutes)*

Out in the sun – Discuss with students how it feels to go out in a black T-shirt on a sunny day. Encourage the use of key scientific language such as absorb, reflect and emit. *(10 minutes)*

Main

- Most students will understand that the inside of a black car feels very hot on a sunny day, so start with these ideas about heating. Focus on energy entering the object and that this is the cause of an increase in temperature.

- Watch out for misunderstanding of the word 'absorb'; many students have the impression that it means that the surface somehow 'sucks in' the energy from its surroundings.

- This topic presents an early opportunity for developing the students' practical skills. You could introduce some of the concepts covered in 'How Science Works' in this lesson, e.g. the nature of different types of variable, how to present results and evaluating the design of investigations. You could also use the first practical as an open-ended planning exercise.

- If time is available, you can try both practical activities with the students. If time is short, then half the students could do one of the practical tasks while the other half does the second. They could share results and ideas at the end.

- After the first practical, check that students actually achieved the results you expected; the difference in temperature can be small and it is not unusual to reach the wrong conclusion. Discuss how to improve the practical to make it fairer or more accurate.

- The second practical may also be performed as a demonstration if equipment or time is limited. Check understanding of both the absorption and emission practicals and, in particular, the correct use of key words.

- A Leslie's cube is ideal to demonstrate that two surfaces at the same temperature can emit different amounts of infrared radiation. An infrared sensor could be used to detect levels of infrared radiation from the cube. The difference is easily felt by placing the back of the hand a few centimetres from the surfaces, but take care that students do not actually touch the surface. Ask a teaching assistant to manage the queue waiting to test out the Leslie's cube while you move on.

Plenaries

Choosing the right colour – Give students a series of simple scenarios, such as 'What colour cup should you use to keep orange juice cold on a hot day?' and ask them to give reasons. Make sure that the reasons are based on the ideas of absorption and emission. *(5 minutes)*

Without words – Ask students to draw illustrations showing why black surfaces are better emitters and absorbers, without using any words on the diagrams. *(10 minutes)*

Practical support

Testing radiation from different surfaces

Equipment and materials required

Kettles or another way of heating water. For each group: drinks cans (or two beakers or boiling tubes) one painted silver and the other matt black, two thermometers (to 0.5 °C), aluminium foil (if beakers are used), stop clock and a measuring cylinder.

Details

The students should add the same volume of hot water to each of the cans and record the temperature every 30 seconds for 5 to 10 minutes. Higher starting temperatures give greater temperature drops in reasonable times, but students will need to be extra careful with hot water. If you use beakers or boiling tubes then you should add foil lids to reduce evaporation.

Absorption tests

Equipment and materials required

Two metal plates (one should have a matt black surface and the other be left shiny and metallic), wax, two small coins and a radiant heater.

Details

Fix the coins onto the plates in advance as shown in the diagram. Place the radiant heater in the middle of the plates and turn on. While the plates are heating you should explain what is happening in terms of absorption and reflection of the energy.

Further teaching suggestions

Leslie's cube

● The Leslie's cube was devised by Sir John Leslie to demonstrate the importance of surface colour on the radiation of energy. By using data-logging equipment, the experiment could be expanded to show that the dull black surface always radiates more energy than the silver one and that the amount of energy radiated depends on the temperature of the water in the cube.

Equipment and materials required

● Leslie's cube, data-logging equipment (including two infrared sensors and a temperature probe), kettle.

Details

● Set up the cube with two infrared sensors, one 5 cm from the matt black surface and another 5 cm from the silver one. Place a temperature probe into the container and add boiling water. (Take care!) Record the cooling of the container and the amount of energy radiated from the surfaces over a period of up to half an hour. Students could then analyse the results and reach conclusions about the relationships. If only one infrared probe is available, students could describe the relationship between the temperature and the amount of energy radiated by each surface separately; to save time record some data in advance for comparison.

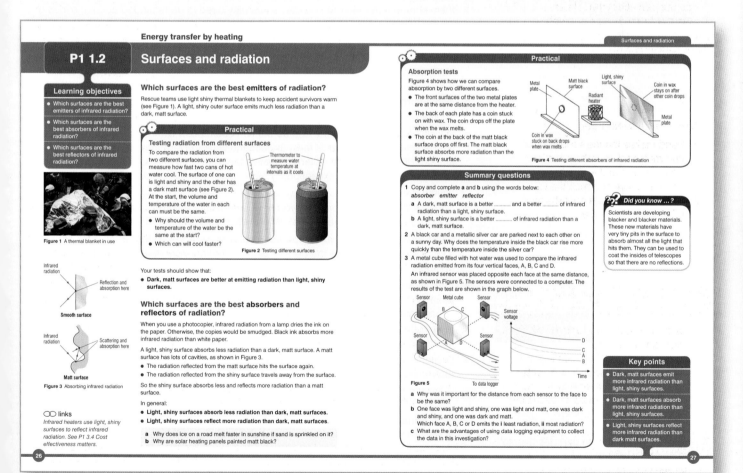

Summary answers

1 a absorber, emitter (absorber and emitter in any order)
  b reflector

2 The black surface absorbs more infrared radiation from the Sun than the silver surface.

3 a To make the test fair. The temperature recorded will differ at different distances from the cube.
  b i D   ii B
  c Greater accuracy, collects multiple sets of data at whatever time intervals you choose.

P1 1.3

States of matter

Learning objectives

Students should learn:

- that solids, liquids and gases have different properties
- that the arrangement of particles in solids, liquids and gases gives rise to their properties, including density and whether they are able to flow.

Learning outcomes

Most students should be able to:

- describe the physical characteristics of solids, liquids and gases
- describe the arrangement and movement of particles in solids, liquids and gases.

Support

- It can be quite time-consuming to draw diagrams of particles, so you may wish to produce a worksheet for students to add their own notes. Be aware that particle diagrams of gases and liquids are often too similarly drawn. For liquids, the particles should be touching with no patterns but gas particles should be very separate.

Extend

- You could go into more detail about the extra phase changes (sublimation) and the fourth state of matter: plasma. What is plasma and why is it different from a basic gas?

Specification link-up: Physics P1.1

- The use of kinetic theory to explain the different states of matter. *[P1.1.2 a)]*
- The particles of solids, liquids and gases have different amounts of energy. *[P1.1.2 b)]*

Lesson structure

Starters

State the facts – Support students by providing a diagram on which they have to label the five changes of state from solid to liquid to gas. Students should describe whether energy is taken into the substances or given out during these changes. A few students might be aware of sublimation [gas to solid directly]. *(5 minutes)*

Property match – Before they use the Student Book, give students some cards describing the properties of solids, liquids and gases. Ask students to match these with other cards describing some example properties including density, fluidity and compressibility. Extend students by challenging them to give explanations of these properties in terms of particle arrangement. *(10 minutes)*

Main

- Students will have looked at the three states of matter during KS3 and the majority of them should remember the basics. Some may need to be reminded about the idea of matter being composed of particles. The 'Modelling states of matter' demonstration is a simple way of doing this.

- The term 'particles' is used throughout the unit but, depending on the ability of students, you might want to talk about atoms and molecules (or ions) as *examples* of these particles.

- Demonstrate the changes of state of dry ice if you have some (see 'Further teaching suggestions').

- Density is tackled later in the course but you could push some students to calculate the density of materials or at least understand what the term means scientifically: the amount of mass in a 'unit' volume. Show a table of some example densities pointing out some materials with exceptionally high or low density (osmium 22.6 g/cm³ and helium 0.000 18 g/cm³).

- Show students some mercury if you have a container holding a few cubic centimetres, to demonstrate that some liquids can be very dense compared with some solids.

- Some students may ask about materials such as expanded polystyrene. This contains a lot of air, which reduces the density. Show some unexpanded polystyrene as a contrast.

- Animations about changes of state are fairly essential at this point in the lesson. Use them to show the behaviour of the particles as a change of state happens. Be careful to use an animation that shows that the particles in a solid are vibrating even when the temperature reaches 0 °C. Some simulations can allow the particles to reach absolute zero (−273 °C) and you could extend students by discussing this idea.

- Demonstrate the reverse change of state as well to show the particles slowing as they lose energy.

Plenaries

Particle behaviour – Students could act out the states of matter. Ask them to behave like particles in a solid [close together and just shaking], liquid [close together and milling around] and gas [zipping about far apart]. Think carefully about the layout of the room if you want to try this. *(5 minutes)*

Particle diagrams – Ask students to make large particle diagrams. Provide them with a lot of small circles to use as the particles (from a hole punch) and let them create a diagram representing the three states and the transition between them. Select the best diagram and display it. You could use this large diagram in future discussions about conduction, convection and evaporation. *(10 minutes)*

Practical support

Changing state

Equipment and materials required
For each group: Bunsen burner, tripod, heatproof mat, gauze, beaker (250 cm³), icy cold spoon or something similar. Optional: ice.

Details
Students could simply heat the water or start from a block of ice if you have a little more time. They need to observe the changes of state and think about the idea of energy being provided to cause the changes. Students should perform a simple risk assessment of the practical before starting. Make sure the glassware is borosilicate and heat carefully at the start if using ice.

Modelling states of matter
This could be a simple demonstration or you might prefer the students to take part, if you have time and enough marbles.

Equipment and materials required
A plastic tray, marbles, ping-pong balls or other small balls.

Details
Place a few balls in the tray and allow them to roll around. This is similar to a gas; the particles can move freely and are generally far apart. Almost fill the bottom layer of the tray; the particles can still move a bit but there are few gaps between them. This situation is similar to a liquid. Finally, fill the tray so that the particles cannot move; they are closely packed together in a manner similar to the particles in a solid. Extend students by discussing the reasons why this is not a good model. [The model is 2-D and there are no representations of the forces between the particles.]

P1 1.3 States of matter

Learning objectives
- How are solids, liquids and gases different?
- How are the particles in a solid, liquid and a gas arranged?
- Why is a gas much less dense than a solid or a liquid?

Everything around us is made of matter in one of three states – solid, liquid or gas. The table below summarises the main differences between the three **states of matter**.

	Flow	Shape	Volume	Density
Solid	no	fixed	fixed	much higher than a gas
Liquid	yes	fits container shape	fixed	much higher than a gas
Gas	yes	fills container	can be changed	low compared with a solid or liquid

a We can't see it and yet we can fill objects like balloons with it. What is it?
b When an ice cube melts, what happens to its shape?

Change of state K
A substance can change from one state to another, as shown in Figure 2. We can make these changes by heating or cooling the substance. For example,
- when water in a kettle boils, the water turns to steam. Steam, also called water vapour, is water in its gaseous state
- when solid carbon dioxide or 'dry ice' warms up, the solid turns into gas directly
- when steam touches a cold surface, the steam condenses and turns to water.

Figure 1 Spot the three states of matter

KEY
Heat →
Cool →

Sublimation · Condensation · Vaporisation or boiling
Melting
Solidifying or freezing

Figure 2 Change of state

c What change of state occurs when hailstones form?

Practical

Changing state
1 Heat some water in a beaker using a Bunsen burner, as shown in Figure 3. Notice that:
- steam or 'vapour' leaves the water surface before the water boils
- when the water boils, bubbles of vapour form inside the water and rise to the surface to release steam.
2 Switch the Bunsen burner off and hold a cold beaker or cold metal object above the boiling water. Observe condensation of steam from the boiling water on the cold object. Take care with boiling water.

Figure 3 Changing state

The kinetic theory of matter
Solids, liquids and gases consist of particles. Figure 4 shows the arrangement of the particles in a solid, a liquid and a gas. When the temperature of the substance is increased, the particles move faster.
- The particles in a solid are held next to each other in fixed positions. They vibrate about their fixed positions so the solid keeps its own shape.
- The particles in a liquid are in contact with each other. They move about at random. So a liquid doesn't have its own shape and it can flow.
- The particles in a gas move about at random much faster. They are, on average, much further apart from each other than in a liquid. So the density of a gas is much less than that of a solid or liquid.
- The particles in solids, liquids and gases have different amounts of energy. In general, the particles in a gas have more energy than those in a liquid, which have more energy than those in a solid.

Figure 4 The arrangement of particles in **a** a solid, **b** a liquid and **c** a gas

Did you know …?
Random means unpredictable. Lottery numbers are chosen at random.

Summary questions
1 Copy and complete **a** to **d** using the words below. Each word can be used more than once.
   gas   liquid   solid
   a A .... has a fixed shape and volume.
   b A .... has a fixed volume but no shape.
   c A .... and a .... can flow.
   d A .... does not have a fixed volume.
2 State the scientific word for each of the following changes.
   a A mist appears on the inside of a window in a bus full of people.
   b Steam is produced from the surface of the water in a pan when the water is heated before it boils.
   c Ice cubes taken from a freezer thaw out.
   d Water put into a freezer gradually turns to ice.
3 Describe the changes that take place in the movement and arrangement of the particles in an ice cube when the ice melts.

Key points
- Flow, shape, volume and density are the properties used to describe each state of matter.
- The particles in a solid are held next to each other in fixed positions.
- The particles in a liquid move about at random and are in contact with each other.
- The particles in a gas move about randomly and are much further apart than particles in a solid or liquid.

Further teaching suggestions

Dry ice
- It may be possible to find a local source of solid carbon dioxide for teacher demonstrations. This can be shown to sublime. You could demonstrate that the mass is reducing by placing a piece on a balance with tongs and noting the decrease in mass over a period of time.

Distillation
- You could show the changes of state from ice to liquid, water to gas and back to liquid water using a distillation apparatus. Start with crushed ice in the round bottomed flask and show the stages, explaining the changes of energy required.

Answers to in-text questions

a Gas.
b It loses its shape.
c Water changes from a liquid to a solid.

Summary answers

1 **a** solid
  b liquid
  c liquid, gas (liquid and gas in any order)
  d gas

2 **a** condensation
  b evaporation/vaporisation
  c melting
  d freezing

3 The particles start to move about each other at random and are no longer in fixed positions.

P1 1.4

Conduction

AQA

Specification link-up: Physics P1.1

- The transfer of energy by conduction … involves particles, and how this transfer takes place. [P1.1.3 a)]
- The rate at which an object transfers energy by heating depends on:
  - surface area and volume
  - the material from which the object is made
  - the nature of the surface with which the object is in contact. [P1.1.3 c)]

Learning objectives

Students should learn:

- that conduction is a process of energy transfer by heating
- that metals are good conductors because they have free electrons that carry energy
- that non-metal solids are generally poor conductors because they rely on atomic vibrations to carry energy.

Learning outcomes

Most students should be able to:

- state that metals are good conductors of energy
- list some poor conductors or insulators.

Some students should also be able to:

- explain why metals are good conductors of energy in terms of electron behaviour.

Lesson structure

Starters

The wooden spoon – Ask students for an explanation of why it is all right to leave a wooden spoon in a pan of soup when heating it, but not a metal spoon. If possible, ask them to draw diagrams of what they think the particles are doing inside the objects. You may want to provide some students with a diagram showing the basic particles in the structure. *(5 minutes)*

A heatproof mat – Is a heatproof mat *really* heatproof? Extend students by asking them to design a reliable experiment to find out just how heat-resistant the material is. You could revisit this idea later in the chapter when discussing U-values. Good ideas should include some system of recording the time for energy to pass through the mat and heat/melt something on the other side. Extend students by asking them to consider how to measure the temperature changes precisely. *(10 minutes)*

Main

- Carry out the 'testing rods' activity. Adding drawing pins attached to the end of the rods with petroleum jelly, so that they fall off when the jelly melts, gives a touch of drama and helps timing. Discuss the accuracy of timings, precision and validity ('How Science Works').

- If you tried the heat-proof mat starter, you could show how slowly the mat conducts, by heating a cube of ice with a Bunsen burner through a mat sitting on a tripod.

- The 'conduction/insulation' practical is a fairly simple concept but is quite fiddly to do successfully. Give students adequate time to set it up carefully and then get readings (5–10 minutes of cooling is required to notice a difference).

- Students should be encouraged to make accurate readings during the experiment and this would be an excellent time to introduce data logging as an alternative to watching a thermometer for a long time. After the practical, students should be able to tell you which material was the best conductor and which was the worst. This practical work gives another opportunity to cover aspects of 'How Science Works', e.g. the reliability of data collected, the nature of variables and experimental design.

- The poor conductivity of air can be shown by holding an ice cube (in tongs) alongside a Bunsen flame, where it melts only slowly, and then a few centimetres above the top of the flame.

- The concept of free electrons will be unfamiliar to many students. A visual approach with animation is ideal for introducing this concept. An analogy, such as students staying in their place (representing ions in a metal) and throwing objects to each other (representing electrons carrying energy), could be used with the right kind of group. After explaining this, students should be able to tell you what the electrons do to move energy from one end of a rod to the other.

- Conduction by lattice vibration again requires clear diagrams to picture this idea. An ionic lattice model (e.g. sodium chloride) can help a lot here. Describe how poor this method of energy transfer is compared with the free electron method. This should reinforce the key point about good and poor conductors.

Answers to in-text questions

a Plastic and wood are poor conductors, so the handle doesn't get hot.

b The material the rods are made from is the independent variable. The dependent variable is the time taken for the wax to melt.

c Felt.

d The starting temperature.

Support

- Compare the student results across groups. You could then provide a graph of the average results (do this 'live' with a spreadsheet if possible) and this will let the students concentrate on explaining the results and evaluating them.

Extend

- The insulation experiment could be expanded to investigate the effectiveness of different thicknesses of materials, e.g. are two layers of felt twice as good as one?

Plenaries

A model for conduction – Extend students by asking them to describe a physical analogy for lattice vibration, to give them a visual idea of what is going on. [They could come up with holding each other at arm's length and passing a shake along a line.] *(5 minutes)*

An electron story – To reinforce the correct use of scientific language including vibration, energy, transfer, diffuse, conductor, support students by asking them to describe their 'experience' as an electron in a metal rod being heated at one end. This use of imagination is often very helpful in cementing abstract ideas. *(10 minutes)*

Practical support

Testing sheets of material as insulators
Equipment and materials required
Kettles or another way of heating water. For each group: two containers (beakers or metal cans), two thermometers (graduated in 0.5 °C), sample materials (cotton wool, felt, paper, foam, etc.), two elastic bands, stop clock and a 100 cm³ measuring cylinder.

Details
It can be difficult to control this experiment because the materials are different thicknesses, and if the materials become wet, a lot of energy is lost through the process of evaporation. Make sure that students take care in lagging the containers and that the containers are on an insulated base, otherwise much of the energy is conducted into the bench. When carrying out practicals using cans of water, it is essential to use covers because heat loss by energy transfer evaporation is significant and will affect the results. The experiment works best with hotter water, but this increases the hazards.

Safety: Take care as some objects remain hot for a considerable time.

Conducting rods
Equipment and materials required
As a demonstration: set of metal rods with wax/petroleum jelly on one end (aluminium, copper, steel, brass and possibly glass), drawing pins, Bunsen burner, tripod, heatproof mat, eye protection.

Details
A specialised conduction demonstration apparatus works better than simple rods. Some metal strips have liquid crystal strips mounted on them and can be placed in hot water; this gives a much more visual demonstration and students can see the temperature gradient through the metals.

Aluminium's melting point is lower than the temperature of a blue Bunsen flame, so be careful not to melt the aluminium rod. A glass rod can be heated strongly until the glass is red hot and yet the other end is still cool, demonstrating just how poor a conductor it is.

Safety: Take care as some objects remain hot for a considerable time.

Energy transfer by heating

| P1 1.4 | Conduction |

Conduction

Learning objectives
- What materials make the best conductors?
- What materials make the best insulators?
- Why are metals good conductors?
- Why are non-metals poor conductors?

When you have a barbecue, you need to know which materials are good **conductors** and which are good **insulators**. If you can't remember, you are likely to burn your fingers!

Testing rods of different materials as conductors
The rods need to be the same width and length for a fair test. Each rod is coated with a thin layer of wax near one end. The uncoated ends are then heated together.

Look at Figure 2. The wax melts fastest on the rod that conducts best.

Figure 2 Comparing conductors

- Metals conduct energy better than non-metals.
- Copper is a better conductor than steel.
- Wood conducts better than glass.

a Why do steel pans have handles made of plastic or wood?
b Name the independent and the dependent variables investigated in Figure 2.

Figure 1 At a barbecue – the steel cooking utensils have wooden or plastic handles

links
For more information on independent and dependent variables, look back at H3 Starting an investigation.

Practical
Testing sheets of materials as insulators
Use different materials to insulate identical cans (or beakers) of hot water. The volume of water and its temperature at the start should be the same.

Use a thermometer to measure the water temperature after a fixed time. The results should tell you which insulator was best.

The table below gives the results of comparing two different materials using the method explained in the practical.

Material	Starting temperature (°C)	Temperature after 300 s (°C)
paper	40	32
felt	40	36

c Which material, felt or paper, was the best insulator?
d Which variable shown in the table was controlled to make this a fair test?

Conduction in metals
Metals contain lots of **free electrons**. These electrons move about at random inside the metal and hold the positive metal ions together. They collide with each other and with the positive ions. (Ions are charged particles.)

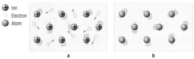

⊕ Ion
○ Electron
● Atom

Figure 4 Energy transfer in a a metal, b a non-metal

When a metal rod is heated at one end, the free electrons at the hot end gain kinetic energy and move faster.
- These electrons **diffuse** (i.e. spread out) and collide with other free electrons and ions in the cooler parts of the metal.
- As a result, they transfer kinetic energy to these electrons and ions.

So energy is transferred from the hot end of the rod to the colder end.

In a non-metallic solid, all the electrons are held in the atoms. Energy transfer only takes place because the atoms vibrate and shake each other. This is much less effective than energy transfer by free electrons. This is why metals are much better conductors than non-metals.

Figure 3 Insulating a loft. The air trapped between fibres make fibreglass a good insulator.

?? Did you know ...?
Materials like wool and fibreglass are good insulators. This is because they contain air trapped between the fibres. Trapped air is a good insulator. We use materials like fibreglass for loft insulation and for lagging water pipes.

Summary questions
1 Copy and complete a to c using the words below:
fibreglass plastic steel wood
a A material called .... is used to insulate a house loft.
b The handle of a frying pan is made of .... or ....
c A radiator in a central heating system is made from ....
2 a Choose a material you would use to line a pair of winter boots. Explain your choice of material.
b How could you carry out a test on three different lining materials?
3 Explain why metals are good conductors of energy.

Key points
- Metals are the best conductors of energy.
- Materials such as wool and fibreglass are the best insulators.
- Conduction of energy in a metal is due mainly to free electrons transferring energy inside the metal.
- Non-metals are poor conductors because they do not contain free electrons.

Further teaching suggestions

Feeling colder
- Why do blocks of cold metal feel colder than blocks of cold wood? Give students some blocks straight from the freezer and ask them to explain the difference. [The answer lies in the rate that energy can leave your hand and enter the material; the faster this happens, the colder the block will feel.]

Home insulation
- List the materials used for insulation in your own home and where they are found. Why are these materials chosen? Which materials are designed to be good conductors and where are these found?

Summary answers

1 a fibreglass
  b wood, plastic (wood and plastic in any order)
  c steel

2 a Felt or synthetic fur could be used, because they are good insulators.
  b Student's plan. Look for design of a fair test.

3 The free electrons that gain kinetic energy diffuse through the metal quickly, passing on energy to other electrons and ions in the metal.

P1 1.5

Convection

Learning objectives

Students should learn:

- that convection currents are the movement of particles in fluids
- how convection currents carry energy in fluids
- how expansion and changes in density cause convection currents.

Learning outcomes

Most students should be able to:

- give examples of where convection currents occur
- describe the process of convection in terms of particle movement in liquids and gases, and explain why convection cannot happen in solids.

Some students should also be able to:

- give a detailed description of convection in terms of particle movement, expansion and density changes.

Support

- Students could use worksheets with the processes in a convection current mixed up. They could cut these up and stick them in their books in the correct sequence.

Extend

- Students should describe the change in the particle behaviour during convection in detail. They should make links between increased temperature and the increase in the kinetic energy of the particles causing the spacing to increase slightly. This should include the speeding up of particles in a gas as the gas is heated.

AQA **Specification link-up: Physics P1.1**

- The transfer of energy by … convection … involves particles, and how this transfer takes place. *[P1.1.3 a)]*
- The rate at which an object transfers energy by heating depends on:
  - surface area and volume
  - the material from which the object is made
  - the nature of the surface with which the object is in contact. *[P1.1.3 c)]*

Lesson structure

Starters

Heat haze – Search an internet image bank for photographs or a video clip of heat haze above a road and ask students to describe what they think is happening. Link this back to the black road absorbing a lot of infrared radiation and becoming very hot. You may be able to demonstrate the effect by heating a metal sheet above a Bunsen burner if the lighting conditions are right in your laboratory. Try it out first to avoid disappointment. *(5 minutes)*

Density demonstration – Demonstrate the expansion of a material when heated (mercury in a thermometer, a ball and chain, etc.) and ask students to explain what is happening in terms of particle behaviour. This should link in closely with the previous lessons. Make sure that students do not think that the particles themselves are expanding! Support students by asking them to draw clear diagrams showing the difference and check that the 'spaces' between the particles are changing but not the particles themselves. *(10 minutes)*

Main

- Emphasise the fact that a **fluid** is a substance where the *particles* can move past each other, so both gases and liquids are fluid. Because gases have completely separated particles, these can flow faster than liquids.

- Demonstrating the chimney effect with the apparatus shown in the Student Book is very helpful. Brown corrugated card produces a lot of fine smoke when it is stubbed out, and the students can see the flow of smoke down the first chimney and up the second. Point out to students that using a fire with a chimney is the cause of some draughts in houses.

- If you have convection heaters, you could demonstrate (or let students have a go at making) spirals of paper hung on string. These move due to the current above the heater. Don't leave big ones up because they could set off motion-sensitive alarms in the middle of the night!

- Convection currents in water can be shown using a small potassium permanganate crystal placed carefully in the bottom of a large beaker, and heating gently using a Bunsen burner directly beneath it; the larger the beaker, the better the effect. A glass convection loop is better than a beaker if available. See 'Practical support'.

- Students need to go through the stages that cause a convection current with emphasis on the use of the correct words at each stage. They could label a diagram or draw a flow chart.

- Make sure that they are using the terms 'expand' and 'contract' correctly before the plenary. A common misconception is that expansion is caused by the particles themselves expanding. This should be addressed directly when explaining convection.

Plenaries

Convection loops – Test understanding of convection, conduction and radiation with a question loop game. Possible questions could include: what happens when a gas is heated? [it expands]; what happens to the particles in the gas as it heats up? [they move further apart]; what happens to the density? [it decreases]; why does the gas rise upwards? [because it is less dense] and so on until the complete convection cycle is covered. *(5 minutes)*

The sea by night – Extend students by asking them to apply the knowledge gained here in similar situations using the ideas from this lesson; students could draw a diagram and give an explanation about why there is a breeze from the land to the sea in the evening at the coast. The diagram should include energy being transferred from the sea causing warming of the air above it. They should then use convection currents to explain the movement of the air. *(10 minutes)*

Practical support

Chimney effect

The chimney-effect apparatus is fairly standard, but could be improvised if necessary. Use smouldering cardboard or matches to produce smoke. The container must have a glass or Perspex front, so that air cannot enter from this route.

Demonstrating convection in liquids

The potassium manganate (VII) can be placed at the bottom of the beaker by the following method so that it does not dissolve as it falls.

Equipment and materials required

Large (100 cm^3) beaker or glass convection loop, Bunsen burner, tripod, gauze, mat, tweezers, glass tube and small crystal of potassium manganate(VII).

Details

Fill the beaker with water. Place your thumb over the end of a glass tube and push it into the beaker so that it touches the bottom and doesn't let any water in. Take your thumb off and, hopefully, the tube will remain empty. Finally drop the crystal down the tube using forceps and remove the tube. Then you should get a perfectly placed crystal.

With a glass convection loop, the crystal should be placed at the top and the tube heated at the bottom. Don't try to get it in the bottom corner.

Safety: CLEAPSS Hazcard 81 Potassium manganate(VII) – harmful and oxidising. Its crystals will stain hands and clothing. Handle crystals with tweezers.

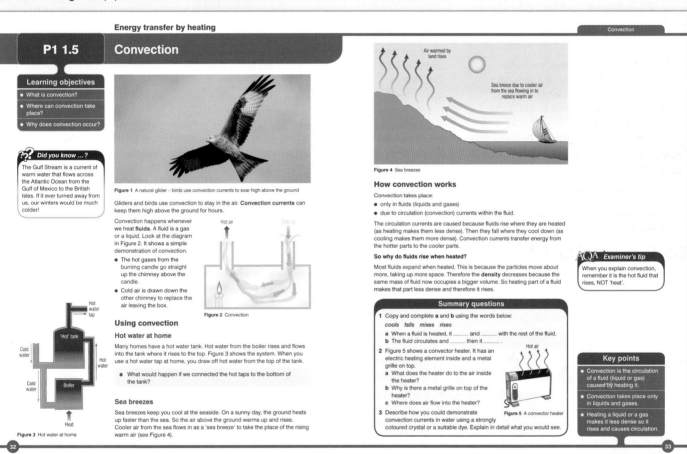

Further teaching suggestions

Convection in a boiling tube

- Demonstrate conduction and convection in water. Hold a small ice cube at the bottom of a boiling tube with a bit of metal gauze and three-quarters fill the tube with water. Heat the water in the middle of the tube with a Bunsen burner; the water at the top will boil while the ice remains frozen. Ask students to explain this in terms of conduction and convection.

Galilean thermometer

- The Galilean thermometer relies on changes of density in liquids and solids to show temperature. Demonstrate one and ask students to explain how it works.

Convection and climates

- Convection currents are very important in the oceans and dramatically affect the weather of the British Isles. Compare London's winter to Moscow's. Students could research the effect of the Gulf Stream and what the weather would be like without it. As an alternative, they could find out about El Niño.

Answers to in-text questions

a The water from the taps would be cold.

Summary answers

1 **a** rises, mixes   **b** cools, falls

2 **a** It heats it and makes it rise.
  b The hot air passes through the grille into the room.
  c Cold air flows into the heater at the bottom.

3 Drop the crystal into a beaker of water through a tube. Heat gently under one corner. The colour rises above point of heating and travels across the top and falls at opposite side of beaker (where density of cooler water is greater). The colour then travels across the bottom of the beaker to replace lower density warmer water that rises above the Bunsen flame.

P1 1.6

Evaporation and condensation

Learning objectives

Students should learn:

- that evaporation is the change of state from a liquid into a gas and condensation is the change of state from a gas into a liquid
- that the rate of evaporation is increased by increasing:
  - the temperature of the liquid
  - the surface area of the liquid
  - the flow of gas above the liquid's surface.
- that during evaporation, the most energetic particles escape reducing the average kinetic energy of the remaining particles and so reducing the temperature.

Learning outcomes

Most students should be able to:

- state the factors that increase the rate of evaporation
- describe the processes of evaporation and the process of condensation in terms of particle behaviour.

Some students should also be able to:

- explain in detail how evaporation has a cooling effect on a liquid.

Support

- Put marks on the watch glasses (or Petri dishes) so that students put in the correct amount of liquid. These marks correspond to selected surface areas, so that the students can avoid doing the calculations. You could then provide a simple table for them to fill in that will allow the plotting of a graph. Alternatively, a qualitative result could be expected.

Extend

- Students could look at the role of evaporation in cooling of humans. Let them find out about why humans sweat and how this helps us cool down. They could also look at the effect of cooling by radiation and why blood is moved to the surface layers. What do furry animals do to cool?

AQA Specification link-up: Physics P1.1

- The transfer of energy by … evaporation and condensation involves particles, and how this transfer takes place. *[P1.1.3 a)]*
- The factors that affect the rate of evaporation and condensation. *[P1.1.3 b)]*

Lesson structure

Starters

Cool demonstration – If you have some alcohol-based hand cleaning gel you could ask a student coat their hands and then use a cool air blower (or just get them to blow) to cause the gel to evaporate. This can have a significant cooling effect on the skin. You might also be able to obtain a cooling spray from the PE department to demonstrate. *(5 minutes)*

Spill – Spill some ethanol onto a non-absorbent surface. Students should watch while it rapidly evaporates. Ask them what they think is happening. Extend students by asking them to draw particle diagrams explaining what is happening. Open the bottle again and ask them why it is not evaporating as quickly even though the ethanol is at the same temperature. [There is a much smaller surface area.] *(10 minutes)*

Main

- An important concept the students need to grasp is that a liquid will evaporate even when it is well below its boiling point. The liquid does not need to be 'hot' to evaporate because some of the particles will have significantly more energy than others. Students will be aware of evaporation but most will not connect it with energy transfer or the particle model.

- Ensure that students are aware that temperature is related to the average kinetic energy of the particles. The higher the temperature, the greater the average kinetic energy the particles have. There will still be some slower particles when the temperature increases but there will be more 'fast' particles.

- Studenst may have difficulty in understanding the cooling effect of evaporation, so take some time describing how the particles with the most energy escape first. This means that the average (mean) energy of the particles decreases, and this means that the temperature falls.

- It is always worth showing the cooling effect of evaporation as detailed in the Student Book. This can be simply achieved by using the 'cool demonstration' starter or simply dipping your finger in ethanol and blowing on it. The ethanol will evaporate quickly and have a significant cooling effect on the surface of your finger. A more detailed example is discussed in 'Practical support'.

- If you have time then the 'Investigating evaporation' practical is well worth trying out (see 'Practical support'). It is simple but can give good results for analysis. It allows students to develop mathematical skills such as calculating surface area, finding change in mass and plotting of graphs with fairly awkward numbers (small masses and areas).

Plenaries

Tropical sweats – Search out some relative humidity figures for different countries. Show students that some places have more water in the air than others and ask them to explain what this will feel like. They should be able to link this with the experiment from earlier and the movement of air. *(5 minutes)*

Evaporation analysis – Provide data for the evaporation of different liquids. Students plot this on the same set of axes and notice that some liquids evaporate more quickly than others for the same temperature and surface area. Can they explain this? Extend students by asking them to develop ideas about the 'size' (mass) of the molecules involved; once this is achieved give them some data about the mass of the particles for them to confirm their ideas. *(10 minutes)*

Practical support

Demonstrating cooling by evaporation

This demonstration shows the cooling effect of evaporation. Enough energy is removed by evaporation, so that water freezes.

Equipment and materials required

Fume cupboard, a small (100 cm³) glass beaker, block of wood, cold water, ethoxyethane (ether) – extremely flammable/harmful.

Details

The experiment must be carried out in a working fume cupboard to make sure that there is a good air flow to cause rapid evaporation and to remove the ether fumes. Wet the wooden block and base of the beaker so that there is a thin 'puddle' between them. Half fill the beaker with ether and rest it on the block inside the fume cupboard. The ether should evaporate and, in doing so, cool the water so much that it freezes. This is a good opportunity to discuss why a good flow of air is required. The water will take a few minutes to freeze, so come back to it later in the lesson.

Safety: CLEAPSS Hazcard 42 Ethoxyethane (ether) – extremely flammable and harmful. Wear eye protection. Make sure there are no naked flames in the same room.

Investigating evaporation

Students could investigate the rate of evaporation using ethanol and watch glasses.

Equipment and materials required

Each group will require a range of watch glasses, ethanol – highly flammable/harmful, stop clock, top-pan balance, ruler.

Details

Students pour some ethanol onto a small watch glass and measure the diameter. They then measure the mass and allow the ethanol to evaporate for a set time (two minutes should be enough if a precise balance is used). They measure the mass again after the time has expired and calculate the mass loss by evaporation. During the two minutes they should calculate the surface area of the ethanol.

Repeat with other surface areas (using the different watch glasses to help). Once the results are collected, students could compare the amount of evaporation that has taken place with the surface area to determine a pattern.

Safety: CLEAPSS Hazcard 40A Ethanol – extremely flammable and harmful. Make sure there are no naked flames in the same room.

Energy transfer by heating

P1 1.6 — Evaporation and condensation ⓚ

Learning objectives

- What is evaporation?
- What is condensation?
- How does evaporation cause cooling?
- What factors affect the rate of evaporation from a liquid?
- What factors affect the rate of condensation on a surface?

Drying off

If you hang wet clothes on a washing line in fine weather, they will gradually dry off. The water in the wet clothes **evaporates**. You can observe evaporation of water if you leave a saucer of water in a room. The water in the saucer gradually disappears. Water molecules escape from the surface of the water and enter the air in the room.

In a well-ventilated room, the water molecules in the air are not likely to re-enter the liquid. They continue to leave the liquid until all the water has evaporated.

Molecule

Liquid

Figure 1 Water molecules escaping from a liquid

Condensation

In a steamy bathroom, a mirror is often covered by a film of water. There are lots of water molecules in the air. Some of them hit the mirror, cool down and stay there. We say water vapour in the air **condenses** on the mirror.

a Why does opening a window in a steamy room clear the condensation?

Cooling by evaporation

If you have an injection, the doctor or nurse might 'numb' your skin by dabbing it with a liquid that easily evaporates. As the liquid evaporates, your skin becomes too cold to feel any pain.

Figure 2 Condensation

Vapour

Fast moving molecule escaping

Forces of attraction between molecules in the liquid

Liquid

Figure 3 Explanation of cooling by evaporation

Demonstration

Cooling by evaporation

Watch your teacher carry out this experiment in a fume cupboard.

- Why is ether used in this experiment?

Fume cupboard

1 A stream of air bubbles through the ether. This liquid vaporises easily

2 The stream of air carries ether vapour out of the beaker. For safety the experiment is done in a fume cupboard as ether is very flammable

3 As ether evaporates, it takes energy from its surroundings. The water between the beaker and the wood freezes

Figure 4 A demonstration of cooling by evaporation

Figure 3 explains why evaporation causes this cooling effect.

- Weak attractive forces exist between the molecules in the liquid.
- The faster molecules, which have more kinetic energy, break away from the attraction of the other molecules and escape from the liquid.
- After they leave, the liquid is cooler because the average kinetic energy of the remaining molecules in the liquid has decreased.

Factors affecting the rate of evaporation ⓚ

Clothes dry faster on a washing line:

- if each item of wet clothing is spread out when it is hung on the line. This increases the area of the wet clothing that is in contact with dry air.
- if the washing line is in sunlight. Wet clothes dry faster the warmer they are.
- if there is a breeze to take away the molecules that escape from the water in the wet clothes.

The example above shows that the rate of evaporation from a liquid is increased by:

- increasing the surface area of the liquid
- increasing the temperature of the liquid
- creating a draught of air across the liquid's surface.

Factors affecting the rate of condensation

In a steamy kitchen, water can often be seen trickling down a window pane. The glass pane is a cold surface so water vapour condenses on it. The air in the room is moist or 'humid'. The bigger the area of the window pane, or the colder it is, the greater the rate of condensation. This example shows that the rate of condensation of a vapour on a surface is increased by:

- increasing the surface area
- reducing the surface temperature.

b Why does washing on a line take longer to dry on a damp day?

Summary questions

1 Copy and complete **a** to **c** using the words below. Each word can be used more than once.

condenses   cools   evaporates

a A liquid .... when its molecules escape into the surrounding air.
b When water .... on glass, water molecules in the air form a liquid on the glass.
c When a liquid ...., it loses its faster-moving molecules and it ....

2 Why do the windows on a bus become misty when there are lots of people on the bus?

3 Explain the following statements.
a Wet clothes on a washing line dry faster on a hot day than on a cold day.
b A person wearing wet clothes on a cold windy day is likely to feel much colder than someone wearing dry clothes.

⁇ Did you know ...?

Air conditioning

An **air conditioning** unit in a room transfers energy from inside the room to the outside. The unit contains a 'coolant' liquid that easily evaporates. The coolant is pumped round a sealed circuit of pipes that go through the unit and the outside.

- The liquid coolant evaporates in the pipes in the room and cools the room.
- The evaporated coolant condenses in the pipes outside and transfers energy to the surroundings.

Figure 5 An air-conditioning unit

Key points

- Evaporation is when a liquid turns into a gas.
- Condensation is when a gas turns into a liquid.
- Cooling by evaporation of a liquid is due to the faster-moving molecules escaping from the liquid.
- Evaporation can be increased by increasing the surface area of the liquid, by increasing the liquid's temperature, or by creating a draught of air across the liquid's surface.
- Condensation on a surface can be increased by increasing the area of the surface or reducing the temperature of the surface.

34

35

Further teaching suggestions

Investigative skills

- Students could plot a graph of the results of the 'Investigating evaporation' practical and reach a conclusion about the results. This could include sharing of results to verify reliability.

Answers to in-text questions

a The molecules in the condensed water can escape into the air and then escape from the room through the window.
b There are lots of water molecules in the air on a damp day and many of them can condense on the clothing.

Summary answers

1 **a** evaporates
   b condenses
   c evaporates, cools

2 The air in the room becomes damp as everyone breathes out water vapour. The water vapour condenses on the inside of the windows.

3 **a** Water evaporates faster from the wet clothes on a hot day than on a cold day because they are warmer.
   b Evaporation of water from the wet clothes on a windy day makes the clothes cooler which makes the wearer colder than someone wearing dry clothes.

P1 1.7

Energy transfer by design

Learning objectives

Students should learn:

- the factors that affect the rate of energy transfer
- ways of controlling the flow of energy
- how we can reduce or increase the rate of energy transfer in a variety of situations
- how to plan an investigation into energy transfer.

Learning outcomes

Most students should be able to:

- investigate factors that affect the rate of energy transfer.

Some students should also be able to:

- explain in detail how the design of a vacuum flask reduces the rate of energy transfer.

AQA Specification link-up: Physics P1.1

- The rate at which an object transfers energy by heating depends on:
  - surface area and volume
  - the material from which the object is made
  - the nature of the surface with which the object is in contact. *[P1.1.3 c)]*
- The bigger the temperature difference between an object and its surroundings, the faster the rate at which energy is transferred by heating. *[P1.1.3 d)]*
- Evaluate the design of everyday appliances that transfer energy by heating … *[P1.1]*

  Controlled Assessment: P4.3 Collect primary and secondary data. *[P4.3.2 a)]*

Lesson structure

Starters

Keeping warm – How could you keep a cup of tea warm? Students should come up with some ideas. They should be able to think of ways of reducing the rate of conduction [change the material of the cup], convection and evaporation [a lid] and radiation [have a white or silver cup]. You might have a travel mug available to show that this had already been designed to keep drinks warm. Extend students by asking them to evaluate each other's designs and move on to consider the cost or practicality of the measures. *(5 minutes)*

Cooling down – How can a substance be cooled quickly? This is the opposite of the above task. Can students design a really good way of cooling by using their knowledge from the last few lessons? *(10 minutes)*

Main

- With students watching, fill a glass beaker and a vacuum flask with the same volume of boiling water at the start of the lesson for later use.
- If a radiator from a small refrigerator is available, this makes an excellent prop to discuss how to design an object to transfer energy quickly. Emphasise the way the surface area is maximised to allow air to flow and transfer energy.
- Discuss how a cup of tea can be cooled by blowing over it, and describe how the energy escapes the tea.
- Students could investigate the difference in cooling for objects with a large surface area and those with a small surface area, as described in 'Practical support'. You could leave this experiment running while you move on to the vacuum flask demonstration. Other students could look at different initial temperatures. All investigative aspects of 'How Science Works' could be covered here.
- Some students will struggle in understanding that the larger beaker has a smaller surface area to volume ratio. Cubic containers may help the students, if some are available.
- Show some vacuum flasks in various states of construction (without the silvering) and explain their features. It is important to emphasise that there is no air between the glass walls. Show students the point where the air has been removed before sealing.
- Show students the difference in temperature of the water in the cup and in the flask to illustrate how good the flask is at keeping water hot. Check that students can describe what each feature of the flask does to prevent energy transfer. Reinforce to students that vacuum flasks also keep cold things cold.

Answers to in-text questions

a To increase the rate of energy transfer by radiation.

b It increases.

c The plastic case, the screw cap lid, the plastic support spring, the sponge pads. The rate at which energy was transferred away from the glass container would increase.

Support

- Work on gaining quantitative results in the practical task. Students should be given containers that are clearly large, medium and small and this will produce a simple pattern.

Extend

- Extend students by asking them to calculate the ratio of surface area to volume for the containers. This will involve measuring the diameter and height of any beaker and then performing the calculations for surface area and volume.

Plenaries

Warming up the lab – Support students by asking them to list or design improvements to reduce the rate of transfer from the laboratory. This will allow you to evaluate their understanding of radiation, conduction, convection and evaporation. They can prioritise these improvements. This links in nicely with the next lesson. *(5 minutes)*

Explorer pack – Students could list and explain the purpose of the clothing they would need to take on a range of scenarios during their exploration of the world. They will be visiting Antarctica, the Sahara, the Amazonian jungle and climbing Mount Everest. Not a bad day out! *(10 minutes)*

Practical support

Investigating the rate of energy transfer

Equipment and materials required

Large (500 cm³) and small (250 cm³) glass beakers, data loggers, temperature sensors, thermometers, Bunsen burners, heatproof mats and tripods, gauzes, aluminium foil for lids, eye protection.

Details

Fill the beakers with hot water and then boil the water with the Bunsen burners to make sure that both beakers start at the same temperature. Turn off the Bunsen burners, carefully remove hot beakers and stand on heatproof mat. Add a foil lid and thermometer and monitor the cooling for 10 minutes. The smaller beaker should cool substantially more than the larger one. These ideas can lead to a more complete investigation of the relationship between surface area and cooling.

Students could then investigate if the temperature difference between the water and its surroundings affects its rate of cooling.

Safety: Wear eye protection. Take care with boiling water.

Demonstrating the effectiveness of a vacuum flask

Equipment and materials required

Vacuum flask, kettle, similarly-sized beaker with lid, two thermometers.

Details

Fill the flask and beaker with the same volume of boiling water. Put the lid on the flask and allow the containers to cool for as long as possible during the lesson. The flask will keep the water very hot, usually above 80 °C, while the water in the beaker will be quite cool. For an even greater difference leave the beaker on a conductive surface.

Safety: Take care with boiling water. Do not drop thermometer into the glass vacuum flask.

P1 1.7 — Energy transfer by design

Learning objectives

- What design factors affect the rate at which a hot object transfers energy?
- What can we do to control the rate of energy transfer to or from an object?

Figure 1 A car radiator

Figure 2 Motorcycle engine fins

Did you know ...?

Some electronic components get warm when they are working, but if they become too hot they stop working. Such components are often fixed to a metal plate to keep them cool. The metal plate increases the effective surface area of the component. We call the metal plate a **heat sink**.

Figure 3 A heat sink in a computer

How Science Works

Cooling by design

Lots of things can go wrong if we don't control energy transfer. For example, a car engine that overheats can go up in flames.

- The cooling system of a car engine transfers energy from the engine to a radiator. The radiator is shaped so it has a large surface area. This increases the rate of energy transfer through convection in the air and through radiation.
- A motorcycle engine is shaped with **fins** on its outside surface. The fins increase the surface area of the engine in contact with air so the engine transfers energy to its surroundings faster than if it had no fins.
- Most cars also have a cooling fan that switches on when the engine is too hot. This increases the flow of air over the surface of the radiator.

a Why do car radiators have a large surface area?
b What happens to the rate of energy transfer when the cooling fan switches on?

The vacuum flask

If you are outdoors in cold weather, a hot drink from a vacuum flask keeps you warm. In the summer the same vacuum flask keeps your drinks cold.

In Figure 4, the liquid you drink is in the double-walled glass container.

- The vacuum between the two walls of the container cuts out energy transfer by conduction and convection between the walls.
- Glass is a poor conductor so there is little energy transfer by conduction through the glass.
- The glass surfaces are silvery to reduce radiation from the outer wall.
- The spring supporting the double-walled container is made of plastic which is a good insulator.
- The plastic cap stops cooling by evaporation as it stops vapour loss from the flask. In addition, energy transfer by conduction is cut down because the cap is made from plastic.

So why does the liquid in the flask eventually cool down?

The above features cut down but do not totally stop the transfer of energy from the liquid. Energy transfer occurs at a very low rate due to radiation from the silvery glass surface and conduction through the cap, spring and glass walls. The liquid transfers energy slowly to its surroundings so it eventually cools.

c List the other parts of the flask that are good insulators. What would happen if they weren't good insulators?

Plastic cap
Double-walled glass (or plastic) container
Plastic protective cover
Hot or cold liquid
Sponge pad (for protection)
Inside surfaces silvered to stop radiation
Vacuum prevents conduction and convection
Plastic spring for support

Figure 4 A vacuum flask

Factors affecting the rate of energy transfer

The bigger the **temperature difference** between an object and its surroundings, the faster the rate at which energy is transferred. In addition, the above examples show that the rate at which an object transfers energy depends on its design. The design factors that matter are:

- the materials the object is in contact with
- the object's shape
- the object's surface area.

In addition, the object's mass and the material it is made from are important. That is because they affect how quickly its temperature changes (and therefore the rate of transfer of energy to or from it) when it loses or gains energy.

How Science Works

Foxy survivors

A desert fox has much larger ears than an arctic fox. Blood flowing through the ears transfers energy from inside the body to the surface of the ears. Big ears have a much larger surface area than little ears so they transfer energy to the surroundings more quickly than little ears.

- A desert fox has big ears so it keeps cool by transferring energy quickly to its surroundings.
- An arctic fox has little ears so it transfers energy more slowly to its surroundings. This helps keep it warm.

Summary questions

1 Hot water is pumped through a radiator like the one in Figure 6. Copy and complete a to c using the words below:

conduction   radiation   convection

a Energy transfer through the walls of the radiator is due to ....
b Hot air in contact with the radiator causes energy transfer to the room by ....
c Energy transfer to the room takes place directly due to ....

Figure 6 A central heating radiator

2 An electronic component in a computer is attached to a heat sink.
a i Explain why the heat sink is necessary.
  ii Why is a metal plate used as the heat sink?
b Plan a test to show that double glazing is more effective at preventing energy transfer than single glazing.

3 Describe, in detail, how the design of a vacuum flask reduces the rate of energy transfer.

links

For more information on factors affecting energy transfer, see P1 1.8 Specific heat capacity.

Practical

Investigating the rate of energy transfer

You can plan an investigation using different beakers and hot water to find out what affects the rate of cooling.

- Write a question that you could investigate.
- Identify the independent, dependent and control variables in your investigation.

Figure 5 Fox ears a A desert fox b An arctic fox

Key points

- The rate of energy transferred to or from an object depends on:
  - the shape, size and type of material of the object
  - the materials the object is in contact with
  - the temperature difference between the object and its surroundings.

Further teaching suggestions

- Use temperature sensors and data logging software to capture more detail and save time plotting the graphs in the experiments.

Heat sinks

- Computer components become exceptionally hot and this energy needs to be removed. The microprocessor will have a cooling system and the case will be designed to allow energy to be dispersed by convection. You could open up the case of a PC and explain how the cooling systems work in terms of conduction, convection and radiation.

  Safety: Ensure the PC cannot be plugged into the mains. (Don't allow any access to a mains lead.)

Vacuum flask

- Sir James Dewar invented the vacuum flask (or Dewar jar). Students could research the history of this and his other important chemical discoveries.

Keeping warm

- Many small animals huddle together to keep warm, famously penguins do this en masse. Can students give a scientific explanation of this behaviour? This is based on the surface area to volume ideas.

Summary answers

1 a conduction
  b convection
  c radiation

2 a i To prevent the component overheating.
    ii Metal is a good conductor. The heat sink is plate-shaped to increase its surface area, so it transfers energy to the surrounding air as effectively as possible.
  b Plan must have a fair system that compares a single plate of glass to a pair of plates, ideally with a sealed air gap between.

3 Student's explanation to include the role played by the plastic cap, double-walled plastic container, silvered inside surfaces, vacuum layer.

P1 1.8 Specific heat capacity

Learning objectives

Students should learn:

- that the greater the mass of an object, the more energy is required to raise its temperature
- the material that an object is made of affects the amount of energy required to raise its temperature and each material has a specific heat capacity
- storage heaters rely on substances to store and transfer energy.

Learning outcomes

Most students should be able to:

- state that more energy is required to raise the temperature of objects with a greater mass
- explain that different materials of the same mass require different amounts of energy to raise their temperatures by the same amount.

Some students should also be able to:

- calculate the energy required to raise a known mass of material by a known temperature.

Answers to in-text questions

a 840 000 J
b The room would heat up quickly then become much cooler.

Support

- Support students with plenty of help with the calculation through this lesson. Provide a worksheet with plenty of examples showing how they are preformed. Make sure the questions do not require any rearrangement of the equation.

Extend

- Students could be extended by looking into why water has such a large specific heat capacity. They may find out about hydrogen bonding between molecules. Ask the student with the best explanation to report to the rest of the class.
- Students may be extended in the 'Hot metal' starter by thinking about the number of particles in the materials and even the energy of each particle.

AQA Specification link-up: Physics P1.1

- The specific heat capacity of a substance is the amount of energy required to change the temperature of one kilogram of the substance by one degree Celsius.
  $E = m \times c \times \theta$ [P1.1.4 d]
- Evaluate different materials according to their specific heat capacities. [P1.1]

  Controlled Assessment: P4.3 Collect primary and secondary data. [P4.3.1 a]

Lesson structure

Starters

Hot metal – Heat a smallish block of metal until it is clearly **very** hot using a Bunsen burner, gauze and tripod. Use tongs to drop it (carefully) into a litre of water and show the increase in temperature; a temperature sensor is easier to see than a thermometer. Why doesn't the water boil when the block was clearly far above 100 °C? Return to this question after the lesson. *(5 minutes)*

Boiling up – Demonstrate the heating of two different masses of water until they boil. You can do this in a kettle or with traditional heating apparatus. Ask students to come up with their own explanation as to why the smaller mass boils first. This demonstrates clearly that the mass of the material is significant.

Main

- You could start the lesson with the boiling demonstration. If you have a data logging apparatus then it is very helpful to record the temperate rise and show that the smaller mass of water has a more rapid rise in temperature.
- This topic contains some of the first mathematics that students will encounter in this part of the course and it is important to take students slowly through the process.
- Go through each of the factors that affect the temperature rise of an object as outlined in the Student Book. If you take each one in turn then students will gain a good understanding. They will easily understand that the more energy you provide, the more the temperature will rise. Then they will find it fairly obvious that the greater the mass of the object the less the temperate will rise. [This is because the energy is shared out between more particles.] Finally, the substance the material is made of is important; you could link this to the way the particles are held together.
- Now you can tackle the idea of specific heat capacity; this can confuse even able students, so describe it carefully. Basically, the specific heat capacity is the amount of energy needed to increase the temperate of 1 kg of a material by 1 °C. Give a few simple examples: it takes 4000 J to make the temperature of 1 kg of water rise by 1 °C. It takes 8000 J to make it rise by 2 °C.
- Discuss the amount of energy required to raise the temperature of 2 kg of water and 0.5 kg and so on. You could then discuss other materials; use aluminium as you will have a sample prop on hand.
- Students should perform a range of calculations based on the equation provided. The more they do, the simpler the idea becomes. You coud also use this as a planning exercise.

Plenaries

Hot water – It takes a lot of energy to heat a small mass of water. Why is water used in central heating systems? Students could come up with a range of reasons why it is chosen. [It is non-toxic, it is cheap, it can flow easily, it can carry a large amount of energy in a small volume.] *(5 minutes)*

Crossword – Students should complete a crossword based on the previous lessons of this chapter. This should form a summary of their learning about energy transfer. Provide differentiated clues to different groups of students: simple questions to support some students and somewhat more difficult ones to extend others. *(10 minutes)*

Practical support

Investigating heating
Equipment and materials required

Per group: low voltage power supply, aluminium heating block, heating element, thermometer, stop clock and beaker (size depends on the mass of the metal block).

Details

Aluminium blocks specifically designed for this experiment should be available; they have one large hole for the heating element to be placed in the top and another for the thermometer. Emphasise that it is important that the thermometer makes good contact with the metal to record an accurate temperature rise.

Students heat the block for a set time; five minutes is enough. They record the temperate each minute to see if the rise is consistent.

They then repeat the process with a beaker of water that has the same mass, so the beaker has to be able to hold sufficient volume. They should compare the two temperature rises and notice that the aluminium's temperature rise is greater.

Measuring the specific heat capacity of a metal
Equipment and materials required

Per group: low voltage power supply, aluminium heating block, heating element, thermometer, joulemeter, connecting leads and stop clock.

Details

In this experiment students need to heat the aluminium block again, but this time they need to know how much energy has been provided to perform the calculation. In their plan they should list their measurements in the correct order.

When students attempt to measure the specific heat capacity of aluminium, it is likely that their value will not match the stated one. They could discuss the reasons that their values are different; this is mainly due to energy transferred to the environment.

Safety: Wear eye protection. Warn students that items will stay hot for a long time after heating.

Energy transfer by heating

Specific heat capacity

P1 1.8 — Specific heat capacity ⓚ

Learning objectives

- How does the mass of a substance affect how quickly its temperature changes when it is heated?
- What else affects how quickly the temperature of a substance changes when it is heated?
- How do storage heaters work?

Joulemeter

To power unit

Heater   Thermometer

Aluminium block

Insulation

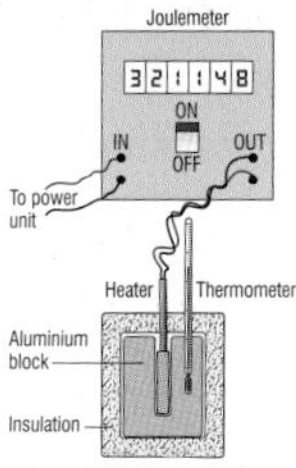

Figure 1 Heating an aluminium block

Did you know ...?

Coastal towns are usually cooler in summer and warmer in winter than towns far inland. This is because water has a very high specific heat capacity. Energy from the Sun (or lack of energy) affects the temperature of the sea much less than the land.

A car in strong sunlight can become very hot. A concrete block of equal **mass** would not become as hot. Metal heats up more easily than concrete. Investigations show that when a substance is heated, its temperature rise depends on:

- the amount of energy supplied to it
- the mass of the substance
- what the substance is.

Practical

Investigating heating

Figure 1 shows how we can use a low voltage electric heater to heat an aluminium block.

Energy is measured in units called joules (J).

Use the energy meter (or joulemeter) to measure the energy supplied to the block. Use the thermometer to measure its temperature rise.

Replace the block with an equal mass of water in a suitable container. Measure the temperature rise of the water when the same amount of energy is supplied to it by the heater.

Your results should show that aluminium heats up more than water.

The following results were obtained using two different amounts of water. They show that:

- 1600 J was used to heat 0.1 kg of water by 4 °C.
- 3200 J was used to heat 0.2 kg of water by 4 °C.

Using these results we can say that:

- 16 000 J of energy would have been needed to heat 1.0 kg of water by 4 °C.
- 4000 J of energy is needed to heat 1.0 kg of water by 1 °C.

More accurate measurements would give 4200 J per kg per °C for water. This is its **specific heat capacity**.

The specific heat capacity of a substance is the energy needed or energy transferred to 1 kg of the substance to raise its temperature by 1 °C.

The unit of specific heat capacity is the joule per kilogram per °C.

For a known change of temperature of a known mass of a substance:

$$E = m \times c \times \theta$$

Where:

E is the energy transferred in joules, J; m is the mass in kilograms, kg; c is the specific heat capacity, J/kg°C; θ is the temperature change in degrees Celsius, °C

To find the specific heat capacity you need to rearrange the above equation:

$$c = \frac{E}{m \times \theta}$$

a How much energy is needed to heat 5.0 kg of water from 20 °C to 60 °C?

Practical

Measuring the specific heat capacity of a metal

Use the arrangement shown in Figure 1 to heat a metal block of known mass. Here are some measurements using an aluminium block of mass 1.0 kg.

Starting temperature = 14 °C
Final temperature = 22 °C
Energy supplied = 7200 J

To find the specific heat capacity of aluminium, the measurements above give:

E = energy transferred = energy supplied = 7200 J
θ = temperature change = 22 °C − 14 °C = 8 °C

Inserting these values into the rearranged equation gives:

$$c = \frac{E}{m \times \theta} = \frac{7200\,J}{1.0\,kg \times 8 °C} = 900\,J/kg°C$$

The table below shows the values for some other substances.

Substance	water	oil	aluminium	iron	copper	lead	concrete
Specific heat capacity (joules per kg per °C)	4200	2100	900	390	490	130	850

Storage heaters

A storage heater uses electricity at night (off-peak) to heat special bricks or concrete blocks in the heater. Energy transfer from the bricks keeps the room warm. The bricks have a high specific heat capacity so they store lots of energy. They warm up slowly when the heater element is on and cool down slowly when it is off.

Electricity consumed at off-peak times is sometimes charged for at a cheaper rate, so storage heaters are designed to be cost effective.

b How would the temperature of the room change if the bricks cooled quickly?

Figure 2 A storage heater

Summary questions

1 A small bucket of water and a large bucket of water are left in strong sunlight. Which one warms up faster? Give a reason for your answer.

2 Use the information in the table above to answer this question.
 a Explain why a mass of lead heats up more quickly than an equal mass of aluminium.
 b Calculate the energy needed
  i to raise the temperature of 0.20 kg of aluminium from 15 °C to 40 °C.
  ii to raise the temperature of 0.40 kg of water from 15 °C to 40 °C.

3 State two ways in which a storage heater differs from a radiant heater.

Key points

- The greater the mass of an object, the more slowly its temperature increases when it is heated.
- The rate of temperature change of a substance when it is heated depends on:
  – the energy supplied to it
  – its mass
  – its specific heat capacity.
- Storage heaters use off-peak electricity to store energy in special bricks.

38

39

Further teaching suggestions

Data logging

- Use temperature sensors and data-logging software to capture more detail and save time plotting the graphs in the experiments.

More calculations

- Students could complete more example questions and calculations until they have perfected the technique.

Summary answers

1 The small bucket warms up faster because the mass of water in it is much less than in the large bucket.

2 a Lead has a lower specific heat capacity than aluminium. Less energy is needed by lead for a given temperature rise.
 b i 4500 J   ii 42 000 J

3 A storage heater contains bricks or concrete that are heated by the heater element. A radiant heater does not contain bricks or concrete.

A storage heater transfers energy to the surroundings gradually. A radiant heater transfers heat instantly.

P1 1.9 Heating and insulating buildings

Learning objectives

Students should learn:

- there are various methods to reduce energy transfer from a house
- how the insulating properties can be measured using U-values
- that solar heating has no fuel costs (expect for pumping systems) but can have high initial costs.

Learning outcomes

Most students should be able to:

- list methods of saving energy in a house and give a brief evaluation of the techniques
- find the payback time of various energy saving measures
- state the general relationship between U-values and insulation properties.

Some students should also be able to:

- explain energy transfers using U-values for materials.

Answers to in-text questions

a The insulation prevents the movement of air, cutting down convection currents.

b 'Staywarm' is twice as good an insulator.

Support

- Use this final energy lesson to link back to all of the previous ideas. You might like to make a giant house diagram and ask students to add the key ideas to it. Select the best explanations of how the energy-saving measures work and add them to the master diagram.

Extend

- Students could find information on modern building design that reduces energy costs. They could find out about the physical design of the structure allowing increased air flow for cooling, or even some of the newer smart materials that can change colour at different temperatures. Why would a brick that changes from white to black when it warms up be useful? How could glass that becomes 'mirrored' in bright sunlight be used?

AQA Specification link-up: Physics P1.1

- U-values measure how effective a material is as an insulator. *[P1.1.4 a)]*
- The lower the U-value, the better the material is as an insulator. *[P1.1.4 b)]*
- Solar panels may contain water that is heated by radiation from the Sun. This water may then be used to heat buildings or provide domestic hot water. *[P1.1.4 c)]*
- Compare ways in which energy is transferred in and out of objects by heating and ways in which the rates of these transfers can be varied. *[P1.1]*
- Evaluate the design of everyday appliances that transfer energy by heating, including economic considerations. *[P1.1]*
- Evaluate the effectiveness of different types of material used for insulation, including U-values and economic factors including payback time. *[P1.1]*

Lesson structure

Starters

Is it worth it? – Swapping over your mobile phone to a new one will cost you £200 but you will be able to enter a new contract for £10 less each month on a two-year contract. Should you swap your phone? What other factors you would have to consider? [Talk time, number of texts, internet access]. *(5 minutes)*

Hot house – Support students by providing a large diagram of a house showing the various locations that heat can be transferred. They could draw on (or label) energy-saving measures. Later in the lesson they could prioritise these improvements. You can differentiate by making the house as simple or complicated as you want. *(10 minutes)*

Main

- This lesson is focused on applying students' knowledge of energy transfer to a real situation: keeping a house warm. You could also look at energy-saving measures in other locations such as your school building or an office block.
- Excluding draughts is often the most cost-effective method of reducing energy costs but the reduced airflow can make some places a bit stuffy.
- The concept of payback time is straightforward when enough examples are understood. Go through each possibility in turn and lead students through the calculation. You can find some costs and savings on a range of energy-saving tips websites. The smaller changes have shorter payback times, as they are relatively cheap. However, once this is achieved, the annual savings are small.
- Show some expanded polystyrene or similar foam when talking about insulation of walls. Although this is not the same as the foam injected, it shows the same idea of preventing the movement of air. New-build houses use this type of foam with aluminium foil on both sides. You can easily obtain this from DIY shops.
- Glass is a reasonable insulator (try passing heat along a glass rod) but windows are thin and have large surface areas, making them worse insulators than thick walls. Make this point to show that the area of a surface is clearly important as to how much energy passes through; this links to some previous experiments.
- The U-value is quite a complex idea because it depends on surface area and a rate of energy transfer. It is appropriate for most students to know that the smaller the value, the better the material is at providing insulation.
- The model house could be used to investigate the effectiveness of materials more fully. There are a range of problems with the model that you could discuss or let students identify. For example, there is only one room and the materials are not brick. You could use this as an open-ended planning exercise.
- If you have time you could demonstrate a solar heating panel, as described in 'Practical support'. It could alternatively be demonstrated later in the course.

Plenary

Energy neutral house – Students can use their knowledge of energy transfer to design an energy neutral house. They can use all of the measures here and may include some of the upcoming ideas on electricity generation. Use their work to help you decide exactly which concepts to focus on in the next chapter. *(10 minutes)*

Practical support

Demonstrating solar heating

It is possible to show solar heating using sunlight or a bright lamp.

Equipment and materials required

Cold water tank and warmed water tank, two temperature sensors attached to a data logger, a pipe clamp, and a large metal plate sprayed matt black with a long thin tube mounted on it in a series of 's' shapes. The tube should also be black but you could leave some gaps, so that students can see the water pass through it.

Details

The cold water tank could be a plastic beaker with a hole drilled in its side near the base, so that a thin rubber tube can be attached. Clamp the tube at the top before starting. Connect the cold reservoir (tank) high up, so that the water pressure will force water down through the long tube. Turn on the lamp to start heating the metal plate and then release a slow trickle of water. The water at the bottom should be warmer than that at the top.

Tips: Turn the lamp on a little in advance to allow the board to heat up a bit. You could also use ice cold water for the top reservoir; this causes the water to heat up due to the room temperature as it flows down the tube – it is cheating but works well.

Safety: Take care if using mains lamps – keep away from water.

Constructing a model house

Students could investigate the effect of insulation using a model house.

Equipment and materials required

Each group will need: A cardboard box to insulate (large enough to contain the heater or lamp (protected e.g. an inspection lamp)), a mains-powered filament lamp or low-voltage heating element, insulating materials (polystyrene, wool, shredded paper, etc.), data loggers or thermometers.

Details

The lamp or heating element is used to provide energy to the inside of the house and make it warmer than the surroundings. The box represents the house and the walls (or roof) can be insulated with one material at a time. Students need to measure the internal temperature of the box, compare it with the external temperature and use this data to evaluate the effectiveness of the insulating material. They will have to turn the heater on and wait a set time to be able to detect energy passing through the walls.

Safety: The lamp or heating element will become hot and should not be in direct contact with combustible material.

Energy transfer by heating

P1 1.9 — Heating and insulating buildings

Learning objectives

- How can we reduce the rate of energy transfer from our homes?
- What are U-values?
- Is solar heating free?

Did you know ...?

A duvet is a bed cover filled with 'down' or soft feathers or some other suitable thermal insulator such as wool. Because the filling material traps air, a duvet on a bed cuts down the transfer of energy from the sleeper. The 'tog' rating of a duvet tells us how effective it is as an insulator. The higher its tog rating is, the more effective it is as an insulator.

How Science Works

Reducing the rate of energy transfers at home

Home heating bills can be expensive. Figure 1 shows how we can reduce the rate of energy transfer at home and reduce our home heating bills.

Figure 1 Saving money

- **Loft insulation** such as fibreglass reduces the rate of energy transfer through the roof. Fibreglass is a good insulator. The air between the fibres also helps to reduce the rate of energy transfer by conduction.
- **Cavity wall insulation** reduces energy loss through the outer walls of the house. The 'cavity' of an outer wall is the space between the two layers of brick that make up the wall. The insulation is pumped into the cavity. It is a better insulator than the air it replaces. It traps the air in small pockets, reducing convection currents.
- **Aluminium foil** between a radiator panel and the wall reflects radiation away from the wall.
- **Double-glazed windows** have two glass panes with dry air or a vacuum between the panes. Dry air is a good insulator so it reduces the rate of energy transfer by conduction. A vacuum cuts out energy transfer by convection as well.

  a Why is cavity wall insulation better than air in the cavity between the walls of a house?

U-values

We can compare different insulating materials if we know their U-values. This is the energy per second that passes through one square metre of material when the temperature difference across it is 1 °C.

The lower the U-value, the more effective the material is as an insulator.

For example, replacing a single-glazed window with a double-glazed window that has a U-value four times smaller would make the energy loss through the window four times smaller.

b The U-value of 'MoneySaver' loft insulation is twice that of 'Staywarm'. Which type is more effective as an insulator?

U-value of the material = energy/s passing per m² for 1°C temperature difference

Figure 2 U-values

Solar heating panels

Heating water at home using electricity or gas can be expensive. A **solar heating panel** uses solar energy to heat water. The panel is usually fitted on a roof that faces south, making the most of the Sun's energy. Figure 3 shows the design of one type of solar heating panel.

The panel is a flat box containing liquid-filled copper pipes on a matt black metal plate. The pipes are connected to a heat exchanger in a water storage tank in the house.

A transparent cover on the top of the panel allows solar radiation through to heat the metal plate. Insulating material under the plate stops energy being transferred through the back of the panel.

On a sunny day, the metal plate and the copper pipes in the box become hot. Liquid pumped through the pipes is heated when it passes through the panel. The liquid may be water or a solution containing antifreeze. The hot liquid passes through the heat exchanger and transfers energy to the water in the storage tank.

Figure 3 A solar heating panel

How Science Works

Payback time

Solar heating panels save money because no fuel is needed to heat the water. But they are expensive to buy and to install.

Suppose you pay £2000 to buy and install a solar panel and you save £100 each year on your fuel bills. After 20 years you would have saved £2000. In other words, the **payback time** for the solar panel is 20 years. This is the time taken to recover the up-front costs from the savings on fuel bills.

links
For more information on payback times, see P1 3.4 Cost effectiveness matters.

Summary questions

1 Copy and complete **a** to **c** using the words below. Each word can be used more than once.

conduction   convection   radiation

a Cavity wall insulation reduces the rate of energy transfer due to ....
b Aluminium foil behind a radiator reduces the rate of energy transfer due to ....
c Closing the curtains in winter reduces the rate of energy transfer due to .... and ....

2 Some double-glazed windows have a plastic frame and a vacuum between the panes.

a Why is a plastic frame better than a metal frame?
b Why is a vacuum between the panes better than air?

3 A manufacturer of loft insulation claimed that each roll of loft insulation would save £10 per year on fuel bills. A householder bought 6 rolls of the loft insulation at £15 per roll and paid £90 to have the insulation fitted in her loft.

a How much did it cost to buy and install the loft insulation?
b What would be the saving each year on fuel bills?
c Calculate the payback time.

Key points

- Energy transfer from our homes can be reduced by fitting:
  – loft insulation
  – cavity wall insulation
  – double glazing
  – draught proofing
  – aluminium foil behind radiators.
- U-values tell us how much energy per second passes through different materials.
- Solar heating panels do not use fuel to heat water but they are expensive to buy and install.

40

41

Further teaching suggestions

Energy efficiency

- Energy efficiency is also a key concern in industry. You can find information about measures that can be taken on numerous business websites.

Energy neutral house

- The energy neutral house task makes a good homework task. Students could be asked to go a lot further and conduct some independent research for their designs.

Summary answers

1 a conduction b radiation c convection and radiation (convection and radiation in any order)

2 a Plastic is a poor conductor. Metal is a good conductor. Energy transfer through a metal frame would therefore be greater than through a plastic frame.
  b Energy transfer due to conduction and convection takes place in the space between the panes if the space is filled with air but not if there is a vacuum there.

3 a £180   b £60   c 3 years.

Summary answers

1 a A matt surface absorbs infrared radiation more easily than a smooth shiny surface does.

  b A smooth shiny surface is better because it would not get as hot in sunlight.

  c It absorbs infrared radiation better and the water gets hotter than with any other surface.

  d A matt black surface is a better emitter of infrared radiation than any other surface.

2 a electrons, collide

  b atoms, vibrate

3 a By conduction through the plate.

  b The larger the surface area, the greater the rate of energy transfer due to radiation and convection from the plate. This stops the metal plate and the component becoming too hot.

4 a convection

  b radiation

  c conduction

  d radiation

5 a Gloves are made of insulating material. The inside of the gloves becomes warm due to infrared radiation and convection from the hand. The glove material is a good insulator and the inside stays warm because it does not conduct energy from the inside.

  b Your ears are warmer than the air around them, so energy will be transferred from your ears to the air. Infrared radiation from your ears would be stopped by covering them.

6 a The metal casing conducts energy from the bearings of the motor to the outside of the case.

  b The warm water in the radiator rises to the top due to convection. The inside of the radiator at the top becomes warm and so conduction takes place from the inside to the outside of the radiator at the top.

  c Infrared radiation from the grill is absorbed by the bread, making the bread hot and toasting its surface.

7 a i The water heated at the bottom rose to the top causing convection in the tube and melting the ice cube at the top.

   ii The water was warmed at the top and stayed there as it is less dense than cold water. Conduction through the water eventually made the water at the bottom warm, and then the ice cube melted.

  b 2. Energy transfer in water is mainly due to convection.

AQA Examiner's tip

For their exam, students will need to understand four mechanisms for energy transfer involving particles: conduction, convection, evaporation and condensation. For instance, condensation will heat a surface on to which a vapour condenses. Students must understand what is happening to the particles in all of these processes.

AQA Practical suggestions

Practicals	AQA	k	📖	⚙
Passing white light through a prism and detecting the infrared radiation with a thermometer.	✓		✓	

Energy transfer by heating: P1 1.1–P1 1.9

Summary questions 🅚

1 a Why does a matt surface in sunshine get hotter than a shiny surface?

  b What type of surface is better for a flat roof – a matt dark surface or a smooth shiny surface? Explain your answer.

  c A solar heating panel is used to heat water. Why is the top surface of the metal plate inside the panel painted matt black?

  d Why is a car radiator painted matt black?

2 Copy and complete **a** and **b** using the words below:

  collide   electrons   atoms   vibrate

  a Energy transfer in a metal is due to particles called .... moving about freely inside the metal. They transfer energy when they .... with each other.

  b Energy transfer in a non-metallic solid is due to particles called .... inside the non-metal. They transfer energy because they ....

3 A heat sink is a metal plate or clip fixed to an electronic component to stop it overheating.

Figure 1 A heat sink

  a When the component becomes hot, how does energy transfer from where it is in contact with the plate to the rest of the plate?

  b Why does the plate have a large surface area?

4 Copy and complete **a** to **d** using the words below. Each word can be used more than once.

  conduction   convection   radiation

  a .... cannot happen in a solid or through a vacuum.

  b Energy transfer from the Sun is due to ....

  c When a metal rod is heated at one end, energy transfer due to .... takes place in the rod.

  d .... is energy transfer by electromagnetic waves.

5 a In winter, why do gloves keep your hands warm outdoors?

  b Why do your ears get cold outdoors in winter if they are not covered?

6 Energy transfer takes place in each of the following examples. In each case, state where the energy transfer occurs and if the energy transfer is due to conduction, convection or radiation.

  a The metal case of an electric motor becomes warm due to friction when the motor is in use.

  b A central heating radiator warms up first at the top when hot water is pumped through it.

  c A slice of bread is toasted under a red-hot electric grill.

7 A glass tube containing water with a small ice cube floating at the top was heated at its lower end. The time taken for the ice cube to melt was measured. The test was repeated with a similar ice cube weighted down at the bottom of the tube of water. The water in this tube was heated near the top of the tube. The time taken for the ice cube to melt was much longer than in the first test.

Weighted lump of ice

Boiling water

Figure 2 Energy transfer in water

  a Energy transfer in the tube is due to conduction or convection or both.

   i Why was convection the main cause of energy transfer to the ice cube in the first test?

   ii Why was conduction the only cause of energy transfer in the second test?

  b Which of the following conclusions about these tests is true?

   1 Energy transfer due to conduction does not take place in water.

   2 Energy transfer in water is mainly due to convection.

   3 Energy transfer in water is mainly due to conduction.

Practicals	AQA	🅚	📖	⚙
Demonstration using balls in a tray to show the behaviour of particles in substances in different states.	✓		✓	
Measuring the cooling effect produced by evaporation; putting wet cotton wool over the bulb of a thermometer or temperature probe.	✓	✓	✓	✓
Plan and carry out an investigation into factors that affect the rate of cooling of a can of water, e.g. shape, volume, and colour of can.	✓		✓	
Using Leslie's cube to demonstrate the effect on radiation of altering the nature of the surface.	✓		✓	
Plan and carry out an investigation using immersion heaters in a metal block to measure specific heat capacity.	✓	✓	✓	
Investigating thermal conduction using rods of different materials.	✓		✓	
Plan and carry out an investigation by constructing a model house, using sensors and data logger to measure temperatures with and without various types of insulation.	✓		✓	

AQA Examination-style questions 🅺

1 Convection takes place in fluids.

Use words from the list to complete each sentence. Each word can be used once, more than once or not at all.

contracts expands rises sinks transfers

When a fluid is heated it ...., becomes less dense, and .... The warm fluid is replaced by cooler, denser, fluid. The resulting convection current .... energy throughout the fluid. (3)

2 There are three states of matter: solid, liquid and gas.

Complete each sentence.

a A solid has
a fixed shape and a fixed volume.
a fixed shape but not a fixed volume.
a fixed volume but not a fixed shape.
neither a fixed shape nor a fixed volume. (1)

b A liquid has
a fixed shape and a fixed volume.
a fixed shape but not a fixed volume.
a fixed volume but not a fixed shape.
neither a fixed shape nor a fixed volume. (1)

c A gas has
a fixed shape and a fixed volume.
a fixed shape but not a fixed volume.
a fixed volume but not a fixed shape.
neither a fixed shape nor a fixed volume. (1)

d Fluids are
solids or liquids.
solids or gases.
liquids or gases. (1)

e The particles in a solid
move about at random in contact with each other.
move about at random away from each other.
vibrate about fixed positions. (1)

3 In an experiment a block of copper is heated from 25 °C to 45 °C.

a Give the name of the process by which energy is transferred through the copper block. (1)

b The mass of the block is 1.3 kg.
Calculate the energy needed to increase the temperature of the copper from 25 °C to 45 °C.
Specific heat capacity of copper = 380 J/kg °C.
Show clearly how you work out your answer. (3)

4 The diagram shows some water being heated with a solar cooker.

The curved mirror reflects the sunlight that falls on it. The sunlight can be focused on to the cooking pot. The energy from the sunlight is absorbed by the pot, heating up the water inside.

a Suggest **one** reason why a matt black pot has been used. (2)

b When the water has been heated, equal amounts of the water are poured into two metal pans. The pans are identical except one has a matt black surface and the other has a shiny metal surface.
Which pan will keep the water warm for the longer time? Explain your answer. (2)

5 The continuous movement of water from the oceans to the air and land and back to the oceans is called the water cycle.

a The Sun heats the surface of the oceans, which causes water to evaporate.
How does the rate of evaporation depend on
i the wind speed (1)
ii the temperature (1)
iii the humidity? (1)

b Explain how evaporation causes a cooling effect. (3)

6 Double-glazed windows are used to reduce the rate of energy transfer from buildings. The diagrams show cross-sections of single-glazed and double-glazed windows.

Single-glazed window   Double-glazed window

Give two reasons why a double-glazed window reduces conduction more effectively than a single-glazed window. (2)

7 *In this question you will be assessed on using good English, organising information clearly and using specialist terms where appropriate.*
Compare the similarities and differences between the process of conduction in metals and non-metals. (6)

43

Kerboodle resources 🅺

Resources available for this chapter on Kerboodle are:

- Chapter map: Energy transfer by heating
- Interactive activity: States of matter and energy transfer (P1 1.3)
- Support: What a state! (P1 1.3)
- How Science Works: Does melting ice expand? (P1 1.3)
- Bump up your grade: Toil, sweat and tears (P1 1.6)
- Practical: Investigating the chill factor (P1 1.6)
- Maths skills: Specific heat capacity (P1 1.8)
- Practical: Measuring specific heat capacity (P1 1.8)
- WebQuest: Solar cells (P1 1.9)
- WebQuest: Home insulation (P1 1.9)
- How Science Works: Solar cells (P1 1.9)
- Extension: Energy in buildings (P1 1.9)
- Revision podcast: Energy transfer by heating
- Test yourself: Energy transfer by heating
- On your marks: Energy transfer by heating
- Examination-style questions: Energy transfer by heating
- Answers to examination-style questions: Energy transfer by heating

---

AQA Examination-style answers

1 When a fluid is heated it **expands**, becomes less dense, and **rises**. The warm fluid is replaced by cooler, denser, fluid. The resulting convection current **transfers** energy throughout the fluid. *(3 marks)*

2 a A solid has **a fixed shape and a fixed volume**. *(1 mark)*

b A liquid has **a fixed volume but not a fixed shape**. *(1 mark)*

c A gas has **neither a fixed shape nor a fixed volume**. *(1 mark)*

d Fluids are **liquids or gases**. *(1 mark)*

e The particles in a solid **vibrate about fixed positions**. *(1 mark)*

3 a conduction *(1 mark)*

b $E = m \times c \times \theta$
$E = 1.3\ \text{kg} \times 380\ \text{J/kg °C} \times 20\ \text{°C}$
$E = 9880\ \text{J}$ *(3 marks)*

4 a A matt black surface is a very good absorber of infrared compared to light, shiny surfaces. *(2 marks)*

b Shiny metal. Shiny surfaces are poor emitters of infrared. Matt black surfaces are good emitters of infrared. *(2 marks)*

5 a i The higher the wind speed, the greater the rate of evaporation. *(1 mark)*

ii The higher the temperature, the greater the rate of evaporation. *(1 mark)*

iii The higher the humidity, the slower the rate of evaporation. *(1 mark)*

b The most energetic molecules leave the surface of the liquid, so the average kinetic energy of the remaining molecules is less.
The temperature depends on the average kinetic energy, so it is reduced. *(3 marks)*

6 There is more glass and glass is a good insulator. The air between the glass is a good insulator. *(2 marks)*

7 Marks awarded for this answer will be determined by the Quality of Written Communication (QWC) as well as the standard of the scientific response.

There is a clear, balanced and detailed description of the similarities and differences in conduction in metals and non-metals. The answer shows almost faultless spelling, punctuation and grammar. It is coherent and in an organised, logical sequence. It contains a range of appropriate or relevant specialist terms used accurately. *(5–6 marks)*

There is a description of a range of similarities and differences in conduction in metals and non-metals. There are some errors in spelling, punctuation and grammar. The answer has some structure and organisation. The use of specialist terms has been attempted, but not always accurately. *(3–4 marks)*

There is a brief description of at least one similarity or difference, which has little clarity and detail. The spelling, punctuation and grammar are very weak. The answer is poorly organised with almost no specialist terms and/or their use demonstrating a general lack of understanding of their meaning. *(1–2 marks)*

No relevant content. *(0 marks)*

Examples of physics points made in the response:
Similarities:
- involve particles
- atoms vibrate causing neighbouring atoms to vibrate, so energy is passed along.

Differences:
- metals have free electrons
- these collide with other free electrons and ions
- passing energy along
- this process much more effective, so metals better conductors.

P1 2.1

Forms of energy

Learning objectives

Students should learn:

- the words commonly used to describe energy in a range of situations
- how energy is transferred in common situations
- that gravitational potential energy and kinetic energy are often transferred, as when objects fall.

Learning outcomes

Most students should be able to:

- state what form of energy is stored in fuels, hot objects and stretched objects
- draw simple energy–transfer diagrams showing changes in energy.

Some students should also be able to:

- describe, in detail, energy transfers involving gravitational, kinetic and energy by heating.

Answers to in-text questions

a Electrical energy.
b It is transferred as light and energy to the surroundings by heating.

Support

- Spend some extra time developing the ideas of energy transfer diagrams; these are a simple way to describe all of the changes students will encounter. Try a few where there is one change followed by another. You can expand on these in future lessons by using Sankey diagrams to show the conservation of energy in a visual way.

Extend

- Extend students by asking them to find out about the question:

  Are sound and energy transferred to heating the surroundings just forms of kinetic energy?

  Encourage students to research and explain the links, then decide if we really need to use the terms 'sound' and 'energy transferred to heating'.

AQA Specification link-up: Physics P1.2

- Energy can be transferred usefully, stored, or dissipated, but cannot be created or destroyed. *[P1.2.1 a)]*

Lesson structure

Starters

Off like a rocket – Show students a video of a firework rocket (search for 'fireworks' at an internet video hosting site). Ask them to draw an energy transfer diagram of what they see happening. Check through their diagrams and show them a good example. [chemical → kinetic + thermal + light + sound + gravitational potential]. *(5 minutes)*

What is energy? – Ask students to express their ideas about what the word 'energy' means. They could produce a mind map to show their prior knowledge. Support students by providing a partially completed map for them to add additional details to. Extend students by providing some more challenging concepts [conservation, efficiency, measurement] that students need to define in their maps. Keep the maps safe; at the end of this chapter, students should redraw their map with the additional information they have learned. *(10 minutes)*

Main

- Fuels are a familiar form of chemical energy and sample fuels should be made available for students to look at in the first part of the lesson. This can lead to a discussion about what you can do with fuels and this leads readily on to the forms of energy you can get from them once burned.

- Most students will already be aware of many of the words used to describe energy. Ask them to write out a complete list of these words with an example showing each one. The key ones required are: 'light, sound, electrical, kinetic, chemical, gravitational potential, elastic strain energy, nuclear'. You should strongly encourage the use of these words and try to make students avoid using any other words in their transfer diagrams. Make sure that all students have constant access to a list like this so that you can enforce the use of correct terms, even if you have to provide a printed one.

- Some students tend to think of 'potential' as a form of energy all on its own and not just a way of describing stored energy, for example, elastic strain energy and chemical energy are both potential energy. This misconception should be addressed at this point.

- Dropping something large to ensure it makes a loud noise shows the energy transfer from gravitational potential to sound and heat. It is hard to demonstrate the transfer of energy to the surroundings, without dropping an object over and over again.

- Energy transfer diagrams (or Sankey diagrams) are very common and students should draw a number of them. It is important that they label these only with the correct terms as listed above.

- After discussing the forms of energy, allow students to explore simple energy transfers in an energy circus as described in 'Practical support'. If you have a teaching assistant, they could supervise some stations in the energy circus. Make sure that students have described the correct energy transfer for each of the devices at the end of the task.

- It is always worth demonstrating the heating effect of a current in a wire. Use a thin constantan or Nichrome wire, and let it ignite a piece of paper on a heat-proof mat. Do not forget to discuss the energy changes in the burning paper.

Plenaries

What's the transfer? – Ask students to describe simple energy transfers going on around the room, e.g. the ticking of a clock, the growth of a plant or the ringing of the bell marking the end of the lesson. They should also look at more complicated ones where the energy may be transferred in one way and then another. *(5 minutes)*

Energy links – Ask students to draw a large circle with all the forms of energy listed around the outside. They must then link the forms of energy together with an arrow, labelled with a device that can transfer the first form to the second form. For example, they could draw an arrow from the word 'electrical' to the word 'kinetic' and have it labelled 'motor', while an arrow going the other way would say 'generator'. *(10 minutes)*

Practical support

Energy transfers

When an object starts to fall freely, it gains kinetic energy, because it speeds up as it falls. So its gravitational potential energy changes to kinetic energy as it falls.

Look at Figure 3 in the Student Book – it shows a box that hits the floor with a thud. All of its kinetic energy is transferred to the surroundings at the point of impact. The proportion of kinetic energy transferred to sound is much smaller than that transferred by heating.

● Draw an energy flow diagram to show the changes in Figure 3.

Demonstrating energy transfers

Throughout this unit, students will see a range of energy transfers. You should challenge them to describe the transfers in each of them using only the recognised terms, avoiding common misconceptions

such as 'steam energy'. Using many small demonstrations reminds students continually that all transfers can be described fairly simply.

Energy circus

Students could carry out a range of simple experiments and describe the energy transfers involved. Some suggested objects/ transfers are:

A yo-yo	A dynamo
A portable radio	An MP3 player
Dropping a steel ball bearing on to a wooden block	
Burning a candle or fuel burner.	

A remote-control car: what energy is reaching the car? [Radio waves reach the car but the energy for movement comes from the chemical energy in the batteries inside the car.]

Safety: Warn students to take care with mains electricity and not to have wet hands. Take care with burning fuels.

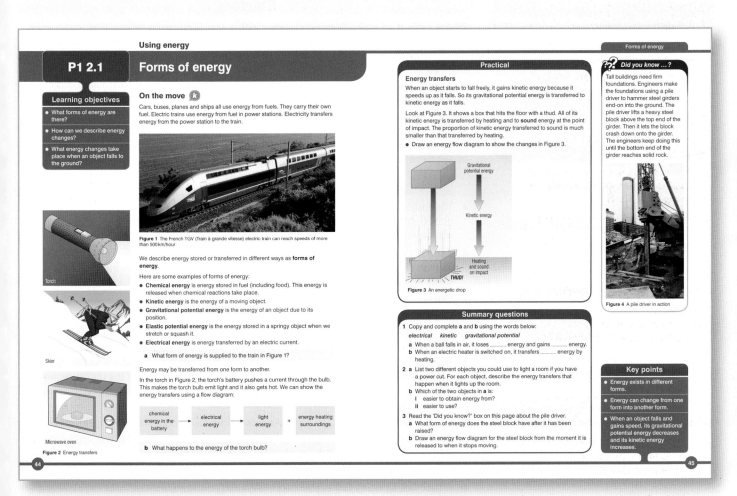

Further teaching suggestions

A pile driver

● You could demonstrate something similar to a pile driver by dropping an iron block onto a nail that has already been partly knocked into a block of wood. Keep students clear and use a safety screen just in case you happen to hit the nail at the wrong angle and knock it out of the wood. Make sure the nail is not so long that it will go all of the way through the block and into the desk!

Energy transfers in the home

● Students should make a list of the energy transfers that take place in devices at home. They should be able to find a wide range of these.

Summary answers

1 a gravitational potential, kinetic
  b electrical

2 a For example: a candle and a torch.
    A candle transfers chemical energy to light and heat. A torch transfers chemical to electrical and then light and heat.
  b i A torch is usually more convenient.
    ii This is a matter of opinion.

3 a gravitational potential energy
  b The diagram should include these transfers:
    gravitational potential energy → kinetic energy of the falling block → sound energy (realised during impact) + kinetic energy of the girder and the block → heat energy in the surroundings and the ground.

P1 2.2

Conservation of energy

Learning objectives

Students should learn:

- that energy is conserved in all energy transfers.

Learning outcomes

Most students should be able to:

- state that energy cannot be created or destroyed
- describe energy transfers between gravitational, kinetic and elastic strain energy.

Some students should also be able to:

- describe, in detail, energy transfers involving gravitational, kinetic and elastic strain energy, taking into account transfer by heating.

Answers to in-text questions

a **i** Kinetic energy is transferred by heating the brakes and the surroundings.

   ii Kinetic energy transfers to gravitational potential energy as it climbs the hill. The gravitational potential energy transfers back to kinetic energy as it descends. Energy transfers by heating to the surroundings due to air resistance and friction throughout.

b It is transferred to kinetic energy and the air resistance heating the surroundings.

c

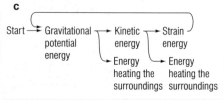

Support

- Students often confuse potential energies and they also resort to using the term 'movement energy', which is not acceptable at GCSE level. Rigorously enforce the correct terms.

Extend

- You may be able to find designs for perpetual motion machines on the internet along with descriptions of how these may work. Extend students by encouraging them to discover the flaws in the designs; some designs are very clever indeed.

AQA Specification link-up: Physics P1.2

- Energy can be transferred usefully, stored, or dissipated, but cannot be created or destroyed. *[P1.2.1 a)]*
- When energy is transferred only part of it may be usefully transferred, the rest is 'wasted'. *[P1.2.1 b)]*

Controlled Assessment: P4.3 Collect primary and secondary data. *[P4.3.2 b) e)]*

Lesson structure

Starters

Where does it all go? – Support students with a simple starter to refresh their ideas: light a candle and ask them to describe what happens to the chemical energy stored in the wax [chemical energy → by heating + light energy]. You could also ask the about the changes in the match. *(5 minutes)*

A plane journey – Ask students to draw a cartoon of an aeroplane journey describing the changes in gravitational, kinetic and chemical energy. The aeroplane lands back at the same place it took off; ask them where the energy in the fuel has gone. To save some time, you could provide a small comic strip for them to add annotations. Use the ideas that they produce here later in the lesson to discuss the idea that energy cannot 'go away'; it is all accounted for. *(10 minutes)*

Main

- The topic opens with a look at the transfer of gravitational potential energy to kinetic and back again. This is a common theme in examinations and time should be taken discussing the aspect with plenty of examples.
- Point out that energy is wasted during each transfer, so a roller coaster can never get as high as it first starts out. This means that the highest point on the track is at the start of the first drop.
- The law of conservation of energy is a **very** important one and must be emphasised very strongly. Try to account for the 'missing' energy in any energy transfer from now on. This is generally energy lost to the surroundings as heat; this is true for both the pendulum and the bungee experiments.
- The 'Practical support' activities may take a bit of time to set up and are fiddly. Students should be thinking about how to improve the accuracy of the measurements (related to 'How Science Works') but it is unlikely they will think of using the shadow idea on their own. You could give hints about this.
- Use a webcam to record the pendulum swinging or you could record a video clip of the pendulum shadow in advance and show it during the lesson. If you project this on a whiteboard, you can mark the heights of the swings as they happen.
- Watch and discuss a video of a bungee jump. Find one at an internet video-hosting site.
- Check that students can explain what is causing the apparent loss of energy in these systems; frictional forces transferring energy by heating. You could demonstrate that the loss is caused by air resistance by attaching a piece of stiff card to the bob and increasing its drag. This rapidly reduces the swing. You could also demonstrate the bungee example using a mass on a spring or, more excitingly, with a toy on a length of fishing elastic.

Plenaries

Measuring the energy in food – Ask students, as a class or in groups, to discuss some of the issues around designing an experiment to measure the energy in a food sample. Students should aim to minimise energy loss to the surroundings. This can be quite a difficult task, so provide a checklist of energy losses that need to be accounted for – for example, waste gases are hot and the energy in them needs to be measured. *(5 minutes)*

Evaluate and improve – Students could be extended by evaluating the results of their experiments ('How Science Works'). They should design improvements to the experiment. This might include the use of ICT or some system that enables them to measure the heights accurately and consistently. Groups could compare results and decide who had the best technique. *(10 minutes)*

Practical support

Investigating energy changes

Pendulum swinging

Equipment and materials required

For each group: retort stand, string with bob (or 50 g mass tied to end), graph paper and some reusable adhesive to mount it, torch, stop clock.

Details

Students could release the pendulum from a fixed height and let it swing for 30 seconds (or just a set number of swings). They then compare the initial height of the swing with the height after this time period. One way to measure the height of a pendulum swing is to shine a bright light on it and measure the position of the shadow.

Position the light so that the shadow falls on a piece of graph paper when the bob is swinging. Students mark where the shadow falls after a number of swings and then look at the pattern in height against time.

Bungee jumping

Equipment and materials required

For each group: retort stand, elastic with mass (or toy tied to end), graph paper and some reusable adhesive to mount it, torch.

Details

A similar shadow technique to the above activity could be used to measure the height of the bounces or video logging technology could be employed if you have it. You could video an experiment in advance so that you can discuss the details with the whole class.

Using energy

Conservation of energy

P1 2.2 Conservation of energy

Learning objectives

● What do we mean by 'conservation of energy'?

● Why is conservation of energy a very important idea?

AQA Examiner's tip

Never use the term 'movement energy' in the exam; you will only gain marks for using 'kinetic energy'.

At the funfair k

Funfairs are very exciting places because lots of energy transfers happen quickly. A roller coaster gains gravitational potential energy when it climbs. This energy is then transferred as the roller coaster races downwards.

As it descends:

its gravitational potential energy → kinetic energy + sound + energy transfer by heating due to air resistance and friction

The energy transferred by heating is 'wasted' energy, which you will learn more about in P1 2.3.

a When a roller coaster gets to the bottom of a descent, what energy transfers happen if:
  i we apply the brakes to stop it
  ii it goes up and over a second 'hill'?

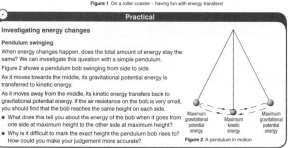

Figure 1 On a roller coaster – having fun with energy transfers!

Practical

Investigating energy changes

Pendulum swinging

When energy changes happen, does the total amount of energy stay the same? We can investigate this question with a simple pendulum.

Figure 2 shows a pendulum bob swinging from side to side.

As it moves towards the middle, its gravitational potential energy is transferred to kinetic energy.

As it moves away from the middle, its kinetic energy transfers back to gravitational potential energy. If the air resistance on the bob is very small, you should find that the bob reaches the same height on each side.

● What does this tell you about the energy of the bob when it goes from one side at maximum height to the other side at maximum height?

● Why is it difficult to mark the exact height the pendulum bob rises to? How could you make your judgement more accurate?

Maximum gravitational potential energy | Maximum kinetic energy | Maximum gravitational potential energy

Figure 2 A pendulum in motion

Conservation of energy

Scientists have done lots of tests to find out if the total energy after a transfer is the same as the energy before the transfer. All the tests so far show it is the same.

This important result is known as the **conservation of energy**.

It tells us that **energy cannot be created or destroyed**.

Bungee jumping

What energy transfers happen to a bungee jumper after jumping off the platform?

● When the rope is slack, some of the gravitational potential energy of the bungee jumper is transferred to kinetic energy as the jumper falls.

● Once the slack in the rope has been used up, the rope slows the bungee jumper's fall. Most of the gravitational potential energy and kinetic energy of the jumper is transferred into elastic strain energy.

● After reaching the bottom, the rope pulls the jumper back up. As the jumper rises, most of the elastic strain energy of the rope is transferred back to gravitational potential energy and kinetic energy of the jumper.

The bungee jumper doesn't return to the same height as at the start. This is because some of the initial gravitational potential energy has been transferred to its surroundings by heating as the rope stretched then shortened again.

b What happens to the gravitational potential energy lost by the bungee jumper?

c Draw a flow diagram to show the energy changes.

Figure 3 Bungee jumping

Practical

Bungee jumping k

You can try out the ideas about bungee jumping using the experiment shown in Figure 4.

Summary questions

1 Copy and complete using the words below:
electrical   gravitational potential   kinetic
A person going up in a lift gains .... energy. The lift is driven by electric motors. Some of the .... energy supplied to the motors is wasted instead of being transferred to .... energy.

2 **a** A ball dropped onto a trampoline returns to almost the same height after it bounces. Describe the energy transfer of the ball from the point of release to the top of its bounce.
  b What can you say about the energy of the ball at the point of release compared with at the top of its bounce?
  c You could use the test in **a** above to see which of three trampolines was the bounciest.
    i Name the independent variable in this test.
    ii Is this variable categoric or continuous?

3 One exciting fairground ride acts like a giant catapult. The capsule, in which you are strapped, is fired high into the sky by the rubber bands of the catapult. Explain the energy transfers taking place in the ride.

Figure 4 Testing a bungee jump

links

For more information on variables, look back at H2 Fundamental ideas about how science works.

Key points

● Energy cannot be created or destroyed.

● Conservation of energy applies to all energy changes.

46

47

Further teaching suggestions

Slow down

● Sometimes we want to get rid of kinetic energy quickly. Students could find out how we slow down planes on landing, or drag racers, and make a booklet or short presentation. This would be good for homework.

ICT link-up

● Use video capture equipment to record the pendulum or 'bungee' for analysis. Some software can calculate speed and displacement.

Measuring the energy in food

● Ask students to design the experiment for homework.

Summary answers

1 gravitational potential, electrical, kinetic

2 **a** **On descent:** Gravitational potential energy → kinetic energy + energy heating the surroundings due to air resistance.
  On impact: Kinetic energy → elastic energy of trampoline + energy heating the surroundings due to impact + sound.
  On ascent: Elastic energy of trampoline → kinetic energy → gravitational potential energy + energy heating the surroundings due to air resistance.
  b The ball has less energy at the top of its bounce than at the point of release.
  c **i** Type of trampoline
    ii Categoric

3 Elastic energy of the rubber straps is transferred to kinetic energy of the capsule. This kinetic energy is transferred to gravitational potential energy as the capsule rises to the top of its flight etc. as with the bungee jumper in the Student Book.

P1 2.3

Useful energy

AQA

Specification link-up: Physics P1.2

- When energy is transferred only part of it may be usefully transferred, the rest is 'wasted'. [P1.2.1 b)]
- Wasted energy is eventually transferred to the surroundings, which become warmer. The wasted energy becomes increasingly spread out and so becomes less useful. [P1.2.1 c)]
- Describe the energy transfers and the main energy wastages that occur with a range of appliances. [P1.2]

Controlled Assessment: P4.3 Collect primary and secondary data. [P4.3.2 b) c) e)]

Learning objectives

Students should learn:

- that energy is wasted heating the surroundings in energy transfers
- that this 'wasted' energy spreads out and is no longer of use.

Learning outcomes

Most students should be able to:

- identify useful and wasted energy in transfers
- describe how friction is the cause of much wasted energy
- understand that energy that escapes to the surroundings by heating is not available for other energy transfers and so is useless.

Answers to in-text questions

a It is gained by the surroundings by heating.
b It is transferred to the surroundings by heating due to friction between its moving parts and in the brakes, and by air resistance.
c The hot water mixes with the cold water. Its energy spreads out and cannot be used again.

Support

- Students can struggle with the idea that energy spreads out and becomes 'useless'. Spend some time discussing the idea that the energy transferred to the surroundings by heating cannot be made to collect together in one place to make it useful again; this would actually take more energy to do than it's worth.

Extend

- What really causes frictional forces? Very smooth surfaces often produce larger frictional effects than rougher ones. Extend students by asking them to come up with a detailed explanation of what is going on. They will need to research how our idea of friction has developed over hundreds of years.

Lesson structure

Starters

Useful or useless? – Show energy transfer diagrams and ask students to identify the useful energy outputs and the useless ones in each case. This will support students and refresh the language of energy transfer. *(5 minutes)*

Overheating – Extend students by asking them to explain why humans become hot when they work hard. How is this excess heat removed from the body? Why do we need to eat less in hot weather? Links can be made to biological processes. This can lead to a discussion about where the energy in our food actually ends up. *(10 minutes)*

Main

- In this unit, avoid the use of the term 'lost' for energy if possible; it implies that the energy disappears. The energy spreads out into the surroundings and becomes useless or 'wasted'.

- A video clip of a car performing an emergency stop (search a video-hosting website) is an excellent way of helping students understand that the kinetic energy of a car has to go somewhere when it stops. A dramatic one with burning rubber works best.

- Frictional effects are best explained using simple diagrams or animations; you should be able to find a range of these. The surfaces rub or catch on each other and this rubbing causes heating. You could show the roughness of 'smooth' surfaces with micrographs or even electron micrographs.

- Rubbing two metal blocks across each other will show frictional heating. Adding oil should make the movement smoother. Check students understand that friction causes heating, because of the forces between the surfaces of objects that rub together.

- Students need to be encouraged to describe exactly where there is friction in a device. They should know about air resistance, drag in water, friction of surfaces in contact and around a pivot.

- If time allows, students could reinforce 'How Science Works' concepts of accuracy and precision by investigating friction themselves. (See 'Practical support'). Stress the progression evident in the concepts needed to tackle an investigation that students will be familiar with. To save time, you could just demonstrate the practical technique described and show what we mean by accuracy and precision.

Plenaries

Sticky problems – Ask students to draw up a table of the ways friction can be reduced and give examples of exactly where this happens. You could provide a table of suggested places and ask students to complete it to explain how the friction could be reduced. *(5 minutes)*

What's wrong? – Support students by asking them to correct some sentences describing energy and friction. This can be used to challenge some misconceptions. Examples can include: 'When a car stops at traffic lights, the speed energy is destroyed by the brakes and is lost.' [Kinetic energy is actually transferred by heating in the tyres and brakes.], 'Rubbing your hands together makes them warmer.' *(10 minutes)*

Practical support

Investigating friction

Many students will have investigated friction before, but you may wish to look in more detail here. The focus should be on improving the technique, focusing on the concepts of accuracy and precision in the specification. (This relates to 'How Science Works'.)

Equipment and materials required

For each group: string, pulley, clamp, 10 × 50 g masses, 1 kg mass (with hoop), three different surfaces to test (desk surface, carpet tiles, rubber mat).

Details

Students place the 1 kg mass on the surfaces and attach it to a mass holder hanging over the desk via the pulley. They then find out what mass is required to start the 1 kg sliding across the surface. To improve the accuracy of the measurements, encourage students to add smaller masses when they get near to the sliding point of the mass, so several runs will be required. Students may find out that their mats or carpet tiles start to move before the mass, so they will need some tape or reusable adhesive to hold it in place. How does this work?

Safety: Protect floor from falling weights and keep feet clear.

Investigating bouncy balls

There are a range of factors that affect how a ball bounces on a surface. In this investigation students could consider the factors and relate the bounce height to energy lessons.

Equipment and materials required

For each group: ping-pong ball, tennis ball, rubber 'bouncy' ball (and others), metre rule, range of surfaces to drop the ball on to.

Details

Students could drop the ping-pong balls from a range of heights on to a solid surface and measure the bounce height. This will be less than the drop height and students could relate this to energy losses using the impact. It can be difficult to measure the bounce height, so students should come up with ideas to do this such as repeating the drops and positioning their heads correctly. They could then move on to exploring what happens with different types of ball before looking at the effect of different surfaces.

This investigation gives ample opportunity for developing planning, recording and analysis skills. You might like to limit the factors that each group investigates and have the groups report back to the class. For example, one group only investigates drop height while another investigates surface. You may also want some students to use video equipment to accurately record the bounces and share the results with the rest of the class.

Safety: Students need to be well-behaved and keep close control of the balls.

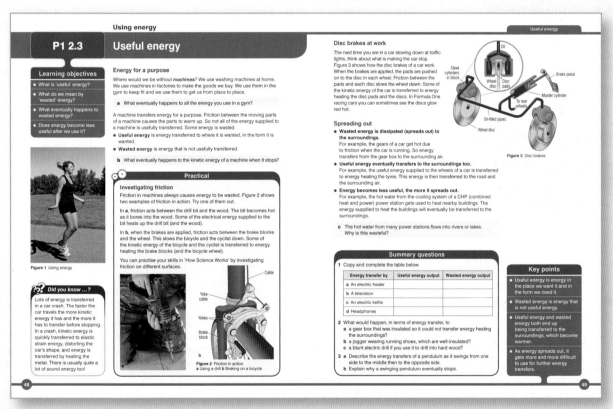

Summary answers

1

	Useful energy output	Wasted energy output
a	energy of the element	energy of the case
b	light energy, sound energy	energy transferred to surroundings as heat
c	energy of the water	energy of steam and of the kettle itself
d	sound energy	energy in the wire

2 a It would heat up. The lubricating oil and the gears would get too hot.

b His feet would get too hot and sweaty.

c The drill would heat up and smoke if it burns the wood.

3 a As the pendulum swings towards the middle, its gravitational potential energy decreases and its kinetic energy increases. As it moves from the middle to the highest position on the opposite side, its kinetic energy transfers back to gravitational potential energy. Air resistance acting causes some of its kinetic energy to be transferred to the surrounding as heat.

b Air resistance causes friction as the pendulum swings. This produces heat and so the pendulum transfers energy to the surroundings and stops.

P1 2.4

Energy and efficiency

Learning objectives

Students should learn:

- that efficiency is a measurement of how effective a device is at transferring energy
- how to measure the efficiency of a motor
- how to calculate the efficiency of a range of devices
- how we can reduce energy consumption.

Learning outcomes

Most students should be able to:

- describe what is meant by the efficiency of a device
- calculate the efficiency of a device.

Some students should also be able to:

- perform calculations including the rearrangement of the efficiency equation. [HT only]

Support

- You might want to use calculation templates to help students learn how to organise their calculations. These are sheets that show the layout of the calculation; students simply put the values from the question into the right places and then perform the calculation. Check the answers to each one until students are confident that they can perform the calculations. For additional support, you could provide an experiment template and results table for the practical task. This could also include a set of appropriately labelled graph axes.

Extend

- Students could try a more complex rearrangement of the equation. For example, they could work out how much electrical energy would be required to do 500 J of work if a motor is only 40% efficient [1250 J]. They could also try multi-stage transfers, where the first stage is 50% efficient and the second stage is 25% efficient; they should find out that the whole process would then only be 12.5% efficient.

AQA Specification link-up: Physics P1.2

- To calculate the efficiency of a device using:

$$\text{efficiency} = \frac{\text{useful energy out}}{\text{total energy in}} \ (\times \ 100\%)$$

$$\text{efficiency} = \frac{\text{useful power out}}{\text{total power in}} \ (\times \ 100\%) \qquad [P1.2.1 \ d)]$$

- Describe the energy transfers and the main energy wastages that occur with a range of appliances. *[P1.2]*
- Interpret and draw a Sankey diagram. *[P1.2]*

  Controlled Assessment: P4.5 Analyse and interpret primary and secondary data. *[P4.5.3 a)]*

Lesson structure

Starters

Staying on – Ask students to explain why some electrical devices of the same type (e.g. two different models of phones or even two torches) last longer than others even though they use the same batteries. Students could be extended by linking this to the efficiency of the device. They should also describe the subtle differences in what the devices do. For example, one phone may have many more functions than another. *(5 minutes)*

Efficiency – What is 'efficiency' and why do we want it? What are the advantages of an efficient device? Form students into groups and ask them to read some energy company literature. Challenge them to agree on a simple description of what efficiency is and why it is important. The groups should share their descriptions. *(10 minutes)*

Main

- Students need to lay out the calculations clearly and show all of the stages of their working; emphasise that they will find it difficult to remember the correct technique and score full marks on a science examination without doing this. Students should also be aware that equations will not be given in questions for this specification. Students will have to pick the equation from an equation sheet.

- The calculations are not particularly challenging, but many students become confused about percentage or fractional efficiency, so tackle first one and then the other. Ensure that all students can complete the basic calculations; lots of practice is needed.

- More mathematically-able students need to perform rearrangement. Even fairly able students of science can struggle with this skill, so it is well worth discussing how this type of calculation is taught in the mathematics department, so that you can be consistent with them.

- It may be difficult to investigate the efficiency of the winch without a lot of equipment. A demonstration may be more effective. Students could still record the results of your demonstration and analyse them. They should find that the motor becomes less efficient, as the weight increases. This introduces concepts of 'How Science Works' involving presentation of data and relationships between variables.

- You may like to discuss how the efficiency of an elevator could be measured. Should the weight of the elevator itself be counted? This could lead to a discussion of why it is not efficient (or cost effective) to drive a large car with only one person in it.

- It is important to explain that sometimes we actually want to transfer electricity by heating and this is an efficient process.

Plenaries

Car efficiency – Give students advertisements for cars and ask them to arrange them in order of energy efficiency, using the fuel consumption figures in the small print. Extend students, by asking them to investigate further and look at the questions of passenger numbers. Is a bus more energy-efficient than a car? *(5 minutes)*

Energy efficiency poster – Students could draw a poster encouraging people to be more energy-efficient in their home. The poster has to include information about why efficiency is important and some suitable suggestions as to what to do. Extend students by asking them to select suitable success or marking criteria for the poster themselves. *(10 minutes)*

Practical support

Investigating efficiency

This investigation can be used to develop and assess students' investigative skills, in particular those related to measurement.

Equipment and materials required
For each group: joulemeter, variable low voltage power supply, connecting leads, small electric winch (motor), 5 × 100 g masses (each weighing 0.1 N), metre rule, clamps to secure the winches to benches, cardboard box or piece of carpet to protect the floor.

Details
Students will lift a range of masses to a fixed height. A full metre is a good height – if the motor were 100% efficient it would require 0.1 J

for each mass. In reality, it will be much less efficient than this. If the winches are quite powerful, you may need to use larger weights to notice the reduction in efficiency.

Safety: Protect the floor and keep feet clear from falling weights. Stop motor before masses reach the pulley.

Electrical heating efficiency
Demonstrate a kettle heating water (a transparent kettle is great). The students could identify energy losses here as sound. Explain that these losses are very small and electrical heating is very efficient. You could mention that the generation of electricity is not very efficient though.

Safety: Take care when using mains electricity and keep hands dry.

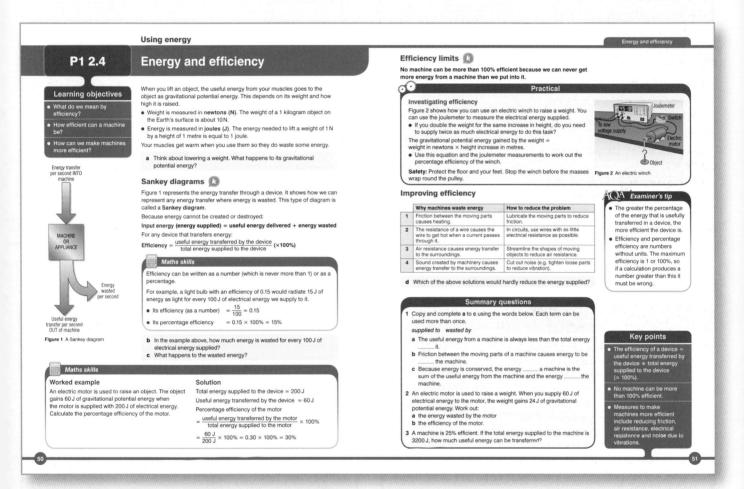

Further teaching suggestions

Car efficiency
- Students could research into car efficiency. A large amount of information is available about the performance of a car; students could find this and produce a graph showing which is the most fuel efficient. Several groups could look into different classes of car to find the 'best in class' and share their findings.

Calculations
- Provide a worksheet with additional calculations. You could provide data from the lifting experiment for students to analyse, if they did not try the task during the lesson.

    The student poster (energy efficiency poster plenary) could also be tacked as a homework task; use the time in the lesson to decide on the success criteria for the work.

Answers to in-text questions

a You use your muscles, so the gravitational potential energy is transferred in them by heating.

b 85 J

c It is transferred by heating the lamp holder and the surroundings.

d Solution 4

Summary answers

1 a supplied to
  b wasted by
  c supplied to, wasted by

2 a 36 J
  b 0.40 (or 40%)

3 800 J

Summary answers

1 1 B   2 C   3 A

2 electrical, light, useful, wasted

3 a 0.15 (or 15%)

b 8500 J

c

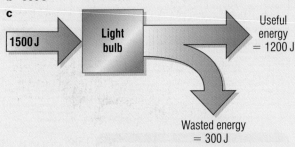

4 a 4.0 J

b 4.0 J

c 1.0 J

d Some of the energy lost was transferred directly to the surroundings as sound and some was eventually transferred to the surroundings by heating.

5 a 1200 J

b 300 J

c

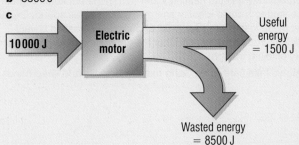

6 a i She loses gravitational potential energy and gains kinetic energy. Some energy may be wasted due to air resistance.

ii She loses some more gravitational potential energy and all her kinetic energy. The energy she loses is mostly transferred into the rope as elastic strain energy. Some of her energy may be wasted due to air resistance.

b 12 000 J

7 a i 1500 J   **ii** 10 500 J   **iii** 12.5%

b Apply oil to the bearings of the motor to reduce friction.

AQA Examiner's tip

Students often do not fully understand the law of energy conservation. Drawing Sankey diagrams to scale helps them understand this concept and this is required in some exam questions.

AQA Examiner's tip

Energy can be transferred usefully, stored or dissipated. Energy is dissipated, for example, when energy is 'wasted' due to friction. This energy is transferred to the surroundings, which become warmer. The student must realise that the wasted energy has not been *destroyed*, and the total energy remains the same throughout.

Summary questions

1 The devices listed below transfer energy in different ways.

1 Car engine   2 Electric bell   3 Electric light bulb

The next list gives the useful form of energy the devices are designed to produce.

Match words A, B and C with the devices numbered 1 to 3.

A Light   B Kinetic energy   C Sound

2 Copy and complete using the words below:

useful   wasted   light   electrical

When a light bulb is switched on, ... energy is transferred into .... energy and energy that heats the surroundings. The energy that radiates from the light bulb is .... energy. The rest of the energy supplied to the light bulb is .... energy.

3 You can use an electric motor to raise a load. In a test, you supply the motor with 10 000 J of electrical energy and the load gains 1500 J of gravitational potential energy.

a Calculate its efficiency.

b How much energy is wasted?

c Copy and complete the Sankey diagram below for the motor.

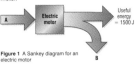

Figure 1 A Sankey diagram for an electric motor

4 A ball gains 4.0 J of gravitational potential energy when it is raised to a height of 2.0 m above the ground. When it is released, it falls to the ground and rebounds to a height of 1.5 m.

a How much kinetic energy did it just before it hit the ground? Assume air resistance is negligible.

b How much gravitational potential energy did it transfer when it fell to the ground?

c The ball gained 3.0 J of gravitational potential energy when it moved from the ground to the top of the rebound. How much energy did it transfer in the impact at the ground?

d What happened to the energy it transferred on impact?

5 A low energy light bulb has an efficiency of 80%. Using an energy meter, a student found the light bulb used 1500 J of electrical energy in 100 seconds.

a How much useful energy did the light bulb transfer in this time?

b How much energy was wasted by the light bulb?

c Draw a Sankey diagram for the light bulb.

6 A bungee jumper jumps from a platform and transfers 12 000 J of gravitational potential energy before the rope attached to her becomes taut and starts to stretch. She then transfers a further 24 000 J of gravitational potential energy before she stops falling and begins to rise.

a Describe the energy changes:

i after she jumps before the rope starts to stretch

ii after the rope starts to stretch until she stops falling.

b What is the maximum kinetic energy she has during her descent?

7 On a building site, an electric winch and a pulley were used to lift bricks from the ground.

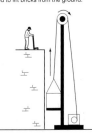

Figure 2 An electric winch and pulley

The winch transferred 12 000 J of electrical energy to raise a load through a height of 3.0 m. The load gained 1500 J of gravitational potential energy when it was raised.

a i How much useful energy was transferred by the motor?

ii Calculate the energy wasted.

iii Calculate the percentage efficiency of the system.

b How could the efficiency of the winch be improved?

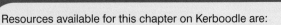

Kerboodle resources

Resources available for this chapter on Kerboodle are:

- Chapter map: Using energy
- Support: Where does it all go? (P1 2.1)
- Interactive activity: Energy transfers and conservation (P1 2.2)
- How Science Works: Falling cupcakes (P1 2.2)
- Practical: Investigating a model bungee jump (P1 2.2)
- Bump up your grade: Using a Sankey diagram (P1 2.4)
- Extension: Using energy conservation (P1 2.4)
- Practical: Investigating the efficiency of an electric motor (P1 2.4)
- Revision podcast: Useful energy
- Test yourself: The efficient use of energy
- On your marks: Using energy
- Examination-style questions: Using energy
- Answers to examination-style questions: Using energy

AQA Examination-style questions

1 A television transfers electrical energy.

Use words from the list to complete each sentence. Each word can be used once, more than once or not at all.

electrical light sound warmer

A television is designed to transfer .... energy into light and .... energy. Some energy is transferred to the surroundings, which become .... (3)

2 A hairdryer contains an electrical heater and a fan driven by an electric motor. The hairdryer transfers electrical energy into other forms.

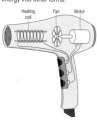

a Apart from energy by heating, name **two** of the other forms of energy. (2)

b Not all of the energy supplied to the fan is usefully transferred. Name **one** form of energy that is wasted by the fan. (1)

c Which of the following statements about the energy wasted by the fan is true?
 A It eventually becomes very concentrated.
 B It eventually makes the surroundings warmer.
 C It is eventually completely destroyed.
 D It is eventually transferred into electrical energy. (1)

d The fan in another hairdryer transfers useful energy at the same rate but wastes more of the energy supplied to it. What does this tell you about the efficiency of this hairdryer? (1)

In a hot water system water is heated by burning gas in a boiler. The hot water is then stored in a tank. For every 111 J of energy released from the gas, 100 J of energy is absorbed by the water in the boiler.

a Calculate the percentage efficiency of the boiler.

Write down the equation you use. Show clearly how you work out your answer. (4)

b The energy released from the gas but **not** absorbed by the boiler is 'wasted'. Explain why this energy is of little use for further energy transfers. (1)

c The tank in the hot water system is surrounded by a layer of insulation. Explain the effect of the insulation on the efficiency of the hot water system. (3)

4 A chairlift carries skiers to the top of a mountain. The chairlift is powered by an electric motor.

a What type of energy have the skiers gained when they reach the top of the mountain? (1)

b The energy required to lift two skiers to the top of the mountain is 240 000 J.
The electric motor has an efficiency of 40%.

Calculate the energy wasted in the motor.

Write down the equation you use. Show clearly how you work out your answer and give the unit. [H] (4)

c Explain why some energy is wasted in the motor. (2)

5 A light bulb transfers electrical energy into useful light energy and wasted energy to the surroundings. For every 100 J of energy supplied to the bulb, 5 J of energy is transferred into light.

Draw and label a Sankey diagram for the light bulb. (3)

6 *In this question you will be assessed on using good English, organising information clearly and using specialist terms where appropriate.*

Explain why an electric heater is the only appliance that can possibly be 100% efficient. (6)

AQA Practical suggestions

Practicals	AQA	k	📖	⚙
An energy 'circus' to demonstrate various energy transfers.		✓		✓

AQA Examination-style answers

1 A television is designed to transfer **electrical** energy into light and **sound** energy. Some energy is transferred to the surroundings, which become **warmer**. *(3 marks)*

2 a Kinetic energy, sound. *(2 marks)*

 b Sound. *(1 mark)*

 c B It eventually makes the surroundings warmer. *(1 mark)*

 d It is less efficient. *(1 mark)*

---

3 a Efficiency

$$= \frac{\text{useful energy transferred by the device}}{\text{total energy supplied to the device}} \ (\times \ 100\%)$$

Efficiency $= \dfrac{100 \text{ J}}{111 \text{ J}} \times 100\%$

Efficiency $= 0.90 \times 100\%$

Efficiency $= 90\%$ *(4 marks)*

 b The energy becomes too spread out to use. *(1 mark)*

 c The insulation reduces the rate at which energy is lost from the tank to the surroundings.
The water in the tank will stay hotter for longer.
This increases the efficiency of the hot water system.
(3 marks)

4 a Gravitational potential energy. *(1 mark)*

 b Efficiency

$$= \frac{\text{useful energy transferred by the device}}{\text{total energy supplied to the device}} \ (\times \ 100\%)$$

total energy supplied $= \dfrac{240\,000 \text{ J}}{0.4}$

total energy supplied $= 600\,000$ J

energy wasted $= 600\,000$ J $- 240\,000$ J

energy wasted $= 360\,000$ J *(4 marks)*

 c Friction between the moving parts of the motor causes some energy to be transferred by heating.
(Or the current flowing in the motor has a heating effect.)
(2 marks)

5

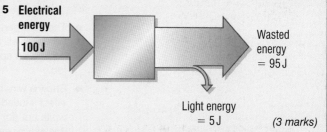

Electrical energy 100 J — Wasted energy = 95 J — Light energy = 5 J *(3 marks)*

6 There is a clear, balanced and detailed description of why an electric heater is the only appliance that can possibly be 100% efficient. The answer shows almost faultless spelling, punctuation and grammar. It is coherent and in an organised, logical sequence. It contains a range of appropriate or relevant specialist terms used accurately. *(5–6 marks)*

There is a partial description of why an electric heater is the only appliance that can possibly be 100% efficient. There are some errors in spelling, punctuation and grammar. The answer has some structure and organisation. The use of specialist terms has been attempted, but not always accurately. *(3–4 marks)*

There is a brief description of why an electric heater is the only appliance that can possibly be 100% efficient, which has little clarity and detail. The spelling, punctuation and grammar are very weak. The answer is poorly organised with almost no specialist terms and/or their use demonstrating a general lack of understanding of their meaning. *(1–2 marks)*

No relevant content. *(0 marks)*

Examples of physics points made in the response:

- all electrical appliances convert some energy by heating
- in most appliances some energy is wasted
- energy is usually wasted by heating
- the useful energy transfer in the heater is by heating
- an appliance is 100% efficient only if all the energy transfer is useful
- the heater can be 100% efficient if no energy is wasted as light.

P1 3.1

Electrical appliances

Learning objectives

Students should learn:

- that electrical appliances are very useful
- about a range of energy transfers that happen in electrical appliances.

Learning outcomes

Most students should be able to:

- describe the energy transfers in a range of electrical appliances
- choose a particular appliance for a particular purpose based on the energy transfer required.

Support

- Ensure students are using the 'official' lists of energy forms. For example, try to encourage the use of 'kinetic energy' instead of movement.

Extend

- Students could be extended by finding out who first discovered how electricity could be used to produce movement. How and where was this first demonstrated? Was its importance realised? This is an important moment in practical science. [Faraday demonstrated a primitive motor but worked with other scientists who were upset that they were not credited.]

AQA Specification link-up: Physics P1.3

- Examples of energy transfers that everyday electrical appliances are designed to bring about. *[P1.3.1 a)]*
- Compare the advantages and disadvantages of using different electrical appliances for a particular application. *[P1.3]*
- Consider the implications of instances when electricity is not available. *[P1.3]*

Lesson structure

Starters

Electricity everywhere – Support students by asking them to list all of the electrical appliances that they use during the day. Include mains-powered and battery-operated. They could then describe how their lives would be more difficult if these appliances did not exist. This should bring home to them how important the discovery of electricity was. *(5 minutes)*

Using energy – Challenge students to design an experiment to compare how much energy is stored in different batteries. Their ideas could include measuring how long a bulb could stay lit for or even how long a toy operates for (as used in many adverts). You could then discuss measuring the energy with a joulemeter as you may have in previous practical tasks. *(10 minutes)*

Main

- The core part of this topic is a discussion of why electricity is so useful in our society. Students will appreciate that electricity can be transferred easily into other forms of energy, so spend some time mentioning and showing the key appliances that do the job.

- Show a wire heating when a current passes through it and ask students what this effect is used in. Use a heatproof mat and turn up the current until the wire becomes white hot (for a moment). Students need to be out of touching distance. Ask: 'What is this effect used in [electrical heating elements] and how do we make sure that the wire does not melt?'

- Show an electric motor operating, pointing out the magnets, and ask how this effect is used. Also ask: 'What is the effect of increasing the current and providing more energy to the motor?' This will be covered in detail if students go on to study GCSE Physics.

- Demonstrate a simple electromagnet and again see if students realise how this effect can be used in loudspeakers (have one handy with a signal generator). With each of the demonstrations, ask students to consider how energy is being wasted to the surroundings.

- Once students are aware of the range of possible energy transfers, they should discuss how to choose a particular appliance for a job. Include a discussion of the clockwork radio – see the 'How Science Works' box in the Student Book.

Plenaries

Making connections – Ask students to complete the paragraph 'Electrical energy is a very convenient form of energy because ...' including these words: 'energy', 'transfer' and 'current'. [For example, 'It is very easy to transfer electrical energy into other forms such as light and movement. The energy can be carried over long distances by the electric current, so we can get the energy to where we need it easily.'] *(5 minutes)*

Electrical energy table – To support students, give them a cut-up table similar to the one in the Student Book and ask them to assemble it to show the useful and wasted energy from more electrical appliances. You could use mobile phone, projector, vacuum cleaner and electric fan. For some students, you could add challenging appliances such as a computer. [The useful energy might only be the light emitted by the monitor and the sound from any speakers.] *(10 minutes)*

Practical support

Energy transfers
This is a simple survey. You could provide students with a supporting worksheet if you think that they will need one.

Demonstrating heating effect of electrical current
You will need a low-voltage power supply (variable), connecting wires, resistance wire, heatproof mat. Make sure that the paper is a small piece so that the fire cannot spread beyond the mat. The plastic insulation of the leads should be kept away from the flames too.

Demonstrating a motor
Ideally, you should use a motor where students can see the moving parts. This way, you can describe the effect the current is having and point out important features, such as the way wires are connected by brushes, so the motor is free to turn without them becoming tangled.

Demonstrating a loudspeaker
The loudspeaker should be a large one, and you should demonstrate that all it is doing is moving in and out by showing some low-frequency vibrations. Connect to a signal generator if required.

Electrical energy

P1 3.1 Electrical appliances

Learning objectives
- Why are electrical appliances so useful?
- What do we use most everyday electrical appliances for?
- How do we choose an electrical appliance for a particular job?

Practical

Energy transfers

Carry out a survey of electrical appliances you find at school or at home.

Record the useful and wasted energy transfers of each appliance.

Everyday electrical appliances

We use **electrical appliances** every day. They transfer electrical energy into useful energy at the flick of a switch. Some of the electrical energy we supply to them is wasted.

Figure 1 Electrical appliances – how many can you see in this photo?

Table 1

Appliance	Useful energy	Energy wasted
Light bulb	Light from the glowing filament.	Energy transfer from the filament heating surroundings.
Electric heater	Energy heating the surroundings.	Light from the glowing element.
Electric toaster	Energy heating bread.	Energy heating the toaster case and the air around it.
Electric kettle	Energy heating water.	Energy heating the kettle itself.
Hairdryer	Kinetic energy of the air driven by the fan. Energy heating air flowing past the heater filament.	Sound of fan motor (energy heating the motor heats the air going past it, so is not wasted). Energy heating the hairdryer itself.
Electric motor	Kinetic energy of object driven by the motor. Potential energy of objects lifted by the motor.	Energy heating the motor and sound energy of the motor.
Computer disc drive	Energy stored in magnetic dots on the disc.	Energy heating the motor that drives the disc.

a What energy transfers happen in an electric toothbrush?

??? Did you know ...?
Unlike high voltage electrical injuries, people do not get many burns when they are struck by lightning. Damage is usually to the nervous system. The brain is frequently damaged as the skull is the most likely place to be struck. Lightning that strikes near the head can enter the body through the eyes, ears and mouth and flow internally through the body.

How Science Works

Clockwork radio

People without electricity supplies can now listen to radio programmes – thanks to the British inventor Trevor Baylis. In the early 1990s, he invented and patented the clockwork radio. When you turn a handle on the radio, you wind up a clockwork spring in the radio. When the spring unwinds, it turns a small electric generator in the radio. It doesn't need batteries or mains electricity. So people in remote areas where there is no mains electricity can listen to their radios without having to walk miles for a replacement battery. But they do have to wind up the spring every time it runs out of energy.

Figure 2 Clockwork radios are now mass-produced and sold all over the world

Choosing an electrical appliance

We use electrical appliances for many purposes. Each appliance is designed for a particular purpose and it should waste as little energy as possible. Suppose you were a rock musician at a concert. You would need appliances that transfer sound energy into electrical energy and then back into sound energy. But you wouldn't want them to produce lots of energy heating the appliance itself and its surroundings. See if you can spot some of these appliances in Figure 3.

Figure 3 On stage

b What electrical appliance transfers:
  i sound energy into electrical energy?
  ii electrical energy into sound energy?
c What other electrical appliance would you need at a concert?

Summary questions

1 Copy and complete using the words below:

electrical   light   heating

When a battery is connected to a light bulb, ... energy is transferred from the battery to the light bulb. The filament of the light bulb becomes hot and so energy transfers to its surroundings by .... and as .... energy.

2 Match each electrical appliance in the list below with the energy transfer A or B it is designed to bring about.
  1 Electric drill
  2 Food mixer
  3 Electric bell

  Energy transfer A Electrical energy → sound energy
                    B Electrical energy → kinetic energy

3 **a** Why does a clockwork radio need to be wound up before it can be used?
  b What energy transfers take place in a clockwork radio when it is wound up then switched on?
  c Give an advantage and a disadvantage of a clockwork radio compared with a battery-operated radio.

Key points
- Electrical appliances can transfer electrical energy into useful energy at the flick of a switch.
- Uses of everyday electrical appliances include heating, lighting, making objects move (using an electric motor) and creating sound and visual images.
- An electrical appliance is designed for a particular purpose and should waste as little energy as possible.

??? Did you know ...?

Electricity and life have been linked ever since scientists noticed that a battery could be used to make dead frogs' legs twitch as if they were alive. Some people thought that electricity might even be used to bring the dead back to life, and this was the idea that inspired the 17-year-old Mary Shelley to write her novel *Frankenstein*. Even today, scientists are accused of trying to produce 'Frankenstein foods' with genetic engineering.

Further teaching suggestions

Applications
- Students could find out where all the electrical effects demonstrated today are used in industry or around the school.

Extended writing
- The 'Electricity everywhere' Starter could be used as the topic of a longer story that students could write, if not used during the lesson. This could be used as homework.

Answers to in-text questions

a Electrical energy transfers to kinetic energy of the brush, heating due to friction between the moving parts and resistance, and sound.
b **i** A microphone.   **ii** A loudspeaker.
c An amplifier.

Summary answers

1 electrical, heating, light

2 1 B, 2 B, 3 A

3 **a** Energy needs to be stored in its spring so that the spring will turn a generator to provide the electricity supply to the radio.
  b Elastic energy in the spring is transferred into kinetic energy of the generator which is transferred into electrical energy + sound + heating due to friction between the moving parts of the generator.
  c E.g. advantage – clockwork radio saves the cost of replacing batteries; disadvantage – needs winding up regularly whereas with batteries you can switch on and listen immediately, as long as the batteries are working.

P1 3.2

Electrical power

AQA Specification link-up: Physics P1.3

- The amount of energy an appliance transfers depends on how long the appliance is switched on and its power. *[P1.3.1 b)]*

Learning objectives

Students should learn:

- that the power rating of an appliance is a measure of how much energy it transfers each second
- how to calculate the power of an appliance
- how to calculate the efficiency of an electrical appliance.

Learning outcomes

Most students should be able to:

- state that the watt is the unit of power
- calculate the power output of appliances using the equation: $P = \dfrac{E}{t}$
- calculate the efficiency of an electrical appliance from power or energy data.

Some students should also be able to:

- perform calculations involving the rearrangement of the equation. [HT only]

Support

- You may need to provide a layout template for the calculations for some students to support and develop their skills. This template may contain partly completed equations.

Extend

- The power output of our Sun, a typical star, is much greater than the power needed for everybody on the Earth. How could we harness this power to meet our energy demands for the next billion years? Students could look into exotic solutions, such as space mirrors, ring worlds and Dyson spheres. The outcome could be a dramatic presentation of the far future.

Lesson structure

Starters

Big numbers – Give students a set of units with SI prefixes and ask them to place the units in order of size. These could be mm, cm, m, km and another set containing mg, g, and kg. You could then add in larger units such as mega (M) and giga (G). Students may not have encountered these before. *(5 minutes)*

Match up – Ask students to sort a range of electrical appliances into order of energy use (power rating). You could do this with real objects or with cards to represent them. The objects could be set up on a long bench and students should add post-it notes for their ranking. Discuss these rankings after everybody has had a go. To extend the task, you could ask students to guess the power ratings (in watts). They could then add post-it notes indicating the useful energy transfers and wasted energy on each. *(10 minutes)*

Main

- Begin with a discussion of power and the clear scientific definition as 'the amount of energy transferred each second'. You could show some appliances and say which has the higher power rating; students should soon get to grips with the idea.

- Recap energy use by electrical appliances using the Practical support 'Measuring energy use'. The unit 'watt' is exactly the same as 'a joule per second' and this is a common concept tested in examinations. Some students seem to struggle with the term 'per' and you might explain this as meaning 'each'. You could also use this practical as an open-ended planning exercise.

- Emphasise that the prefix 'kilo' just means 'one thousand'. Check that students understand numbers like 2.4 kW and 0.5 kW, as some have difficulty; if they are struggling it is sometimes best to say the 'kilo' means 'multiply the number by one thousand'. Similarly, some students will need the prefix 'mega' explained to them carefully.

- Provide plenty of example calculations as students need to develop a clear layout for their calculations. Adhere to a rigorous method, and check that students are reaching the correct answers with their method.

- Extend students by encouraging them to rearrange the equation. As before, to ensure consistency, check with the mathematics department how this rearrangement is usually tackled.

- The efficiency of weightlifters is not very good. Although the weightlifter may be producing a useful power output of 600 W, they may actually be using chemical energy at 1000 W. This is more than an electrical fire – so it is no wonder that they get hot!

- The efficiency calculation links back to the previous chapter. This time you are using power statistics but the techniques should be exactly the same as you used last time to ensure consistency.

Plenaries

Matching the power – Give students a set of pictures of household electrical appliances and a set of power ratings. Ask them to match the ratings with the appliances. [Examples could include: kettle 2 kW, washing machine 0.5 kW, desktop computer 200 W, dishwasher 1.5 kW, electric clock 1 W, iron 1 kW, CD player 30 W, blender 300 W]. *(5 minutes)*

Calculation loop – This is similar to most loop games, but students have to match calculation questions with numerical answers to match. There should be a set of calculations and only one card with the correct answer. Students work out the correct answer and then ask the question on their card. Repeat until all of the questions are answered. This should ensure plenty of practice at the calculations from the lesson. Prepare a slideshow of the calculations, so that you can show the right approach at the end of each question. *(10 minutes)*

Practical support

Measuring energy use

You could demonstrate the energy use of electrical appliances using a joulemeter, if you have not already done so in previous practical work. Connect up appliances to a low-voltage power supply and measure the energy using the joulemeter. Demonstrate a range of bulbs so students can link the energy use to the brightness. Then move on to motors, showing larger motors requiring more energy. You could even show the low power heating elements again.

Electrical energy

P1 3.2   Electrical power

Learning objectives

- What do we mean by power?
- How can we calculate the power of an appliance?
- How can we calculate the efficiency of an appliance in terms of power?

Figure 1 A lift motor

When you use a lift to go up, a powerful electric motor pulls you and the lift upwards. The lift motor transfers energy from electrical energy to gravitational potential energy when the lift goes up at a steady speed. We also get electrical energy transferred to wasted energy heating the motor and the surroundings, and sound energy.

- The energy we supply per second to the motor is the **power** supplied to it.
- The more powerful the lift motor is, the faster it moves a particular load.

In general, we can say that:

the more powerful an appliance, the faster the rate at which it transfers energy.

We measure the power of an appliance in watts (W) or kilowatts (kW).

1 **watt** is a rate of transfer of energy of 1 joule per second (J/s).

1 **kilowatt** is equal to 1000 watts (i.e. 1000 joules per second or 1 kJ/s).

You can calculate power using:

$$P = \frac{E}{t}$$

Where:

P is the power in watts, W

E is the energy transferred to the appliance in joules, J

t is the time taken for the energy to be transferred in seconds, s.

Maths skills

Worked example

A motor transfers 10 000 J of energy in 25 s. What is its power?

Solution

$P = \frac{E}{t}$

$P = \frac{10\,000\,J}{25\,s} = 400\,W$

a What is the power of a lift motor that transfers 50 000 J of energy from the electricity supply in 10 s?

Power ratings

Here are some typical values of power ratings for different energy transfers:

Appliance	Power rating
A torch	1 W
An electric light bulb	100 W
An electric cooker	10 000 W = 10 kW (where 1 kW = 1000 watts)
A railway engine	1 000 000 W = 1 megawatt (MW) = 1 million watts
A Saturn V rocket	100 MW
A very large power station	10 000 MW
World demand for power	10 000 000 MW
A star like the Sun	100 000 000 000 000 000 000 MW

Figure 2 Rocket power

b How many 100 W electric light bulbs would use the same amount of power as a 10 kW electric cooker?

Muscle power

How powerful is a weightlifter?

A 30 kg dumbbell has a weight of 300 N. Raising it by 1 m would give it 300 J of gravitational potential energy. A weightlifter could lift it in about 0.5 seconds. The rate of energy transfer would be 600 J/s (= 300 J ÷ 0.5 s). So the weightlifter's power output would be about 600 W in total!

c An inventor has designed an exercise machine that can also generate 100 W of electrical power. Do you think people would buy this machine in case of a power cut?

Efficiency and power

For any appliance

- its useful power out (or output power) is the useful energy **per second** transferred by it.
- its total power in (or input power) is the energy **per second** supplied to it.

In P1 2.4 Energy and efficiency, we saw that the efficiency of an appliance

$= \frac{\text{useful energy transferred by the device}}{\text{total energy supplied to it}}$ ($\times$ 100%)

Because power = energy **per second** transferred or supplied, we can write the efficiency equation as:

Efficiency $= \frac{\text{useful power out}}{\text{total power in}}$ ($\times$ 100%)

For example, suppose the useful power out of an electric motor is 20 W and the total power in is 80 W, the percentage efficiency of the motor is:

$\frac{\text{useful power out}}{\text{total power in}} \times 100\% = \frac{20\,W}{80\,W} \times 100\% = 25\%$

Figure 3 Muscle power

Summary questions

1 **a** Which is more powerful?
   i A torch bulb or a mains filament bulb.
   ii A 3 kW electric kettle or a 10 000 W electric cooker.
  b There are about 20 million occupied homes in England. If a 3 kW electric kettle was switched on in 1 in 10 homes at the same time, how much power would need to be supplied?

2 The total power supplied to a lift motor is 5000 W. In a test, it transfers 12 000 J of electrical energy to gravitational potential energy in 20 seconds.
  a How much electrical energy is supplied to the motor in 20 s?
  b What is its efficiency in the test?

3 A machine has an input power rating of 100 kW. If the useful energy transferred by the machine in 50 seconds is 1500 kJ, calculate
  a its output power in kilowatts
  b its percentage efficiency.

Key points

- Power is rate of transfer of energy.
- $P = \frac{E}{t}$
- Efficiency $= \frac{\text{useful power out}}{\text{total power in}}$ ($\times$ 100%)

56

57

Further teaching suggestions

Measuring energy output of a battery

- The energy output of a battery can be measured using data logging techniques. Connect up two simple circuits containing a battery and a light bulb with a current sensor. In one circuit, use normal batteries and in the other, use long-life batteries. Use the data logging software to record how the current changes over a long period of time, and present the graphs to students during the next lesson for discussion. Do the long-life batteries last up to four times as long?

Equipment and materials required

Batteries (two types), light bulbs and holders, connecting leads, battery holders, current sensors, data loggers.

Horsepower

- Further calculations may be useful. Students could look into the origin of the term 'horsepower' and find out how many watts are equivalent to one horsepower. This could be done as a piece of homework.

Answers to in-text questions

a 5000 W (5 kW)
b 100 light bulbs
c Probably not, as 100 W would keep one or two light bulbs on, but only when you pedal.

Summary answers

1 **a** **i** A mains filament bulb.
    ii A 10 000 W electric cooker.
  b 6 million kilowatts.

2 **a** 100 000 J
  b 0.12 (or 12%)

3 **a** 30 kW
  b 30%

P1 3.3

Using electrical energy

Learning objectives

Students should learn:

- how to calculate the energy transferred by mains-supplied electrical appliances
- how to calculate the cost of operating electrical appliances.

Learning outcomes

Most students should be able to:

- calculate the amount of energy used by a mains appliance (in kW h)
- calculate the cost of the electricity used.

Some students should also be able to:

- carry out rearrangement of the appropriate equations. [HT only]

$\mathcal{AQA}$ **Specification link-up: Physics P1.3**

- To calculate the amount of energy transferred from the mains using: $E = P \times t$ *[P1.3.1 c)]*
- To calculate the cost of mains electricity given the cost per kilowatt-hour. *[P1.3.1 d)]*

Lesson structure

Starters

Paying for electricity – Students should list the reasons that electricity should be paid for, e.g. the cost of materials, the workforce and the meter readers. Students could be extended by considering how these production costs could be reduced. They should realise that different productions techniques will have different costs associated with them. *(5 minutes)*

True cost – Show students a few electricity bills from different companies, so that they understand that different companies use different rates. They should get an appreciation of the complexity including different rates at different times of the day, standing charges, VAT and so on. They should check that the bills are correct. *(10 minutes)*

Main

- This is another quite mathematical concept with important calculations. You might like to start with some basic cost calculations of simple things like food to make sure students can complete them.

- The most common difficulty is the name of the units. Students really need to understand that a 'kilowatt-hour' is a measure of an amount of energy, so spend some time going through this.

- Students should be reminded that the amount of energy an appliance uses is linked to the power it uses and time the appliance is activated for.

- Make sure that students can work out how many kilowatt-hours have been used when given two different meter readings. It is a simple subtraction, but some students just choose one of the two meter readings and think that this is the number of units used.

- Some students struggle when talking about immaterial things like 'kilowatt-hours', and you may need to give analogies like 'how many gobstoppers could you buy for £2 if they cost 12p each' and so on.

- Students now have two methods of calculating energy use: kilowatt-hours and joules. Students need not translate between the two.

- Extend students by asking them to work out how many kilowatt-hours could be bought with a set amount of money. How long can they keep a TV running for if they have £1?

Plenaries

Big bill – Show students a copy of the school electricity bill and ask them to think of ways they could reduce it. They should gain an appreciation of running all of the equipment they use every day. They could also try out the calculations to see if they come up with the same answer as the electricity company. *(5 minutes)*

Choosing the best supplier – Extend students by giving them copies of two pricing structures: one with a standing charge, and one without a standing charge but with a higher price per kilowatt-hour. Ask students to find out which company each of three different families should use. (For example: Ultra-Elec has a standing charge of 20 pence per day and a cost of 10 pence per kW h. Top-Power has no standing charge but cost of 12 pence per kW h. If the Bauer family use 300 kW h in a period of 90 days, which company is cheaper for them to use?) You will return to this idea in the next lesson. *(10 minutes)*

Support

- As in previous lessons, provide students with a layout template for calculations to help them with the work presented here.

Extend

- Extend students by asking them to calculate the energy use from a 100 W bulb left running for a year, in joules. They could then compare low energy bulbs that sometimes cost more to buy but are much cheaper to run each year. This may lead on to the idea of 'payback time'.

Practical support

The cost of electricity

Students could check the weekly usage of electricity from their own electricity meters and note it in a diary over a few months. They need to ensure that this is safe, so get them to check with their parents and then record the reading every week at a fixed time. The data would have to be collected over a fairly long period (several months) and then students could analyse their usage patterns. As an example, they could plot a graph showing their weekly use against the weekly temperature (either recorded or from records from the internet) to see if there is a correlation between the two, and discuss questions such as 'Do we use more electricity when it is colder?'

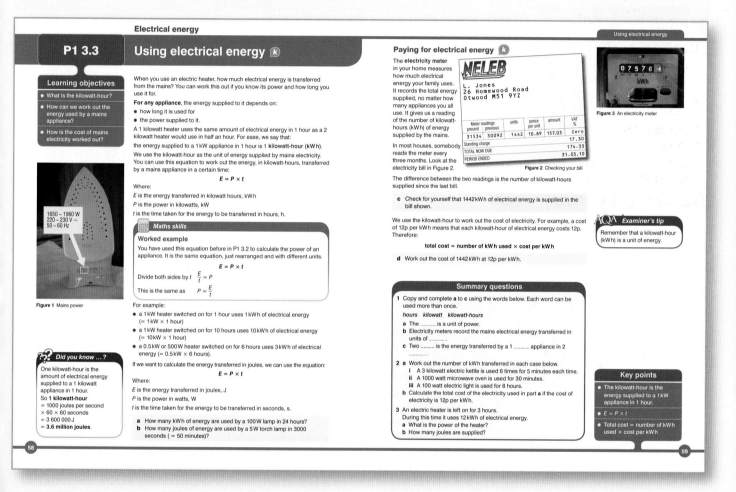

Electrical energy

P1 3.3

Using electrical energy

Learning objectives
- What is the kilowatt-hour?
- How can we work out the energy used by a mains appliance?
- How is the cost of mains electricity worked out?

When you use an electric heater, how much electrical energy is transferred from the mains? You can work this out if you know its power and how long you use it for.

For any appliance, the energy supplied to it depends on:
- how long it is used for
- the power supplied to it.

A 1 kilowatt heater uses the same amount of electrical energy in 1 hour as a 2 kilowatt heater would use in half an hour. For ease, we say that:
the energy supplied to a 1 kW appliance in 1 hour is 1 **kilowatt-hour (kWh)**.

We use the kilowatt-hour as the unit of energy supplied by mains electricity. You can use this equation to work out the energy, in kilowatt-hours, transferred by a mains appliance in a certain time:

$$E = P \times t$$

Where:
E is the energy transferred in kilowatt hours, kWh
P is the power in kilowatts, kW
t is the time taken for the energy to be transferred in hours, h.

Maths skills

Worked example

You have used this equation before in P1 3.2 to calculate the power of an appliance. It is the same equation, just rearranged and with different units.

$$E = P \times t$$

Divide both sides by t $\quad \dfrac{E}{t} = P$

This is the same as $\quad P = \dfrac{E}{t}$

Figure 1 Mains power

1650 – 1960 W
220 – 230 V ~
50 – 60 Hz

For example:
- a 1 kW heater switched on for 1 hour uses 1 kWh of electrical energy (= 1 kW × 1 hour)
- a 1 kW heater switched on for 10 hours uses 10 kWh of electrical energy (= 10 kW × 1 hour)
- a 0.5 kW or 500 W heater switched on for 6 hours uses 3 kWh of electrical energy (= 0.5 kW × 6 hours).

If we want to calculate the energy transferred in joules, we can use the equation:

$$E = P \times t$$

Where:
E is the energy transferred in joules, J
P is the power in watts, W
t is the time taken for the energy to be transferred in seconds, s.

a How many kWh of energy are used by a 100 W lamp in 24 hours?
b How many joules of energy are used by a 5 W torch lamp in 3000 seconds (= 50 minutes)?

?? Did you know …?

One kilowatt-hour is the amount of electrical energy supplied to a 1 kilowatt appliance in 1 hour.
So **1 kilowatt-hour**
= 1000 joules per second
× 60 × 60 seconds
= 3 600 000 J
= **3.6 million joules**.

Paying for electrical energy

The **electricity meter** in your home measures how much electrical energy your family uses. It records the total energy supplied, no matter how many appliances you all use. It gives us a reading of the number of kilowatt-hours (kWh) of energy supplied by the mains.

In most houses, somebody reads the meter every three months. Look at the electricity bill in Figure 2.

NELEB

L. Jones
26 Homewood Road
Otwood M51 9YZ

Meter readings present	previous	units	pence per unit	amount	VAT %
31534	30092	1442	10.89	157.03	Zero
Standing charge				17.30	
TOTAL NOW DUE				174.33	
PERIOD ENDED		31.03.10			

Figure 2 Checking your bill

The difference between the two readings is the number of kilowatt-hours supplied since the last bill.

c Check for yourself that 1442 kWh of electrical energy is supplied in the bill shown.

We use the kilowatt-hour to work out the cost of electricity. For example, a cost of 12p per kWh means that each kilowatt-hour of electrical energy costs 12p. Therefore:

total cost = number of kWh used × cost per kWh

d Work out the cost of 1442 kWh at 12p per kWh.

Figure 3 An electricity meter

07576 4
kWh

AQA Examiner's tip

Remember that a kilowatt-hour (kWh) is a unit of energy.

Summary questions

1 Copy and complete **a** to **c** using the words below. Each word can be used more than once.

hours   kilowatt   kilowatt-hours

a The .... is a unit of power.
b Electricity meters record the mains electrical energy transferred in units of ....
c Two .... is the energy transferred by a 1 .... appliance in 2 ....

2 **a** Work out the number of kWh transferred in each case below.
   i A 3 kilowatt electric kettle is used 6 times for 5 minutes each time.
   ii A 1000 watt microwave oven is used for 30 minutes.
   iii A 100 watt electric light is used for 8 hours.
   b Calculate the total cost of the electricity used in part **a** if the cost of electricity is 12p per kWh.

3 An electric heater is left on for 3 hours. During this time it uses 12 kWh of electrical energy.
   a What is the power of the heater?
   b How many joules are supplied?

Key points
- The kilowatt-hour is the energy supplied to a 1 kW appliance in 1 hour.
- $E = P \times t$
- Total cost = number of kWh used × cost per kWh

58 | 59

Further teaching suggestions

ICT link-up

- This is a great opportunity for students to use a simple spreadsheet to calculate the cost of the electricity used. They could then very easily find out what would happen to the price if the cost per kWh increased or decreased by altering just one number. You could design the sheet or ask students confident with ICT to make one of their own.

?? Did you know …?

In standby mode, a large TV operates at 10 W. If it is left on standby for 12 hours, it will use 0.12 kWh. That means it costs 0.84p per night or £3 per year.

Around the world, machines in standby mode consume 4 TWh of energy in standby mode each year. (£280 million at UK prices.)

Answers to in-text questions

a 2.4 kWh
b 15 000 J
c Students to check answer.
d £173.04

Summary answers

1 **a** kilowatt
  b kilowatt-hours
  c kilowatt-hours, kilowatt, hours

2 **a** **i** 1.5 kWh
     ii 0.5 kWh
     iii 0.8 kWh
  b 33.6p

3 **a** 4 kW
  b 43.2 million joules (4000 × 3 × 60 × 60)

P1 3.4

Cost effectiveness matters

Specification link-up: Physics P1.2

- Compare the efficiency and cost effectiveness of methods used to reduce 'energy consumption'. [P1.2]

Learning objectives

Students should learn:

- that a cost-effective appliance is efficient and provides good value for money
- that the cost effectiveness can be compared by looking at the efficiency of the appliance and the original (capital) cost.

Learning outcomes

Most students should be able to:

- compare appliances or techniques to find out which is most cost effective based on running costs and capital costs
- take into account other cost factors such as environmental impact in their assessments.

Lesson structure

Starters

Cosy home – Before students look at the Student Book, support students by giving them a diagram of a house and ask them to think of all the ways that energy is being wasted. They should suggest ways that the house could be made more energy efficient. They should be able to come up with all of the ways mentioned in this spread and possibly more. [For example, draught excluders, cavity wall insulation, loft insulation, double glazing, carpeted floors.] *(5 minutes)*

Value pack – Show students some cornflake packets (or similar) of different sizes along with the price. They then have to work out a fair comparison of value (e.g. cost per 100 g). Then show them a supermarket brand in different-sized packages and ask them to find the best value. They could discuss if the supermarket brand is exactly the same as the better-known brand. This could link into the central idea of cost effectiveness during the lesson. *(10 minutes)*

Main

- Begin this lesson by clearly defining the terms you are going to use. Capital cost is the original cost of purchasing. Running costs are more difficult, as you may need to go back and review the previous calculations. Interest costs are usually not considered by most students, but you will have to introduce them here. The environmental costs are harder to work out in monetary value; you could deal with them as a discussion later.

- There are four sections to the lesson, each looking in detail at a particular example:

- The first activity focuses on the idea of payback time in a house. You could expand on this by incorporating other measures. For example, fitting draught excluders may cost £10 and save £20 each year. This gives a very short payback time. Double glazing costs £4000 and saves only £200 each year, giving a payback time of 20 years (although it reduces noise levels too).

- For the shop-around task, you could use the plenary from the previous lesson if it was not attempted, or you could make up a few more scenarios. Tailor these to the ability of the students; add standing charges if you want to make the task more demanding.

- The low energy light bulb task is one about which most students should have some prior knowledge. You could point out the lighting systems in your school that are most likely low energy fluorescent tubes and explain the reasons the school uses them. You should look at the cost of LED lighting; this is changing quickly and the costs may have fallen a great deal each year.

- The final activity is a straightforward choice; students need to consider what makes a 'good' heater in this scenario.

Plenaries

Truthful advertising – Ask students to come up with some ideas for an advertisement poster for a hybrid car pointing out the advantages in terms of fuel efficiency and environmental impact. They could do this by brainstorming as a class or by individually sketching their ideas. *(5 minutes)*

I'll waste if I want to! – Do you have the right to waste energy? The government have restricted the sale of filament light bulbs but shouldn't people with enough money be able to use whatever amount of energy they want to? Similarly, cars with larger engines are more heavily road-taxed even though the petrol itself is taxed anyway. Is it fair to tax people who want to use more fuel, even more money? Students could discuss issues such as larger families needing bigger cars, car-sharing, and family cars that may carry six people at weekends but only one during the week. Extend students by asking them to discuss this concept in some depth or to write a letter of complaint to the government. They will need to use persuasive argument and include scientific facts. *(10 minutes)*

Support

- There are a few mathematical concepts here, so check students' calculations carefully and provide extra assistance where necessary.

Extend

- There is plenty of scope here to discuss improvements in energy efficiency in detail. Students could research emerging technology like hydrogen fuel cells for cars.

Further teaching suggestions

Different rates: Are they fair?
- Most electricity companies charge more per unit for pre-pay meters. This means that the poorest people actually pay more for each unit. You could have a discussion about whether this is a fair practice. Be careful to respect the privacy or feelings of some students who may be using these meters.

Truthful advertising
- Students could complete their advertisement poster as homework. They could make the the poster more honest by incorporating all of the disadvantages of the technology: cost, range, speed.

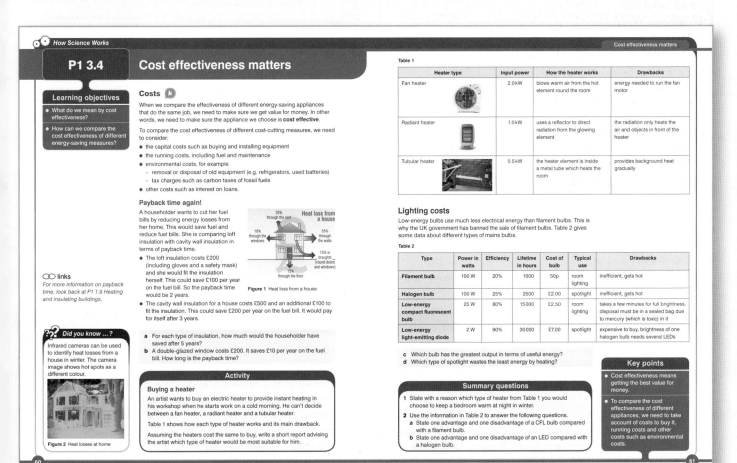

P1 3.4 — Cost effectiveness matters

Learning objectives
- What do we mean by cost effectiveness?
- How can we compare the cost effectiveness of different energy-saving measures?

Costs
When we compare the effectiveness of different energy-saving appliances that do the same job, we need to make sure we get value for money. In other words, we need to make sure the appliance we choose is **cost effective**.

To compare the cost effectiveness of different cost-cutting measures, we need to consider:
- the capital costs such as buying and installing equipment
- the running costs, including fuel and maintenance
- environmental costs, for example
  - removal or disposal of old equipment (e.g. refrigerators, used batteries)
  - tax charges such as carbon taxes of fossil fuels
- other costs such as interest on loans.

Payback time again!
A householder wants to cut her fuel bills by reducing energy losses from her home. This would save fuel and reduce fuel bills. She is comparing loft insulation with cavity wall insulation in terms of payback time.
- The loft insulation costs £200 (including gloves and a safety mask) and she would fit the insulation herself. This could save £100 per year on the fuel bill. So the payback time would be 2 years.
- The cavity wall insulation for a house costs £500 and an additional £100 to fit the insulation. This could save £200 per year on the fuel bill. It would pay for itself after 3 years.

a For each type of insulation, how much would the householder have saved after 5 years?
b A double-glazed window costs £200. It saves £10 per year on the fuel bill. How long is the payback time?

Figure 1 Heat loss from a house

links
For more information on payback time, look back at P1 1.9 Heating and insulating buildings.

Did you know ...?
Infrared cameras can be used to identify heat losses from a house in winter. The camera image shows hot spots as a different colour.

Figure 2 Heat losses at home

Activity
Buying a heater
An artist wants to buy an electric heater to provide instant heating in his workshop when he starts work on a cold morning. He can't decide between a fan heater, a radiant heater and a tubular heater.

Table 1 shows how each type of heater works and its main drawback.

Assuming the heaters cost the same to buy, write a short report advising the artist which type of heater would be most suitable for him.

Table 1

Heater type	Input power	How the heater works	Drawbacks
Fan heater	2.0 kW	blows warm air from the hot element round the room	energy needed to run the fan motor
Radiant heater	1.0 kW	uses a reflector to direct radiation from the glowing element	the radiation only heats the air and objects in front of the heater
Tubular heater	0.5 kW	the heater element is inside a metal tube which heats the room	provides background heat gradually

Lighting costs
Low-energy bulbs use much less electrical energy than filament bulbs. This is why the UK government has banned the sale of filament bulbs. Table 2 gives some data about different types of mains bulbs.

Table 2

Type	Power in watts	Efficiency	Lifetime in hours	Cost of bulb	Typical use	Drawbacks
Filament bulb	100 W	20%	1000	50p	room lighting	inefficient, gets hot
Halogen bulb	100 W	25%	2500	£2.00	spotlight	inefficient, gets hot
Low-energy compact fluorescent bulb	25 W	80%	15000	£2.50	room lighting	takes a few minutes for full brightness, disposal must be in a sealed bag due to mercury (which is toxic) in it
Low-energy light-emitting diode	2 W	90%	30000	£7.00	spotlight	expensive to buy, brightness of one halogen bulb needs several LEDs

c Which bulb has the greatest output in terms of useful energy?
d Which type of spotlight wastes the least energy by heating?

Summary questions
1 State with a reason which type of heater from Table 1 you would choose to keep a bedroom warm at night in winter.
2 Use the information in Table 2 to answer the following questions.
  a State one advantage and one disadvantage of a CFL bulb compared with a filament bulb.
  b State one advantage and one disadvantage of an LED compared with a halogen bulb.

Key points
- Cost effectiveness means getting the best value for money.
- To compare the cost effectiveness of different appliances, we need to take account of costs to buy it, running costs and other costs such as environmental costs.

Answers to in-text questions
a Loft insulation £300; cavity wall insulation £400
b 20 years
c The halogen bulb.
d The LED.

Summary answers
1 The tubular heater, as the room would be too hot with either of the other two heaters on throughout the night.

2 a The CFL bulb uses much less electrical energy than the filament bulb. However, it contains mercury and needs to be disposed of carefully.
  b The LED uses less electrical energy. However, you need several LEDs for the same brightness as a halogen bulb and they are much more expensive than a single halogen bulb.

Summary answers

1 a i A TV or visual display unit (VDU).
   ii An electric motor.
  b i sound, wasted
     ii kinetic, sound

2 a joule, kilowatt-hour
  b C, B, A, D

3 a i The higher one.
     ii 243 kWh
    iii £29.16
  b i 10 kWh
     ii 5 hours

4 a 500 kWh
  b £60
  c £12

5 a The heater
  b A 4.0 kWh   B 1.0 kWh   C 1.5 kWh
  c 78p

6 a i 0.12 kWh
     ii 432 000 J
  b Electrical energy to sound and light and energy transfer by heating.
  c Some energy is always wasted when a battery is used or recharged. Less energy would be used overall by using the computer with the charging unit connected to it, because the battery would not be used.

7 a 3.6 kWh
  b 43.2p

Summary questions 🄚

1 a Name an appliance that transfers electrical energy into:
   i light and sound energy
   ii kinetic energy.
  b Complete the sentences below.
   i In an electric bell, electrical energy is transferred into useful energy in the form of .... energy, and .... energy.
   ii In a dentist's drill, electrical energy is transferred into useful energy in the form of .... energy and sometimes as .... energy.

2 a Which two words in the list below are units that can be used to measure energy?
   joule kilowatt kilowatt-hour watt
  b Rank the electrical appliances below in terms of energy used from highest to lowest.
   A a 0.5 kW heater used for 4 hours
   B a 100 W lamp left on for 24 hours
   C a 3 kW electric kettle used 6 times for 10 minutes each time
   D a 750 W microwave oven used for 10 minutes.

3 a The readings of an electricity meter at the start and the end of a month are shown below.

0	9	3	7	2
0	9	6	1	5

   i Which is the reading at the end of the month?
   ii How many kilowatt-hours of electricity were used during the month?
   iii How much would this electricity cost at 12p per kWh?
  b A pay meter in a holiday home supplies electricity at a cost of 12p per kWh.
   i How many kWh would be supplied for £1.20?
   ii How long could a 2 kW heater be used for after £1.20 is put in the meter slot? [H]

4 An escalator in a shopping centre is powered by a 50 kW electric motor. The escalator is in use for a total time of 10 hours every day.
  a How much electrical energy in kWh is supplied to the motor each day?
  b The electricity supplied to the motor costs 12p per kWh. What is the daily cost of the electricity supplied to the motor?
  c How much would be saved each day if the motor was replaced by a more efficient 40 kW motor?

5 The data below show the electrical appliances used in a house in one evening.
   A a 1.0 kW heater for 4 hours
   B a 0.5 kW television for 2 hours
   C a 3 kW electric kettle three times for 10 minutes each time.
  a Which appliance uses most energy?
  b How many kWh of electrical energy is used by each appliance?
  c Each kWh costs 12p. How much did it cost to use the three appliances?

6 The battery of a laptop computer is capable of supplying 60 watts to the computer circuits for 2 hours before it needs to be recharged.
  a Calculate the electrical energy the battery can supply in two hours in:
   i kilowatt-hours
   ii joules.
  b Describe the energy transfers that take place when the computer is being used.
  c A mains charging unit can be connected to the computer when in use to keep its battery fully charged. Would the computer use less energy with the charging unit connected than without it connected?

7 A student has an HD television at home that uses 120 watts of electrical power when it is switched on. He monitors its usage for a week and finds it is switched on for 30 hours.

Figure 1 An HD TV in use

  a How many kilowatt-hours of electrical energy are supplied to it in this time?
  b Calculate the cost of this electrical energy at 12p per kilowatt-hour.

AQA Examiner's tip

Students often do not grasp the fact that joules and kilowatt-hours are alternative units for energy. The presence of the 'W' in kWh often persuades the student that it is a unit of power. Kilowatt-hours are used by energy companies because a kWh is a fairly typical amount of energy used when a fairly typical appliance is left on for 1 hour. The numbers are easy to work with and understand. They sometimes even drop the kWh and call it a 'unit'. The irony is, that in GCSE Physics, having this alternative unit and then calling it a 'unit' causes more confusion than it prevents!

AQA Examiner's tip

To keep things simple in calculating kWh, students can be encouraged to express the number of hours as a fraction, e.g. 15 minutes can be written as 15/60 hours.

AQA Examiner's tip

Students need to understand that the same equation for power (power = energy × time) is being used. However, no rearrangement of the equation will be asked for when dealing with the cost of electricity.

Kerboodle resources 🄚

Resources available for this chapter on Kerboodle are:
- Chapter map: Electrical energy
- Maths skills: Electrical energy (P1 3.3)
- Support: Power to the kitchen (P1 3.3)
- Bump up your grade: Read a meter (P1 3.3)
- Interactive activity: Electrical energy calculations (P1 3.4)
- Extension: The best rates (P1 3.4)
- Revision podcast: Electricity costs
- Test yourself: Electrical energy
- On your marks: Electrical energy
- Examination-style questions: Electrical energy
- Answers to examination-style questions: Electrical energy

AQA Examination-style questions

1 The pictures show six different household appliances.

Fan heater   Vacuum cleaner   Washing machine

Iron   Kettle   Blender

Name the **four** appliances in which electrical energy is usefully transferred into kinetic energy. (4)

2 An electric motor is used to lift a load. The useful power output of the motor is 30 W. The total input power to the motor is 75 W.

Calculate the efficiency of the motor.

Write down the equation you use. Show clearly how you work out your answer. (3)

3 Which **two** of the following units are units of energy?

a J

b J/s

c kWh

d W (1)

4 The diagram shows the readings on a household electricity meter at the beginning and end of one week.

| 5 | 2 | 3 | 4 | 0 | | 5 | 2 | 5 | 5 | 5 |

Beginning of the week   **End of the week**

a How many kWh of electricity were used during the week? (1)

b On one day 35 kWh of electricity were used. The total cost of this electricity was £5.25.

Calculate how much the electricity cost per kWh.

Write down the equation you use. Show clearly how you work out your answer and give the unit. [H] (3)

c During the week a 2.4 kW kettle was used for 2 hours.

Calculate how much energy was transferred by the kettle.

Write down the equation you use. Show clearly how you work out your answer and give the unit. (3)

5 A student uses some hair straighteners.

a The hair straighteners have a power of 90 W.

What is meant by *a power of 90 W*? (2)

b Calculate how many kilowatt-hours of electricity are used when the straighteners are used for 15 minutes.

Write down the equation you use. Show clearly how you work out your answer and give the unit. (3)

c The electricity supplier is charging 14p per kWh.

Calculate how much it will cost to use the straighteners for 15 minutes a day for one year.

Write down the equation you use. Show clearly how you work out your answer and give the unit. (2)

6 Filament bulbs are being replaced by compact fluorescent bulbs.

A compact fluorescent bulb costs £12, a filament bulb costs 50p.

A 25 W compact fluorescent bulb gives out as much light as a 100 W filament bulb.

A filament bulb lasts for about 1000 hours; a compact fluorescent bulb lasts for about 8000 hours, although this time is significantly shorter if the bulb is turned on and off very frequently.

A compact fluorescent bulb contains a small amount of poisonous mercury vapour.

a Explain how a 25 W compact fluorescent bulb provides the same amount of light as a 100 W filament bulb but use less electricity. (2)

b *In this question you will be assessed on using good English, organising information clearly and using specialist terms where appropriate.*

Compare the advantages and disadvantages of buying compact fluorescent bulbs rather than filament bulbs. (6)

63

AQA Practical suggestions

Practicals	AQA	k	📖	⚙
Candidates reading the electricity meter at home on a daily or weekly basis. They could then look for trends in usage and try to explain these, e.g. in terms of weather conditions.		✓		✓
Plan and carry out an investigation using an electrical joulemeter to measure the energy transferred by low voltage bulbs of different powers, low voltage motors and low voltage immersion heaters.		✓		✓

AQA Examination-style answers

1 Fan heater
Washing machine
Blender
Vacuum cleaner *(4 marks)*

2 $\text{Efficiency} = \dfrac{\text{useful power out}}{\text{total power in}} \times 100\%$

$\text{Efficiency} = \dfrac{30\,\text{W}}{75\,\text{W}} \times 100\%$

$\text{Efficiency} = 40\%$ *(3 marks)*

3 a (J) and **c** (kWh) – both required *(1 mark)*

4 a 215 *(1 mark)*

b Total cost = number of kWh used × cost per kWh
cost per kWh = total cost/number of kWh used
cost per kWh = 525p/35
cost per kWh = 15p *(3 marks)*

c $E = P \times t$
$E = 2.4\,\text{kW} \times 2\,\text{h}$
$E = 4.8\,\text{kWh}$ *(3 marks)*

5 a 90 joules of energy are transferred each second *(2 marks)*

b $E = P \times t$
$E = 0.09\,\text{kW} \times 0.25\,\text{h}$
$E = 0.0225\,\text{kWh}$ *(3 marks)*

c cost = number of kWh used × cost per kWh
cost per day = 0.0225 kWh × 14p = 0.315p
cost for the year = 0.315p × 365 = 115p or £1.15 *(2 marks)*

6 a Compact fluorescent bulb is more efficient than the filament bulb.

A bigger proportion of the energy supplied to the compact fluorescent bulb is transferred to light and less wasted to the surroundings by heating. *(2 marks)*

b There is a clear, balanced and detailed description of the advantages and disadvantages of buying compact fluorescent bulbs rather than filament bulbs. The answer shows almost faultless spelling, punctuation and grammar. It is coherent and in an organised, logical sequence. It contains a range of appropriate or relevant specialist terms used accurately. *(5–6 marks)*

There is a description of a range of the advantages and disadvantages of buying compact fluorescent bulbs rather than filament bulbs. There are some errors in spelling, punctuation and grammar. The answer has some structure and organisation. The use of specialist terms has been attempted, but not always accurately. *(3–4 marks)*

There is a brief description of at least two advantages and disadvantages of buying compact fluorescent bulbs rather than filament bulbs, which has little clarity and detail. The spelling, punctuation and grammar are very weak. The answer is poorly organised with almost no specialist terms and/or their use demonstrating a general lack of understanding of their meaning. *(1–2 marks)*

No relevant content. *(0 marks)*

Examples of physics points made in the response:

Advantages of compact fluorescent bulbs:
• more efficient/4 times more efficient
• cheaper to use
• last longer/lasts 8 times as long
• better for the environment.

Disadvantages of compact fluorescent bulbs:
• more expensive to buy/cost 24 times as much to buy
• disposal a problem because of mercury vapour
• shortened lifespan if turned on and off very frequently.

P1 4.1

Fuel for electricity

Learning objectives

Students should learn:

- how a fossil fuel-based power station operates
- the differences between using fossil fuels and nuclear fuels in electricity generation
- that other fuels (e.g. biofuel) can also be used to generate electricity.

Learning outcomes

Most students should be able to:

- draw a flow chart showing the stages of electricity generation in a power station
- describe the similarities and differences between different power stations.

Some students should also be able to:

- evaluate in detail the advantages and disadvantages of nuclear power in comparison with fossil fuels.

Answers to in-text questions

a It is condensed to water and goes back to the boiler.

b It is carried away by the hot water from the cooling tower, escaping into the air.

Support

- Students could be provided with a diagram of a power station and complete the labelling of the important components. This will allow them to concentrate on how the parts behave.

Extend

- Students can find out a lot more about the internal working of a power station by visiting appropriate websites. They should be able to find some statistics about fuel use, employment, pollution and sustainability.

AQA Specification link-up: Physics P1.4

- In some power stations an energy source is used to heat water. The steam produced drives a turbine that is coupled to an electrical generator. Energy sources include:
  - the fossil fuels (coal, oil and gas) which are burned to heat water or air
  - uranium and plutonium, when energy from nuclear fission is used to heat water
  - biofuels that can be burned to heat water. *[P1.4.1 a)]*
- Evaluate different methods of generating electricity. *[P1.4]*

Lesson structure

Starters

Fossil fuels – Get the students to describe how coal, oil and natural gas have formed. Support students by giving them pictures of some of the stages and ask them to put them into order. They can annotate these diagrams. Have some samples to show the students. *(5 minutes)*

Burning? – What is burning? The students should draw a spider diagram or mind map covering what they know about combustion of fuels. They can do this while watching a birthday candle burn; they have to stop when the candle is finished; choose a candle that will last for a few minutes. Support students by providing some example fuels for them to describe and expect then to produce a clear, and general, word equation. Extend students by expecting them to give an example symbol equation. *(10 minutes)*

Main

- Start by demonstrating the combustion of some fuel. This could be a simple Bunsen flame or a spirit burner. Discuss energy being released during oxidation of carbon linking back to the first starter if possible. You could demonstrate that water is being produced too with a cold sheet of glass or metal. You could extend this demonstration by putting a conical flask of water above the flame and letting it boil. Add a bung with a delivery tube to show steam generation; this is a vital process in power stations.

- Link these ideas to electricity generation; an animation of the processes involved in a power station gets the stages across clearly. Emphasise the difference in scale and the high pressure and temperature of the steam in a power station in comparison with your earlier demonstration. The students need to be able to state what each part of the power station does, so it is best to go through them thoroughly and check understanding at each stage.

- Demonstrate a turbine using the apparatus above or as outlined in 'Practical support'. You could use a biofuel to heat the water at this stage to introduce the concept. Show wood but use a spirit burner with ethanol in it as it burns cleanly and is easy to control.

- The carbon neutrality of biofuel is an important issue. Point out that the growing plant takes in the same amount of carbon as it released during burning. However, you can bring in the idea of energy being wasted during farming, processing and transporting the crop/biofuel to show that even biofuels have a carbon cost.

- When discussing the amount of energy produced by a kilogram of fuel, use a kilogram of coal to give a visual clue. There is enough energy in a kilogram of coal to keep a bright (100 W) light bulb running for 1000 hours; that is over 41 days. There is enough energy released by 1 kg of uranium to keep the same bulb running for 10 million hours. That's over a thousand years.

Plenaries

Anagrams – Ask students to decipher anagrams of important key words from this spread. These could be ['lace run: nuclear, be foul I: biofuel, I lo: oil, cola: coal, aural tangs: natural gas, a ruin um: uranium, clue sun: nucleus.] You can add some more about energy resources too and see if the students can figure them out [bend ruin wit: wind turbine, hamlet ogre: geothermal]. Obviously you can differentiate, extending or supporting, by using single words or more complex phrases. *(5 minutes)*

Lightning (brain) storm – Some people suggest harnessing the electricity from lightning strikes for power. The students could brainstorm the advantages and disadvantages of this idea. They should come up with the ideas that the energy would be 'free' but unreliable. They could then go on to research how much energy is actually provided by a lightning strike as part of a homework task. [~500 MJ] *(10 minutes)*

Practical support

Turbines

It is possible to buy turbine-demonstrating apparatus, but even if you haven't got any then the general principle is simple enough to show.

Equipment and materials required

Metal can with bung and glass delivery tube to let out steam, paper turbine or one of those fairground windmills on a stick, Bunsen, tripod and heatproof mat, a piece of metal, conical flask, spirit burner, ethanol.

Details

Half-fill the can with water and put the bung and glass delivery tube in. Heat on a medium flame to get a decent flow of steam and then place the windmill in the flow and watch it turn. It is important to point out that the steam is invisible and can cause severe burns.

Tips: Keep the glass delivery tube short so that energy is not wasted and boil the water in a kettle beforehand to save a bit of time. You might get a faster flow of steam if you taper the end of the glass delivery tube, but sometimes this just causes the steam to condense, so it is best to experiment beforehand to get the results you want.

Safety: Take care with hot water and steam. Wear eye protection. CLEAPSS Hazcard XOA Ethanol – highly flammable/harmful.

Generating electricity

P1 4.1 Fuel for electricity 🄺

Learning objectives

- How is electricity generated in a power station?
- Which fossil fuels do we burn in power stations?
- How do we use nuclear fuels in power stations?
- What other fuels can be used to generate electricity?

Inside a power station

Figure 1 Inside a fossil fuel power station

Figure 2 Inside a gas-fired power station

Almost all the electricity you use is generated in power stations.

- In **coal-** or **oil-fired power stations**, and in most **gas-fired power stations**, the burning fuel heats water in a boiler. This produces steam. The steam drives a **turbine** that turns an electricity **generator**. Coal, oil and gas are fossil fuels, which are fuels obtained from long-dead biological material.

a What happens to the steam after it has been used?
b What happens to the energy of the steam after it has been used?

- In some gas-fired power stations, we burn natural gas directly in a gas turbine engine. This heats the air drawn into the engine. It produces a powerful jet of hot gases and air that drives the turbine. A gas-fired turbine can be switched on very quickly.

Biofuels 🄺

We can get methane gas from cows or animal manure and from sewage works, decaying rubbish and other sources. It can be used in small-scale gas-fired power stations. Methane is an example of a **biofuel**.

A biofuel is any fuel obtained from living or recently living organisms such as animal waste or woodchip. Other biofuels include ethanol (from fermented sugar cane), straw, nutshells and woodchip.

A biofuel is:

- **renewable** because its biological source continues to exist and never dies out as a species
- **carbon-neutral** because, in theory, the carbon it takes in from the atmosphere as carbon dioxide can 'balance' the amount released when it is burned.

Practical

Turbines

See how we can use water to drive round the blades of a turbine.

- Why is steam better than water?

Figure 3 Using biofuel to generate electricity

Nuclear power 🄺

Figure 4 shows you that every atom contains a positively charged nucleus surrounded by electrons. The **atomic nucleus** is composed of two types of particles: neutrons and protons. Atoms of the same element can have different numbers of neutrons in the nucleus.

How is electricity obtained from a nuclear power station?

The fuel in a nuclear power station is uranium (or plutonium). The uranium fuel is in sealed cans in the core of the reactor. The nucleus of a uranium atom is unstable and can split in two. Energy is released when this happens. We call this process **nuclear fission**. Because there are lots of uranium atoms in the core, it becomes very hot.

The energy of the core is transferred by a fluid (called the 'coolant') that is pumped through the core.

- The coolant is very hot when it leaves the core. It flows through a pipe to a 'heat exchanger', then back to the reactor core.
- The energy of the coolant is used to turn water into steam in the heat exchanger. The steam drives turbines that turn electricity generators.

Figure 4 The structure of the atom

🄺 How Science Works

Comparing nuclear power and fossil fuel power

	Nuclear power station	Fossil fuel power station
Fuel	Uranium or plutonium	Coal, oil or gas
Energy released per kg of fuel	1 000 000 kWh (= about 10 000 × energy released per kg of fossil fuel)	100 kWh
Waste	Radioactive waste that needs to be stored for many years	Non-radioactive waste
Greenhouse gases	No – because uranium releases energy without burning	Yes – because fossil fuels produce gases such as carbon dioxide when they burn

Summary questions

1 Copy and complete **a** to **c** using the words below:
coal gas oil uranium
  a The fuel that is not a fossil fuel is ....
  b Power stations that use .... as the fuel can be switched on very quickly.
  c Greenhouse gases are produced in a power station that uses coal, gas or .... as fuel.

2 **a** State one advantage and one disadvantage of:
   i an oil-fired power station compared with a nuclear power station
   ii a gas-fired power station compared with a coal-fired power station.
  b Look at the table above.
   How many kilograms of fossil fuel would give the same amount of energy as 1 kilogram of uranium fuel?

3 **a** Explain why ethanol is described as a biofuel.
  b Ethanol is also described as carbon-neutral. What is a carbon-neutral fuel?

Key points

- Electricity generators in power stations are driven by turbines.
- Coal, oil and natural gas are burned in fossil fuel power stations.
- Uranium or plutonium are used as the fuel in a nuclear power station. Much more energy is released per kg from uranium or plutonium than from fossil fuel.
- Biofuels are renewable sources of energy. Biofuels such as methane and ethanol can be used to generate electricity.

Further teaching suggestions

ICT link-up

- Many of the energy generating companies have websites with information about power stations. Students can explore these to get a better idea of what is going on.

Is nuclear power the future?

- Many countries are developing nuclear programmes to generate electricity, but is this the way forward? There are clear advantages and disadvantages of nuclear power and fossil fuels, so the students could produce a booklet allowing people to vote on which of the two methods should be developed further in the UK. The booklet should contain all of the facts from both sides of the argument and a detachable voting slip. This activity could be set as homework, giving the students clear guidelines on how much time to spend on this task.

Summary answers

1 **a** uranium
  b gas
  c oil

2 **a** **i** E.g. advantage of oil-fired power station: no radioactive waste; disadvantage: produces greenhouse gases.
   ii E.g. advantage of gas-fired power station: can be started quicker; disadvantage: gas supplies will run out before coal supplies.
  b 10 000 kg

3 **a** A biofuel is any fuel from a biological source. Ethanol can be obtained from sugar cane.
  b Burning the ethanol from a sugar plant puts carbon dioxide into the atmosphere. The growth of a sugar cane plant takes the same amount of carbon dioxide from the atmosphere. Thus ethanol is described as carbon-neutral. Any fuel that, in theory, can 'balance' its intake and output of carbon dioxide is described as a carbon-neutral fuel.

P1 4.2

Energy from wind and water

Learning objectives

Students should learn:

- how wind turbines can be used to generate electricity
- how water can be used to generate electricity in a variety of ways
- the advantages and disadvantages of the above methods of electricity generation.

Learning outcomes

Most students should be able to:

- describe how wind turbines generate electricity
- describe the different ways in which the flow of water can generate electricity
- list some advantages and disadvantages of these methods of electricity generation.

Some students should also be able to:

- evaluate in detail the advantages and disadvantages of these methods of electricity generation.

Support

- Try to use models for all of the explanations, so that the students can see them in action. You can use a ripple tank to show the idea of wave generators, emphasising the changes in energy taking place.

Extend

- Provide the students with some data about the power output of different-sized wind turbines in different wind conditions. Can they find any patterns? There should be a relationship between the area the blades sweep out and the power output. There should also be a relationship between the wind speed and power output. These patterns can be found by plotting graphs of the data and analysing the shape.

AQA
Specification link-up: Physics P1.4

- Water and wind can be used to drive turbines directly. [P1.4.1 b)]
- Evaluate different methods of generating electricity. [P1.4]

Lesson structure

Starters

Wind and convection currents – Support students by giving them a set of cards describing how wind is caused and ask them to put them in the correct order. This links back to their previous studies. Cards can include: sunlight warms the ground, energy is radiated and warms up the air near the ground, the air expands and rises, when the hot air rises cooler air is drawn into the gap, the movement of this cooler air is the wind. Students can be extended by asking them to explain the causes of the flow of air themselves in terms of expansion and density changes. *(5 minutes)*

Water cycle recap – To support students, ask them to draw a diagram explaining the water cycle. You may need to provide a basic diagram showing an ocean, land, mountains and a river for the students to annotate. The students should use scientific language including evaporation, condensation and precipitation. Link this cycle to hydroelectricity later. *(10 minutes)*

Main

- You may want to show the students the ideas behind a turbine and generator. It can be difficult to light up a bulb with wind power. Try using a large desk fan, as the source of wind, and a large bladed demonstration wind turbine connected to a low voltage lamp. You could try an LED if you can't get enough energy to light the bulb. Obviously, this is a very inefficient way of lighting a bulb, so you can revise energy transfer and efficiency here. You might want to get some students to design or carry out an investigation into the efficiency of wind power with a set-up similar to this.

- A video clip of a wind farm in operation gives a good idea of the scale of these structures and may also highlight the noise issue. Search for 'wind farm' at an internet video-hosting site. If you want to impress the noise problem on the students, play a sample in a continuous loop while they try to work through some of the summary questions. If you have an exercise cycle with a dynamo, you can illustrate that turning the wheel more quickly produces more electrical energy.

- There are several alternative designs for wave-powered generators; you could ask the students how they think they work. As usual, discuss changes in energy.

- The idea behind a hydroelectric scheme can be shown simply by letting water flow down a pipe from a raised reservoir. This can be directed onto a paddle wheel, causing it to spin. You may need to show students accelerated video clips of a tide coming in or out, as they may not have seen the effect before. If you have access to the internet, you may be able to find a webcam showing a real-time image of a major estuary. Is the tide in or out? Search the internet for 'webcam estuary'.

- Compare and contrast advantages/disadvantages of the energy sources covered in this lesson as a class discussion.

Plenaries

Designing a tidal barrier – You could extend students by asking them to design a tidal barrier that generates electricity, allows traffic to cross the river, and lets boats through when necessary. This could be made into quite a complicated task or left at a simple level, depending whether students require more support. Students could discuss their ideas as a group, and complete the task as homework. *(5 minutes)*

Wind farm advertisement – Design a poster to persuade a local community to allow a wind farm in the vicinity. Other students could design an 'anti' poster. The poster could include information about new jobs, noise, reliability, cheaper or more expensive electricity. You might like to extend students to set their own marking criteria for the task such as what data is required and how many images can be used. They can then evaluate each other's work. For extra support, you can provide some of the information in the form of brochures or resident interviews. *(10 minutes)*

Practical support

Demonstrating a water turbine

There are a range of water turbine kits that can be attached to a tap and simple generator. It can be hard to get a big enough power output from one, so test a few bulbs connected to the generator first to see what it is capable of. Be careful to test the fittings as high water pressure can spray everywhere.

Pumped storage

It is difficult to demonstrate this with improvised equipment, but with the correct kit, it should be possible. You may wish to demonstrate it as two separate phases: pumping water uphill and then generating electricity as the water flows back.

Equipment and materials required

A 12 V electric water pump, rubber tubing and two reservoirs (buckets). Water turbine and generator, connecting leads, low voltage bulb and holder.

Details

Fill the lower reservoir with water and place one end of the tubing in it. Place the other in a second reservoir on a desk. You should be able to pump water to this height; if the second bucket is placed higher up you can also show the difficulty of pumping water 'uphill'. To drive a turbine is more difficult; you will need a specialised water turbine and generator connected to a lamp or similar. You will also need an upper reservoir with a hole to let water flow out and downhill to the generator.

Generating electricity

P1 4.2 — Energy from wind and water

Learning objectives

- What does a wind turbine consist of?
- How do we use waves to generate electricity?
- What type of power station uses water running downhill to generate electricity?
- How can we use the tides to generate electricity?

Strong winds can cause lots of damage on a very stormy day. Even when the wind is much weaker, it can still turn a wind turbine. Energy from the wind and other natural sources such as **waves** and **tides** is called **renewable energy**. That's because such natural sources of energy can never be used up.

In addition, no fuel is needed to produce electricity from these natural sources so they are carbon-free to run.

Wind power

A wind turbine is an electricity generator at the top of a narrow tower. The force of the wind drives the turbine's blades around. This turns a generator. The power generated increases as the wind speed increases.

a What happens if the wind stops blowing?

Wave power

A wave generator uses the waves to make a floating generator move up and down. This motion turns the generator so it generates electricity. A cable between the generator and the shore delivers electricity to the grid system.

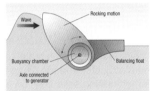

Figure 2 Energy from waves

Wave generators need to withstand storms and they don't produce a constant supply of electricity. Also, lots of cables (and buildings) are needed along the coast to connect the wave generators to the electricity grid. This can spoil areas of coastline. Tidal flow patterns might also change, affecting the habitats of marine life and birds.

b What could happen if the waves get too high?

Figure 1 A wind farm – why do some people oppose these developments?

How Science Works

When electricity demand is low, we can use electricity from wind turbines, wave generators and other electricity generators to pump water uphill into a reservoir. When demand is high, we can let the water run downhill through a hydroelectric generator.

Hydroelectric power

We can generate hydroelectricity when rainwater collected in a reservoir (or water in a pumped storage scheme) flows downhill. The flowing water drives turbines that turn electricity generators at the foot of the hill.

c Where does the energy for hydroelectricity come from?

Tidal power

A tidal power station traps water from each high tide behind a barrage. We can then release the high tide into the sea through turbines. The turbines drive generators in the barrage.

One of the most promising sites in Britain is the Severn estuary. This is because the estuary rapidly becomes narrower as you move up-river away from the open sea. So it funnels the incoming tide and makes it higher.

d Why is tidal power more reliable than wind power?

Figure 3 A hydroelectric scheme

Figure 4 A tidal power station

Summary questions

1 Copy and complete **a** to **d** using the words below:

hydroelectric tidal wave wind

a .... power does not need water.
b .... power does not need energy from the Sun.
c .... power is obtained from water running downhill.
d .... power is obtained from water moving up and down.

2 **a** Use the table below for this question. The output of each source is given in millions of watts (MW).
   i How many wind turbines would give the same total power output as a tidal power station?
   ii How many kilometres of wave generators would give the same total output as a hydroelectric power station?
b Use the words below to fill in the location column in the table.

coastline estuaries hilly or coastal areas mountain areas

	Output	Location	Total cost in £ per MW
Hydroelectric power station	500 MW per station		50
Tidal power station	2000 MW per station		300
Wave power generators	20 MW per kilometre of coastline		100
Wind turbines	2 MW per wind turbine		90

3 The last column of the table above shows an estimate of the total cost per MW of generating electricity using different renewable energy sources. The total cost for each includes its running costs and the capital costs to set it up.
a The capital cost per MW of a tidal power station is much higher than that of a hydroelectric power station. Give one reason for this difference.
b **i** Which energy resource has the lowest total cost per MW?
   ii Give two reasons why this resource might be unsuitable in many areas.

Key points

- A wind turbine is an electricity generator on top of a tall tower.
- Waves generate electricity by turning a floating generator.
- Hydroelectricity generators are turned by water running downhill.
- A tidal power station traps each high tide and uses it to turn generators.

Further teaching suggestions

Pumped storage
- You can demonstrate this concept if you have the correct equipment; see 'Practical support'.

Tidal barrages
- Why not build a tidal barrage across the Severn or the Mersey? These rivers are ideal for generating lots of electrical energy, but what are the problems involved? Get the students to debate the issue. This can be done in class or the research can be completed at home before the discussion.

Answers to in-text questions

a No electricity is generated.
b The wave would flow over the top of the generator reducing it's efficiency significantly.
c From the gravitational potential energy of water in the reservoirs.
d The tides are very predictable whereas the wind isn't.

Summary answers

1 **a** wind
  b tidal
  c hydroelectric
  d wave

2 **a** **i** 1000
     ii 25 km
  b From top to bottom: mountain areas, estuaries, coastline, hilly or coastal areas.

3 **a** The area of the trapped water needs to be much greater in a tidal power station than in a hydroelectric station, as the water drops much less. So the barrage needs to be much longer in a tidal power station.
  b **i** The hydroelectric power station.
     ii Hydroelectricity is only suitable in mountainous areas where there is plenty of rainfall. Many areas do not have enough rainfall or do not have mountains.

P1 4.3 — Power from the Sun and the Earth

AQA — Specification link-up: Physics P1.4

- Electricity can be produced directly from the Sun's radiation. [P1.4.1 c)]
- In some volcanic areas hot water and steam rise to the surface. The steam can be tapped and used to drive turbines. This is known as geothermal energy. [P1.4.1 d)]
- Evaluate different methods of generating electricity. [P1.4]

Learning objectives

Students should learn:

- how solar cells can be used to generate electricity at high cost and in relatively small amounts
- how geothermal energy can be used to generate electricity in a variety of ways
- the advantages and disadvantages of the above methods of electricity generation.

Learning outcomes

Most students should be able to:

- describe how a solar cell can be used to produce electricity
- describe the different ways in which geothermal energy can generate electricity
- list some advantages and disadvantages of these methods of electricity generation.

Some students should also be able to:

- evaluate in detail the advantages and disadvantages of these methods of electricity generation.

Lesson structure

Starters

Old Faithful – Show a video clip of 'Old Faithful' (search for 'Old Faithful' at an internet video-hosting site). Ask students if they have ever seen a geyser and if they know what causes them. Try to get them to explain where the heat comes from; they may assume that there are chemical reactions whereas the truth is that the energy is due to radioactive decay. *(5 minutes)*

To the centre of the Earth – The students should draw a simple diagram showing the structure and properties of the layers of the Earth (crust, mantle and core). You can provide the basic diagram for support. Extend the students by asking for a more detailed description of the properties of the layers such as the idea of density. They should be aware that the core has a molten layer and that the centre of the Earth is very hot. *(10 minutes)*

Main

- Demonstrate a solar cell being used to turn a small fan; you may need a bright bulb to do this. If you have a data projector and are using this during the lesson, it is also a great light source for demonstrating solar cells on a dreary day. You can even show that some solar cells work better in different coloured light; just use coloured backgrounds to blank slides. You can show how inefficient the cells are by using a very bright light shining on a panel that is lighting up a small bulb.

- If students are not investigating how the amount of light falling on the cell affects the output, they can simply show this idea by moving the cell further from the bulb; the small bulb should grow visibly dimmer. Students can develop concepts of 'How Science Works' by considering how to gather quantitative data when investigating solar cells.

- Small solar-powered garden lights are available from garden centres quite cheaply. Charge one of these up during the day and then cover the light sensor during the lesson, to show that it has been charged by collecting energy from the Sun. Link this to the idea that solar panels are far more useful when coupled with a battery, as they can then provide the energy when needed (in the dark in this case). However adding a battery to the system will increase the expense even more. Show some images of solar cells used on satellites and discuss why they are an ideal solution for electricity generation in space. Here the solar panels are the cheapest solution.

- Demonstrating geothermal energy is not easy, so use video clips and diagrams to get the ideas across. The focus should be on understanding that the energy comes from hot rocks. You may mention that the source of the heat is radioactivity, explain that this will be covered later in the course or extend students by asking them to find out more about this source of heat.

Support

- Geothermal energy is the most difficult concept and the most difficult to demonstrate. Use video clips of hot springs or even volcanoes to show that the inside of the Earth is very hot.

Extend

- Ask students to find out about the source of the Earth's internal heat. They will have to find some facts about radioactive decay and its role in providing this energy over billions of years.

Plenaries

Solar car – Search the internet for 'solar car video' to show the students a video clip of a solar car in action; you might be able to find a toy one too. Ask them to list the advantages and disadvantages of the design. They can discuss whether solar-powered transport is a possibility in the future. You can tell them that solar-powered planes have also been developed but these can only transport one person at a time so far. *(5 minutes)*

Keep cool – Ask the students to come up with a design for a device that keeps you cooler, the brighter the Sun is. They could produce an advertisement explaining how it works. A solar-powered fan is a typical design but colour-changing clothing is a possibility with smart materials (white on the side that faces the Sun, but black on the opposite side). You could extend the students by asking them to build a prototype of a design if it is feasible or support some by providing example smart materials or components. *(10 minutes)*

Practical support

Solar cells

A solar cell can be demonstrated with a low-power electric motor.

Equipment and materials required

Solar cell, motor and bulb. Rechargeable solar garden lamp.

Details

A low-power motor will be required; complete kits containing a matched solar panel and motor are available. The students should be able to discover that the motor will turn faster the closer the bulb is to the cell. They might like to compare the speed of the motor in bright sunlight to that produced by a bulb. Covering part of the solar panel will reduce the energy output too.

Generating electricity

P1 4.3 Power from the Sun and the Earth

Learning objectives

- What are solar cells and how do we use them?
- What is the difference between a panel of solar cells and a solar heating panel?
- What is geothermal energy?
- How can we use geothermal energy to generate electricity?

Figure 2 A solar-powered vehicle. Think of some advantages and disadvantages of this car.

links

For more information on solar heating panels, look back at P1 1.9 Heating and insulating buildings.

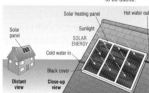

Figure 3 Solar water heating

Solar radiation transfers energy to you from the Sun. That can sometimes be more energy than you want if you get sunburnt. But we can use the Sun's energy to generate electricity using **solar cells**. We can also use the Sun's energy to heat water directly in solar heating panels.

a Which generates electricity – a solar cell or a solar heating panel?

Practical

Solar cells

Use a solar cell panel to drive a small electric motor.

- See what happens if you gradually cover the solar cells with a card.

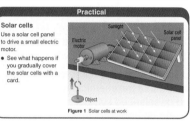

Figure 1 Solar cells at work

Solar cells at present convert less than 10% of the solar energy they absorb into electrical energy. We can connect them together to make solar cell panels.

- They are useful where we only need small amounts of electricity (e.g. in watches and calculators) or in remote places (e.g. on small islands in the middle of an ocean).
- They are very expensive to buy even though they cost nothing to run.
- We need lots of them – and plenty of sunshine – to generate enough power to be useful.

A **solar heating panel** heats water that flows through it. Even on a cloudy day in Britain, a solar heating panel on a house roof can supply plenty of hot water.

b If the water stopped flowing through a solar heating panel, what would happen?

A **solar power tower** uses thousands of flat mirrors to reflect sunlight on to a large water tank at the top of a tower. The mirrors on the ground surround the base of the tower.

- The water in the tank is turned to steam by the heating effect of the solar radiation directed at the water tank.
- The steam is piped down to ground level where it turns electricity generators.
- The mirrors are controlled by a computer so they track the Sun.

A solar power tower in a hot dry climate can generate more than 20 MW of electrical power.

c The solar furnace shown in Figure 3 in P1 1.1 uses 63 flat tracking mirrors to reflect solar radiation on to the giant reflector. Why does the solar power tower in Figure 4 opposite collect much more solar radiation than this solar furnace?

Geothermal energy

Geothermal energy comes from energy released by radioactive substances, deep within the Earth.

- The energy released by these radioactive substances heats the surrounding rock.
- As a result, energy is transferred by heating towards the Earth's surface.

We can build **geothermal power stations** in volcanic areas or where there are hot rocks deep below the surface. Water gets pumped down to these rocks to produce steam. Then the steam produced drives electricity turbines at ground level.

In some areas, we can heat buildings using geothermal energy directly. Heat flow from underground is called **ground heat**. It can be used to heat water in long lengths of underground pipes. The hot water is then pumped round the building. Ground heat is used as under-floor heating in some large 'eco-buildings'.

d Why do geothermal power stations not need energy from the Sun?

Summary questions

1 Copy and complete **a** to **c** using the words below:
   geothermal   solar   radiation   radioactivity
   a A suitable energy resource for a calculator is .... energy.
   b .... inside the Earth releases .... energy.
   c .... from the Sun generates electricity in a solar cell.

2 A satellite in space uses a solar cell panel for electricity. The panel generates 300 W of electrical power and has an area of 10 m².
   a Each cell generates 0.2 W. How many cells are in the panel?
   b The satellite carries batteries that are charged by electricity from the solar cell panels. Why are batteries carried as well as solar cell panels?

3 A certain geothermal power station has a power output of 200 000 W.
   a How many kilowatt-hours of electrical energy does the power station generate in 24 hours?
   b State one advantage and one disadvantage of a geothermal power station compared with a wind turbine.

Figure 4 A solar power tower

AQA Examiner's tip

Make sure you know the difference between a solar cell panel (in which sunlight is used to make electricity) and a solar heating panel (in which sunlight is used to heat water).

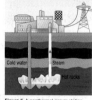

Figure 5 A geothermal power station

Key points

- Solar cells are flat solid cells that convert solar energy directly into electricity.
- Solar heating panels use the Sun's energy to heat water directly.
- Geothermal energy comes from the energy released by radioactive substances deep inside the Earth.
- Water pumped into hot rocks underground produces steam to drive turbines that generate electricity.

Further teaching suggestions

Investigating solar panels

- The students could investigate the energy output of solar panels. This provides an important opportunity to develop or assess investigative skills; the students should be encouraged to form their own detailed plans. There are two main variants:
  - Investigating how the energy output is related to the area of the panel.
  - Investigating how the energy output is related to the distance of the light source from the panel. These students can measure the output voltage (pd) from the panel instead of the actual energy output.
  Equipment required for each group: solar panel, bright bulb, sensitive ammeter and voltmeter, leads, metre rule or tape measure, black card to cover parts of panel.

Power plants

- As a research project, the students can find out where the best places to site geothermal power plants and solar power plants are. They should be reminded that the plants should not be too far from civilisation.

Answers to in-text questions

a A solar cell.

b The water in the panel would continue to heat up and possibly increase the pressure in the system damaging it.

c The power tower has many more flat mirrors tracking the Sun than the solar furnace has.

d The energy is from radioactive substances inside the Earth.

Summary answers

1 **a** solar
  b radioactivity, geothermal
  c radiation

2 **a** 1500
  b To supply electricity when the solar panels are in darkness.

3 **a** 4800 kW h
  b Geothermal energy does not depend on the weather like the wind; geothermal energy is not available in many areas.

P1 4.4

Energy and the environment

Learning objectives

Students should learn:

- about how burning fossil fuels affects the environment
- that there are severe potential hazards associated with the use of nuclear power and the disposal of nuclear waste.

Learning outcomes

Most students should be able to:

- describe how burning fossil fuels affects the environment
- describe the ways in which using renewable energy resources affect the environment.

Some students should also be able to:

- explain the issues relating to nuclear power and renewable energy sources.

Support

- To develop mathematical skills, you might like to find the most recent data of energy resources used in the UK (or even the world) and have the students produce a pie chart or other form of graph.

Extend

- What is the real cost of building and decommissioning nuclear power stations? Ask the students to find out if any nuclear power stations have actually been fully dismantled and how much this has cost. Where has the waste from this decommissioning process been stored and for how long will it be kept? What happens in countries that have nuclear power stations but are unable to afford to decommission them?

Specification link-up: Physics P1.4

- Small-scale production of electricity may be useful in some areas and for some uses, e.g. hydroelectricity in remote areas and solar cells for roadside signs. *[P1.4.1 e)]*
- Using different energy resources has different effects on the environment. These effects include:
  - the release of substances into the atmosphere
  - the production of waste materials
  - noise and visual pollution
  - the destruction of wildlife habitats. *[P1.4.1 f)]*
- Evaluate different methods of generating electricity. *[P1.4]*
- Evaluate ways of matching supply with demand, either by increasing supply or decreasing demand. *[P1.4]*

Lesson structure

Starters

Renewable or not? – Give the students a list of energy resources and ask them to place them in either pile. You can use these non-renewable ones: coal, oil, natural gas, uranium and these renewable ones: tidal, solar, geothermal, wind, wave, biofuel. *(5 minutes)*

Acid rain – Ask students to explain what acid rain is and what causes it. Extend students by expecting them to explain some of the chemical reactions that lead to the formation of the acid; these could be word or balanced symbol equations. Students can be supported by recapping what an acid is and demonstrate that rainwater is slightly acidic using universal indicator and some freshly collected (or made up) rainwater. *(10 minutes)*

Main

- This topic lends itself well to debate and students will wish to put their ideas forward.
- In the context of the lesson the term 'reliable' should be used to mean a resource that produces electricity in a predictable and fairly constant way.
- Many students rule nuclear power out as a possible source of energy almost immediately without considering its benefits. You may need to point out these benefits to the students to make sure that they put a bit of thought into the issue. Remind the students that most nuclear power stations operate safely and some countries have many nuclear power stations. You can also mention that there have been a large number of deaths due to coal-mining and that, if global warming estimates are correct, the number of deaths caused by burning fossil fuels would far outweigh those caused by nuclear power.
- Check again that the students do not think that nuclear fuel is renewable. This is a common error because students are aware that the fuel is not burned but is reprocessed, and some of them assume that this is the same as recycling.
- A tidal barrage is reliable, in that it will always be able to produce electricity in a well-understood pattern but the output varies from day to day. The damage to wildlife in the estuary, or to a habitat in flooded valleys, is the main environmental concern and is frequently tested in examinations. This is also true for hydroelectricity and the flooding of valleys. Wind, wave and solar are less reliable and we could not guarantee a constant or predictable amount of electricity from them.
- The disadvantages of the renewable sources of energy should lead the students to the idea that it is unwise to rely on a single type of energy resource. We will need to rely on a combination of the resources in future and this is likely to include large-scale power plants (fossil fuel or nuclear) alongside smaller-scale, more local, renewable operations.

Plenaries

What's the problem? – Support students by showing cards (or photographs) of environmental problems and ask the students to write down an energy resource that causes this problem. Students can be extended by asking them to offer solutions to the problems and evaluate the impact of the solutions themselves. *(5 minutes)*

Energy resource crossword – Let the students complete a crossword of all of the key words from this chapter so far. You can provide differentiated clues to the students enabling suitable support or extension. *(10 minutes)*

Further teaching suggestions

Chernobyl disaster
- The students may like to research the details of the Chernobyl disaster. A lot of material is available on the internet from a simple search, but they will have to be careful to find information at the correct level for them to understand.

A field trip
- It may be possible to arrange a field trip to visit a nearby fossil fuel power station or a nuclear one. This may be run in conjunction with another department, such as geography.

If students go on such a trip make sure that they produce a suitable report: a few digital cameras or a video camera would help with this.

Safety: Follow local guidelines for out-of-school activities.

Saving energy at home
- Ask the students to work out how much money they could save each year if they replaced all of the light bulbs in their house with energy-saving ones. They need to find the power rating of the bulbs to do this.

Generating electricity

P1 4.4   Energy and the environment

Learning objectives
- What do fossil fuels do to our environment?
- Why are people concerned about nuclear power?
- How do renewable energy resources affect our environment?

Can we get energy without creating any problems? Look at the pie chart in Figure 1.

It shows the energy sources we use at present to generate electricity. What effect does each one have on our environment?

How Science Works

When a popular TV programme ends, lots of people decide to put the kettle on. The national demand for electricity leaps as a result. Engineers meet these surges in demand by switching gas turbine engines on in gas-fired power stations.

Fossil fuel problems
- When we burn coal, oil or gas, greenhouse gases such as carbon dioxide are released. We think that these gases cause global warming. We get some of our electricity from oil-fired power stations. We use much more oil to produce fuels for transport.
- Burning fossil fuels can also produce sulfur dioxide. This gas causes **acid rain**. We can remove the sulfur from a fuel before burning it to stop acid rain. For example, natural gas has its sulfur impurities removed before we use it.
- Fossil fuels are non-renewable. Sooner or later, we will have used up the Earth's reserves of fossil fuels. We will then have to find alternative sources of energy. But how soon? Oil and gas reserves could be used up within the next 50 years. Coal reserves will last much longer.
- **Carbon capture and storage** (CCS) could be used to stop carbon dioxide emissions into the atmosphere from fossil fuel power stations. Old oil and gas fields could be used for storage.

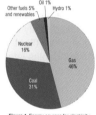

Figure 1 Energy sources for electricity

a Burning fossil fuels in power stations pollutes our atmosphere. Which gas contributes towards:
  i   global warming?
  ii   acid rain?

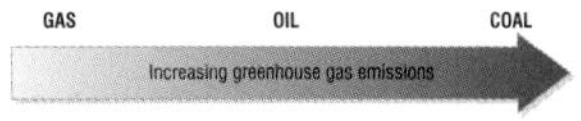

GAS   OIL   COAL
Increasing greenhouse gas emissions

Figure 2 Greenhouse gases from fossil fuels

Nuclear v. renewable

We need to cut back on our use of fossil fuels to stop global warming. Should we rely on nuclear power or on renewable energy in the future?

Nuclear power
Advantages
- No greenhouse gases (unlike fossil fuel).
- Much more energy from each kilogram of uranium (or plutonium) fuel than from fossil fuel.

?? Did you know ... ?
The Gobi Desert is one of the most remote regions on Earth. Many areas do not have mains electricity. Yet people who live there can watch TV programmes – just as you can. All they need is a solar panel and satellite TV.

Disadvantages
- Used fuel rods contain radioactive waste, which has to be stored safely for centuries.
- Nuclear reactors are safe in normal operation. However, an explosion at one could release radioactive material over a wide area. This would affect these areas for many years.

  b   Why is nuclear fuel non-renewable?

Renewable energy sources and the environment
Advantages
- They will never run out.
- They do not produce greenhouse gases or acid rain.
- They do not create radioactive waste products.
- They can be used where connection to the National Grid is uneconomic. For example, solar cells can be used for road signs and hydroelectric can be used in remote areas.

Disadvantages
- Wind turbines create a whining noise that can upset people nearby and some people consider them unsightly.
- Tidal barrages affect river estuaries and the habitats of creatures and plants there.
- Hydroelectric schemes need large reservoirs of water, which can affect nearby plant and animal life. Habitats are often flooded to create dams.
- Solar cells would need to cover large areas to generate large amounts of power.

  c   Do wind turbines affect plant and animal life?

Summary questions

1 Copy and complete a to c using the words below:
  acid rain fossil fuels greenhouse gas plant and animal life
  radioactive waste
  a   Most of Britain's electricity is produced by power stations that burn ....
  b   A gas-fired power station does not produce .... or much ....
  c   A tidal power station does not produce .... as a nuclear power station does but it does affect .... locally.

2 Match each energy source with a problem it causes.
Energy source	Problem
i Coal	A Noise
ii Hydroelectricity	B Acid rain
iii Uranium	C Radioactive waste
iv Wind power	D Takes up land

3 a   List three possible renewable energy resources that could be used to generate electricity for people on a remote flat island in a hot climate.
  b   List three types of power stations that do not release greenhouse gases into the atmosphere.

?? Did you know ... ?
In 1986, some nuclear reactors at Chernobyl in Ukraine overheated and exploded. Radioactive substances were thrown high into the atmosphere. Chernobyl and the surrounding towns were evacuated. Radioactive material from Chernobyl was also deposited on parts of Britain.

Figure 3 Chernobyl, the site of the world's most serious accident at a nuclear power station

Figure 4 The effects of acid rain

Key points
- Fossil fuels produce increased levels of greenhouse gases which could cause global warming.
- Nuclear fuels produce radioactive waste.
- Renewable energy resources can affect plant and animal life.

70   71

?? Did you know ... ?

After the Chernobyl disaster, some radioactive caesium fell onto UK farmland and contaminated the grassland. Over 4 million sheep feeding off this grass became contaminated and dangerous for human consumption, so their slaughter was banned. Were the sheep lucky or unlucky? The final UK bans probably won't be lifted until 2026; that's 40 years after the accident.

Summary answers

1   a   fossil fuels
    b   acid rain, greenhouse gas
    c   radioactive waste, plant and animal life
2   i   B
    ii   D
    iii   C
    iv   A
3   a   solar cell panels, wave generators, wind turbines
    b   nuclear, hydroelectric, tidal

Answers to in-text questions

a   i   Carbon dioxide.
   ii   Sulfur dioxide.
b   It turns into radioactive waste when it is used.
c   They affect birds and can upset humans.

P1 4.5

The National Grid

Learning objectives

Students should learn:

- how the National Grid is used to distribute electricity around the country
- why transformers are used to increase and decrease the voltage of alternating current.

Learning outcomes

Most students should be able to:

- explain the advantages of providing electricity via a National Grid
- describe the role of pylons, cables and transformers in the National Grid
- explain why electricity is transferred at very high voltage.

Support

- You could revisit the idea of electrical conduction by using a circuit to test materials to see if they conduct. A simple circuit in which a test component is used to bridge a gap and light a bulb is sufficient. You can then let the students test long pieces of thin wire to show that these do not conduct as well. This brings home the idea that energy is lost when current travels through long thin wires.

Extend

- Resistance and power. The electrical power transferred by a wire is given by $P = I^2R$. This comes from combining the two key electrical equations $P = VI$ and $V = IR$, where P is power, I is current, V is voltage and R is the resistance of the wire. This power, and hence energy wasted in the wire, is dependent on the square of the current, so a small increase in current will dramatically increase the power of the wire. This is why the current is kept as small as possible and the voltage is kept very high.

AQA Specification link-up: Physics P1.4

- Electricity is distributed from power stations to consumers along the National Grid. *[P1.4.2 a)]*
- The uses of step-up and step-down transformers in the National Grid. *[P1.4.2 c)]*
- For a given power increasing the voltage reduces the current required and this reduces the energy losses in the cables. *[P1.4.2 b)]*

Lesson structure

Starters

Danger of death 1 – Show the students a picture of the 'Danger of death' icon used on transformer sub-stations. Ask them what they think the danger is and what the icon is showing. You could also check the students' knowledge of other hazard symbols here or even introduce the different categories. The icons are readily available from CLEAPSS. *(5 minutes)*

Choosing wisely – Give the students samples of a range of materials and a list of their properties. Ask them to choose which materials would be suitable for particular jobs and to explain why. Extend students by asking for clear descriptions of the properties of the materials themselves, not just particular objects. Jobs could include conducting electricity [copper], electrical insulation [plastic], making jewellery [gold], cutting [hardened steel] and so on. You may support students by asking them to link materials directly to properties using a worksheet or card-matching. Use the properties of aluminium (light, corrosion-resistant, good conductor) to explain why it can be used in power cables later in the lesson. *(10 minutes)*

Main

- Discussing the National Grid would be best with props. It may be possible to find a ceramic insulator or even a short length of pylon cable. Local electrical engineering companies may have off-cuts or broken parts. The thicker the cable you can find, the better.

- If you don't have a ceramic insulator, then you can discuss how the high voltage leads are insulated from the pylons by showing some pottery and describing that it is a particularly good insulator. You could extend students by linking to the idea that there are no free electrons and so conduction cannot occur.

- If a sample of aluminium cable is not available, then use sample blocks of aluminium and steel to compare the density of the two materials. The students will easily see the advantage of using aluminium. It also helps if the steel is a bit on the rusty side, so that you can show the aluminium is also easier to maintain.

- It is possible to demonstrate the saving in energy at higher voltages. See 'Practical support'; make sure you try it out in advance as it can be fiddly to get just right.

- The calculation is straightforward. Students may be confused about why you would bother to raise the voltage and lower the current if the power you get is the same anyway. You could extend students by introducing the equation mentioned in the Support and extension box.

Plenaries

Electrical flow – Support students by giving them a set of cards describing the passage of electricity from the generator to the light bulb, and ask them to sort the cards into order. You could use: 'The generator produces a voltage', 'The voltage causes a current in wires in the power station', 'A step-up transformer is used to increase the voltage and decrease the current', 'The electrical energy is transmitted through the National Grid system', 'A step-down transformer is used to reduce the voltage to 230 V and increase the current', 'The electrical energy is transmitted through the wires in a house to a plug socket'. Extend students by asking them to come up with a detailed description of their own. *(5 minutes)*

Danger of death 2 – Can the students produce an improved design for the hazard symbol? They should use the standard hazard symbol colours [yellow and black] and shape [triangle] but can change the design in any other way. You could discuss why safety symbols must have a standard appearance and colour scheme. *(10 minutes)*

Demonstration support

Modelling the National Grid

To demonstrate that high voltages are more efficient at transferring electrical energy, the following method can be used. It is fiddly to get just right, so make sure that you have tested it first.

Equipment and materials needed

Two matched transformers with a step-up or step-down ratio of about five (e.g. 100 turns input and 500 turns output). Two 2 m lengths of thin wire with high resistivity (nichrome or constantan work well), a 1.25 V lamp and a low voltage (1–1.5 V) ac power supply.

Details

Connect the power supply directly to the bulb through the long wires. The bulb should light dimly at best. This is because most of the energy is being wasted in heating the wires. Don't leave this set-up on for long, or the wires could overheat.

Next, connect the wires to the step-up transformer at the power supply end and the step-down transformer at the bulb end. The voltage in the wires will increase by a factor of five and the current will be reduced by a similar amount. This will lead to a twenty-fifth of the heating effect and energy wastage, so the lamp should be much brighter.

To make the demonstration more like the National Grid, you could suspend the wires on retort stands.

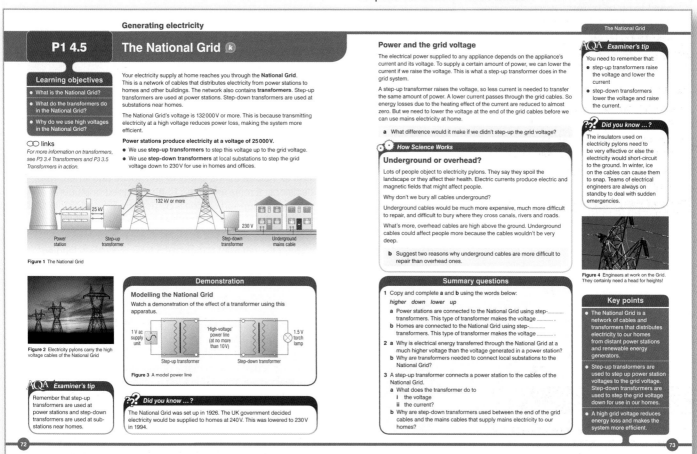

Further teaching suggestions

Do pylons affect our health?

- Some groups believe that the electromagnetic fields produced by electrical cables seriously affect our health. The students can try to find out if there is any evidence supporting this position. It is important that the students understand the nature and quality of the evidence presented to them, so they can judge the validity of any conclusions drawn (this relates to 'How Science Works' Analysing secondary data).This can lead to a discussion about the nature of anecdotal evidence.

Underground/overhead

- There are a number of reasons for choosing which method and there is plenty of information available about how the decisions are made. The students could be given a scenario (or several) and choose which method to use to transfer electricity. The National Grid has its own website which is a good place to start the research.

Hazards

- If the students did not redesign the 'danger of death' symbol, they could do this on a larger scale at home. They could produce a booklet warning of the hazards of messing with electricity pylons.

Answers to in-text questions

a Electrical energy would be wasted in the cables. Less electrical power would be supplied to the consumers.

b Faults would be harder to find. The ground would need to be dug up to make the repair.

Summary answers

1 **a** up, higher
  b down, lower

2 **a** To reduce the energy wasted in transmitting the electricity.
  b To reduce the voltage to a safer level for cables inside towns and cities.

3 **a** **i** It increases the voltage.
     ii It reduces the current.
  b Mains devices operate at 230 V. The grid voltage needs to be stepped down by transformers from 132 000 V to 230 V for safe use in our homes.

P1 4.6

Big energy issues

Learning objectives

Students should learn:

- how we utilise our electricity supplies to meet our demands
- that there are a range of factors that need to be considered when deciding on how to meet future energy needs.

Learning outcomes

Most students should be able to:

- describe the advantages and disadvantages of producing electricity by different techniques
- evaluate the possible resources and come to a conclusion about which are viable options for generation of electricity in the future.

AQA

Specification link-up: Physics P1.4

- Evaluate different methods of generating electricity. *[P1.4]*
- Evaluate ways of matching supply with demand, either by increasing supply or decreasing demand. *[P1.4]*
- Compare the advantages and disadvantages of overhead power lines and underground cables. *[P1.4]*
- Small-scale production of electricity may be useful in some areas and for some uses, e.g. hydroelectricity in remote areas and solar cells for roadside signs. *[P1.4.1 e)]*

Lesson structure

Starters

Not the right room for an argument – In this lesson the students are going to discuss energy issues. This could become a chaotic argument without proper ground rules. Extend the students by getting them to work on a set of rules that will let the discussion progress effectively. Rules need to include things like who can speak and when, who is recording discussions or decisions, if roles are going to be assigned or students are free to take on any position they want. Support students by defining these ground rules yourself. *(5 minutes)*

Getting the facts straight – Before the debate the students prepare fact sheets summarising the information about the different energy resources they have studied. You could support students by providing sheets with tables on for the students to complete, or extend students by asking them to design their own fact sheets. *(10 minutes)*

Main

- Start the lesson by recapping the possible energy resources. You will need to give extra information about start-up times (fairly simple) and the concept of 'base load' (a bit harder). You can show a graph showing electricity demand through a typical day and point out that there is always a demand so many power stations are fully active all of the time to cover this. Nuclear power stations are left running all of the time. Extra stations are turned on to meet times of increased demand.

- The rest of this lesson is centred about a debate about how to meet future energy needs. The debate is relevant because the students present will probably not have access to 'unlimited' fossil fuel supplies as the last few generations have. This could be as a result of shortages or commitments to reduce carbon emissions by the government. The result of this is an energy gap that needs to be filled by new resources.

- Before starting any debate, set the ground rules. You could do this with the starter activity or you could show a set of your own. Explain the purpose of the debate and the outcomes that are needed (a set of proposals) so the students know that they have to reach conclusions. Give timings and establish roles within the groups if they are needed. You can chair or you can split the class into smaller groups so that more students will take an active part.

- Success criteria could include:
  - Everybody has had their say and taken part.
  - We have used scientific facts to reach our conclusions.
  - We have discussed the costs of our suggestions and are willing to accept them.
  - We have produced two suggestions to go forward to the class.

- At the end of the discussion, the students will need to have produced a clear set of proposals about what to do. You need at least four suggestions to vote on really. If you are not certain that the groups will give suitable suggestions, you can prepare a few of your own as back up. You can then use these in the 'democracy in action' plenary to end the lesson and reach consensus.

Support

- Some students find it very difficult to discuss ideas or debate as they lack the confidence to express scientific ideas. You can provide prompt sheets that describe the role each person is playing in the discussion. These should contain relevant facts and figures that can help the student take an active role in the discussion. For example, you could provide a sheet describing the advantages and disadvantages of wind farms along with the current level of energy produced by this resource.

Extend

- The students can expand the issues here onto a global scale. They should consider the increasing demand from developing countries and discuss the effect that this demand would have on limited resources and prices.

Plenaries

Democracy in action – The students vote on a range of proposals for energy production. You can make this an anonymous vote with ballot papers giving various options. The results can be declared immediately by a nominated returning officer or you can deliver them next lesson. If you have several classes, you can keep a running total and declare this at an opportune point. *(5 minutes)*

You work for me – The students can write a letter to their MP outlining the decision they have reached. They need to explain what they have decided to do and ask the MP to act on the decision. This should be a formal letter if possible; you can even post the letters or deliver them by hand the next time your MP comes to visit the school. Students can be extended by giving them clear success criteria about the content of the letter, including how many facts and figures are required. You may like to support students with the start of the letter leading up to the point where the scientific facts are introduced. *(10 minutes)*

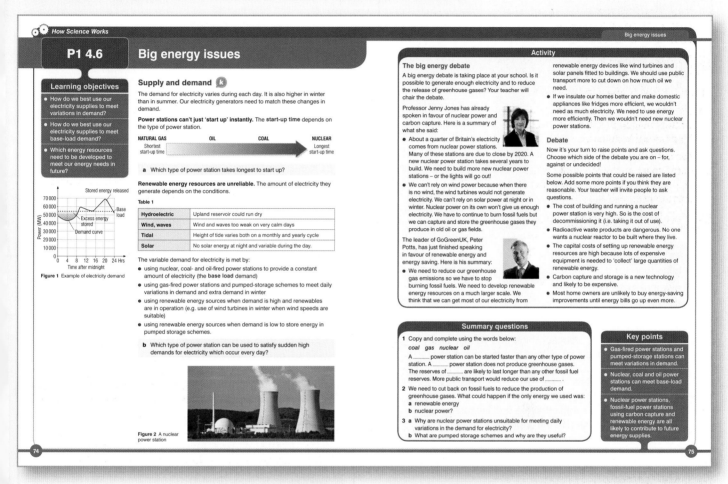

How Science Works

Big energy issues

P1 4.6 Big energy issues

Learning objectives

- How do we best use our electricity supplies to meet variations in demand?
- How do we best use our electricity supplies to meet base-load demand?
- Which energy resources need to be developed to meet our energy needs in future?

Figure 1 Example of electricity demand

Supply and demand

The demand for electricity varies during each day. It is also higher in winter than in summer. Our electricity generators need to match these changes in demand.

Power stations can't just 'start up' instantly. The start-up time depends on the type of power station.

NATURAL GAS — OIL — COAL — NUCLEAR
Shortest start-up time → Longest start-up time

a Which type of power station takes longest to start up?

Renewable energy resources are unreliable. The amount of electricity they generate depends on the conditions.

Table 1

Hydroelectric	Upland reservoir could run dry
Wind, waves	Wind and waves too weak on very calm days
Tidal	Height of tide varies both on a monthly and yearly cycle
Solar	No solar energy at night and variable during the day.

The variable demand for electricity is met by:

- using nuclear, coal- and oil-fired power stations to provide a constant amount of electricity (the base load demand)
- using gas-fired power stations and pumped-storage schemes to meet daily variations in demand and extra demand in winter
- using renewable energy sources when demand is high and renewables are in operation (e.g. use of wind turbines in winter when wind speeds are suitable)
- using renewable energy sources when demand is low to store energy in pumped storage schemes.

b Which type of power station can be used to satisfy sudden high demands for electricity which occur every day?

Figure 2 A nuclear power station

Activity

The big energy debate

A big energy debate is taking place at your school. Is it possible to generate enough electricity and to reduce the release of greenhouse gases? Your teacher will chair the debate.

Professor Jenny Jones has already spoken in favour of nuclear power and carbon capture. Here is a summary of what she said:

- About a quarter of Britain's electricity comes from nuclear power stations. Many of these stations are due to close by 2020. A new nuclear power station takes several years to build. We need to build more new nuclear power stations – or the lights will go out!
- We can't rely on wind power because when there is no wind, the wind turbines would not generate electricity. We can't rely on solar power at night or in winter. Nuclear power on its own won't give us enough electricity. We have to continue to burn fossil fuels but we can capture and store the greenhouse gases they produce in old oil or gas fields.

The leader of GoGreenUK, Peter Potts, has just finished speaking in favour of renewable energy and energy saving. Here is his summary:

- We need to reduce our greenhouse gas emissions so we have to stop burning fossil fuels. We need to develop renewable energy resources on a much larger scale. We think that we can get most of our electricity from renewable energy devices like wind turbines and solar panels fitted to buildings. We should use public transport more to cut down on how much oil we need.
- If we insulate our homes better and make domestic appliances like fridges more efficient, we wouldn't need as much electricity. We need to use energy more efficiently. Then we wouldn't need new nuclear power stations.

Debate

Now it's your turn to raise points and ask questions. Choose which side of the debate you are on – for, against or undecided!

Some possible points that could be raised are listed below. Add some more points if you think they are reasonable. Your teacher will invite people to ask questions.

- The cost of building and running a nuclear power station is very high. So is the cost of decommissioning it (i.e. taking it out of use).
- Radioactive waste products are dangerous. No one wants a nuclear reactor to be built where they live.
- The capital costs of setting up renewable energy resources are high because lots of expensive equipment is needed to 'collect' large quantities of renewable energy.
- Carbon capture and storage is a new technology and likely to be expensive.
- Most home owners are unlikely to buy energy-saving improvements until energy bills go up even more.

Summary questions

1 Copy and complete using the words below:
   coal   gas   nuclear   oil
   A .... power station can be started faster than any other type of power station. A .... power station does not produce greenhouse gases. The reserves of .... are likely to last longer than any other fossil fuel reserves. More public transport would reduce our use of ....

2 We need to cut back on fossil fuels to reduce the production of greenhouse gases. What could happen if the only energy we used was:
   a renewable energy
   b nuclear power?

3 **a** Why are nuclear power stations unsuitable for meeting daily variations in the demand for electricity?
   b What are pumped storage schemes and why are they useful?

Key points

- Gas-fired power stations and pumped-storage stations can meet variations in demand.
- Nuclear, coal and oil power stations can meet base-load demand.
- Nuclear power stations, fossil-fuel power stations using carbon capture and renewable energy are all likely to contribute to future energy supplies.

Further teaching suggestions

Cut back

- Demand for electricity is increasing, as more electrical devices are produced. One way to preserve resources is to cut back on waste and to stop using some things altogether. As an alternative to the main discussion, students can look at where they would cutback on a personal and then national level. They should be able to find lots of suggestions from environmental campaign groups.

Answers to in-text questions

a Nuclear power stations.

b Hydroelectric power stations.

Summary answers

1 gas, nuclear, coal, oil

2 **a** Our energy sources may not be reliable (available when we need them). For example, we may not have enough energy during the summer months if we only relied on wind power.

b Our electricity supplies would be reliable but people would be concerned about the storage of radioactive waste.

3 **a** Nuclear power stations have a very long start-up time and could not be started or stopped quickly to match daily variations in demand.

b A pumped storage scheme is a hydroelectric scheme with electricity generators that can be reversed to act as pumps. When demand is low, surplus electricity from the National Grid is used to pump water uphill in an upland reservoir. When demand is high, the water flow is reversed, so it runs downhill and the generators generate electricity.

Summary answers

1 a coal, oil and natural gas

b coal and oil

c coal, oil, natural gas and wood

d uranium

e uranuium

2 a **i** tidal

ii hydroelectric

iii wave

iv wind

b **i** wind

ii hydroelectricity

iii waves

3 a **i** geothermal

ii hydroelectric

iii coal-fired

iv nuclear

b **i** renewable

ii non-fossil

4 a 1 Wind energy

2 Hydroelectricity

3 Solar energy

b **i** Hydroelectricity

ii Solar energy

5 a cheaper, cheaper

b longer

c more expensive

d shorter

6 a **i** To change the voltage from the power station generator to a suitably high grid voltage and reducing the grid voltage to a suitable mains voltage for our homes.

ii A step-up transformer.

b **i** The grid voltage is much higher.

ii The current supplied to the grid is much smaller.

iii Power is wasted in the cables due to the heating effect of the current. The less the current, the less the power that is wasted.

AQA Examiner's tip

Many students have some background knowledge of the issues surrounding electricity generation. However, make sure they are able to evaluate the different methods particularly with regard to building costs, decommissioning, reliability and start-up time. All data will be given.

AQA Examiner's tip

Also be aware of methods of storing and distributing electricity by suggesting when pumped storage systems could be used and comparing underground and overhead power cables.

AQA Examiner's tip

Students need to understand the similarities and differences in how electricity is generated from different resources and their different effects on the environment.

Summary questions 🅚

1 Answer **a** to **e** using the list of fuels below:

coal   natural gas   oil   uranium   wood

a Which fuels from the list are fossil fuels?

b Which fuels from the list cause acid rain?

c Which fuels release chemical energy when they are used?

d Which fuel releases the most energy per kilogram?

e Which fuel produces radioactive waste?

2 a Copy and complete **i** to **iv** using the words below:

hydroelectric   tidal   wave   wind

i .... power stations trap sea water.

ii .... power stations trap rain water.

iii .... generators must be located along the coastline.

iv .... turbines can be located on hills or offshore.

b Which renewable energy resource transfers:

i the kinetic energy of moving air to electrical energy

ii the gravitational potential energy of water running downhill into electrical energy

iii the kinetic energy of water moving up and down to electrical energy?

3 a Copy and complete **i** to **iv** using the words below:

coal-fired   geothermal   hydroelectric   nuclear

i A .... power station does not produce greenhouse gases and uses energy which is from inside the Earth.

ii A .... power station uses running water and does not produce greenhouse gases.

iii A .... power station releases greenhouse gases.

iv A .... power station does not release greenhouse gases but does produce waste products that need to be stored for many years.

b Wood can be used as a fuel. State whether it is

i renewable or non-renewable

ii a fossil fuel or a non-fossil fuel.

4 a Figure 1 shows a landscape showing three different renewable energy resources, numbered 1 to 3. Match each type of energy resource with one of the labels below.

Figure 1 Renewable energy

Hydroelectricity   Solar energy   Wind energy

b Which of the three resources shown is not likely to produce as much energy as the others if the area is

i hot, dry and windy

ii wet and windy?

5 Copy and complete **a** to **d** using the words below. Each word or phrase can be used more than once.

cheaper   more expensive   longer   shorter

a Wind turbines are .... to build than nuclear power stations and .... to run.

b Nuclear power stations take .... to decommission than fossil fuel power stations.

c Solar cells are .... to install than solar heating panels.

d A gas-fired power station has a .... start-up time compared to a nuclear power station.

6 a **i** What are transformers used for in the National Grid?

ii What type of transformer is connected between generators in the power station and the cables of the grid system?

b **i** What can you say about the voltage of the cable the grid system compared with the voltages at th power station generator and at the mains cables into the home?

ii What can you say about the current through the grid cables compared with the current from the power station generator?

iii What is the reason for making the grid voltage different from the generator voltage?

Kerboodle resources 🅚

Resources available for this chapter on Kerboodle are:

- Chapter map: Generating electricity
- Interactive activity: How are fuels used to produce electricity? (P1 4.1)
- WebQuest: Biofuels (P1 4.1)
- Viewpoint: Is nuclear power the answer to the world's energy crisis? (P1 4.4)
- How Science Works: Wind turbines (P1 4.2)
- Revision podcast: Energy and the environment (P1 4.4)
- Animation: The National Grid (P1 4.5)
- Extension: Power lines (P1 4.5)
- Bump up your grade: The big issue (P1 4.6)
- Test yourself: Methods we use to generate electricity
- On your marks: Methods we use to generate electricity
- Teacher notes: Generating electricity
- Examination-style questions: Generating electricity
- Answers to examination-style questions: Generating electricity

AQA Examination-style questions 🄺

1 Electricity may be generated in a coal-fired power station.

Copy and complete the following sentences using words from the list below. Each word can be used once, more than once or not at all.

electricity fuel generator steam turbine water wood

In a coal-fired power station, ... is burned to heat .... This produces .... at high pressure which makes a .... spin round. This then drives a .... that produces .... (6)

2 Various power sources can be used to generate electricity.

Match the power sources in the list with the statements 1 to 4 in the table.

A falling water
B tides
C waves
D wind

	Statement
1	the source of hydroelectric power
2	used with a floating generator
3	very unpredictable and at times may stop altogether
4	will produce a predictable cycle of power generation during the day

(4)

3 A solar cell panel and a solar heating panel work in different ways.

Which statement below is correct?

A A solar cell produces light when it is supplied with electricity.

B A solar cell generates electricity when it is supplied with light.

C A solar heating panel produces heat when it is supplied with electricity.

D A solar heating panel produces electricity when it is supplied with heat. (1)

4 Gas-fired power stations have a shorter start-up time than other power stations. Give **one** reason why is it important to have power stations with a short start-up time. (1)

5 During the night, when demand for electricity is low, a wind farm may be generating a large amount of power. Explain how, by using another type of power station, this power could be stored and used when it is needed. (3)

6 Explain why step-up transformers are used in the National Grid. (2)

7 Palm oil can be used to make a biofuel called biodiesel. Biodiesel can be used instead of the normal type of diesel obtained by refining crude oil.

a Suggest **two** advantages of using biodiesel rather than normal diesel. (2)

b Suggest **two** disadvantages of using biodiesel rather than normal diesel. (2)

8 The pie chart shows the main sources of energy used in power stations in a country last year.

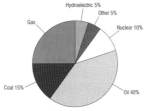

a What fraction of the energy used in power stations was obtained from gas? (2)

b Name **one** source of energy shown that is a fossil fuel. (1)

c Name **one** source of energy shown that is renewable. (1)

d Name **one** source of energy that could be included in the label 'other'. (1)

e Name **one** source of energy that does not cause carbon dioxide to be released when it is used. (1)

9 *In this question you will be assessed on using good English, organising information clearly and using specialist terms where appropriate.*

Power stations that burn fossil fuels produce waste gases that can cause pollution.

Describe the effect that these gases could have on the environment and what could be done to reduce the amount of these gases emitted by power stations. (6)

77

AQA Practical suggestions

Practicals	AQA⤴	🄺	📖	⚙
Investigating the effect of changing different variables on the output of solar cells, e.g. distance from the light source, the use of different-coloured filters and the area of the solar cells.	✓		✓	
Planning and carrying out an investigation into the effect of changing different variables on the output of model wind turbines, e.g. the number or pitch of the blades, the wind velocity.	✓	✓		✓
Demonstrating a model water turbine linked to a generator.	✓		✓	
Modelling the National Grid.	✓		✓	

AQA Examination-style answers

1 In a coal-fired power station, **fuel** is burned to heat **water**. This produces **steam** at high pressure, which makes a **turbine** spin round. This then drives a **generator** that produces **electricity**. *(6 marks)*

2 **A** falling water   1
B tides   4
C waves   2
D wind   3 *(4 marks)*

3 **B** A solar cell generates electricity when it is supplied with light. *(1 mark)*

4 To increase power quickly to meet changing demand or to prevent power cuts. *(1 mark)*

5 Pumped storage; electric pumps pump water into a high reservoir and this is later released through a turbine. *(3 marks)*

6 To increase the voltage on the cables and reduce power losses. *(2 marks)*

7 **a** Any **two** from the following:
conserves crude oil reserves;
is a renewable resource;
is carbon neutral *(2 marks)*

b Any **two** from the following:
may lead to deforestation;
reduces land available for growing food;
may lead to soil erosion *(2 marks)*

8 **a** All other sources account for 75%;
gas is 25% or $\frac{25}{100}$ or 0.25 *(2 marks)*

b Gas/coal/oil *(1 mark)*

c Hydroelectric *(1 mark)*

d Any sensible answer, e.g. wood burning. *(1 mark)*

e Nuclear or hydroelectric *(1 mark)*

9 There is a clear, balanced and detailed description of the effect that gases could have on the environment and what could be done to reduce the gas emitted. The answer shows almost faultless spelling, punctuation and grammar. It is coherent and in an organised, logical sequence. It contains a range of appropriate or relevant specialist terms used accurately. *(5–6 marks)*

There is a description of at least 2 effects that gases could have on the environment and at least one example of what could be done to reduce the gas emitted. There are some errors in spelling, punctuation and grammar. The answer has some structure and organisation. The use of specialist terms has been attempted, but not always accurately. *(3–4 marks)*

There is a brief description of at least one effect that gases could have on the environment or one example of what could be done to reduce the gas emitted. The answer has little clarity and detail. The spelling, punctuation and grammar are very weak. The answer is poorly organised with almost no specialist terms and/or their use demonstrating a general lack of understanding of their meaning. *(1–2 marks)*

No relevant content. *(0 marks)*

Examples of physics points made in the response:
- carbon dioxide/greenhouse gas
- can contribute to global warming
- carbon dioxide may be removed by CCS
- sulfur dioxide (named)
- dissolves in rain water
- to form acid rain
- which can destroy vegetation/cause leaf loss in trees, etc.
- sulfur may be removed from fuels before burning.

P1 5.1

The nature of waves

Learning objectives

Students should learn:

- that waves transfer energy from one point to another without the transfer of matter
- that waves are categorised as mechanical or electromagnetic
- that electromagnetic waves are transverse and mechanical waves may be transverse or longitudinal.

Learning outcomes

Most students should be able to:

- give examples of mechanical and electromagnetic waves
- give examples of longitudinal waves and transverse waves and describe the differences between them.

Some students should also be able to:

- explain the motion of particles in longitudinal and transverse mechanical waves.

Support

- The students struggle with the terms longitudinal and transverse; you will need to repeat these terms and demonstrate the motion many times in this lesson and a few of the future lessons too. Keep showing that parallel means in the same direction the wave is moving and perpendicular means at right angles to the direction.

Extend

- The particles in a longitudinal and transverse wave appear to be doing very different things, but their behaviour is actually very similar. If you have simulations, let the students observe the behaviour of a single particle over a period of time. They should be able to see that the particles are both actually moving in the same way; they are following a repeating sinusoidal pattern around a fixed point. It is this simple motion that defines the wave.

AQA Specification link-up: Physics P1.5

- Waves transfer energy. *[P1.5.1 a)]*
- Waves may be either transverse or longitudinal. *[P1.5.1 b)]*
- Electromagnetic waves are transverse, sound waves are longitudinal and mechanical waves may be either transverse or longitudinal. *[P1.5.1 c)]*
- All types of electromagnetic waves travel at the same speed through a vacuum (space). *[P1.5.1 d)]*
- Longitudinal waves show areas of compression and rarefaction. *[P1.5.1 f)]*

Lesson structure

Starters

Aftershock value – There is a great deal of footage of tsunami and recent earthquakes. You can use some of this to demonstrate the power of an 'uncontrolled' wave. Point out the regular vibration in earthquakes; shaking buildings and so on. *(5 minutes)*

Wave – Start with a simple task to support the students in revisiting their basic wave knowledge; ask the student to list as many types of wave as possible. Check through a few lists with the class and then ask the students to explain what a wave actually does. Use some of the examples to get them to realise that waves move energy but not material. When doing this, watch out for things like waves at the beach; these are moving water and are more complicated than the simple waves covered in this unit. Students can be extended by describing why these waves are not simple, by comparing them with the definition in the Student Book. *(10 minutes)*

Main

- During the lesson you should show off as many types of wave as you can; you will be revisiting some kinds during this chapter and the next, but it is a good idea to show the variety. Show water waves with video clips or a ripple tank, show sound waves with an obviously vibrating loudspeaker, use the rope to show transverse and the slinky to show longitudinal waves (and also transverse – See 'Practical support'). You can even show light and explain that it is transferring energy without material and you will demonstrate that it is a wave in a later lesson (using diffraction).

- Mechanical waves are fairly easy for the students to grasp; make sure they note the wave shape in transverse waves and emphasise that the particles in the material may be vibrating but they are returning back to their starting positions. You can use the ribbon or a sticky label to mark points on the wave.

- It's difficult to see the wave's shape in longitudinal waves; you can just watch the motion back and forth. A simulation of wave motion is very helpful indeed. There is a good range available for free that can be found on the internet. These can show the motion of an individual particle in the wave which is very helpful in demonstrating that the particle doesn't end up going anywhere; it just vibrates back and forth around a fixed point.

- The key phrases about longitudinal and transverse waves are obviously important; repeat them several times when describing the waves and check that all of the students can restate them.

Plenaries

The same but different – The students can conclude the lesson by creating a summary of the two types of wave (mechanical and electromagnetic) and the two types of wave motion (longitudinal and transverse). These should emphasise the similarities and differences in the waves. If you have a wave wall then select the best work and add it immediately. *(5 minutes)*

Mexican brain wave – Put the students into three or four rows all seated. Select one student to be the questioner in each row and give them a set of questions and answers about waves. The student asks the first person in the row a question; if they get the answer right then all of the people that have answered correctly stand up, wave, sit down and the questioner moves on. If they don't answer correctly, the second question is asked. The first row that waves all the way to the end is the winner. You could also do this in one big circle with smaller classes. You can differentiate by giving different sets of questions to each group of students. *(10 minutes)*

Practical support

Observing mechanical waves

Equipment and materials required

A slinky spring and piece of ribbon (or some sticky tape).

Details

To demonstrate longitudinal waves, stretch the spring out slightly and then move one end of the slinky in and out while keeping the other end still. The emphasis should be on the vibrations of the particles without them actually progressing. Sticking a bit of ribbon on a point on the spring can show this more effectively.

Transverse waves can be produced by moving the spring from side to side, showing the particles vibrating at right angles to the direction of propagation of the wave.

● Answer: The ribbon vibrates (moves) back and forth but ends up in the same place once the wave has passed.

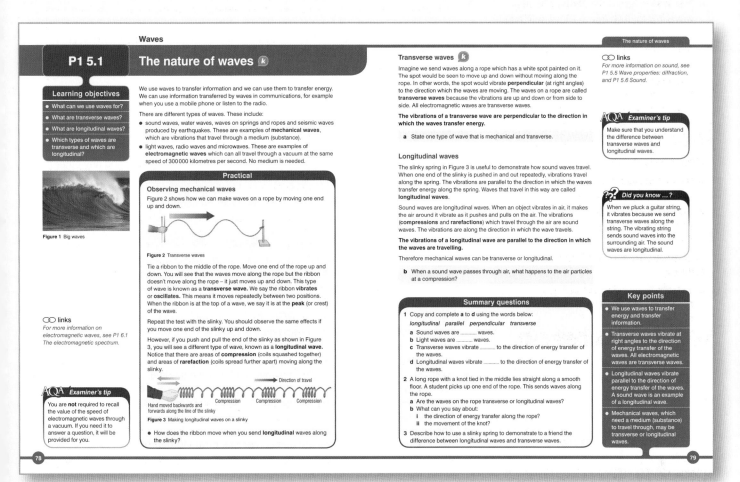

The nature of waves

Waves

P1 5.1 The nature of waves

Learning objectives

● What can we use waves for?
● What are transverse waves?
● What are longitudinal waves?
● Which types of waves are transverse and which are longitudinal?

We use waves to transfer information and we can use them to transfer energy. We can use information transferred by waves in communications, for example when you use a mobile phone or listen to the radio.

There are different types of waves. These include:

● sound waves, water waves, waves on springs and ropes and seismic waves produced by earthquakes. These are examples of **mechanical waves**, which are vibrations that travel through a medium (substance).

● light waves, radio waves and microwaves. These are examples of **electromagnetic waves** which can all travel through a vacuum at the same speed of 300 000 kilometres per second. No medium is needed.

Figure 1 Big waves

links

For more information on electromagnetic waves, see P1 6.1 The electromagnetic spectrum.

AQA Examiner's tip

You are **not** required to recall the value of the speed of electromagnetic waves through a vacuum. If you need it to answer a question, it will be provided for you.

Practical

Observing mechanical waves

Figure 2 shows how we can make waves on a rope by moving one end up and down.

Figure 2 Transverse waves

Tie a ribbon to the middle of the rope. Move one end of the rope up and down. You will see that the waves move along the rope but the ribbon doesn't move along the rope – it just moves up and down. This type of wave is known as a **transverse wave**. We say the ribbon **vibrates** or **oscillates**. This means it moves repeatedly between two positions. When the ribbon is at the top of a wave, we say it is at the **peak** (or crest) of the wave.

Repeat the test with the slinky. You should observe the same effects if you move one end of the slinky up and down.

However, if you push and pull the end of the slinky as shown in Figure 3, you will see a different type of wave, known as a **longitudinal wave**. Notice that there are areas of **compression** (coils squashed together) and areas of **rarefaction** (coils spread further apart) moving along the slinky.

Direction of travel

Hand moved backwards and forwards along the line of the slinky

Compression   Compression   Compression

Figure 3 Making longitudinal waves on a slinky

● How does the ribbon move when you send **longitudinal** waves along the slinky?

Transverse waves

Imagine we send waves along a rope which has a white spot painted on it. The spot would be seen to move up and down without moving along the rope. In other words, the spot would vibrate **perpendicular** (at right angles) to the direction which the waves are moving. The waves on a rope are called **transverse waves** because the vibrations are up and down or from side to side. All electromagnetic waves are transverse waves.

The vibrations of a transverse wave are perpendicular to the direction in which the waves transfer energy.

a State one type of wave that is mechanical and transverse.

Longitudinal waves

The slinky spring in Figure 3 is useful to demonstrate how sound waves travel. When one end of the slinky is pushed in and out repeatedly, vibrations travel along the spring. The vibrations are parallel to the direction in which the waves transfer energy along the spring. Waves that travel in this way are called **longitudinal waves**.

Sound waves are longitudinal waves. When an object vibrates in air, it makes the air around it vibrate as it pushes and pulls on the air. The vibrations (**compressions** and **rarefactions**) which travel through the air are sound waves. The vibrations are along the direction in which the wave travels.

The vibrations of a longitudinal wave are parallel to the direction in which the waves are travelling.

Therefore mechanical waves can be transverse or longitudinal.

b When a sound wave passes through air, what happens to the air particles at a compression?

Summary questions

1 Copy and complete a to d using the words below:
longitudinal   parallel   perpendicular   transverse
a Sound waves are .... waves.
b Light waves are .... waves.
c Transverse waves vibrate .... to the direction of energy transfer of the waves.
d Longitudinal waves vibrate .... to the direction of energy transfer of the waves.

2 A long rope with a knot tied in the middle lies straight along a smooth floor. A student picks up one end of the rope. This sends waves along the rope.
a Are the waves on the rope transverse or longitudinal waves?
b What can you say about:
i the direction of energy transfer along the rope?
ii the movement of the knot?

3 Describe how to use a slinky spring to demonstrate to a friend the difference between longitudinal waves and transverse waves.

links

For more information on sound, see P1 5.5 Wave properties: diffraction, and P1 5.6 Sound.

AQA Examiner's tip

Make sure that you understand the difference between transverse waves and longitudinal waves.

Did you know …?

When we pluck a guitar string, it vibrates because we send transverse waves along the string. The vibrating string sends sound waves into the surrounding air. The sound waves are longitudinal.

Key points

● We use waves to transfer energy and transfer information.

● Transverse waves vibrate at right angles to the direction of energy transfer of the waves. All electromagnetic waves are transverse waves.

● Longitudinal waves vibrate parallel to the direction of energy transfer of the waves. A sound wave is an example of a longitudinal wave.

● Mechanical waves, which need a medium (substance) to travel through, may be transverse or longitudinal waves.

78   79

Further teaching suggestions

Slow-motion waves

● You can show the motion of waves more clearly if you use video clips. If you have video logging equipment, you can record your own clips to show. Alternatively look for some slow motion clips of vibrations using the internet; here you should be able to see the vibrations of a guitar string, detailed motion of water waves and so on.

Wave wall

● If you have space, create a 'wave wall'. Add large diagrams to this throughout this chapter starting with ones that show the difference between transverse and longitudinal waves. Keep the text large and use the minimum number of words, so most of the students can review it when needed.

Answers to in-text questions

a Waves on a rope or on a string.

b The particles become closer together.

Summary answers

1 a longitudinal
  b transverse
  c perpendicular
  d parallel

2 a transverse
  b i Along the rope away from the student.
    ii The knot moves repeatedly up and down along a line that is perpendicular to the direction of energy transfer along the rope (which is along original line of the rope).

3 Hold the slinky at one end and ask the friend to hold the other end. Move away from each other to stretch the slinky. To demonstrate a longitudinal wave, push your end of the slinky towards and away from your friend repeatedly to send compression waves along the slinky. To demonstrate a transverse wave, move the end of the slinky repeatedly from one side to the other side or up and down. This will send waves along the slinky that are always at right angles to the line of the undisturbed slinky.

P1 5.2

Measuring waves

Learning objectives

Students should learn:

- that waves can be described by their wavelength, frequency, amplitude and speed
- the relationship between the wave speed, frequency and wavelength.

Learning outcomes

Most students should be able to:

- label a diagram of a wave to show the wavelength and amplitude
- calculate the wave speed when given the frequency and speed.

Some students should also be able to:

- apply the wave speed equation in a range of situations including rearrangement of the equation. [HT only]

Answers to in-text questions

a amplitude: 9 mm; wavelength: 34 mm

Support

- The students can have calculation templates for the first few wave calculations. For the practical task, you can provide the student with a couple of methods that they can use or ask them to come up with a plan on their own.

Extend

- The students investigate the relationship between the depth of water and the wave speed as described in the 'Practical support' feature.

AQA
Specification link-up: Physics P1.5

- The terms frequency, wavelength and amplitude. *[P1.5.1 i)]*
- All waves obey the wave equation: $v = f \times \lambda$ *[P1.5.1 j)]*

Lesson structure

Starters

Speed up – Ask the students to perform some simple speed calculations to remind them of this work from KS3. Make sure that they are using the correct units for speed, distance and time. Extend students by asking them to rearrange the equation and given more challenging data to use. You might need to support students by going through the stages of the calculations and units in more detail. *(5 minutes)*

Light on knowledge – The students need to list the properties of light and any other facts that they know about it. They should be able to come up with a range of facts from KS3, possibly including these: [it's very fast, travels in straight lines, white light can be split into colours, it can be reflected and refracted, filters can be used to allow only certain colours through]. *(10 minutes)*

Main

- Start with a study of a wave's shape, point out the crests and troughs clearly. It is very common for students to mark the amplitude incorrectly. Students often label amplitude as the full 'height' of the wave from peak to trough, as mentioned in the Examiner's tip. Watch out for this and emphasise its correction when it occurs.

- Demonstrate what frequency is with a signal generator and big loudspeaker, a ripple tank or animation. Simply put, frequency is just the 'number of waves each second'. Show the wide range of possible frequencies if you use a signal generator; you can test the range of student hearing.

- Sketching waves can be surprisingly difficult for some students, especially if you want to keep the wavelength consistent. Squared paper is a good idea as this allows some consistency. You can also ask students to make measurements of waves by looking at the squares.

- The students can try to verify the relationship between frequency and wavelength with the 'skipping rope' practical or you can get one group to demonstrate to the class.

- Ripple tanks can be fiddly to set up so that the waves can be seen clearly. The exact set-up will depend on the model that you have but it's always wise to test everything out before the lesson to make sure it is capable of showing wave motion clearly.

- Performing the second practical task in one way or another is a really good way of reinforcing wave movement. You could just provide the equipment and ask the students to come up with a plan to measure the speed; this is a fairly straightforward task. To extend them more, they could look into the relationship between wavelength and frequency, or even the water depth and speed of the wave. This can be linked back to the tsunami of the previous lesson; is it important to know the speed of the wave? Does the wave get faster or slower when it approaches the coast?

- The wave speed calculation is a simple multiplication. You should try to encourage the students to convert lengths to metres and times to seconds so that you can have a speed consistently measured in m/s. Plenty of practice is recommended. Extend students by asking them to calculate the frequency or wavelength when given the other two values.

- Don't forget to add some of the best examples of calculations to the wave wall and refer back to them now and again to drive the calculation home.

Plenaries

Wave taboo – Split the students into groups and give them some cards with key words written on (transverse, longitudinal, reflect, speed, etc.) and a list of words they can't use in describing the key word. How many can the group get in a set time limit? An example card could be [reflect: can't use bounce, rebound, ponder]. *(5 minutes)*

Kinaesthetic maths challenge – Provide the students with cards labelled wavelength, wave speed, frequency, times and equals. Each card has a number on it too. The students must form themselves into living equations by standing in groups of five making a correct equation. Extend students by providing more difficult numbers and questions that require rearrangements. An example set could be ['wave speed (30 m/s)', '=' 'wavelength (1.5 m)' '×', 'frequency (20 Hz)']. To support students, you can use coloured cards to make it easier to match them up. *(10 minutes)*

Practical support

Frequency and wavelength

Equipment and materials required
A skipping rope for each group (longish), stop clock, meter ruler.

Details
The students stretch the rope out but not too taut. One student oscillates the rope up and down smoothly while the others observe the wavelength of the wave formed. As the frequency of the oscillation increases, they should see that the wavelength decreases. The students can measure the frequency with a stop clock and the wavelength with the meter ruler.

Making straight (plane) waves
This can be performed as a demonstration if there is not enough equipment or you can use simple trays and have the students make their own waves.

Equipment and materials required
Ripple tank, stop watch, ruler and a tray, signal generator, loudspeaker, connecting leads.

Details
The experiment is as described in the Student Book. If you don't have a wave tank, then the students can make do with waterproof trays. Most laboratories have lots of these. The students can fill the tray to about 1 cm depth; moving the ruler at one end should send a wave along the tray and this can be measured. Alternatively, a sharp tap on the outside of the tray can send a good quality wave pulse. Students can be extended by using this technique to see if altering the depth of the water increases or decreases the wave speed. The changes to depth should only be by 1 mm at a time between 1 and 2 cm.

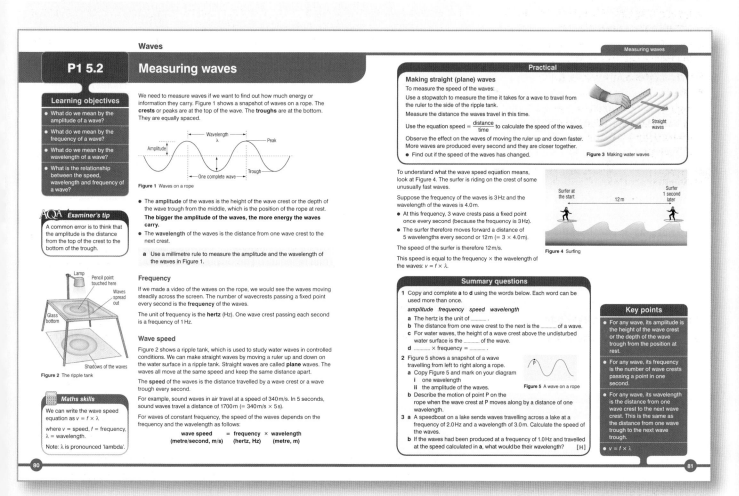

Further teaching suggestions

Drawing and labelling waves
- Wavelength is a reasonably simple concept, but many mistakes are made drawing and labelling waves in examinations. Point out that the wavelength can also be measured from trough to trough, or in fact any point in a wave to the next point that is doing exactly the same thing. Watch out for students who draw the wavelength incorrectly; this is usually from the point where the wave crosses zero displacement to the next zero, i.e. half a wavelength. A similar problem arises when labelling the amplitude on wave diagrams. This must be from the peak to the zero displacement position, i.e. half of the 'height' of the wave, not the full 'height' as many students draw.

Summary answers

1 a frequency
  b wavelength
  c amplitude
  d wavelength, speed

2 a i The wavelength should be from one wave crest to the next.
    ii The amplitude should be from a wave crest directly down to the mid-point between the wave crest and the wave trough.
  b As the wave moves across, P moves down to the bottom of the wave then back to the top as the next wave crest arrives.

3 a 6.0 m/s
  b 6.0 m

P1 5.3 | Wave properties: reflection

AQA Specification link-up: Physics P1.5

- Waves can be reflected … *[P1.5.1 g)]*
- The normal is a construction line perpendicular to the reflecting surface at the point of incidence. *[P1.5.2 a)]*
- The angle of incidence is equal to the angle of reflection. *[P1.5.2 b)]*
- The image produced in a plane mirror is virtual, upright and laterally inverted. *[P1.5.2 c)]*

   Controlled Assessment: P4.5 Analyse and interpret primary and secondary data. *[P4.5.2 a) b) c) d)]*

Learning objectives

Students should learn:

- what the normal is in a ray diagram
- that the angle of incidence is the angle between the normal and the incident ray of light
- that the angle of reflection is the angle between the reflected ray and the normal
- that the angle of incidence and the angle of reflection are equal for plane mirrors.

Learning outcomes

Most students should be able to:

- draw a diagram showing reflection by a plane mirror which shows the angle of incidence, the angle of reflection and the normal
- explain that the image in a mirror is virtual; it cannot be projected onto a screen.

Some students should also be able to:

- draw a diagram to show the formation of the image of a point object in a plane mirror.

Answers to in-text questions

a i 20°
   ii 40°
b virtual

Support

- Use a worksheet with the mirror position and incident rays marked on. This can also have a normal and protractor printed on if necessary. Make sure students are familiar with angular measurements by asking them to take some measurements of known angles first. Place extra emphasis on the terms **incident ray** and **reflected ray** and make sure the students are measuring the angles to the normal line; it is common for students to be measuring the angle to the surface of the mirror by mistake.

Extend

- There are two laws of reflection. The students should find out what the other law is and explain what it means. This states that the reflected ray is in the same plane as the incident plane.

Lesson structure

Starters

Virtually real – Ask: 'What does the word 'virtual' mean?' The students should give several examples of its use. What about the word 'real'? Many will have heard of virtual reality; point out that the terms have a specific meaning in optics. *(5 minutes)*

Ray diagram – Ask the students to draw a ray diagram showing how they can see a non-luminous object, such as the writing in their books. Make sure that the students are using a ruler to draw rays of light and that the rays are reflecting cleanly from the surface. Be fussy about gaps in the rays; this is a common error and leads to lost marks in examinations. Extend students by asking them to critique each other's work and advise each other how to correct the work to make it the highest possible standard. To support students you can start to form a set of rules about how to draw ray diagrams and add it to a prominent list displayed on the wall for the next series of lessons. *(10 minutes)*

Main

- The students need to be aware of the difference between diffuse reflection, where no image is formed, and normal reflection. The difference is obvious when showing them a mirror and a sheet of paper. When discussing the position of the image in the mirror, use the 'image distance' activity in 'Further teaching suggestions'.

- The normal is a very important part of ray diagrams and the students must draw it on all such diagrams. Return to the ray diagram the students drew in the starter (or get them to draw a diagram now). Introduce the idea of the normal and make sure the students adapt their diagrams.

- All angles are measured from the normal, so make sure that the students are not measuring them from the surface of the mirror to the incident or reflected ray. Many students remember the law of reflection, but the experiment allows them to become familiar with the equipment that they may not have used for several years. Check that they are forming and directing the rays correctly and that they are drawing a normal to aim the rays at.

- Getting across the ideas of real and virtual images can be tricky; a real image is formed when the light rays really pass a point but a virtual image is formed when the light rays seem to have come from a point; they never actually meet at the point.

- Demonstrate lateral inversion using some mirror writing and have the students read it 'through' a mirror.

- If you have time available, the construction of periscopes is a good activity for some groups requiring more support.

Plenaries

Pepper's ghost – Show students this simple but classic optical illusion and ask them to come up with an explanation of how it works. This leads to the idea of partial reflection; an effect they often see when looking through glass. The students should be challenged to draw ray diagrams explaining the effect. *(5 minutes)*

Mirror maze – Support students in checking their understanding of the law of reflection by asking them to add mirrors to a simple maze diagram so that a light ray can pass through it to the centre. They can do this by simply drawing the mirror positions on to a worksheet or you could demonstrate a solution using a laser. You can extend students by asking them to design a similar maze that may be solved using a set of five mirrors with precise positioning. *(10 minutes)*

Practical support

A reflection test

The students may have carried out similar experiments during KS3, but it is worthwhile to get them used to the equipment again. The experiment is best carried out in a darkened lab, but full blackout is not required.

Equipment and materials required

Power supply, ray box, single slit, ray box stops, plane mirror, ruler, protractor and a sheet of A3 paper.

Details

The students set up the ray box so that it produces a single ray. The mirror is fixed to the back of the paper using a holder or sticky-tac, so that the ray can be reflected by it. Then the students shine rays at the centre of the mirror from a range of angles and measure the angles of incidence and reflection. This is best done by marking the path of each ray at two points with a cross and then joining these with a ruler. The lines should be drawn to the back of the mirror where reflection takes place. You might find that the experiment works best if the mirror is tilted downwards very slightly.

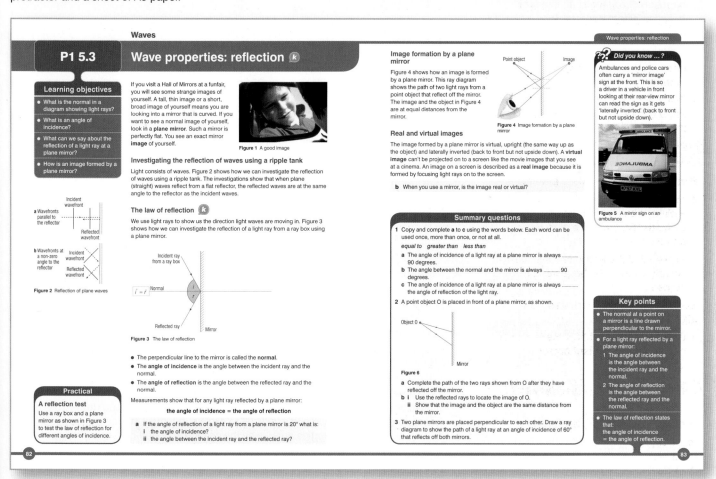

Further teaching suggestions

Image distance

- A quick way to show that the image lies the same distance behind the mirror as the object is in front of it, is to place a 30 cm ruler pointing out from just beneath your nose. Place the plane mirror at the 30 cm point and look at your reflection. You can clearly see that the mirror is 30 cm away and that your reflected image appears 30 cm further away than that.

Mirror writing

- The students can try to write a message backwards without the help of a mirror. Check the results. Add some backwards writing to your 'Wave wall' started in P1 5.1.

??? Did you know ... ?

One of the first movies to shock people was the moving image of a train coming towards the camera. The film *Arrival of a Train*, by the Lumière brothers, is just a 50 s clip of a train arriving at a station. You should be able to find a copy of this clip by searching for 'trainarrival.mov' on the internet. Somehow it's not as frightening as it used to be. There are plenty of other early clips around to show how cinema has developed.

Summary answers

1. **a** less than
   b equal to
   c equal to

2. **a**, **b i** **ii**

   Object O .... Image

   Mirror

3. 60°

P1 5.4

Wave properties: refraction

Learning objectives

Students should learn:

- that refraction is the changing of direction of a wave at an interface between different materials
- that refraction occurs because light changes speed when it moves from one medium to another
- that a prism disperses white light into a spectrum because each frequency is refracted by a different amount.

Learning outcomes

Most students should be able to:

- draw diagrams showing how light is refracted when entering and leaving a transparent substance.

Some students should also be able to:

- explain why refraction takes place
- draw a diagram showing the refraction of light by a prism and explain the process that causes this effect.

Answers to in-text questions

a yes

Support

- As with the reflection experiments, you may want to use worksheets that have the position of the glass block and incident rays marked on to save some time.

Extend

- The speed that light travels in a material and how much refraction takes place at its surface are determined by something called the 'refractive index' of the material. Can the students find out why diamond separates out light into different colours so well?

AQA — Specification link-up: Physics P1.5

- Waves can be refracted… [P1.5.1 g)]
- Waves undergo a change of direction when they are refracted at an interface. [P1.5.1 h)]

Lesson structure

Starters

It's just a broken pencil – Place a pencil in a beaker of water. Can the students come up with an explanation of why the pencil looks broken? This is quite difficult; make sure that the students see the effect clearly (have a big photograph on the interactive whiteboard if needed). The explanations may include rays of light bending. (5 minutes)

See through – Support students' understanding of transmission and absorption by giving them definitions of three words: 'transparent', 'opaque', and 'translucent'. They can then sort an example set of materials into these three groups. Include some awkward materials that are just about transparent and some coloured filters, so that the students will have to come up with explanations like: 'The red filter is transparent to red light but it is opaque to other colours'. Students can be extended by not giving them the categories but asking them to come up with criteria and examples of their own. (10 minutes)

Main

- Make sure that, when the students are using the term 'bending' when talking about refraction, they are not thinking that the light is 'following a curved path'. Most of the refraction here is a clear and sudden change of direction, so you might want to restrict your use of the word as far as possible.

- During the initial investigation, watch out for the students marking out and then drawing the rays correctly. They should notice that the ray leaves the block parallel to the direction it entered. The students may also notice some total internal reflection and you might like to remind them of the uses of this phenomenon.

- If possible, demonstrate the changing of wave speed with a ripple tank or use a simulation. You can't beat seeing the waves speeding up and slowing down. The reason for the change in speed is difficult to explain, but most students just accept it. There are several analogies about why the change in speed causes a change in direction; a column of soldiers marching from a road into mud, a four-wheel drive vehicle doing the same. Use whichever one the students are comfortable with.

- Refraction from a prism can be shown as a demonstration, or you might like the class to have a go. You can get an excellent spectrum using your data projector as a white light source. This 'spreading' of the different colours is called dispersion and it occurs because the different frequencies of light all travel at different speeds in the glass, so refract at slightly different angles.

- Getting a good recombination of a spectrum into white light is almost impossible, but it is worth trying to give the idea of recombining, so that you can tell the story of Newton and his work on light.

Plenaries

Reflect or refract – Students to make a big diagram for the wave wall to show the difference between these two words, so that nobody gets it wrong again. The best diagram goes up on the wall for future reference. You can have the students come up with clear criteria for what 'best' means in a diagram of this sort. (5 minutes)

The magic penny – Place a penny at the bottom of an opaque cup so that you just about can't see it. Pour water into the cup and it reappears. The students should explain why, using a diagram. To support students, you can provide a partial diagram of the scenario and ask them to complete it. This should be a ray diagram showing the reflection of light off the coin, travelling in straight lines and refraction at the surface. Students should also draw a normal line at the refraction point. Students can be extended by asking them to consider why a swimming pool looks shallower than it actually is, a ray diagram of this scenario should also be drawn. (10 minutes)

Practical support

Investigating refraction of light

The students may have performed a similar experiment during KS3, but here the emphasis should be placed on taking measurements from the normal.

Equipment and materials required

For each group: low voltage power supply, ray box, single slit, ray box stops, rectangular glass block, ruler, protractor and a sheet of A3 paper.

Details

The glass block should be placed in the centre of the A3 sheet of paper. It's a good idea to draw around it in case it gets knocked. The students can shine rays into the block from a range of angles aiming for a fixed point on the front surface. They should draw small crosses to mark the path and then measure the angles of incidence and refraction. The angles must be measured from the normal. As in P1 5.3, this provides an opportunity to discuss the accuracy of measurements and errors involved in the experiment. Examine the protractors to show that measurement to the nearest degree may not always be possible, have several students measure the same angle and see if they come up with the same measurement. ('How Science Works'.)

Investigating refraction by a prism

This can be run as a simple demonstration or you can let the students have a quick go.

Equipment and materials required

For each group: low voltage power supply, ray box, single slit, ray box stops, prism.

Details

Simply shine the ray through the prism and rotate the prism until a spectrum is produced. Newton was able to recombine the dispersed rays back into a ray of white light with a second prism, but this takes a great deal of skill. Use a data projector as a source of light if a larger spectrum is needed.

Refraction of water waves

Equipment and materials required

Ripple tank with wave generator, thin glass block.

Details

Set up the ripple tank with enough water in it to cover the glass block. It should be strongly illuminated from below so that the shadow of waves can be seen on the ceiling (or the board if you have a mirror). Show the students the behaviour of simple waves and then place the glass block in to show that wave speed changes above the block. Rotating the block will show that the wave direction is different when the block is at an angle. This show the waves are being refracted.

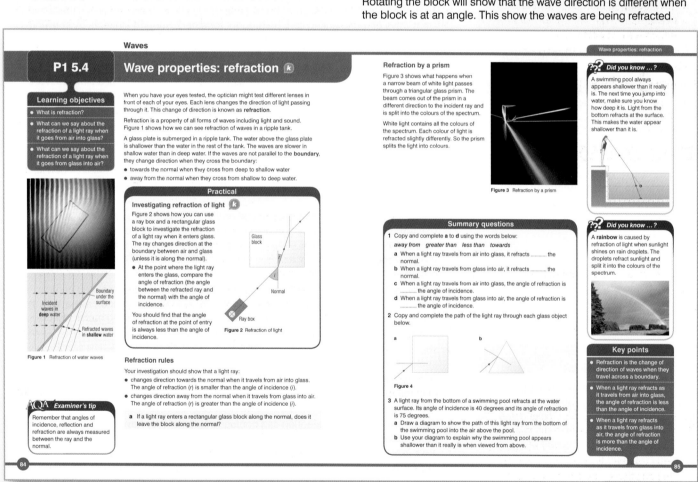

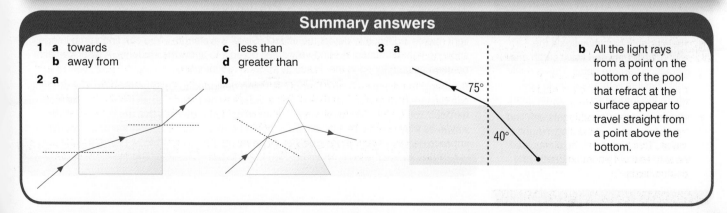

P1 5.5

Wave properties: diffraction

Learning objectives

Students should learn:

- that diffraction is the spreading effect of waves produced when they pass through a gap or past an obstacle
- that the diffraction effect is greatest when the waves are of a similar size to the gaps.

Learning outcomes

Most students should be able to:

- draw a diagram showing how waves diffract when they pass through gaps
- list and describe the factors that affect the amount of diffraction that takes place
- give examples of diffraction of mechanical and electromagnetic waves.

Answers to in-text questions

a The light waves are transverse and the ultrasonic sound waves are longitudinal.

b radiowaves

Support

- The students can make thought balloons. They blow up a balloon (can be any shape) and make notes on it about reflection, refraction and diffraction using permanent pen. This can be put on the wall or deflated for ease of transport.

Extend

- The students can investigate the relationship between wavelength and diffraction in more detail. This is really only possible with a real ripple tank where the frequency can be adjusted.

- What's waving? The students can find out about what is oscillating in light waves. This high-level topic may lead them to find out about magnetic and electric fields.

AQA Specification link-up: Physics P1.5

- Waves can be … diffracted. *[P1.5.1 g)]*

Lesson structure

Starters

Safe harbour – Show some video footage of water waves passing through a harbour entrance. Ask students to sketch a diagram of what is happening to the waves. Look for the different designs they come up with and chose one that shows the wave peaks clearly. This is the kind of diagram you will be asking students to use, so show the best one to the whole class and add it to the 'Wave wall' started in P1 5.1 The nature of waves. *(5 minutes)*

Ray or wave – Show the students a traditional diagram showing a light ray, then ask them to show the rays coming from a light bulb. Show them the ripples caused by a pebble being dropped into water. Discuss the fact that this is wave motion. How can these two different ways of representing light be brought together? Support students by showing them that the rays are straight paths that connect the wave fronts by showing diagrams or simulations of this motion. Students can be extended by considering what happens to the waves and the idea of rays once they pass through gaps or even reflect. They may consider the wave front explanation of reflection (using a simulation) at a simple level so that they can compare models of light behaviour. *(10 minutes)*

Main

- Start the lesson with a basic demonstration of the effect of diffraction; use both water and light. Make sure you show the shape of the spreading pattern and the fact that the extent of this spreading can be changed by adjusting the gap. You can look at the effect of changing the wavelength of the wave on the diffraction pattern if you want to extend the students.

- Simulations of diffraction are easy to find and make this topic far easier to understand. Use them to show the waves spreading as they pass through the gaps. You should be able to adjust the size of the gaps to see the effect. Most simulations also let you alter the wavelength or frequency too. You can return to the simulation at key points in the lesson to reinforce the learning.

- There are plenty of diagrams and video clips of ultrasound scans that you can use to discuss the use of ultrasound. Go beyond the usual foetal scans and have a look at a heart beating; you could even show some industrial uses; checking metal objects for cracks is a suitable example.

- You can then demonstrate the test with microwaves. Some students still find it hard to appreciate that there are actually waves being transmitted and received. Start with a large gap between the metal plates; show how far they spread with the detector and then decrease the gap size and repeat. You should find the waves spread in nearly all directions when the gap size reaches 3 cm.

- The explanation of TV reception can confuse students; they have probably not realised how houses in hilly areas have poor reception unless they actually live in such an area. You can discuss the use of satellite or cable TV in these areas to overcome the problem.

Plenaries

Does light diffract? – Why don't we notice light diffract around objects? What property of light makes it difficult to detect the effect? [Small wavelength.] You can find some images showing light diffracting around very small objects to show the students. A laser can also be used as mentioned in the 'Practical support'. *(5 minutes)*

Breaking the waves – A new harbour is being designed to keep boats safer. The students can design the features that would cause waves to be broken up as they enter the harbour. You could support students by showing some designs that are used to break waves as they reach a beach. Students could be extended by asking them to suggest improvements to existing designs. *(10 minutes)*

Practical support

Investigating diffraction

This may have to be a demonstration unless you have a large stock of equipment. You can also use simulations as described in the main lesson plan.

Equipment and materials required

For each group: ripple tank (or large tray), metal or glass blocks.

Details

The students can use a full ripple tank set-up; this will have a suitable source of waves produced by a vibrating motor. If this is unavailable, they can improvise by producing water waves as described in the previous lesson. It is difficult to get consistent waves though.

They should notice that changing the gap size changes the amount of diffraction that takes place. When the gap size reaches the wavelength, the diffraction should be very large.

Diffraction of laser light

Diffraction is one of the fundamental processes that shows light behaving like a wave, so it is important to try to demonstrate this effect to the students.

Equipment and materials required

A laser (LED lasers are fine), a narrow slit for the laser light to pass through.

Details

Most laser kits come with an adjustable narrow slit. Pass the beam through the slit and adjust it so show that the narrow beam spreads. By adjusting the slit, the beam spreads more or less. Explain that this is showing that light is spreading just like water waves and this can only be explained if light is behaving like a wave.

Safety: Do not look directly at a laser light beam – see CLEAPSS P5 5.2 or Handbook 12.12.

Tests using microwaves

Microwaves are good examples of electromagnetic waves that can be seen to noticeably diffract around simple objects.

Equipment and materials required

Microwave transmitter, receiver and metal plates. One of the plates should have a gap of 1 cm to allow diffraction of the microwaves.

Details

Demonstrate that the receiver can detect a microwave signal from the transmitter. You can then allow the waves to pass through the gap and move the detector in a semicircular arc detector to show that the microwaves have diffracted.

You should also demonstrate that the microwaves diffract when they pass the **edge** of the metal plate and so a signal can be detected behind the plate. Point the transmitter at the edge of the plate and move the detector in an arc again; the signal should be detectable behind the plate.

- Answer: The microwaves from the transmitter are reflected by the metal plates.

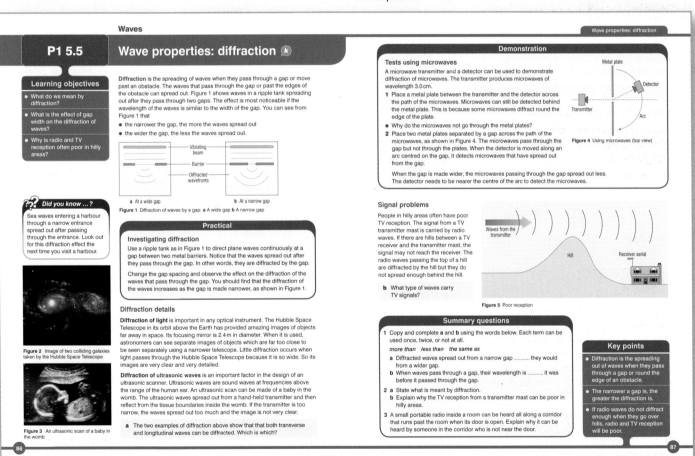

Summary answers

1. **a** more than   **b** the same as

2. **a** Diffraction is the spreading out of waves when they pass through a gap or round an obstacle.
   b Where TV reception is poor, radio waves carrying the TV signal from the transmitter mast do not diffract enough when they travel over hills. TV receivers which are much below the diffracted waves will not receive a strong enough signal to give a good TV picture.

3. The sound waves from the portable radio diffract when they pass through the open door and some of the waves travel along the corridor.

P1 5.6

Sound

AQA
Specification link-up: Physics P1.5
- Sound waves are longitudinal waves and cause vibrations in a medium, which are detected as sound. [P1.5.3 a)]
- Echoes are reflections of sounds. [P1.5.3 c)]

Learning objectives

Students should learn:

- that the human ear can detect a range of frequencies from 20 to 20 000 Hz
- that sound is a mechanical wave that requires a medium to travel through and so cannot pass through a vacuum (space)
- about the difference between a sound wave and a light wave.

Learning outcomes

Most students should be able to:

- state the range of hearing for a typical human
- describe the properties of a sound wave, including its longitudinal nature
- describe the behaviour of a sound wave, including reflection and refraction.

Some students should also be able to:

- explain why mechanical vibrations produce sound waves.

Lesson structure

Starters

Sound facts – Give the students a set of 'facts' about sound and let them use traffic light cards to indicate if they agree (green), don't know (amber) or disagree (red). Facts can include these correct ones: sound needs particles to travel; the speed of sound in air is 300 m/s, and sound travels faster in more dense materials. You can also use these incorrect ones: we hear sounds when particles travel from a source to our ears; sound travels as fast as light; we can hear all sound waves. The facts provided can be differentiated to allow extra support or extension. *(5 minutes)*

Good vibrations – How do different instruments produce sound waves? The students should describe what is going on for five different ways of producing a sound. Try to demonstrate a drum, guitar, flute or recorder, loudspeaker and singing. This should show that vibrations are needed to produce sound waves. *(10 minutes)*

Main

- The contents of this lesson are mostly revision for the students, so you can spend a bit of time clearing up any misconceptions. The initial practical/demonstration should remind the students of the basics of sound, and allow you to describe the operation of a signal generator and loudspeaker in more detail. If possible, use a bell jar to show that particles are required for sound waves to travel. Use a safety screen in case glass implodes.

- Remind the students of the nature of mechanical longitudinal waves using a slinky. They will have to be able to describe what is happening to the particles in air. Students should know that sound can be reflected and this is simply called an 'echo'. Go through this again when you use the slinky.

- The behaviour of particles in air is actually more complex than the students might think. The particles actually *are* moving around from place to place quite rapidly but in a random way. A sound wave is a vibration superimposed on top of this random motion. Some simulations will show this, but others will show the particles vibrating around fixed positions for simplicity. You can discuss the limitations of the models.

- It can be worth discussing sound-absorbing materials and the lengths sound recording studios will go to in order to prevent reflections.

- You can investigate the reflection of sound waves in more detail using 'Investigating sound waves' from the 'Practical support', if you feel it is appropriate.

- Refraction of sound is very hard to show, but the students should be aware that things like distant traffic sounds are louder at night. This is due to the sound waves being refracted in the atmosphere similar to light waves in a mirage.

- In the next lesson, the students will need some musical instruments, so ask them to bring some in if they can play them.

Support

- The students may need extra support with the oscilloscopes. Squared paper helps students a lot with sketching accurate waveforms.

Extend

- Ask: 'Is there any relationship between the physical size of an animal's ear and the range of frequencies it can detect?' The students will need to find information from reference books or, more likely, the internet.

Plenaries

Oscilloscope guide – Can the students write their own guide to using an oscilloscope so that they can always find the trace? This will help them learn the names of the controls and allow them to write in a scientific way. The guide can have some example traces drawn, for example a trace where the waves' peaks are too close together to see clearly, and measures to fix the problems (reduce the time base). *(5 minutes)*

Let's hear it then – The students need to design a simple experiment that will show that sound travels faster in solid materials than it does in air. This could be a basic plan or a more detailed one. Students can be supported by providing some suggested equipment and recording techniques. Extend students by asking them carry out the tests along these lines: Place the microphones a measured distance apart separated by the material, and connected to a timing system. Make a sound that triggers the first microphone and then the second. Use the speed equation to measure the speed from the distance and time. They can then evaluate the success of the experiment or perhaps consider a link between density and the speed of sound. *(10 minutes)*

Practical support

Investigating sound waves

This makes a better demonstration than a student practical, but if you have lots of equipment it can be useful to get the students used to it for the next topic.

Equipment and materials required

Signal generator and loudspeaker. Connecting leads, paper discs.

Details

At the start of the investigation, you will need to show the students how to operate the signal generator and how it should be connected to the loudspeaker. Some generators have several outputs, so make sure that the students are using the right one if they are having a go. To see the vibrations of the loudspeaker clearly, they can drop some paper discs from a hole punch on to it – these will bounce around. To test the hearing limits of the students, it is better to get them to raise their hands at the start and put them down when they can no longer hear the noise. Some students can still hear the high frequency sounds when you secretly turn the power off; truly amazing!

Waves

P1 5.6   Sound

Learning objectives

- What range of frequencies can be detected by the human ear?
- What are sound waves?
- What are echoes?

Figure 1 Making sound waves

?? Did you know …?

When you blow a round whistle, you force a small ball inside the whistle to go round and round inside. Each time it goes round, its movement draws air in then pushes it out. Sound waves are produced as a result.

⊂⊃ links

For more information on alternating current, see P2 5.1 Alternating current.

Sound waves at frequencies above 20000 Hz are called ultrasound. For more information on the use of ultrasound in medicine, see P3 1.2 Ultrasound.

Investigating sound waves 🄺

Sound waves are easy to produce. Your vocal cords vibrate and produce sound waves every time you speak. Any object vibrating in air makes the layers of air near the object vibrate. These layers make the layers of air further away vibrate. The vibrating object pushes and pulls repeatedly on the air. This sends out the vibrations of the air in waves of compressions and rarefactions. When the waves reach your ears, they make your eardrums vibrate in and out so you hear sound as a result.

The vibrations travelling through the air are sound waves. The waves are longitudinal because the air particles vibrate along the direction in which the waves transfer energy.

Practical

Investigating sound waves

You can use a loudspeaker to produce sound waves by passing alternating current through it. Figure 2 shows how to do this using a signal generator. This is an alternating current supply unit with a variable frequency dial.

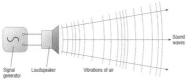

Signal generator   Loudspeaker   Vibrations of air   Sound waves

Figure 2 Using a loudspeaker

- If you observe the loudspeaker closely, you can see it vibrating. It produces sound waves as it pushes the surrounding air backwards and forwards.
- If you alter the frequency dial of the signal generator, you can change the frequency of the sound waves.

Find out the lowest and the highest frequency you can hear. Young people can usually hear sound frequencies from about 20 Hz to about 20000 Hz. Older people in general can't hear frequencies at the higher end of this range.

a   Which animal produces sound waves at a higher frequency, an elephant or a mouse?

Sound waves cannot travel through a vacuum. You can test this by listening to an electric bell in a bell jar. As the air is pumped out of the bell jar, the ringing sound fades away.

b   What would you notice if the air is let back into the bell jar?

Reflection of sound

Have you ever created an echo? An **echo** is an example of reflection of sound. Echoes can be heard in a large hall or gallery which has bare, smooth walls.

- If the walls are covered in soft fabric, the fabric will absorb sound instead of reflecting it. No echoes will be heard.
- If the wall surface is uneven (not smooth), echoes will not be heard because the reflected sound is 'broken up' and scattered.

c   What happens to the energy of the sound waves when they are absorbed by a fabric?

Refraction of sound

Sound travels through air at a speed of about 340 m/s. The warmer the air is, the greater the speed of sound. At night you can hear sound a long way from its source. This is because sound waves refract back to the ground instead of travelling away from the ground. Refraction takes place at the boundaries between layers of air at different temperatures. In the daytime, sound refracts upwards, not downwards, because the air near the ground is warmer than air higher up.

Figure 4 Refraction of sound

Wires to battery

Air removed using a vacuum pump

Bell jar

Bell works but cannot be heard

Figure 3 A sound test

Summary questions

1 Copy and complete **a** and **b** using the words below:

    absorbed   reflected   scattered

   a   An echo is heard when sound is .... from a bare, smooth wall.
   b   Sound waves are .... by a rough wall and .... by soft fabric.

2 a   What is the highest frequency of sound the human ear can hear?
   b   Why does a round whistle produce sound at a constant frequency when you blow steadily into it?

3 a   A boat is at sea in a mist. The captain wants to know if the boat is near any cliffs so he sounds the horn and listens for an echo. Why would hearing an echo tell him he is near the cliffs?
   b   Explain why someone in a large cavern can sometimes hear more than one echo of a sound.

Key points

- The frequency range of the normal human ear is from about 20 Hz to about 20000 Hz.
- Sound waves are vibrations that travel through a medium (substance). They cannot travel through a vacuum (as in space).
- Echoes are due to sound waves reflected from a smooth, hard surface.

88   89

Further teaching suggestions

Particle behaviour

- Yet again, there are some fine simulations of the behaviour of sound waves showing particle behaviour. These are very handy when discussing what is happening to these invisible particles.

Answers to in-text questions

a   A mouse.

b   The ringing sound can be heard again.

c   The sound energy is transferred by heating and the fabric warms up.

Summary answers

1   a   reflected
    b   scattered, absorbed

2   a   About 20 000 Hz.
    b   When the whistle is blown, a small ball in the whistle goes round the inside of the whistle at high speed and makes the air inside vibrate. This makes the air outside the whistle vibrate and creates sound waves in the air outside the whistle.

3   a   Cliffs nearby would reflect the sound waves from the horn as their surfaces are hard and smooth.
    b   Sound waves reflecting from the wall of the cavern would then reflect elsewhere on the cavern wall. Someone in the cavern would hear echoes due to these different reflections.

P1 5.7

Musical sounds

AQA

Specification link-up: Physics P1.5

- The pitch of a sound is determined by its frequency and loudness by its amplitude. [P1.5.3 b)]

Learning objectives

Students should learn:

- that the pitch of a sound increases as the frequency increases
- that the loudness of the sound increases as the amplitude increases.

Learning outcomes

Most students should be able to:

- describe the properties of a sound wave in terms of frequency and amplitude.

Some students should also be able to:

- explain how sound is produced by different types of musical instruments and compare the sounds they produce, including pitch and loudness.

Answers to in-text questions

a An ambulance, a police vehicle, a fire engine, an ice cream van.

b The waves are not as tall.

c The waves would be smaller in height and stretched out more.

Support

- Focus on the use of the oscilloscope to trace waves. You may have to recap how to adjust the control so that the waveform is clear. Make sure the students understand that making changes to the oscilloscope only affects how the wave is displayed so that it is easier to see; it is not changing the original wave.

Extend

- Ask: 'What happens when two notes are played together?' The students should look at the waveform generated when two tuning forks are used at the same time. The effect can also be generated by putting two loudspeakers playing at slightly different frequencies next to each other. This beat phenomenon is very important in music.

Lesson structure

Starters

It's music to my ears – Play some short extracts of music, from classical to punk and ask the students to list the instruments they can hear. Ask: 'Which music is the best?' Get the students to discuss what 'musical' is. Play some example of white noise and other sounds too. *(5 minutes)*

The intro round – Using a personal music player (through headphones on low volume so the rest of the class cannot hear it), a student listens to the introductions of some songs and has to reproduce them using only their vocal skills. Simple tunes can be used to support students or you can make the task more challenging by having students work together in groups. You can select a variety of modern tunes and slip in a few sounds that are fairly impossible for humans to make. *(10 minutes)*

Main

- The analysis of sound waves is made much easier if you have a digital oscilloscope that allows capture of waveforms. These can be used to store data about the waveform directly into a computer system and so the waves can be projected for all the class to see. If you have a system like this then, with a bit of practice, you can get it to find frequency and amplitude quite easily.

- The investigation is quite extensive and it may be difficult for all of the students to have a go. At the end of it, make sure that the students have all reached the correct conclusions.

- If you want the students to sketch out some of the waveforms, then give them some squared paper to help them out as you have done in previous lessons. Make sure that the students are using the appropriate words clearly (amplitude, loudness, frequency, pitch) correctly when describing the waves.

- After consolidating the students' findings, show some additional musical instruments to show how complex waveforms can quickly become.

- Voice recognition systems are improving all of the time, but you may want to show the limitations of the current technology. The operating system of your computer, or some of your applications, will probably have voice recognition built in, so give it a try and see how it does. Try to confuse it with sentences like: 'Which witches wear our weather predicting watches?'

- Resonance is an important phenomena; showing the structure of instruments will show how they are designed to resonate at certain key frequencies. You should be able to use a signal generator and loudspeaker to make an acoustic guitar resonate. Play about with the frequency until the guitar starts humming. The sound box is now resonating. You could also use a violin.

Plenaries

Perfect pitch – Which of the students can produce the purest note according to the oscilloscope? Connect a microphone directly to the 'scope and the students can try to see who is best able to produce a sine wave. Try whistling compared to singing. *(5 minutes)*

Compare traces – The students must compare three oscilloscope traces in terms of frequency, amplitude and quality of the note. They describe the differences and explain how they will sound different when produced by a musical instrument. Extend students by asking them to use real instruments to provide traces on the oscilloscope and then provide a detailed description of the traces. Students can be supported by providing relatively simple traces marked out on a grid showing amplitude and time period. Provide the formula to convert time period to frequency so that it is easier to determine the frequency. *(10 minutes)*

Practical support

Investigating different sounds

You may well not have enough equipment to let the students carry this out as a full class practical, but it is worth considering letting them use it in small groups one at a time, so that they can appreciate the techniques involved.

Equipment and materials required

For each group: signal generator, loudspeaker, microphone, oscilloscope, tuning forks and some musical instruments.

Details

The main problems you may have are the background noise in the classroom and lack of experience with the oscilloscope. A teaching assistant or helpful technician may help with the latter, but the background noise will always distort the waveforms from instruments in a class practical; you may want to show what the waves should look like with a demonstration at the end of the practical. Most signal generators have two outputs, so you can connect one to the loudspeaker and one to the cathode ray oscilloscope (CRO). This removes the background noise completely. Make sure that you mark the cm/s dial so that the students know which one to adjust. They should not need to alter any other settings to display the wave. Musically-inclined students should be able to use a range of instruments and compare the waveform with the pure wave of the tuning forks.

Musical instruments

Equipment and materials required

As above.

Details

The students will have to use a microphone and oscilloscope to capture the waveform. It can be very difficult for them to adjust the oscilloscope to the correct settings to see the wave clearly. If you have a digital oscilloscope, you can have some pre-recorded waveforms to display in case the students can't record them clearly.

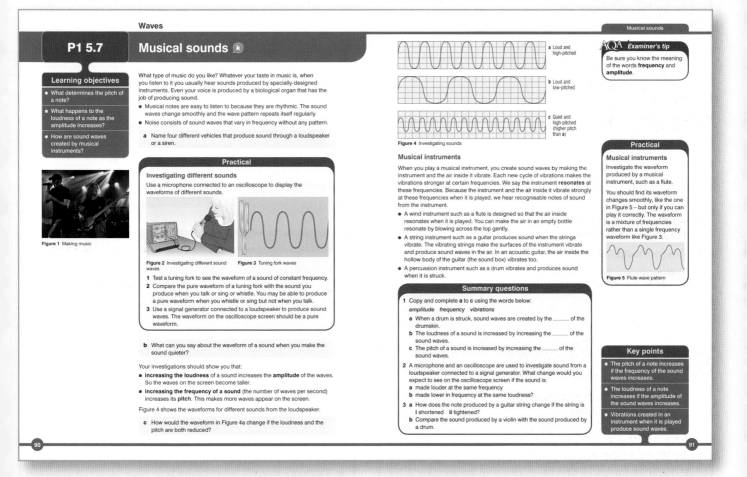

Further teaching suggestions

Scientific instruments

- Why not make some pan pipes with test tubes? Just fill a set up with differing amounts of water and give them a play.

Pop idle

- Does listening to music make you work better or put you off? Can the students come up with an experiment? This can be quite a demanding task. They could look at the effect of noise on concentration; try working when listening to annoying background noises. They can look at the differences that ambient music has in comparison with some heavy metal.

Summary answers

1   **a**   vibrations

     b   amplitude

     c   frequency

2   **a**   The waves would be taller but would have the same spacing.

     b   The waves would be more stretched out but would have the same height.

3   **a**   **i**   The note has a higher pitch (frequency).

         ii   The note has a higher pitch (frequency).

     b   The sound of a violin (played correctly) lasts as long as the violin bow is in contact with a string. The sound of a drum dies away after the drum skin has been struck. A drum note is less rhythmical than a violin note.

Summary answers

1 a They are the same.

b

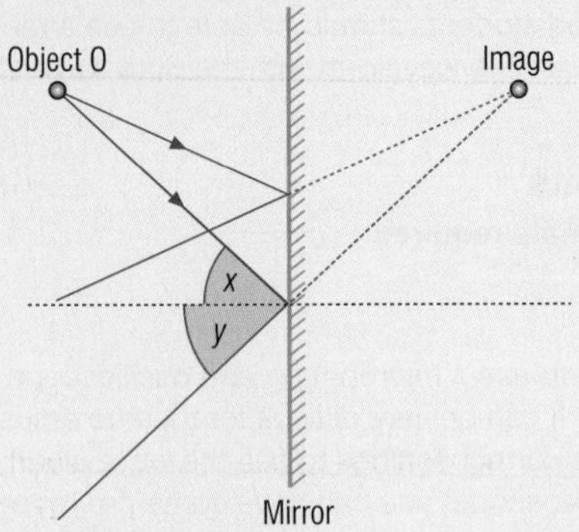

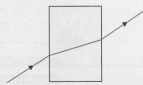

Object 0   Image

x
y

Mirror

c They are the same.

2 a i

ii The light ray bends towards the normal, where it enters the block and bends away from the normal where it leaves the block. Its direction on leaving the block is the same as before it entered the block.

b i refraction

ii diffraction

iii reflection

3 a light, radio (light and radio in any order)

b sound

c sound

4 a 3.0 m/s

b speed = frequency × wavelength

3.0 m/s = frequency × 1.5 m

frequency = $\frac{3.0}{1.5}$ = 2.0 Hz.

5 a The sound waves spread out as they travel away from the loudspeaker, so the sound becomes fainter and the amplitude becomes smaller.

b i The waves on the screen become taller.

ii The waves on the screen become more stretched out across the screen, so fewer waves appear on the screen.

6 a reflected, smooth

b rough, scattered

c soft, absorbed

7 a Approximately 20 000 Hertz.

b Keep the frequency and the loudness of the sound from the loudspeaker the same throughout. Keep the loudspeaker, the board or cushion and the sound meter in the same positions throughout.

With the board in position, measure the sound meter reading.

Replace the board with the cushion and measure the sound meter reading again.

If the reading for the board is higher than the reading for the cushion, the board reflects more sound than the cushion.

AQA Examiner's tip

Students may be required to draw ray diagrams in their exams. Most students throw away marks because they don't think straight lines, accuracy and direction arrows are at all important!

Summary questions

1 Figure 1 shows an incomplete ray diagram of image formation by a plane mirror.

Object 0

x

Mirror

Figure 1

a What can you say about the angles *x* and *y* in the diagram?

b Complete the ray diagram to locate the image.

c What can you say about the distance from the image to the mirror compared with the distance from the object to the mirror?

2 a Figure 2 shows a light ray directed into a glass block.

Figure 2

i Sketch the path of the light ray through the block.

ii Describe how the direction of the light ray changes as it passes into and out of the block.

b Copy and complete **i** to **iii** using the words below:

diffraction   reflection   refraction

i The change of the direction of a light ray when it enters a glass block from air is an example of ....

ii The spreading of waves when they pass through a gap is an example of ....

iii The image of an object seen in a mirror is formed because the mirror causes light from the object to undergo ....

3 Copy and complete **a** to **c** using the words below. Each word can be used more than once.

light   radio   sound

a .... waves and .... waves travel at the same speed through air.

b .... waves are longitudinal waves.

c .... waves cannot travel through a vacuum.

4 Waves travel a distance of 30 m across a pond in 10 seconds. The waves have a wavelength of 1.5 m.

a Calculate the speed of the waves.

b Show that the frequency of the waves is 2.0 Hz.

5 a A loudspeaker is used to produce sound waves. In terms of the amplitude of the sound waves, explain why the sound is fainter further away from the loudspeaker.

b A microphone is connected to an oscilloscope. Figure 3 shows the display on the screen of the oscilloscope when the microphone detects sound waves from a loudspeaker.

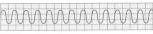

Figure 3

Describe how the waveform displayed on the oscilloscope screen changes if the sound from the loudspeaker is

i made louder

ii reduced in pitch.

6 Copy and complete **a** to **c** using the words below.

absorbed   reflected   scattered   smooth   soft   rou[gh]

a An echo is due to sound waves that are .... from .... wall.

b When sound waves are directed at a .... surface, they are broken up and ....

c When sound waves are directed at a wall covered wi[th] a .... material, they are .... and not reflected.

7 a What is the highest frequency the human ear can hea[r]

b A sound meter is used to measure the loudness of t[he] sound reflected from an object. Describe how you would use the meter and the arrangement shown in Figure 4 to test if more sound is reflected from a boa[rd] than from a cushion in place of the board. The contr[ol] knob and a frequency dial can be used to change th[e] loudness and the frequency of the sound from the loudspeaker. List the variables that you would need [to] keep constant in your test.

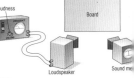

Loudness

Board

Loudspeaker   Sound me[ter]

Figure 4

Kerboodle resources

Resources available for this chapter on Kerboodle are:

- Chapter map: Waves
- Animation: Waves (P1 5.1)
- Interactive activity: The properties of transverse and longitudinal waves (P1 5.1)
- Support: Waves – knowing the words is half the battle (P1 5.1)
- Practical: Investigating the reflection of light (P1 5.3)
- Simulation: Refraction (P1 5.4)
- Practical: Investigating refraction (P1 5.4)
- Bump up your grade: Wave diagrams (P1 5.5)
- How Science Works: Measuring sound (P1 5.6)
- Extension: Waves (P1 5.7)
- Revision podcast: Wave properties
- Test yourself: Waves
- On your marks: Waves
- Examination-style questions: Waves
- Answers to examination-style questions: Waves

AQA Examiner's tip

Diffraction is often poorly understood at GCSE level. Diffraction effects are only significant when the gap/obstacle is of the same order of magnitude as the wavelength. Students should understand that this means the diffraction effect is not considered significant if the gap is more than 10 times the wavelength or the wavelength is more than 10 times the size of the gap.

AQA Examination-style questions

1 Draw labelled diagrams to explain what is meant by
  a a transverse wave. (2)
  b a longitudinal wave. (2)

2 Match the words in the list with the descriptions **1** to **4** in the table.

A amplitude
B frequency
C wave speed
D wavelength

	Description
1	The distance travelled by a wave crest every second.
2	The distance from one crest to the next.
3	The height of the wave crest from the rest position.
4	The number of crests passing a fixed point every second. (4)

3 Which of the following is a correct description of the image in a plane mirror?

A It is a virtual image
B It can be focused on to a screen
C It is on the surface of the mirror
D It is upside down (1)

4 When a ray of light passes from air into glass it usually changes direction.

a What is the name given to this effect? (1)
b Which diagram correctly shows what happens to a ray of light as it passes through a glass block?

(1)

5 The diagram represents some water waves passing through a narrow gap.

Give the name of the effect being shown by the waves. When is it most significant? (2)

6 Give one similarity and one difference between a sound wave and a light wave. (2)

7 A sound wave in air has a frequency of 256 Hz. The wavelength of the wave is 1.3 m.

Calculate the speed of sound in air. Write down the equation you use. Show clearly how you work out your answer and give the unit. (2)

8 a Give **one** example of each of the following from everyday life.
  i reflection of light (1)
  ii reflection of sound (1)
  iii refraction of light (1)
  iv diffraction of sound (1)

b We do not normally see diffraction of light in everyday life.

Suggest a reason for this. (2)

9 Electromagnetic waves travel at a speed of 300 000 000 m/s.

BBC Radio 4 is transmitted using a wavelength of 1500 metres.

Calculate the frequency of these waves.

Write down the equation you use. Show clearly how you work out your answer and give the unit. [H] (3)

10 *In this question you will be assessed on using good English, organising information clearly and using specialist terms where appropriate.*

The diagram shows an oscilloscope trace of the sound wave produced by a musical instrument.

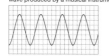

Explain, in detail, how the wave form would change if the instrument produced a sound which was louder and at a higher pitch. (6)

93

AQA Practical suggestions

Practicals	AQA	k	📖	⚙
Reflecting light off a plane mirror at different angles.	✓	✓	✓	
Using a class set of skipping ropes to investigate frequency and wavelength.	✓		✓	
Demonstrating transverse and longitudinal waves with a slinky spring.	✓		✓	
Carrying out refraction investigations using a glass block.	✓	✓	✓	
Carrying out investigations using ripple tanks, including the relationship between depth of water and speed of wave.	✓		✓	

AQA Examiner's tip

There are a lot of terms that need to be defined and understood. It is important for students to practice correctly identifying and sketching situations involving reflection, refraction and diffraction. These terms often get students in a muddle.

AQA Examination-style answers

1 a Diagram must show direction of wave travel.
Diagram must show direction of vibration perpendicular to direction of wave travel. *(2 marks)*

b Diagram must show direction of wave travel.
Diagram must show direction of vibration parallel to direction of wave travel. *(2 marks)*

2 A amplitude   3
  B frequency   4
  C wave speed   1
  D wavelength   2 *(4 marks)*

3 A It is a virtual image. *(1 mark)*

4 a refraction *(1 mark)*
  b Diagram B *(1 mark)*

5 Diffraction, when the gap is of the same order of magnitude as the wavelength. *(2 marks)*

6 **Similarity**: They can both be reflected, refracted, diffracted.
Difference: Light waves are much faster/sound waves are much slower OR light waves are transverse/sound waves are longitudinal. *(2 marks)*

7 $v = f \times \lambda$ so $256 \times 1.3 = 333$ m/s *(2 marks)*

8 a   **i** Any example using a mirror/water or a shiny smooth surface. *(1 mark)*
  ii Any example of an echo. *(1 mark)*
  iii Any example using a lens, e.g. spectacles, cameras. *(1 mark)*
  iv Any example of hearing a sound around a corner. *(1 mark)*

b The wavelength of light is very small, so diffraction only occurs when light passes through a very narrow gap.
OR
The wavelength of light is very small, so the diffraction effect is very small. *(2 marks)*

9 Wave speed = frequency × wavelength
$$\text{Frequency} = \frac{\text{speed}}{\text{wavelength}}$$
$$\text{Frequency} = \frac{300\,000\,000 \text{ m/s}}{1500 \text{ m}}$$
Frequency = 200 000 Hz *(3 marks)*

10 There is a clear, balanced and detailed description of how the wave form would change including increased amplitude and frequency. The answer shows almost faultless spelling, punctuation and grammar. It is coherent and in an organised, logical sequence. It contains a range of appropriate or relevant specialist terms used accurately. *(5–6 marks)*

There is a description of at least one of the ways in which the wave form would change. There are some errors in spelling, punctuation and grammar. The answer has some structure and organisation. The use of specialist terms has been attempted, but not always accurately. *(3–4 marks)*

There is a brief description of at least one way in which the wave form would change, which has little clarity and detail. The spelling, punctuation and grammar are very weak. The answer is poorly organised with almost no specialist terms and/or their use demonstrating a general lack of understanding of their meaning. *(1–2 marks)*

No relevant content. *(0 marks)*

Examples of physics points made in the response:
- louder sound means larger amplitude
- so height of crests increases
- depth of troughs increases
- speed is constant
- higher pitch means higher frequency
- so wavelength becomes smaller
- crests are closer together.

P1 6.1

The electromagnetic spectrum

$\mathcal{AQA}$ Specification link-up: Physics P1.5

- All types of electromagnetic waves travel at the same speed through a vacuum (space). *[P1.5.1 d)]*
- Electromagnetic waves form a continuous spectrum. *[P1.5.1 e)]*
- All waves obey the wave equation: $v = f \times \lambda$ *[P1.5.1 j)]*

Learning objectives

Students should learn:

- the names of the regions of the electromagnetic spectrum
- that all electromagnetic waves travel at the same speed through a vacuum
- how to calculate the wavelength or frequency of an electromagnetic wave. **[HT only]**

Learning outcomes

Most students should be able to:

- state the parts of the electromagnetic spectrum in order of wavelength
- state that all electromagnetic waves travel at the same speed through a vacuum.

Some students should also be able to:

- rearrange and use the wave speed equation. **[HT only]**

Support

- For extra support, you can give the students a large diagram of the electromagnetic spectrum to annotate over the next few lessons. They can add uses in communications and dangers to it as they go. You should also provide templates to help the students perform the calculations.

Extend

- Extend students by asking them to find out about electromagnetic waves in other media; they have been told that electromagnetic waves all travel at the same speed in a vacuum, but is this true of other media? They can find out about how the speed depends on the wavelength and how this leads to dispersion in prisms and lenses.

Lesson structure

Starters

The visible spectrum – Students should be familiar with the visible spectrum already. Let them use this knowledge to outline their understanding by asking them to show how light is reflected, transmitted or refracted. Move on to see if they can explain reflection from coloured surfaces; this includes reflection and absorption. This can be accompanied by a demonstration. *(5 minutes)*

Calculating speed – Can the students remember how to calculate the speed of something? Ask them to write down the equation and answer a couple of simple speed questions. This will lead into the wave equation later in the lesson. Start with some easy questions to support those that find calculations difficult. You can use some 'difficult' numbers and calculations needing rearrangement to extend others. For example, what is the speed of light if it takes 1.3 s to travel from the Earth to the Moon, a distance of 390 000 km [300 000 km/s^{-1} or 300 000 000 m/s]. *(10 minutes)*

Main

- Throughout these next few topics, it will be useful to have a large diagram of the electromagnetic spectrum on the wall so that you can refer to it regularly. You could put up a giant poster and have the students add notes to it throughout the chapter. Photograph this at the end and give copies to everybody.

- The students will have studied the electromagnetic spectrum at KS3, but many will be unfamiliar with the word 'electromagnetic'. You might like to simply explain that these waves are caused by changes in electric and magnetic fields. These are similar to the fields around a bar magnet, which they should remember. The most important thing, however, is that the students understand that no matter (material) is transferred from place to place.

- It is important to get across the idea that the electromagnetic waves travel best through empty space: a vacuum. When doing this, they all travel at the same speed (which is the maximum speed at which anything can travel). Also emphasise that the spectrum is continuous: there are ranges of each of the regions. This idea can be shown by discussing the range of different wavelengths of red, pointing out that there is not just one 'red'.

- The main difficulty in any calculations will be the rather difficult numbers that electromagnetic waves present. You may find that some calculators cannot cope with them. Standard eight-digit calculators cannot display 300 000 000; so you may have to remind students of how to cancel out some of the zeros. With students that are more mathematically able, you may wish to use numbers in standard form, e.g. 3.00×10^8 m/s.

- You can then move through the spectrum pointing out the behaviour of waves when they interact with materials or cross boundaries. The focus is on the group of waves used in communications (visible, IR, microwave and radio) but you can mention that other waves behave in a similar manner.

Plenary

RMIVUXG? – The students may know an acronym to give the order of electromagnetic waves within the spectrum (ROYGBIV). Can they think up a method of remembering the regions of the electromagnetic spectrum? They need to use this to remember the order of the spectrum and so cannot change the order of the letters. An example could be 'Really Massive Iguanas Viciously Upset Xenophobic Gorillas'. As you can see the VUX part can be a bit of a problem. *(5 minutes)*

Further teaching suggestions

The wave equation

- The students can reinforce their understanding of the wave equation by trying some further calculations. This work could be set as homework.

Electromagnetic waves

P1 6.1   The electromagnetic spectrum 🄺

Learning objectives

- What are the parts of the electromagnetic spectrum?
- How can we calculate the frequency or wavelength of electromagnetic waves?

🔗 links

For more information on the use of X-rays in medicine, see P3 1.1 X-rays.

We all use waves from different parts of the **electromagnetic spectrum**. Figure 1 shows the spectrum and some of its uses.

Electromagnetic waves are electric and magnetic disturbances that transfer energy from one place to another.

Electromagnetic waves do not transfer matter. The energy they transfer depends on the **wavelength** of the waves. This is why waves of different wavelengths have different effects. Figure 1 shows some of the uses of each part of the electromagnetic spectrum.

| Radio | Microwaves | Infrared | Light | Ultraviolet radiation | X-rays and gamma radiation |

1 kilometre   1 millimetre   1 nanometre   1 picometre

Wavelength

(1 nanometre = 0.000 001 millimetres, 1 picometre = 0.001 nanometres)

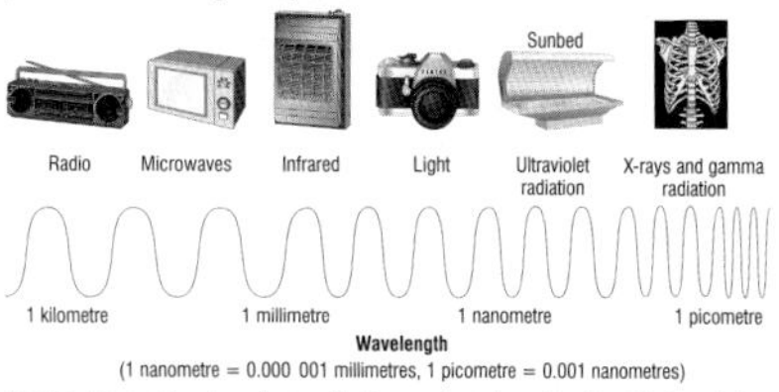

Figure 1 The spectrum is continuous. The frequencies and wavelengths at the boundaries are approximate as the different parts of the spectrum are not precisely defined.

Waves from different parts of the electromagnetic spectrum have different wavelengths.

- Long-wave radio waves have wavelengths as long as 10 km.
- X-rays and gamma rays have wavelengths as short as a millionth of a millionth of a millimetre (= 0.000 000 000 001 mm).

  a Where in the electromagnetic spectrum would you find waves of wavelength 10 millimetres?

The spectrum of visible light covers just a very tiny part of the electromagnetic spectrum. The wavelength decreases from radio waves to gamma rays.

The speed of electromagnetic waves

All electromagnetic waves travel at a speed of 300 million m/s through space or in a vacuum. This is the distance the waves travel each second.

We can link the speed of the waves to their frequency and wavelength using the **wave speed** equation:

$$v = f \times \lambda$$

Where:

v = wave speed in metres per second, m/s
f = frequency in hertz, Hz
λ = wavelength in metres, m

🔗 links

For more information on the wave speed equation, look back at P1 5.2 Measuring waves.

b Work out the wavelength of electromagnetic waves of frequency 200 million Hz.

c Work out the frequency of electromagnetic waves of wavelength 1500 m.

📱 Maths skills

Higher

We can work out the wavelength if we know the frequency and the wave speed. To do this, we rearrange the equation into:

$$\lambda = \frac{v}{f}$$

We can work out the frequency if we know the wavelength and the wave speed. To do this, we rearrange the equation into:

$$f = \frac{v}{\lambda}$$

Where:

v = speed in metres per second, m/s
f = frequency in hertz, Hz
λ = wavelength in metres, m.

Worked example

A mobile phone gives out electromagnetic waves of frequency 900 million Hz. Calculate the wavelength of these waves. The speed of electromagnetic waves in air = 300 million m/s.

Solution

wavelength λ (in metres) = $\dfrac{\text{wave speed } v \text{ (in m/s)}}{\text{frequency } f \text{ (in Hz)}}$ = $\dfrac{300\,000\,000\,\text{m/s}}{900\,000\,000\,\text{Hz}}$ = 0.33 m

Energy and frequency

The wave speed equation shows us that the shorter the wavelength of the waves, the higher their frequency is. The energy of the waves increases as the frequency increases. The energy and frequency of the waves therefore increases from radio waves to gamma rays as the wavelength decreases.

Summary questions

1 Copy and complete **a** to **c** using the words below:
  greater than   smaller than   the same as
  a The wavelength of light waves is .... the wavelength of radio waves.
  b The speed of radio waves in a vacuum is .... the speed of gamma rays.
  c The frequency of X-rays is .... the frequency of infrared radiation.

2 Fill in the missing parts of the electromagnetic spectrum in the list below.
  radio ...a... infrared visible ...b... X-rays ...c...

3 Electromagnetic waves travel through space at a speed of 300 million metres per second. Calculate:
  a the wavelength of radio waves of frequency 600 million Hz
  b the frequency of microwaves of wavelength 0.30 m.

4 A distant star explodes and emits light and gamma rays simultaneously. Explain why the gamma rays and the light waves reach the Earth at the same time.

Key points

- The electromagnetic spectrum (in order of decreasing wavelength, increasing frequency and energy) is:
  – radio waves
  – microwaves
  – infrared radiation
  – light
  – ultraviolet radiation
  – gamma radiation and X-rays.
- The wave speed equation is used to calculate the frequency or wavelength of electromagnetic waves.

Answers to in-text questions

a microwaves

b 1.5 m

c 200 000 Hz

Summary answers

1 **a** smaller than
  b the same as
  c greater than

2 **a** microwaves
  b ultraviolet radiation
  c gamma rays

3 **a** 0.5 m
  b 1000 million Hz

4 They are emitted at the same time. They travel the same distance at the same speed, so they arrive at the Earth together at a later time.

P1 6.2

Light, infrared, microwaves and radio waves

Learning objectives

Students should learn that:

- the ways in which infrared, microwaves and radio waves are used in communication systems.

Learning outcomes

Most students should be able to:

- state the uses of infrared, microwaves and radio waves in communication.

Some students should also be able to:

- explain how infrared, microwaves and radio waves are used in communication.

Support

- Provide a plan for the testing of infrared radiation. After completing this task, the students can make their own plan to test the range of the signal from a remote or even if the infrared rays follow the same laws of reflection as visible light.

Extend

- If you carry out the microwave experiment (and the transmitter is a polarised one, as it usually is) you may like to challenge the students to find an explanation for polarisation. Point the transmitter and receiver directly at each other and switch on to show the maximum signal. Position a metal diffraction grille (a set of vertical wires) between the transmitter and receiver and rotate it. The signal should vary from maximum to zero just by rotating the plate.

AQA

Specification link-up: Physics P1.5

- Radio waves, microwaves, infrared and visible light can be used for communication. *[P1.5.1 k)]*
- Compare the use of different types of waves for communication. *[P1.5]*

Lesson structure

Starters

Radio 'gaga' – Give the students a set of mixed-up sentences about radio waves and ask them to sort the words into the right order to produce correct sentences. Examples could include: atmosphere are used through waves television radio the transmit to signals [Radio waves are used to transmit television signals through the atmosphere; microwaves can be used for communicating with satellites]. *(5 minutes)*

Colour filters – Shine a bright white light through a series of filters and ask the students to explain what is happening with a diagram. Extend students by asking them to consider the use of multiple filters. Support students by reminding them that white light is composed of bands of colours and give and example of the effect of a filter before asking them to try some of their own. Ask the students if they think that there will be a similar effect for the non-visible parts of the spectrum. This leads into the absorption of electromagnetic energy as it passes through materials, so you can show the effect again to enhance that point later. *(10 minutes)*

Main

- Using a data projector at the beginning of this lesson is very handy. You can use it as a bright light source to show dispersion through a prism producing a very bright spectrum. If the projector is ceiling mounted, then mount the prism on a stick. A bit of fiddling should produce a clear spectrum somewhere in the room.

- You can show a film camera and a digital camera. If you have any old ones that can be taken apart, you can show the places where the film of CCD would sit and let the students look through the lens system.

- The students should already be familiar with the heating effect of IR from 'P1 1.1 Energy transfer by heating', but it is worth showing an IR heater again as reinforcement. Demonstrating an infrared remote control should be fairly simple but the students may not be aware that the infrared can be reflected, so try turning some equipment, like the data projector, on or off by reflecting the signal off the whiteboard.

- If you have a microwave oven available, you can use it to demonstrate the heating effect by cooking something. The cooking can be very uneven and you might want to discuss why this is with some students. You could also discuss shielding. The front door should contain a metal mesh used to absorb microwaves so that none leak out. These would be dangerous to people, as they would cause heating of the water in tissues. Simple microwave detectors are available.

- It is worth demonstrating a radio, especially one with a dial to adjust the frequency received. It is even better if you have a very old radio with the wavelength and frequency on the dial; so that you can discuss the connection between the two.

Plenaries

EM wave summary – The students should produce a summary about all of the areas of the electromagnetic spectrum they have studied so far. This can be in the form a table, brief summary phrases or a mind map. *(5 minutes)*

What's the frequency? – Give the students the frequency of some local radio stations and ask them to work out the wavelengths (and vice versa). This recaps the calculations from earlier. Some stations are listed here for the Orkney Islands, you can add more: Radio 1 98.9 MHz [3.03 m], Radio 2 89.3 MHz [3.36 m], Radio 3 91.5 MHz [3.28 m]. Students should be extended by tackling rearrangement of the necessary equation or supported by the use of calculation templates. *(10 minutes)*

Practical support

Testing infrared radiation

Infrared signals are able to pass through several paper sheets as long as the batteries on the remote are in good order.

Equipment and materials required

Infrared remote control and device. A TV is fine, as is a data projector.

Details

Simply place layers of paper over the transmitter one at a time to find out how many layers are needed to block the signal. You should find that larger transmitters, such as those for TVs, can send a signal through at least three sheets. Low-power transmitters, such as those operated by a button cell, struggle to get a signal through two sheets.

Demonstrating microwaves

If you have low-power microwave equipment, you may like to look at the laws of reflection for microwave radiation.

Equipment and materials required

Low-power microwave transmitter and receiver, aluminium screen, large protractor, A3 paper and ruler.

Details

Position the aluminium screen towards the back of the paper and mark its position. Draw a normal to the screen to measure angles from. Now position the transmitter so that it is off the normal and pointing to the centre of the screen. Move the receiver in an arc, always pointing to the centre of the screen, until a maximum reflected signal is found. Compare the angle of incidence and reflection for a few points to show that the law of reflection is obeyed. During the experiment, discuss why aluminium is used as opposed to paper.

You may also like to investigate the penetrating power of the microwaves by seeing if they pass through various thicknesses of paper or card. Does making the paper wet make a difference? Why? (You can choose from a range of 'How Science Works' to develop in this investigation, e.g. collecting primary data.)

The polished metal surface reflects the microwaves. The direction of the reflected waves is at the same angle to the metal plate as the direction of incident waves.

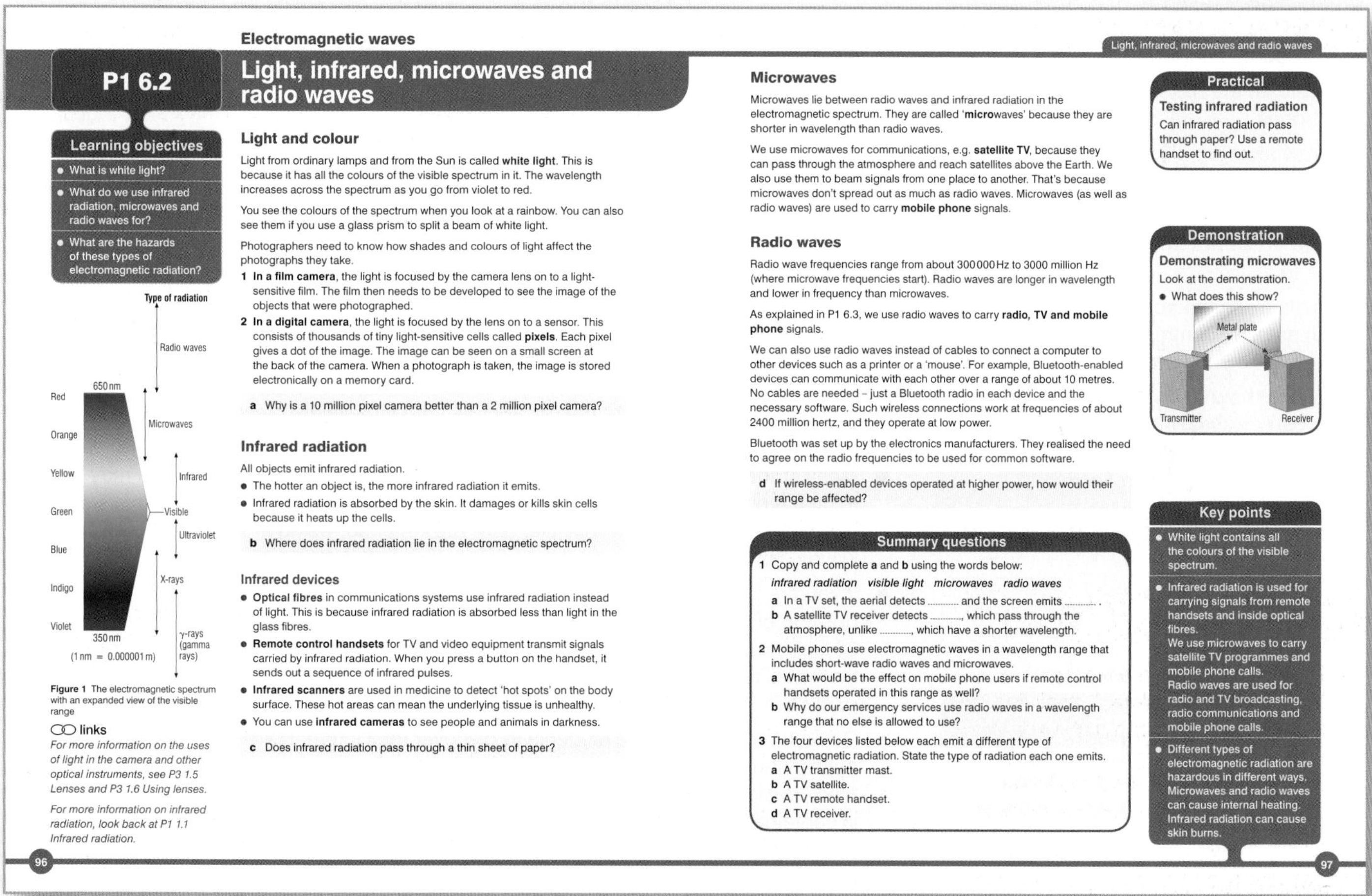

Electromagnetic waves

Light, infrared, microwaves and radio waves

P1 6.2 — Light, infrared, microwaves and radio waves

Learning objectives

- What is white light?
- What do we use infrared radiation, microwaves and radio waves for?
- What are the hazards of these types of electromagnetic radiation?

Type of radiation

Red — 650 nm
Orange
Yellow
Green
Blue
Indigo
Violet — 350 nm
(1 nm = 0.000001 m)

Radio waves
Microwaves
Infrared
Visible
Ultraviolet
X-rays
γ-rays (gamma rays)

Figure 1 The electromagnetic spectrum with an expanded view of the visible range

links

For more information on the uses of light in the camera and other optical instruments, see P3 1.5 Lenses and P3 1.6 Using lenses.

For more information on infrared radiation, look back at P1 1.1 Infrared radiation.

Light and colour

Light from ordinary lamps and from the Sun is called **white light**. This is because it has all the colours of the visible spectrum in it. The wavelength increases across the spectrum as you go from violet to red.

You see the colours of the spectrum when you look at a rainbow. You can also see them if you use a glass prism to split a beam of white light.

Photographers need to know how shades and colours of light affect the photographs they take.

1 **In a film camera**, the light is focused by the camera lens on to a light-sensitive film. The film then needs to be developed to see the image of the objects that were photographed.

2 **In a digital camera**, the light is focused by the lens on to a sensor. This consists of thousands of tiny light-sensitive cells called **pixels**. Each pixel gives a dot of the image. The image can be seen on a small screen at the back of the camera. When a photograph is taken, the image is stored electronically on a memory card.

a Why is a 10 million pixel camera better than a 2 million pixel camera?

Infrared radiation

All objects emit infrared radiation.
- The hotter an object is, the more infrared radiation it emits.
- Infrared radiation is absorbed by the skin. It damages or kills skin cells because it heats up the cells.

b Where does infrared radiation lie in the electromagnetic spectrum?

Infrared devices

- **Optical fibres** in communications systems use infrared radiation instead of light. This is because infrared radiation is absorbed less than light in the glass fibres.
- **Remote control handsets** for TV and video equipment transmit signals carried by infrared radiation. When you press a button on the handset, it sends out a sequence of infrared pulses.
- **Infrared scanners** are used in medicine to detect 'hot spots' on the body surface. These hot areas can mean the underlying tissue is unhealthy.
- You can use **infrared cameras** to see people and animals in darkness.

c Does infrared radiation pass through a thin sheet of paper?

Microwaves

Microwaves lie between radio waves and infrared radiation in the electromagnetic spectrum. They are called 'microwaves' because they are shorter in wavelength than radio waves.

We use microwaves for communications, e.g. **satellite TV**, because they can pass through the atmosphere and reach satellites above the Earth. We also use them to beam signals from one place to another. That's because microwaves don't spread out as much as radio waves. Microwaves (as well as radio waves) are used to carry **mobile phone** signals.

Radio waves

Radio wave frequencies range from about 300 000 Hz to 3000 million Hz (where microwave frequencies start). Radio waves are longer in wavelength and lower in frequency than microwaves.

As explained in P1 6.3, we use radio waves to carry **radio, TV and mobile phone** signals.

We can also use radio waves instead of cables to connect a computer to other devices such as a printer or a 'mouse'. For example, Bluetooth-enabled devices can communicate with each other over a range of about 10 metres. No cables are needed – just a Bluetooth radio in each device and the necessary software. Such wireless connections work at frequencies of about 2400 million hertz, and they operate at low power.

Bluetooth was set up by the electronics manufacturers. They realised the need to agree on the radio frequencies to be used for common software.

d If wireless-enabled devices operated at higher power, how would their range be affected?

Summary questions

1 Copy and complete **a** and **b** using the words below:

infrared radiation visible light microwaves radio waves

a In a TV set, the aerial detects .... and the screen emits ....

b A satellite TV receiver detects ...., which pass through the atmosphere, unlike ...., which have a shorter wavelength.

2 Mobile phones use electromagnetic waves in a wavelength range that includes short-wave radio waves and microwaves.

a What would be the effect on mobile phone users if remote control handsets operated in this range as well?

b Why do our emergency services use radio waves in a wavelength range that no else is allowed to use?

3 The four devices listed below each emit a different type of electromagnetic radiation. State the type of radiation each one emits.

a A TV transmitter mast.

b A TV satellite.

c A TV remote handset.

d A TV receiver.

Practical

Testing infrared radiation
Can infrared radiation pass through paper? Use a remote handset to find out.

Demonstration

Demonstrating microwaves
Look at the demonstration.
- What does this show?

Metal plate
Transmitter — Receiver

Key points

- White light contains all the colours of the visible spectrum.
- Infrared radiation is used for carrying signals from remote handsets and inside optical fibres. We use microwaves to carry satellite TV programmes and mobile phone calls. Radio waves are used for radio and TV broadcasting, radio communications and mobile phone calls.
- Different types of electromagnetic radiation are hazardous in different ways. Microwaves and radio waves can cause internal heating. Infrared radiation can cause skin burns.

Answers to in-text questions

a The image has more fine detail.

b Between microwaves and light.

c Yes.

d The range would be increased.

Summary answers

1 **a** radio waves, visible light

b microwaves, infrared radiation

2 **a** A remote handset used when pointed at a mobile phone user would disrupt the mobile phone's reception if it operated at the same wavelength.

b So that there will be no interference with their communications systems.

3 **a** radio waves

b microwaves

c infrared radiation

d visible light

P1 6.3

Communications

Specification link-up: Physics P1.5

- Radio waves, microwaves, infrared and visible light can be used for communication. [P1.5.1 k)]
- Evaluate the possible risks involving the use of mobile phones. [P1.5]

Learning objectives

Students should learn:

- that microwaves and short-wave radio waves are used in mobile phone networks
- how the atmosphere affects the range that different waves can travel
- that there are risks and benefits associated with the use of mobile phones
- how optical fibres can be used to carry waves.

Learning outcomes

Most students should be able to:

- state that satellite TV signals are carried by microwaves
- evaluate the risks of using mobile phones
- draw a diagram to show how light or infrared waves travel along an optical fibre.

Some students should also be able to:

- explain why microwaves can be used for satellite communications but not terrestrial TV signals
- explain how optical fibres can be used to carry waves, allowing them to be contained and travel around bends due to total internal reflection.

Support

- The experiment to discover total internal reflection is a very good one for students to carry out. You can provide a sheet for it that has the incident rays, normal and the location for the glass block already printed on it. This makes the experiment considerably more reliable.

Extend

- What is the fastest way of sending a signal to the opposite side of the Earth? Sending a signal via a satellite or sending the signal through optical fibres? The students can find out about this and the way optical fibre networks are at the core of the internet.

Lesson structure

Starters

Mb fns – How does mobile phone texting work? Ask the students to explain how a text message gets from one phone to another phone in the same room. Can they write their answers in txt? You should extend students by insisting that they draw a flow chart of the process and include key words that you provide. Support some students by providing the stages and asking them to place them into a flow chart. *(5 minutes)*

Get the message across – The students must think up as many ways as possible to communicate with each other and pass on a simple message, like 'I am hungry' or 'I am thirsty'. [Speech, mime, semaphore, passing a note, Morse code, texting, using a social networking site and so on]. Which methods are best in which situations? *(10 minutes)*

Main

- You can get a complete breakdown of the radio frequency spectrum from Ofcom (www.ofcom.org.uk/radiocomms/isu/ukfat). This is a comprehensive document so you might just want to select a bit of it but it shows the importance of allocating particular parts of the spectrum for particular uses. You could discuss with the students what would happen if there was a 'free for all'.

- The debate about the safely of mobile phones seems to have receded. No reliable evidence of damage has been found. However, there are still occasional campaigns about wireless computer networks in schools and the placement of transmitter masts. The intensity of the radiation from the mast could be much higher than that from a phone if the students were nearby and, as some masts are placed on schools, parents groups are worried about this. Is there a mast in your school?

- Many students will not be aware that the atmosphere has many layers; you may wish to take a bit of time and show them a diagram of its structure from the Earth's surface to space. Emphasise how thin it is; only 100 km or so. Using a globe to explain how the waves can reach places below the horizon is very helpful.

- If you are talking about satellite TV, you may wish to briefly mention the geostationary position of the satellites and the distances involved. With a typical globe (diameter 30 cm) the satellite would be nearly 1 m above the surface. This is part of the reason that satellite transmissions for communications show a 'time lag'. The microwaves are partly absorbed by the atmosphere but most of the distance is empty space.

- Demonstrate or allow the students to discover total internal reflection and then the optical fibre, see 'Practical support'. If you have a model optical fibre (a large curvy block designed to show multiple total internal reflections), you can show how the ray is contained within the glass; no energy leaves the glass. Optical fibres are used in endoscopes in medicine and also by spies and the military for seeing through walls or around corners. You may be able to find video clips of their use.

Plenaries

Round the bend – Give the students a diagram of an optical fibre with a reasonably contorted path and ask them to draw the path of a ray that is shown entering the fibre. It is possible to extend students by providing them with a more convoluted fibre and insist on proper construction of the reflection (normal included and accurate angles.) You can also support students by providing a diagram where some of the reflection points are already marked with normals, making the diagram easier to complete accurately. *(5 minutes)*

Sorry for the inconvenience – The students should design a leaflet from a TV or satellite TV company explaining why the television signal has been poor recently. It should explain how the TV signal is transmitted to the house and what kinds of things can affect the signal (rain, snow, sunspots). *(10 minutes)*

Practical support

Demonstrating an optical fibre
Optical fibres are easy to demonstrate in a laboratory, even in fairly bright conditions.

Equipment and materials required
A length of optical fibre (anywhere between 2–10 m) a bright light source (preferably one that can be switched on and off quickly).

Details
Bend the fibre around several objects (perhaps the whole room). Don't bend it too much though, or the glass might crack; anything smaller than a 10 cm radius is dodgy. Allow one student to observe the distant end while you flash a torch into the near end. Even with the thinnest of fibres, the transmitted light should be obvious. The students can pass the fibre end along while the light is flashing.

Total internal reflection
The students may well be aware of this effect, but if they are not then it is simple to discover.

Equipment and materials required
For each group: ray box, power supply, single slit, blanking plates, rectangular glass or Perspex block (or semicircular), protractor, ruler, pencil and A3 paper.

Details
The students position the block on the paper and draw around it to mark its position, in case it moves. They shine a ray of light at the front surface of the block at a small angle to the normal and mark the direction the ray enters and leaves the block. This is best done by marking the path of the ray with two small crosses, and then joining them with a straight line with the ruler. They then increase the angle and repeat the process. They should find that at a certain point, the ray is reflected by the surface of the block; it is totally internally reflected.

P1 6.3 Communications 🔘

Learning objectives
- Why do we use radio waves of different frequencies for different purposes?
- Which waves do we use for satellite TV?
- How can we evaluate whether or not mobile phones are safe to use?
- What are optical fibres?

Figure 1 Sending microwave signals to a satellite

❓❓❓ Did you know ...?
Satellite TV signals are carried by microwaves. We can detect the signals on the ground because they pass straight through a layer of ionised gas in the upper atmosphere. This layer reflects lower-frequency radio waves.

Figure 2 A mobile phone mast

Radio communications
Radio waves are emitted from an aerial when we apply an alternating voltage to the aerial. The frequency of the radio waves produced is the same as the frequency of the alternating voltage.

When the radio waves pass across a receiver aerial, they cause a tiny alternating voltage in the aerial. The frequency of the alternating voltage is the same as the frequency of the radio waves received. The aerial is connected to a loudspeaker. The alternating voltage from the aerial is used to make the loudspeaker send out sound waves.

The radio and microwave spectrum is divided into **bands** of different wavelength ranges. This is because the shorter the wavelength of the waves:
- the more information they can carry
- the shorter their range (due to increasing absorption by the atmosphere)
- the less they spread out (because they diffract less).

Radio wavelengths
Microwaves and radio waves of different wavelengths are used for different communications purposes. Examples are given below.
- **Microwaves** are used for satellite phone and TV links and satellite TV broadcasting. This is because microwaves can travel between satellites in space and the ground. Also, they spread out less than radio waves do so the signal doesn't weaken as much.
- **Radio waves of wavelengths less than about 1 metre** are used for TV broadcasting from TV masts because they can carry more information than longer radio waves.
- **Radio waves of wavelengths from about 1 metre up to about 100 m** are used by local radio stations (and for the emergency services) because their range is limited to the area round the transmitter.
- **Radio waves of wavelengths greater than 100 m** are used by national and international radio stations because they have a much longer range than shorter wavelength radio waves.

a Why do microwaves spread out less than radio waves do?

Mobile phone radiation 🔘
A mobile phone sends a radio signal from your phone. The signal is picked up by a local mobile phone mast and is sent through the phone network to the other phone. The 'return' signal goes through the phone network back to the mobile phone mast near your phone and then on to you. The signals to and from your local mast are carried by radio waves of different frequencies.

The radio waves to and from a mobile phone have a wavelength of about 30 cm. Radio waves at this wavelength are not quite in the microwave range but they do have a similar heating effect to microwaves. So they are usually referred to as microwaves.

b Why should signals to and from a mobile phone be at different frequencies?

🔘 How Science Works

Is mobile phone radiation dangerous?
The radiation is much weaker than the microwave radiation in an oven. But when you use a mobile phone, it is very close to your brain. Some scientists think the radiation might affect the brain. As children have thinner skulls than adults, their brains might be more affected by mobile phone radiation. A UK government report published in May 2000 recommended that the use of mobile phones by children should be limited.

Mobile phone hazards
Here are some findings by different groups of scientists:

The short-term memory of volunteers using a mobile phone was found to be unaffected by whether the phone was on or off.

The brains of rats exposed to microwaves were found to respond less to electrical impulses than the brains of unexposed rats.

Mice exposed to microwaves by some scientists developed more cancers than unexposed mice. Other scientists were unable to confirm this effect.

A survey of mobile phone users in Norway and Sweden found they experienced headaches and fatigue. No control group of people who did not use a mobile phone was surveyed.
- What conclusions do you draw from the evidence above?
- Suggest how researchers could improve the validity of any conclusions we can draw.

Optical fibre communications
Optical fibres are very thin glass fibres. We use them to transmit signals carried by light or infrared radiation. The light rays can't escape from the fibre. When they reach the surface of the fibre, they are reflected back into the fibre. In comparison with radio waves and microwaves:
- optical fibres can carry much more information – this is because light has a much smaller wavelength than radio waves so can carry more pulses of waves
- optical fibres are more secure because the signals stay in the fibre.

c Why are signals in an optical fibre more secure than radio signals?

Summary questions
1 Copy and complete **a** to **c** using the words below. Each term can be used more than once.

infrared radiation   microwaves   radio waves

a Mobile phone signals are carried by ....

b Optical fibre signals are carried by ....

c A beam of .... can travel from the ground to a satellite but a beam of .... cannot if its frequency is below 30 MHz.

2 **a** Why could children be more affected by mobile phone radiation than adults?

b Why can light waves carry more information than radio waves?

3 Explain why microwaves are used for satellite TV and radio waves for terrestrial TV.

🔗 links
For more information on how optical fibres are used in the endoscope, see P3 1.4 The endoscope.

Demonstration

Demonstrating an optical fibre
Observe light shone into an optical fibre. You should see the reflection of light inside an optical fibre. This is known as total internal reflection.

Figure 3 Optical fibres

Key points
- Radio waves of different frequencies are used for different purposes because the wavelength (and therefore frequency) of waves affects:
  – how far they can go
  – how much they spread
  – how much information they can carry.
- Microwaves are used for satellite TV signals.
- Further research is needed to evaluate whether or not mobile phones are safe to use.
- Optical fibres are very thin transparent fibres that are used to transmit signals by light and infrared radiation.

98 | 99

Further teaching suggestions

A guest speaker
- One of your network technicians, or IT teachers, could present a brief talk about the school network, discussing all of the components (bridges, routers, modems, etc.) and what they do. They can put particular emphasis on the wireless part of the network.

Answers to in-text questions

a They spread out less because their wavelength is less.

b If the mast-to-phone signal reflected back to the mast, it would disrupt the signal from the phone.

c Radio waves spread out and can be detected by any radio receiver. Signals in an optical fibre stay in the fibre until they reach the receiver at the end of the fibre.

Summary answers

1 **a** radio waves
  b infrared radiation
  c microwaves, radio waves

2 **a** Children have thinner skulls than adults and mobile phone radiation could pass through their skulls more easily than through adult skulls.

  b The light has a much shorter wavelength so can carry more pulses than radio waves.

3 The distance satellite TV signals travel is much greater than the distance terrestrial signals travel. The signals spread out and weaken more the further they travel. Microwaves spread out less than radio waves, so they don't weaken as much as radio waves do.

P1 6.4

The expanding universe

Learning objectives

Students should learn:

- that the universe is a vast collection of billions of galaxies each containing billions of stars
- that the velocity of distant galaxies can be measured by analysis of the red-shift of light from those galaxies
- that the evidence gained from red-shift analysis shows that the universe is expanding.

Learning outcomes

Most students should be able to:

- state that the universe contains a vast number of galaxies and stars
- describe why the light from distant galaxies is shifted in wavelength
- explain that red-shift evidence shows that the universe is expanding.

Support

- The numbers involved in this topic are well out of the range that most students can grasp. Present as much of this visually as you can; students don't need to know the numbers just the order of sizes.

Extend

- Students can be extended by asking them to look at emission spectra. If you have a set of gas emission spectrum tubes, you can demonstrate the emission spectra of different hot gases. With a suitable diffraction grating and spectroscope, you can clearly see the distinct lines produced by different elements. If you don't have a spectroscope, you can still show the different colours from different elements.

AQA Specification link-up: Physics P1.5

- If a wave source is moving relative to an observer, there will be a change in the observed wavelength and frequency. This is known as the Doppler effect. *[P1.5.4 a)]*
- There is an observed increase in the wavelength of light from most distant galaxies. The further away the galaxies are, the faster they are moving, and the bigger the observed increase in wavelength. This effect is called 'red-shift'. *[P1.5.4 b)]*

Lesson structure

Starters

How many stars? – Give the class estimates on the number of stars in a galaxy and the number of galaxies. Ask them to work out how many stars they could have each if they shared them out among the class. This should give a quick impression of just how large the universe is. There are estimated to be 100 billion stars in a galaxy like ours and 125 billion galaxies, so that should give around 417 billion stars each for a class of 30 students. *(5 minutes)*

Stars and planets – Make the students define the properties of stars and planets. To support them, you can give them sets of cards describing the properties and behaviours of stars and planets, and ask them to sort them into two piles, one corresponding to stars and one to planets. You can extend students by asking them to work out the properties themselves and then make cards to sort (you can use these with other groups later). *(10 minutes)*

Main

- You might like to ask the students why there are no photographs of the complete Milky Way galaxy; they should realise that we could never get a probe to sufficient distance. If you want to show a model galaxy, try using a blank CD with a small bulge of plasticine in the centre. You can draw the spiral arms on the label. It's about the right proportions (according to NASA). We are on the western spiral arm about 1 cm from the rim. You can then show the separation of galaxies. Our neighbour Andromeda would be about 1 m away on this scale; other galaxies would most likely be outside your room.

- A Doppler effect for sound can be demonstrated with a tube (or hose) with a funnel in the end. Blow through the tube while spinning it and the students should hear changes in the pitch (or wavelength) of the note as the funnel end approaches or recedes from them. The students may be familiar with the effect when hearing sirens on cars passing by. It is useful to show the students several simple examples of absorption spectra to show what these lines would look like. They can then show the effect of shifting the lines to the red part of the spectrum.

- Hubble's two conclusions are very important and lead to the conclusion that the universe is expanding. The students really need to be able to state these conclusions and link them to the supporting evidence; they are a common concept on examination papers.

- The idea of an expanding universe that has no centre is a bit strange. The closest simple analogy is the surface of an expanding balloon. It is worth showing this. Blow up a balloon with galaxies drawn on its surface and they all move further apart from one another and none of them are in the middle. The universe is a bit like this.

Plenaries

True or false – Give the students a set of 'facts' about galaxies and the universe, and ask them to say if they are true or false. You might have some 'unknown' ones too. *(5 minutes)*

Space is big – Give the students a list of distances and ask them to put them in order (e.g. your school to France, your school to New York, the Earth to the Moon, the Earth to the Sun, the Earth to Pluto, the Sun to the nearby star Alpha Centauri, the Sun to the centre of the Milky Way (or galaxy), the Milky Way to Andromeda, the Milky Way to the edge of the observable universe). Students can be asked to match up distance cards given in kilometres. Extend students by asking them to convert the numbers into standard form and discuss why this is generally used for large numbers. Students can be supported by making this task a card sort activity; matching up the distances with the descriptions. *(10 minutes)*

Practical support

Doppler and sound

Demonstrate Doppler shift in sound. This can look a bit silly, but it works.

Equipment and materials required

A 1.5 m length of hosepipe (narrower tubes do not work as well) with a large funnel securely attached to one end.

Details

Simply swing the funnel end of the hosepipe around your head (in a lasso style) while blowing into the other end. The pitch (and frequency and wavelength of the sound) changes as it swings towards and away from the students. When it is moving away, the wavelength is increased so the sound is lower pitched and vice versa.

Electromagnetic waves

The expanding universe

P1 6.4 — The expanding universe

Learning objectives

- What do we mean by red-shift of a light source?
- How does red-shift depend on speed?
- How do we know the distant galaxies are moving away from us?
- Why do we think the universe is expanding?

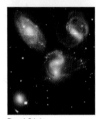

Figure 1 Galaxies

The Doppler effect

The **Doppler effect** is the change in the observed wavelength (and frequency) of waves due to the motion of the source of the waves. Christian Doppler discovered the effect in 1842 using sound waves. He demonstrated it by using an open railway carriage filled with trumpeters. The spectators had to listen to the pitch of the trumpets as they sped past. Another example, explained below, is the red-shift of the light from a distant galaxy moving away from us.

Red-shift

We live on the third rock out from a middle-aged star on the outskirts of a big galaxy we call the Milky Way. The galaxy contains about 100000 million stars. Its size is about 100000 light years across. This means that light takes 100000 years to travel across it. But it's just one of billions of galaxies in the universe. The furthest galaxies are about 13000 million light years away!

a Why do stars appear as points of light?

We can find out lots of things about stars and galaxies by studying the light from them. We can use a prism to split the light into a spectrum. The wavelength of light increases across the spectrum from blue to red. We can tell from its spectrum if a star or galaxy is moving towards us or away from us. This is because:

- the light waves are stretched out if the star or galaxy is moving away from us. The wavelength of the waves is increased. We call this a **red-shift** because the spectrum of light is shifted towards the red part of the spectrum.
- the light waves are squashed together if the star or galaxy is moving towards us. The wavelength of the waves is reduced. We call this a **blue-shift** because the spectrum of light is shifted towards the blue part of the spectrum.

The dark spectral lines shown in Figure 2 are caused by absorption of light by certain atoms such as hydrogen that make up a star or galaxy. The position of these lines tells us if there is a shift and if so, whether it is a red-shift or a blue-shift.

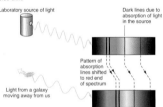

Laboratory source of light

Dark lines due to absorption of light in the source

Pattern of absorption lines shifted to red end of spectrum

Light from a galaxy moving away from us

Figure 2 Red-shift

The bigger the shift, the more the waves are squashed together or stretched out. So the faster the star or galaxy must be moving towards or away from us. In other words:

the faster a star or galaxy is moving (relative to us), the bigger the shift is.

b What do you think happens to the wavelength of the light from a star that is moving towards us?

Expanding universe

In 1929, Edwin Hubble discovered that:

1 the light from distant galaxies was red-shifted
2 the further a galaxy is from us, the bigger its red-shift is.

He concluded that:

- the distant galaxies are moving away from us (i.e. receding)
- the greater the distance a galaxy is from us, the greater the speed at which it is moving away from us (its speed of recession).

Why should the distant galaxies be moving away from us? We have no special place in the universe, so all the distant galaxies must be moving away from each other. In other words, **the whole universe is expanding**.

c Galaxy X is 2000 million light years away. Galaxy Y is 4000 million light years away. Which galaxy, X or Y, has the bigger red-shift?

Summary questions

1 Copy and complete **a** to **d** using the words below:
   approaching   expanding   orbiting   receding
   a The Earth is .... the Sun.
   b The universe is ....
   c The distant galaxies are ....
   d A blue-shift in the light from a star would tell us it is ....

2 **a** Put these objects in order of increasing size:
      Andromeda galaxy   Earth   Sun   universe
   b Copy and complete **i** and **ii** using the words below:
      galaxy   star   red-shift   planet
      i The Earth is a .... in orbit round a .... called the Sun.
      ii There is a .... in the light from a distant ....

3 Galaxy X has a larger red-shift than galaxy Y.
   a Which galaxy, X or Y, is
      i nearer to us
      ii moving away faster?
   b The light from the Andromeda galaxy is not red-shifted. What does this tell you about Andromeda?

Did you know ... ?

You can hear the Doppler effect when an ambulance with its siren on goes speeding past.

- As it approaches, the sound waves it sends out are squashed up so their frequency is higher (and the wavelength shorter) than if the siren was stationary. So you hear a higher pitch.
- As it travels away from you, the sound waves it sends out are stretched out so their frequency is lower (and the wavelength longer) than if the siren was stationary. So you hear a lower pitch.

Key points

- The red-shift of a distant galaxy is the shift to longer wavelengths of the light from it because the galaxy is moving away from us.
- The faster a distant galaxy is moving away from us, the greater its red-shift is.
- All the distant galaxies show a red-shift. The further away a distant galaxy is from us, the greater its red-shift is.
- The distant galaxies are all moving away from us because the universe is expanding.

Further teaching suggestions

ICT link-up

- Why do scientists need more and more powerful computers? Simulations of galaxies smashing together may look nice, but it takes a lot of computing power to work out when a billion stars meet another billion stars. Many of the simulations online have been carried out by 'supercomputers' thousands of times more powerful than a simple PC.

Matching spectra

- Can the students discover what elements are present in real stellar spectra? Give the students a card showing the absorption spectrum of the Sun and a set of spectra for different elements, some of which are present in the Sun. Ask the students to work out which ones match. Make sure the cards are printed to the same scale though.

Andromeda ascendant

- The Andromeda galaxy is one of our nearest galactic neighbours and it is getting nearer all the time. It's moving towards us at about half a million kilometres per hour and may eventually collide in three to four billion years' time. The students could look into the possible outcomes of this collision, and collisions on this scale generally. There are numerous excellent computer simulations, and Hubble Space Telescope images of real collisions, available on the internet.

Answers to in-text questions

a Because they are so far away.

b It is blue-shifted because its wavelength is reduced.

c Galaxy Y.

Summary answers

1 **a** orbiting
  b expanding
  c receding
  d approaching

2 **a** Earth, Sun, Andromeda galaxy, universe.
  b **i** planet, star
       ii red-shift, galaxy

3 **a** **i** Y
       ii X
  b It is not moving away from us. It is much nearer to us than the galaxies with red-shifts.

P1 6.5
The Big Bang

Learning objectives

Students should learn:

- that the universe is thought to have begun in an awesome event called the Big Bang
- that the expansion of the universe supports the Big Bang theory
- that the cosmic microwave background radiation is a primary piece of evidence supporting this theory.

Learning outcomes

Most students should be able to:

- state that the Big Bang generated the universe
- describe the evidence for the expansion of the universe and how it supports the Big Bang theory
- state the evidence for this conclusion.

Some students should also be able to:

- describe limitations in the Big Bang theory.

Support

- As in the last lesson, the concepts can be difficult to grasp without careful explanations. The key idea to put across is that the universe was very different early on and there is strong evidence that there was a beginning. Don't worry if the students think that this was just a big explosion but make sure that they do not think that the Earth was formed in this explosion.

Extend

- Students can be extended by asking: Just how small is 'small'? These students may wish to look into the concept of singularities: objects of zero volume and infinite density; it is from one of these that the universe is thought to have originated. The ideas are closely linked to black holes, which the students will study if they take GCSE Physics; you may wish to leave this until then and link the two ideas together.

AQA Specification link-up: Physics P1.5

- How the observed red-shift provides evidence that the universe is expanding and supports the 'Big Bang' theory (that the universe began from a very small initial 'point'). [P1.5.4 c)]
- Cosmic microwave background radiation (CMBR) is a form of electromagnetic radiation filling the universe. It comes from radiation that was present shortly after the beginning of the universe. [P1.5.4 d)]
- The 'Big Bang' theory is currently the only theory that can explain the existence of CMBR. [P1.5.4 e)]
- Consider the limitations of the model that scientists use to explain how the universe began and why the universe continues to expand. [P1.5]

Lesson structure

Starters

Heat death – Remind students that all energy transfers lead to energy being transferred by heating. Ask them to describe what will happen when all of the energy the universe started with is 'wasted'. This is quite a high-level concept and can lead to quite a detailed discussion about the eventual fate of the universe. You might want to back this idea up with a short video clip outlining the possibilities. *(5 minutes)*

Your history – Give the students a list of historical events reaching back through human history, and then to the formation of the Earth. Ask them to put the events in order. You can support students by giving some example dates to match up with the events. You can then add other events such as the formation of the solar system, start of life on Earth and the start of the universe to this. Extend the students by giving the correct times of the events and get the students to lay out the card separated by a correctly scaled distance (they may try 1 cm representing 1000 years). This will be impossible but they will understand the idea that the universe is very old compared to civilisation. *(10 minutes)*

Main

- This lesson is all about big ideas and how scientists have to provide evidence for them. (It is ideal for teaching aspects of 'How Science Works' issues.)
- Many students may ask what was before the Big Bang. The best approach is to talk about the meaning of 'before'. As scientists believe that time only started with the Big Bang there was no time before it, so it is meaningless to ask questions about what happened.
- Students may also be a bit confused by the term 'explosion'. The Big Bang is better described as a sudden expansion and the production of a lot of energy. As the universe continues to expand, this energy gets more and more dissipated and so the universe cools down.
- The main thrust of the lesson is to explain to the students that an idea like the Big Bang needs to have *evidence* before it is accepted by scientists. It is not enough to come up with the best sounding explanations. This links to the 'Fundamental ideas' section of 'How Science Works'. Those that did not accept the theory were right to question it, until they were given evidence of the *cosmic microwave background radiation*. They should then accept the new model, or come up with an alternative explanation that takes the new evidence into account.
- Changes to ideas like this are important to science; the students need to know that scientists will analyse new ideas and accept them if they explain the evidence better than the old ideas. This process ensures that scientific knowledge develops and becomes a better description of the universe. You should also point out that recent discoveries, such as the possible speeding up of the expansion, will also have to be explained by scientists over the coming years; we do not have a complete description of the universe and may never have.
- Conditions in the very early universe were **very** different than they are now. The temperatures were so high that atoms could not exist, and even protons and neutrons could not form.
- The end of the universe is still open to debate but it is a long way off, and students should not worry too much about it. We have a few billion years to go before a 'Big Crunch' or a 'Big Yawn'.

Plenaries

The Lords of Time – If time travel were possible, we could go back and get conclusive evidence about the early universe, formation of the solar system and so on. The students can speculate about the advantages and dangers of using this apparently impossible technology for scientific research. Extend the students by suggesting some of the potential hazards and seeing if they can come up with some practical rules to avoid them. You may want to support some students by making up some rules of your own (no visiting your own family) and discussing why you think they would be needed by the Time Agency. *(5 minutes)*

Sceptic – Understanding the Big Bang is very difficult and the course can only cover the simplest ideas. Can the students summarise the evidence about the expanding universe and cosmic background microwave information in order to explain it to a reasonably intelligent but sceptical person? *(10 minutes)*

Electromagnetic waves

P1 6.5 — The Big Bang Ⓚ

Learning objectives

- What is the Big Bang theory of the universe?
- Why is the universe expanding?
- What is cosmic microwave background radiation?
- What evidence is there that the universe was created in a Big Bang?

Figure 1 The Big Bang

Did you know …?

You can use an analogue TV to detect cosmic microwave radiation very easily – just disconnect your TV aerial. The radiation causes lots of fuzzy spots on the screen.

Figure 2 A microwave image of the universe from, the Cosmic Background Explorer satellite

The universe is expanding, but what is making it expand? The **Big Bang theory** was put forward to explain the expansion. This states that:

- the universe is expanding after exploding suddenly in a Big Bang from a very small initial point
- space, time and matter were created in the Big Bang.

Many scientists disagreed with the Big Bang theory. They put forward an alternative theory, the Steady State theory. The scientists said that the galaxies are being pushed apart. They thought that this is caused by matter entering the universe through 'white holes' (the opposite of black holes).

Which theory is weirder – everything starting from a Big Bang or matter leaking into the universe from outside? Until 1965, most people supported the Steady State theory.

How Science Works

Evidence for the Big Bang

Scientists had two conflicting theories about the evolution of the universe: it was in a Steady State or it began at some point in the past with a Big Bang. Both theories could explain why the galaxies are moving apart, so scientists needed to find some way of selecting which theory was correct. They worked out that if the universe began in a Big Bang then there should have been high-energy electromagnetic radiation produced. This radiation would have 'stretched' as the universe expanded and become lower-energy radiation. Experiments were devised to look for this trace energy as extra evidence for the Big Bang model.

It was in 1965 that scientists first detected microwaves coming from every direction in space. The existence of this **cosmic microwave background radiation** can only be explained by the Big Bang theory.

The cosmic microwave background radiation is not as perfectly even spread as scientists thought it should be. Their model of the early universe needs to be developed further by gathering evidence and producing theories to explain this 'unevenness' in the early universe.

a How do scientists decide between two conflicting theories?

Cosmic microwave background radiation

- It was created as high-energy gamma radiation just after the Big Bang.
- It has been travelling through space since then.
- As the universe has expanded, it stretched out to longer and longer wavelengths and is now microwave radiation.
- It has been mapped out using microwave detectors on the ground and on satellites.

b What will happen to cosmic microwave background radiation as the universe expands?

How Science Works

The future of the universe

Will the universe expand forever? Or will the force of gravity between the distant galaxies stop them from moving away from each other? The answer to this question depends on their total mass and how much space they take up – in other words, the density of the universe.

- If the density of the universe is less than a certain amount, it will expand forever. The stars will die out and so will everything else as the universe heads for a Big Yawn!
- If the density of the universe is more than a certain amount, it will stop expanding and go into reverse. Everything will head for a Big Crunch!

Recent observations by astronomers suggest that the distant galaxies are accelerating away from each other. These observations have been checked and confirmed by other astronomers. So astronomers have concluded that the expansion of the universe is accelerating. It could be we're in for a Big Ride followed by a Big Yawn.

The discovery that the distant galaxies are accelerating is puzzling astronomers. Scientists think some unknown source of energy, now called 'dark energy', must be causing this accelerating motion. The only known force on the distant galaxies, the force of gravity, can't be used to explain 'dark energy' as it is an attractive force and so acts against their outward motion away from each other.

c What could you say about the future of the universe if the galaxies were slowing down?

d i An object released above the ground accelerates as it falls. What makes it accelerate?

ii Why are scientists puzzled by the observation that the distant galaxies are accelerating?

Summary questions

1 Copy and complete **a** to **d** using the words below:
   created   detected   expanded   stretched
   a The universe was .... in an explosion called the Big Bang.
   b The universe .... suddenly in and after the Big Bang.
   c Microwave radiation from space can be .... from all directions.
   d Radiation created just after the Big Bang has been .... by the expansion of the universe and is now microwave radiation.

2 Put the following events A–D in the correct time sequence:
   A The distant galaxies were created.
   B Cosmic microwave background radiation was first detected.
   C The Big Bang happened.
   D The expansion of the universe began.

3 **a** Why do astronomers think that the expansion of the universe is accelerating?
   b What would have been the effect on the expansion of the universe if its density had been greater than a certain value?

links

For more information on how the chemical elements formed after the Big Bang, see P2 7.6 How the chemical elements formed.

Figure 3 The future of the universe?

Key points

- The universe started with the Big Bang, a massive explosion from a very small point.
- The universe has been expanding ever since the Big Bang.
- Cosmic microwave background radiation (CMBR) is electromagnetic radiation created just after the Big Bang.
- CMBR can only be explained by the Big Bang theory.

102   103

Further teaching suggestions

ICT link-up

- There are several websites explaining the Big Bang and theories about possible ends to the universe. Some are a bit technical, but students may wish to find out more from them. Search at www.nasa.gov or www.bbc.co.uk.

Improving evidence

- Ever since the discovery of the cosmic microwave background radiation, scientists have been trying to find

improved ways of measuring it, so that they can find out the structure of the early universe. The students can find out how satellites, including the COBE mentioned in the Student Book, have been used to map the radiations and find variations in it. There are several satellites that have been used, or are due for launch in the coming years, all with dedicated websites.

Answers to in-text questions

a They weigh up the evidence they have and design experiments to collect more evidence until a clear decision can be made.

b It will be stretched even more to longer wavelengths.

c The expansion might reverse or it might just gradually stop.

d i The force of the Earth's gravity on the object causes it to accelerate.

ii The force of gravity on the distant galaxies from the rest of the universe could not make them accelerate.

Summary answers

1 **a** created   **c** detected
  b expanded   **d** stretched

2 CDAB

3 **a** The distant galaxies are accelerating away from each other.
  b The universe would stop expanding and go into reverse, ending in a Big Crunch.

Summary answers

1 a D, A, B, C.

  b i $v = f \times \lambda$

    ii 300 million m/s

2 A: light   B: X-rays   C: microwaves   D: radio

3 a microwave, radio waves

  b mobile phone, TV (mobile phone and TV in any order)

4 a Radio waves.

  b Light and infrared radiation.

  c i Mobile phone radiation can penetrate the skull. Too much radiation may affect the brain. The tests are to ensure they do not cause too much radiation to be absorbed by the head.

    ii Phone A is safer, because less radiation is absorbed from A than from B.

5 a an increase

  b a red-shift

  c away from us

  d It would be shifted to smaller wavelengths.

6 a i Galaxy A.

    ii Galaxy C is further away than galaxy A.

  b i It is expanding.

    ii We are not in any special place.

7 a i X, because it appears smaller than Y, as seen from the Earth.

    ii X, because it is further away than Y, so it is moving faster and has a larger red-shift than Y.

  b i Z is moving away faster than X is because Z has a larger red-shift.

    ii Z is further away than X because we know it is moving faster than X and the greater the speed of a galaxy is, the further away it must be.

Electromagnetic waves: P1 6.1–P1 6.5

Summary questions

1 a Place the four different types of electromagnetic waves listed below in order of increasing wavelength.

    A Infrared waves

    B Microwaves

    C Radio waves

    D Gamma rays

  b The radio waves from a local radio station have a wavelength of 3.3 metres in air and a frequency of 91 million Hz.

    i Write down the equation that links frequency, wavelength and wave speed.

    ii Calculate the speed of the radio waves in air.

2 In P1 6.1 you will find the typical wavelengths of electromagnetic waves. Give the type of electromagnetic wave for each of the wavelengths given.

    A 0.0005 mm

    B 1 millionth of 1 millionth of 1 mm

    C 10 cm

    D 1000 m

3 Copy and complete a and b using the words below:

    microwave   mobile phone   radio waves   TV

  a A .... beam can travel from a ground transmitter to a satellite, but a beam of .... cannot if its frequency is below 30 MHz.

  b .... signals and .... signals always come from a local transmitter.

4 Mobile phones send and receive signals using electromagnetic waves near or in the microwave part of the electromagnetic spectrum.

  a Name the part of the electromagnetic spectrum which has longer wavelengths than microwaves.

  b Which two parts of the electromagnetic spectrum may be used to send information along optical fibres?

  c New mobile phones are tested for radiation safety and given an SAR value before being sold. The SAR is a measure of the energy per second absorbed by the head while the phone is in use. For use in the UK, SAR values must be less than 2.0 W/kg. SAR values for two different mobile phones are given below.

    Phone A   0.2 W/kg

    Phone B   1.0 W/kg

    i What is the main reason why mobile phones are tested for radiation safety?

    ii Which phone, A or B, is safer? Give a reason for your answer.

5 Light from a distant galaxy has a change of wavelength due to the motion of the galaxy.

  a Is this change of wavelength an increase or a decrease?

  b What is the name for this change of wavelength?

  c Which way is the galaxy moving?

  d What would happen to the light it gives out if it were moving in the opposite direction?

6 a Galaxy A is further from us than galaxy B.

    i Which galaxy, A or B, produces light with a greater red-shift?

    ii Galaxy C gives a bigger red-shift than galaxy A. What can we say about the distance to galaxy C compared with galaxy A?

  b All the distant galaxies are moving away from each other.

    i What does this tell us about the universe?

    ii What does it tell us about our place in the universe?

7 The diagram shows two galaxies X and Y, which have the same diameter.

  a i Which galaxy, X or Y, is further from Earth? Give a reason for your answer.

    ii Which galaxy, X or Y, produces the larger red-shift?

  b A third galaxy Z seen from Earth appears to be the same size as X but it has a larger red-shift than X.

    i What can you say about the speed at which Z is moving away from us, compared with the speed at which X is moving away?

    ii What can you deduce about the distance to Z compared with the distance to X? Give a reason for your answer.

AQA Examiner's tip

Waves transfer energy without transferring material. Students need to understand that this is the key to why waves are such useful (and interesting!) things.

AQA Examiner's tip

Knowledge of the properties and applications of electromagnetic waves used for communications are important. Much of this is 'learning facts' and should be a source of fairly easy marks in examinations. For example, wavelengths of electromagnetic spectrum range from 10–15 m to 104 m or more, all travel at the same speed in a vacuum, etc.

AQA Examiner's tip

Two key pieces of evidence that support the Big Bang theory must be known: The 'red-shift' and the Cosmic Microwave Background Radiation.

Kerboodle resources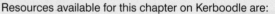

Resources available for this chapter on Kerboodle are:

- Chapter map: Electromagnetic waves
- Viewpoint: Do mobile phones cause a risk to our health? (P1 6.1)
- Bump up your grade: Communicate – stay in touch (P1 6.3)
- How Science Works: Bluetooth range (P1 6.3)
- Animation: Doppler effect (P1 6.4)
- Data Handling Skills: The expanding universe (P1 6.4)
- Extension: Small things lead to large things (P1 6.5)
- How Science Works: Before the Big Bang (P1 6.5)
- Interactive activity: Electromagnetic waves and communication consolidation
- Interactive activity: The origins of the universe consolidation
- Revision podcast: Communications
- Revision podcast: The Big Bang
- Test yourself: Electromagnetic waves
- On your marks: Electromagnetic waves
- Examination-style questions: Electromagnetic waves
- Answers to examination-style questions: Electromagnetic waves

AQA Examination-style questions

1 Electromagnetic waves can travel through the vacuum of space.

Copy and complete the following sentences using words from the list below. Each word can be used once, more than once or not at all.

energy   frequency   speed   wavelength

All electromagnetic waves travel at the same .... in a vacuum. They do not carry material, but they do carry .... Gamma waves have the greatest .... and the smallest .... *(4)*

2 Different types of electromagnetic waves have different uses in communications.

Match the type of electromagnetic wave in the list with its use **1** to **4** in the table.

A infrared
B microwaves
C radio waves
D visible light

	These waves are used for
1	producing images in a video camera
2	mobile phone communication
3	television remote controls
4	carrying terrestrial television signals

(4)

Microwaves are used for communications. They can be used to send signals to other parts of the world by means of a satellite.

a Give **one** reason why the receiver shown in the diagram can only pick up the signal if a satellite is used. *(1)*

b Explain why microwaves are used rather than:
  i long wave radio waves *(1)*
  ii visible light *(2)*

4 The diagram shows a ray passing through an optical fibre.

a Name **two** types of electromagnetic wave that can travel along an optical fibre. *(2)*

b Suggest **two** advantages of sending signals along an optical fibre rather than using electrical signals in a metal wire. *(2)*

5 Scientists have developed a theory about the universe called the 'Big Bang' theory. This theory is supported by evidence. Part of this evidence is the existence of cosmic background microwave radiation.

a What does the 'Big Bang' theory state?
  A The universe began with a massive explosion.
  B The universe will end with a massive explosion.
  C The universe began from a very small initial point.
  D The universe will end at a very small initial point. *(1)*

b Where does cosmic background microwave radiation come from?
  A people who use microwave ovens to heat food
  B gamma radiation created just after the Big Bang
  C mobile phone transmitters
  D radioactive rocks in the Earth's crust. *(1)*

c If a scientist finds new evidence that does not support the Big Bang theory what should other scientists do?
  A Change the theory immediately.
  B Check the new evidence to make sure it is reproducible.
  C Ignore the new evidence.
  D Try to discredit the scientist who found the new evidence. *(1)*

6 Red-shift from distant galaxies provides evidence for the Big Bang theory.

What is meant by red-shift? *(2)*

7 *In this question you will be assessed on using good English, organising information clearly and using specialist terms where appropriate.*

Explain how red-shift provides evidence for the Big Bang theory. *(6)*

AQA Practical suggestions

Practicals	AQA	k	📖	⚙
Investigating the range of Bluetooth or infrared communications between mobile phones and laptops.	✓	✓		✓
Demonstrating the Doppler effect for sound.	✓		✓	

AQA Examination-style answers

1 All electromagnetic waves travel at the same **speed** in a vacuum. They do not carry material, but they do carry **energy**. Gamma waves have the greatest **frequency** and the smallest **wavelength**. *(4 marks)*

2 **A** infrared   3
  B microwaves   2
  C radio waves   4
  D visible light   1 *(4 marks)*

3 a No direct line of sight due to Earth's curvature. *(1 mark)*

  b **i** Microwaves can carry more information. Microwaves spread out less than radio waves/signal doesn't weaken so much. *(1 mark)*
    ii More difficult for visible light to penetrate atmosphere/a lot of energy would be absorbed. *(2 marks)*

4 a visible light
    infrared *(2 marks)*

  b can carry more information;
    more secure/less energy lost *(2 marks)*

5 a **C** The universe began from a very small initial point. *(1 mark)*

  b **B** Gamma radiation created just after the Big Bang. *(1 mark)*

  c **B** Check the new evidence to make sure it is reproducible. *(1 mark)*

6 The wavelength of light from a galaxy is shifted towards the red end of the spectrum and the galaxy is moving away from us. *(2 marks)*

7 There is a clear, balanced and detailed description of how red-shift provides evidence for the Big Bang theory. The answer shows almost faultless spelling, punctuation and grammar. It is coherent and in an organised, logical sequence. It contains a range of appropriate or relevant specialist terms used accurately. *(5–6 marks)*

There is a description of how red-shift provides evidence for the Big Bang theory. There are some errors in spelling, punctuation and grammar. The answer has some structure and organisation. The use of specialist terms has been attempted, but not always accurately. *(3–4 marks)*

There is a brief description of at least one way in which the red-shift provides evidence for the Big Bang theory. There is little clarity and detail. The spelling, punctuation and grammar are very weak. The answer is poorly organised with almost no specialist terms and/or their use demonstrating a general lack of understanding of their meaning. *(1–2 marks)*

No relevant content. *(0 marks)*

Examples of physics points made in the response:
- light from (most) galaxies is red-shifted
- the further the galaxy the bigger the red-shift
- the furthest galaxies are moving fastest
- (this shows that) the universe is expanding
- if the universe has always been expanding
- it must have once been very small.

AQA Examination-style answers

1 There is a **transparent** cover on top of the panel that allows infrared **radiation** through to heat the metal plate. The metal plate is coloured **black** for maximum absorption. There is a sheet of **insulation** under the plate to stop heat loss by **conduction** through the back of the panel. *(5 marks)*

2 a i radio *(1 mark)*
　　ii energy *(1 mark)*

　b i $v = f \times \lambda$
　　　$\lambda = \dfrac{v}{f}$
　　　　$= \dfrac{300\,000\,000}{24\,000\,000\,000}$
　　　　$= 0.0125\,\text{m}$ *(2 marks)*
　　ii It raises its temperature. It heats it. *(2 marks)*
　　iii The wavelength is shorter. The frequency is higher. *(2 marks)*

3 a i The National Grid. *(1 mark)*
　　ii It increases the voltage. *(1 mark)*
　　iii (Stepping up the voltage) reduces the current, which means less power loss. *(2 marks)*

　b Any one of the following: climate change; global warming; greenhouse effect; acid rain; smoke; smog. *(1 mark)*

　c i less pollution than fossil fuels, nuclear; help stop global warming; does little harm to habitats; energy costs may be reduced; no waste *(2 marks)*
　　ii noise pollution; visual pollution ('eyesore'); hazard to birds; intermittent supply *(2 marks)*

4 There is a clear, balanced and detailed description of how the flask reduces heat transfer by conduction, convection and radiation. The answer shows almost faultless spelling, punctuation and grammar. It is coherent and in an organised, logical sequence. It contains a range of appropriate or relevant specialist terms used accurately. *(5–6 marks)*

There is a description of a range of the ways in which the flask reduces heat transfer by conduction, convection and radiation. There are some errors in spelling, punctuation and grammar. The answer has some structure and organisation. The use of specialist terms has been attempted, but not always accurately. *(3–4 marks)*

There is a brief description of at least two ways in which the flask reduces heat transfer by conduction, convection and radiation, which has little clarity and detail. The spelling, punctuation and grammar are very weak. The answer is poorly organised with almost no specialist terms and/or their use demonstrating a general lack of understanding of their meaning. *(1–2 marks)*

No relevant content. *(0 marks)*

Examples of physics points made in the response:
- conduction requires particles
- convection requires particles
- vacuum does not contain particles
- so stops energy transfer by conduction and convection
- silvered surfaces reflect radiation
- so prevents radiation into and out of the flask
- plastic support and stopper are poor conductors.

---

1 The diagram shows a solar heating panel on the roof of a house.

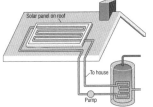

The solar heating panel consists of a flat box backed by a metal plate. The box contains copper pipes filled with a liquid. Liquid pumped through the pipes is heated as it passes through the panel.
Copy and complete the following sentences using words from the list below. Each word can be used once, more than once or not at all.
black   white   transparent   conduction   convection   insulation   radiation
There is a .... cover on top of the panel that allows infrared .... through to heat the metal plate. The metal plate is coloured .... for maximum absorption. There is a sheet of .... under the plate to stop heat loss by .... through the back of the panel.
(5)

2 a Microwaves are one type of electromagnetic wave.
　　i Which type of electromagnetic wave has a lower frequency than microwaves? (1)
　　ii What do all types of electromagnetic wave transfer from one place to another? *(1)*

　b The picture shows a tennis coach using a speed gun to measure how fast the player serves the ball.

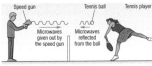

　　i The microwaves transmitted by the speed gun have a frequency of 2.4×10^{10} Hz and travel through the air at 3.0×10^8 m/s.
　　　Calculate the wavelength in metres of the microwaves emitted from the speed gun. Write down the equation you use. Show clearly how you work out your answer and give the unit. *(2)*
　　ii Some of the microwaves transmitted by the speed gun are absorbed by the ball. What effect will the absorbed microwaves have on the ball? *(2)*
　　iii Some of the microwaves transmitted by the speed gun are reflected from the moving ball back towards the speed gun. Describe how the wavelength and frequency of the microwaves change as they are reflected from the moving ball. *(2)*
AQA, 2009

AQA Examiner's tip
Read through the whole passage first, to get the sense of it, before trying to put the words in.

AQA Examiner's tip
Make sure you have a way of remembering the order of the waves in the electromagnetic spectrum. For example, **g**ood **x**ylophones **u**pset **v**iolins **i**n **m**usical **r**ecitals for **g**amma, **X**-ray, **u**ltraviolet, **v**isible, **i**nfrared, **m**icrowave, **r**adio wave.

AQA Examiner's comments

Question 2 covers a wide range of subject content on electromagnetic waves. It is a good assessment of the electromagnetic waves topic. Higher Tier candidates should be able to rearrange the wave equation. They should also be familiar with using numbers written in standard form.

Students often struggle with the idea that a high frequency corresponds to a short wavelength. This idea is effectively demonstrated with a slinky spring or with a microphone, oscilloscope and tuning forks.

AQA Examiner's comments

The vacuum flask question is an old standard and one every student should practise! Set this question as a starter activity before teaching energy transfer and again at the end of the topic. This will assess pupil progress in understanding conduction, convection, radiation and evaporation.

Show the inside of a vacuum flask. Some students may never have seen a vacuum flask of the type shown in the diagram where it is possible to remove the glass vessel.

Ask pupils to bring in flasks and compare their effectiveness in maintaining the temperature of hot or cold water over the course of the lesson or perhaps a whole day.

3 The diagram shows how electricity is distributed from power stations to consumers.

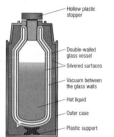

Power station | Step-up transformer | Transmission cables | Step-down transformer | Consumer

a i What name is given to the network of cables and transformers that links power stations to consumers? (1)

ii What does a step-up transformer do? (1)

iii Explain why step-up transformers are used in the electricity distribution system. (2)

b Most of the world's electricity is generated in power stations that burn fossil fuels. State **one** environmental problem that burning fossil fuels produces. (1)

c Electricity can be generated using energy from the wind. A company wants to build a new wind farm. Not everyone thinks that this is a good idea.

i What arguments could the company give to persuade people that a wind farm is a good idea? (2)

ii What reasons may be given by the people who think that wind farms are **not** a good idea? (2)

AQA, 2007

AQA *Examiner's tip*

There are pros and cons to the use of any source for generating electricity, even the renewable ones. Make sure you know what they are.

4 *In this question you will be assessed on using good English, organising information clearly and using specialist terms where appropriate.*

The diagram shows a vacuum flask. The flask can be used to keep hot liquids hot and cold liquids cold.

AQA *Examiner's tip*

Make sure you understand that a vacuum is a completely empty space.

Hollow plastic stopper

Double-walled glass vessel

Silvered surfaces

Vacuum between the glass walls

Hot liquid

Outer case

Plastic support

Explain how the flask reduces energy transfer by conduction, convection and radiation. (6)

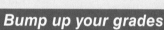

Bump up your grades

The P1 unit contains four equations. Foundation Tier candidates will not have to change the subject of the equations. So, for instance, they will only need to practise using the specific heat capacity equation to find the energy transferred. Higher Tier candidates will need to practise rearranging the specific heat capacity equation and the equation for wave speed. Higher Tier candidates should be encouraged to use their maths skills to carry out the change of subject rather than the 'triangle' method.

Bump up your grades

Some students struggle to identify the equation required to perform a calculation. It can help if they are encouraged at an early stage to write down a list of the symbol, quantity and unit for each piece of data and also the symbol of the quantity they are looking for.

Numerical skills are also required in extracting and interpreting information from graphs, charts and tables. This includes calculations involving 'payback time' which many Foundation Tier students find very tricky.

Bump up your grades

The 'Maths skills' boxes in the Student Book can be used to illustrate mathematical techniques. They should also serve as exemplars to guide students on how to lay out calculations. Encourage students to write down each stage of their calculation. They should firstly write down the equation as it is given, then rearrange it, substitute the numbers and then calculate the answer. The final answer should be on the answer line and should normally be rounded to two or three significant figures.

Once the calculation is complete, a unit may be required. Learning all the units will guarantee at least one easy mark on an exam paper. Higher Tier candidates should be also be familiar with using numbers written in standard form.

P2 1.1

Distance–time graphs

AQA

Specification link-up: Physics P2.1

- The gradient of a distance–time graph represents speed. [P2.1.2 b)]

Learning objectives

Students should learn:

- how to interpret the gradient of a distance–time graph
- how to calculate the speed of an object using the speed formula
- how to use a distance–time graph to compare the speeds of different objects.

Learning outcomes

Most students should be able to:

- state that the gradient of a distance–time graph represents the speed
- use the speed formula to calculate the average speed of an object.

Some students should also be able to:

- rearrange and use the speed formula
- compare the speed of different objects using the gradient of a distance–time graph.

Answers to in-text questions

a The gradient would have been less steep.

b 30 m/s

c 500 s

d 13.3 m/s

Support

- Construct graphs one section at a time so that the students can fully understand one part of the graph before moving on to the next part of the motion. Build up the complexity of the graphs as the lessons in this section of the course continue.

Extend

- Using the details from the train timetable (see 'Further teaching suggestions' for 'Calculating speeds'), the students can plot graphs to compare the speeds of local trains and express trains.

Lesson structure

Starters

Understanding graphs – Show the students slides of a range of graphs showing the relationship between two variables and ask them to describe what is happening. Use this activity to support students and ensure that they understand the key terms used in describing a graph (the axes and gradient). You can extend students by giving more complex examples leading to ideas such as an increase in rate (changes of gradient). *(5 minutes)*

Speedy start – Give the students a set of cards showing different moving objects and ask them to put them in order from fastest to slowest. Add some data on the objects so that the students can actually work out the speed of the objects using the speed formula. Examples could be a worm (0.5 cm/s), human walking (0.5 m/s), bicycle (5 m/s), car (20 m/s), passenger jet (200 m/s), and missile (1 km/s). *(10 minutes)*

Main

- Some students have difficulty understanding what you mean by the term 'object' and you will have to exemplify this idea by talking about cars, trains or runners. Students can also have difficulty with the whole idea of a 'time axis'. You might like to show time as moving on by revealing the graph from left to right, and discussing what is happening to the distance the object has moved over each second.

- There are quite a few who fail to understand that the horizontal portions of the graph show that the object is stationary. Emphasise that the distance isn't changing, even though time is; 'the object hasn't got any further away during this second so it must be still'. You should use additional simple graphs to discuss the motion of several objects until you are sure that the students can identify when the objects are moving fastest.

- The students should be familiar with the speed equation, but it may have been some time since they used it in KS3. A few practice questions should remind them of the basic idea. Be very cautious of students using inappropriate units for speed such as 'mph' or even 'm/s' (metres per second). If students find 'per' difficult, then just use 'each'.

- To extend students, you can get them to read information off the graphs to calculate speed, although this is covered in detail in a later lesson at an appropriate level. They should be able to calculate the overall average speed and the speed during individual phases of the motion.

- You should also extend students by discussing displacement instead of distance, or you could leave this until you are discussing velocity in the next topic.

- The practical activity is a good way to round off the lesson, and it can be as brief as 10 minutes long if bicycles are not involved.

Plenaries

Record breakers – The students should analyse data about the 100 m sprint records (or other records such as swimming). They can try to find out if there appears to be a continuous improvement in running speeds or if there are leaps where the records change suddenly. They can also discuss the precision of the records and link this to improvements in timing technology. *(5 minutes)*

A driving story – Give the students a paragraph describing the motion of a car through a town, including moving at different speeds and stopping at traffic lights, etc. Ask them to sketch a graph of the described motion. Students can be supported by giving them the graph and asking for them to generate the story or extended by providing numerical information that has to be plotted accurately. *(10 minutes)*

Practical support

Be a distance recorder!

Measuring speed is a simple activity and livens up what can be a fairly dry start to the 'Motion' chapter.

Equipment and materials required

For each group: stopwatch, metre wheel. Clipboards and marker cones are also useful.

Details

The students should measure out distances first and then time each other walking, running, hopping or riding over these fixed distances. An outdoor netball court, or similar, can provide a set of straight and curved lines for the students to follow. You may like to see if the students travel faster along the straight edges or if they follow the curves on the court. If you intend to use bicycles, then a lot more space will be needed and the students must wear the appropriate safety gear. Check with the PE department to see if they have cones to mark out the distances and if they mind bicycles on their running tracks or shoes on their indoor courts!

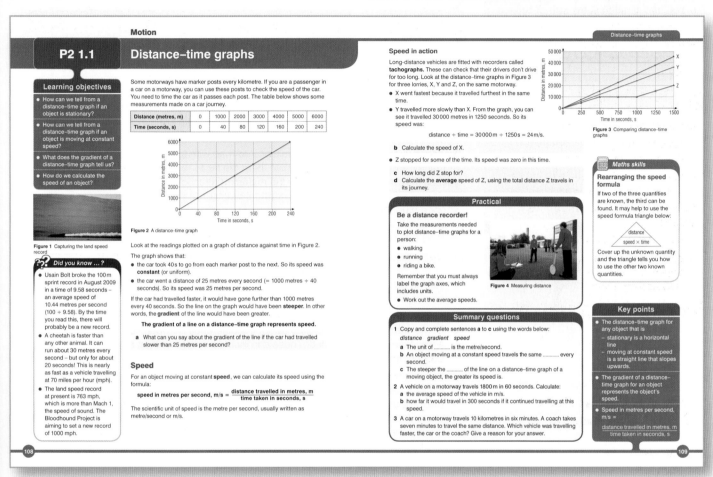

Motion

Distance–time graphs

P2 1.1 Distance–time graphs

Learning objectives

- How can we tell from a distance–time graph if an object is stationary?
- How can we tell from a distance–time graph if an object is moving at constant speed?
- What does the gradient of a distance–time graph tell us?
- How do we calculate the speed of an object?

Figure 1 Capturing the land speed record

??? Did you know ... ?

- Usain Bolt broke the 100 m sprint record in August 2009 in a time of 9.58 seconds – an average speed of 10.44 metres per second (100 ÷ 9.58). By the time you read this, there will probably be a new record.
- A cheetah is faster than any other animal. It can run about 30 metres every second – but only for about 20 seconds! This is nearly as fast as a vehicle travelling at 70 miles per hour (mph).
- The land speed record at present is 763 mph, which is more than Mach 1, the speed of sound. The Bloodhound Project is aiming to set a new record of 1000 mph.

Some motorways have marker posts every kilometre. If you are a passenger in a car on a motorway, you can use these posts to check the speed of the car. You need to time the car as it passes each post. The table below shows some measurements made on a car journey.

Distance (metres, m)	0	1000	2000	3000	4000	5000	6000
Time (seconds, s)	0	40	80	120	160	200	240

Figure 2 A distance–time graph

Look at the readings plotted on a graph of distance against time in Figure 2.

The graph shows that:

- the car took 40 s to go from each marker post to the next. So its speed was **constant** (or uniform).
- the car went a distance of 25 metres every second (= 1000 metres ÷ 40 seconds). So its speed was 25 metres per second.

If the car had travelled faster, it would have gone further than 1000 metres every 40 seconds. So the line on the graph would have been **steeper**. In other words, the **gradient** of the line would have been greater.

The gradient of a line on a distance–time graph represents speed.

a What can you say about the gradient of the line if the car had travelled slower than 25 metres per second?

Speed

For an object moving at constant **speed**, we can calculate its speed using the formula:

$$\text{speed in metres per second, m/s} = \frac{\text{distance travelled in metres, m}}{\text{time taken in seconds, s}}$$

The scientific unit of speed is the metre per second, usually written as metre/second or m/s.

Speed in action

Long-distance vehicles are fitted with recorders called **tachographs**. These can check that their drivers don't drive for too long. Look at the distance–time graphs in Figure 3 for three lorries, X, Y and Z, on the same motorway.

- X went fastest because it travelled furthest in the same time.
- Y travelled more slowly than X. From the graph, you can see it travelled 30 000 metres in 1250 seconds. So its speed was:

$$\text{distance} \div \text{time} = 30\,000\,\text{m} \div 1250\,\text{s} = 24\,\text{m/s}.$$

b Calculate the speed of X.

- Z stopped for some of the time. Its speed was zero in this time.

c How long did Z stop for?
d Calculate the **average** speed of Z, using the total distance Z travels in its journey.

Figure 3 Comparing distance–time graphs

Practical

Be a distance recorder!

Take the measurements needed to plot distance–time graphs for a person:

- walking
- running
- riding a bike.

Remember that you must always label the graph axes, which includes units.

- Work out the average speeds.

Figure 4 Measuring distance

Summary questions

1 Copy and complete sentences a to c using the words below:

distance gradient speed

a The unit of .... is the metre/second.
b An object moving at a constant speed travels the same .... every second.
c The steeper the .... of the line on a distance–time graph of a moving object, the greater its speed is.

2 A vehicle on a motorway travels 1800 m in 60 seconds. Calculate:
a the average speed of the vehicle in m/s.
b how far it would travel in 300 seconds if it continued travelling at this speed.

3 A car on a motorway travels 10 kilometres in six minutes. A coach takes seven minutes to travel the same distance. Which vehicle was travelling faster, the car or the coach? Give a reason for your answer.

Maths skills

Rearranging the speed formula

If two of the three quantities are known, the third can be found. It may help to use the speed formula triangle below:

distance
speed × time

Cover up the unknown quantity and the triangle tells you how to use the other two known quantities.

Key points

- The distance–time graph for any object that is
  - stationary is a horizontal line
  - moving at constant speed is a straight line that slopes upwards.
- The gradient of a distance–time graph for an object represents the object's speed.
- Speed in metres per second, m/s = $\frac{\text{distance travelled in metres, m}}{\text{time taken in seconds, s}}$

108
109

Further teaching suggestions

Detailed speed measurements

- To make more detailed measurements of the speed of an object, a distance sensor can be used.

Equipment and materials required

- Distance sensor, data logger and a simple moving object.

Details

- The distance sensor should be mounted in a fixed position and the object moves in front of it while the data logger records. You can use this to measure your distance in front of the meter while you walk back and forth at different speeds. The students can then analyse the graphs and see if they can describe the motion from them.

A need for speed

- The students could find out about how the land speed record has changed over the past 150 years (from trains to rocket cars). They could plot a graph of the record speed against the year and see if they can extrapolate to find what the record will be in 50 years' time. A similar activity can be carried out for the air and water speed records.

Calculating speeds

- Provide the students with a graph and ask them to describe the motion of the object. Students who complete this quickly should also calculate the speed of the object during each stage of the motion. Alternately, ask the students to get a bus or train timetable and a map. They should use the information in these to work out the average speed of the trains or buses between different locations.

Summary answers

1 a speed   b distance   c gradient

2 a 30 m/s   b 9000 m

3 The car travels faster because it takes less time to travel the same distance as the coach.

P2 1.2

Velocity and acceleration

Learning objectives

Students should learn:

- that velocity is the speed in a particular direction
- that acceleration is the rate of change of velocity.

Learning outcomes

Most students should be able to:

- explain the difference between the velocity of an object and the speed
- calculate the acceleration of an object using the acceleration equation.

Some students should also be able to:

- rearrange and use the acceleration equation.

AQA Specification link-up: Physics P2.1

- The velocity of an object is its speed in a given direction. *[P2.1.2 d)]*
- The acceleration of an object is given by the equation: $a = \dfrac{v - u}{t}$. *[P2.1.2 e)]*

  Controlled Assessment: P4.3 Collect primary and secondary data. *[P4.3.2 d)]*

Lesson structure

Starters

Getting nowhere fast – A racing driver completes a full circuit of a 3 km racetrack in 90 seconds. Ask: 'What is his average speed? Why isn't he 3 km away from where he started?' Demonstrate this idea to explain the difference between distance travelled and displacement. Lead on to a discussion about objects that are moving but do not get further away from the origin as they are following closed paths. *(5 minutes)*

Treasure island – Give the students a scaled map with a starting point, hidden treasure, protractor and a ruler. At first, only give them the times they have to walk for, then the speeds they must go at, and finally the matching directions. See which group can find the treasure first. This shows how important direction is when describing movement. Support students by starting with very simple examples. Extend students by asking them to produce a set of instructions to get to a treasure chest while avoiding a set of obstacles such as the 'pit of peril'. *(10 minutes)*

Main

- Talking about fairground rides or roundabouts helps to get across the idea that you can be moving at a constant speed but be feeling a force. You can link this experience into the idea that unbalanced forces cause acceleration, see later topics.

- Some students will not be clear about the difference between speed and velocity, and a few examples are needed. These can include simply walking around the room and describing your velocity as you go in one direction or another.

- You might like to discuss a collision between two cars travelling at 45 and 50 km/h. If they collide while travelling in opposite directions the impact will be devastating, because the relative velocity is 95 km/h. If they collide when they are travelling in the same direction only a 'nudge' will be felt, because their relative velocity is only 5 km/h. Clearly, the direction is very important. Check that all of the students can give an example of a velocity.

- Velocity–time graphs look similar enough to distance–time graphs to cause a great deal of confusion for students. Because they have just learned that the horizontal region on a distance–time graph shows that the object is stationary, they will probably feel that this is true for the velocity–time graph too. Time should be taken to explain that the object is moving at a steady velocity.

- As usual, some students will take the calculations in their stride while you may need to provide extra support for others. When using *v* and *u* as symbols in equations, be very careful that the students are discriminating between them clearly.

- Many students are unclear on the units for acceleration (m/s^2) and ask what the 'squared bit' is. If they are mathematically strong, you might like to show where the unit comes from, using the equation, but otherwise they should not worry about it. Always check that they are applying the unit correctly.

- There may be some confusion with the terms 'acceleration', 'deceleration' and 'negative acceleration', especially if you consider objects that move backwards as well as forwards. To extend students, you can show a graph of the motion of an object moving forwards then backwards, and describe the acceleration in detail.

Support

- The difference between speed–time and distance–time graphs should be reinforced. You might want to use different colour sets to plot the graphs to make them visually different.

Extend

- Extend students by asking them to look into the details of the concepts of displacement and velocity. Ask: 'What is the average speed of a Formula One car over one whole lap? What is the average velocity for the complete lap?' The students could draw a diagram to explain the difference.

Plenaries

Comparing graphs – Ask the students to make a comparison of what a distance–time graph and a velocity–time graph show. They should produce a chart/diagram that could be used to show another group of students the similarities and differences, highlighting the distinctions between what the gradients of these graphs represent. *(5 minutes)*

Accelerated learning – The students should try a few additional acceleration questions. They might be supported using simple structured questions, or extended by asking for calculations involving the rearrangement of the basic acceleration equation. *(10 minutes)*

Further teaching suggestions

Acceleration, power and mass in vehicles

- The students could find out about what makes a vehicle good at accelerating. By finding out the power output (bhp or kW) and mass of some vehicles (include motorcycles), they could investigate if there is a relationship between mass, power and acceleration. They could explain how well the data fits any pattern.

ICT link-up

- Distance sensors need to be used to measure velocity and changes in velocity accurately. Motion can also be monitored with video equipment and frame by frame playback. (This relates to How Science Works: making measurements.)

Motion

P2 1.2 — Velocity and acceleration

Learning objectives

- What is the difference between speed and velocity?
- What is acceleration and what is its unit?
- How can we calculate the acceleration of an object?
- What is deceleration?

Figure 2 You experience plenty of changes in velocity on a corkscrew ride!

links

For more information on circular motion, see P3 2.6 Circular motion.

Figure 3 On a test circuit

When you visit a fairground, do you like the rides that throw you round? Your speed and your direction of motion keep changing. We use the word **velocity** for speed in a given direction. An exciting ride would be one that changes your velocity often and unexpectedly!

Velocity is speed in a given direction.

- An object moving steadily round in a circle has a constant speed. Its direction of motion changes continuously as it goes round so its velocity is not constant.

Direction of motion

Figure 1 Speed and velocity

- Two moving objects can have the same speed but different velocities. For example, a car travelling north at 30 m/s on a motorway has the same speed as a car travelling south at 30 m/s. But their velocities are not the same because they are moving in opposite directions.

  a How far apart are the two cars 10 seconds after they pass each other?

Acceleration

A car maker claims their new car 'accelerates more quickly than any other new car'. A rival car maker is not pleased by this claim and issues a challenge. Each car in turn is tested on a straight track with a velocity recorder fitted.

The results are shown in the table:

Time from a standing start (seconds, s)	0	2	4	6	8	10
Velocity of car X (metre per second, m/s)	0	5	10	15	20	25
Velocity of car Y (metre per second, m/s)	0	6	12	18	18	18

Which car has a greater **acceleration**? The results are plotted on the velocity–time graph in Figure 4. You can see the velocity of Y goes up from zero faster than the velocity of X does. So Y accelerates more in the first 6 seconds.

The acceleration of an object is its change of velocity per second. The unit of acceleration is the metre per second squared, abbreviated to m/s².

Any object with a changing velocity is accelerating. We can work out its acceleration using the equation:

Acceleration

$$\text{Acceleration (metres per second squared, m/s}^2) = \frac{\text{change in velocity in metres per second, m/s}}{\text{time taken for the change in seconds, s}}$$

For an object that accelerates steadily from an initial velocity u to a final velocity v, its change of velocity = final velocity – initial velocity = $v - u$.

Therefore, we can write the equation for acceleration as:

$$\text{acceleration, } a = \frac{v - u}{t}$$

Where:

v = the final velocity in metres per second,
u = the initial velocity in metres per second,
t = time taken in seconds.

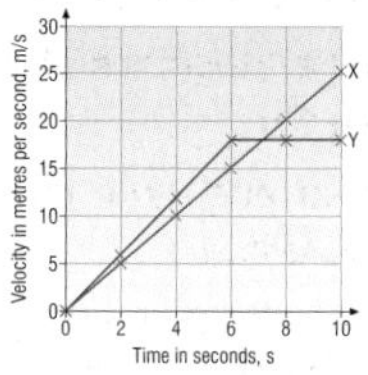

Maths skills

Worked example

In Figure 4, the velocity of Y increases from 0 to 18 m/s in 6 seconds. Calculate its acceleration.

Solution

Change of velocity = $v - u$ = 18 m/s – 0 m/s = 18 m/s

Time taken, t = 6 s

$$\text{Acceleration, } a = \frac{\text{change in velocity in metres per second, m/s}}{\text{time taken for the change in seconds, s}} = \frac{v - u}{t}$$

$$= \frac{18 \text{ m/s}}{6 \text{ s}} = 3 \text{ m/s}^2$$

b Calculate the acceleration of X in Figure 4.

Deceleration

A car decelerates when the driver brakes. We use the term **deceleration** or **negative acceleration** for any situation where an object slows down.

Summary questions

1 Copy and complete **a** to **c** using the words below:
   acceleration speed velocity
   a An object moving steadily round in a circle has a constant ....
   b If the velocity of an object increases by the same amount every second, its .... is constant.
   c Deceleration is when the .... of an object decreases.

2 The velocity of a car increased from 8 m/s to 28 m/s in 8 s without change of direction. Calculate:
   a its change of velocity
   b its acceleration.

3 The driver of a car increased the speed of the car as it joined the motorway. It then travelled at constant velocity before slowing down as it left the motorway at the next junction.
   a i When did the car decelerate?
   ii When was the acceleration of the car zero?
   b When the car joined the motorway, its velocity increased from 5.0 metres per second to 25 metres per second in 10 seconds. What was its acceleration during this time?

Figure 4 Velocity–time graph

Key points

- Velocity is speed in a given direction.
- Acceleration is change of velocity per second. The unit of acceleration is the metre per second squared (m/s²).
- Acceleration = change of velocity ÷ time taken.
- Deceleration is the change of velocity per second when an object slows down.

110

111

Answers to in-text questions

a 600 m

b 2.5 m/s²

Summary answers

1 **a** speed
  b acceleration
  c velocity

2 **a** 20 m/s
  b 2.5 m/s²

3 **a i** The car decelerated as it left the motorway.
   ii The acceleration of the car was zero when it was travelling on the motorway at constant velocity.
  b 2.0 m/s²

P2 1.3

More about velocity–time graphs

AQA

Specification link-up: Physics P2.1

- The gradient of a velocity–time graph represents acceleration. *[P2.1.2 f)]*
- Calculation of the acceleration of an object from the gradient of a velocity–time graph. *[P2.1.2 g)]* **[HT only]**
- Calculation of the distance travelled by an object from a velocity–time graph. *[P2.1.2 h)]* **[HT only]**

Controlled Assessment: P4.3 Collect primary and secondary data. *[P4.3.2 a)]*; P4.5 Analyse and interpret primary and secondary data. *[P4.5.3 a)]*

Learning objectives

Students should learn:

- how to interpret the gradient of a velocity–time graph
- how to calculate the distance travelled by an object from the area under a velocity–time graph. **[HT only]**

Learning outcomes

Most students should be able to:

- explain how data-logging equipment can be used to measure the velocity of an object
- describe the acceleration of an object from a velocity–time graph.

Some students should also be able to:

- use velocity–time graphs to compare accelerations
- use velocity–time graphs to compare distance travelled. **[HT only]**

Lesson structure

Starters

Late again? – Give the students the distance from their last class to the laboratory and ask them to work out their speed on the journey to you, using the time it took them to arrive. You can provide some example distances from other likely rooms if they have no idea about how far it is between places (surprisingly common). Anybody travelling at less than 1 m/s clearly isn't keen enough! *(5 minutes)*

Finding areas – Get the students to calculate the total area of a shape made up of rectangles and triangles. Students can be extended by asking them to find the total areas of more complex graphs, while others can be supported by providing graphs in which the shape has already been broken down into basic rectangles and triangles. *(10 minutes)*

Main

- Demonstrate the results produced for test A in the Student Book. If you do not get a straight line, you might want to discuss air resistance as a force opposing the movement of the trolley.
- The investigation into the motion of an object is a good one if you have sufficient equipment. Alternatives using light gates do not give a simple comparison of the accelerations, but you may be able to demonstrate that the velocity has increased. (This relates to: How Science Works: types of variable; fair testing; relationships between variables.)
- As before, time should be taken to ensure that the students understand what the gradients of the different graphs mean. They should be encouraged to break the graph down and just look at one section at a time, in order to explain what is happening between these sections. Real motion may not produce straight lines and simple gradients, but these are the best to use in examples for now.
- There should be no difficulty explaining that braking will reduce the velocity of the car, but you might like to ask what braking would look like on the graph if the car was in reverse. The change can confuse some students.
- Using the area under the graph to find the distance travelled is commonly forgotten, so try a couple of examples and refer back to it in later lessons. When calculating the area, ensure that the students are not giving their answers as 'distance = 15 cm², or similar. This can happen when they 'count boxes' or do their calculations based on the area being measured in centimetres. Make sure that they are reading the distances and times off the graph, not the actual dimensions of the shapes. **[HT only]**
- Finally, you could show what would happen if the deceleration took longer, by superimposing the new gradient over the old one and showing that the area is greater.

Answers to in-text questions

a Less steep.

b It would not be as steep.

c Greater.

Support

- Focus on the basics of measuring the area, reminding the students of the calculations needed to find the area of the triangular parts. Watch out for students reading incorrect values from the graphs; instead of reading the changes they can often just read the higher value.

Extend

- The students should look at the effect of aerodynamics on motion; it is air resistance that makes the motion of objects much more complex. They should find out about how these effects are investigated.

Plenaries

Busy teacher – Wear a pedometer throughout the lesson, calculate your average step distance and then ask the students to work out how far you have moved and your average speed. A typical example stride distance is 0.5 m with somewhere between 400 and 600 paces per lesson, giving a distance of 200 to 300 m in 1 h. The students could estimate their average daily speed too. *(5 minutes)*

Comparing graphs – Ask the students to describe the differences in the movement of three cars as shown on the same velocity–time graph. You can also use distance–time graphs. These comparisons should cover the speeds at different times and even the acceleration of the cars over periods by comparing the gradients. Support students by taking them through the examples step by step. Students can be extended by asking them to read data from the graphs (such as starting speed and final speed) and attempt to calculate the acceleration. *(10 minutes)*

Practical support

Investigating acceleration

Dynamics trolleys are an excellent way of studying motion, but class sets are very expensive. If none are available, then fairly large toy cars can be used for the basic experiments. Velocity sensors are also expensive and you may need to modify this experiment into a demonstration.

Equipment and materials required

Dynamics trolley, adjustable slope, protractor and data-logging equipment including a velocity sensor.

Details

Set up the equipment so that the angle of the ramp can be adjusted and easily measured. Make sure that the sensor is pointing along the path of the slope as otherwise the velocity will not be measured accurately. The students activate the sensor and then release the trolley.

Repeating this for a range of slope angles should give the result that the steeper the slope the greater the acceleration.

Alternative equipment

Light gates

As an alternative to a velocity sensor, a set of light gates can be used in experiments. This involves mounting a card of known length on top of the trolley, so that it interrupts the beam and the sensor measures the time for this to take place. This data can be used to determine the velocity; some software will do this for you directly. To determine acceleration, you can use a slotted card that interrupts the beam twice. This allows you to determine acceleration by looking at the speed at which the trolley was travelling when it first interrupted the beam and the speed the second time. Several sets of light gates can be used to measure the velocity at different stages of the motion.

Distance sensors

These use ultrasound or infrared to measure the distance to an object. Some software will convert these distance values into speed values and plot the required graphs.

Safety: Make sure trolley does not shoot off the end of the runway. Protect feet and bench.

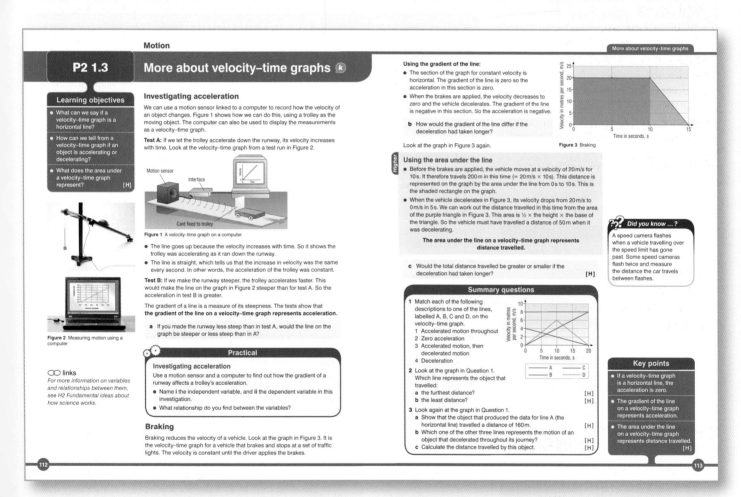

Further teaching suggestions

Calculating distance

● The students could calculate the distance travelled by an object using a velocity–time graph. **[HT only]**

ICT link-up

● Using route planner software, the students can find the distances between points on their journey to school or other locations. They can time themselves travelling between these points and work out their average speed. Sharing this information will allow them to compare different modes of transport.

Summary answers

1 1 B   2 A   3 D   4 C

2 a A

   b C

3 a 8 m/s (velocity) × 20 s (time) = 160 m (distance)

   b C

   c 40 m

P2 1.4

Using graphs

AQA Specification link-up: Physics P2.1

- Calculation of the speed of an object from the gradient of a distance–time graph. *[P2.1.2 c)]* [HT only]
- The gradient of a velocity–time graph represents acceleration. *[P2.1.2 f)]*
- Calculation of the acceleration of an object from the gradient of a velocity–time graph. *[P2.1.2 g)]* [HT only]
- Calculation of the distance travelled by an object from a velocity–time graph. *[P2.1.2 h)]* [HT only]
- Interpret data from tables and graphs relating to speed, velocity and acceleration. *[P2.1]*

Learning objectives

Students should learn:

- how to calculate the speed from a distance–time graph [HT only]
- how to calculate the distance travelled from a velocity–time graph [HT only]
- how to calculate the acceleration of an object from a velocity–time graph. [HT only]

Learning outcomes

Most students should be able to:

- calculate the gradient of a distance–time graph and relate this to the speed of an object [HT only]
- calculate the gradient of a velocity–time graph and hence the acceleration [HT only]
- find the area under a velocity–time graph for constant velocity and use this to calculate the distance travelled by an object [HT only]
- find the area under a velocity–time graph for constant acceleration and use this to calculate the distance travelled by an object. [HT only]

Support

- Although the content of this lesson is Higher Tier, not all students working on this topic will be mathematically strong. Some will need support with any form of rearrangement of the equations. Use additional worked examples for finding acceleration and distance travelled.

Extend

- Students can be challenged with more complex examples of motion calculations including ones requiring rearrangement of the basic equations. They could also look at more realistic motion graphs involving non-constant acceleration, and discuss what the shapes in these graphs indicate. Although they do not need to be able to describe or explain graphs like this, it can be useful to push them beyond the limits of the specification to enhance their understanding and analytical skills.

Lesson structure

Starters

Graph matching – The students have to match the description of the movement of objects with graphs of distance–time and velocity–time. Provide three different descriptions of journeys and three graphs that represent the movement for the students to match them with. The descriptions can contain numerical values such as 10 m/s so that the students can find this value from one of the graphs. *(5 minutes)*

Plot – Give the students a set of velocity–time data for a moving object, and ask them to plot a graph of displacement–time. Check the graphs for accuracy of plotting and clear labelling of the axes. You can make this more challenging by asking the students to plot several graphs on to the same axes, leading to a discussion about why you would want all of the data on one set of axes (ease of comparison). Students can be supported by providing partially completed graphs to add points to. *(10 minutes)*

Main

- This topic is for Higher Tier students only.
- As 'gradient' is the correct term, it should be encouraged; if the students are used to 'slope', then gently correct them through the lesson to help them change their ways. They need to know that the examination questions will always be using the term gradient.
- With a bit of practice, students should have no difficulty determining gradients. Watch out for students reading off the total distance and total time instead of the change in distance and change in time.
- Get the students to describe what is happening to the speed of a range of objects. You might like to show graphs, followed by video clips of objects doing what was shown in the graph, e.g. cars accelerating from 0–100 km/h or balls bouncing, etc. (Search an internet video hosting site). Some unusual, and funny, changes in motion can make the lesson livelier.
- When you move on to velocity–time graphs, yet again emphasise that these show something different than the speed-time ones. Hopefully, the students will never get the two types of graph confused after your constant reminders. The students should be reading the changes in velocity and time from the graphs, but some may make the same mistakes as mentioned previously.
- After numerous examples, the students should have a firm grip. Additional homework questions should be used to consolidate their learning.

Plenaries

Dynamic definitions – The students should provide detailed definitions of speed, velocity, distance, displacement and acceleration, including how they are represented on graphs. This should form a one page summary of all of the material from this set of four lessons. Support students by giving them definitions to match up with the key terms. *(5 minutes)*

Stretch – Take the opportunity to stretch the students' skills by giving a challenging set of questions involving several levels of complexity. Look for them to change units, identify and read values off a graph, and rearrange the acceleration equation. All of these things may be needed by Higher Tier candidates so push them to their limits. *(10 minutes)*

Further teaching suggestions

The students should have found the distance travelled by an object from a velocity–time graph in the last topic, so challenge them with more difficult graphs of motion.

You may want to see if they can find the distance travelled when the acceleration is not uniform. This would involve square-counting techniques (see 'Counting squares' below).

For additional challenge, look into graphs showing the object moving back towards the origin. You could try some velocity–time graphs in which the velocity becomes negative, and see if the students can calculate the distance the object ends up from the origin.

Graph work

- Follow-up work can be set on analysing or plotting a range of graphs of motion.

ICT link-up

- Simulation software can be used to investigate motion and to plot graphs of the behaviour. These can be either quite simple or rather complex, so you should be able to find something suitable for all ranges of ability.

Counting squares

- One common technique for working out the area under a line on a graph is to count the squares on the graph paper. Anything less than half a square doesn't count, and anything more than half a square counts as a complete square. This works reasonably well for simple graphs including those with straight gradients. You could discuss how to improve the accuracy of the method by using smaller and smaller squares on the graph paper. Make sure that the students know the distance each square of the graph paper represents.

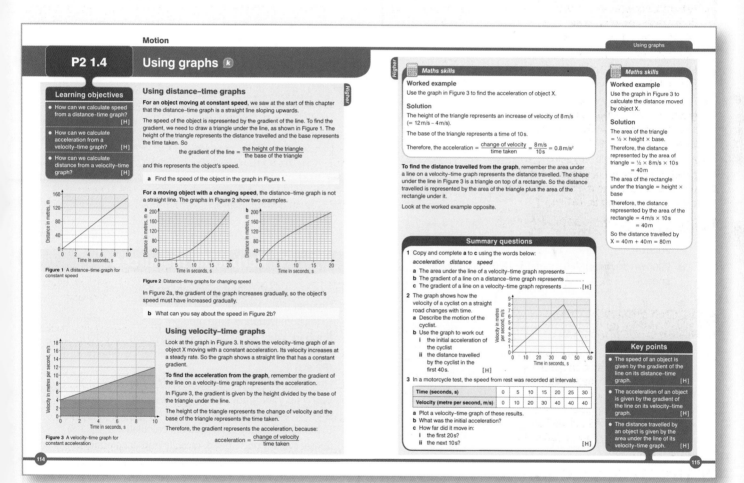

Answers to in-text questions

a 15 m/s.

b The speed decreased gradually and became constant.

Summary answers

1 a distance

  b speed

  c acceleration

2 a The cyclist accelerates with a constant acceleration for 40 s, and then decelerates to a standstill in 20 s.

  b i 0.2 m/s^2

   ii 160 m

3 a Student's graph, accurately drawn.

  b 2 m/s^2

  c i 400 m

   ii 400 m

Summary answers

1 a i Start the stopwatch when the car passes the marker and stop it when the car has completed 10 laps.

ii Take the car off the track and bend the tape measure round the track along the path the car takes. Use the tape measure to measure the distance of one lap. Multiply this distance by 10 to get the distance for 10 laps.

b 1.2 m/s

2 a 700 m

b 40 s

3 a A to B

b i 2000 m, 100 s

ii 20 m/s

4 a i 20 m/s

ii 2.5 m/s^2

b −1.2 m/s^2

5 a 3.0 m/s^2

b 2400 m

6 a

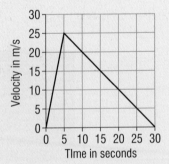

b 0.25 m/s^2, 0, −0.50 m/s^2

c 2000 m

d 2000 m (distance)/160 s (time) = 12.5 m/s (average speed)

7 a

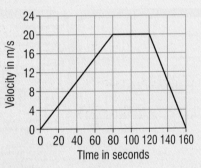

b 25 m/s (velocity)/5 s (time) = 5.0 m/s^2 (acceleration)

c −25 m/s (velocity)/25 s (time) = −1.0 m/s^2 (deceleration)

d 62.5 m + 312.5 m = 375 m

Summary questions

1 A model car travels round a circular track at constant speed.

a If you were given a stopwatch, a marker, and a tape measure, how would you measure:

i the time taken by the car to travel 10 laps

ii the distance the car travels in 10 laps.

b If the car travels 36 metres in 30 seconds, calculate its speed.

2 A train travels at a constant speed of 35 m/s. Calculate:

a how far it travels in 20 s

b how long it takes to travel a distance of 1400 m.

3 The figure shows the distance–time graph for a car on a motorway.

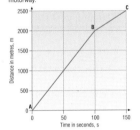

a Which part of the journey was faster, A to B or B to C?

b i How far did the car travel from A to B and how long did it take?

ii Calculate the speed of the car between A and B.

4 a A car took 8 s to increase its velocity from 8 m/s to 28 m/s. Calculate:

i its change of velocity

ii its acceleration.

b A vehicle travelling at a velocity of 24 m/s slowed down and stopped in 20 s. Calculate its deceleration.

5 The figure shows the velocity–time graph of a passenger jet before it took off.

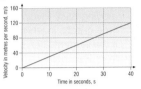

a Calculate the acceleration of the jet.

b Calculate the distance it travelled before it took off.

6 The table below shows how the velocity of a train changes as it travelled from one station to the next.

Time (seconds)	0	20	40	60	80	100	120	140	16
Velocity (m/s)	0	5	10	15	20	20	20	10	0

a Plot a velocity–time graph using this data.

b Calculate the acceleration in each of the three parts of the journey.

c Calculate the total distance travelled by the train.

d Show that the average speed for the train's journey was 12.5 m/s.

7 A motorcyclist started from rest and accelerated steadily to 25 m/s in 5 seconds then slowed down steadily to a halt 30 seconds after she started.

a Draw a velocity–time graph for this journey.

b Show that the acceleration of the motorcyclist in the first 5 seconds was 5.0 m/s^2.

c Calculate the deceleration of the motorcyclist in the last 25 seconds.

d Use your graph to show that the total distance travelled by the motorcyclist was 375 metres.

116

Kerboodle resources

Resources available for this chapter on Kerboodle are:

- Chapter map: Motion
- Extension: Distance–time gradient calculations (P2 1.1)
- Support: What is my distance–time graph? (P2 1.1)
- Bump up your grade: What is my distance–time graph? (P2 1.1)
- How science works: Acceleration of a trolley (P2 1.2)
- Bump up your grade: Velocity–time graph: Using motion graphs to show how fast things move (P2 1.3)
- Extension: Velocity–time gradient calculations (P2 1.3)
- Interactive activity: Speed, velocity and acceleration on graphs
- Revision podcast: Velocity and acceleration
- Test yourself: Motion
- On your marks: Motion
- Examination-style questions: Motion
- Answers to examination-style questions: Motion

AQA Examination-style questions

1 The table gives values of distance and time for a child travelling along a straight track competing in an egg and spoon race.

Time (seconds)	0	5	10	15	20	25
Distance (metres)	0	8	20	20	24	40

a Copy the graph axes below on to graph paper. Plot a graph of distance against time for the child. (3)

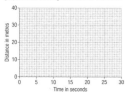

b Name the dependent variable shown on the graph. (1)
c What type of variable is this? (1)
d Use your graph to estimate the distance travelled in 22 seconds. (1)
e Use your graph to estimate the time taken for the child to travel 15 metres. (1)
f Describe the motion of the child between 10 seconds and 15 seconds.
Give a reason for your answer. (2)

2 The graph shows how far a runner travels during a charity running race.

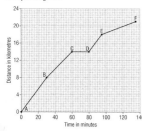

a What was the distance of the race? (1)
b How long did it take the runner to complete the race? (1)
c For how long did the runner rest during the race? (1)
d Between which two points was the runner moving the fastest?
Give a reason for your answer. (2)
e Between which two points did the runner travel at the same speed as they did between A and B? (1)
f Calculate the speed of the runner between B and C in metres per second.
Write down the equation you use. Show clearly how you work out your answer. (3)

3 A cyclist is travelling along a straight road. The graph shows how the velocity changes with time for part of the journey.

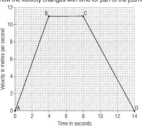

a Explain how the acceleration can be found from a velocity–time graph. (1)
b Copy and complete the following sentences using the list of words and phrases below. Each one can be used once, more than once or not at all.

is stationary   travels at a constant speed
accelerates   decelerates

i Between A and B the cyclist .... (1)
ii Between B and C the cyclist .... (1)
iii Between C and D the cyclist .... (1)
c i Use the graph to find the maximum speed of the cyclist. (1)
ii Use the graph to calculate the distance travelled in metres between 4 and 8 seconds. Show clearly how you work out your answer. (2)
iii Use the graph to calculate the total distance travelled in metres.
Show clearly how you work out your answer. [H] (3)

AQA Examination-style answers

1 a
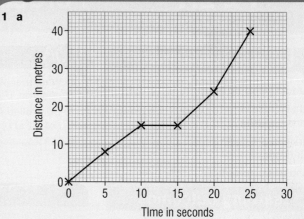
(3 marks)

b distance (1 mark)
c continuous (1 mark)
d 30 to 31 metres (1 mark)
e 7.5 to 8.5 seconds (1 mark)
f stationary; no change in distance/gradient is zero (2 marks)

2 a 21 km (1 mark)
b 135 minutes (2 hours 15 minutes) (1 mark)
c 20 minutes (1 mark)
d A to B or D to E; steepest gradient (2 marks)
e D to E (1 mark)
f speed = gradient = $\dfrac{(14\,000 - 8000)}{(30 \times 60)}$

$\quad = \dfrac{6000}{1800}$

$\quad = 3.3\,\text{m/s}$ (3 marks)

3 a gradient = acceleration (1 mark)
b i Between A and B the cyclist **accelerates** (1 mark)
ii Between B and C the cyclist **travels at a constant speed** (1 mark)
iii Between C and D the cyclist **decelerates** (1 mark)
c i 11 m/s (1 mark)
ii $(8 - 4) \times 11 = 44\,\text{m}$ (2 marks)
iii $\dfrac{44}{2} + \dfrac{44 + (6 \times 11)}{2} = 99\,\text{m}$ (3 marks)

AQA Examiner's tip

These questions cover most of the skills needed to answer questions on motion graphs. Candidates may have to plot a graph from a table of data and will need plenty of practice. Only Higher Tier candidates will need to find the gradient of a distance–time or a velocity–time graph, or find the area of a velocity–time graph. However, the Foundation Tier will need to know what the respective gradients represent without calculating them. They could also be asked to calculate the acceleration using the equation if they are given the initial and the final velocity.

AQA Examiner's tip

It is very common for students to get confused between distance–time and velocity–time graphs. It is therefore a good exercise to get pupils to sketch both types of graph for several made up journeys that involve acceleration, deceleration and constant velocity. These graphs can be sketched with the same time axis to enable a comparison. This will help to highlight the difference between sloping sections and horizontal sections for each type of graph.

P2 2.1

Forces between objects

AQA
Specification link-up: Physics P2.1

- Whenever two objects interact, the forces they exert on each other are equal and opposite. *[P2.1.1 a)]*
  Controlled Assessment: P4.3 Collect primary and secondary data. *[P4.3.2 a) b) c) d) e) f)]*

Learning objectives

Students should learn:

- that forces between objects are equal and opposite
- friction is a contact force between surfaces
- the unit of force is the newton (N).

Learning outcomes

Most students should be able to:

- state the unit of force and that forces occur in equal and opposite pairs
- describe how frictional forces act between objects.

Some students should also be able to:

- explain examples of equal and opposite forces acting when two objects interact.

Lesson structure

Starters

It's a drag – Show a video clip of a drag racer (do an online video search for 'drag racer') deploying parachutes to assist in braking. Ask the students to explain how the parachutes help to slow it down. Try and draw out the key concepts of forces and friction. You can also check that the students use force arrows appropriately. *(5 minutes)*

Picture the force – Show a set of diagrams of objects standing still or in motion and ask the students to mark on all of the forces. Check that the students are using 'force arrows' and that they are marked clearly onto the point at which the force acts. *(10 minutes)*

Main

- Some of the material here checks the students' understanding of basic forces; they need to be encouraged to draw clear diagrams of the forces acting on objects. Look for force arrows in the right directions and see if the students draw them of differing lengths and are trying to represent the magnitude.

- It will help if the students have a clear understanding of what a one newton force feels like, so pass around a 100 g mass so they can get a feel for it. You could also give examples of very large forces (e.g. the force between the Sun and Earth) and very small forces (e.g. the force of attraction between adjacent students) to show the vast range of forces scientists deal with.

- The idea of equal and opposite forces needs to be reinforced with plenty of examples. Show a range of objects in equilibrium such as a boat, see-saw, car rolling, and identify the pairs of forces on diagrams. (Search for pictures online.)

- The car stuck in mud situation is one where the forces do not appear to be equal and opposite. The force in the rope is clear (you can show this with a model) but this is not the only force at work. To analyse the situation more fully would require including the frictional forces and the forces exerted by the tractor on the Earth. As the car and tractor accelerate, the Earth is accelerated in the opposite direction by a tiny amount.

- You can demonstrate equal and opposite forces using skates (see 'Practical support') or by dragging objects along the floor with a string with newtonmeters at each end. It can be difficult to read moving newtonmeters, but the students will get the hang of it with practice. (This relates to 'How Science Works: making measurements, repeatability and reproducibility'.)

- When discussing the operation of wheels, you might like to go through some of the stages of the force being transferred to the wheel from the engine; especially with those interested in automotive engineering.

- To round off, you could show a car trying to accelerate too rapidly and skidding; this provides a visual answer to in-text question **c**. (Search for 'racing' or 'car skid' at a video hosting site.)

Answers to in-text questions

a 50 N upwards.

b 200 N.

c The wheels slip on the ground.

Support

- Start with some simple reminders of forces and force diagrams. Provide some diagrams with some of the forces already marked on with indications of their direction and magnitude and ask the students to complete them.

Extend

- Ask: 'What is the ideal launch angle of a projectile? Can you discover the ideal angle to fire a projectile and make it travel the furthest distance?' They need to design a launch system to make this investigation work. Alternatively you can look at the forces required to drag objects; when the objects are accelerating, the force is larger than that at constant speed. The students can look into why this happens and perhaps the relationship force = mass × acceleration.

Plenaries

Pulling power – Support students understanding of balanced forces by giving the students cards describing ten (or more) players and ask them to assign them to two tug-of-war teams, so that the teams are balanced. There may be several solutions. Have players with force strengths of 50 N, 100 N, 150 N, 200 N, 250 N, 300 N, 350 N, 400 N, 450 N, 500 N. You can use more complicated numbers if you want to extend some students more. *(5 minutes)*

The force is strong in which one? – Give the students a set of cards showing the size of the forces between objects (e.g. force on a person due to the gravity of Earth, force produced by a tug of war team) and a description of the objects and ask them to match up the cards. *(10 minutes)*

Practical support

Action and reaction

Equipment and materials required

Two sets of roller skates or skateboards, full sets of safety equipment (helmet, pads, etc.) a connecting rope, two newtonmeters.

Details

The students should firstly demonstrate the effect of pushing each other. If student A pushes student B forwards gently, then student A should move backwards. If the students are roughly the same size and the skates are similar, then you could show that they both move the same distance before friction stops them. One student can then try to pull the other with a rope; they should both move closer. Measuring the forces to show that they are identical in size is trickier; the rope becomes slack. You might want to pull a skater around instead and take force measurements at both ends of the rope.

Safety: Make sure there is enough room for students to move around safely.

Forces

P2 2.1   Forces between objects

Learning objectives

● What can forces do?

● What is the unit of force?

● When two objects interact, what can we say about the forces acting?

??! Did you know …?

Quicksand victims sink because they can't get enough support from the sand. The force of gravity on the victim (acting downwards) is greater than the upwards force of the sand on the victim. People caught in quicksand should not struggle but flatten themselves on the surface and crawl to a safe place.

⊙⊙ links

For more information on how forces make objects turn, see P3 2.1 Moments.

When you apply a **force** to a tube of toothpaste, be careful not to apply too much force. The force you apply to squeeze the tube changes its shape and pushes toothpaste out of the tube. If you apply too much force, the toothpaste might come out too fast.

A force can change the shape of an object or change its state of rest or its motion.

Equal and opposite forces

Whenever two objects push or pull on each other, they exert equal and opposite forces on one another. The unit of force is the newton (abbreviated as N).

● A boxer who punches an opponent with a force of 100 N experiences a reverse force of 100 N from his opponent.

● Two roller skaters pull on opposite ends of a rope. The skaters move towards each other. This is because they pull on each other with equal and opposite forces. Two newtonmeters could be used to show this.

Figure 1 Equal and opposite forces

⚙ Practical

Action and reaction

Test this with a friend if you can, using roller skates and two newtonmeters. Don't forget to wear protective head gear!

● What did you find out?

● Comment on the precision of your readings.

a A hammer hits a nail with a downward force of 50 N. What is the size and direction of the force of the nail on the hammer?

In the mud

A car stuck in mud can be difficult to shift. A tractor can be very useful here. Figure 2 shows the idea. At any stage, the force of the rope on the car is equal and opposite to the force of the car on the rope.

To pull the car out of the mud, the force of the ground on the tractor needs to be greater than the force of the mud on the car. These two forces aren't necessarily equal to one another because the objects are not the same.

Pull of rope on car = Pull of car on rope

Force of ground on tractor is greater than force of mud on car

Figure 2 In the mud

b A lorry tows a broken-down car. When the force of the lorry on the tow rope is 200 N, what is the force of the tow rope on the lorry?

Friction in action

The driving force on a car is the force that makes it move. This is sometimes called the engine force or the **motive force**. This is due to **friction** between the ground and the tyre of each drive wheel. Friction acts where the tyre is in contact with the ground.

When the car moves forwards:

● the force of friction of the ground on the tyre is in the forward direction

● the force of friction of the tyre on the ground is in the reverse direction.

The two forces are equal and opposite to one another.

Direction of car

Force of tyre on road   Force of road on tyre

Figure 3 Driving force

c What happens if there isn't enough friction between the tyre and the ground?

Summary questions

1 **a** When the brakes of a moving car are applied, what is the effect of the braking force on the car?

b When you sit on a cushion, what is the effect of your weight on the cushion?

c When you kick a football, what is the effect of the force of your foot on the ball?

2 Copy and complete **a** and **b** using the words below:

downwards   equal   opposite   upwards

a The force on a ladder resting against a wall is .... and .... to the force of the wall on the ladder.

b A book is at rest on a table. The force of the book on the table is .... The force of the table on the book is ....

3 When a student is standing at rest on bathroom scales, the scales read 500 N.

a What is the size and direction of the force of the student on the scales?

b What is the size and direction of the force of the scales on the student?

Key points

● A force can change the shape of an object or change its motion or its state of rest.

● The unit of force is the newton (N).

● When two objects interact, they always exert equal and opposite forces on each other.

Further teaching suggestions

Investigating quicksand

● Slowly adding water to a bowl of cornstarch will produce a substance similar to quicksand. It's a bit hit and miss to get the consistency just right. When it is stirred gently, it will flow, but when it is hit, it will become solid. You could try to float objects on top of the mixture and see if vibrations (produced by a signal generator and loudspeaker) will cause them to sink. You could also measure the size of the force needed to pull out objects slowly or quickly.

Equipment and materials required

● Cornstarch (cornflour), 250 cm³ beaker, signal generator, loudspeaker.

Applying forces

● Have the students describe how forces are used in various simple devices such as doors, tin openers, bicycles, etc.

??? Did you know …?

Quicksand

On average, quicksand is actually denser than the human body, so it is difficult to sink in it further than your chest even if you panic. Survival guides suggest the following method of escape. Stay calm; if you don't struggle you *will* float. Slowly adjust your position so you are lying on your back and then wiggle your legs gently in a circular motion. You will crawl towards the edge. Don't get your friends to pull you out vertically; this apparently takes a very large force. It may be possible to investigate this with a cornflour-based practical.

Summary answers

1 **a** It slows the car down.

b It squashes the cushion.

c It squashes the ball for a short time and makes it move.

2 **a** equal, opposite

b downwards, upwards

3 **a** 500 N downwards.

b 500 N upwards.

P2 2.2 | Resultant force

Learning objectives

Students should learn:

- how to find the resultant force on an object
- that a zero resultant force does not cause acceleration
- that a non-zero resultant force causes acceleration.

Learning outcomes

Most students should be able to:

- find the resultant force acting on an object when there are two forces acting in the same direction or in opposite directions
- describe how the resultant force will affect the movement of the object
- describe examples where an object acted on by two forces is at rest or in uniform motion.

Some students should also be able to:

- explain examples where the motion of an object acted on by two forces along the same line is changed by the action of the forces.

Support

- Provide diagrams of objects so that the students can add force arrows and information about how the forces affect movement. For the basic mathematics of adding forces, show a clear methodology; treat the forces in each direction separately before finding the resultant.

Extend

- Some students will have studied vectors in mathematics and they could be challenged to find the resultant of two forces that are not in line. Start with a pair of perpendicular forces and see if the students can determine the magnitude and direction of the resultant using Pythagoras' theorem. Those talented in mathematics may be able to look into sets of forces that are not perpendicular.

AQA | Specification link-up: Physics P2.1

- A number of forces acting at a point may be replaced by a single force that has the same effect on the motion as the original forces all acting together. This single force is called the resultant force. *[P2.1.1 b)]*
- A resultant force acting on an object may cause a change in its state of rest or motion. *[P2.1.1 c)]*
- If the resultant force acting on a stationary object is:
  - zero, the object will remain stationary
  - not zero, the object will accelerate in the direction of the resultant force. *[P2.1.1 d)]*
- If the resultant force acting on a moving object is:
  - zero, the object will continue to move at the same speed and in the same direction
  - not zero, the object will accelerate in the direction of the resultant force. *[P2.1.1 e)]*

Controlled Assessment: P4.5 Analyse and interpret primary and secondary data. *[P4.5.3 a)]*

Lesson structure

Starters

Mad maths – Before stating to look at forces, you can provide some additional support for students with their mathematical skills. Give the students several addition sums that include negative numbers to check their understanding. Link this to the idea that forces are added together but ones in opposite directions are treated as negative. The students need to be able to add together accurately. The sizes of forces are often measured in kilo-newton so you might like to have the students handle larger numbers too. *(5 minutes)*

Balanced forces – Show the students a toy boat floating on water and ask them to draw a diagram of all of the forces on the boat. Add small masses, one at a time, until the boat sinks. Ask them to draw a diagram showing the forces at the time when the boat was sinking. This leads to the concept of balanced and unbalanced forces, but you can also discuss density. Extend the students by asking why the upward thrust of the water increases as the load does. They should be able to make observations that the boat is lower in the water and connect this to a greater force acting upwards. *(10 minutes)*

Main

- The calculation of resultant forces is generally easy when limited to one direction. The students must take care about the directions of the forces as some can get confused and simply add all of the numbers together. This is more likely when there are more than two forces. It is best to get the students to add all of the forces in one direction, then all of the forces in the other direction and then subtract these totals.

- It is well worth making the hovercraft (described in the 'Practical support'), but remember that the glue will take some time to cool so do this bit early in the lesson and give it 30 minutes to set thoroughly.

- Demonstrating a linear air track is a good way of showing motion without friction, and it can help the students get to grips with the idea that objects only slow down because of the friction.

- If you have footage of a jet plane taking off, use it to discuss the forces involved. If it is of an aircraft carrier launch system, you can point out the extra force applied by the steam catapult and ask why this is necessary. (Search for 'jet plane' at an internet video hosting site). The heavily loaded fighter planes often seem to dip as they leave the short runway as they are still not travelling quite fast enough to give sufficient uplift.

- An aeroplane cruising is a good example of balanced forces. The students can draw a diagram and discuss the sensations they feel when they are in a plane like this. Because the forces are balanced, the students should feel no acceleration. If they close their eyes they would not be able to tell they were moving at all. Make sure that you explain that the engines need to be generating a force as there is a substantial amount of air resistance.

- When discussing braking, be careful that the students do not think that the force applied to the pedal is the actual braking force applied to the wheels. If this were the case, then a car would take a lot longer to stop.

- If the glue is set, then this is a good time to go back to the hovercraft. The hovercrafts should glide well on flat desks. Get the students to explain why they float; include a diagram.

Plenaries

Hovercraft tests – The hovercraft should be finished so you can have a range of simple competitions. Which travels furthest from the starting point, which stays hovering for longest, which can move a 50 g mass, and so on? *(5 minutes)*

An uphill struggle – Challenge students to come up with some explanations about forces and link the ideas to energy transfer. Example questions could include: 'Why is it harder to push a car uphill rather than on a flat road?' [You have to overcome friction and part of the weight of the object, you are also increasing its potential energy] and 'Is it easier to drag a piano up a ramp rather than upstairs? Why?' [You have to lift the object up each step so overcoming its weight]. How can an aeroplane maintain speed if the engines are turned off [Some of the potential energy is transferred to kinetic as the plane reduces its height]. *(10 minutes)*

Practical support

Investigating forces

Hovercrafts are fun to make. There are various designs but this one uses an old CD.

Equipment and materials required
Balloons and balloon pump, old CD, thick paper, 'sports bottle' top and glue gun.

Details
Glue the sports bottle top on to the centre of the CD with the glue gun so that it covers the hole, making sure that the seal around the edge is good. Let this cool for at least 10 minutes. Blow up the balloon and carefully pull the end over the bottle top so that the air will be released through the base of the CD. The CD will act like a hovercraft. It is vastly improved by fixing a cylinder of paper around the top edge of the CD so that it holds the balloon vertically and stops it dragging on the desk. You should be able to blow up the balloon while it is still attached to the CD. Searching the internet will yield a range of designs and pictures to help with this activity.

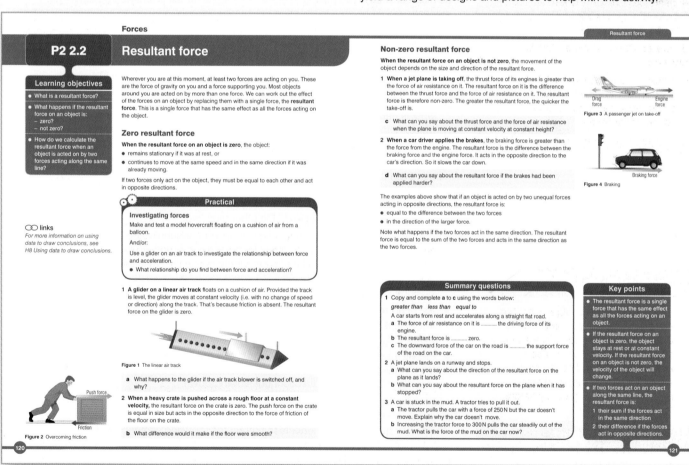

Answers to in-text questions

a It stops because friction between the glider and the track is no longer zero.

b The crate would slide across the floor after being given a brief push.

c They are equal and opposite to each other.

d The resultant force would have been greater.

Summary answers

1 **a** less than   **b** greater than   **c** equal to

2 **a** It acts in the opposite direction to the direction in which the plane moves.
  b It is zero.

3 **a** The tractor force is less than or equal to the force of the mud on the car so the car remains stationary.
  b The force of the mud on the car is now 300 N.

P2 2.3

Force and acceleration

Learning objectives

Students should learn:

- the relationship between the resultant force on an object and its acceleration
- how to use the equation $F = ma$ to determine the acceleration of an object.

Learning outcomes

Most students should be able to:

- calculate the force required to produce a given acceleration of an object of known mass
- state that objects of larger mass require greater forces to produce a given acceleration
- determine the direction of the acceleration on an object.

Some students should also be able to:

- rearrange and use the equation $F = ma$.

Answers to in-text questions

a 640 N

b 4.0 m/s^2

Support

- Give students plenty of examples for the calculations to provide extra support.

Extend

- See the more detailed acceleration investigation in the 'Further teaching suggestions' box. 'Why doesn't the snooker table move when a ball hits the cushion?'

AQA **Specification link-up: Physics P2.1**

- The acceleration of an object is determined by the resultant force acting on the object and the mass of the object. $a = \frac{F}{m}$ or $F = m \times a$ [P2.1.2 a)]

  Controlled Assessment: P4.4 Select and process primary and secondary data. *[P4.4.2 b)]*; P4.5 Analyse and interpret primary and secondary data. *[P4.5.3 a)]*

Lesson structure

Starters

Accelerator – Ask: 'What does the accelerator in a car do? How do you think it works?' Use this question to link back to energy, fuels and forces. [The pedal causes more fuel to be fed to the engine; this is burnt releasing energy at a greater rate; the energy generates a force – by exerting a pressure in the cylinder – and this force is transferred by a mechanical system to the wheels.] You should be able to find an animation of the process with a simple internet search. With some students you might like to move on to a discussion about the advantages of maintaining a constant speed instead of accelerating and braking between junctions. Significantly less energy is wasted. *(5 minutes)*

Lift off – Show the students footage of a chemical rocket launch and ask them to describe as much of what is happening as possible using accurate scientific language. The students should be able to describe the energy changes happening and then link to the ideas of this change, producing forces. You can support some students by providing a list of key words that must be incorporated into their descriptions including: fuel, combustion, thrust, kinetic energy, potential energy. *(10 minutes)*

Main

- A DVD showing a snooker match is a very useful resource. You can use it to discuss what is happening to the balls during impact and their movement across the green baize. Remind the students that there are frictional forces at work which is one of the reasons the balls slow.

- Pause the play and discuss the forces at work at each stage. With a data projector you can even draw force arrows over the action on your whiteboard. Show clips where the balls are moving in opposite directions and hit each other causing them to recoil. This can be used to illustrate forces in the opposite direction to motion, causing objects to decelerate or even accelerate in the other direction.

- The experiments can be simple or quite detailed depending on the time you have available. They produce quite a bit of data and can produce an excellent analysis task. The students should be encouraged to notice the limitations of the experiments and suggest improvements. As such, there are plenty of opportunities to cover 'How Science Works' concepts.

- As this is another fairly mathematically intensive topic, you will have to spend time on checking the students' ability to use the equation. As usual, encourage students to use a rigorous layout to increase the chances of a correct answer.

- Finally, watch out for students thinking that a moving object will always be moving in the direction of the resultant force. They need to understand that the object could be moving in the opposite direction, but slowing down.

Plenaries

What's wrong? – Ask the students to correct the following sentence that describes a common misconception: 'Objects always move in the direction of the resultant force.' [Students need to understand the forces will cause an acceleration that will speed up or slow down the object but this does not mean that it will instantly move in the direction of the force.] *(5 minutes)*

I'm snookered – The students must draw a series of diagrams showing the forces involved in getting out of a 'snooker', where the object ball, the blue, is behind the pink. They draw each of the stages of the movements, showing the forces as the ball is first hit and the collisions with the cushions. Obviously you can differentiate this task by having some simple and some complex situations. With some students you might want to make sure that the angles are accurately plotted. You might be able to use a snooker or pool simulation game to describe the effects too; these are more interactive and more fun for the students. *(10 minutes)*

Practical support

Investigating force and acceleration

This is a simple experiment, except for keeping the force constant; the alternative (see 'Further teaching suggestions') is more accurate but needs more equipment.

Equipment and materials required

For each group: dynamics trolley, string, masses (similar to trolley mass), stopwatch and possibly motion sensor or light gates.

Details

The students pull the trolley along attempting to use a constant force by watching the newtonmeter. They should pull the trolley along a track of known distance, so that they can compare the acceleration easily. If insufficient trolleys are available to double up, then just let the students add masses roughly equivalent to that of the trolley.

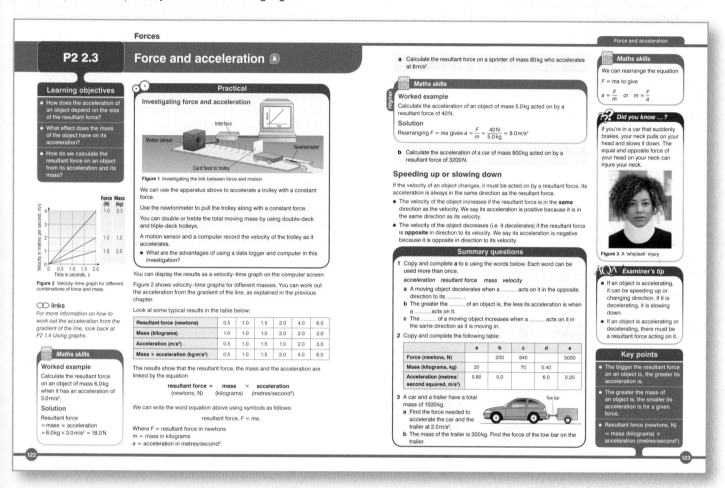

Forces

P2 2.3 Force and acceleration (k)

Learning objectives

- How does the acceleration of an object depend on the size of the resultant force?
- What effect does the mass of the object have on its acceleration?
- How do we calculate the resultant force on an object from its acceleration and its mass?

Figure 2 Velocity–time graph for different combinations of force and mass

Figure 2 Velocity-time graph for different combinations of force and mass

links

For more information on how to work out the acceleration from the gradient of the line, look back at P2 1.4 Using graphs.

Maths skills

Worked example

Calculate the resultant force on an object of mass 6.0 kg when it has an acceleration of 3.0 m/s².

Solution

Resultant force
= mass × acceleration
= 6.0 kg × 3.0 m/s² = 18.0 N

Practical

Investigating force and acceleration

Figure 1 Investigating the link between force and motion

We can use the apparatus above to accelerate a trolley with a constant force.

Use the newtonmeter to pull the trolley along with a constant force.

You can double or treble the total moving mass by using double-deck and triple-deck trolleys.

A motion sensor and a computer record the velocity of the trolley as it accelerates.

- What are the advantages of using a data logger and computer in this investigation?

You can display the results as a velocity–time graph on the computer screen.

Figure 2 shows velocity–time graphs for different masses. You can work out the acceleration from the gradient of the line, as explained in the previous chapter.

Look at some typical results in the table below:

Resultant force (newtons)	0.5	1.0	1.5	2.0	4.0	6.0
Mass (kilograms)	1.0	1.0	1.0	2.0	2.0	2.0
Acceleration (m/s²)	0.5	1.0	1.5	1.0	2.0	3.0
Mass × acceleration (kg m/s²)	0.5	1.0	1.5	2.0	4.0	6.0

The results show that the resultant force, the mass and the acceleration are linked by the equation

resultant force = mass × acceleration
(newtons, N)   (kilograms)   (metres/second²)

We can write the word equation above using symbols as follows:

resultant force, $F = ma$,

Where F = resultant force in newtons
m = mass in kilograms
a = acceleration in metres/second².

a Calculate the resultant force on a sprinter of mass 80 kg who accelerates at 8 m/s².

Maths skills

Worked example

Calculate the acceleration of an object of mass 5.0 kg acted on by a resultant force of 40 N.

Solution

Rearranging $F = ma$ gives $a = \dfrac{F}{m} = \dfrac{40\,N}{5.0\,kg} = 8.0\,m/s^2$

b Calculate the acceleration of a car of mass 800 kg acted on by a resultant force of 3200 N.

Speeding up or slowing down

If the velocity of an object changes, it must be acted on by a resultant force. Its acceleration is always in the same direction as the resultant force.

- The velocity of the object increases if the resultant force is in the **same** direction as the velocity. We say its acceleration is positive because it is in the same direction as its velocity.
- The velocity of the object decreases (i.e. it decelerates) if the resultant force is **opposite** in direction to its velocity. We say its acceleration is negative because it is opposite in direction to its velocity.

Summary questions

1 Copy and complete **a** to **c** using the words below. Each word can be used more than once.

acceleration   resultant force   mass   velocity

a A moving object decelerates when a .... acts on it in the opposite direction to its ....
b The greater the .... of an object is, the less its acceleration is when a .... acts on it.
c The .... of a moving object increases when a .... acts on it in the same direction as it is moving in.

2 Copy and complete the following table:

	a	b	c	d	e
Force (newtons, N)		200	840		5000
Mass (kilograms, kg)	20		70	0.40	
Acceleration (metres/ second squared, m/s²)	0.80	5.0		6.0	0.20

3 A car and a trailer have a total mass of 1500 kg.
a Find the force needed to accelerate the car and the trailer at 2.0 m/s².
b The mass of the trailer is 300 kg. Find the force of the tow bar on the trailer.

Maths skills

We can rearrange the equation

$F = ma$ to give

$a = \dfrac{F}{m}$ or $m = \dfrac{F}{a}$

Did you know ... ?

If you're in a car that suddenly brakes, your neck pulls on your head and slows it down. The equal and opposite force of your head on your neck can injure your neck.

Figure 3 A 'whiplash' injury

AQA Examiner's tip

- If an object is accelerating, it can be speeding up or changing direction. If it is decelerating, it is slowing down.
- If an object is accelerating or decelerating, there must be a resultant force acting on it.

Key points

- The bigger the resultant force on an object is, the greater its acceleration is.
- The greater the mass of an object is, the smaller its acceleration is for a given force.
- Resultant force (newtons, N) = mass (kilograms) × acceleration (metres/second²)

122   123

Further teaching suggestions

ICT link-up

- A range of good simulations of force experiments are available.

More investigating force and acceleration

- In this experiment, the students can discover the effect of different forces on acceleration or the effect of the objects mass.

Equipment and materials required

For each group: dynamics trolley (or similar), string, pulley, clamp, 10 × 20 g masses and mass holder, stopwatch and possibly motion sensor or light gates.

Details

The students mount the pulley over the end of the desks. One end of the string is attached to the mass holder (which hangs down) and the other to the trolley. The mass is released and

falls to the floor pulling the trolley with a constant force. With larger masses, you will need to protect the floor and students' feet.

The movement of the trolley can be monitored by a motion sensor, or the time it takes to move between two marked points can be recorded. The students can load the mass holder with different masses to increase the force on the trolley in order to investigate the effect of the size of the force on the acceleration. (This relates to: 'How Science Works': relationships between variables.) Some may even look into the effect of the mass of the trolley by loading it up with increasing mass and accelerating it with a fixed force. By analysing graphs and discovering that a is proportional to F and a is also inversely proportional to m, some students should be able to link the concepts together to reach $F = ma$.

Summary answers

1 **a** resultant force, velocity
  b mass, resultant force
  c acceleration, resultant force

2 **a** 16 N   **c** 12 m/s²   **e** 25 000 kg
  b 40 kg   **d** 2.4 N

3 **a** 3000 N   **b** 600 N

P2 2.4

On the road

Learning objectives

Students should learn:

- that the resultant force on a vehicle travelling at constant velocity is zero
- about the factors that affect the thinking distance of vehicles
- about the factors that affect the braking distance of moving vehicles.

Learning outcomes

Most students should be able to:

- use a chart to find the stopping distance, the braking distance and the thinking distance at a given speed
- list and describe the factors that affect the stopping distance of a vehicle
- explain which are the most important factors for cars moving at a range of speeds.

Some students should also be able to:

- differentiate between factors that affect the thinking distance, braking distance or both distances.

Support

- Allow the students to use an experiment template with clear instructions and a results table during the practical task.

Extend

- Concentrate on the links between forces, acceleration and mass using $F = ma$ calculations. You can challenge some students to tackle realistic-sized objects (cars of mass 1000 kg) and accelerations. Discuss the idea that the fast-moving cars have large amounts of kinetic energy.

AQA   Specification link-up: Physics P2.1

- When a vehicle travels at a steady speed the resistive forces balance the driving force. *[P2.1.3 a)]*
- The greater the speed of a vehicle the greater the braking force needed to stop it in a certain distance. *[P2.1.3 b)]*
- The stopping distance of a vehicle is the sum of the distance the vehicle travels during the driver's reaction time (thinking distance) and the distance it travels under the braking force (braking distance). *[P2.1.3 c)]*
- A driver's reaction time can be affected by tiredness, drugs and alcohol. *[P2.1.3 d)]*
- When the brakes of a vehicle are applied, work done by the friction force between the brakes and the wheel reduces the kinetic energy of the vehicle and the temperature of the brakes increase. *[P2.1.3 e)]*
- A vehicle's braking distance can be affected by adverse road and weather conditions and poor condition of the vehicle. *[P2.1.3 f)]*

Lesson structure

Starters

Chances – You should be able to find information on government safety sites about car collisions. You can extend this to cover bicycle crashes and simple accidents in the home. Link these results to the idea of speed restrictions in your area, especially around primary schools. Overall, students should realise that greater speed significantly increases the injury. *(5 minutes)*

Stop! – To support students in understanding the wide range of factors that can affect the stopping distance of cars, ask the students to sort a set of cards about things which may or may not affect stopping distances. Correct ones can include the physical properties of the car, the tyres, the driver and weather conditions along with a lot of incorrect ones. You can extend students by asking them to discuss and describe how the factor affects the stopping distance and construct well-formed descriptions like 'The greater the mass of a car, the more kinetic energy it will have when moving at a fixed speed. This means that a more massive car will be more difficult to stop.' *(10 minutes)*

Main

- Video clips of vehicles braking and skidding make this topic more visually stimulating. (Search for videos of crash tests at an internet video site.)
- When discussing reaction times, you could try a simple experiment in concentration. At the beginning of the lesson give the students an unusual key word that won't usually crop up in the lesson ('banana') and ask them to put their hands up as quickly as possible whenever they hear it. Early in the lesson they will be quite quick but later, as their concentration flags, they will struggle. If you are using a digital projector, slip in a banana slide somewhere in the lesson and see how the students react; are they faster at reacting to visual stimuli?
- You could ask the students to evaluate the data used to produce the stopping distance chart. It is based on an alert driver, driving a medium-sized car, but it does not take into account the improved braking systems of modern cars and the increase in the size (mass) of the average car. This can lead to a discussion of whether large cars are safer or more dangerous to passengers and pedestrians.
- The students should understand the factors affecting overall stopping distance, but they need to be clear which affects the thinking distance and which affects the braking distance. You can link these concepts with $F = ma$ from the previous topic and again with kinetic energy in previous lessons. Note that the speed of the car affects thinking and braking distance, so it is usually the most important factor overall.
- Testing reaction time rounds the lesson off well, you can try the simple version or driving simulation software.

Plenaries

Expect the unexpected – Use the unusual key word one more time as the students are packing away. Reaction times will be dramatically reduced as they are paying attention to other things. *(5 minutes)*

I said stop! – Using the cards from the Starter, students have to separate those that were correct into ones that affect thinking distance and ones that affect braking distance. This task should solidify their understanding of the two phases of stopping. Ask: 'Do some factors affect both?' [e.g. speed] Students could put them in order of importance for a car travelling at 30 mph. Push the students further by showing them a detailed graph of stopping distances for different speeds; this should have the braking distance and thinking distances separate. Ask the students to describe the relationships. *(10 minutes)*

Practical support

Reaction times

This is a fairly simple activity only requiring a stopwatch with separate start and lap-time buttons.

Equipment and materials required

Stopwatches.

Details

The students can try the simple activity and see the wide range of response times. They should appreciate that the times improve with practice and when they are fully concentrating on the clock. In a real car situation, the driver would not be able to focus on one simple task, so the times would be significantly greater.

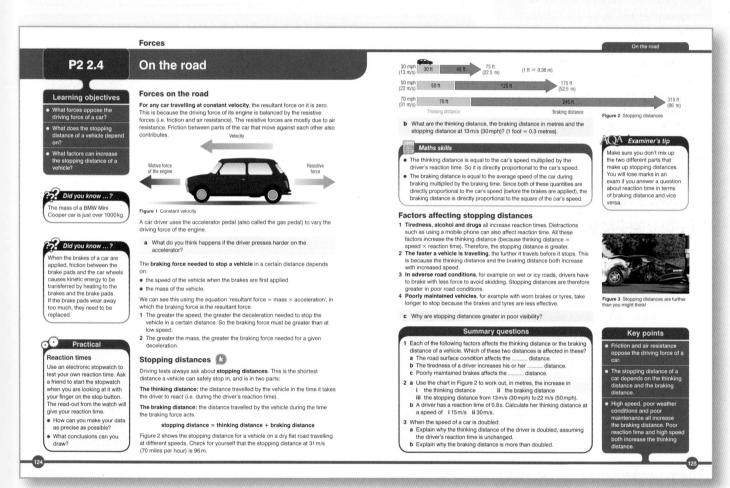

Forces

On the road

P2 2.4 On the road

Learning objectives

- What forces oppose the driving force of a car?
- What does the stopping distance of a vehicle depend on?
- What factors can increase the stopping distance of a vehicle?

Did you know …?

The mass of a BMW Mini Cooper car is just over 1000 kg.

Did you know …?

When the brakes of a car are applied, friction between the brake pads and the car wheels causes kinetic energy to be transferred by heating to the brakes and the brake pads. If the brake pads wear away too much, they need to be replaced.

Practical

Reaction times

Use an electronic stopwatch to test your own reaction time. Ask a friend to start the stopwatch when you are looking at it with your finger on the stop button. The read-out from the watch will give your reaction time.

- How can you make your data as precise as possible?
- What conclusions can you draw?

Forces on the road

For any car travelling at constant velocity, the resultant force on it is zero. This is because the driving force of its engine is balanced by the resistive forces (i.e. friction and air resistance). The resistive forces are mostly due to air resistance. Friction between parts of the car that move against each other also contributes.

Figure 1 Constant velocity

A car driver uses the accelerator pedal (also called the gas pedal) to vary the driving force of the engine.

a What do you think happens if the driver presses harder on the accelerator?

The braking force needed to stop a vehicle in a certain distance depends on:

- the speed of the vehicle when the brakes are first applied
- the mass of the vehicle.

We can see this using the equation 'resultant force = mass × acceleration', in which the braking force is the resultant force.

1 The greater the speed, the greater the deceleration needed to stop the vehicle in a certain distance. So the braking force must be greater than at low speed.
2 The greater the mass, the greater the braking force needed for a given deceleration.

Stopping distances

Driving tests always ask about **stopping distances**. This is the shortest distance a vehicle can safely stop in, and is in two parts:

The thinking distance: the distance travelled by the vehicle in the time it takes the driver to react (i.e. during the driver's reaction time).

The braking distance: the distance travelled by the vehicle during the time the braking force acts.

stopping distance = thinking distance + braking distance

Figure 2 shows the stopping distance for a vehicle on a dry flat road travelling at different speeds. Check for yourself that the stopping distance at 31 m/s (70 miles per hour) is 96 m.

Figure 2 Stopping distances

b What are the thinking distance, the braking distance in metres and the stopping distance at 13 m/s (30 mph)? (1 foot = 0.3 metres).

Maths skills

- The thinking distance is equal to the car's speed multiplied by the driver's reaction time. So it is directly proportional to the car's speed.
- The braking distance is equal to the average speed of the car during braking multiplied by the braking time. Since both of these quantities are directly proportional to the car's speed (before the brakes are applied), the braking distance is directly proportional to the square of the car's speed.

Factors affecting stopping distances

1 **Tiredness, alcohol and drugs** all increase reaction times. Distractions such as using a mobile phone can also affect reaction time. All these factors increase the thinking distance (because thinking distance = speed × reaction time). Therefore, the stopping distance is greater.
2 **The faster a vehicle is travelling**, the further it travels before it stops. This is because the thinking distance and the braking distance both increase with increased speed.
3 **In adverse road conditions**, for example on wet or icy roads, drivers have to brake with less force to avoid skidding. Stopping distances are therefore greater in poor road conditions.
4 **Poorly maintained vehicles**, for example with worn brakes or tyres, take longer to stop because the brakes and tyres are less effective.

c Why are stopping distances greater in poor visibility?

Examiner's tip

Make sure you don't mix up the two different parts that make up stopping distances. You will lose marks in an exam if you answer a question about reaction time in terms of braking distance and vice versa.

Figure 3 Stopping distances are further than you might think!

Summary questions

1 Each of the following factors affects the thinking distance or the braking distance of a vehicle. Which of these two distances is affected in these?
  a The road surface condition affects the .... distance.
  b The tiredness of a driver increases his or her .... distance.
  c Poorly maintained brakes affects the .... distance.
2 a Use the chart in Figure 2 to work out, in metres, the increase in
    i the thinking distance   ii the braking distance
    iii the stopping distance from 13 m/s (30 mph) to 22 m/s (50 mph).
  b A driver has a reaction time of 0.8 s. Calculate her thinking distance at a speed of   i 15 m/s   ii 30 m/s.
3 When the speed of a car is doubled:
  a Explain why the thinking distance of the driver is doubled, assuming the driver's reaction time is unchanged.
  b Explain why the braking distance is more than doubled.

Key points

- Friction and air resistance oppose the driving force of a car.
- The stopping distance of a car depends on the thinking distance and the braking distance.
- High speed, poor weather conditions and poor maintenance all increase the braking distance. Poor reaction time and high speed both increase the thinking distance.

124

125

Answers to in-text questions

a The car speeds up.

b 9 m, 13.5 m, 22.5 m.

c The reaction time of the driver is longer because the road ahead is more difficult to see.

Summary answers

1 a braking   b thinking   c braking
2 a i 6 m   ii 24 m   iii 30 m
   b i 12 m   ii 24 m
3 a The thinking distance is equal to the speed of the car multiplied by the driver's reaction time. So if the speed is doubled, the thinking distance is doubled.
   b The braking distance is equal to the average speed of the car during braking multiplied by the time taken for the brakes to stop the car. If the speed is doubled, the average speed is doubled and the time taken is increased, so the braking distance more than doubles. The time taken actually doubles as well, so the braking distance becomes four times greater.

P2 2.5 Falling objects

AQA

Learning objectives

Students should learn:

- the difference between mass and weight
- the mass of the object is a constant value whereas the weight depends on the strength of the gravitational field it is in
- why an object falling through a fluid accelerates until it reaches its terminal velocity.

Learning outcomes

Most students should be able to:

- explain the difference between mass and weight
- calculate the weight of an object of a given mass
- describe the forces acting on an object falling through a fluid such as air or water, and how these forces affect the acceleration of the object
- describe how the velocity of an object released from rest in a fluid changes as it falls
- explain why an object reaches a terminal velocity and describe some of the factors that determine this velocity.

Some students should also be able to:

- explain the motion of an object released from rest falling through a fluid including how the acceleration decreases and becomes zero at terminal velocity.

Support

- Allow the students to use an experiment template with clear instructions and a results table during the practical task. They then concentrate on reaching a conclusion and explain it in terms of the forces acting on the parachute.

Extend

- Ask the students about objects falling on other planets and moons. Show them footage of a coin experiment on the Moon; does it fall faster than on the Earth? Ask the students to describe the motion in detail.

Specification link-up: Physics P2.1

- The faster an object moves through a fluid the greater the frictional force that acts on it. *[P2.1.4 a)]*
- An object falling through a fluid will initially accelerate due to the force of gravity. Eventually the resultant force will be zero and the object will move at its terminal velocity (steady speed). *[P2.1.4 b)]*
- Draw and interpret velocity–time graphs for objects that reach terminal velocity, including a consideration of the forces acting on the object. *[P2.1.4 c)]*
- Calculate the weight of an object using the force exerted on it by a gravitational force:

  $W = m \times g$ *[P2.1.4 d)]*

  Controlled Assessment: P4.1 Plan practical ways to develop and test candidates' own scientific ideas. *[P4.1.1 a) b) c)]*

Lesson structure

Starters

Fluid facts – Support students by giving them cards with information (including diagrams) about the physical properties and the explanations in terms of particle behaviour for solids, liquids and gases and ask them to match them up. This should help them revise the states of matter and the particle theory in particular. *(5 minutes)*

Air resistance – What causes air or water resistance? The students need to use their understanding of particles and forces to give a description. They should sketch the movement of objects and label the forces on them and then try to show the particles being pushed out of the way and pushing back. Extend the students by trying to draw out the idea that moving faster through a fluid will require a greater force as more particles will need to be pushed out of the way each second. They may also be able to explain that the particles will need to be pushed 'harder' to get them out of the way faster. *(10 minutes)*

Main

- Video clips of falling objects are ideal for this topic, in particular clips of parachutists or bird flight. (Search for video clips at an internet video hosting site.)
- Weight and mass are commonly confused. Let the students handle a 1 kg mass and emphasise that the '1 kg' is the material in the block and this will not change just because you take it to the Moon. It has weight because it is attracted towards the Earth. Weigh the mass and explain that the weight is the force that is pulling it towards the centre of the Earth. If there were less gravity, then this force would be less.
- There are a couple of phrases used to describe 'the strength of gravity' and these are sometimes interchanged. Try to stick to 'gravitational field strength' and explain that there is a 'field' around the Earth where its gravity affects other objects. The students should accept this field idea after discussing the effect of a magnetic field.
- Remind students that all liquids and gases are fluids, so all motion we see on the Earth is motion through fluids.
- Air resistance is easy to show by throwing around bits of paper of various sizes, some scrunched, some not.
- When discussing terminal velocity, point out that this depends on the shape, or aerodynamics, of the object falling. A skydiver can adjust his shape and change speeds. Also point out that with the parachute opens, there is still a terminal velocity but this is much less than the one without the parachute opened.

Plenaries

Top speed – Show the students a list of top speeds for cars along with some other information such as engine power and a photograph. They can discuss why the cars have a maximum speed [there is a limit to the size of the force the engine can produce to overcome air resistance]. They should also realise that doubling the engine power does not double the terminal velocity [top speed]. *(5 minutes)*

Falling forces – The students should draw a comic strip with stick figures showing the forces at various stages of a parachute jump. This should summarise the concepts and demonstrate the changing size of the forces. You can support students by providing the images in the correct order and label them. Extend students by asking them to draw the force arrows to scale (they should have some appreciation of their own weight). *(10 minutes)*

Practical support

⚙ Investigating falling

This investigation can be trickier than it sounds, mainly because many objects don't fall straight down. Parachutes are particularly tricky as they take some time to unfurl, so you might want to miss them out if you don't have a suitable location.

Parachutes

For each group (parachutes): small mass (20 g), string or cotton, scissors, approximately 15 cm by 15 cm square of cloth.

Give the students a few minutes to make a parachute. The higher the parachutes are dropped from, the more effective they are, so find somewhere with sufficient height; a wide stairwell can be good if proper supervision can be arranged. It is just possible to notice the effect if you drop objects when standing on the desk, but great care must be taken. (This relates to 'How Science Works': designing investigations.) It would be safer to pick one responsible student to do this rather than the whole class.

Other objects

For each group: paper and a paper clip to make spinners or small paper cones, bun cases (or muffin cases).

The students drop the objects from a fixed height as with the parachutes; this does not need to be as high. The results will vary quite a bit as there will be timing errors and some variation due to draughts, so use the opportunity to discuss the importance of repeating and finding an average value. You could also use this as an open-ended planning exercise.

Feather and coin

You can demonstrate the effect of air resistance on falling objects with this traditional demonstration.

Equipment and materials required

Vacuum pump, sturdy acrylic tube containing a feather and metal coin, sealed and connected to the pump.

Details

With air in the tube you should be able to show that the coin falls faster than the feather as students would expect. Remove as much air as possible and the two objects fall at the same rate.

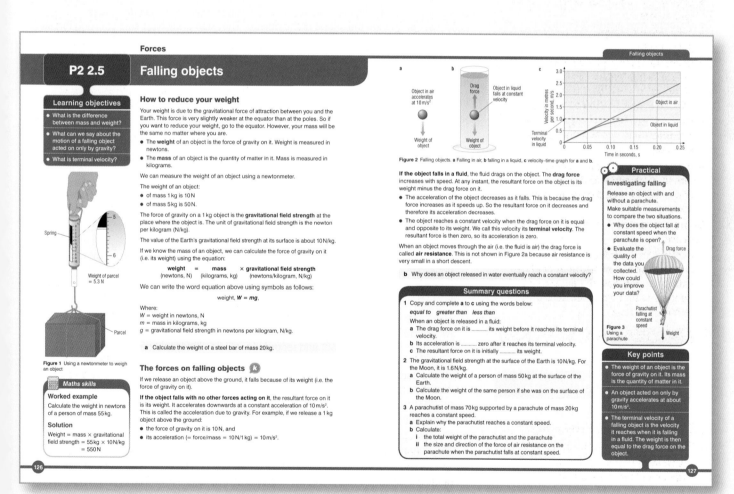

Answers to in-text questions

a 200 N

b The drag force on it increases (as its velocity increases) until it is equal and opposite to its weight. The resultant force on it is then zero and its acceleration is zero.

Summary answers

1 a less than   **b** equal to   **c** equal to

2 a 500 N   **b** 80 N

3 a As the parachutist falls, the drag force increases, so the resultant force decreases. The resultant force is zero when the drag force becomes equal and opposite to the weight of the parachutist and the parachute. The speed is then constant.

  b i 900 N   **ii** 900 N upwards

P2 2.6

Stretching and squashing

Learning objectives

Students should learn:

- that the extension of an object is the change in length due to a force being applied
- the extension of a spring is proportional to the force applied to it up to the spring's limit of proportionality
- the spring constant is the force per unit extension needed to extend the spring.

Learning outcomes

Most students should be able to:

- describe how a spring extends in terms of the force acting on it and 'Hooke's law'
- calculate the force required to extend a spring of known spring constant.

Some students should also be able to:

- use the spring constant and load to calculate the extension of a spring.

Answers to in-text questions

a An overloaded plastic shopping bag usually gives way at the handles first.

b 2.5 N

Support

- Provide a clear results table demonstrating how to calculate the extension of the objects for the experiment. This will let the students concentrate on the plotting and analysis of the graph.

Extend

- Challenge the students to investigate the stretching of elastic as described in 'Practical support'. They should calculate the cross-sectional area and see if it is related to the extension. After this they can look into the reasons why materials stretch and return to their original shape by considering the forces between the particles on the material.

Specification link-up: Physics P2.1

- A force acting on an object may cause a change in shape of the object. *[P2.1.5 a)]*
- A force applied to an elastic object such as a spring will result in the object stretching and storing elastic potential energy. *[P2.1.5 b)]*
- For an object that is able to recover its original shape, elastic potential energy is stored in the object when work is done on the object to change its shape. *[P2.1.5 c)]*
- The extension of an elastic object is directly proportional to the force applied, provided that the limit of proportionality is not exceeded:

$F = k \times e$ *[P2.1.5 d)]*

Controlled Assessment: P4.5 Analyse and interpret primary and secondary data. *[P4.5.3 a)]*

Lesson structure

Starters

Distortion – Get the students to list the basic things that forces can do (cause acceleration, change the shape of the object). They can draw diagrams showing forces acting on objects that cause these things to happen. Concentrate on the forces in the diagrams that cause objects to compress or stretch, and use these to discuss if these changes are permanent or can be reversed. You can then show the behaviour of elastic material compared to the behaviour of material that is not elastic (e.g. plastic). *(5 minutes)*

In proportion – In this lesson the students will be finding a relationship that is proportional, so start the lesson by asking the students to compare some graphs and the relationship between them. Use their descriptions to come up with the idea of proportionality. This can be quite difficult for some students, so support them with a simple graph such as one showing the amount of money earned compared to hours worked. They should be able to see the relationship that if paid at an hourly rate then the money you earn is proportional to the length of time you work. Extend students by discussing the gradient of graphs and what it means in particular examples. *(10 minutes)*

Main

- Demonstrate elastic behaviour and the property of returning to its original dimensions. You can show other objects that return to their original shapes and explain that the term 'elastic' in science has a specific meaning. Check that the students also understand the term 'deforming'.

- You can now demonstrate the extension of a spring and show the students how to make measurements. Take time to explain the problems with measuring the length (where do you measure from and to) and show the basic process. The students can then try out the experiment and record the results clearly including the calculation of extension as shown in the Student Book. For some students, you might like to try the elastic band version of the experiment as described in the 'Practical support'. The term 'directly proportional' can be confusing to the students; explain what it means using a graph. (How Science Works: relationships between variables.) You could also use this as a planning exercise.

- Now link back to the idea of elastic energy and the transfers involved when loading and unloading the spring.

- The 'Hooke's law' definition is very important; the trickiest part is the idea of the limit of proportionality. If some of your students have overloaded the spring, you can show this point on graphs of their data. If not, then you can overload the spring yourself and show this proportionality limit or the elastic limit.

- The spring constant can be explained by showing the students a range of springs, some stiffer than others.

- Finally, the students can investigate the energy stored by testing out some catapults as described in the 'Practical support' section.

Plenaries

Graphical analysis – Give the students a graph showing the extension of different springs and ask them to describe the differences. They should look at the limit of proportionality and the spring constants. To extend students and check their graph plotting skills, you could just provide the raw data and ask the students to plot the graphs. Expect all of the students to use the correct terms in their descriptions. *(5 minutes)*

Cushions – The students can design basic impact protection systems using springs and other elastic materials. These could be for vehicles or personal protection. You can then demonstrate the effects springs can have using dynamics trolleys. *(10 minutes)*

Practical support

Stretch tests

This investigation can be used to verify Hooke's law for a spring or to look at how other materials extend.

Equipment and materials required
For each group: set of masses and holder (50 g), retort stand, clamp, spring, rulers (you will likely need 30 cm, 50 cm and 1 m), G-clamp (to hold the retort stand on the bench if needed).

Details
The students could plan their investigation after setting up the equipment as shown in Figure 1 from the Student Book. They need to measure the initial length of the spring and record this. They can then load the spring by placing 50 g masses on it and record the new length leading to the extension. The results should indicate the relationship for Hooke's law.

You can extend the practical by investigating the stretching of elastic. Elastic bands are fine to use but you should try fishing pole elastic. You can easily get this from a fishing supplier. It comes in a range of diameters (each of a different colour) so you can actually investigate the relationship between cross-sectional area and the

way the elastic stretches. Other materials such as strips of plastic can also be investigated.

Catapult
The students can build catapults to investigate the energy that can be stored in them.

Equipment and materials required
Elastic bands (or fishing pole elastic), wooden stakes, rulers and tape measure, small projectiles.

Details
Students should construct a simple catapult from a piece of elastic (bands or similar) and the wooden stakes. They can then stretch the elastic by measured distances and fire projectile to find the distance the projectile travels. This leads to a discussion about the amount of energy stored in the bands and how it is transferred into kinetic energy as the band contracts. You can then try different thicknesses of bands to see if more energy is stored when they are stretched by the same length.

Safety: Ensure students behave responsibly and do not stand in firing line of the projectiles.

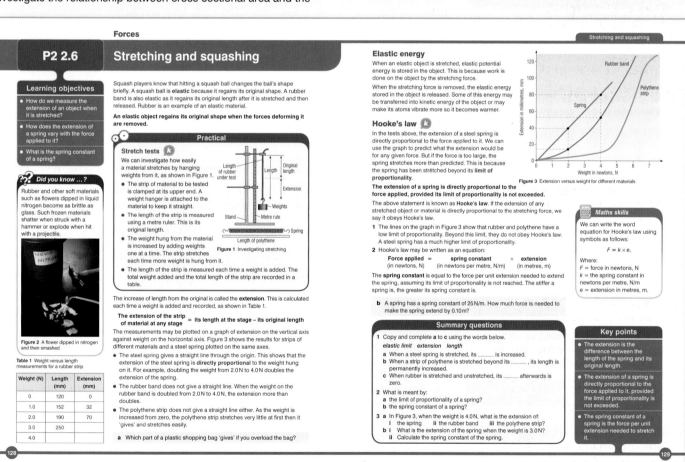

Summary answers

1 a length
  b elastic limit
  c extension

2 a The limit of proportionality of a spring is the point at which the extension is no longer directly proportional to the force applied when the spring is stretched.

  b The spring constant of a spring is the force per unit extension needed to stretch the spring, assuming its limit of proportionality is not exceeded.

3 a i 80 mm   ii 52 mm   iii 12 mm
  b i 60 mm   ii 0.05 N/mm

P2 2.7

Force and speed issues

AQA

Specification link-up: Physics P2.1

- The greater the speed of a vehicle the greater the braking force needed to stop it in a certain distance. [P2.1.3 b)]
- The stopping distance of a vehicle is the sum of the distance the vehicle travels during the driver's reaction time (thinking distance) and the distance it travels under the braking force (braking distance). [P2.1.3 c)]
- When the brakes of a vehicle are applied, work done by the friction force between the brakes and the wheel reduces the kinetic energy of the vehicle and the temperature of the brakes increase. [P2.1.3 e)]
- A vehicle's braking distance can be affected by adverse road and weather conditions and poor condition of the vehicle. [P2.1.3 f)]
- Evaluate the effects of alcohol and drugs on stopping distances. [P2.1]
- Evaluate how the shape and power of a vehicle can be altered to increase the vehicle's top speed. [P2.1]

Learning objectives

Students should learn:

- that fuel use can be reduced by a range of measures including reducing average speed
- that an average speed camera calculates the average speed of a vehicle using timing and distance information
- how to judge the effectiveness of anti-skid surfaces.

Learning outcomes

Most students should be able to:

- discuss a range of speed and travel-related issues linking their discussions to scientific knowledge and understanding.

Answers to in-text questions

a The engine force is greater than the air resistance.

b Students' discussion.

Lesson structure

Starters

The Tufty Club – Show a few road safety films, these can be current ones and a few historical examples (Green cross code, Clunk-click, Tufty, and so on). Discuss how some of these advertisements have changed over time to make them appeal to each new generation. Have they become too scary? *(5 minutes)*

Transport survey – The students survey themselves to try to find out the total number of kilometres they travel by foot, car, bus and so on during a week. To support students, you should provide a worksheet for this so that the calculations are relatively simple. You could also provide them with some example data to use instead. Students can be extended further by asking them to find the total distances travelled and even average distances per student per year. You can then discuss the results and see if the students are willing to make changes to their travel arrangements. *(10 minutes)*

Main

- This lesson is based around a range of speed-related issues and leads to discussions or debates between the students. You can choose to focus on one or two of the issues or go through them all. You can assign different discussion topics to different groups.

- Students could test different shapes of deflectors, including a V-shaped deflector with the 'V' horizontal then vertical, and a curved deflector with sloped sides. A curved deflector fitted to the lorry trailer is sometimes referred to as a 'nose cone' deflector. About half the fuel consumption of a fast-moving HGV is used to overcome air resistance. Friction and tyre resistance (referred to as 'rolling resistance') accounts for the other half. Average fuel usage for a lorry in the United Kingdom is about 3 litres per kilometre. A 20% reduction in the force of air resistance would therefore reduce fuel consumption by about 0.3 litres per kilometre. Measurements by transport engineers have shown that a wind deflector like the one shown in P2 2.7 could reduce fuel usage by about 0.3 litres per kilometre and a nose cone deflector could reduce fuel usage by about 0.5 litres per kilometre. Students could be asked to use the current price of diesel to work out the annual saving of a wind deflector on a lorry that travels 100 000 km per year – a very significant figure!

- If you are discussing speed limits and choose not to use the Starter, you can look at some safety footage during the lesson. With some extra time, you can actually record radio or even TV adverts.

- Speed cameras are meant to save lives but some people regard them as revenue sources. Discuss the statistics but include some recent revenue information to present the other side of the argument. You should be able to find recent data using the internet.

- The students can discuss anti-skid surfaces. They can request a new surface to be laid outside the school in a letter to the council. Any letter about anti-skid surfaces should contain the scientific arguments about how the material works and economic arguments about how it will save money in the long run. You might also want to discuss other traffic-calming measures such as speed bumps.

Support

- Provide some templates or fact sheets for all of the debates and discussions. Assign individual research roles to the students and give them time to prepare their arguments.

Extend

- Students could find out how much a human life is worth in monetary terms. Risk assessors look into various safety measures and decide if the cost is worth the benefit. Billions of pounds are spent on safety features every year; however, many billions more could be spent but are not because the benefits are not significant enough. It should be possible for the students to find out information about this idea and to see if all industries put the same value on a single life.

Plenaries

Safety signage – You could use a slideshow of the symbols drivers are meant to recognise and see how many of them the students know. An automatic slideshow can be set up showing the symbols for a few seconds each and you could see which student identifies the most. *(5 minutes)*

Positive solutions – The students have looked at a range of issues and now should make firm decisions on them. Set up a vote on any issue you have discussed. To support students, you may have to provide a range of options if the students have difficulty selecting items to vote on. To extend students further, you may want to ask them to produce more formal recommendations about what action to take instead of a simple yes or no vote. *(10 minutes)*

Did you know … ?

Columbus's journey took 43 days and so his effective velocity was around 6.7 km/h. This isn't fast, but he did not go in a straight line. The Apollo 11 crew travelled at an average speed of nearly 4000 km/h. Accelerating at $2\,m/s^2$ for a year is not very realistic and a huge amount of fuel would be required. As an alternative, a 'light sail' could give accelerations of $0.5\,mm/s^2$ which could get you to Pluto in around 5 years.

Forces

P2 2.7 — Force and speed issues

Learning objectives

● How can the fuel economy of road vehicles be improved?

● What is an average speed camera?

Speed costs

Reducing the speed of a vehicle reduces the fuel it uses. This is because air resistance at high speed is much greater than at low speed. So more fuel is used. Lorry drivers can reduce their fuel usage by fitting a wind deflector over the cab. The deflector reduces the air resistance on the lorry. This means that less engine force and less power are needed to maintain a certain speed. So fuel costs are reduced because less fuel is needed.

Figure 1 A wind deflector on a lorry

a When a vehicle is accelerating, what can you say about the engine force and the air resistance?

Activity

The shape of a wind deflector on a lorry affects air resistance. Investigate the effect of the deflector shape by testing a trolley with a box on (or a toy lorry) without a deflector then fitted with deflectors of different shapes. You could use a hairdryer to blow air at the 'lorry' and use a newtonmeter to measure the force needed to stop it being blown backwards. (See P2 3.1 Figure 2.)

Speed kills!

● At 20 mph, the stopping distance of a car is 12 metres.
● At 40 mph, the stopping distance is 36 metres.
● At 60 mph, the stopping distance is 72 metres.

If someone walks across a road in front of a car, a driver travelling slowly is much more likely to stop safely than a speeding driver. The force on a person struck by a car increases with speed. Even at 20 mph, it can be many times the person's weight. A speed limit of 20 mph is in place outside many schools now.

Speed cameras

Speed cameras are very effective in discouraging motorists from speeding. A speeding motorist caught by a speed camera is fined and can lose his or her driving licence. On some motorways.

● Speed limits can vary according to the amount of traffic on the motorway.
● Speed cameras may be linked. These can catch out motorists who slow down for a speed camera then speed up.

In some areas, residents are supplied with 'mobile' speed cameras to catch speeding motorists. Some motorists think this is going too far and that speed cameras should not be used in this way. Lots of motorists say speed cameras are being used by local councils to increase their income.

Are speed cameras effective?

A report from one police force said that where speed cameras had been introduced:

● average speeds fell by 17%
● deaths and serious injuries fell by 55%.

Did you know … ?

Epic journeys

Figure 2 On the Moon

1 Christopher Columbus and his three ships left the Canary Islands on the 8th of September 1492. He reached the Bahama Islands on the 12th of October after a 5500 km journey across the Atlantic Ocean.

2 In 1969, Neil Armstrong, Buzz Aldrin and Michael Collins were the first astronauts to land on the Moon. They spent 22 hours on the Moon. The 380 000 km journey to the Moon took four days.

3 If a space rocket accelerated for a year at $2\,m/s^2$ (about the same as a car starting from rest), the rocket would reach a speed of 60 000 km/s – about a fifth of the speed of light.

Another police force reported that, in their area, as a result of installing more speed cameras in 2003:

● There were no child deaths in road accidents for the first time since 1927.
● 420 fewer children were involved in road accidents compared with the previous year.

b Discuss whether or not the statements above prove the argument that speed cameras save lives.

Anti-skid surfaces

Have you noticed that road surfaces near road junctions and traffic lights are often different from normal road surfaces?

● The surface is rougher than normal. This gives increased friction between the surface and a vehicle tyre, so it reduces the chance of skidding when a driver in a car applies the brakes.
● The surface is lighter in colour so it is marked out clearly from a normal road surface.

Skidding happens when the brakes are applied too harshly. The wheels lock and the tyres slide on the road as a result. Increased friction between the tyres and the road allows more force to be applied without skidding happening, so the stopping distance is reduced.

Figure 3 A speed camera

Figure 4 An anti-skid surface

Summary questions

1 The legal limit for a driver with alcohol in the blood is 80 milligrams per litre. Above this level, reaction times become significantly longer. The thinking distance of a normal car driver (i.e. one with no alcohol in the blood) travelling at 30 mph is 9.0 m (30 feet).
  a **i** What would this distance be for a driver whose reaction time is 20% longer than that of a normal driver?
  ii Drivers at the legal limit are 80% more likely to be in a road accident than normal drivers. Researchers think that a reduction of the legal limit to 40 milligrams per litre would cut the risk from 80% to 20%. Discuss whether or not the present legal limit should be reduced.
  b The braking distance for a car at 30 mph is 13.5 m and 6.0 m at 20 mph.
  i Thinking distance is directly proportional to speed. Show that the thinking distance at 20 mph is 6.0 m.
  ii Calculate the reduction in the stopping distance.
  c Many parents want the speed limit outside schools to be reduced to 20 mph. Explain why this would reduce road accidents outside schools significantly.

2 Campaigners in the village of Greystoke want the council to resurface the main road at the traffic lights in the village. A child was killed crossing the road at the traffic lights earlier in the year. The council estimates it would cost £45 000. They say they can't afford it. Campaigners have found some more data to support their case.
  ● There are about 50 000 road accidents each year in the UK.
  ● The cost of road accidents is over £8 billion per year.
  ● Anti-skid surfaces have cut accidents by about 5%.
  a Estimate how much each road accident costs.
  b Imagine you are one of the campaigners. Write a letter to your local newspaper to challenge the council's response that they can't afford to resurface the road.

Key points

● Fuel economy of road vehicles can be improved by reducing the speed or fitting a wind deflector.

● Average speed cameras are linked in pairs and they measure the average speed of a vehicle.

● Anti-skid surfaces increase the friction between a car tyre and the road surface. This reduces skids, or even prevents skids altogether.

130 / 131

Summary answers

1 a i 10.8 m (= 9.0 m + 20% of 9.0 m)

ii The research evidence needs to be confirmed by other researchers. If confirmed, many people would argue for a reduction on the grounds that a risk that is 80% greater than 'normal' would be unacceptable in many other situations where the public are involved. In addition, if the limit were to be reduced, the number of other road casualties caused by drivers would be reduced.

b i Thinking distance = speed × reaction time. A reduction of speed from 30 mph to 20 mph would therefore reduce the normal thinking distance of 9 m at 30 mph by a third which is a reduction of 3.0 metres.

ii In addition to the 3.0 m reduction of thinking distance, the braking distance would be reduced by 7.5 m. Therefore the stopping distance would be reduced by 10.5 m (from 22.5 m to 12 metres).

c Anyone stepping in front of a car within its stopping distance would be hit by the car. So a reduction of more than 10 metres in the stopping distance would greatly reduce the number of road accidents to children and adults crossing a road or stepping into a road unexpectedly.

2 a £160 000

b Students' letters

Summary answers

1 a i in the opposite direction to

   ii in the same direction as

   b i Away from the door

   ii Away from the door

2 a i 1.6 N/kg

   ii 1000 N

   b i 8 m/s², 640 N

   ii −0.4 m/s², 28 000 N

3 a The acceleration of X is constant and equal to 10 m/s².

   b The object accelerates at first. The drag force on it increases with speed, so the resultant force on it and its acceleration decreases. When the drag force is equal to the weight of the object, the resultant force is zero. The acceleration is then zero, so the velocity is constant.

4 a decreasing

   b increasing

   c terminal

5 a i The braking distance is increased because friction between the tyres and the road is reduced by the driver, otherwise the car would skid. Therefore the stopping distance is increased.

   ii The reaction time is increased, so the distance travelled in this time (the thinking distance) is increased. Therefore the stopping distance is increased.

   b i 12.6 m

   ii 3.4 m

6 a 79, 121, 160, 201, 239

   b

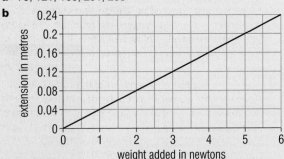

   c 280 mm

   d i 0.025 N/mm or 25 N/m

   ii 3.5 N

7 a i 225 N

   ii 450 N

   b The cyclist exerts a constant force driving her forward. Crouching reduces the force of air resistance (the drag force). The drag force increases with speed. So the cyclist can get to a higher speed before the drag force becomes equal to the driving force.

Summary questions

1 A student is pushing a box across a rough floor. Friction acts between the box and the floor.

   a Copy and complete sentences i and ii using the words below:

   in the same direction as   in the opposite direction to

   i The force of friction of the box on the floor is .... the force of friction of the floor on the box.

   ii The force of the student on the box is .... the force of friction of the box on the floor.

   b The student is pushing the box towards a door. Which direction, towards the door or away from the door, is:

   i the force of the box on the student?

   ii the force of friction of the student on the floor?

2 a The weight of an object of mass 100 kg on the Moon is 160 N.

   i Calculate the gravitational field strength on the Moon.

   ii Calculate the weight of the object on the Earth's surface.
   The gravitational field strength near the Earth's surface is 10 N/kg.

   b Calculate the acceleration and the resultant force in each of the following situations.

   i A sprinter of mass 80 kg accelerates from rest to a speed of 9.6 m/s in 1.2 s.

   ii A train of mass 70 000 kg decelerates from a velocity of 16 m/s to a standstill in 40 s without change of direction.

3 The figure shows the velocity–time graphs for a metal object X dropped in air and a similar object Y dropped in a tank of water.

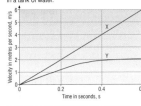

   a What does the graph for X tell you about its acceleration?

   b In terms of the forces acting on Y, explain why it reached a constant velocity.

4 Copy and complete a to c using the words below:
   decreasing   increasing   terminal

   a When the resultant force on an object is not zero and acts in the opposite direction to the object's velocity, its velocity is ....

   b When an object falls in a fluid and the drag force on it is less than its weight, its velocity is ....

   c When the drag force on an object falling in a fluid is equal to its weight, the object moves at its .... velocity.

5 a Explain why the stopping distance of a car is increased if:

   i the road is wet instead of dry

   ii the driver is tired instead of alert.

   b A driver travelling at 18 m/s takes 0.7 s to react when a dog walks into the road 40 m ahead. The braking distance for the car at this speed is 24 m.

   i Calculate the distance travelled by the car in the time it takes the driver to react.

   ii How far in front of the dog does the car stop?

6 In a Hooke's law test on a spring, the following results were obtained.

Weight (N)	Length (mm)	Extension (mm)
0	245	0
1.0	285	40
2.0	324	
3.0	366	
4.0	405	
5.0	446	
6.0	484	

   a Copy and complete the third column of the table.

   b Plot a graph of the extension on the vertical axis against the weight on the horizontal axis.

   c If a weight of 7.0 N is suspended on the spring, what would be the extension of the spring?

   d i Calculate the spring constant of the spring.

   ii An object suspended on the spring gives an extension of 140 mm. Calculate the weight of the object.

7 a A racing cyclist accelerates at 5 m/s² when she start from rest. The total mass of the cyclist and her bicy is 45 kg. Calculate:

   i the resultant force that produces this acceleratio

   ii the total weight of the cyclist and the bicycle.

   b Explain why she can reach a higher speed by crouching than by staying upright.

Kerboodle resources

Resources available for this chapter on Kerboodle are:

- Chapter map: Forces
- Support: Resultant forces (P2 2.2)
- Extension: Making sense of resultant forces (P2 2.2)
- Bump up your grade: What is the resultant force? (P2 2.2)
- Maths skills: Force, mass and acceleration (P2 2.3)
- Practical: Does the force on a trolley affect acceleration? (P2 2.3)
- WebQuest: Safe driving (P2 2.4 & 2.7)
- Extension: Finding the stopping distance of a vehicle (P2 2.4)
- How Science Works: Reaction time challenge (P2 2.4)
- Support: Stop that bike! (P2 2.4)
- Animation: Skydiver (P2 2.5)
- Support: Let's hope that chute opens! (P2 2.5)
- Extension: Weight and mass – planets apart! (P2 2.5)
- Practical: Terminal velocity of a ball in a liquid (P2 2.5)
- Data handling skills: Investigating Hooke's law using springs (P2 2.6)
- Support: Stretching your grades! (P2 2.6)
- Practical: Does a stretched spring obey Hooke's law? (P2 2.6)
- Interactive activity: Stopping distances and motive forces
- Revision podcast: Forces
- Test yourself: Forces
- On your marks: Forces
- Examination-style questions: Forces
- Answers to examination-style questions: Forces

AQA Examination-style questions

1 a The tractor is pulling a trailer. The force acting on the trailer is labelled A, and the force acting on the tractor is labelled B.

Copy and complete the following sentences using the list of words and phrases below. Each one can be used once, more than once or not at all.

A and B are the same   A is greater than B
B is greater than A

i If the tractor and trailer are accelerating .... (1)
ii If the tractor and trailer are moving at a constant speed .... (1)

b The driving force from the tractor is 12 000 N and the total resistive forces are 10 000 N.
i Calculate the resultant force. (1)
ii Calculate the acceleration of the tractor and trailer. Mass of the tractor and trailer = 2300 kg
Write down the equation you use. Show clearly how you work out your answer and give the unit. (3)

2 A car is travelling at 30 m/s when the vehicle in front suddenly stops. The car travels 19 m before the driver applies the brake.
a What is the name given to this distance? (1)
b Calculate the reaction time of the driver. Write down the equation you use. Show clearly how you work out your answer. (2)
c The driver applies the brakes and stops 6 seconds later. Calculate the deceleration of the car. Write down the equation you use. Show clearly how you work out your answer. (2)
d The braking distance is 81 m. What is the total stopping distance in metres? (1)
e Give two factors that would increase reaction time. (2)

3 The diagram shows the forces acting on a dragster just before it reaches its top speed. The resistive forces are represented by arrow **X**. The driving force is shown by arrow **Y**.

a What is the main type of resistive force acting on the dragster? (1)
b If the driving force remains the same, what will happen to force X?
Give a reason for your answer. (2)
c The dragster slows down by applying its brakes and using a parachute. The velocity–time graph shows the motion of the dragster from a stationary start until it stops.

Explain, in terms of energy changes, the shape of the graph when the brakes are applied. (3)

4 A student carries out an experiment to find if extension is proportional to the force applied for an elastic hair bobble. She measures the extension with one and then two 0.1 kg masses. She holds the bobble with one hand and the ruler in the other.

a If the extension is proportional to the force applied, what value should the student expect to obtain for distance X? (1)
b Give the name of the form of energy stored in the stretched hair bobble. (1)
c Calculate the weight of one of the 0.1 kg masses. (g = 10 N/kg) (2)
d *In this question you will be assessed on using good English, organising information clearly and using specialist terms where appropriate.*
The student is unable to draw a valid conclusion because she has not carried out the investigation with sufficient precision. Describe the improvements she could make in order to carry out the investigation more precisely and gain sufficient data to draw a valid conclusion. (6)

AQA Examination-style answers

1 a i If the tractor and trailer are accelerating **A is greater than B**. *(1 mark)*
ii If the tractor and trailer are moving at a constant speed **A and B are the same** *(1 mark)*

b i $12\,000 - 10\,000 = 2000\,N$ *(1 mark)*
ii $a = \dfrac{F}{m} = 2000/2300 = 0.87\,m/s^2$ *(3 marks)*

2 a Thinking distance *(1 mark)*
b time = distance/speed = 19/30 = 0.63 s *(2 marks)*
c $-5\,m/s^2$ *(2 marks)*
d 100 m *(1 mark)*
e Any two relevant factors, for example, consuming alcohol/drugs/medicine/fatigue/old age/illness *(2 marks)*

3 a Air resistance/drag *(1 mark)*
b Increase (until it equals the driving force); air resistance increases with speed *(2 marks)*
c Work done by friction force/friction between the brakes and the wheel;
reduces kinetic energy; temperature of brakes increases and the dragster slows to a stop *(3 marks)*

4 a 20 mm *(1 mark)*
b elastic potential energy *(1 mark)*
c $W = m \times g = 0.1 \times 10 = 1\,N$ *(2 marks)*
d Marks awarded for this answer will be determined by the Quality of Written Communication (QWC) as well as the standard of the scientific response.

There is a clear, balanced and detailed description of the improvements she could make in order to carry out the investigation more precisely and gain sufficient data to draw a valid conclusion. The answer shows almost faultless spelling, punctuation and grammar. It is coherent and in an organised, logical sequence. It contains a range of appropriate or relevant specialist terms used accurately. *(5–6 marks)*

There is a description of a range of the ways in which improvements could be made in order to carry out the investigation more precisely and gain sufficient data to draw a valid conclusion. There are some errors in spelling, punctuation and grammar. The answer has some structure and organisation. The use of specialist terms has been attempted, but not always accurately. *(3–4 marks)*

There is a brief description of at least two ways in which improvements could be made in order to carry out the investigation more precisely and gain sufficient data to draw a valid conclusion, which has little clarity and detail. The spelling, punctuation and grammar are very weak. The answer is poorly organised with almost no specialist terms and/or their use demonstrating a general lack of understanding of their meaning. *(1–2 marks)*

No relevant content. *(0 marks)*

Examples of physics points made in the response:
- use a boss/clamp/stand
- ruler in fixed position
- method to reduce parallax, e.g. use a set square
- repeats measurements
- use a larger range of masses
- and smaller intervals.

AQA Practical suggestions

Practicals	AQA	k	📖	⚙️
Dropping a penny and a feather in a vacuum and through the air to show the effect of air resistance.	✓		✓	
Plan and carry out an investigation into 'Hooke's law'.	✓	✓	✓	
Catapult practicals to compare stored energy.	✓		✓	
Measurement of acceleration of trolleys using known forces and masses.	✓	✓	✓	✓
Timing objects falling through a liquid, e.g. wallpaper paste or glycerine, using light gates or stop clocks.	✓	✓		
Plan and carry out an investigation to measure the effects of air resistance on parachutes, paper spinners, cones or bun cases.	✓		✓	
Measuring reaction time with and without distractions, e.g. iPod 'off' and then 'on'.	✓	✓	✓	✓

P2 3.1

Energy and work

AQA
Specification link-up: Physics P2.2

Learning objectives

Students should learn:

- that the term 'work' means the amount of energy transferred to an object
- that when a force is used to move an object, work is done against friction and this is transferred as heat.

- When a force causes an object to move through a distance work is done. *[P2.2.1 a)]*
- Work done, force and distance are related by the equation:
  $W = F \times d$. *[P2.2.1 b)]*
- Energy is transferred when work is done. *[P2.2.1 c)]*
- Work done against frictional forces. *[P2.2.1 d)]*

Controlled Assessment: P4.3 Collect primary and secondary data. *[P4.3.2 c) d) e)]*

Learning outcomes

Most students should be able to:

- state that the 'work done' is the amount of energy transferred
- calculate the work done when a force moves an object through a distance.

Some students should also be able to:

- perform calculations including the rearrangement of the work done equation.

Lesson structure

Starters

Hard at work – Give the students a list of activities involving the use of forces and ask them to put them in order of the amount of energy transferred. They should identify that the energy transferred depends on the size of the force used and the distance moved. A simple example would be pushing a block across a desk by 1 m and then 2 m, followed by pushing a much larger block 1 m and then 3 m. *(5 minutes)*

Energy transfer – The students should draw energy transfer diagrams for a range of machines and identify useful energy output. They should reinforce the ideas of describing energy and energy transfer including concepts such as the conservation of energy and amounts of energy wasted through this process. To support students, you can provide partially completed diagrams and word lists of the 'forms' of energy, so that they are using the correct terms. To extend the students, concepts such as efficiency can be revised so that the students can calculate the amounts of wasted energy. *(10 minutes)*

Main

- The term 'work done' has a very particular meaning in physics and the students will have to accept that it does not mean the same as its everyday usage. Two main types of work can be done: work done against a force (as covered in this topic) and work done in heating. The examples when people are holding up a heavy object (but are doing no mechanical work) should be discussed in terms of energy being transferred to heat by the muscles.

- The calculation is relatively straightforward, but check that the students are confident with it and that they remember to use the correct units. Try a few examples with large or small transfers to reinforce the use of kilojoules (or megajoules).

- In the main practical activity, the students should quickly realise the limitations of data collected; it is not easy to measure the amount of useful work done and very difficult to even estimate how much energy is being wasted. If the meter is not horizontal, then the force also acts at an angle to the movement. This gives the opportunity to teach students the 'How Science Works' concepts of resolution, precision and accuracy.

- The heating effect due to friction should be demonstrated in some way, even if it is simple hand rubbing. You may be able to find footage of Formula One cars braking, where the brake discs literally glow red-hot. This can lead to a discussion about how frictional forces can be reduced.

Answers to in-text questions

a Energy transferred to the surroundings by heating and as sound.

b 80 000 J

c Friction between the box and the surface is greater with the rubber bands in place. More force is needed to overcome the frictional force.

Support

- Before you start the topic, refresh the students' knowledge by providing a partially completed mind map that they can complete. This should cover the key points they would have learned in the earlier topic.

Plenaries

All work – Give the students some scenarios and let them decide if mechanical work is being done. They must explain why work is being done or not. Include scenarios where there is no movement (pushing against a brick wall) and ones where there is movement (pushing a car). Discuss the idea that energy might be being transferred but as there is no movement, there is no effective work done. Is writing in a book doing work? *(5 minutes)*

Demonstrating friction – The students design their own demonstration to show that doing work against friction has a heating effect. This should be aimed at primary school children so should only involve equipment readily available to them. Support can be provided by giving the students some suggested materials and diagrams while extension opportunities can include asking the students to show that it is possible to start a fire with sufficient frictional forces. *(10 minutes)*

Extend

- You could extend students by asking them to look into the more formal definition of work done. This is 'that the work done is equal to the force required multiplied by the distance travelled **in the direction** of the force'. This can lead to analysis of an object moving up slopes, where the direction travelled and direction of the force are not the same.

Practical support

Doing work

In this task, the students measure the work done in moving an object across a surface.

Equipment and materials required

Range of Newton meters, box or metal block that can be dragged, string, metre rule and some elastic bands.

Details

The task is straightforward; the students simply drag the box with or without elastic bands. A measured distance of a metre is the simplest, and provides an easy calculation. The bands will increase the frictional forces so more work will be done. The quality of the

results will depend on the students moving the object at a steady speed, so that a constant force is used. Check that they can easily read the newtonmeters during the experiment. This experiment should reveal the value of repeat measurements. Remind students that precision can be judged by the range in a set of repeat measurements and that resolution is the smallest detectable change that can be measured by a particular instrument.

The work can be extended by moving an object up slopes; this will link to gravitational potential energy in later lessons.

You might like to link to power, getting the students to measure the time it takes to do the task and sort out the power output, using the equation power = work done divided by time. If the students move the object faster, does the force change?

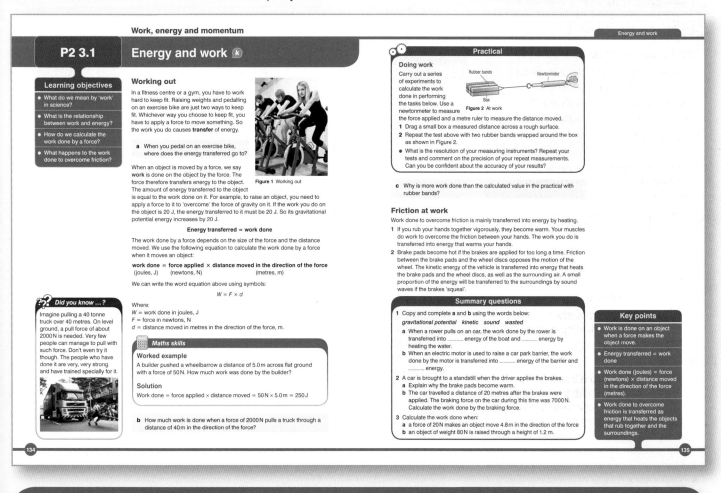

Work, energy and momentum

P2 3.1

Energy and work (k)

Learning objectives

- What do we mean by 'work' in science?
- What is the relationship between work and energy?
- How do we calculate the work done by a force?
- What happens to the work done to overcome friction?

Working out

In a fitness centre or a gym, you have to work hard to keep fit. Raising weights and pedalling on an exercise bike are just two ways to keep fit. Whichever way you choose to keep fit, you have to apply a force to move something. So the work you do causes **transfer** of energy.

a When you pedal on an exercise bike, where does the energy transferred go to?

When an object is moved by a force, we say **work** is done on the object by the force. The force therefore transfers energy to the object. The amount of energy transferred to the object is equal to the work done on it. For example, to raise an object, you need to apply a force to it to 'overcome' the force of gravity on it. If the work you do on the object is 20 J, the energy transferred to it must be 20 J. So its gravitational potential energy increases by 20 J.

Figure 1 Working out

Energy transferred = work done

The work done by a force depends on the size of the force and the distance moved. We use the following equation to calculate the work done by a force when it moves an object:

work done = force applied × distance moved in the direction of the force
(joules, J)   (newtons, N)   (metres, m)

We can write the word equation above using symbols:

$$W = F \times d$$

Where:
W = work done in joules, J
F = force in newtons, N
d = distance moved in metres in the direction of the force, m.

Did you know ...?

Imagine pulling a 40 tonne truck over 40 metres. On level ground, a pull force of about 2000 N is needed. Very few people can manage to pull with such force. Don't even try it though. The people who have done it are very, very strong and have trained specially for it.

Maths skills

Worked example

A builder pushed a wheelbarrow a distance of 5.0 m across flat ground with a force of 50 N. How much work was done by the builder?

Solution

Work done = force applied × distance moved = 50 N × 5.0 m = 250 J

b How much work is done when a force of 2000 N pulls a truck through a distance of 40 m in the direction of the force?

Practical

Doing work

Carry out a series of experiments to calculate the work done in performing the tasks below. Use a newtonmeter to measure the force applied and a metre ruler to measure the distance moved.

Figure 2 At work

1 Drag a small box a measured distance across a rough surface.
2 Repeat the test above with two rubber bands wrapped around the box as shown in Figure 2.
● What is the resolution of your measuring instruments? Repeat your tests and comment on the precision of your repeat measurements. Can you be confident about the accuracy of your results?

c Why is more work done than the calculated value in the practical with rubber bands?

Friction at work

Work done to overcome friction is mainly transferred into energy by heating.

1 If you rub your hands together vigorously, they become warm. Your muscles do work to overcome the friction between your hands. The work you do is transferred into energy that warms your hands.
2 Brake pads become hot if the brakes are applied for too long a time. Friction between the brake pads and the wheel discs opposes the motion of the wheel. The kinetic energy of the vehicle is transferred into energy that heats the brake pads and the wheel discs, as well as the surrounding air. A small proportion of the energy will be transferred to the surroundings by sound waves if the brakes 'squeal'.

Summary questions

1 Copy and complete **a** and **b** using the words below:
  gravitational potential   kinetic   sound   wasted
  a When a rower pulls on an oar, the work done by the rower is transferred into .... energy of the boat and .... energy by heating the water.
  b When an electric motor is used to raise a car park barrier, the work done by the motor is transferred into .... energy of the barrier and .... energy.
2 A car is brought to a standstill when the driver applies the brakes.
  a Explain why the brake pads become warm.
  b The car travelled a distance of 20 metres after the brakes were applied. The braking force on the car during this time was 7000 N. Calculate the work done by the braking force.
3 Calculate the work done when:
  a a force of 20 N makes an object move 4.8 m in the direction of the force
  b an object of weight 80 N is raised through a height of 1.2 m.

Key points

- Work is done on an object when a force makes the object move.
- Energy transferred = work done
- Work done (joules) = force (newtons) × distance moved in the direction of the force (metres).
- Work done to overcome friction is transferred as energy that heats the objects that rub together and the surroundings.

134   135

Further teaching suggestions

Work done against friction

- To show that the work done against frictional force causes heating. You can use a bicycle.

Equipment and materials required

A bicycle that will stand upside down, gloves.

Details

Turn the bicycle upside down and get the wheel spinning by turning the pedal by hand. Don't go too fast because you now need to stop the wheel by slowing it down with the palm of your gloved hand against the tyre. Once you

know the right speed to cause a noticeable heating effect but no hand damage, you can get a volunteer to have a go. As an alternative, you could lift the rear wheel and drive it very quickly before applying the brakes gently. Repeat this until the smell of burning rubber is obvious.

Spy plane

- The frictional forces on rapidly moving objects are very high. The SR-71 'Blackbird' spy plane used to leak quite a bit of fuel when on the ground, but when it was at full speed it became hotter and the metal expanded and sealed up the gaps. Ask: 'What colour was the plane and why?'

Summary answers

1 a kinetic, wasted   **b** gravitational potential, sound

2 a Friction between the brake pads and the wheel discs make the pads and the discs hot because they slide against each other until the car stops.
   b 140 000 J

3 a 96 J
   b 96 J

P2 3.2

Gravitational potential energy

Learning objectives

Students should learn:

- that the gravitational potential energy of an object depends on its weight and height
- how to calculate gravitational potential energy from the appropriate equation.

Learning outcomes

Most students should be able to:

- state that the gravitational potential energy of an object depends on its weight and height above 'ground'
- calculate changes in gravitational potential energy.

Some students should also be able to:

- perform calculations including the rearrangement of the gravitational potential energy equation.

AQA Specification link-up: Physics P2.2

- Power is the work done or energy transferred in a given time.

  $P = \dfrac{E}{t}$ [P2.2.1 e)]

- Gravitational potential energy is the energy that an object has by virtue of its position in a gravitational field.

  $E_p = m \times g \times h$ [P2.2.1 f)]

Lesson structure

Starters

Lifting work – Remind the students of the idea of work being done by a force when an object moves a distance. Demonstrate lifting things from the floor to a desk and ask them to explain where the energy 'used' has gone. Some should realise that the objects have gained gravitational potential energy. Now ask them to explain what factors affect the amount of energy; they should be able to identify the height and weight. You can move on to ask about what affects the weight (mass and the strength of gravity). *(5 minutes)*

Power recap – The students have studied power in the first section of the course (P1 3.2) and will need to use the equation again here. Ask them to define or explain what power is and then calculate the power of some simple mechanical systems. Students can be supported by calculation frames and the use of straightforward questions while others can be pushed further by asking questions that require rearrangement of the equations and the use of more 'difficult' numbers (kilojoules, megajoules, etc.). *(10 minutes)*

Main

- Start with some form of demonstration of lifting either by you or a video clip of something extraordinary being lifted. This should lead to the idea that energy is required to move the object and link this concept back to the equation for work done from the last lesson. In lifting, work is being done because a force is being used to move an object through a distance. You can identify the distance the object is lifted and then ask about the force that was required. It should be clear that the force is actually the weight of the object. In this way you can lead the students to discover the equation itself using the idea of conservation of energy: the energy you use to lift the object is stored in the object.

- You can now talk about the object moving through heights and the changes in energy that are occurring. Use props, for example, have a set of 1 kg masses (weighing 10 N each), move them up and down to different heights and get the students to explain how much energy is being transferred. Move two or three masses at a time until the simple calculation comes naturally.

- Introduce the symbol E_p (for gravitational potential energy) as quickly as you can, so the students start using it and save time. Let them try a couple of calculations with more difficult numbers to get used to it.

- You can now move on to the second form of the equation (where weight is replaced with mass × gravitational field strength). The idea is just that the weight of an object is the product of the mass and gravitational field strength, so you can replace weight to give this new equation but some students can struggle with this simple substitution. It is worth spending some time with the units here as there are four of them to get to grips with.

- After the maths, the practical task is short but it will give the students something physical to do. You can get some to walk up a flight of stairs if no boxes are suitable.

Support

- There are a couple of calculations in this topic that students might need extra support with. As usual, plenty of examples and templates showing how to lay out the calculations would be of great benefit.

Extend

- Students should consider why we measure changes in gravitational potential energy instead of amounts of gravitational potential energy. This is because of the difficulty in defining a place where the gravitational potential energy would be zero. For most purposes we would consider the ground level to have no gravitational potential but what about when objects fall down mines? The students could look into where the place at which an object would have zero gravitational potential energy actually is.

Plenaries

How high – Finish with a calculation that looks at something big that travels quite high. A jumbo jet is about 400 000 kg with a cruising altitude of 10 700 m. The E_p is 41 986 800 000 J (~42 GJ). All students should be capable of handling larger numbers although they may need support as this figure is larger than most calculators can display in 'normal' notation. *(5 minutes)*

A hard day – The students can estimate the energy they expend by climbing stairs when moving between lessons during a typical day by estimating the height changes and their weight. They can work out how much energy they would need if they were to climb to the top of a tall tower (Burj Khalifa in the United Arab Emirates is 800 m). To support students, provide some suitable estimates of the numbers; they may have a mass of 50 kg giving an approximate weight of 500 N and travel upwards through 15 m each day. This gives a total work done of 7.5 kJ. To extend students, have them consider walking; when a step is taken the centre of gravity of your body rises slightly (you may be able to find a video clip demonstrating this). This means that work is being done during each step. Ask them to estimate the energy transfer for a day. If needed, provide some suitable estimates such as: if they take 5000 steps each day (while their centre of gravity is raised by 5 cm) each step and the person weighs 600 N, this would be 150 kJ. *(10 minutes)*

Practical support

Stepping up

Any tasks preformed should be relatively simple and non-strenuous. Make sure that the students have no medical conditions that could be triggered by the activities.

Equipment and materials required

Scales that measure weight in newtons, objects to step on to. The objects should be robust enough to pose no significant hazards; you might just want to use steps or your PE department may still have a few benches that are appropriate.

Details

The practical should only take a few minutes. Some students may be sensitive about their weight but you could ask them to move objects onto shelves or up some stairs as an alternative task.

Work, energy and momentum

P2 3.2 — Gravitational potential energy

Learning objectives

- What does the gravitational potential energy of an object depend on?
- What happens to the gravitational potential energy of an object when it moves up or down?
- How can we calculate the change of gravitational potential energy of an object when it moves up or down?

Gravitational potential energy transfers

Every time you lift an object up, you do some work. Some of your muscles transfer chemical energy from your muscles into **gravitational potential energy** of the object.

Gravitational potential energy is energy stored in an object because of its position in the Earth's gravitational field.

The force you need to lift an object steadily is equal and opposite to the force of gravity on the object. Therefore, the upward force you need to apply to it is equal to its weight. For example, a force of 80 N is needed to lift a box of weight 80 N.

Figure 1 Using joules

- When an object is moved up, its gravitational potential energy increases. The increase of its gravitational potential energy is equal to the work done by the lifting force.
- When an object moves down, its gravitational potential energy decreases. The decrease of its gravitational potential energy is equal to the work done by the force of gravity acting on it.

The work done when an object moves up or down depends on:
1 how far it is moved vertically (its change of height)
2 its weight.

Using the formula $W = F \times d$ (work done = force applied × distance moved in the direction of the force), we can therefore say:

the change of its gravitational potential energy (in joules) = its weight (in newtons) × its change of height (in metres)

a Read the 'Did you know?' box. What happens to the energy supplied to the muscles to keep them contracted?

Gravitational potential energy and mass

Astronauts on the Moon can lift objects much more easily than they can on the Earth. This is because, at their surfaces, the gravitational field strength of the Moon is only about a sixth of the Earth's gravitational field strength.

In P2 2.5, 'Falling objects', we saw that the weight of an object in newtons is equal to its mass × the gravitational field strength.

Therefore, when an object is lifted or lowered, because its change of gravitational potential energy is equal to its weight × its change of height:

change of gravitational potential energy (in J) = mass (in kg) × gravitational field strength (in N/kg) × change of height (in metres)

Maths skills

Worked example

A student of weight 300 N climbs on a platform which is 1.2 m higher than the floor. Calculate the increase of her gravitational potential energy.

Solution

Increase of GPE = 300 N × 1.2 m
= 360 J

Note: We often use the abbreviation 'GPE' or E_p for gravitational potential energy.

Did you know ...?

You use energy when you hold an object stationary in your outstretched hand. The biceps muscle of your arm is in a state of contraction. Energy must be supplied to keep the muscles contracted. No work is done on the object because it doesn't move. The energy supplied heats the muscles and is transferred by heating to the surroundings.

We can write the word equation on the previous page using symbols:
$$E_p = m \times g \times h$$
Where:
E_p = change of GPE in joules, J
m = mass in kilograms, kg
g = gravitational field strength in newtons per kilogram, N/kg
h = change in height in metres, m.

Maths skills

Worked example

A 2.0 kg object is raised through a height of 0.4 m. Calculate the gain of gravitational potential energy of the object. The gravitational field strength of the Earth at its surface is 10 N/kg.

Solution

Gain of GPE = mass × gravitational field strength × height gain
= 2.0 kg × 10 N/kg × 0.4 m
= 8.0 J

Power and energy

Power is the rate of transfer of energy. If energy E (in joules) is transferred in time t (in seconds):

$$\text{power, } P \text{ (in watts)} = \frac{E}{t}$$

b A weightlifter raises a 20 kg metal bar through a height of 1.5 m.
 i Calculate the gain of gravitational potential energy. The gravitational field strength of the Earth at its surface is 10 N/kg.
 ii The bar is raised by the weightlifter in 0.5 seconds. Calculate the power of the weightlifter.

Summary questions

1 Copy and complete **a** to **c** using the words below. Each word can be used more than once.

decreases   increases   stays the same

 a When a ball falls, its gravitational potential energy ....
 b When a car travels along a level road, the gravitational potential energy of the car ....
 c When a child on a swing moves from one extreme to the opposite extreme, her gravitational potential energy .... then ....

2 A student of weight 450 N steps on a box of height 0.20 m.
 a Calculate the gain of gravitational potential energy of the student.
 b Calculate the work done by the student if she steps on and off the box 50 times.

3 a A weightlifter raises a steel bar of mass 25 kg through a height of 1.2 m. Calculate the change of gravitational potential energy of the bar. The gravitational field strength at the surface of the Earth is 10 N/kg.
 b The weightlifter then drops the bar and it falls vertically to the ground. Assume air resistance is negligible. What is the change of its gravitational potential energy in this fall?

Activity

Stepping up

Measure your mass in kilograms using floor scales.

Step on and off a sturdy box or low platform.

Measure the height of the box.

- Use the formula change of GPE = $m \times g \times h$ where g = 10 N/kg to calculate how much potential energy you gained when you stepped on the box.

Key points

- The gravitational potential energy of an object depends on its weight and how far it moves vertically.
- The gravitational potential energy of an object increases when the object goes up and decreases when the object goes down.
- The change of gravitational potential energy of an object is equal to its mass × the gravitational field strength × its change of height.

136   137

Further teaching suggestions

- These are important calculations and homework should be used to reinforce the work done in the lesson.

Answers to in-text questions

a It heats the muscles then is transferred by heating directly (or indirectly via the blood system) from the muscles to the surroundings.

b i 300 J ii 600 W

Summary answers

1 a decreases
 b stays the same
 c decreases, increases

2 a 90 J
 b 4500 J

3 a an increase of 300 J
 b a decrease of 300 J

P2 3.3 Kinetic energy

Learning objectives

Students should learn:

- that kinetic energy is the energy a moving object has
- that the kinetic energy of an object increases when the object is travelling faster or is more massive
- how to calculate the kinetic energy of a moving object
- that elastic potential energy is energy stored in an object when work is done to change the shape of the object.

Learning outcomes

Most students should be able to:

- explain how the kinetic energy of an object depends on the speed and mass of the object
- perform calculations using the kinetic energy equation
- describe situations where elastic potential energy is stored.

Some students should also be able to:

- perform calculations using the kinetic energy equation including those that involve rearrangement of the equation.

Support

- This is the most difficult calculation the students will attempt in the course. Take extra care with the equation going through each stage in a very formal way. Even if the students don't fully understand the maths, a methodical technique will always lead them to the correct answer.

Extend

- Challenge students to build their own elastic-powered vehicles and hold a competition on whose can go the furthest. The vehicles should all have identical elastic bands and could be cars, boats or aeroplanes. The results can lead to a discussion about which of the modes of transport is the most efficient. You might want to consider transfers involving kinetic energy and E_p; these can be quite demanding.

AQA Specification link-up: Physics P2.2

- A force applied to an elastic object such as a spring will result in the object stretching and storing elastic potential energy. *[P2.1.5b)]*
- For an object that is able to recover its original shape, elastic potential energy is stored in the object when work is done on the object to change its shape. *[P2.1.5c)]*
- The kinetic energy of an object depends on its mass and its speed:
  $E_k = \frac{1}{2} \times m \times v^2$ *[P2.2.1 g)]*
- Evaluate the benefits of different types of braking system, such as regenerative braking. *[P2.2]*

  Controlled Assessment: P4.3 Collect primary and secondary data. *[P4.3.2 c) d) e)]*; P4.5 Analyse and interpret primary and secondary data. *[P4.5.3 a)]*

Lesson structure

Starters

Mass and velocity – Using mini-whiteboards, the students must give accurate definitions of mass and velocity. Ask: 'What are the units of each?' make sure that the students are comfortable with kilograms (show them one) and metres per second (walk at 1 m/s). In addition, check the way they are writing the units; are they using m/s or m s^{-1}? *(5 minutes)*

Kinetic cards – Give the students a set of cards with pictures of various moving objects. Each card shows the mass and the velocity; the students have to put them into order from least kinetic energy to most. Possible cards include a marble (0.01 kg, 5 m/s), tennis ball (0.2 kg, 25 m/s), bullet (0.02 kg, 200 m/s), car (750 kg, 20 m/s), and train (100 000 kg, 15 m/s). Support the students by identifying the factors that affect kinetic energy beforehand through discussion. Extend students by showing them the kinetic energy of an object of mass 10 kg moving at 2 m/s and then the effect of doubling the mass and then the velocity. Can they identify which factors are most significant? *(10 minutes)*

Main

- The students should remember that moving objects have energy and this is called 'kinetic energy'. Some will still be using the term 'movement energy', but it is time to leave this behind and get them to use the correct term as 'movement energy' will not be credited on the exam. Be tough on this point as it's an easy way to lose a mark even though the student understands the ideas involved.
- The 'Investigating kinetic energy' 'Practical support' works well with light gates. If you don't have them, then the modified version is a reasonable alternative. There are a few sources of error in the results and this would be a good opportunity to look into the nature of taking measurements ('How Science Works') and how repeating readings can improve the quality of the data. You could have a set of results in a spreadsheet table so that you can show the relationship graphically, or let the students enter data as they go along. (This relates to 'How Science Works': relationships between variables.)
- Clearly, many students will not come up with the relationship themselves, although most will see that the relationship is not a simple linear one. It is more important to show that the data fits a pattern that we already know.
- Some of the students will have a problem with the '$\{\frac{1}{2}\}$' in the kinetic energy equation and ask you: 'half of what?' This is tricky to explain without going into the derivation, so tell the students that they will find out if they go on to study A-level physics. The kinetic energy equation is the most difficult equation that students need to rearrange, and you should lead them through this carefully.
- The elastic potential energy ideas are a bit simpler, but the students will need to be able to give a reasonable definition like the one in the Student Book. This should be easier when linked back to the lesson on stretching (P2 2.6 'Stretching and squashing'). Making elastic band toys is a good endpoint and shows another important energy transfer. The models can also be tested by applying concepts from 'How Science Works' in another lesson.

Plenaries

Higher/lower – Go through a series of objects with different masses and velocities and ask the students to say (or calculate) if the kinetic energy is higher or lower than the previous one. You can use some of the values from the Starter activity or throw in some gravitational potential energy calculations too. *(5 minutes)*

Kinetic cards revisited – Try the same activity as in the Starter, but the students now have to calculate the energy to check their order. Use this task to make sure that the students are treating the calculations correctly. To support the students' calculation, frames can be provided for some of the cards. To extend, you can provide some additional cards that show the mass and kinetic energy and request that the students find the velocity. *(10 minutes)*

Answers to in-text questions

a The impact area of the foot becomes hot due to the impact and the rest of the foot and the shoe therefore gains energy due to heating.

b The missing speed values are 1.39 and 1.75 m/s. For each column, the square of each speed value divided by the height drop is the same. This shows that the speed squared is directly proportional to the height drop.

Practical support

Investigating kinetic energy

This experiment can be demonstrated with a ball and motion sensor or with a dynamics trolley and light gates.

Equipment and materials required (ball)

A ramp (or drainpipe), tennis ball, velocity or distance sensor, balance to measure mass of object.

Details

If you don't have a velocity sensor, then the software may be able to convert the distance measurements into speed measurements. Some velocity sensors have two parts; one of which needs to be mounted on the moving object. Clearly a ball won't do, so a trolley can be used.

Equipment and materials required (trolley)

Long ramp, dynamics trolley, card of known length, light gate, balance to measure mass of object.

Details

Mount the card on the trolley so that it interrupts the light gate when it passes through. Position the trolley at various measured heights on the track so that it rolls down the track and its speed is measured at the bottom. The ramp works well at an angle of around 30°.

Alternative equipment

It is possible to measure the speed of the object by letting it pass through a measured distance and timing it with a stopwatch. For this, you will need to ensure that the object isn't travelling very fast, so shallow launch angles will be needed.

Safety: Protect bench and feet from falling trolleys.

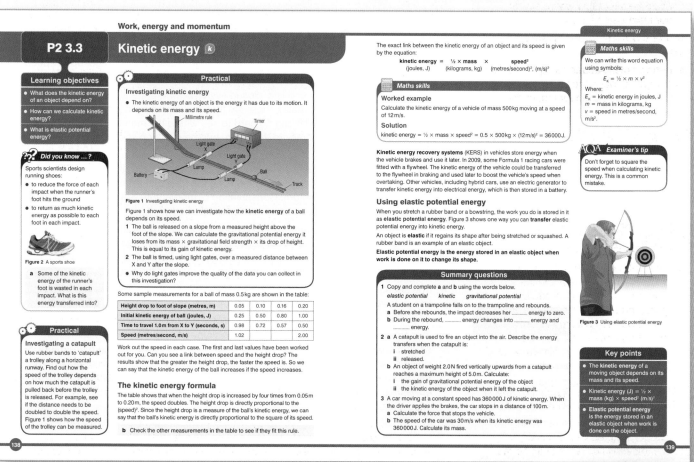

Summary answers

1 a kinetic

b elastic potential, kinetic, gravitational potential

2 a i Chemical energy in the muscles is transferred into elastic energy of the bow and energy due to heating in the muscles.

ii Elastic potential energy of the bow is transferred into kinetic energy and gravitational potential energy of the arrow.

b i 10 J **ii** 10 J

3 a 3600 N **b** 800 kg

P2 3.4

Momentum

Learning objectives

Students should learn:

- that the momentum of an object is the product of the mass and velocity of the object
- that the unit of momentum is the kilogram metre/second (kg m/s)
- that momentum is conserved in any collision provided no external forces act on the colliding objects.

Learning outcomes

Most students should be able to:

- calculate the momentum of an object of known mass and velocity
- state that momentum is conserved in any collision in a closed system (one where no external forces act on the colliding bodies).

Some students should also be able to:

- apply and rearrange the appropriate equations to two bodies that collide in a straight line.

Answers to in-text questions

a 240 kg m/s
b 0.48 m/s

Support

- Students might have difficulty remembering the mass of an object is not the same as the weight. Use props to remind the students of the difference; the mass is the amount of matter in the object.

Extend

- Who came up with the ideas about forces and momentum? What is inertia? The students can look up and explain Newton's laws of motion. Ask why conservation of momentum is considered a very important part of physics.

AQA Specification link-up: Physics P2.2

- Momentum is a property of moving objects
  $p = m \times v$ [P2.2.2 a)]
- In a closed system, the total momentum before an event is equal to the total momentum after the event. This is called conservation of momentum. [P2.2.2 b)]

Lesson structure

Starters

Trying to stop – The students should explain why it takes an oil tanker several kilometres to stop, but a bicycle can stop in only a few metres. You can point out that they may be travelling at the same speed and this will lead to the conclusion that it is something to do with the mass (size). Discuss if this is always the case; larger objects are more difficult to stop. *(5 minutes)*

Stopping power – Give the students a set of cards with various sports balls on them. Ask the students to put them in order of difficulty to stop, and then explain what properties make the balls more difficult. They should be able to links the 'stopability' to the speed and mass of the balls. To make the activity more stimulating borrow a real set of balls so that the students can compare them. They should realise that even though a table tennis ball can travel as fast as a cricket ball, it isn't going to be as hard to stop. *(10 minutes)*

Main

- It is best to begin with a discussion about trying to stop something moving or start something off. Trains are a good example of something with a large mass that can travel quickly. The students can find out how long it takes a train to get up to speed and how long it takes it to stop, even in an emergency.

- The students are looking at basic 'closed systems' where there are no external forces applied to the objects. In reality, there are frictional forces acting, so the situation can be more complicated and it can be hard to see where the momentum 'goes' when the objects stop. This is generally to the Earth, but the effect on such a large object is not noticeable.

- The demonstration will take a little time to explain, but should give good results. Any discrepancies should be accounted for using the idea that external forces (frictional) have changed the momentum. Conservation of momentum is a **fundamental** concept in physics; just as important as conservation of energy.

- You could talk about the famous 'everybody in China jumping at the same time' idea. It is a scientific myth that this would cause an earthquake or even change the orbit of the Earth. This would actually have no real effect on the Earth at all as the mass of all of the people combined is tiny when compared to the mass of the Earth.

- The shunting effect can be demonstrated by a Newton's cradle. This can be improvised from a set of ping-pong balls on wire, or similar, if a real one is not available. You could always resort to a video clip if you can't get one to work.

- The calculation is a multi-stage one and this type of calculation often confuses students. Make sure students have plenty of practice calculating the momentum of objects before they try to work out velocities after collisions. To extend students, you can look at collisions where both of the trolleys are moving before the collision or collisions where the trolleys 'bounce off' and end up travelling in opposite directions.

Plenaries

The skate escape – Two people are trapped on a **perfectly** friction-free circular surface just out of reach of each other. They are both 10 m from the edge and all that they have to help them escape is a tennis ball. Ask: 'How do they both escape?' [All they need to do is throw something from one to the other, this will give them momentum in opposite directions and they will slowly drift to the sides. If they repeatedly throw the ball to each other they will speed up.] *(5 minutes)*

Impossibly super – In several films, superheroes stop cars or trains by standing in front of them and letting them crash into them. The cars stop dead and the costumed hero doesn't move an inch. Ask: 'What's wrong with the science here?' The students should come up with an explanation using the conservation of momentum. Students can be supported by watching the clip; pause it before the collision and ask them what is going to happen and to compare it with what would happen in reality. Extend students by having them perform a calculation of the collision. They should note that a superhero of mass 100 kg attempting to stop a train of mass 100 000 kg travelling at 50 m/s will have very little effect. They can then consider what forces would do to the system (do they think that the friction of the feet on the ground would make any significant difference?) *(10 minutes)*

Practical support

Investigating collisions

This activity can be carried out with dynamics trolleys or a linear air track. Two light gates are required.

Equipment and materials required
Two or three dynamics trolleys or gliders on a linear air track, card of known length, two light gates.

Details
Mount the card on the first trolley so that it passes through a light gate before the collision. The trolleys can be made to stick together using velcro or a pin and bit of cork. After the collision, they should pass through the second light gate to measure the new velocity. Keep the light gates close to the collision point, so that the trolleys do not slow down too much. If the trolleys have the same mass then the velocity should simply halve after the collision. If frictional forces are affecting the result, it is possible to tilt the track slightly, so that the frictional force is balanced by a small component of the weight of the trolleys. It is important to try this if a detailed investigation is taking place.

Safety: Protect feet and bench from falling trolleys.

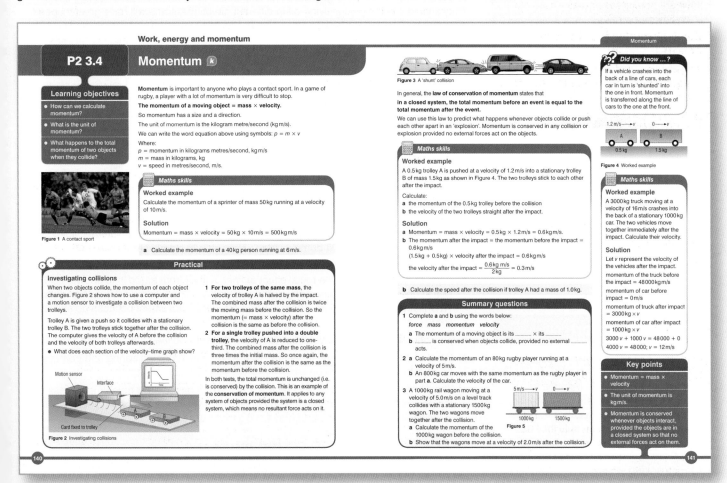

Further teaching suggestions

ICT link-up
● Detailed models are available to simulate these collisions. These can be used as a demonstration for individual student use. Snooker or pool games can also be used. There are several commercial and free simulations available ranging widely in their complexity.

Summary answers

1 a mass, velocity   b momentum, force
2 a 400 kg m/s   b 0.5 m/s
3 a 5000 kg m/s
    b Total momentum after collision = (1000 kg + 1500 kg) × v = 2500 v, where v is the final velocity to be calculated. Using conservation of momentum, 2500 v = 5000. Therefore v = 5000 ÷ 2500 = 2 m/s.

P2 3.5

Explosions

AQA Specification link-up: Physics P2.2

- Momentum is a property of moving objects
  $p = m \times v$ [P2.2.2 a)]
- In a closed system, the total momentum before an event is equal to the total momentum after the event. This is called conservation of momentum. [P2.2.2 b)]
  Controlled Assessment: P4.5 Analyse and interpret primary and secondary data. [P4.5.2 a) b)]

Learning objectives

Students should learn:

- that momentum has size and direction, and the direction of travel is important in collisions
- that there is no change in momentum in an explosion (momentum is always conserved).

Learning outcomes

Most students should be able to:

- state that the total momentum before and after an explosion is the same, provided no external forces act
- describe how the launching of a bullet causes recoil.

Some students should also be able to:

- explain that momentum is conserved in all interactions that do not include external forces
- apply the conservation of momentum to perform calculations where an explosion occurs causing two objects to recoil from each other.

Lesson structure

Starters

Jumping frogs – Position a few spring-loaded jumping frog toys on the desk and set them off. The students have to explain the energy transfers before they all go off. They need to mention elastic potential, kinetic, gravitational potential and sound. They should also account for where the energy finally ends up. *(5 minutes)*

Slow motion – Show a video of a simple explosion frame-by-frame and ask the students to explain what is happening. (Search for 'explosion' at an internet video hosting site.) They should see the pieces flying off in different directions; some will have greater speed than others. Support students by providing key words or a set of cartoon diagrams showing the stages of the explosion. Students can be extended by insisting that they incorporate the idea of conservation of momentum into their descriptions. *(10 minutes)*

Main

- Students may only think of explosions as chemical explosions instead of simple spring ones. Talk about an explosion being caused when some kind of stored energy (chemical or elastic) is suddenly transferred into kinetic. You can show a few basic chemical explosions and point out that too much is going on to explain clearly, so you are going to stick with some simple ones during the lesson.

- The explosion experiment usually works well, but you might want to repeat it a couple of times and analyse the mean results. This gives an opportunity for the students to consider the errors inherent in these measurements and why repeat readings are so important. This is an excellent opportunity to explore concepts in 'How Science Works'.

- Show the students some footage of crash-test dummies. Search an internet video hosting site for 'crash-test dummy video'. They should clearly see the area of impact in a collision.

- A good way of showing the recoil effect of firing a shell from a gun is to show a field gun in operation. These are really quite large and are knocked backwards significantly. When firing a '21-gun salute', there is little backwards movement because no shell is fired.

- The calculation can be very difficult for many students, so lead them through it carefully.

- You can discuss the energy transfers involved with the damping spring and perhaps link this to the suspension on cars.

- The students should be made to realise that the gun has to have much more mass that the projectile, otherwise it would recoil at very high velocities. A modern shell is fired at velocities of up to 1000 m/s and may have a mass of 100 kg.

Support

- Momentum conservation questions are best posed as a set of diagrams showing the situation before and after the collisions. The students can be led through the calculations with a calculation template until they are more comfortable with the technique.

Extend

- Ask: 'Why doesn't momentum change?' The students could try to link the idea of conservation of momentum to equal and opposite forces. Ask: 'What exactly is a force? What is the scientific definition?' Mathematically skilled students could look at collisions in two dimensions and calculate the resulting velocities.

Plenaries

It's against the frog – Have a set of quick questions handy and use the jumping frogs again. A student has the time it takes for the frog to go off in which to answer a question. Play this as a knockout game with teams if needed. You can differentiate by setting different levels of question to provide support or extension material. *(5 minutes)*

Boating – Discuss what happens when somebody steps on to a boat but falls in the water because the boat moves away. (There are plenty of video clips showing this effect.) Ask the students to explain what happened, perhaps with diagrams. They should understand that the person is actually pushing the boat away; when they move left, the boat will always be forced to the right as a consequence of the conservation of momentum. The effect is clearly greatest when the mass of the boat is similar to the mass of the person. *(10 minutes)*

Practical support

Investigating a controlled explosion

This demonstration can be used to show that momentum is conserved in explosions.

Equipment and materials required

Four dynamics trolleys, two light gates or velocity sensors or wooden blocks.

Details

This experiment can be carried out with wooden blocks as shown in the Student Book or with light gates or velocity sensors to measure the speed. If the sensors are used, then use cards as in previous experiments to interrupt light beams. The momentum of the objects can be calculated using the equation.

You should make sure that the sensors are positioned close to the explosion point, so that not too much energy is lost due to friction. The same kind of experiment can be carried out with a linear air track.

Safety: Protect feet and bench from falling trolleys.

Work, energy and momentum

P2 3.5 — Explosions

Learning objectives

- Why does momentum have a direction as well as size?
- When two objects push each other apart
  - do they move away at different speeds?
  - why is their total momentum zero?

If you are a skateboarder, you will know that the skateboard can shoot away from you when you jump off it. Its momentum is in the opposite direction to your own momentum. What can we say about the total momentum of objects when they fly apart from each other?

Practical

Investigating a controlled explosion

Figure 1 shows controlled explosion using trolleys. When the trigger rod is tapped, a bolt springs out and the trolleys recoil (spring back) from each other.

Figure 1 Investigating explosions

Using trial and error, we can place blocks on the runway so the trolleys reach them at the same time. This allows us to compare the speeds of the trolleys. Some results are shown in Figure 2.

$\frac{\text{Speed of A}}{\text{Speed of B}} = 1$

$\frac{\text{Speed of A}}{\text{Speed of C}} = 2$

$\frac{\text{Speed of A}}{\text{Speed of D}} = 3$

Figure 2 Using different masses

- Did your results agree exactly with the ones above? If not, try to explain why.

- Two single trolleys travel equal distances in the same time. This shows that they recoil at equal speeds.
- A double trolley only travels half the distance that a single trolley does. Its speed is half that of the single trolley.

In each test:

1 the mass of the trolley × the speed of the trolley is the same, and
2 they recoil in opposite directions.

So momentum has size and direction. The results show that the trolleys recoil with equal and opposite momentum.

a Why does a stationary rowing boat recoil when someone jumps off it?

Conservation of momentum 🔑

In the trolley examples:

- momentum of A after the explosion = (mass of A × velocity of A)
- momentum of B after the explosion = (mass of B × velocity of B)
- total momentum before the explosion = 0 (because both trolleys were at rest).

Using conservation of momentum gives:

(mass of A × velocity of A) + (mass of B × velocity of B) = 0

Therefore

(mass of A × velocity of A) = − (mass of B × velocity of B)

The minus sign after the equal sign tells us that the momentum of B is in the opposite direction to the momentum of A. The equation tells us that A and B move apart with equal and opposite amounts of momentum. So the total momentum after the explosion is the same as before it.

Momentum in action

When a shell is fired from an artillery gun, the gun barrel recoils backwards. The recoil of the gun barrel is slowed down by a spring. This lessens the backwards motion of the gun.

b In the worked example, if the mass of the gun had been much greater than 2000 kg, why would the speed of the shell have been greater?

Summary questions

1 A 60 kg skater and a 80 kg skater standing in the middle of an ice rink push each other away. Copy and complete a to c using the words below:

force momentum velocity

a They move apart with equal and opposite ....
b The 60 kg skater moves away with a bigger .... than the other skater.
c They push each other with equal and opposite ....

Figure 4

2 In Question 1, the 60 kg skater moves away at 2.0 m/s. Calculate:
a her momentum
b the velocity of the other skater.

3 A 600 kg cannon recoils at a speed of 0.5 m/s when a 12 kg cannon ball is fired from it.
a Calculate the velocity of the cannon ball when it leaves the cannon.
b Calculate the kinetic energy of:
i the cannon
ii the ball.

Maths skills

Worked example

An artillery gun of mass 2000 kg fires a shell of mass 20 kg at a velocity of 120 m/s. Calculate the recoil velocity of the gun.

Solution

Applying the conservation of momentum gives:

mass of gun × recoil velocity of gun = − (mass of shell × velocity of shell)

If we let *V* represent the recoil velocity of the gun,

$2000\,\text{kg} \times V = -(20\,\text{kg} \times 120\,\text{m/s})$

$V = \frac{2400\,\text{kg m/s}}{2000\,\text{kg}} = -1.2\,\text{m/s}$

Figure 3 An artillery gun in action

Key points

- Momentum is mass × velocity and velocity is speed in a certain direction.
- When two objects push each other apart, they move apart:
  - with different speeds if they have unequal masses
  - with equal and opposite momentum so their total momentum is zero.

Further teaching suggestions

Crash-test dummies

- If you have a few old toys you can improvise crash-test dummies. These can lead to a discussion about the limitations of the model. Ask: 'How close are the crash-test dummies to people?' Use a full-sized skeleton to discuss the joints a more realistic dummy should have, and point out the weak spots in impact such as the neck. You can discuss why the dummies are simplified; only certain data is needed to estimate the effect on humans. The extra data generated by a more realistic dummy would not be useful. It would cause more difficulties in the study and would make the dummies even more expensive than they already are.

Answers to in-text questions

a The boat has equal and opposite momentum to the jumper after the jump, so it moves in the opposite direction to the jumper.

b The gun would recoil much less, so more of the energy released would have been transferred into kinetic energy of the shell.

Summary answers

1 a momentum
  b velocity
  c force

2 a 120 kg m/s
  b 1.5 m/s

3 a 25 m/s
  b i 75 J
    ii 3750 J

P2 3.6

Impact forces

Learning objectives

Students should learn:

- how the force during an impact will depend on the change in momentum and the time over which the impact takes place
- that forces are equal and opposite during impacts.

Learning outcomes

Most students should be able to:

- state that a resultant force will change the momentum of an object
- describe the factors that affect the size of a force in an impact.

Some students should also be able to:

- calculate the force produced in a collision using the equations:

$a = \dfrac{v - u}{t}$ and $F = ma$

Answers to in-text questions

a If a child falls off the swing, the impact force is lessened because the rubber mat increases the duration of the impact.

b The wearer's kinetic energy is reduced over a greater distance if a seat belt is worn. (Or the wearer's momentum is reduced over a longer time if a seat belt is worn.)

c 1800 N

Support

- This can be a challenging set of calculations as there are two separate stages needed to determine the forces. Provide a set of layout templates to guide the students through the calculations until they get into the habit of laying out their work correctly. Check that the students are calculating the deceleration correctly before moving on to the calculation of the force.

Extend

- There is plenty of scope for looking at the impact forces calculations in more depth and in more complex situations. You can look at collisions between two moving cars, in opposite or the same directions linking this into the safety features designed for these situations described in the next lesson.

AQA Specification link-up: Physics P2.1, P2.2

- The acceleration of an object is determined by the resultant force acting on the object and the mass of the object.

$a = \dfrac{F}{m}$ or $F = m \times a$ [P2.1.2 a)]

- The acceleration of an object is given by the equation:

$a = \dfrac{v - u}{t}$ [P2.1.2 e)]

- Evaluate the benefits of air bags, crumple zones, seat belts and side impact bars in cars. [P2.2]

Lesson structure

Starters

Skids – Why does a car take longer to stop in wet weather? Show students some pictures of cars stopping suddenly and discuss the sizes of the forces. What reduces the forces and why does this mean that the car takes a greater distance to stop? Extend students by asking them to provide equations for acceleration and then for an equation linking force and acceleration, link these to change of momentum. Extra support can be provided by revising the ideas of friction as a force beforehand. *(5 minutes)*

Sudden impact – Arrange some bathroom tiles on the floor (inside a tray and wear safety glasses). Drop some objects onto the tiles to see if they break. These can include heavy but soft objects and a hammer. Ask the students to explain why the tiles break or why they do not. *(10 minutes)*

Main

- Calculating the forces involved in collisions requires the use of two equations and so is quite a tricky concept, and some students will struggle with the mathematics. A good starting point is to show a video clip of crash testing. (Search the internet for a 'crash testing' video); there are a few available. You should emphasise the large amount of energy that is transferred during the collision and ask the students where they think it is transferred to.

- The 'Investigating impacts' practical clearly shows that the forces involved in impact are reduced by using a material that distorts. These plastic materials absorb some of the energy of the impact. You might like to show what happens if a spring (an elastic material) is used instead.

- A key element to understanding the impacts and forces involved is that the size of the force can be reduced by extending the time of the impact. Discuss how materials that can compress (foam, crumple zones and so on) mean that the impact is taking place over a significantly longer time so the forces acting can be much smaller. This is why 'padding' can make impact less painful or damaging.

- The calculations will take a bit of explaining and the students will most likely need to go through the ideas a couple of times. Use plenty of examples including ones involving the trolleys or toys that you have been using. Impact times tend to be very short, so you may like to start with longer-lasting collisions before moving on to the bullet example.

- After the maths, either demonstrate the egg-throwing or let the students have a go at the egg-hurling competition (see 'Further reading suggestions').

Plenaries

Bouncy castles – Small children often cry when they fall over, but not on bouncy castles. The students should draw a diagram showing why not. Check that they are identifying the forces and the timings involved. *(5 minutes)*

'Owwzatt!' – How should cricketers catch fast-moving cricket balls? The students should write out instructions explaining the science behind their ideas. This should include the reasons why gloves are used to 'cushion' the catch. Students can extend their explanations by explaining the hand motion of the fielders when they catch the ball (show some video footage). The fielders move their hands in the direction the ball is travelling. Again this increases the impact time (and reduces the chances of the ball bouncing off their hands). Support can be provided by demonstrating the actions and properties of the ball and glove in the laboratory. Borrow some props from the PE department if they have them. *(10 minutes)*

Practical support

Investigating impacts

The impacts can be investigated on a simple or more detailed level depending on time available.

Equipment and materials required

Dynamics trolley, plasticine, motion sensor, launch ramp.

Details

You can compare the two impacts just by observing them or by monitoring the movement with a distance sensor. The trolleys should be launched from the same height on the ramp; firstly onto the brick directly and then with a round blob of plasticine. With the motion sensor, you can then compare the two impacts, and you should be able to show that the second impact took place over a longer time. The first impact should make a nice thud, and this helps you to discuss what happened to the kinetic energy.

Safety: Protect feet and bench from falling bricks and trolleys. Wear eye protection.

Work, energy and momentum

Impact forces

P2 3.6 — Impact forces

Learning objectives

- When vehicles collide, what does the force of the impact depend on?
- How does the impact force depend on the impact time?
- What can we say about the impact forces and the total momentum when two vehicles collide?

Figure 2 A crash test. Car makers test the design of a crumple zone by driving a remote control car into a brick wall.

Figure 3 Impact force

Did you know ...?

Scientists at Oxford University have developed new lightweight material for bulletproof vests. The material is so strong and elastic that bullets bounce off it.

Crumple zones at the front end and rear end of a car are designed to lessen the force of an impact. The force changes the momentum of the car.

- In a front-end impact, the momentum of the car is reduced.
- In a rear-end impact (where a vehicle is struck from behind by another vehicle), the momentum of the car is increased.

In both cases the effect of a crumple zone is to increase the impact time and so lessen the impact force.

Practical

Investigating impacts

We can test an impact using a trolley and a brick, as shown in Figure 1. When the trolley hits the brick, the plasticine flattens on impact, making the impact time longer. This is the key factor that reduces the impact force.

Trolley pushed towards brick

Brick

Plasticine

Figure 1 Investigating impacts

a Why is rubber matting under a child's swing a good idea?

Impact time

Let's see why making the impact time longer reduces the impact force.

Suppose a moving trolley hits another object and stops. The impact force on the trolley acts for a certain time (the impact time) and causes it to stop. A soft pad on the front of the trolley would increase the impact time and would allow the trolley to travel further before it stops. The momentum of the trolley would be lost over a longer time and its kinetic energy would be transferred over a greater distance.

1 The kinetic energy of the trolley is transferred to the pad as work done by the impact force in squashing the pad.
2 Since work done = force × distance, the impact force is therefore reduced because the distance is increased.

The longer the impact time is, the more the impact force is reduced.

If we know the impact time, we can calculate the impact force as follows:

- From P2 1.2, since acceleration = change of velocity ÷ time taken, we can work out the deceleration by dividing the change of velocity by the impact time.
- From P2 2.3, since force = mass × acceleration, we can now calculate the impact force by multiplying the mass of the trolley by the deceleration.

The above method shows how much the impact force can be reduced by increasing the impact time. Car safety features such as crumple zones and side bars increase the impact time and so reduce the impact force.

b In a car crash, why does wearing a car seat belt reduce the impact force on the wearer?

Maths skills

Worked example

A bullet of mass 0.004 kg moving at a velocity of 90 m/s is stopped by a bulletproof vest in 0.0003 s.
Calculate **a** the deceleration and **b** the impact force.

Solution

a Initial velocity of bullet = 90 m/s
Final velocity of bullet = 0
Change of velocity = final velocity − initial velocity
= 0 − 90 m/s = −90 m/s
(where the minus sign tells us the change of velocity is a decrease)
Deceleration = $\frac{\text{change of velocity}}{\text{impact time}} = \frac{-90\,\text{m/s}}{0.0003\,\text{s}} = -300\,000\,\text{m/s}^2$

b Using 'force = mass × acceleration', impact force = 0.004 kg × −300 000 m/s² = −1200 N

c Calculate the impact force if the impact time had been 0.0002 s.

Two-vehicle collisions

When two vehicles collide, they exert equal and opposite impact forces on each other at the same time. The change of momentum of one vehicle is therefore equal and opposite to the change of momentum of the other vehicle. The total momentum of the two vehicles is the same after the impact as it was before the impact, so momentum is conserved – assuming no external forces act.

For example, suppose a fast-moving truck runs into the back of a stationary car. The impact decelerates the truck and accelerates the car. Assuming the truck's mass is greater than the mass of the car, the truck loses momentum and the car gains momentum.

Summary questions

1 Copy and complete **a** to **c** using the words below:
equal   greater   smaller
 a The greater the mass of a moving object is the .... the force needed to stop it in a certain time.
 b When two objects collide, they exert .... forces on each other.
 c When two vehicles collide, the vehicle with the .... mass has a greater change of velocity.

2 **a** An 800 kg car travelling at 30 m/s is stopped safely when the brakes are applied. What deceleration and braking force is required to stop it in **i** 6.0 s? **ii** 30 s?
 b If the vehicle in part **a** had been stopped in a collision lasting less than a second, explain why the force on it would have been much greater.

3 A 2000 kg van moving at a velocity of 12 m/s crashes into the back of a stationary truck of mass 10 000 kg. Immediately after the impact, the two vehicles move together.
 a Show that the velocity of the van and the truck immediately after the impact was 2 m/s.
 b The impact lasted for 0.3 seconds. Calculate the **i** deceleration of the van **ii** force of the impact on the van.

Did you know ... ?

We sometimes express the effect of an impact on an object or person as a force to weight ratio. We call this the **g-force**. For example, a g-force of 2g means the force on an object is twice its weight. You would experience a g-force of:

- about 3–4g on a fairground ride that whirls you round
- about 10g in a low-speed car crash
- more than 50g in a high-speed car crash. You would be lucky to survive!

Key points

- When vehicles collide, the force of the impact depends on mass, change of velocity, and the duration of the impact.
- The longer the impact time is, the more the impact force is reduced.
- When two vehicles collide,
  - they exert equal and opposite forces on each other
  - their total momentum is unchanged.

144   145

Further teaching suggestions

Egg hurling

- The students can be provided with some simple equipment; cardboard tubes, sponge tape, etc. Ask the students to design egg safety capsules. You can then see which work by dropping eggs or throwing them. If there is no time in the lesson, the students could construct their egg safety capsule at home for testing next lesson.

Summary answers

1 **a** greater
 b equal
 c smaller

2 **a** **i** 5.0 m/s², 4000 N
  ii 1 m/s², 800 N
 b The deceleration is greater because the impact time is shorter and the change of velocity is the same. The impact force is equal to the mass × the deceleration, so the impact force is greater.

3 **a** Initial momentum = 24 000 kg m/s;
  velocity after impact = $\frac{\text{momentum}}{\text{mass}} = \frac{24\,000}{12\,000} = 2$ m/s.
 b **i** 33 m/s²
  ii 330 000 N

P2 3.7

Car safety

AQA Specification link-up: Physics P2.1, P2.2

- The acceleration of an object is determined by the resultant force acting on the object and the mass of the object. *[P2.1.2 a)]*
- Evaluate the benefits of air bags, crumple zones, seat belts and side impact bars in cars. *[P2.2]*
- Evaluate the benefits of different types of braking system, such as regenerative braking. *[P2.2]*

Learning objectives

Students should learn:

- that seat belts and air bags reduce the force of an impact by extending the duration of the impact
- that energy can be absorbed by distorting material during impacts
- that detailed calculation of damage can be used to assess the speed of a collision.

Learning outcomes

Most students should be able to:

- describe the safety features of a modern car and their effects
- describe how a safety feature works in relation to reducing the forces of impacts by extending the duration of the impact
- describe how road traffic accidents can be investigated using the evidence from the scene.

Answers to in-text questions

a The wearer would not be stopped until his or her head hit the windscreen.

b The seat belt would go across the body above the chest. The child might slip through the seat belt in an accident.

Support

- Students should relate well to demonstrations and videos before constructing their own devices to crash together. Lego constructions can work well.

Extend

- There is plenty of scope here to look at the details of collisions. You may like to see if the students can design a crumple zone for the trolley out of paper or aluminium foil. Give each student a small amount of sticky tape and a single sheet of A4 paper, and ask them to try to make a crumple zone that they can attach to the front of a trolley to absorb the kinetic energy. The trolley can be rolled from a fixed height on a ramp to make the test fair, and the collisions observed or even measured with a motion sensor. This should give an indication of the effectiveness.

Lesson structure

Starters

Crash flashback – Give the students a momentum problem to solve to refresh the ideas from the last topic. Include cars or other large things as the objects involved in the collision. You can differentiate by providing a straightforward calculation to support some students while also providing a more complex situation requiring rearrangement of the basic equation to extend others. *(5 minutes)*

Crumpled cars – Show the students selected photographs of crashed cars (search the internet for images) and ask them to describe the damage they see. They should notice the crumpling effect; especially at the front or rear of the car, but may not realise that this is a deliberate design. Point this out to them and ask them to think of reasons why a designer would deliberately want this effect. Give them clues by linking back to plastic and elastic materials. The key is to understand that forces have been used to stop the car and the kinetic energy of the car has partly gone into distorting the car's shape. *(10 minutes)*

Main

- The students need to understand that a fast-moving car will have a great deal of kinetic energy and to stop, this energy needs to be transferred. This is done when a force acts on the car so a rapid change in kinetic energy is accompanied by very large forces causing very large accelerations. It is the large forces that have to be handled as they cause the damage to the car and passengers. The reduction of the forces is generally achieved by making the impacts last longer.

- The pressures involved in collisions can also be reduced by making the forces act over a wider area, (hence the wide seatbelts and large airbags).

- You might be able to find a seatbelt from a scrap car so that you can explain why it is not totally rigid and is so wide. If not, you will have to settle for photographs. Video clips of crash tests can be easily found and these show the behaviour of a body and seatbelt in a car crash. You can also find examples of the dummies not wearing a seatbelt.

- Similarly, you can find slow motion footage of the effect of air bags in crashes. Emphasise the effect of increasing the collision time and spreading the force over a much larger area of the body. The impact time can be increased tenfold and the area of impact by a similar amount, reducing the pressure on the body one hundred times.

- You can discuss the idea of child safety seats. If you (or another member of staff) have one, you can look at the side impact padding and the extensive belting to secure the child. Seats facing backwards are safer that those facing forwards, so should passenger seats on cars, buses and trains be facing backwards?

- If you have access to computers, the students can find out about the improved safety features of cars and complete a summary of the costs and benefits. If not then a range of brochures are usually available from the dealers.

Plenaries

Best car – Give the students pictures and information about cars through the ages and get them to identify the innovations that have taken place. They can produce a timeline showing the changes. You can also include information about changes to maximum speeds and road types like the introduction of motorways. You can support some students by providing a blank timeline and some articles (to find information from) to add to the timeline. To extend other students, you might ask them to continue at home and evaluate the origin and success of a particular new safety idea (for example who invented airbags and how successful have they been?). *(5 minutes)*

Hard sell – The students must produce an advertisement for the expensive safety features in a new car. This could be hard hitting or more subtle in its persuasiveness. Most safety features started off as expensive accessories but as their benefits were proven, they became required by law. *(10 minutes)*

Practical support

Investigating impacts

The impacts can be investigated on a simple or more detailed level depending on time available.

Equipment and materials required

Dynamics trolley, plasticine, motion sensor, launch ramp.

Details

You can compare the two impacts just by observing them or by monitoring the movement with a distance sensor. The trolleys should be launched from the same height on the ramp; firstly onto the brick directly and then with a round blob of plasticine. With the motion sensor, you can then compare the two impacts, and you should be able to show that the second impact took place over a longer time. The first impact should make a nice thud, and this helps you to discuss what happened to the kinetic energy.

You may like to see if the students can design a crumple zone for the trolley out of paper. Give each student a small amount of sticky tape and a single sheet of A4 paper, and ask them to try to make a crumple zone that they can attach to the front of a trolley to absorb the kinetic energy. The trolley can be rolled from a fixed height on a ramp to make the test fair, and the collisions observed or even measured with a motion sensor. This should give an indication of the effectiveness.

Safety: Protect feet and bench from falling trolleys and bricks. Wear eye protection.

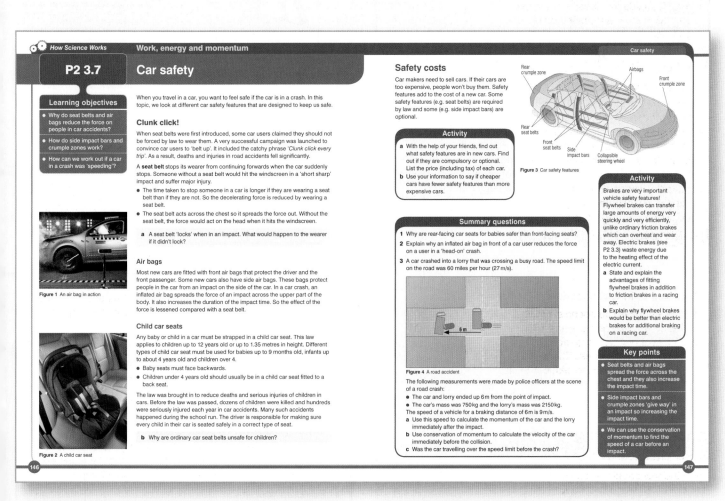

Activity answers

Braking systems

a Advantages:

- Less fuel is used because kinetic energy is stored in the flywheel when the brakes are applied and returned to the vehicle when it accelerates.
- The initial acceleration at the start is greater because the engine and the flywheel can both be used to accelerate the vehicle.
- Energy can be transferred rapidly and efficiently to and from the flywheel when the vehicle slows down at a bend and speeds up on leaving the bend.
- Less energy is wasted as the flywheel brake does not heat up like the ordinary friction brake.

b Electric brakes would waste more energy. Also, the wires carrying the electric current might overheat.

Summary answers

1 In an accident where the car suddenly stopped, the child would press against the back of the car seat. This would prevent the child from being thrown forwards.

2 The air bag increases the time taken to stop the person it acts on. This reduces the force of the impact. Also, the force is spread out across the chest by the air bag, so its effect is lessened again.

3 **a** 26 100 kg m/s

 b 35 m/s

 c yes

Summary answers

1 a i equal to
   ii less than

  b i 180 J
   ii 11 N × 20 m = 220 N m = 220 J
   iii Friction between the trolley and the slope causes some of the energy from the student to be transferred to the surroundings by braking.

2 a $\dfrac{700\,kg \times (20\,m/s)}{2} = 140\,000\,J$

  b 1750 N

3 a 12 kg m/s

  b 6 m/s

4 Initial velocity $u = 4\,m/s$, final velocity $v = 0$ (because the crash stops the car), time taken $t = 1.8\,s$.
   Acceleration, $a = (v - u) \div t = (0 - 4) \div 1.8 = 2.2\,m/s^2$

5 a i elastic potential energy
   ii kinetic energy

  b i 3.0 J
   ii Some of the kinetic energy of the stone was transferred to the surroundings by air resistance; the stone was still moving horizontally at maximum height, so it still had kinetic energy due to this movement.

6 a i 3600 kg m/s
   ii 1200 kg m/s

  b i 2400 kg m/s
   ii 3.0 m/s

  c i 5400 J
   ii 600 J
   iii 3600 J

  d Some of the kinetic energy was transferred into sound and by heating (due to friction) to the wagons and the surroundings.

Summary questions

1 a Copy and complete **i** and **ii** using the words below. Each term can be used once, twice or not at all.

   equal to   greater than   less than

   When a braking force acts on a vehicle and slows it down,
   i the work done by the force is .... the energy transferred from the object
   ii the kinetic energy after the brakes have been applied is .... the kinetic energy before they were applied.

  b A student pushes a trolley of weight 150 N up a slope of length 20 m. The slope is 1.2 m high.

   i Calculate the gravitational potential energy gained by the trolley.
   ii The student pushed the trolley up the slope with a force of 11 N. Show that the work done by the student was 220 J.
   iii Give one reason why all the work done by the student was not transferred to the trolley as gravitational potential energy.

2 A 700 kg car moving at 20 m/s is stopped in a distance of 80 m when the brakes are applied.

  a Show that the kinetic energy of the car at 20 m/s is 140 000 J.
  b Calculate the braking force on the car.

3 A student of mass 40 kg standing at rest on a skateboard of mass 2.0 kg jumps off the skateboard at a speed of 0.30 m/s. Calculate:

  a the momentum of the student
  b the recoil velocity of the skateboard.

4 A car bumper is designed not to bend in impacts at less than 4 m/s. It was fitted to a car of mass 900 kg and tested by driving the car into a wall at 4 m/s. The time of impact was measured and found to be 1.8 s.
   Show that the deceleration of the car was 2.2 m/s².

5 a Copy and complete **i** and **ii** using the words below. Each term can be used once, twice or not at all.

   elastic potential energy   kinetic energy
   gravitational potential energy

   An object is catapulted from a catapult.
   i .... is stored in the catapult when it is stretched.
   ii The object has .... when it leaves the catapult.

  b A stone of mass 0.015 kg is catapulted into the air and it reaches a height of 20 m before it descends and hits the ground some distance away.

   i Calculate the increase of gravitational potential energy of the stone when it reached its maximum height ($g = 10\,N/kg$).
   ii State two reasons why the catapult stored more energy than that calculated in part **b i**?

6 a A 1200 kg rail wagon moving at a velocity of 3.0 m/s on a level track collides with a stationary wagon of mass 800 kg. The 1200 kg truck is slowed down to a velocity of 1.0 m/s as a result of the collision.

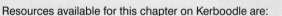

  a Calculate the momentum of the 1200 kg wagon
   i before the collision
   ii after the collision.
  b Calculate
   i the momentum, and
   ii the velocity of the 800 kg wagon after the collision
  c Calculate the kinetic energy of:
   i the 1200 kg wagon before the collision
   ii the 1200 kg wagon after the collision
   iii the 800 kg wagon after the collision.
  d Give a reason why the total kinetic energy after the collision is not equal to the total kinetic energy before the collision.

Kerboodle resources

Resources available for this chapter on Kerboodle are:

- Chapter map: Work, energy and momentum
- Bump up your grade: Meteor fall (P2 3.1)
- Interactive activity: Calculating kinetic energy (P2 3.3)
- Practical: Finding the elastic energy of springs (P2 3.3)
- Video: Momentum in sports (3.4)
- Simulation: Momentum (P2 3.4)
- Bump up your grade: Momentum calculations – understanding conservation of momentum (P2 3.4)
- How Science Works: Momentum in action (P2 3.4)
- Bump up your grade: What a bang! (P2 3.5)
- Revision podcast: Kinetic energy and momentum (P2s 3.7 & 3.8)
- Test yourself: Work, energy and momentum
- On your marks: Work, energy and momentum
- Examination-style questions: Work, energy and momentum
- Answers to examination-style questions: Work, energy and momentum

Examination-style questions

1 a Copy and complete the following sentences using the list of words and phrases below. Each one can be used once.

kinetic energy   work   power
gravitational potential energy

 i Energy is transferred when .... is done. (1)
 ii .... is the energy that an object has by virtue of its position in a gravitational field. (1)
 iii The .... of an object depends on its mass and speed. (1)
 iv .... is the energy transferred in a given time. (1)

b Explain why a meteorite 'burns up' as it enters the Earth's atmosphere. Use ideas about work and energy. (3)

2 The diagram shows three cars, **A**, **B** and **C**, travelling along a straight, level road.

A   Speed 40 m/s

650 kg

B   18 m/s

1250 kg

C   15 m/s

1500 kg

a Calculate the momentum of each of the vehicles and explain which one has the greatest momentum. Write down the equation you use. Show clearly how you work out your answer and give the unit. (3)

b Car **C**, travelling at 15 m/s, crashes into the back of car **A** when car **A** is stationary. The cars move together after the collision.
 i Calculate the total momentum of the cars just after the collision. (1)
 ii Calculate the speed of the two cars just after the collision. (2)

c Explain, using ideas about momentum changes, how the crumple zone at the front of car **C** may reduce the chance of injury to the occupants during the collision. (3)

3 When ploughing a field a horse and plough move 170 m and the horse pulls with a force of 800 N.

a Calculate the work done by the horse.
Write down the equation you use. Show clearly how you work out your answer and give the unit. (3)

b i The horse takes 3 minutes to plough 170 m.
Calculate the power of the horse.
Write down the equation you use. Show clearly how you work out your answer and give the unit. (3)
 ii Calculate the kinetic energy of the horse.
Write down the equation you use. Show clearly how you work out your answer and give the unit.
Mass of horse = 950 kg (3)

c Explain why the horse has to do more work if the field slopes uphill than it would do on level ground. (2)

4 The picture shows a catapult.

Stone   Elastic   Catapult

When a force is applied to the stone, work is done in stretching the elastic and the stone moves backwards.

a Calculate the work done if the average force applied to the stone is 20 N. The force moves it backwards 0.15 m. Write down the equation you use. Show clearly how you work out your answer and give the unit. (3)

b Calculate the maximum speed of the stone after the catapult is released. The mass of the stone is 0.049 kg. Assume all the work done is transferred to the stone as kinetic energy when the catapult is released. Write down the equation you use. Show clearly how you work out your answer and give the unit. (3)

149

Examination-style answers

1 a i Energy is transferred when **work** is done. *(1 mark)*
 ii **Gravitational potential energy** is the energy that an object has by virtue of its position in a gravitational field. *(1 mark)*
 iii The **kinetic energy** of an object depends on its mass and speed. *(1 mark)*
 iv **Power** is the energy transferred in a given time. *(1 mark)*

b work is done on the meteorite; energy transferred by heating; kinetic energy transferred by heating *(3 marks)*

2 a $p = m \times v$
A: $= 650 \times 40 = 26\,000$ kg m/s
B: $= 1250 \times 18 = 22\,500$ kg m/s
C: $= 1500 \times 15 = 22\,500$ kg m/s
A is greatest because although it has the smallest mass, it has a much larger velocity. *(3 marks)*

b i 22 500 kg m/s *(1 mark)*
 ii $(1500 + 650) \times v = 22\,500$
$v = 22\,500 / 2150 = 10.5$ m/s *(2 marks)*

c The crumple zone causes the change in momentum to happen over a longer time;
This means the maximum force on the occupants is reduced;
This reduces chance of injury. *(3 marks)*

3 a $WD = F \times d = 800 \times 170$
$= 136\,000$ J *(3 marks)*

b i $P = \dfrac{E}{t} = (800 \times 170)/180$
$= 756$ W *(3 marks)*
 ii $E_k = \frac{1}{2} \times m \times v^2 = \frac{1}{2} \times 950 \times (170/180)^2$
$= 424$ J *(3 marks)*

c work done against gravitational force; when an object is raised vertically *(2 marks)*

4 a $W = F \times d = 20 \times 0.15$
$= 3.0$ J *(3 marks)*

b $E_k = \frac{1}{2} \times m \times v^2$
$3 = 0.5 \times 0.049 \times v^2$
$v^2 = 122$
$v = 11$ m/s *(3 marks)*

Practical suggestions

Practicals	AQA	k	📖	⚙
Investigating the transfer of E_p to E_k by dropping a card through a light gate.	✓		✓	
Plan and carry out an investigation to measure velocity using trolleys and ramps.	✓		✓	
Running upstairs and calculating work done and power, lifting weights to measure power.	✓		✓	
A motor lifting a load to show how power changes with load.	✓		✓	
Stretching different materials before using as catapults to show the different amounts of energy transferred, indicated by speed reached by the object or distance travelled.	✓	✓		

Examiner's tip

Question 2 shows that the greatest momentum can be possessed by the least massive vehicle if it is travelling sufficiently fast. Students may enjoy a practical illustration of this idea: 'The momentum challenge'. This involves pupils sprinting (in a suitable area) and then multiplying their velocity by their mass. The class results can be displayed in a bar chart. The fastest runner is often not the winner.

Examiner's tip

Calculations based on conservation of momentum for collisions and explosions need to be practised by Higher Tier and Foundation Tier students alike. Question 2 can be repeated for different combinations of cars colliding. Some students could be extended by investigating collisions where both cars are initially moving. The students can assume that each car's clutch is disengaged and the brakes are not applied.

P2 4.1

Electrical charges

Learning objectives

Students should learn:

- that when insulating materials are rubbed together, charge can be transferred from one to the other
- that objects become electrically charged when electrons move from one material to the other
- that when charged objects are brought together, like charges repel and unlike charges attract.

Learning outcomes

Most students should be able to:

- state that there are two types of electrical charge and that electrons carry a negative charge whereas protons carry a positive charge
- draw diagrams showing how charge can be transferred from one object to another indicating the fact that charges are equal and opposite
- describe the forces that act between charged objects.

Some students should also be able to:

- provide a detailed description of the transfer of charge in terms of electron movement.

Support

- The concepts discussed here are best shown through a range of demonstrations, each one supported by clear diagrams showing the charge on the objects. You can provide diagrams without the charges shown and ask students to add this feature after each demonstration.

Extend

- Ask: 'Is it actually friction that charges up objects?' Apparently objects of different materials can become charged up just by being left in contact with each other, and rubbing objects together just increases the area of contact. The students can find out about this explanation.

AQA Specification link-up: Physics P2.3

- When certain insulating materials are rubbed against each other, they become electrically charged. Negatively charged electrons are rubbed off one material and onto the other. *[P2.3.1 a)]*
- The material that gains electrons becomes negatively charged. The material that loses electrons is left with an equal positive charge. *[P2.3.1 b)]*
- When two electrically charged objects are brought together they exert a force on each other. *[P2.3.1 c)]*
- Two objects that carry the same type of charge repel. Two objects that carry different types of charge attract. *[P2.3.1 d)]*

Lesson structure

Starters

Laws of attraction – Give the students a set of three cards with pictures of bar magnets on them and ask them to arrange them so that they all attract each other or all repel each other. Use real magnets to check the answers. Students should come up with some kind of triangular arrangement. *(5 minutes)*

Invisible force fields – Give the students two bar magnets and ask them to balance them so that the end of one is floating above the end of the other. Ask: 'Can they balance two magnets above one another?' Demonstrate magnet rings on a pole if you have them and ask the students to explain what is happening. You should reach the idea that there are invisible, non-contact forces. Students needing support should be able to draw diagrams demonstrating the effects. Extend students by asking them to state what factors affect the size of the forces and to consider gravitational forces too. Compare these with the electric force later in the lessons and discuss the factors that affect the size of this force. *(10 minutes)*

Main

- Start by demonstrating the balloon-sticking effect; it should be fairly easy to get the balloon to stick to a wall or to your own body. You may also be able to show that two charged balloons repel each other. You can discuss the static build up on a TV screen by talking about the amount of dust that builds up on it.

- The use of a 'Van de Graaff' generator is fairly essential. Students tend to get excited and some volunteer to receive a shock. Try some of the demonstrations in 'Practical support'. Make sure that you do not shock any students who have medical problems.

- The students should be familiar with the structure of the atom by now and you should be able to go through this part quickly. Highlight the idea of an ion; this will be used in later explanation around resistance.

- Emphasis needs to be placed on the idea that it is only the electrons that are free to move. When electrons leave an object, it becomes positively charged and when they enter a neutral object it becomes negatively charged. Some students struggle with the idea that adding electrons makes something negative. They need to grasp that the electron has a negative charge and so if you have more electrons, you have more negative charge.

- To demonstrate the effect that charged objects have on each other, the students can carry out the simple practical activity, 'The force between two charged objects' from the Student Book. They should have no trouble finding that like charges repel and opposites attract.

- At the end, the students should be able to tell you the simple attraction/repulsion rules.

Plenaries

Static force – Support students by giving them a set of diagrams with charged objects on them, two or more on each card, and ask them to draw force arrows. Some students can be extended by asking them to try to draw the direction of the resultant force. *(5 minutes)*

Forever amber – The students should write a brief newspaper report for the ancient Greek newspaper $\nu\Sigma\langle, \Sigma\iota\delta\eta\sigma\Sigma\int$ announcing the discovery and properties of static electricity. It was first discovered using amber or 'electrum' as they called it. This could be extended as homework in which the ancient Greeks might like to speculate about future uses of this mysterious 'electricity'. *(10 minutes)*

Practical support

The 'Van de Graaff' generator
This is an impressive and fun piece of equipment that can be used to demonstrate many of the aspects of static electricity. It is not just for giving shocks!

Equipment and materials needed
A 'Van de Graaff' generator (VDG) and accessory kit.
(See CLEAPSS Handbook, Section 12.9).

Details
- A VDG is a very temperamental device. Some days it will work very well but on others you will barely get a crackle. Dry days are best, and it is advisable to polish the dome to make it shiny. Keep computers (and mobile phones) away from the VDG.
- It is traditional to start by showing the sparks that the VDG can produce. Connect the discharging wand (or discharging dome) to earth and switch on the generator. Give the dome a couple of minutes to build up charge while you explain what the VDG is doing. Bring the wand close to the dome and with luck you will get reasonably big sparks.
- Hair standing on end can be demonstrated easily, and works best if the student stands on an insulating box. Make sure that the dome is discharged before the student steps off the insulator. If you don't want to use a student, then you may have a hair

sample that can be attached to the top of the dome or use a set of polystyrene balls in a container.
- Other demonstrations can include bringing a fluorescent tube close to the dome or demonstrating a current as a flow of charge.

Safety: Make sure students do not have any heart conditions.

The force between two charged objects
With this simple experiment, the students should be able to find that there are two types of charge and investigate how they affect each other.

Equipment and materials needed
For each group: retort stand with boss and clamp, cotton, two perspex rods, two polythene rods and a dry cloth.

Details
The students first need to make a 'hammock' from the cotton to be able to suspend one of the rods from the retort stand; they might find this easier if they use some light card as a base. They then rub one of the rods vigorously with the dry cloth and place it in the hammock. Next, they rub one of the other rods and bring it close to the suspended one and note the interaction; the suspended rod should rotate towards or away. They continue this procedure for all of the combinations of rods. If there seems to be little movement, it is probably because the cloth is not dry enough.

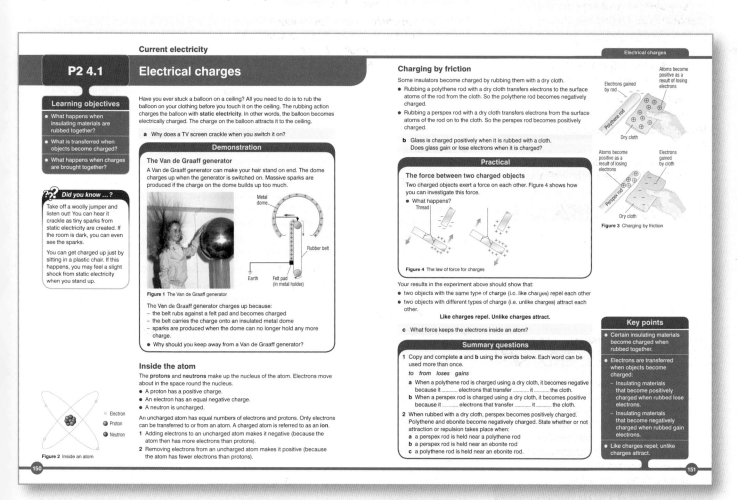

Answers to in-text questions
a Static electricity builds up on the screen.
b Glass loses electrons when it is charged.
c The electron is negative. The nucleus is positive. There is a force of (electrostatic) attraction between them.

Summary answers
1 a gains, to, from
  b loses, from, to
2 a attraction
  b attraction
  c repulsion

Electric circuits

Learning objectives

Students should learn:

- that electrical circuits are drawn using standard symbols
- the difference between a cell and a battery
- the size of an electric current is measured in amperes using an ammeter
- the symbols used to represent common circuit components.

Learning outcomes

Most students should be able to:

- recognise and draw the circuit symbols for a cell, a battery, a switch, an indicator, a resistor, a variable resistor, a diode, a fuse, a voltmeter, an ammeter and an LED
- describe the function of each of the above components
- state the difference between a cell and a battery
- draw circuit diagrams using the above symbols.

Answers to in-text questions

a So current passes through it and through the torch bulb.
b A battery formed from two cells, a switch and a heater.
c No.

Support

- Some students have particular difficulties with connecting up electronic circuits correctly because they cannot match the neat circuit diagrams with the jumble of wires they are given. You can support students by using fixed boards, such as the Locktronic ones. It is a good idea to write the names of the component on them until the students can match the symbol and name correctly.

Extend

- For the circuit-building exercise, extend students by asking them to look at the currents through the different branches of the circuit and find any relationships. They could even look into the potential differences and see if they can come up with the relationship before you discuss it in future lessons.

Specification link-up: Physics P2.3

- Electrical charges can move easily through some substances, e.g. metals. *[P2.3.1 e)]*
- Electric current is a flow of electric charge. The size of the electric current is the rate of flow of electric charge. The size of the current is given by the equation:

  $I = \dfrac{Q}{t}$ *[P2.3.2 a)]*

- Circuit diagrams using standard symbols. The following standard symbols should be known: (*See Student Book pages 210 and 215 for symbols*). *[P2.3.2 c)]*

Lesson structure

Starters

It's symbolic – Show a set of slides/diagrams to the students containing common symbols and ask them to say what they mean. Use road signs, hazard symbols, washing symbols, etc. This should help them to understand that symbols are a simple way of representing information clearly. You can use symbols used in countries where the language is very different. *(5 minutes)*

Describe the circuit – Give the students diagrams of two circuits containing cells, switches and bulbs, one series and one parallel, and ask them to describe them both in a paragraph. The student can demonstrate their understanding of circuit symbols this way and you can check their prior knowledge of concepts such as current, voltage, series and parallel. Support students by providing simple circuits with the minimal number of components. Students can be extended by asking them to draw a circuit when given a description of it. *(10 minutes)*

Main

- The students should be familiar with the basic ideas of circuits and circuit symbols from KS3. You can use this topic to check the students' circuit-building skills, so that you can be sure that they can carry out the investigations later.

- Start by showing the components and asking 'Do symbols have to look like what they represent?' When introducing each symbol, show the students a real device represented by that symbol. You could show them that there are several physically-different looking devices that match each symbol. For example, there are a range of different ammeters represented by the same symbol and a wide range of resistors.

- Most students cope well with the basic symbols for bulbs, switches and batteries. You may find that they struggle more with the various types of resistors because they are so similar. The best way to describe resistors is to discuss what is added to the basic resistor symbol.
  - The variable resistor has an arrow through it showing that you can adjust it.
  - The LDR has arrows going towards it representing light.
  - The fuse has a thin line representing the thin wire that runs inside it.

- Point out the difference between a cell and a battery. Many students still do not understand that a battery is a series of cells. It helps to physically show a 1.5 V cell and then put two or more together to produce a battery. You can point out that the word 'battery' means 'a collection put close together' as in 'battery hens' and a 'battery of guns'.

- The concept of current needs to be covered in some detail. The students need to work with the formal definition shown in the book; it's a bit like measuring the rate of flow of water in a pipe; the water current would be the mass of water passing each second. Simulation software really helps students to visualise the charges moving through the wire, discuss the charge moving around the circuit from positive to negative carrying energy with it. You will explain this energy transfer in more detail in future lessons.

- With the remaining time, you should let the students build a couple of circuits. Those in the 'Circuit tests' practical support are fine, or you could extend students further (see 'Extend' idea).

Plenaries

Current calculations – The students have a few calculations based on the equation to perform. You can extend the students by asking them to perform a calculation based on rearrangements of the equation and using unusual quantities (a time of 1 hour and a current of 40 mA when recharging a mobile phone for example). Support can be provided by sticking to relatively simple quantities and calculations requiring no rearrangement. *(5 minutes)*

Symbol domino loop – Give the students a set of cards showing circuit symbols and descriptions of their functions. Each card would have a symbol and a description that matches the symbol on a different card but when they are placed together correctly, the whole set would make a complete loop. Can the students name them all? *(10 minutes)*

Practical support

Circuit tests

This is a simple introduction to building circuits allowing the students to refresh their skills.

Equipment and materials needed

Cells (1.5 V), torch bulb (1.5 V), leads, diode, variable resistor.

Details

The students set up a simple circuit with the variable resistor and the bulb. They should find that the variable resistor can be used to alter the brightness of the bulb and be told that this is due to the current being changed. The students then include a diode in the circuit. They should then reverse the diode. This will show that the diode only allows the current in one direction.

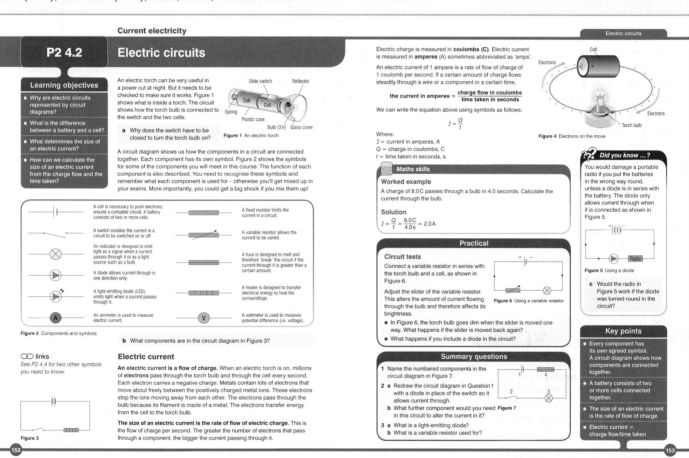

Further teaching suggestions

Circuit building

- This is more of a support activity to help students remember how to build basic circuits.

  ### Equipment and materials required
  Battery pack (3 V), three torch bulbs (3 V), leads, ammeter.

  ### Details
  Ask the students to set up a simple series circuit with two bulbs, and then a parallel one with a bulb on each branch. Can they make a parallel circuit with one bulb on one branch and two on the other? What can they say about the brightness of the bulbs? They should draw circuit diagrams of all these circuits before they construct them.

Summary answers

1 cell, switch, indicator, fuse

2 a
  b A variable resistor.

3 a A light-emitting diode is a diode that emits light when current passes through it.
  b A variable resistor is used to change the current in a circuit.

P2 4.3

Resistance

Learning objectives

Students should learn:

- how to use an ammeter and voltmeter
- how to measure the resistance of a component
- that a wire at a constant temperature obeys Ohm's law
- that the resistance of a metal wire does not depend on the direction of the current.

Learning outcomes

Most students should be able to:

- measure the resistance of a resistor using an ammeter and voltmeter
- calculate the resistance of a device from the current through it and the potential difference across it
- state Ohm's law for a metal wire.

Some students should also be able to:

- perform calculations that involve rearrangement of the resistance equation.

Answers to in-text questions

a $8.0\,\Omega$

b $10\,\Omega$

Support

- For resistance calculations, provide the students with a question sheet that has templates for the layout for equations, so that they go through the process step-by-step.

Extend

- The current–potential difference graphs shown in the Student Book all show constant resistance and no error in the measurements as the gradients are perfectly straight lines. Show the students some graphs produced from real measurements (containing some degree of error in readings) and discuss how the students would determine the resistance in this case. A gradient is often used to find resistance so they may like to calculate this after determining a best fit.

AQA   Specification link-up: Physics P2.3

- The potential difference (voltage) between two points in an electric circuit is the work done (energy transferred) per coulomb of charge that passes between the points:

  $V = \dfrac{W}{Q}$ *[P2.3.2 b)]*

- Current–potential difference graphs are used to show how the current through a component varies with the potential difference across it. *[P2.3.2 d)]*
- The current–potential difference graphs for a resistor at constant temperature … . *[P2.3.2 e)]*
- The resistance of a component can be found by measuring the current through, and potential difference across, the component. *[P2.3.2 f)]*
- The current through a resistor (at a constant temperature) is directly proportional to the potential difference across the resistor. *[P2.3.2 g)]*
- Calculate current, potential difference or resistance using the equation: $V = I \times R$. *[P2.3.2 h)]*

  Controlled Assessment: P4.5 Analyse and interpret primary and secondary data. *[P4.5.3 a)]*

Lesson structure

Starters

Resistors – Show the students the circuit symbols for all of the different types of resistor and ask them to describe the similarities in the symbols. Ask: 'What do they think the other parts of the symbols mean?' This is a simple recap. *(5 minutes)*

Reading the meter – Show the students some pictures of analogue meters and ask them to read off the value shown. Use a variety of different scales for the meters. Some students may need to be supported when trying to read digital scales; for example 0.21 is often read as 'nought point twenty one' or even just 'twenty one', so go through some examples of this. To extend students, you can ask them to design suitable scales (by making choices of suitable ranges and precision) for displaying sets of values clearly. For example, what set of scales could be used to display 0.55, 0.78 and 0.49 mV most clearly. *(10 minutes)*

Main

- It is very important that the students understand how to use an ammeter and voltmeter, and they have a good opportunity to do that in this lesson. Currents through components are often less than 1 ampere, so the students will have to get used to using 'milliamperes' (most people just use 'milliamps') in a lot of their work. The terms potential difference and voltage are often used interchangeably, try to enforce the use of potential difference (pd) as this will be used in examination questions.

- When a charge is moved through a potential difference, energy is transferred and so work is done. This is slightly similar to a force doing work when it moves an object. For some students, the equation defining potential difference will make more sense if it is stated as $W = VQ$ (work done = charge × pd moved through). In the end, some students may not be able to grasp exactly what pd is; this can be OK as long as they can use the equation.

- A simple analogy explaining resistance is a student moving along a packed corridor with his eyes closed. Other students in the corridor will get in the way, resisting his progress. If all of the other students are moving about a lot, the resistance will be higher – a bit like the wire heating up. During the movement, the electrons will lose energy as they collide with the ions in the metal. Link this idea to earlier energy transformation work. It is always important to check that the students do not think that electrons are used up as they move. They just lose (transfer) energy. Some computer simulations of electron movement show that the electrons are losing energy as they move through the potential difference. These are very useful.

- The students may be more comfortable just using word equations but they have to be able to recognise the symbols, so give them some questions that use them; they are quicker to write anyway.

- The practical activity in the Student Book is a good way of checking the students' skills in using the meters and using the equation. It will also give opportunities for students to manipulate variables, and discuss the 'directly proportional' relationship between variables (this relates to 'How Science Works').

Plenaries

An electron's tale – Students write a paragraph about the journey of an electron around a circuit containing a bulb and resistor. They should write about the energy changes that are going on in the circuit. A good description should also reference the collisions that take place. *(5 minutes)*

Reinforced resistance – The students have met two calculations in the lesson and plenty of reinforcement is required to ensure that they use the equations correctly. Give some additional ones, differentiating as appropriate. Students can be further extended by looking at combining the equations (or using one after another) to solve more complex problems. *(10 minutes)*

Practical support

Investigating the resistance of a wire

The students can investigate if the resistance of a wire depends on the current flowing through it. Constantan wires work well, as these do not change resistance as much when they heat up. It is also advisable to use battery packs or power packs with lockable voltage outputs, as the wires can heat up and cause burns if high currents are used.

Equipment and materials required

For each group: a power supply or battery pack, connecting leads, switch, crocodile clips, variable resistor, length of wire (30–50 cm), heatproof mat, ammeter and voltmeter.

Details

The students connect up the circuit with the variable resistor and test wire in series. The ammeter is also placed in series and the voltmeter in parallel across the test wire. Some students will struggle to set this up, so check the circuits before they are switched on. Using the variable resistor, the students can control the current through the test wire and measure both the current and the potential difference. In general, they should find that the resistance stays constant unless the wire heats up too much. The experiment shouldn't get too hot if low pd's are used, but use a heatproof mat anyway.

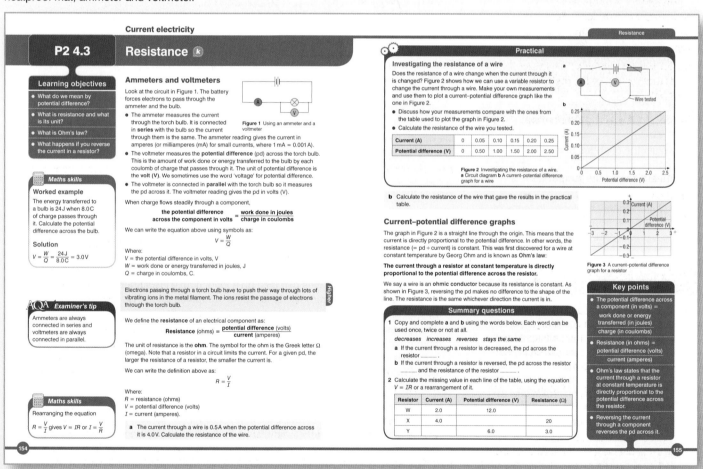

Further teaching suggestions

ICT link-up

- If you get different groups to investigate the current–potential different characteristics of different lengths (or diameters) of wire, then the data can be collected in a spreadsheet. This can be used to calculate the mean resistance of the wire from the data, and then to check for a relationship between the length (or diameter) and the resistance by quickly plotting a graph.

Summary answers

1 a decreases
  b reverses, stays the same
2 W: 6.0 Ω; X: 80 V; Y: 2.0 A

P2 4.4

More current–potential difference graphs

Learning objectives

Students should learn that:

- that the resistance of a filament bulb increases as the temperature rises
- how the resistance of a diode depends on the pd applied across it
- how the resistance of a thermistor decreases when its temperature increases
- how the resistance of an LDR decreases when the light level increases.

Learning outcomes

Most students should be able to:

- draw current–pd graphs for a resistor, a filament bulb and a diode
- describe how the resistance of a filament bulb changes depending on the current through it
- describe how the resistance of a diode depends on which way round it is connected in a circuit
- describe how the resistance of a thermistor and light-dependent resistor (LDR) depend on the temperature and light level, respectively.

Some students should also be able to:

- explain the changes that take place in a series circuit including a thermistor or a LDR when the temperature or the light level changes
- explain resistance change in terms of ions and electrons. [HT only]

Support

- Using data logging equipment is a very good way of collecting data for current–potential difference graphs. Once set up, the students just have to adjust the variable resistor, press the space bar to take readings and then repeat until all the data is collected. The graphs can be displayed in seconds.

Extend

- Students could be asked to read values accurately off graphs and use these values in further calculations. For example, the students can read the resistance of a thermistor at a certain temperature and then calculate what current would pass through it at certain potential differences. They could see if the operation of a thermistor is independent of the pd across it.

Specification link-up: Physics P2.3

$\mathcal{AQA}$

- Current–potential difference graphs are used to show how the current through a component varies with the potential difference across it. *[P2.3.2 d)]*
- The resistance of a filament bulb increases as the temperature of the filament increases … . *[P2.3.2 m)]*
- The current through a diode flows in one direction only. The diode has a very high resistance in the reverse direction … . *[P2.3.2 n)]*
- An LED emits light when a current flows through it in the forward direction. *[P2.3.2 o)]*
- The resistance of a light-dependent resistor (LDR) decreases as light intensity increases. *[P2.3.2 p)]*
- The resistance of a thermistor decreases as the temperature increases. *[P2.3.3 q)]*
- Apply the principles of basic electrical circuits to practical situations. *[P2.3]*
  Controlled Assessment: P4.5 Analyse and interpret primary and secondary data. *[P4.5.3 a)]*

Lesson structure

Starters

Three switches – Ask: 'You are outside a room with three switches that control three light bulbs inside the room; one switch for each light. How can you work out which switch controls which light if you are only allowed to open the door and go into the room once?' This is a test of deduction (quite an old one at that); it involves leaving one switch on, one off and turning one on for a minute then off again before entering the room. *(5 minutes)*

Pop! – Set up a circuit with a filament bulb that will have too high a current. Switch it on when the room is silent (so that they can hear the 'tink' sound) and ask the students to explain what happened. Their descriptions should mention the heating effect causing the wire to melt. If they don't, then demonstrate again by slowly increasing the current so that the students can appreciate the wire getting hotter and hotter. To support students, you may need to provide a brief recap of the effect of high resistance. Extend students by asking for a description in terms of electrons and ions and then ask what happens to the ions as the wire heats up and what this would do to the resistance. *(10 minutes)*

Main

- Start this topic with a reminder of the practical work from last lesson. Demonstrate how to build a circuit component-by-component in a logical way so that the students will follow this technique.
- The initial practical activities can take up a lot of time if the students wish to take plenty of measurements. You may like to let some groups do one of the experiments while the rest do the other, and then get them to share the results.
- The results should show that the filament bulb does not have a straight line on its current–potential difference graph. This is because it is heating up and the resistance is increasing, the greater the current in the wire. Link this back to the students' ideas about what happens to a metal when it gets hotter. The ions are vibrating more and the electrons are having more collisions with them. This increases the resistance. Higher Tier candidates should be able to explain this point in examinations.
- A diode is a more complex device. It behaves in a non-ohmic way. The reasons for its behaviour are beyond KS4. Some students will have heard of light-emitting diodes and think that all diodes give out light. You could demonstrate one of these in a circuit, showing that it only lights up if it is placed in the circuit the right way. The arrow on the symbol shows the direction of the current.
- As with the initial practical task, you might like to set different groups different tasks for the thermistor and LDR. They can then share the results with the other groups. These two devices can be investigated to focus on one of the many of the investigative aspects of 'How Science Works'.

Plenaries

Inside the black box – An electrical component has been placed inside a black box with only the two connections visible. The students should design an experiment to find out what it is. Support candidates by giving them some suggested equipment that includes a voltmeter and ammeter. *(5 minutes)*

Electrical evaluation – The students should evaluate the results of their experiments by comparing sets of data collected by different groups. This will allow them to assess the reliability of their techniques and suggest some improvements. Extend students by asking them to calculate values such as the resistance of the thermistor at a certain temperature; they should be able to suggest that collecting more data over a narrow range around this temperature may lead to a more reliable and precise result. For additional support you should demonstrate how to read values of the graph to determine the resistance. *(10 minutes)*

Practical support

Investigating different components

The students can investigate how the resistance of a filament bulb and a diode change when the potential difference across them is changed.

Equipment and materials required
For each group: a power supply or battery pack, connecting leads, variable resistor, ammeter, voltmeter, filament bulb, fixed resistor and diode.

Details
The students connect up the circuit with the component under test in series with the variable resistor. The ammeter is also placed in series

and the voltmeter is placed in parallel with the test component. Using the variable resistor, the students change the pd across the component and record the current and pd. From the results, the students produce a current–potential difference graph. They should also try the circuit with the current flowing in the opposite direction, to show that this does not affect the bulb, but is very important for the diode.

Thermistors and light-dependent resistors (LDRs)
The students can investigate an LDR by finding out how its resistance is related to the distance it is from a bright light. Sensitive thermistors can have a significant change in resistance from just placing them between finger and thumb to warm them up. With low voltage electrical supplies, it is possible to set up circuits in which a thermistor can be attached by crocodile clips and placed in a beaker of hot water (from a kettle) and the resistance can be measured as the water cools.

Current electricity

P2 4.4 — More current–potential difference graphs

Have you ever switched a light bulb on only to hear it 'pop' and fail? Electrical appliances can fail at very inconvenient times. Most electrical failures are because too much current passes through a component in the appliance.

Learning objectives
- What happens to the resistance of a filament bulb as its temperature increases?
- How does the current through a diode depend on the potential difference across it?
- What happens to the resistance of a thermistor as its temperature increases and of an LDR as the light level increases?

Practical
Investigating different components

We can use the circuit in Figure 2 on the previous page to find out if the resistance of a component depends on the current. We can also see if reversing the component in the circuit has any effect.

Make your own measurements using a resistor, a filament bulb and a diode.

Plot your measurements on a current–potential difference graph. Plot the 'reverse' measurements on the negative section of each axis.
- Why can you use a line graph to display your data? (See H3 Using data.)

Using current–potential difference graphs
A filament bulb

Figure 1 shows the graph for a torch bulb (i.e. a low-voltage filament bulb).
- The line **curves** away from the current axis. So the current is *not* directly proportional to the potential difference. The filament bulb is a non-ohmic conductor.
- The resistance (= potential difference/current) increases as the current increases. So the resistance of a filament bulb increases as the filament temperature increases.

The resistance of the metal filament increases as its temperature increases. This is because the ions in the metal filament vibrate more as the temperature increases. So they resist the passage of the electrons through the filament more.

- Reversing the potential difference makes no difference to the shape of the curve. The resistance is the same for the same current, regardless of its direction.

a Calculate the resistance of the filament bulb at **i** 0.1 A **ii** 0.2 A.

Figure 1 A current–potential difference graph for a filament bulb

The diode
Look at Figure 2, a graph for a diode.
- In the 'forward' direction, the line curves towards the current axis. So the current is not directly proportional to the potential difference. A diode is not an ohmic conductor.
- In the reverse direction, the current is negligible. So its resistance in the reverse direction is much higher than in the forward direction.

Note that a light-emitting diode (LED) emits light when a current passes through it in the forward direction.

b What can we say about the forward resistance of a diode as the current increases?

Figure 2 A current–potential difference graph for a diode

Practical
Thermistors and light-dependent resistors (LDRs)

We use thermistors and LDRs in sensor circuits. A thermistor is a temperature-dependent resistor. The resistance of an LDR depends on how much light is on it.

Test a thermistor and then an LDR in series with a battery and an ammeter.
- What did you find out about each component tested?

Figure 3 a A thermistor and its circuit symbol **b** An LDR and its circuit symbol

Current–potential difference graphs for a thermistor and an LDR
For a thermistor, Figure 4 shows the current–potential difference graph at two different temperatures.
- At constant temperature, the line is straight so its resistance is constant.
- If the temperature is increased, its resistance decreases.

For a light-dependent resistor, Figure 5 shows the current–potential difference graph in bright light and in dim light.

c What does the graph tell us about an LDR's resistance if the light intensity is constant?
d If the light intensity is increased, what happens to the resistance of the LDR?

Figure 4 Thermistor graph
Figure 5 LDR graph

Summary questions
1 Copy and complete sentences **a** to **d** using the words below:
diode filament bulb resistor thermistor
a The resistance of a .... decreases as its temperature increases.
b The resistance of a .... depends on which way round it is connected in a circuit.
c The resistance of a .... increases as the current through it increases.
d The resistance of a .... does not depend on the current through it.

2 A thermistor is connected in series with an ammeter and a 3.0 V battery, as shown.
a At 15 °C, the current through the thermistor is 0.2 A and the potential difference across it is 3.0 V. Calculate its resistance at this temperature.
b State and explain what happens to the ammeter reading if the thermistor's temperature is increased.

Figure 6

3 The thermistor in Figure 6 is replaced by a light-dependent resistor (LDR). State and explain what happens to the ammeter reading when the LDR is covered.

Did you know ...?
When a light bulb fails, it usually happens when you switch it on. Because resistance is low when the bulb is off, a large current passes through it when you switch it on. If the current is too large, it burns the filament out.

Key points
- *Filament bulb:* resistance increases with increase of the filament temperature.
- *Diode:* 'forward' resistance low; 'reverse' resistance high.
- *Thermistor:* resistance decreases if its temperature increases.
- *LDR:* resistance decreases if the light intensity on it increases.

Did you know ...?
The longest lasting light bulb has been on for more than 110 years. It is in a fire station in Livermore, USA, and was installed in 1901. It is never off, except in power cuts and when it was moved to the new fire station. You might like to check if it is still going!

Answers to in-text questions
a i 5 Ω **ii** 10 Ω
b It decreases.
c The resistance is constant.
d The resistance decreases.

Summary answers
1 **a** thermistor
  b diode
  c filament bulb
  d resistor

2 **a** 15 Ω
  b The ammeter reading increases because the resistance of the thermistor decreases.

3 When the LDR is covered, its resistance increases. The current decreases because the resistance of the LDR increases and the pd across the LDR is still 3.0 V.

P2 4.5

Series circuits

AQA

Specification link-up: Physics P2.3

- The potential difference provided by cells connected in series is the sum of the potential difference of each cell (depending on the direction in which they are connected). [P2.3.2 j)]
- For components connected in series:
  - the total resistance is the sum of the resistance of each component
  - there is the same current through each component
  - the total potential difference of the supply is shared between the components. [P2.3.2 k)]
- Apply the principles of basic electrical circuits to practical situations. [P2.3]

  Controlled Assessment: P4.5 Analyse and interpret primary and secondary data. [P4.5.2 a) b)]

Learning objectives

Students should learn that:

- in a series circuit the same current passes through all components
- the pd of the voltage supply is shared across the components in a series circuit
- cells in series add their potentials to give the total voltage
- the total resistance in a series circuit is the sum of the component resistances.

Learning outcomes

Most students should be able to:

- state that the current through components in series is the same
- find the total potential difference across several components in series, given the potential difference across each component
- find the total potential difference of a group of cells connected in series
- calculate the total resistance in a series circuit.

Some students should also be able to:

- analyse a series circuit to find the current and pd across components.

Answers to in-text questions

a 0.12 A
b 0.4 V
c 1.1 V
d 5 Ω

Support

- Provide the students with a printed set of circuit rules containing the ones from this topic and the next, to help them remember them all.

Extend

- There are a set of rules about the current and potentials in a circuit called Kirchhoff's laws. These are basically an electrical statement of the laws of conservation of energy, and the students should be able to find out what they are.

Lesson structure

Starters

Duff battery – Ask the students to correct this information: 'A chemical reaction in a battery makes electrons. These move quickly around a circuit and go through the components until there are no electrons left. The battery "runs out" when there are no chemicals left in it to make electrons from.' [e.g. 'A chemical reaction in the battery provides electrons with energy. These electrons move slowly around the circuit and push other electrons through it. As the electrons move through the components of the circuit, they lose energy until they reach the cell again when they have transferred all of the energy they were provided with. The battery "runs out" when all of the chemicals in it have reacted together and it cannot provide the electrons with any more energy.'] (5 minutes)

One way only – Ask: 'In what situation are we allowed only one way through something?' Let the students think for a few moments. Ask: 'If there is only one way to go on a tour, do the same number of people come out as go in?' Link the idea to the conservation of a property such as the cars on a motorway. To extend students, ask them to think about what happens if the pathway gets narrower. For extra suppor,t use animation of flow to show that the same number of objects must leave as enter. (10 minutes)

Main

- When discussing series and parallel circuits, many teachers use the analogy of a central heating system with the water representing the electrons, a pump representing the battery, etc. There are limitations with this concept, but it can help some students. The students need to be reminded that the current is the rate of **flow** of electrons. The larger the current, the more electrons are passing a point each second. The electrons cannot be destroyed and they do not escape from the circuit.

- As noted in the practical, there can be some minor errors produced by the meters so you will have to explain them to the students. This is a useful opportunity to consider 'How Science Works': variation in data and sources of error.

- Simulation software can be used to show the measurement of the pd across many bulbs connected in series. It is also easy to add more cells to show that the total pd drop across the components always matches the pd of the battery.

- Many students will simply accept that the total resistance of a set of components in series is just the same as the individual resistances without the need for calculations. Test their understanding by showing them a set of resistors in series, and asking for the total resistance. Students should have no problems with this.

- You might like to show some more difficult resistors such as 1.5 MΩ or 33 mΩ to get the students used to them. They should see that the physical size of a resistor is not always an indication of how much resistance it represents.

Plenaries

Controlling current – Give the students a set of cards representing cells (1.5 V) and resistors (1 Ω, 2 Ω, 5 Ω, etc.) and ask them to put some of them together to produce a current of 1 A, then a current of 0.5 A. There should be a number of ways to do this. You can extend the students by providing more difficult values to use or a situation where they must use a LED or select a suitable thermistor using its resistance characteristics. Support can be provided by giving only simple possibilities. (5 minutes)

Circuit rules – The students should start making a list of circuit rules that help them work out the currents, potential differences and resistances in series and parallel circuits. *(10 minutes)*

Practical support

 Investigating potential differences in a series circuit

This experiment helps to verify the rule about potential differences in series circuits.

Equipment and materials required

For each group: a power supply or battery pack (1.5 V), connecting leads, variable resistor, 1.5 V bulb and three voltmeters.

Details

The students connect up a bulb and variable resistor in series. Connect up one voltmeter across the bulb (with voltage, V_1) and one across the variable resistor (with voltage, V_2). When the circuit is switched on, the students should find that $V_1 + V_2 = V_{tot}$ when the variable resistor is set to any position. You may find that the voltmeters don't quite show this, and so it is a good time to discuss errors and limitations of the equipment (this relates to 'How Science Works'). In the discussion, students could observe the circuit again with a third voltmeter connected across the cell. This should demonstrate that the cell pd is always shared between the bulb and the variable resistor, even if the cell pd changes.

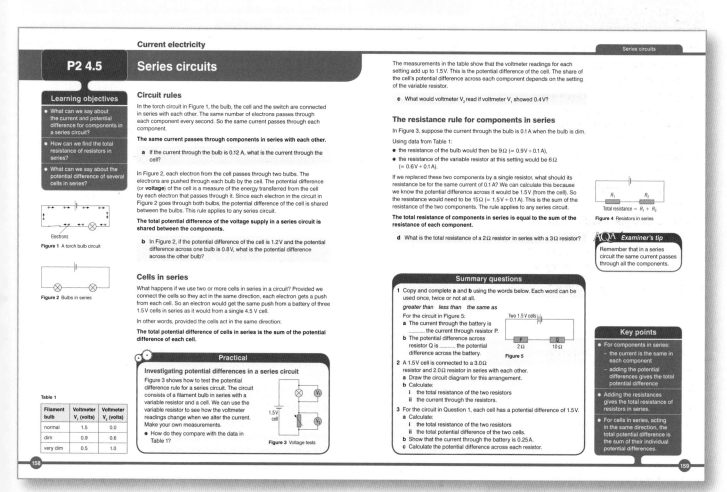

Current electricity

Series circuits

P2 4.5 Series circuits

Learning objectives

- What can we say about the current and potential difference for components in a series circuit?
- How can we find the total resistance of resistors in series?
- What can we say about the potential difference of several cells in series?

Electrons

Figure 1 A torch bulb circuit

Figure 2 Bulbs in series

Table 1

Filament bulb	Voltmeter V_1 (volts)	Voltmeter V_2 (volts)
normal	1.5	0.0
dim	0.9	0.6
very dim	0.5	1.0

Circuit rules

In the torch circuit in Figure 1, the bulb, the cell and the switch are connected in series with each other. The same number of electrons passes through each component every second. So the same current passes through each component.

The same current passes through components in series with each other.

  a If the current through the bulb is 0.12 A, what is the current through the cell?

In Figure 2, each electron from the cell passes through two bulbs. The electrons are pushed through each bulb by the cell. The potential difference (or **voltage**) of the cell is a measure of the energy transferred from the cell by each electron that passes through it. Since each electron in the circuit in Figure 2 goes through both bulbs, the potential difference of the cell is shared between the bulbs. This rule applies to any series circuit.

The total potential difference of the voltage supply in a series circuit is shared between the components.

  b In Figure 2, if the potential difference of the cell is 1.2 V and the potential difference across one bulb is 0.8 V, what is the potential difference across the other bulb?

Cells in series

What happens if we use two or more cells in series in a circuit? Provided we connect the cells so they act in the same direction, each electron gets a push from each cell. So an electron would get the same push from a battery of three 1.5 V cells in series as it would from a single 4.5 V cell.

In other words, provided the cells act in the same direction:

The total potential difference of cells in series is the sum of the potential difference of each cell.

Practical

Investigating potential differences in a series circuit

Figure 3 shows how to test the potential difference rule for a series circuit. The circuit consists of a filament bulb in series with a variable resistor and a cell. We can use the variable resistor to see how the voltmeter readings change when we alter the current. Make your own measurements.

- How do they compare with the data in Table 1?

Figure 3 Voltage tests

The measurements in the table show that the voltmeter readings for each setting add up to 1.5 V. This is the potential difference of the cell. The share of the cell's potential difference across each component depends on the setting of the variable resistor.

  c What would voltmeter V_2 read if voltmeter V_1 showed 0.4 V?

The resistance rule for components in series

In Figure 3, suppose the current through the bulb is 0.1 A when the bulb is dim.

Using data from Table 1:
- the resistance of the bulb would then be 9 Ω (= 0.9 V ÷ 0.1 A),
- the resistance of the variable resistor at this setting would be 6 Ω (= 0.6 V ÷ 0.1 A).

If we replaced these two components by a single resistor, what should its resistance be for the same current of 0.1 A? We can calculate this because we know the potential difference across it would be 1.5 V (from the cell). So the resistance would need to be 15 Ω (= 1.5 V ÷ 0.1 A). This is the sum of the resistance of the two components. The rule applies to any series circuit.

The total resistance of components in series is equal to the sum of the resistance of each component.

  d What is the total resistance of a 2 Ω resistor in series with a 3 Ω resistor?

R_1 R_2

Total resistance = $R_1 + R_2$

Figure 4 Resistors in series

AQA *Examiner's tip*

Remember that in a series circuit the same current passes through all the components.

Summary questions

1 Copy and complete **a** and **b** using the words below. Each word can be used once, twice or not at all.

  greater than less than the same as

For the circuit in Figure 5:

  a The current through the battery is .... the current through resistor P.

  b The potential difference across resistor Q is .... the potential difference across the battery.

Two 1.5 V cells

| P | Q |
| 2 Ω | 10 Ω |

Figure 5

2 A 1.5 V cell is connected to a 3.0 Ω resistor and 2.0 Ω resistor in series with each other.

  a Draw the circuit diagram for this arrangement.

  b Calculate:

    i the total resistance of the two resistors

    ii the current through the resistors.

3 For the circuit in Question 1, each cell has a potential difference of 1.5 V.

  a Calculate:

    i the total resistance of the two resistors

    ii the total potential difference of the two cells.

  b Show that the current through the battery is 0.25 A.

  c Calculate the potential difference across each resistor.

Key points

- For components in series:
  - the current is the same in each component
  - adding the potential differences gives the total potential difference
- Adding the resistances gives the total resistance of resistors in series.
- For cells in series, acting in the same direction, the total potential difference is the sum of their individual potential differences.

158 / 159

Further teaching suggestions

ICT link-up

- If at all possible, show a simulation of electron movement through the circuit to show that the electrons pass all the way around the circuit and are not used up. The simulation should also have some way of showing that the electrons are transferring energy as they go.

Missing values

- Give the students some series circuit diagrams with missing pd's, currents or resistances. Ask them to find the missing values. This should test their knowledge of the current–pd–resistance relationship and the total resistance rule.

Summary answers

1 a the same as   **b** less than

2 a

1.5 V

3.0 Ω   2.0 Ω

  b i 5.0 Ω **ii** 0.3 A

3 a i 12 Ω **ii** 3.0 V

  b $\dfrac{3\,V}{12\,\Omega} = 0.25\,A$ **c** P = 0.5 V, Q = 2.5 V

P2 4.6

Parallel circuits

Learning objectives

Students should learn:

- that the potential difference across components in parallel is the same
- that the total current in a parallel circuit is the sum of the currents in the individual branches.

Learning outcomes

Most students should be able to:

- recognise components in parallel with each other
- calculate the current in a branch of a parallel circuit, given the total current and the current in the other branches
- identify, for resistors of known resistance in parallel, which resistor has the most current passing through it and which has the least.

Some students should also be able to:

- analyse parallel circuits to find the current through branches and the potential difference across components.

Support

- There are some more tricky circuits here and the students may need a step-by-step guide to assemble them: 'connect the positive end of the battery to the ammeter', etc. You might also think about attaching labels A_1, A_2 to the ammeters to reduce confusion.

Extend

- The light that shines twice as bright lasts half as long. If two bulbs are connected to a battery in parallel, they will shine more brightly than if they were connected in series but they will only last half as long. Can the students explain why? Explanations should include the idea that more energy is being transferred, so the battery will not last as long and there should be an explanation of why the bulbs are brighter in the first place (there is a large current and greater pd across them).

AQA   Specification link-up: Physics P2.3

- The current through a component depends on its resistance. The greater the resistance, the smaller the current for a given potential difference across the component. *[P2.3.2 i)]*
- For components connected in parallel:
  - the potential difference across each component is the same
  - the total current through the whole circuit is the sum of the currents through the separate components. *[P2.3.2 l)]*
- Apply the principles of basic electrical circuits to practical situations. *[P2.3]*
  Controlled Assessment: P4.5 Analyse and interpret primary and secondary data. *[P4.5.2 a) b)]*

Lesson structure

Starters

Circuit jumble – Show the students a diagram of a parallel circuit with three branches and several components on each branch. The wires and components are jumbled up and the students have to redraw the circuit properly. This should be a clear diagram with no gaps in the connections. *(5 minutes)*

The river – Show the students a picture of a river that branches and rejoins. Ask them to explain what happens to the current in the river before, during and after the split. Support students by showing clips of the flow or demonstrating the same idea with pipes (transparent ones work best). They should realise that the current divides and then rejoins, meaning that the total current is unchanged after the merger. Less obvious is that fact that each kilogram of water that went down one branch has travelled by the same distance **downhill** as each kilogram that went the other way. This concept is similar to the ideas of pd and energy transfer in different branches of a circuit. Students can be extended by asking them to identify the limitations of this model of current and pd at the end of the lesson. *(10 minutes)*

Main

- The initial investigation is straightforward and the students should be able to find the rule easily. A discussion of errors involved in the ammeter readings helps to get across concepts involving single measurements from 'How Science Works'.
- A simulation can be used if there are not enough ammeters, but you should show the results in a real circuit too.
- Spend a bit of time explaining that at the junction of a branch some of the electrons go one way, whereas the rest go the other way, but they all come from and go back to the battery.
- The bypass idea helps some students realise that because there are more paths for the current, a larger current can flow.
- The second simple circuit should confirm that the potential difference is the same across both of the resistors. If the resistors are the same size, then the currents should also be the same through each branch. To extend students, ask them to investigate a circuit that has two resistors on one branch and one on the other. Ask: 'Does the potential difference across the first branch match that across the second?'
- The circuit analysis will show if the students have got a firm grip of the equations. You may have to lead them through the analysis one step at a time. Try a couple more circuits if time permits.

Plenaries

Parallel analogies – Can the students come up with any more analogies for a parallel circuit besides the ones from the 'Did you know' box in the Student Book? They should explain them to each other to decide which is best. *(5 minutes)*

Stair lights – Can the students design a simple circuit that can be used to turn the lights on and off from the top and bottom of a set of stairs? If time permits, they could build one. This would involve a pair of switches; one at the bottom of the stairs. The students can then explain how the lights operate. For support you can demonstrate the circuit and show the diagram asking the students to explain how it operates. For extension the students can see if it is possible to control a circuit like this from three or more switches; is there a general pattern to the design? *(10 minutes)*

Practical support

⚙ Investigating parallel circuits

This experiment shows that that the current is divided through parallel branches.

Equipment and materials required
For each group: a power supply or battery pack (1.5 V), connecting leads, variable resistor, two 1.5 V bulbs and three ammeters.

Details
The students set up the circuit with two parallel branches, each with an ammeter. The third ammeter is placed in series with the power supply or battery to measure total current, and the variable resistor is used in series with the battery to control the current. The readings from the two ammeters on the branches (A_2 and A_3) should be equal to the total current from the battery (A_1). As in the experiment from the last lesson, there can be inaccuracies in the readings so go through the results with the students and discuss the reasons for these errors (this relates to 'How Science Works').

Potential difference in a parallel circuit
This is another simple circuit used to verify that the potential difference across parallel components is the same.

Equipment and materials required
For each group: a power supply or battery pack (1.5 V), connecting leads, a 2 Ω resistor and a 5 Ω resistor, a variable resistor, and two voltmeters.

Details
The students connect up the circuit as shown and measure the pd across the two resistors. This should be the same. To show that this fact does not change, replace one of the resistors with a variable one and alter its resistance.

Current electricity

Parallel circuits

P2 4.6　Parallel circuits

Learning objectives
- What can we say about the currents in the components in a parallel circuit?
- What can we say about the potential differences across the components in a parallel circuit?
- How can we calculate current through a resistor in a parallel circuit?

❓ Did you know …?
A bypass is a parallel route. A heart bypass is another route for the flow of blood. A road bypass is a road that passes a town centre instead of going through it. For components in parallel, charge flows separately through each component. The total flow of charge is the sum of the flow through each component.

Practical
Investigating parallel circuits
Figure 1 shows how you can investigate the current through two bulbs in parallel with each other. You can use ammeters in series with the bulbs and the cell to measure the current through each component.

Figure 1 At a junction

Set up your own circuit and collect your data.
- How do your measurements compare with the ones for different settings of the variable resistor shown in Table 1 below?
- Discuss if your own measurements show the same pattern.

Look at the sample data below.

Table 1

Ammeter A_1 (A)	Ammeter A_2 (A)	Ammeter A_3 (A)
0.50	0.30	0.20
0.30	0.20	0.10
0.18	0.12	0.06

In each case, the reading of ammeter A_1 is equal to the sum of the readings of ammeters A_2 and A_3.

This shows that the current through the cell is equal to sum of the currents through the two bulbs. This rule applies wherever components are in parallel.

a If ammeter A_1 reads 0.40 A and A_2 reads 0.1 A, what would A_3 read?

The total current through the whole circuit is the sum of the currents through the separate components.

Potential difference in a parallel circuit
Figure 2 shows two resistors X and Y in parallel with each other. A voltmeter is connected across each resistor. The voltmeter across resistor X shows the same reading as the voltmeter across resistor Y. This is because each electron from the cell either passes through X or through Y. So it delivers the same amount of energy from the cell, whichever resistor it goes through. In other words:

For components in parallel, the potential difference across each component is the same.

Figure 2 Components in parallel

Calculations on parallel circuits
Components in parallel have the same potential difference across them. The current through each component depends on the resistance of the component.
- The bigger the resistance of the component, the smaller the current through it. The resistor which has the largest resistance passes the smallest current.
- We can calculate the current using the equation:

$$\text{current (amperes)} = \frac{\text{potential difference (volts)}}{\text{resistance (ohms)}}$$

b A 3 Ω resistor and a 6 Ω resistor are connected in parallel in a circuit. Which resistor passes the most current?

🖩 Maths skills
Worked example
The circuit diagram shows three resistors $R_1 = 1\,\Omega$, $R_2 = 2\,\Omega$ and $R_3 = 6\,\Omega$ connected in parallel to a 6 V battery.
Calculate:
a the current through each resistor
b the current through the battery

Solution

a $I_1 = \dfrac{V_1}{R_1} = \dfrac{6}{1} = 6\,A$

$I_2 = \dfrac{V_2}{R_2} = \dfrac{6}{2} = 3\,A$

$I_3 = \dfrac{V_3}{R_3} = \dfrac{6}{6} = 1\,A$

Figure 3

b The total current from the battery = $I_1 + I_2 + I_3 = 6\,A + 3\,A + 1\,A = 10\,A$

Summary questions
1 Copy and complete **a** and **b** using the words below:
　current　potential difference
　a Components in parallel with each other have the same ....
　b For components in parallel, each component has a different ....

2 A 1.5 V cell is connected across a 3 Ω resistor in parallel with a 6 Ω resistor.
　a Draw the circuit diagram for this circuit.
　b Show that the current through:
　　i the 3 Ω resistor is 0.50 A　**ii** the 6 Ω resistor is 0.25 A.
　c Calculate the current passing through the cell.

3 The circuit diagram shows three resistors $R_1 = 2\,\Omega$, $R_2 = 3\,\Omega$ and $R_3 = 6\,\Omega$ connected to each other in parallel and to a 6 V battery.
Calculate:
　a the current through each resistor
　b the current through the battery

Figure 4

Key points
- For components in parallel:
  - the total current is the sum of the currents through the separate components
  - the bigger the resistance of a component, the smaller its current is.
- In a parallel circuit the potential difference is the same across each component.
- To calculate the current through a resistor in a parallel circuit, use this equation:
  $$\text{current (amperes)} = \frac{\text{potential difference (volts)}}{\text{resistance (ohms)}}$$

160　161

Further teaching suggestions

ICT link-up
- A range of software is available to simulate circuit construction and measure current and potential differences. This can be much easier to use than assembling larger parallel circuits with a number of voltmeters and ammeters.

Analysing circuits
- Give the students some series and parallel circuits to analyse. They should find the missing currents, potential differences and resistances.

Answers to in-text questions
a 0.30 A
b The 3 Ω resistor.

Summary answers

1 **a** potential difference
　b current

2 **a**

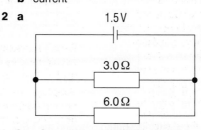

1.5 V

3.0 Ω

6.0 Ω

　b　**i** current = 1.5 V/3 Ω = 0.50 A
　　　ii current = 1.5 V/6 Ω = 0.25 A
　c cell current = 0.5 + 0.25 = 0.75 A

3 **a** R_1: 3 A; R_2: 2 A; R_3: 1 A
　b 6 A

Summary answers

1 a

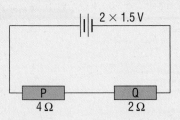

b

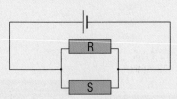

2 a filament bulb   **b** resistor
   c thermistor   **d** diode

3 a

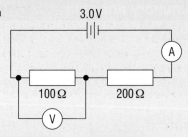

$2 \times 1.5\,V$

P $4\,\Omega$ Q $2\,\Omega$

   b   **i** $3.0\,V$
     ii $6\,\Omega$
     iii $0.5\,A$
     iv P: $2.0\,V$; Q: $1.0\,V$

4 a

R

S

   b   **i** $1.0\,A$
     ii $0.5\,A$
     iii $1.5\,A$

5 a different from
   b equal to

6 a   **i** $2.0\,V$
    ii pd across the LDR = battery pd − pd across the
      $200\,\Omega$ resistor = $3.0 - 2.0 = 1.0\,V$
   b The resistance of the LDR increases when it is
    covered, so the total resistance of the circuit increases.
    Therefore, the current decreases, so the ammeter
    reading decreases.

7 a

$3.0\,V$

A

$100\,\Omega$ $200\,\Omega$

V

   b   **i** $300\,\Omega$ **ii** $0.010\,A$
    iii $1.0\,V$ **iv** $2.0\,V$

8 a   **i** The battery pd of $3.0\,V$ is shared between the LED
     and the resistor. Since the potential difference
     across the LED is $0.6\,V$ when it emits light,
     the potential difference across the resistor is
     $3.0 - 0.6 = 2.4\,V$.
    ii $0.024\,A$

Current electricity: P2 4.1–P2 4.6

Summary questions

1 Sketch a circuit diagram to show:
   a a torch bulb, a cell and a diode connected in series so
     that the torch bulb is on
   b a variable resistor, two cells in series and a torch bulb
     whose brightness can be varied by adjusting the
     variable resistor.

2 Match each component in the list to each statement **a** to
   d that describes it.
   diode   filament bulb   resistor   thermistor
   a Its resistance increases if the current through it
     increases.
   b The current through it is proportional to the potential
     difference across it.
   c Its resistance decreases if its temperature is
     increased.
   d Its resistance depends on which way round it is
     connected in a circuit.

3 a Sketch a circuit diagram to show two resistors P and Q
    connected in series to a battery of two cells in series
    with each other.
   b In the circuit in part **a**, resistor P has a resistance of
     $4\,\Omega$, resistor Q has a resistance of $2\,\Omega$ and each cell
     has a potential difference of $1.5\,V$. Calculate:
     i the total potential difference of the two cells
     ii the total resistance of the two resistors
     iii the current in the circuit
     iv the potential difference across each resistor.

4 a Sketch a circuit diagram to show two resistors R and S
    in parallel with each other connected to a single cell.
   b In the circuit in part **a**, resistor R has a resistance of
     $2\,\Omega$, resistor S has a resistance of $4\,\Omega$ and the cell has
     a potential difference of $2\,V$. Calculate:
     i the current through resistor R
     ii the current through resistor S
     iii the current through the cell in the circuit.

5 Copy and complete **a** and **b** using the phrases below.
   Each option can be used once, twice or not at all.
   different from   equal to
   a For two components X and Y in series, the potential
     difference across X is usually .... the potential
     difference across Y.
   b For two components X and Y in parallel, the potential
     difference across X is .... the potential difference
     across Y.

6 Figure 1 shows a light-dependent resistor is series with
   $200\,\Omega$ resistor, a $3.0\,V$ battery and an ammeter.

$3.0\,V$

LDR $200\,\Omega$

Figure 1

   a With the LDR in daylight, the ammeter reads $0.010\,A$.
     i Calculate the potential difference across the $200\,\Omega$
      resistor when the current through it is $0.010\,A$.
     ii Show that the potential difference across the LDR
      is $1.0\,V$ when the ammeter reads $0.010\,A$.
   b If the LDR is then covered, explain whether the
     ammeter reading increases or decreases or stays the
     same.

7 In Figure 1 in Question 6, the LDR is replaced by a 100
   resistor and a voltmeter connected in parallel with this
   resistor.
   a Draw the circuit diagram for this circuit.
   b Calculate:
     i the total resistance of the two resistors in the circu
     ii the current through the ammeter
     iii the voltmeter reading
     iv the potential difference across the $200\,\Omega$ resistor.

8 Figure 2 shows a light-emitting diode (LED) in series wi
   a resistor and a $3.0\,V$ battery.

$3.0\,V$

LED $1000\,\Omega$

Figure 2

   a The LED in the circuit emits light. The potential
     difference across it when it emits light is $0.6\,V$.
     i Explain why the potential difference across the
      $1000\,\Omega$ resistor is $2.4\,V$.
     ii Calculate the current in the circuit.
   b If the LED in the circuit is reversed, what would be th
     current in the circuit? Give a reason for your answer.

9 State and explain how the resistance of a filament
   bulb changes when the current through the filament is
   increased.

---

   b The current would be (almost) zero as the 'reverse'
     resistance of the LED is very high. The total resistance
     of the LED and the resistor would therefore be much
     greater than it was when the LED was in its 'forward'
     direction so the current would be much less than
     $0.024\,A$.

9 The resistance increases when the current is increased.
   This is because the increase of current makes the bulb
   hotter. As a result, the metal ions of the filament vibrate
   more, so they resist the passage of electrons through the
   filament more.

Kerboodle resources

Resources available for this chapter on Kerboodle are:
- Chapter map: Current electricity
- Maths skills: Potential difference, current and resistance
  (P2 4.3)
- How Science Works: What's the potential (P2 4.3)
- Practical: Resistance in a wire (P2 4.3)
- Interactive activity: Circuit symbols and resistance
- Revision podcast: Series and parallel circuits
- Test yourself: Current electricity
- On your marks: Current electricity
- Examination-style questions: Current electricity
- Answers to examination-style questions: Current electricity

AQA Examination-style questions

1 A plastic rod is rubbed with a dry cloth.

  a Explain how the rod becomes negatively charged. (3)

  b What charge is left on the cloth? (1)

  c What happens if the negatively charged rod is brought close to another negatively charged rod? (1)

2 a Copy and complete the table of circuit symbols and their names. (5)

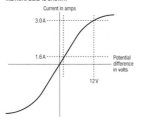

Circuit symbol	Name
(V)	i
ii	ammeter
(variable resistor symbol)	iii
iv	LDR
(cell symbol)	v

  b Copy and complete the following sentences using the list of words and phrases below. Each word can be used once, more than once or not at all.

energy transferred   charge   resistance   voltage

Electric current is a flow of ....

The potential difference between two points in a circuit is the .... per unit of .... that passes between the points.

The greater the .... the lower the current for a given potential difference. (4)

Complete the following calculations. Write down the equation you use. Show clearly how you work out your answer and give the unit.

  a i Calculate the potential difference between A and B. (1)

    ii The potential difference across the 15 Ω resistor is 5 V.
Calculate the potential difference across the 12 Ω resistor. (1)

  b i Calculate the combined resistance of the 12 Ω and the 15 Ω resistors in series. (1)

    ii Calculate the current that flows through the circuit at X. (2)

    iii Calculate the current flowing through the circuit at Y. (1)

  c Calculate the resistance of the resistor labelled R. (2)

  d Calculate the charge that flows through resistor R in 2 minutes. (3)

  e Calculate the work done (energy transferred) by the cell if the total charge that has flowed through it is 3000 C. (2)

4 a Sketch and label a graph of current against potential difference for a diode. (3)

  b The graph of current against potential difference for a filament bulb is shown.

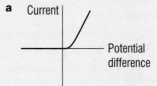

  i Calculate the potential difference when the resistance of the filament bulb is 2 Ω when the current is 1.6 A. Write down the equation you use. Show clearly how you work out your answer and give the unit. (2)

  ii Calculate the resistance at a potential difference of 12 V. Write down the equation you use. Show clearly how you work out your answer and give the unit. (3)

  c *In this question you will be assessed on using good English, organising information clearly and using specialist terms where appropriate.*

Explain the change in resistance of the filament bulb in terms of ions and electrons. [H] (6)

AQA Examination-style answers

1 a electrons move from cloth to rod; electrons have negative charge *(3 marks)*

  b positive *(1 mark)*

  c repels *(1 mark)*

2 a i voltmeter *(1 mark)*

    ii (A) *(1 mark)*

    iii variable resistor *(1 mark)*

    iv (LDR symbol) *(1 mark)*

    v battery/power supply *(1 mark)*

  b Electric current is a flow of **charge**. The potential difference between two points in a circuit is the **energy transferred** per unit of **charge** that passes between the points.

The greater the **resistance** the lower the current for a given potential difference. *(4 marks)*

3 a i 9 V *(1 mark)*

    ii 4 V *(1 mark)*

  b i 27 Ω *(1 mark)*

    ii $I = \dfrac{V}{R} = 9/27 = 0.33\,A$ *(2 marks)*

    iii $0.33 + 0.5 = 0.83\,A$ *(1 mark)*

  c $I = \dfrac{V}{R} = 9/0.5 = 18\,Ω$ *(2 marks)*

  d $Q = I \times t = 0.5 \times 120 = 60\,C$ *(3 marks)*

  e $W = V \times Q = 9 \times 3000 = 27\,000\,J$ *(2 marks)*

4 a

(graph of Current against Potential difference for a diode)

(3 marks)

  b i $V = I \times R = 1.6 \times 2 = 3.2\,V$ *(2 marks)*

    ii $R = \dfrac{V}{I} = 12/3 = 4\,Ω$ *(3 marks)*

  c There is a clear, balanced and detailed description of how the change in resistance of the filament bulb occurs. The answer shows almost faultless spelling, punctuation and grammar. It is coherent and in an organised, logical sequence. It contains a range of appropriate or relevant specialist terms used accurately. *(5–6 marks)*

There is a description of a range of the ways in which the change in resistance of the filament bulb occurs. There are some errors in spelling, punctuation and grammar. The answer has some structure and organisation. The use of specialist terms has been attempted, but not always accurately. *(3–4 marks)*

There is a brief description of at least two ways in which the change in resistance of the filament bulb occurs, which has little clarity and detail. The spelling, punctuation and grammar are very weak. The answer is poorly organised with almost no specialist terms and/or their use demonstrating a general lack of understanding of their meaning. *(1–2 marks)*

No relevant content. *(0 marks)*

Examples of physics points made in the response:

- as the voltage increases, the current increases
- this increases the collisions
- between electrons and ions
- the ions vibrate with a greater amplitude
- and this increases the temperature
- and the resistance.

AQA Practical suggestions

Practicals	AQA	(k)	(book)	(gears)
Using filament bulbs and resistors to investigate potential difference/current characteristics.	✓	✓	✓	✓
Investigating potential difference/current characteristics for LDRs and thermistors.	✓		✓	
Setting up series and parallel circuits to investigate current and potential difference.	✓		✓	
Plan and carry out an investigation to find the relationship between the resistance of thermistors and their temperatures.	✓			
Investigating the change of resistance of LDRs with light intensity.	✓		✓	

P2 5.1

Alternating current

Learning objectives

Students should learn:

- that direct current involves the flow of electrons in one direction and can be provided by cells or batteries
- that alternating current involves the rapid change in direction of the current
- that UK mains electricity is alternating current with a frequency of 50 Hz
- to use oscilloscope traces to compare (ac) and (dc) supplies.

Learning outcomes

Most students should be able to:

- distinguish between alternating and direct current
- state the frequency of UK mains electricity
- describe how the potential of the live wires varies with each cycle
- use oscilloscope traces to compare direct and alternating potential differences and measure the peak voltage of an ac source.

Some students should also be able to:

- measure the period and frequency of an ac source using an oscilloscope or diagrams of oscilloscope traces. [HT only]

Support

- Provide a diagram comparing an (ac) source to a (dc) source and ask the students to mark on the amplitude (voltage) and the period of the waveforms. You will most likely need a classroom assistant or technician to demonstrate the oscilloscope to small groups at a time.

Extend

- Ask: 'Why is our mains electricity frequency 50 Hz?' 'What is the physical reason for this and is it the same in all countries?' 'How was this frequency and voltage decided on and why?' They should find out information about the speed of rotation of the generators and the decisions made.

AQA Specification link-up: Physics P2.4

- Cells and batteries supply current that always passes in the same direction. This is called direct current (dc). [P2.4.1 a)]
- An alternating current (ac) is one that is constantly changing direction. [P2.4.1 b)]
- Mains electricity is an ac supply. In the UK it has a frequency of 50 cycles per second (50 hertz) and is about 230 V. [P2.4.1 c)]

Lesson structure

Starters

Wave forms – Show the students a wave diagram (e.g. picture from the Student Book) and ask them to discuss it. They should recognise the sine wave shape and perhaps the wavelength (or period) and amplitude. *(5 minutes)*

Mains facts – Ask the students some true/false questions about mains electricity to see what they already know. These should include some basic questions that have already been covered [A dc conventional current travels from positive to negative, the current through series circuits is the same in each component] and some testing of their mains knowledge (Mains voltage is 240 V [false], the three pins in a mains plug are positive, negative and neutral [false]). You can differentiate to support or extend by selecting appropriately challenging questions. *(10 minutes)*

Main

- Many of the students will have been wondering what the other two outputs on a power supply are for. Show them that a bulb will light up from a dc source and also from the ac source. The dc outputs are colour coded for positive and negative, but the ac ones are not: ask the students why they think this is.

- In a dc circuit the electrons eventually make it around the complete circuit. In an ac circuit they just oscillate back and forth a few centimetres. Describe this to the students pointing out that the electrons are still transferring energy. Make sure that the students know that mains electricity supply is 230 V ac at 50 Hz. This is frequently asked for in examination papers. Don't use these high voltages in demonstrations.

- Some students may know that fluorescent lamps in some buildings flicker or buzz. Let them hear a 50 Hz signal using a signal generator and loudspeaker, and they will probably recognise the noise.

- The oscilloscope is a complex device, but the students only need to know about the time base and the Y-gain. (See 'Practical support'.) Higher Tier students will need to be able to take measurements from CRO traces. Make sure that they are only using the controls that they need. You can explain what some of the other buttons do, but make sure that the students know that they only have to be able to read the traces.

- If you have a computer-based oscilloscope, it is much better to use this for demonstrations rather than a small CRO. Connect it up to a signal generator or ac power supply to show the traces. The whole class should be able to see it at once if you use a data projector too. Most of them allow you to capture ('freeze') the signal and this makes measurement easier.

Plenaries

ac/dc? – Give the students a set of electrical appliances and ask them to stack them in two piles: ac operation and dc operation. If you want to extend the students, you can ask 'What about appliances such as laptops that have transformers and rectifiers to convert?' You can then discuss what the connecting box does. *(5 minutes)*

Traces – Show the students a series of oscilloscope traces and ask them to say if the peak pd is higher or lower, and the frequency higher or lower, than the previous one. They could read off the time period and the voltage from the traces. Extend students by asking them to read exact values of peak pd and time period from the traces; they should then calculate the frequency (make sure that different diagrams have different time bases). For support, you should use a single time-base setting for most of the diagrams. *(10 minutes)*

Practical support

The oscilloscope

Oscilloscopes can be fiddly to use and are expensive, but they are essential to understanding alternating current. If not enough equipment is available, let the students use what there is, one group at a time.

Equipment and materials needed

Per group: cathode ray oscilloscope, low voltage ac source, battery and leads.

Details

The greatest problem the students will have with this experiment is setting the time base and volts per centimetre (Y-gain) dials on the CRO. If these are incorrectly set, then the students will not get a useful trace. To make things easier for them, put small blobs of paint on the scale around the dials showing the correct setting to show a 2 V, 50 Hz trace clearly. This will be a common function, so don't worry too much about defacing the scopes. If you want to show what would happen to the trace if the frequency of the pd is changed, you can set up a signal generator instead of the ac source.

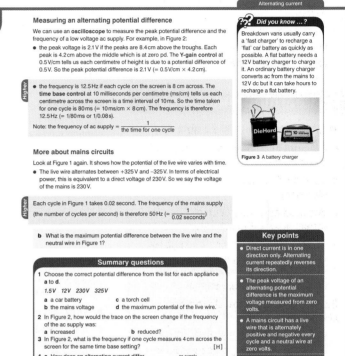

Did you know ... ?

A rapid car battery recharge can produce currents of over 100 A for short periods. At 12 V, this means that it is transferring 1200 J each second. For comparison, a normal AA battery operates at 1.5 V and produces a current of only 100 mA, so transfers 0.15 J each second.

Further teaching suggestions

ICT link-up

- There are excellent computer-based oscilloscopes that can display traces (e.g. picoscope). These are very useful for demonstrations, because the display can be projected so that everybody can see it at once. It is still worth showing the students an old-fashioned one too. Simulations are also available online; search the web for 'oscilloscope' simulation.

Answers to in-text questions

a The bulb would flicker continuously.

b 325 V

Summary answers

1. **a** 12 V
   b 230 V
   c 1.5 V
   d 325 V

2. The number of cycles on the screen would:
   a increase
   b decrease

3. 25 Hz

4. **a** A direct current in a circuit is in one direction only; an alternating current repeatedly reverses its direction.
   b The diode only allows current through when the polarity of the ac supply is such that the diode conducts. This happens every other half-cycle when the polarity of the supply is such that diode is 'forward-biased' (i.e. in its 'forward' direction relative to the ac supply).

P2 5.2

Cables and plugs

Learning objectives

Students should learn:

- that mains plugs and sockets are made from robust insulating materials
- that mains cables are made from copper conductive wires insulated by flexible plastic
- the names and colours of the wires in a three-pin plug
- the structure of a mains three-pin plug and the functions of the live wire, the neutral wire and the earth wire.

Learning outcomes

Most students should be able to:

- describe the design and function of a three-pin mains plug, including the materials and the colours of the wires
- explain why it is important that appliances are double-insulated
- explain why it is necessary to connect some appliances to the earth via the earth wire
- explain, in terms of safety, why the fuse in the plug of an appliance and the switch of an appliance are on the live side of the appliance.

Some students should also be able to:

- explain in detail the choice of materials used for the mains parts of a three-pin mains plug.

Answers to in-text questions

a So each one can be switched on or off without affecting the others.

b Brass is harder than copper or zinc.

c The live wire could be exposed where the cable is worn away or damaged.

d The green and yellow wire.

Support

- Provide the students with a large diagram of plug wiring. They should then label the parts, colour the wires and describe the materials used for each part.

Extend

- Get the students to write a 'How to wire a plug' guide as found in some DIY stores. The guide should contain idiot-proof step-by-step instructions of what equipment you need and what you should do.

Specification link-up: Physics P2.4

- Most electrical appliances are connected to the mains using cable and a three-pin plug. *[P2.4.1 d)]*
- The structure of electrical cable. *[P2.4.1 e)]*
- The structure and wiring of a three-pin plug. *[P2.4.1 f)]*
- Understand the principles of safe practice and recognise dangerous practice in the use of mains electricity. *[P2.4]*
- Evaluate and explain the need to use different cables for different appliances. *[P2.4]*

Lesson structure

Starters

Mystery object – Put a mains plug in a bag and ask one student to describe it to the rest of the class, but only using shape and texture. This can be made more difficult by using a continental plug. They should describe the materials used and the shape; later this leads to reasons for these design features. *(5 minutes)*

Material sorting – Give each group of students a bag containing a range of materials and ask them to sort the materials in any way they wish. They must explain how they sorted them to other groups in terms of the properties. To support students, you can give them a list of properties to use during the sorting process. Extend the students by selecting materials that require additional discussion and ask them to define what they mean by the category they have chosen. You should make sure that you ask them to sort information into groups including conductors, insulators, hard and flexible, as these are good ways of describing why particular materials are chosen for plugs and cables. *(10 minutes)*

Main

- Only use appliances that have been safety-checked for this lesson!
- If you have a metal electric heater, then use it to introduce the idea of earthing an appliance. Discuss the materials used in a plug and cable by actually showing them. If you have very old appliances you might like to show how these have improved over the years. The students need to be able to explain why each material has been chosen.
- Emphasise the importance of the insulating properties of plastic and how this is linked to the idea of double insulation. You should be able to show a few appliances with the appropriate symbol on.
- The colour coding is usually well understood, but some students will know the black and red wires used in mains circuits in houses – this can lead to some confusion. (All new wiring now uses the new colours.)
- The students need to know that the diameter of the wires in the plug is important as thicker wires can carry a larger current without overheating. Link this back to their knowledge of resistance; thicker wires have lower resistance and so heat up less for the same current.
- Show the students some badly wired plugs. This works best if the plugs are real, but use diagrams if necessary. Make sure these can not be plugged in by using a plug-wiring board. Some of the faults should be hard to spot. One commonly missed mistake is the cable grip gripping the wires instead of the larger cable.
- You may have plugs for different countries, electrical systems or adapters for them. Showing them to students will emphasise that each country has its own designs for plugs.
- A tip for wiring a plug is: When looking down on to a plug as it is being wired the **BR**own wire connects to the **B**ottom **R**ight, the **BL**ue wire connects to the **B**ottom **L**eft. The other wire goes to the other pin!

Plenaries

Materials summary – The students should make a table listing the parts of a plug and cable, the materials used and the reasons for those choices. This should be centred on ideas about good conductors and insulators along with flexibility or rigidity. *(5 minutes)*

Wonky wiring – Show the students incorrectly wired plugs and ask them to describe the problems. You can also include some cartoons of bad habits in wiring including too many plugs in one socket, wires taped together, leads trailing across the floor and water near electrical appliances. Students can be supported by asking them to match known problems with particular pictures of plugs. Some can be extended by showing appliances with multiple problems. *(10 minutes)*

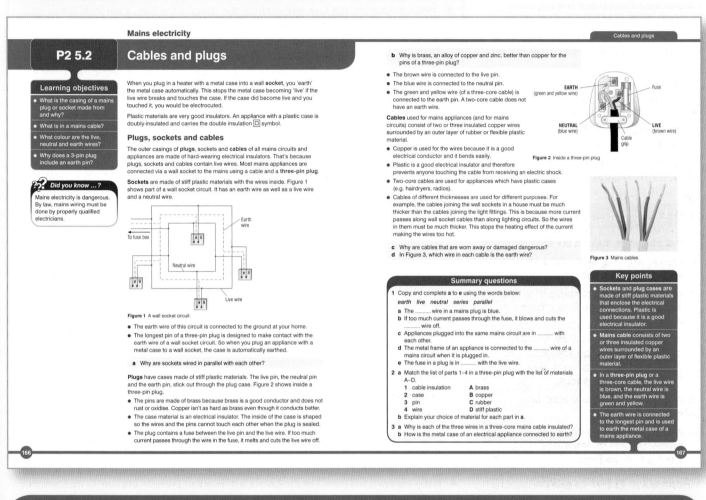

P2 5.2 Cables and plugs

Learning objectives

- What is the casing of a mains plug or socket made from and why?
- What is in a mains cable?
- What colour are the live, neutral and earth wires?
- Why does a 3-pin plug include an earth pin?

Did you know ...?

Mains electricity is dangerous. By law, mains wiring must be done by properly qualified electricians.

When you plug in a heater with a metal case into a wall **socket**, you 'earth' the metal case automatically. This stops the metal case becoming 'live' if the live wire breaks and touches the case. If the case did become live and you touched it, you would be electrocuted.

Plastic materials are very good insulators. An appliance with a plastic case is doubly-insulated and carries the double insulation ⧈ symbol.

Plugs, sockets and cables

The outer casings of **plugs**, sockets and **cables** of all mains circuits and appliances are made of hard-wearing electrical insulators. That's because plugs, sockets and cables contain live wires. Most mains appliances are connected via a wall socket to the mains using a cable and a **three-pin plug**.

Sockets are made of stiff plastic materials with the wires inside. Figure 1 shows part of a wall socket circuit. It has an earth wire as well as a live wire and a neutral wire.

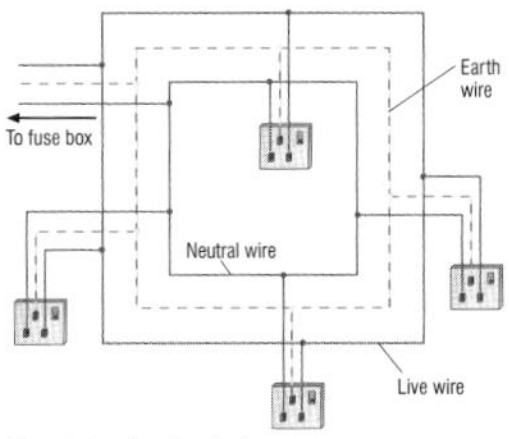

Figure 1 A wall socket circuit

- The earth wire of this circuit is connected to the ground at your home.
- The longest pin of a three-pin plug is designed to make contact with the earth wire of a wall socket circuit. So when you plug an appliance with a metal case to a wall socket, the case is automatically earthed.

a Why are sockets wired in parallel with each other?

Plugs have cases made of stiff plastic materials. The live pin, the neutral pin and the earth pin, stick out through the plug case. Figure 2 shows inside a three-pin plug.

- The pins are made of brass because brass is a good conductor and does not rust or oxidise. Copper isn't as hard as brass even though it conducts better.
- The case material is an electrical insulator. The inside of the case is shaped so the wires and the pins cannot touch each other when the plug is sealed.
- The plug contains a fuse between the live pin and the live wire. If too much current passes through the wire in the fuse, it melts and cuts the live wire off.

b Why is brass, an alloy of copper and zinc, better than copper for the pins of a three-pin plug?

- The brown wire is connected to the live pin.
- The blue wire is connected to the neutral pin.
- The green and yellow wire (of a three-core cable) is connected to the earth pin. A two-core cable does not have an earth wire.

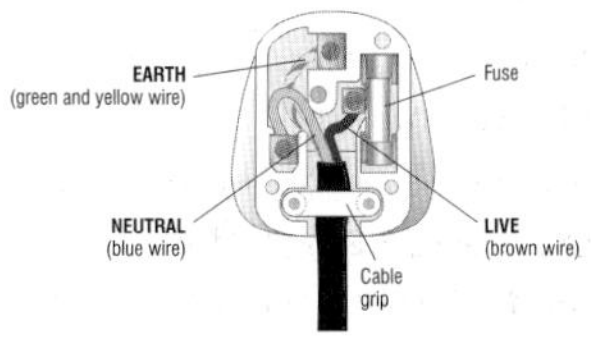

Figure 2 Inside a three-pin plug

Cables used for mains appliances (and for mains circuits) consist of two or three insulated copper wires surrounded by an outer layer of rubber or flexible plastic material.

- Copper is used for the wires because it is a good electrical conductor and it bends easily.
- Plastic is a good electrical insulator and therefore prevents anyone touching the cable from receiving an electric shock.
- Two-core cables are used for appliances which have plastic cases (e.g. hairdryers, radios).
- Cables of different thicknesses are used for different purposes. For example, the cables joining the wall sockets in a house must be much thicker than the cables joining the light fittings. This is because more current passes along wall socket cables than along lighting circuits. So the wires in them must be much thicker. This stops the heating effect of the current making the wires too hot.

c Why are cables that are worn away or damaged dangerous?
d In Figure 3, which wire in each cable is the earth wire?

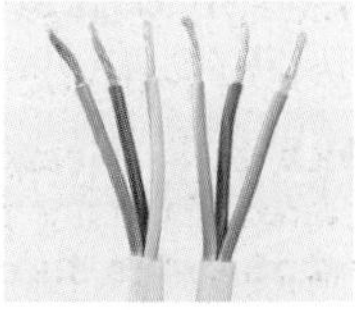

Figure 3 Mains cables

Summary questions

1 Copy and complete **a** to **e** using the words below:

earth live neutral series parallel

- **a** The .... wire in a mains plug is blue.
- **b** If too much current passes through the fuse, it blows and cuts the .... wire off.
- **c** Appliances plugged into the same mains circuit are in .... with each other.
- **d** The metal frame of an appliance is connected to the .... wire of a mains circuit when it is plugged in.
- **e** The fuse in a plug is in .... with the live wire.

2 **a** Match the list of parts 1–4 in a three-pin plug with the list of materials A–D.

1 cable insulation	**A** brass
2 case	**B** copper
3 pin	**C** rubber
4 wire	**D** stiff plastic

b Explain your choice of material for each part in **a**.

3 **a** Why is each of the three wires in a three-core mains cable insulated?
b How is the metal case of an electrical appliance connected to earth?

Key points

- **Sockets** and **plug cases** are made of stiff plastic materials that enclose the electrical connections. Plastic is used because it is a good electrical insulator.
- **Mains cable** consists of two or three insulated copper wires surrounded by an outer layer of flexible plastic material.
- In a **three-pin plug** or a three-core cable, the live wire is brown, the neutral wire is blue, and the earth wire is green and yellow.
- The earth wire is connected to the longest pin and is used to earth the metal case of a mains appliance.

Further teaching suggestions

Plug wiring board

- If you have concerns about the safety of plug wiring in your laboratory, then you can pass around a plug board for the students to see faulty wiring.

Equipment and materials required

A plank of wood with six incorrectly wired plugs mounted on it.

Details

All that is involved is mounting six plugs onto a board with the pins sticking through it, so that they cannot be plugged in. Drill or chisel out the board, stick the cases down with strong glue and wire up the six plugs in incorrect ways so that the students can try to explain what has been done wrong. You might like to glue the pins into the wood to make sure that they don't fall out. Here are some examples of problems: wires stripped all the way back to the cable grip so that they short, live and neutral wire swapped, wires not tightened at the pins, fuse replaced with metal pin or similar, cable gripping wires not cable, cracked case (glue it down, then whack it with a screwdriver). If you have a bigger board then add others.

Summary answers

1 a neutral **b** live **c** parallel
d earth **e** series

2 a 1 **C**; 2 **D**; 3 **A**; 4 **B**
b **1** Rubber is flexible and is an insulator.
2 Stiff plastic is an insulator, it doesn't wear and it can't be squashed.
3 Brass is a good conductor and doesn't deteriorate.
4 Copper is an excellent conductor and copper wires bend easily.

3 a The three wires must be insulated from each other otherwise there would be a dangerously large current in the cable due to the very low resistance between the live wire and the other wires where they touch.
b The earth wire of the cable is connected to a terminal fixed to the metal case. The other end of the earth wire is connected to the earth pin in the three-pin plug attached to the cable. When the plug is connected to a three-pin wall socket, the metal case is therefore connected via the earth wire to the ground.

P2 5.3

Fuses

- If an electrical fault causes too great a current, the circuit is disconnected by a fuse or a circuit breaker in the live wire. *[P2.4.1 g)]*
- When the current in a fuse wire exceeds the rating of the fuse, it will melt, breaking the circuit. *[P2.4.1 h)]*
- Some circuits are protected by Residual Current Circuit Breakers (RCCBs). *[P2.4.1 i)]*
- Appliances with metal cases are usually earthed. *[P2.4.1 j)]*
- The earth wire and fuse together protect the wiring of the circuit. *[P2.4.1 k)]*
- Understand the principles of safe practice and recognise dangerous practice in the use of mains electricity. *[P2.4]*
- Compare the uses of fuses and circuit breakers. *[P2.4]*
- Evaluate and explain the need to use different cables for different appliances. *[P2.4]*

Learning objectives

Students should learn:

- that fuses and circuit breakers are devices that cut off electrical circuits when too large a current flows
- about the advantages of using circuit breakers to cut off circuits instead of fuses
- how to choose the correct rating of fuse for an appliance
- why it is important that appliances are earthed
- that double insulated appliances have a shell made of insulating materials and so do not need to be earthed.

Learning outcomes

Most students should be able to:

- explain how and why a fuse cuts off an electrical circuit
- explain why the fuse in the plug of an appliance protects the appliance
- list the advantages of a circuit breaker over a fuse.

Some students should also be able to:

- explain in detail why earthing the metal case of an appliance protects the user.

Answers to in-text questions

a The fuse wire would melt.

b The mains voltage is across less resistance because only part of the element is between the live and the neutral wire and so the current is bigger.

c The fault has not been put right so consult an electrician.

Support

- For the 'Electromagnets' Starter, give the students a set of cards to put in order.

Extend

- The students can look at the internal action of a circuit breaker and explain how it works in terms of electromagnetism. You should be able to find some suitable diagrams or animations to help the discussion along.

Lesson structure

Starters

Heating effect – Ask: 'Why do wires get hot when a current passes through them?' The students should explain the effect in terms of electron collisions with ions in the wire. Check that the students know that the wire is full of free electrons even when there is no current. To support students, you can show an animation of the effect to revise the key ideas. Extend students by asking them to describe all of the factors they think will cause heating in the wires and why they think this is. *(5 minutes)*

Electromagnets – Demonstrate an electromagnetic switch or relay and get the students to draw a flow chart of what is happening. This should describe electrical currents and the magnetic field and the effect of the field on other objects. You could expand this by looking at an electric bell causing motion and link this into the circuit breaker idea later in the lesson. *(10 minutes)*

Main

- Fuses are a bit dull without demonstrations, so try to fit in a few of the ones in the practical. If you are showing a fuse melting, use one with a glass casing, so that the students can see the wire becoming hot and then melting. This will disappoint some students who think a fuse actually explodes in some way.

- Many students will think that the fuse is a device that protects the user of an appliance. It is important to point out that the fuse really prevents an appliance from catching fire through overheating. Emphasise that it only takes a small current to kill and a 3.5 A appliance with a 5 A fuse in it can provide a current of 1.5 A without troubling the fuse.

- Earthing confuses some, but just point out that the basic idea is to provide an easy path for the current to take if there is a fault. Usually, if the appliance is earthed, then a large current would flow if the live wire touched the case and the fuse should melt and cut off the appliance. This is the common reason why an appliance keeps melting fuses. If the students see this happen, they should realise that the live wire is disconnected.

- Even if the fuse does not melt (usually because of putting 13 A fuses in everything), the earth wire provides a low resistance path for the current and the user would not be electrocuted by touching the case.

- You can demonstrate the use of circuit-breakers as outlined in the 'Further teaching suggestions' box. The students should realise the advantages fairly quickly. If you want to go into extra detail, then you can show a large model circuit-breaker. They should be able to link the idea of a current creating a magnetic field and pulling open a switch, therefore cutting off the current.

- Finally the students can look at a RCCB. They should note that no earth wire is needed. If there is a difference in the current between the live and neutral wire, there must be a current leak indicating a fault in the appliance.

Plenaries

Mains safety – The students produce a jingle, catchphrase or slogan to encourage people to use mains electricity safely. It should cover the dangers but also remind people that electricity is perfectly safe when used correctly. *(5 minutes)*

Dump your fuses – The students can produce an outline of an advertisement from a company that manufactures circuit-breakers and is trying to convince householders to swap their fuse boxes for breaker boxes. They should concentrate on the advantages of using a circuit-breaker in comparison with a fuse. Students can be extended by insisting that a full explanation of how a circuit-breaker works is included. Others can be supported by asking them to complete a simple comparison instead. *(10 minutes)*

Practical support

Demonstrating fuses

This is a simple demonstration to show that 1 A fuses melt before they allow excess current through them, then 3 A and so on.

Equipment and materials required
Power supply, leads, crocodile clips, fuses (1 A, 3 A, 5 A).

Details
You can show the students the differences between fuses, by showing them the fuse wire that is found in them. Connect up some

1 A, 3 A and 5 A fuse wire together in series with an ammeter and variable resistor, and pass an increasing current through it to show that the 1 A fuse wire melts first. You should reconnect the circuit (without the 1 A fuse) and increase the current again until the 3 A fuse melts, and finish with the 5 A melting. Discuss the thickness of the wires; the greater the diameter the greater the current required to melt the fuse wire. Hopefully this will be when a current of 1 A passes through it, but just how accurately is fuse wire manufactured? This would give a good opportunity to discuss aspects of 'How Science Works' on making measurements.

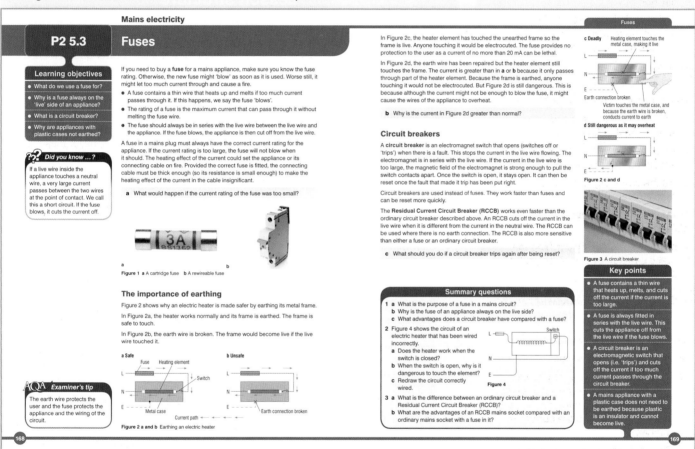

Summary answers

1 a A fuse protects an appliance or a circuit.
b So it cuts off the live wire if too much current passes through it.
c It is faster than a fuse and doesn't need to be replaced after it 'trips'.

2 a Yes.
b The element is live.
c

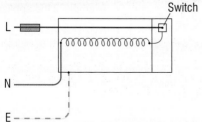

3 a An ordinary circuit-breaker switches the current in the live wire off if the current is greater than a certain value. An RCCB switches the current in the live wire if the current in the live wire and the neutral wire differ.
b An RCCB cuts off the current in the live wire faster than a fuse does. Also, an RCCB is more sensitive than a fuse.

P2 5.4

Electrical power and potential difference

Learning objectives

Students should learn that:

- that the power of an electrical appliance is the rate at which it transfers energy
- how to calculate the electrical power of an appliance using the current and potential difference
- how to select an appropriate fuse for an electrical appliance.

Learning outcomes

Most students should be able to:

- state that the power of an appliance is the amount of energy it transfers each second
- calculate the power of an electrical appliance from the current and the potential difference
- find the fuse required for an appliance based on its electrical power rating.

Some students should also be able to:

- perform calculations involving the rearrangement of the electrical power equation.

Answers to in-text questions

a About 1 W

b 1150 W

c The normal current through the lamp is much less than 13 A. A 13 A fuse may not blow if there is a fault in the lamp.

Support

- The calculations here can be very confusing to some students, and they should be provided with a template to encourage them to lay them out correctly.

Extend

- Can the students produce a comparison between electrical potential difference and gravitational potential difference? This is a tricky task, but one that can cement understanding of what a potential difference represents.

$\mathcal{AQA}$ Specification link-up: Physics P2.4

- The rate at which energy is transferred by an appliance is called the power.

$P = \dfrac{E}{t}$ [P2.4.2 b)]

- Power, potential difference and current are related by the equation:

$P = I \times V$ [P2.4.2 c)]

Controlled Assessment: P4.3 Collect primary and secondary data. [P4.3.2 a) b) c) d) e) f)]; P4.2 Assess and manage risks when carrying out practical work. [P4.2.1 a) b)]

Lesson structure

Starters

Power – Can the students give a scientific definition of the word power? Can they remember any equations? You could even set them a mechanical power question involving gravitational or kinetic energy. Once a formal definition had been made, you can ask how this could be connected to electrical energy where no force is apparently causing anything to move. *(5 minutes)*

Electrical units – The students match up electrical quantities, with their definitions, abbreviations and units. Include current (I, ampere), voltage (V, volts), resistance (Ω, ohms), power (P, watts), energy (E, joule). Can they provide any definitions for these units? To extend the students, ask them to describe how these factors are interrelated by giving equations or describing the links in sentences. Students can be supported by forming the activity as a jigsaw puzzle that can be assembled to produce a complete table of the information. *(10 minutes)*

Main

- Start with a brief recap about power; the students should remember how to calculate the power of a mechanical device. Point out that if energy is being transferred by a device, then some form of work must be being done, so there is a power output. With electricity, there is no force or distance moved, so there must be another way of finding the power output.

- The next section involves a derivation of an equation; you will have to provide extra support and spend a little more time demonstrating what to do with the equations for some students. Take some time to go through what each of the phrases means and to come up with the final equation; some students will find this difficult. The definition of potential difference as 'electrical energy per unit charge' is one that many students will find particularly hard to understand. In the end, most students will happily accept that the power is the current times the potential difference, even if they don't thoroughly understand why.

- The calculations are not difficult but the students should have quite a bit of practice. Get them to work out the power of several appliances before moving on to rearrangement. Sometimes examiners ask the students to work out the power of a mains appliance without giving the voltage. Students are expected to remember that mains voltage is 230 V.

- The practical task serves as reinforcement in the use of the calculation of current and power.

- Show the students real fuses and point out that they are all the same physical size, so it is easy to select the wrong one without thinking. They might like to see the 30 A fuses used for cookers. Ask: 'Why are these physically larger?' and link back to the diameter of the wire needed for a larger current.

- When choosing a fuse, always choose one that is slightly higher than the operating current, otherwise it will melt during normal operation. For example, if the appliance needs exactly 3 A, then a 5 A fuse should be used.

Plenaries

Electrical error – 'I'm sick of all my stuff fusing; I'm going to put a 13 A fuse in all of my things, so that they'll all keep working.' Ask: 'Is this a good plan or not?' Discuss the hazards associated with doing this. *(5 minutes)*

Match the fuse – The students need to find the correct fuse for an electrical appliance after being told the power rating. This involves calculating the current and then choosing the fuse that is slightly higher. Use 3 A, 5 A, 13 A and 30 A fuses. To extend, you can ask the students to select fuses for circuits where there are several appliances connected (e.g. a four-socket extension). For additional support, you can turn this activity into a simple matching one with only one fuse suitable for each appliance. *(10 minutes)*

Practical support

Comparing electrical power

The students can measure the electrical power of a range of 12 V appliances and make a comparison using a joulemeter or an ammeter and voltmeter combination. There are a wide range of 12 V appliances available designed to fit into a car electrical socket or for camping, and these can easily be adapted for the practical. Search online for '12 V appliance' and you will find some suggestions.

You may want the students to assess the risk of the experiment ('How Science Works') and discuss why you are using 12 V appliances instead of the cheaper mains ones.

Equipment and materials required

Per group: power supply (12 V), joulemeter (or ammeter and voltmeter combination), leads and a few appliances that operate at 12 V. The appliances could be a lamp, clocks, a small heater, and so on.

Details

The students can connect up the power supply to the appliance along with the joulemeter and determine the electrical power by measuring the energy transfer over a minute. Alternatively, they can connect the ammeter in series and voltmeter in parallel and determine the power rating using the electrical equation power = current × potential difference. Different groups can compare their results to establish if there is any variation.

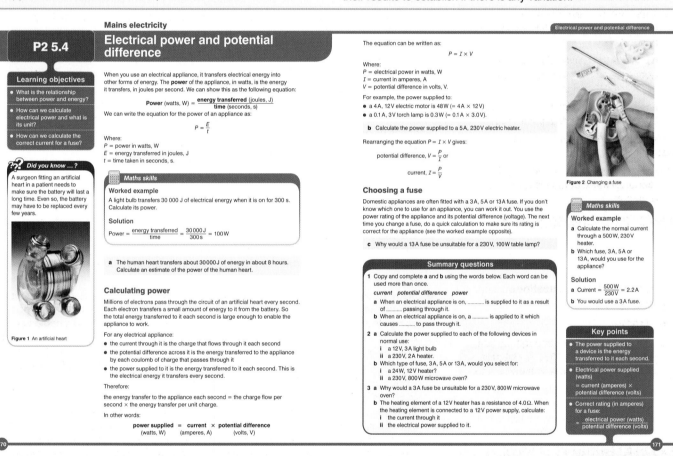

Further teaching suggestions

Enlightenment

- This is a simple way to show that the higher the power rating of an appliance, the more energy it transfers.

Equipment and materials required

Three identical lamps except that one has a 40 W bulb, the others have 60 W and 100 W. As with all mains appliances, these should have passed safety tests.

Details

Just plug all of the lamps in and turn them on. The students should easily see the difference in brightness and relate this to the amount of energy being transferred. Explain that all are operating at 230 V; the students should then calculate the current in each lamp. [0.17 A, 0.26 A, 0.43 A] Ask: 'What fuse should each of the lamps have?'

Summary answers

1 a power, current
   b potential difference, current

2 a i 36 W   ii 460 W
   b i 3 A   ii 5 A

3 a The current supplied to the microwave oven
      = 800 W/230 V = 3.5 A. A 3 A fuse would blow when the oven is switched on (at full power).
   b i 3.0 A   ii 36 W

P2 5.5

Electrical energy and charge

Learning objectives

Students should learn:

- that an electric current is a flow of charge; in metal wires this charge is carried by electrons
- that the unit of charge is the coulomb where one ampere represents a flow of charge of one coulomb per second **[HT only]**
- that charge transferred is current × time, that potential difference is energy transferred per unit charge **[HT only]**
- that a resistor transfers electrical energy by heating to the surroundings.

Learning outcomes

Most students should be able to:

- state that an electrical current is a flow of charge
- describe how a resistor transfers electrical energy by heating to the surroundings.

Some students should also be able to:

- calculate the energy transferred using the pd and the charge transferred **[HT only]**
- perform calculations involving rearrangement of the charge = current × time equation and the potential difference = energy transferred per unit charge equation. **[HT only]**

Support

- Use calculation templates to help the students through the equations and to make sure that they are laying out their calculations clearly.

Extend

- Ask: 'How many electrons are passing each second at a point, if there is a current of 1 A and each electron carries a charge of 1.6×10^{-19} C?' [The students should be able to figure out that 1 C of charge passes each second, so the number of electrons is given by $1\,C/1.6 \times 10^{-19}$ C which is 6.25×10^{18} electrons. This shows just how small the charge on a single electron is.] These numbers are impossible for a calculator to handle without using scientific notation, so it is a good opportunity to improve these skills.

AQA Specification link-up: Physics P2.3, P2.4

- Electric current is a flow of electric charge. The size of the electric current is the rate of flow of electric charge. The size of the current is given by the equation:
  $$I = \frac{Q}{t} \ [P2.3.2 \ a)]$$
- When an electrical charge flows through a resistor, the resistor gets hot. *[P2.4.2 a)]*
- Energy transferred, potential difference and charge are related by the equation:
  $$E = V \times Q \ [P2.4.2 \ d)] \ \textbf{[HT only]}$$

Lesson structure

Starters

Stuck for words? – Pair up the students and give one of them cards with electrical words including charge, current, pd, power, resistance, etc. Ask them to mime the words to the other students. This is remarkable difficult as they are quite abstract ideas but it can lead to students using their imagination of what the words mean. *(5 minutes)*

Electrical energy transfer – How many electrical appliances can the students draw energy transfer diagrams for? Provide some example appliances if you can. The students could even estimate the electrical efficiency of the appliances once they are clear about which form of energy is useful. Differentiate by providing some simple appliances (and possible starting points for the diagrams) to give extra support while asking about more challenging appliances to extend the students. *(10 minutes)*

Main

- This is another fairly mathematically intense topic with two important equations; keep the emphasis on the electrons carrying charge from place to place and in doing so, carrying energy. Much of the spread is only needed for students taking the Higher Tier examination.

- The first equation comes from the definition of current and charge. The size of the electric current is just how much charge passes each second (just as the size of a water current is how many litres of water pass each second). Use water flowing down a tube into a big measuring cylinder if you want a visual illustration.

- Many students struggle to remember the unit coulomb, so say it a lot. Some students are more apt with the word equations than the symbols, so give them plenty of practice using the symbol form, since this will be needed in the exam. Students should learn to use $Q = It$.

- The second part of the spread contains material for Higher Tier students only.

- The derivation of the energy-transferred equation will again be confusing for some. For these students, just concentrate on the end equation. Using the equation is fairly straightforward after a few examples. Check that the students are using the correct units. With so many equations, it it is easy for them to pick the wrong one. A reference wall display is very handy.

- There may be situations on higher level examination papers where the students are expected to combine the equations, so give these students some examples; e.g. 'How much energy is transferred when a current of 2 A passes through a potential difference of 4 V for 1 minute'? [480 J]

- The last section deals with energy transfer. You should go through the description of the energy being provided to the electrons, then carried by them and transferred to the bulb and resistor, carefully. The students should be picturing electrons as energy carriers by now, and then thinking of a coulomb as the charge carried by a big bunch of electrons. Remember that there is conservation of energy; the electrons can only release the amount of energy they have been provided with in the battery.

- Try more examples of this, making sure that the students are picking up the idea that **each** coulomb of charge (bunch of electrons) is getting the same number of joules as the battery potential difference. It's actually the changes in the electric field that the charge produces that transfers the energy, but the students need not worry about this.

Plenaries

Electrical spelling – Hold a spelling competition about electrical words using mini-whiteboards. If a student gets a word wrong, they get knocked out. Start with simple words like charge and then get more difficult. The last one in wins the competition. 'Coulomb' eliminates a fair few! *(5 minutes)*

Electric crossword – The students have nearly finished this look into current and mains electricity, so let them have a go at a crossword with answers based on this (and the previous) chapter. It's easy to give differentiated clues to cover a range of abilities for support and extension. For example 'the rate of flow of charge, and 'the movement of charge through a wire' are both clues to 'electric current'. *(10 minutes)*

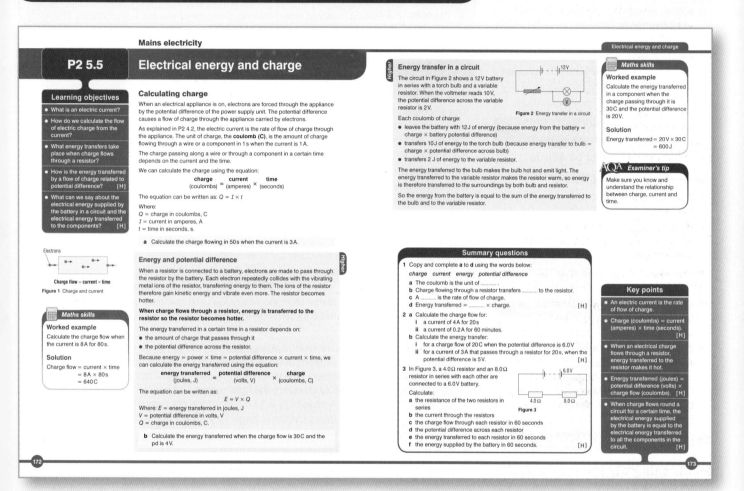

Mains electricity

Electrical energy and charge

P2 5.5 — Electrical energy and charge

Learning objectives

- What is an electric current?
- How do we calculate the flow of electric charge from the current?
- What energy transfers take place when charge flows through a resistor?
- How is the energy transferred by a flow of charge related to potential difference? [H]
- What can we say about the electrical energy supplied by the battery in a circuit and the electrical energy transferred to the components? [H]

Figure 1 Charge and current

Electrons

Charge flow = current × time

Maths skills

Worked example

Calculate the charge flow when the current is 8A for 80s.

Solution

Charge flow = current × time
$$= 8A \times 80s$$
$$= 640C$$

Calculating charge

When an electrical appliance is on, electrons are forced through the appliance by the potential difference of the power supply unit. The potential difference causes a flow of charge through the appliance carried by electrons.

As explained in P2 4.2, the electric current is the rate of flow of charge through the appliance. The unit of charge, the **coulomb (C)**, is the amount of charge flowing through a wire or a component in 1 s when the current is 1 A.

The charge passing along a wire or through a component in a certain time depends on the current and the time.

We can calculate the charge using the equation:

$$\text{charge (coulombs)} = \text{current (amperes)} \times \text{time (seconds)}$$

The equation can be written as: $Q = I \times t$

Where:
Q = charge in coulombs, C
I = current in amperes, A
t = time in seconds, s.

a Calculate the charge flowing in 50 s when the current is 3 A.

Energy and potential difference

When a resistor is connected to a battery, electrons are made to pass through the resistor by the battery. Each electron repeatedly collides with the vibrating metal ions of the resistor, transferring energy to them. The ions of the resistor therefore gain kinetic energy and vibrate even more. The resistor becomes hotter.

When charge flows through a resistor, energy is transferred to the resistor so the resistor becomes hotter.

The energy transferred in a certain time in a resistor depends on:

- the amount of charge that passes through it
- the potential difference across the resistor.

Because energy = power × time = potential difference × current × time, we can calculate the energy transferred using the equation:

$$\text{energy transferred (joules, J)} = \text{potential difference (volts, V)} \times \text{charge (coulombs, C)}$$

The equation can be written as:

$$E = V \times Q$$

Where: E = energy transferred in joules, J
V = potential difference in volts, V
Q = charge in coulombs, C.

b Calculate the energy transferred when the charge flow is 30 C and the pd is 4 V.

Energy transfer in a circuit

The circuit in Figure 2 shows a 12 V battery in series with a torch bulb and a variable resistor. When the voltmeter reads 10 V, the potential difference across the variable resistor is 2 V.

Figure 2 Energy transfer in a circuit

Each coulomb of charge:

- leaves the battery with 12 J of energy (because energy from the battery = charge × battery potential difference)
- transfers 10 J of energy to the torch bulb (because energy transfer to bulb = charge × potential difference across bulb)
- transfers 2 J of energy to the variable resistor.

The energy transferred to the bulb makes the bulb hot and emit light. The energy transferred to the variable resistor makes the resistor warm, so energy is therefore transferred to the surroundings by both bulb and resistor.

So the energy from the battery is equal to the sum of the energy transferred to the bulb and to the variable resistor.

Maths skills

Worked example

Calculate the energy transferred in a component when the charge passing through it is 30 C and the potential difference is 20 V.

Solution

Energy transferred = 20 V × 30 C
$$= 600 J$$

AQA Examiner's tip

Make sure you know and understand the relationship between charge, current and time.

Summary questions

1 Copy and complete **a** to **d** using the words below:

charge   current   energy   potential difference

a The coulomb is the unit of ....
b Charge flowing through a resistor transfers .... to the resistor.
c A .... is the rate of flow of charge.
d Energy transferred = ... × charge. [H]

2 **a** Calculate the charge flow for:
  i a current of 4 A for 20 s
  ii a current of 0.2 A for 60 minutes.
 b Calculate the energy transfer:
  i for a charge flow of 20 C when the potential difference is 6.0 V
  ii for a current of 3 A that passes through a resistor for 20 s, when the potential difference is 5 V. [H]

3 In Figure 3, a 4.0 Ω resistor and an 8.0 Ω resistor in series with each other are connected to a 6.0 V battery. Calculate:
 a the resistance of the two resistors in series
 b the current through the resistors
 c the charge flow through each resistor in 60 seconds
 d the potential difference across each resistor
 e the energy transferred to each resistor in 60 seconds
 f the energy supplied by the battery in 60 seconds. [H]

Figure 3

Key points

- An electric current is the rate of flow of charge.
- Charge (coulombs) = current (amperes) × time (seconds). [H]
- When an electrical charge flows through a resistor, energy transferred to the resistor makes it hot.
- Energy transferred (joules) = potential difference (volts) × charge flow (coulombs). [H]
- When charge flows round a circuit for a certain time, the electrical energy supplied by the battery is equal to the electrical energy transferred to all the components in the circuit. [H]

172   173

Further teaching suggestions

Map it out

- The students should produce a summary or mind map of the information about current electricity, mains electricity and electrical energy calculations. This has been quite a lot of information, so encourage the use of small diagrams on the map to enhance the readability. For example, a little diagram of where to place a voltmeter in a circuit should be present. Mind mapping only really works if the students review and refine the map **regularly**. You might want them to do this at home and check the improved version after a week.

Calculations

- Use this opportunity to give the students some additional calculations to check their understanding and ability.

Summary answers

1 **a** charge
 b energy
 c current
 d potential difference

2 **a** **i** 80 C
   ii 720 C
 b **i** 120 J
   ii 300 J

3 **a** 12.0 Ω
 b 0.50 A
 c 30 C
 d 4 Ω: 2.0 V; 8.0 Ω: 4.0 V
 e 4 Ω: 60 J (= 30 C × 2.0 V); 8.0 Ω: 120 J (= 30 C × 4.0 V)
 f 180 J

Answers to in-text questions

a 150 C
b 120 J

P2 5.6 Electrical issues

- Apply the principles of basic electrical circuits to practical situations. [P2.3]
- Evaluate the use of different forms of lighting, in terms of cost and energy efficiency. [P2.3]
- Understand the principles of safe practice and recognise dangerous practice in the use of mains electricity. [P2.4]
- Evaluate and explain the need to use different cables for different appliances. [P2.4]
- Consider the factors involved when making a choice of electrical appliances. [P2.4]

Learning objectives

Students should learn:

- that electrical faults can lead to electrocution or fires and even small currents through the body are potentially lethal
- how to recognise and prevent electrical faults
- how the efficiency of electrical appliances is rated to help customers make an informed choice of appliance
- why energy efficiency is important and the advances in lighting technology.

Learning outcomes

Most students should be able to:

- recognise a wide range of electrical hazards
- describe the range of lighting available and compare its efficiency
- describe how the efficiency of an electrical appliance is shown
- compare the electrical systems in other countries to that in the UK.

Answers to in-text questions

a i The new fuse would blow when the appliance is switched on.
   ii A three-core cable.
b i 30
   ii 11
   iii Number of kilowatt hours
     $= 0.1\,kW \times 30\,000$ hours
     $= 3000\,kW\,h$
     Cost $= 3000\,kW\,h \times 10\,p/kW\,h$
     $= £300$
   iv £172 (= £234 saving on electricity costs − £62 extra 'capital' cost).

Support

- This lesson is far easier to understand if you have props, so seek out some adaptors, efficiency-rating cards and different light bulbs. You could get students to bring in some ones they have used on holiday.

Extend

- Students could find out about the wiring of ring mains in houses. They should find the specification of the wires needed, colours, fuses used and so on. They can present this information to the rest of the class.

Lesson structure

Starters

The shocking truth – There are a number of electrical-safety videos that can be found, many to do with railways. Show the students one (have a good look first to see it is suitable) and discuss what happens. There are several thousands of electrical injuries every year many from DIY work. (5 minutes)

Spot the hazards – The hazard-spotting task is a good way to start the lesson. Most students should be able to spot the hazards in Shockem Hall. You should ask them to explain how they could be fixed too. The students could then perform a safely check of the laboratory and other classrooms they visit during the school day. Students can be extended by asking them to design an appropriate checklist for room inspections or supported by providing one. It is also a good time to explain why not to stick pencils into the plug socket or unscrew the covers. (10 minutes)

Main

- Take the opportunity to revise all of the safety features mentioned in the previous lessons and how these need to be taken into account when wiring appliances and mains circuits.
- When you move on to discussing lighting, you can demonstrate each of the three bulbs mentioned in the Student Book in a mains socket. If you have a mains-rated joule meter you can compare how much energy each consumes within a 1 minute period. It is more difficult to compare the light output, but see if the students can come up with a suitable idea. A possibility is to measure the pd output from a solar panel placed a fixed distance away, but don't forget to subtract the background reading from the ambient light in the room.
- You should have some efficiency labelling to hand.
- It took a lot of effort for the government to regulate electrical work in the same way as gas has been regulated for many years. The students can discuss why this was necessary (there were lots of fires or accidents). Many 'DIYers' were unhappy at the decision. What would happen if the homeowner did their own work and sold the house only to have it burn down due to a fault? Will the law make it too expensive to do simple jobs in the home?
- You should be able to find a range of adapters (or photographs of them) for different purposes to show the students. Spanish mains supply is 220 V and 50 Hz, so most appliances will work but kettles will take a little longer to boil. You can ask the student why this is [power = current × voltage]. The sockets only have two holes for pins but can have an earth connection at the edge.
- You can also discuss the electrical systems in the USA. Here the frequency of the mains is 60 Hz and the voltage is 110 V. Larger currents are needed to provide the same power as UK systems. This would require thicker wires to achieve the same level of safety.

Plenaries

Overall efficiency – Buildings are rated for their overall efficiency and so your school building may have such a report. Show the students the report and overall rating and discuss it. What could be done to improve the rating? (5 minutes)

Setting standards – There are a range of electrical standards around the World but which is best? The students can compare the systems in terms of pd, frequency and design of cables and sockets, and make a decision about which would be best as a 'World standard'. Extend the students by asking them to define what 'best' means; i.e. let them set the criteria. To support others, you can make the task more of a comparison and then have a discussion about which pd is best or plug design is safest. The students can expand on this task as homework through independent research. *(10 minutes)*

P2 5.6   Electrical issues

Learning objectives

- Why are electrical faults dangerous?
- How can we prevent electrical faults?
- When choosing an electrical appliance, what factors in addition to cost should we consider?
- How do different forms of lighting compare in terms of cost and energy efficiency?

Activity

Spot the hazards!

How many electrical faults and hazards can you find in Shockem Hall? See how many you can spot in the main hall.

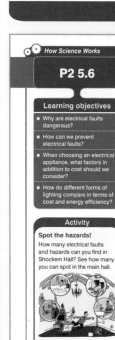

Figure 1 Shockem Hall

?? Did you know ...?

What kills you – current or voltage? Mains electricity is dangerous. A current of no more than about 0.03 A through your body would give you a severe shock and might even kill you. Your body has a resistance of about 1000 Ω including contact resistance at the skin. If your hands get wet, your resistance is even lower.

An electrical fault is dangerous. It could give someone a nasty shock or even electrocute them, resulting in death. Also, a fault can cause a fire. This happens when too much current passes through a wire or an appliance and heats it up.

Fault prevention

Electrical faults can happen if sockets, plugs, cables or appliances are damaged. Users need to check for loose fittings, cracked plugs and sockets and worn cables. Any such damaged items need to be repaired or replaced by a qualified electrician.

- If a fuse blows or a circuit breaker trips when a mains appliance is in use, switch the appliance off. Then don't use it until it has been checked by a qualified electrician.
- If an appliance (or its cable or plug or socket) overheats and/or you get a distinctive burning smell from it, switch it off. Again, don't use it until it has been checked.

Too many appliances connected to a socket may cause the socket to overheat. If this happens, switch the appliances and the socket off and disconnect the appliances from the socket.

Smoke alarms and infrared sensors connected to an alarm system are activated if a fire breaks out. An electrical fault could cause an appliance or a cable to become hot and could set fire to curtains or other material in a room. Smoke alarms and sensors should be checked regularly to make sure they work properly.

An electrician selecting a cable for an appliance needs to use:

- a two-core cable if the appliance is 'double-insulated' and no earth wire is needed
- a three-core cable if an earth wire is needed because the appliance has a metal case
- a cable with conductors of suitable thickness so the heating effect of the current in the cable is insignificant.

a   i   If a mains appliance suddenly stops working, why is it a mistake to replace the fuse straightaway?
     ii   Should the cable of an electric iron be a two-core or a three-core cable?

New bulbs for old

When choosing an electrical appliance, most people compare several different appliances. The cost of the appliance is just one factor that may need to be considered. Other factors might include the power of the appliance and its efficiency.

If you want to replace a bulb, a visit to an electrical shop can present you with a bewildering range of bulbs.

A filament bulb is very inefficient. The energy from the hot bulb gradually makes the plastic parts of the bulb socket brittle and they crack.

Low energy bulbs are much more efficient so they don't become hot like filament bulbs do. Different types of low energy bulb are now available:

- **Low-energy compact fluorescent bulbs (CFLs)** are now used for room lighting instead of filament bulbs.
- **Low-energy light-emitting diodes (LEDs)** used for spotlights are usually referred to as high-power LEDs. They operate at low voltage and low power. They are much more efficient than filament bulbs or halogen bulbs and they last much longer.

This table gives more information about these different bulbs.

Type	Power	Efficiency	Lifetime in hours	Cost of bulb	Typical use
Filament bulb	100 W	20%	1000	50p	room lighting
Halogen bulb	100 W	25%	2500	£2.00	spotlight
Low-energy compact fluorescent bulb (CFL)	25 W	80%	15 000	£2.50	room lighting
Low-energy light-emitting diode (LED)	2 W	90%	30 000	£7.00	spotlight

b   A householder wants to replace a 100 W room light with a row of low-energy LEDs with the same light output. Use the information in the table above to answer the following questions.
   i   How many times would the filament bulb need to be replaced in the lifetime of an LED?
   ii   How many LEDs would be needed to give the same light output as a 100 W filament bulb?
   iii   The householder reckons the cost of the electricity for each LED at 10p per kWh over its lifetime of 30 000 hours would be £6. Show that the cost of the electricity for a 100 W bulb over this time would be £300.
   iv   Use your answers above to calculate how much the householder would save by replacing the filament bulb with LEDs.

Summary questions

1 An 'RCCB' socket should be used for mains appliances such as lawnmowers where there is a possible hazard when the appliance is used. Such a socket contains a residual current circuit breaker instead of a fuse. This type of circuit breaker switches the current off if the live current and the neutral current differ by more than 30 mA. This can happen, for example, if the blades of a lawnmower cut into the cable.

Create a table to show a possible 'electrical' hazard for each of these appliances: lawnmower, electric drill, electric saw, hairdryer, vacuum cleaner. The first entry has been done for you.

Appliance	Hazard
Lawnmower	The blades might cut the cable.

?? Did you know ...?

All new appliances like washing machines and freezers sold in the EU are labelled clearly with an efficiency rating. The rating is from A (very efficient) to G (lowest efficiency). Light bulbs are also labelled in this way on the packaging.

Figure 2 Efficiency measures

Key points

- Electrical faults are dangerous because they can cause electric shocks and fires.
- Never touch a mains appliance (or plug or socket) with wet hands. Never touch a bare wire or a terminal at a potential of more than 30 V.
- Check cables, plugs and sockets for damage regularly. Check smoke alarms and infrared sensors regularly.
- When choosing an electrical appliance, the power and efficiency rating of the appliance need to be considered.
- Filament bulbs and halogen bulbs are much less efficient than low energy bulbs.

Further teaching suggestions

Investigating lighting efficiency

- You can turn the activity of assessing different lighting types into a full investigation. The students would need to plan ways to measure the energy input to the lamp and some form of measurement of the brightness of the bulb. Leave this relativity open for the students to plan. Include cost implications of each type of lighting.

Make your own test

- The students can devise their own test questions and compile an examination for each other. You can set the criteria such as number of questions and time it takes to complete and then the students make a set of questions in teams. The students can sit the best test next lesson.

Electricians

- Students interested in becoming electricians can find out about the training and qualifications.

Mind maps

- Mind mapping only really works if the students review and refine the map regularly; get them to do this with their previous map.

ICT link-up

- There are plenty of opportunities here for ICT-based research. As usual, a list of suitable websites should be provided along with some form of research template.

Summary answers

1 An example of each possible electrical hazard is given in the table.

Appliance	Hazard
Electric drill	The drill might 'hit' a live wire in a cable in the wall.
Electric saw	The saw might cut the cable (or cut a limb).
Hairdryer	Anyone with wet hands using a hairdryer would be at risk.
Vacuum cleaner	The vacuum cleaner might run over and damage its cable.

Summary answers

1 a i The neutral wire.

   ii The live wire.

  b i The waves on the screen would be taller.

   ii There would be more waves on the screen.

2 a live, neutral

  b i neutral

   ii live

   iii earth

3 a i parallel

   ii series, live

  b i A fuse has a wire that melts if too much current passes through it. A circuit breaker has a switch that is pulled open if too much current passes through it.

   ii A circuit breaker is faster. Also a circuit breaker does not need to be replaced, but a fuse does.

4 a i 10.8 A

   ii 13 A

  b 920 W

5 a

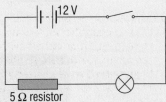

5 Ω resistor

  b i 432 J

   ii 108 J

   iii 324 J

  c i 30 Ω

   ii $I = V/R = 12/30 = 0.4$ A

   iii battery = 4.8 W, 5 Ω resistor = 0.8 W, 25 Ω resistor = 4.0 W

6 a i 2.5 A

   ii 2.4 Ω

  b The current through the lamp is less at 3 V than at 6 V, so the lamp filament is not as hot. Therefore, its resistance is less.

7 a i 3.0 A

   ii 600 C

  b i Energy = power × time
            = 36 W × 200 s = 7200 J

   ii 12 J/C

8 a 28.7 A

  b i D, because the maximum safe current through D is greater than the current that would pass through it when the oven operates at full power. So D would not overheat. E would not overheat either but it would be more expensive than D.

   ii Cables A, B and C would overheat as their maximum safe current is less than the current that would pass through them when the oven is at full power. The overheated cable might cause a fire. Also, the cable insulation could melt and cause a short-circuit that may start a fire.

Summary questions

1 a In a mains circuit, which wire:

  i is earthed at the local sub-station

  ii alternates in potential?

b An oscilloscope is used to display the potential difference of an alternating voltage supply unit. How would the trace change if:

  i the pd is increased

  ii the frequency is increased?

2 Copy and complete **a** and **b** using the words below. Each word can be used more than once.

earth live neutral

a When a mains appliance is switched on, current passes through it via the .... wire and the .... wire.

b In a mains circuit:

  i the .... wire is blue

  ii the .... wire is brown

  iii the .... wire is green and yellow.

3 a Copy and complete the following sentences:

  i Wall sockets are connected in .... with each other.

  ii A fuse in a mains plug is in .... with the appliance and cuts off the .... wire if too much current passes through the appliance.

b i What is the main difference between a fuse and a circuit breaker?

  ii Give two reasons why a circuit breaker is safer than a fuse.

4 a i Calculate the current in a 230 V, 2.5 kW electric kettle.

  ii Which fuse, 3 A, 5 A or 13 A, would you fit in the kettle plug?

b Calculate the power supplied to a 230 V electric toaster when the current through it is 4.0 A.

5 A 5 Ω resistor is in series with a bulb, a switch and a 12 V battery.

a Draw the circuit diagram.

b When the switch is closed for 60 seconds, a direct current of 0.6 A passes through the resistor. Calculate:

  i the energy supplied by the battery

  ii the energy transferred to the resistor

  iii the energy transferred to the bulb. [H]

c The bulb is replaced by a 25 Ω resistor.

  i Calculate the total resistance of the two resistors.

  ii Show that a current of 0.4 A passes through the battery.

iii Calculate the power supplied by the battery and the power delivered to each resistor.

6 When a 6 V bulb operates normally, the electrical power supplied to it is 15 W.

a Calculate:

  i the current through the bulb when it operates normally

  ii the resistance of the bulb when it operates normally.

b If the bulb is connected to a 3 V battery, state and explain why its resistance is less than at 6 V.

7 A 12 V 36 W bulb is connected to a 12 V supply.

a Calculate:

  i the current through the bulb.

  ii the charge flow through the bulb in 200 s.

b i Show that 7200 J of electrical energy is delivered the bulb in 200 s.

  ii Calculate the energy delivered to the bulb by each coulomb of charge that passes through it.

8 An electrician has the job of connecting a 6.6 kW electric oven to the 230 V mains supply in a house.

a Calculate the current needed to supply 6.6 kW of electrical power at 230 V.

b The table below shows the maximum current that can pass safely through five different mains cables. For each cable the cross-sectional area (csa) of each conductor is given in square millimetres (mm²).

	Cross-sectional area of conductor (mm²)	Maximum safe current (A)
A	1.0	14
B	1.5	18
C	2.5	28
D	4.0	36
E	6.0	46

  i To connect the oven to the mains supply, which cable should the electrician choose? Give a reason for your answer.

  ii State and explain what would happen if she chose a cable with thinner conductors?

Kerboodle resources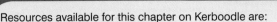

Resources available for this chapter on Kerboodle are:

- Chapter map: Mains electricity
- Practical: ac/dc display (P2 5.1)
- How Science Works: Are you energy smart? (P2 5.4)
- WebQuest: Light bulbs (P2 5.6)
- Interactive activity: Electrical power
- Revision podcast: Electric charge and electric power
- Test yourself: Mains electricity
- On your marks: Mains electricity
- Examination-style questions: Mains electricity
- Answers to examination-style questions: Mains electricity

AQA Examiner's tip

It is important in Question 1 that candidates describe the fault fully and explain the possible consequences in sufficient detail, i.e. 'It's dangerous' is not enough. Encourage answers more along the lines of: 'The knife may touch the live wires in the toaster, the knife conducts electricity, and therefore the person may get electrocuted'.

AQA Examiner's tip

In Question 3 candidates are expected to recall that UK mains voltage is about 230 V. Look out for questions where this voltage is not given but the value is needed for the calculation.

End of chapter questions

AQA Examination-style questions

1 The pictures show situations in which electricity is not being used safely.

For each picture **a**, **b** and **c**, explain how electricity is not being used safely.

a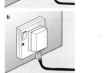

(2)

b

c

(2)

d The colour of the earth wire in a plug is .... (1)

e The pins of the plug are made of brass because it is a good .... (1)

f The voltage on the neutral wire is about .... V. (1)

g RCCB stands for .... (1)

Most domestic appliances are connected to the 230 V mains supply with a 3-pin plug containing a fuse. 3 A, 5 A and 13 A fuses are available.

a A bulb for a desk lamp has a normal current of 0.26 A.
  i Which of the three fuses should be used? (1)
  ii Calculate the power of the lamp. (2)
  iii Calculate how many coulombs of charge pass through the lamp if it is left on for 1 hour. [H] (3)

b i Calculate the current passing through a 1.15 kW electric fan heater. (2)
  ii Which fuse should be used in the plug for this heater? (1)

c Calculate how much electrical energy is transferred when the fan heater is left on for 30 minutes. Write down the equation you use. Show clearly how you work out your answer and give the unit. (3)

d *In this question you will be assessed on using good English, organising information clearly and using specialist terms where appropriate.*

The heater is made of metal and has an earth wire connected to it. Explain how the fuse and earth wire together protect the wiring of the circuit. (6)

3 A kettle is connected to the UK mains supply and boiled. An energy monitoring device measures that 420 000 J has been transferred to the kettle in the time it takes to boil.

a Calculate how much charge has flowed through the kettle. Write down the equation you use. Show clearly how you work out your answer and give the unit. [H] (3)

b The power of the kettle is 2.2 kW. How long did the kettle take to boil? (3)

4 An oscilloscope is connected to a power supply. The trace is shown on a centimetre grid.

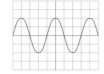

a Explain how you know that it is an ac supply being measured. (1)

b Give the peak voltage if each division on the y-axis is 2 V/cm. (1)

c Each x-axis division is 0.01 s/cm.
  i Calculate the time period of the supply. (1)
  ii Calculate the frequency of the supply. [H] (2)

d Describe the position and appearance of the trace on the screen if the supply was switched to 6 V dc. (2)

AQA Examination-style answers

1 a Too many plugs in one socket. The current may be too large in the socket and cause a fire. *(2 marks)*

b The cable has been repaired with tape. This tape could come off and leave a bare live wire. *(2 marks)*

c A knife is being pushed into the toaster. The knife may touch the live heating element inside the toaster and the person could be electrocuted. *(2 marks)*

d green and yellow *(1 mark)*

e electrical conductor *(1 mark)*

f 0 volts *(1 mark)*

g Residual Current Circuit Breaker *(1 mark)*

2 a i 3 A *(1 mark)*
  ii $P = I \times V = 0.26 \times 230$
    $= 59.8\,\text{W}$ *(2 marks)*
  iii $Q = I \times t = 0.26 \times 3600 = 936\,\text{C}$ *(3 marks)*

b i $I = \dfrac{P}{V} = 1150/230 = 5\,\text{A}$ *(2 marks)*
  ii 13 A *(1 mark)*

c $E = P \times t = 1150 \times 30 \times 60$
  $= 2.1\,\text{MJ}$ *(3 marks)*

d There is a clear, balanced and detailed description of how the fuse and earth wire together protect the wiring of the circuit. The answer shows almost faultless spelling, punctuation and grammar. It is coherent and in an organised, logical sequence. It contains a range of appropriate or relevant specialist terms used accurately. *(5–6 marks)*

There is a description of how the fuse and earth wire together protect the wiring of the circuit. There are some errors in spelling, punctuation and grammar. The answer has some structure and organisation. The use of specialist terms has been attempted, but not always accurately. *(3–4 marks)*

There is a brief description of how the fuse and earth wire together protect the wiring of the circuit, which has little clarity and detail. The spelling, punctuation and grammar are very weak. The answer is poorly organised with almost no specialist terms and/or their use demonstrating a general lack of understanding of their meaning. *(1–2 marks)*

No relevant content. *(0 marks)*

Examples of physics points made in the response:
- a fault may cause the live wire to touch the metal casing
- the metal casing is connected to the earth wire
- a large current will flow through the live wire to earth
- due to the low resistance of the earth wire
- the large current will blow the fuse which is in the live wire
- this disconnects the circuit
- which prevents the circuit being damaged by the large current.

3 a $Q = \dfrac{E}{V} = 420\,000/230 = 1826\,\text{C}$ *(3 marks)*

b $t = \dfrac{E}{P} = 420\,000/2\,200$
  $= 191\,\text{seconds}$ *(3 marks)*

4 a The trace goes above and below the central line (positive and negative). *(1 mark)*

b 4 V or 4.1 V *(1 mark)*

c i 0.04 seconds *(1 mark)*
  ii Frequency $= \dfrac{I}{t} = 1/0.04 = 25\,\text{Hz}$ *(2 marks)*

d A horizontal line on the third division below the centre. *(2 marks)*

AQA Practical suggestions

Practicals	AQA	k	📖	⚙
Measuring oscilloscope traces.	✓	✓	✓	
Demonstrating the action of fuse wires.	✓		✓	
Using fluctuations in light intensity measurements from filament bulbs to determine the frequency of ac.		✓		
Measuring the power of 12 V appliances by measuring energy transferred (using a joulemeter or ammeter and voltmeter) in a set time.		✓		✓

AQA Examiner's tip

Question 4 illustrates an oscilloscope trace of an ac supply. Note that ac and dc wave forms can easily be displayed on an oscilloscope as a demonstration. There are many 'PC oscilloscopes' on the market that are more compact than a cathode ray oscilloscope (CRO) and relatively inexpensive. To demonstrate a 'traditional' CRO, a flexible camera attached to a projector can be employed with great effect.

P2 6.1

Observing nuclear radiation

AQA

Specification link-up: Physics P2.5

- The basic structure of an atom is a small central nucleus composed of protons and neutrons surrounded by electrons. *[P2.5.1 a)]*
- Some substances give out radiation from the nuclei of their atoms all the time, whatever is done to them. These substances are said to be radioactive. *[P2.5.2 a)]*
- The origins of background radiation. *[P2.5.2 b)]*

Learning objectives

Students should learn:

- that unstable nuclei decay and emit invisible radiation when the structure of the nucleus changes to become more stable
- that this radiation can be detected in a number of ways including by a GM tube
- that background radiation is present everywhere due to cosmic rays and decay of unstable isotopes in rocks (among other sources).

Learning outcomes

Most students should be able to:

- draw a diagram illustrating the structure of an atom (nuclear model)
- state what we mean by a 'radioactive' substance and describe the types of radiation emitted from these substances
- describe the origins of background radiation.

Some students should also be able to:

- explain how radioactive materials were discovered.

Answers to in-text questions

a No, the salts give out radiation all the time.

b Yes.

c Because it is emitted from the nucleus of an atom.

Support

- Building atoms and nuclei is a really good way of cementing the idea of the particles that make up the nucleus. Have some circular component cut out in advance. If you want to go further, you can use polystyrene balls stuck together with cocktail sticks or use marbles held together with modelling clay.

Extend

- Introduce nuclear notation and the formal definitions of atomic number, mass number and focus on the layout. The students should be shown some recently discovered elements and find out how there are produced. They can also look into the discovery of radiation a little more.

Lesson structure

Starters

'Lookie likey' – What does an atom look like? Ask the students to draw and label one before showing them our current (nuclear) model. Does an atom really *look* like this? Show the students some caricatures of famous people to see if these capture the 'essence' of the person. Use this to point out that sometimes images are not realistic but they capture the important information, just like the pictures of atoms and nuclei used throughout this chapter. *(5 minutes)*

Atom models – Ask students to draw some simple atomic models. You can support the students by giving them a set of cut-out protons, neutrons and electrons to use. Give them some specifications like carbon: 6 protons, 6 neutrons and 6 electrons to see if they arrange the particles correctly. Extend students by asking them to present a range of atoms and insisting that they use the correct electron configurations (providing the rules if needed). Ask students to note any of the properties of the components that they already know. *(10 minutes)*

Main

- Before carrying out any demonstrations involving radioactive material, make certain that you are familiar with local handling rules. (See 'Practical support'.)

- Start by checking knowledge of atomic structure, protons, neutrons and electrons, as this is essential in discussing isotopes later. You can then discuss the history of the discovery of radioactivity. You should point out that although the initial discovery was accidental; the investigation into the cause was a thorough scientific one. Marie Curie died aged 67 partly because of her work. Similar things happened with early researchers into X-rays. This shows that even scientists underestimated the hazards of their research.

- Show the presence of radiation due to the sources by using a GM tube or spark detector. (See 'Practical support'.) If you have a video camera and projector, you may want to use it to show the detail of the experiment without getting the students too close.

- Emphasise that nuclear radiation is caused by changes in the nucleus. You might ask the students to draw a nucleus and describe the parts. If you do this, it is worth reminding them that the nucleus is really spherical; not just a disc. Show a model made of marbles stuck together; if one falls off, then attribute it to nuclear decay.

- Demonstrate background radiation by letting the Geiger counter run without any sources present. Explain that it is normal for there to be a low level of radiation, this is 'background radiation', and go through some of the sources. Explain that the contributions vary from place to place depending on things like the rock type (e.g. fresh igneous rocks are more active than sandstone).

- Some students may like to know more about why the nucleus decays. The reason for the nucleus changing is linked to energy. The nucleus changes so that it has less energy; the parts that make it up have become more tightly bound; this is yet another example of energy spreading out.

Plenaries

Murder mystery – The body of a press photographer has been found in a sealed room, and all of the film in her camera has gone black even though it hasn't been used. Write a letter to the police explaining what you think happened and how you know. [Hopefully students will come up with the idea that they have been blasted by a large amount of ionising radiation.] *(5 minutes)*

Comparing locations – Provide the students with some data about the sources of background radiation in different locations. They must produce a pie chart of this information and compare the risks in each of the locations. To support students, you can provide pie chart drawing apparatus (percentage wheels). To extend students, you can provide extra information including the actual values (instead of percentages) and ask them to calculate percentages from the source information. *(10 minutes)*

Practical support

Using a GM tube and ratemeter

The usual way of showing the presence of ionising radiation is by using a Geiger–Müller tube and ratemeter. This has the advantage that the count rate is proportional to the activity, and some of the students will be familiar with the device from films and television. Many modern devices have the counter and tube components combined and so are simpler to use.

Equipment and materials needed

Geiger–Müller tube, ratemeter (and possibly high voltage power supply), large plastic tray, tongs, radioactive sources, laboratory coat.

Details

The operating voltage of the GM tube is usually 400 V and this is usually provided by the ratemeter, but you may need an external supply for tubes that connect to computers. Check with the manual. Position the detector in the tray and switch it on. Bring the sources close to the tube window (and above the tray) and the ratemeter should count. If you can find a ratemeter that clicks, the demonstration is a lot more fun.

If you do not want the student to get too close to the sources, then you could connect a small video camera to a data projector to show the demonstrations more clearly.

Radioactivity

P2 6.1 — Observing nuclear radiation

Learning objectives

- What is a radioactive substance?
- What types of radiation are given out from a radioactive substance?
- When does a radioactive source give out radiation (radioactive decay)?
- Where does background radiation come from?

A key discovery

Figure 1 Becquerel's key

If your photos showed a mysterious image, what would you think? In 1896, the French physicist, **Henri Becquerel**, discovered the image of a key on a film he developed. He remembered the film had been in a drawer under a key. On top of that there had been a packet of uranium salts. The uranium salts must have sent out some form of radiation that passed through paper (the film wrapper) but not through metal (the key).

Marie Curie

Becquerel asked a young research worker, **Marie Curie**, to investigate. She found that the salts gave out radiation all the time. It happened no matter what was done to them. She used the word **radioactivity** to describe this strange new property of uranium.

She and her husband, Pierre, did more research into this new branch of science. They discovered new radioactive elements. They named one of the elements **polonium**, after Marie's native country, Poland.

Figure 2 Marie Curie 1867–1934

a You can stop a lamp giving out light by switching it off. Is it possible to stop uranium giving out radiation?

Becquerel and the Curies were awarded the Nobel Prize for the discovery of radioactivity. When Pierre died in a road accident, Marie went on with their work. She was awarded a second Nobel Prize in 1911 for the discovery of polonium and radium. She died in 1934 from leukaemia, a disease of the blood cells. It was probably caused by the radiation from the radioactive materials she worked with.

Practical

Investigating radioactivity

We can use a **Geiger counter** to detect radioactivity. Look at Figure 3. The counter clicks each time a particle of radiation from a radioactive substance enters the Geiger tube.

Figure 3 Using a Geiger counter

What stops the radiation? Ernest Rutherford carried out tests to answer this question about a century ago. He put different materials between the radioactive substance and a detector.

He discovered two types of radiation:

- One type (**alpha radiation**, symbol α) was stopped by paper.
- The other type (**beta radiation**, symbol β) went through the paper.

Scientists later discovered a third type, **gamma radiation** (symbol γ), even more penetrating than beta radiation.

b Can gamma radiation go through paper?

A radioactive puzzle

Why are some substances radioactive? Every atom has a nucleus made up of protons and neutrons. Electrons move about in energy levels (or shells) surrounding the nucleus.

Most atoms each have a stable nucleus that doesn't change. But the atoms of a radioactive substance each have a nucleus that is unstable. An unstable nucleus becomes stable by emitting alpha, beta or gamma radiation. We say an unstable nucleus **decays** when it emits radiation.

We can't tell when an unstable nucleus will decay. It is a **random** event that happens without anything being done to the nucleus.

c Why is the radiation from a radioactive substance sometimes called 'nuclear radiation'?

The origins of background radiation

A Geiger counter clicks even when it is not near a radioactive source. This effect is due to **background radiation**. This is radiation from radioactive substances:

- in the environment (e.g. in the air or the ground or in building materials), or
- from space (cosmic rays), or
- from devices such as X-ray tubes.

Some of these radioactive substances are present because of nuclear weapons testing and nuclear power stations. But most of it is from naturally occurring substances in the Earth. For example, radon gas is radioactive and is a product of the decay of uranium found in the rocks in certain areas.

Figure 4 Radioactive decay

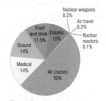

Figure 5 The origins of background radiation

Summary questions

1 Copy and complete **a** and **b** using the words below. Each word can be used more than once.

protons   neutrons   nucleus   radiation

a The .... of an atom is made up of .... and ....
b When an unstable .... decays, it emits ....

2 **a** The radiation from a radioactive source is stopped by paper. What type of radiation does the source emit?
b The radiation from a different source goes through paper. What can you say about this radiation?

3 **a** Explain why some substances are radioactive.
b State two sources of background radioactivity.

Key points

- A radioactive substance contains unstable nuclei that become stable by emitting radiation.
- There are three main types of radiation from radioactive substances – alpha, beta and gamma radiation.
- Radioactive decay is a random event – we cannot predict or influence when it will happen.
- Background radiation is from radioactive substances in the environment or from space or from devices such as X-ray machines.

Further teaching suggestions

ICT link-up

- The students cannot handle radioactive material, but simulations allow them to explore ideas safely. These are an excellent way to visualise the behaviour of the particles and waves and to study absorption. They can also demonstrate the half-life of materials, a process that is too difficult to show with real substances in class. However, it is best to use these simulations alongside real apparatus if possible, to show that the models are linked to physical reality.

Summary answers

1 **a** nucleus, protons, neutrons
  b nucleus, radiation

2 **a** alpha radiation
  b This radiation is either beta or gamma radiation.

3 **a** Because they have an unstable nucleus that can become more stable by emitting radiation.
  b Any two from radioactive isotopes in the air, the ground or in building materials; X-ray machines; cosmic radiation.

P2 6.2 The discovery of the nucleus

Learning objectives

Students should learn:

- that alpha-scattering experiments led Rutherford to deduce the nuclear model of the atom
- that the nuclear model of the atom was accepted because it could explain alpha scattering much better than the previous models could
- that this led to the replacement of the 'plum pudding' model of the atom by the nuclear model.

Learning outcomes

Most students should be able to:

- describe the Rutherford scattering experiment and the evidence it produced
- explain how this evidence leads to the nuclear model of the atom
- describe the 'plum pudding' model and explain why this model proved to be inadequate.

Some students should also be able to:

- draw and explain in detail the paths of alpha particles scattered by a nucleus.

Answers to in-text questions

a It had hit something much heavier.

b Rutherford's model would have been incorrect.

Support

- Provide a diagram of the experiment including the paths taken by the alpha particles so that the students can add the conclusions to the evidence presented.

Extend

- Ask: 'How was the neutron discovered?' Because it has no electrical charge, it is much more difficult to detect than the electron or proton. The students should find out who discovered it and how. Point out that the neutron was referred to in science books before its actual discovery – scientists were so convinced of its existence.

AQA Specification link-up: Physics P2.5

- The basic structure of an atom is a small central nucleus composed of protons and neutrons surrounded by electrons. *[P2.5.1 a)]*
- Explain how results from the Rutherford and Marsden scattering experiments led to the 'plum pudding' model being replaced by the nuclear model. *[P2.5]*

Lesson structure

Starters

What's in the tin? – Peel the label off a tin of sponge pudding. Show the unmarked tin to the students and ask them to describe ways they could find out about what's inside without opening it. [They should consider X-rays, weighing and measuring it to find the density. They might even suggest drilling and sampling.] Discuss how sometimes, scientists have to investigate things that cannot be simply observed; they need to use techniques beyond what we can see. *(5 minutes)*

Believe it or not? – What does it take to change the students' minds about something? How much evidence would be needed to convince them that NASA has really sent men to the Moon? Discuss how difficult it is to change people's strongly held beliefs and point out that scientists are the same; they won't want to change ideas that they have been working with for many years. To support students give them a set of cards showing possible evidence and have them prioritise them (e.g. photographs, testimony, rock samples, radio communications). To extend the students you can have them come up with counter arguments to the evidence. *(10 minutes)*

Main

- This topic is all about a famous experiment and it should be built up as such. Through hard work and brilliant ideas, our idea of 'what an atom is' was developed. You might want to establish the context; electrons (cathode rays) had not long been discovered and Rutherford had discovered that one element could change into another when it emitted an 'alpha particle'.

- The actual experiment took weeks in a very dark laboratory where Geiger or Marsden had to count tiny flashes of light through a microscope. Each flash was one alpha particle hitting the fluorescent screen. If you have electron tubes, you can show a little bit of what this would be like (see 'Further teaching suggestions' box).

- The most important result of the experiment was the few particles that bounced back. These showed that there was something massive at the centre of the atom. One possible analogy would be to spread a large sheet of paper out vertically and behind it fix a small metal disc held firmly by a stand. If you threw darts at it, most would go straight through but one in a thousand may hit the metal disc and bounce back.

- It will be impossibly difficult for the students to imagine the size of an atom and then the relative size of the nucleus. You might like to point out that 99.99% of the chair they are sitting on is just empty space; then again so is 99.99% of their bodies!

- The problem with plum puddings is that nobody eats them any more, so many students don't understand what you are referring to (a Christmas pudding is a good substitute). Try illustrating with a real plum pudding. They are cheap and you can always eat it afterwards.

- This whole topic links in neatly with 'How Science Works' and the section on 'Observation as a stimulus to investigation'. This relates to how data and observations from testing a prediction can either support or refute existing theories and models.

Plenaries

It's not like a solar system – Some people think of an atom as being a bit like a solar system. The students should make a list of similarities but, more importantly, the differences. [The nucleus is not much like a star, it is made up of different bits (protons and neutrons) and the electrons don't actually orbit in ellipses]. *(5 minutes)*

I don't believe it – Can the students write a letter to an unconvinced scientist who wants to hold on to the plum pudding model? This will help them reinforce their understanding by explaining the concepts to others. They need to include all of the evidence and then the explanations that are used. Differentiate by asking for different levels of detail for different students or by providing some sample phrases describing pieces of evidence that must be included. *(10 minutes)*

Practical support

Lucky strike

This practical really needs no additional explanation. A more advanced version is outlined in the 'Further teaching suggestions' box.

Hot cross buns

A hot cross bun can be used to give an impression of the 'plum pudding' model for students who are not familiar with a plum pudding. The currants represent the electrons spread throughout the positive dough. The big cross is a handy reminder of the fact the bun is positive.

Radioactivity

P2 6.2   The discovery of the nucleus

Learning objectives

- How was the nuclear model of the atom established?
- Why was the plum pudding model of the atom rejected?
- Why was the nuclear model accepted?

?? Did you know ... ?

Ernest Rutherford was awarded the Nobel Prize in 1908 for his discoveries on radioactivity. His famous discovery of the nucleus was made in 1913. He was knighted in 1914 and made a member of the House of Lords in 1931. He hoped that no one would discover how to release energy from the nucleus until people learned to live at peace with their neighbours. He died in 1937 before the discovery of nuclear fission.

Figure 2 Ernest Rutherford

Practical

Lucky strike!

Fix a small metal disc about 2 cm thick at the centre of a table. Hide the disc under a cardboard disc about 20 cm in diameter. See if you can hit the metal disc with a rolling marble.

Ernest Rutherford made many important discoveries about radioactivity. He discovered that alpha and beta radiation consists of different types of particles. He realised alpha (α) particles could be used to probe the atom. He asked two of his research workers, Hans Geiger and Ernest Marsden, to investigate. They used a thin metal foil to scatter a beam of alpha particles. Figure 1 shows the arrangement they used.

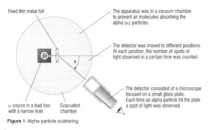

The apparatus was in a vacuum chamber to prevent air molecules absorbing the alpha (α) particles.

The detector was moved to different positions. At each position, the number of spots of light observed in a certain time was counted.

The detector consisted of a microscope focused on a small glass plate. Each time an alpha particle hit the plate a spot of light was observed.

Figure 1 Alpha particle scattering

They measured the number of alpha particles deflected per second through different angles. The results showed that:

- most of the alpha particles passed straight through the metal foil
- the number of alpha particles deflected per minute decreased as the angle of deflection increased
- about 1 in 10000 alpha particles were deflected by more than 90°.

a If you kicked a football at an empty goal and the ball bounced back at you, what would you conclude?

Rutherford was astonished by the results. He said it was like firing 'naval shells' at tissue paper and discovering the occasional shell rebounds. He knew that α particles are positively charged. He deduced from the results that there is a nucleus at the centre of every atom that is:

- positively charged because it repels α particles (remember that like charges repel and unlike charges attract)
- much smaller than the atom because most α particles pass through without deflection
- where most of the mass of the atom is located.

Using this model, Rutherford worked out the proportion of α particles that would be deflected for a given angle. He found an exact agreement with Geiger and Marsden's measurements. He used his theory to estimate the diameter of the nucleus. He found it was about 100000 times smaller than the atom.

Rutherford's nuclear model of the atom was quickly accepted because:

- It agreed exactly with the measurements Geiger and Marsden made in their experiments.
- It explains radioactivity in terms of changes that happen to an unstable nucleus when it emits radiation.
- It predicted the existence of the neutron, which was later discovered.

b What difference would it have made if Geiger and Marsden's measurements had not fitted Rutherford's nuclear model?

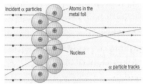

Figure 3 Alpha (α) particle paths

Goodbye to the plum pudding model!

Before the nucleus was discovered in 1914, scientists didn't know what the structure of the atom was. They did know atoms contained electrons and they knew these are tiny negatively charged particles. But they didn't know how the positive charge was arranged in an atom, although there were different models in circulation. Some scientists thought the atom was like a 'plum pudding' with:

- the positively charged matter in the atom evenly spread about (as in a pudding), and
- electrons buried inside (like plums in the pudding).

Rutherford's discovery meant farewell to the 'plum pudding' atom.

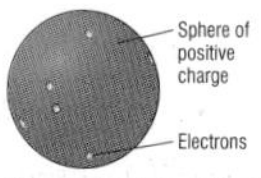

Figure 4 The plum pudding atom

?? Did you know ... ?

Almost all the mass of an atom is in its nucleus. The density of the nucleus is about a thousand million million times the density of water. A matchbox of nuclear matter would weigh about a million million tonnes!

Summary questions

1 Copy and complete **a** to **c** using the words below:

charge diameter mass

  a A nucleus has the same type of .... as an alpha particle.
  b A nucleus has a much smaller .... than the atom.
  c Most of the .... of the atom is in the nucleus.

2 **a** Figure 5 shows four possible paths, labelled A, B, C and D, of an alpha particle deflected by a nucleus. Which path would the alpha particle travel along?
  b Explain why each of the other paths in part **a** is not possible.

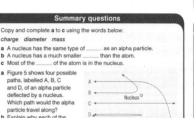

Figure 5

3 **a** Describe two differences between the nuclear model of the atom and the plum pudding model.
  b Explain why the alpha-scattering experiment led to the acceptance of the nuclear model of the atom and the rejection of the plum pudding model.

Key points

- Rutherford used the measurements from alpha-scattering experiments to prove that an atom has a small positively charged central nucleus where most of the mass of the atom is located.
- The plum pudding model could not explain why some alpha particles were scattered through large angles.
- The nuclear model of the atom correctly explained why the alpha particles are scattered and why some are scattered through large angles.

Further teaching suggestions

A scattering experiment

- It is possible to model the scattering experiment of Rutherford using a hidden cone and marbles. The marbles are rolled at the cone and scatter in directions similar to those in the original experiment. You should find a kit available in a good science equipment catalogue. This is really only suitable for small groups though. More useful animations can be found at various websites on the internet.

Electron tubes

- These are generally only used at A-level, but you could use them here to extend the students.

  #### Details

  Use the manual for the tube to set it up. It will require an extremely high-tension power supply and some proper connecting leads. These shouldn't be able to provide a dangerous current but take care with any high voltages. With the tube you should be able to show the phosphorescence effect of a charged particle and some magnetic deflection if you wish.

??? Did you know ... ?

There are objects made up of purely nuclear material. A neutron star is made up of neutrons packed together as tightly as the protons and neutrons in a nucleus.

Summary answers

1 **a** charge   **b** diameter   **c** mass

2 **a** Path B.
  b A is wrong because it is attracted by the nucleus; C is wrong because it is unaffected by the nucleus; D is wrong because it is repelled by the nucleus through too great an angle.

3 **a** Any two of the following three points:
   1 In the nuclear model, all the positive charge is concentrated in a nucleus that is much smaller than the atom. In the 'plum pudding' atom, the positive charge is spread out throughout the atom.
   2 In the nuclear model, most of the mass of the atom is concentrated in the nucleus. In the 'plum pudding' atom, most of the mass is spread out throughout the atom.
   3 In the nuclear model, most of the atom is empty space. In the 'plum pudding' model, there is no empty space in the atom.
  b The nuclear model explains why some of the alpha particles are scattered through large angles. According to the 'plum pudding' model, such large-angle scattering should not be observed.

P2 6.3

Nuclear reactions

Learning objectives

Students should learn:

- that isotopes are atoms of the same element with different mass numbers
- that when a nucleus emits an alpha particle, its mass number is reduced by 4 and its proton number is reduced by 2
- that when a nucleus decays by beta emission, its mass number stays the same but its proton number increases by 1.

Learning outcomes

Most students should be able to:

- state the relative charge and mass of the constituents of an atom
- state how many protons and neutrons are in a nucleus, given its mass number and its atomic number
- describe what happens to an isotope when it undergoes alpha or beta decay.

Some students should also be able to:

- write nuclear equations to represent alpha or beta decay given appropriate data. [HT only]

Answers to in-text questions

a 92 p, 143 n

b $^{228}_{90}$Th = 90 p + 138 n
$^{224}_{88}$Ra = 88 p + 136 n

c $^{40}_{19}$K = 19 p + 21 n; $^{40}_{20}$Ca = 20 p + 20 n

Support

- Support students by providing a list of the terms and symbols used in this topic, along with diagrams representing the basic decays for them to label.

Extend

- Alchemists dreamed for thousands of years that lead could be transformed into gold. With nuclear physics, this can now actually be achieved. The students should find out who has done this and why the market has not been flooded with this artificial gold.

Specification link-up: Physics P2.5

- The relative masses and relative electric charges of protons, neutrons and electrons. [P2.5.1 b)]
- In an atom the number of electrons is equal to the number of protons in the nucleus. The atom has no overall electrical charge. [P2.5.1 c)]
- Atoms may lose or gain electrons to form charged particles called ions. [P2.5.1 d)]
- The atoms of an element always have the same number of protons, but have a different number of neutrons for each isotope. The total number of protons in an atom is called its atomic number. The total number of protons and neutrons in an atom is called its mass number. [P2.5.1 e)]
- Identification of an alpha particle as 2 neutrons and 2 protons, the same as a helium nucleus, a beta particle as an electron from the nucleus and gamma radiation as electromagnetic radiation. [P2.5.2 c)]
- Nuclear equations to show single alpha and beta decay. [P2.5.2 d)] **[HT only]**

Lesson structure

Starters

Fact or fiction – The students use red, amber and green cards to decide if a series of statements about radioactivity are false, they don't know, or true. These can include things like: radioactive materials glow [mostly false], radioactive material are all metals [false], there is no safe dose of nuclear radiation [true], radioactivity is artificial [false] and so on. (5 minutes)

Chemical change – Give the students a demonstration of a chemical reaction (magnesium + oxygen → magnesium oxide, or magnesium + hydrochloric acid → magnesium chloride + hydrogen. Ask the students to describe what is happening in terms of particles and see if they understand basic conservation of particles in this experiment. Use the idea later to help discuss conservation of protons and neutrons in nuclear decay. Support students by providing them with simple atom diagrams showing the process and ask them to describe the making or breaking of bonds. To extend the students, you should require descriptions of energy changes. (10 minutes)

Main

- There is quite a lot of information in this spread and students are likely to become confused if they move too quickly through it. The main source of confusion is often with the large number of scientific terms.
- Start with a reminder of the structure of an atom, but do not dwell on it too long because this will be the fifth or sixth time the students have been through it. There are alternative terms for the number of protons and total number of nucleons (proton number and nucleon number) but the AQA specifications sticks to 'atomic number' and 'mass number' and so should you. Watch out for students getting confused about finding the number of neutrons. Some think that there is *always* the same number of neutrons as protons (as there often are in smaller atoms of elements).
- Some students find it very difficult to write out the superscript and subscripts on the isotopes in the correct positions. Try to encourage them to be precise and write out plenty of examples. It may be difficult to write these on an interactive whiteboard too.
- Higher Tier students need to be able to understand the format of decay equations so that they can find the missing values when needed. Give them a few extra ones with missing numbers.
- You will find animations of nuclear decays helpful, as the students can see the alpha or beta particle leave the nucleus and how it is changed by the process. Somebody might ask where the electron comes from in beta decay. They may think that a neutron is an electron and a proton stuck together, and it just splits; you should point out that this is not the case but you won't be explaining it until the students opt for advanced-level physics.
- Gamma ray emission is really just the release of excess energy by the nucleus after another form of decay leaves it with a bit too much energy. As there are no particles emitted and there is no change to the nucleus.

Plenaries

Name that isotope – Provide the students with a table describing different isotopes with gaps in and ask them to complete the table. They need to fill in missing details such as element name, proton number, mass number and number of electrons using the information provided. They will need a periodic table to help. *(5 minutes)*

Definitions – The students must give accurate definitions of the terms: 'proton, neutron, electron, ion, mass number, atomic number, alpha particle, beta particle and gamma ray.' These should be linked to the learning that has taken place already in this chapter. Select the best and use these definitions on a wall display to remind the students. To support students, you can make this activity a simple phrase or card-matching task. To extend students, you can insist on illustrations demonstrating the ideas. *(10 minutes)*

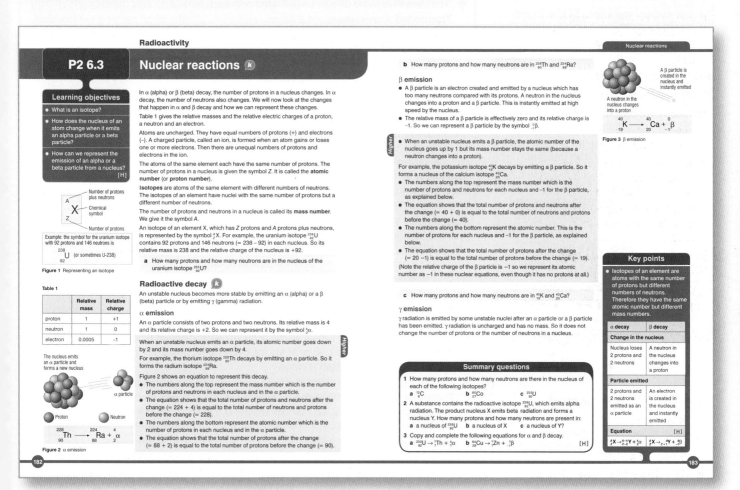

Radioactivity

P2 6.3 — Nuclear reactions ⓚ

Learning objectives

- What is an isotope?
- How does the nucleus of an atom change when it emits an alpha particle or a beta particle?
- How can we represent the emission of an alpha or a beta particle from a nucleus? [H]

In α (alpha) or β (beta) decay, the number of protons in a nucleus changes. In α decay, the number of neutrons also changes. We will now look at the changes that happen in α and β decay and how we can represent these changes.

Table 1 gives the relative masses and the relative electric charges of a proton, a neutron and an electron.

Atoms are uncharged. They have equal numbers of protons (+) and electrons (−). A charged particle, called an ion, is formed when an atom gains or loses one or more electrons. Then there are unequal numbers of protons and electrons in the ion.

The atoms of the same element each have the same number of protons. The number of protons in a nucleus is given the symbol Z. It is called the **atomic number** (or **proton number**).

Isotopes are atoms of the same element with different numbers of neutrons. The isotopes of an element have nuclei with the same number of protons but a different number of neutrons.

The number of protons and neutrons in a nucleus is called its **mass number**. We give it the symbol A.

An isotope of an element X, which has Z protons and A protons plus neutrons, is represented by the symbol $^A_Z X$. For example, the uranium isotope $^{238}_{92}U$ contains 92 protons and 146 neutrons (= 238 − 92) in each nucleus. So its relative mass is 238 and the relative charge of the nucleus is +92.

a How many protons and how many neutrons are in the nucleus of the uranium isotope $^{235}_{92}U$?

Radioactive decay ⓚ

An unstable nucleus becomes more stable by emitting an α (alpha) or a β (beta) particle or by emitting γ (gamma) radiation.

α emission

An α particle consists of two protons and two neutrons. Its relative mass is 4 and its relative charge is +2. So we can represent it by the symbol $^4_2 \alpha$.

When an unstable nucleus emits an α particle, its atomic number goes down by 2 and its mass number goes down by 4.

For example, the thorium isotope $^{228}_{90}Th$ decays by emitting an α particle. So it forms the radium isotope $^{224}_{88}Ra$.

Figure 2 shows an equation to represent this decay.

- The numbers along the top represent the mass number which is the number of protons and neutrons in each nucleus and in the α particle.
- The equation shows that the total number of protons and neutrons after the change (= 224 + 4) is equal to the total number of neutrons and protons before the change (= 228).
- The numbers along the bottom represent the atomic number which is the number of protons in each nucleus and in the α particle.
- The equation shows that the total number of protons after the change (= 88 + 2) is equal to the total number of protons before the change (= 90).

b How many protons and how many neutrons are in $^{228}_{90}Th$ and $^{224}_{88}Ra$?

β emission

- A β particle is an electron created and emitted by a nucleus which has too many neutrons compared with its protons. A neutron in the nucleus changes into a proton and a β particle. This is instantly emitted at high speed by the nucleus.
- The relative mass of a β particle is effectively zero and its relative charge is −1. So we can represent a β particle by the symbol $^0_{-1} \beta$.

- When an unstable nucleus emits a β particle, the atomic number of the nucleus goes up by 1 but its mass number stays the same (because a neutron changes into a proton).

For example, the potassium isotope $^{40}_{19}K$ decays by emitting a β particle. So it forms a nucleus of the calcium isotope $^{40}_{20}Ca$.

- The numbers along the top represent the mass number which is the number of protons and neutrons for each nucleus and +1 for the β particle, as explained below.
- The equation shows that the total number of protons and neutrons after the change (= 40 + 0) is equal to the total number of neutrons and protons before the change (= 40).
- The numbers along the bottom represent the atomic number. This is the number of protons for each nucleus and −1 for the β particle, as explained below.
- The equation shows that the total number of protons after the change (= 20 −1) is equal to the total number of protons before the change (= 19). (Note the relative charge of the β particle is −1 so we represent its atomic number as −1 in these nuclear equations, even though it has no protons at all.)

c How many protons and how many neutrons are in $^{40}_{19}K$ and $^{40}_{20}Ca$?

γ emission

γ radiation is emitted by some unstable nuclei after an α particle or a β particle has been emitted. γ radiation is uncharged and has no mass. So it does not change the number of protons or the number of neutrons in a nucleus.

Figure 1 Representing an isotope

Table 1

	Relative mass	Relative charge
proton	1	+1
neutron	1	0
electron	0.0005	−1

Figure 2 α emission

Figure 3 β emission

A β particle is created in the nucleus and instantly emitted

A neutron in the nucleus changes into a proton

$^{40}_{19}K \rightarrow {}^{40}_{20}Ca + {}^{0}_{-1}\beta$

Key points

- Isotopes of an element are atoms with the same number of protons but different numbers of neutrons. Therefore they have the same atomic number but different mass numbers.

	α decay	β decay
Change in the nucleus		
	Nucleus loses 2 protons and 2 neutrons	A neutron in the nucleus changes into a proton
Particle emitted		
	2 protons and 2 neutrons emitted as an α particle	An electron is created in the nucleus and instantly emitted
Equation		[H]
	$^A_Z X \rightarrow {}^{A-4}_{Z-2}Y + {}^4_2\alpha$	$^A_Z X \rightarrow {}^{A}_{Z+1}Y + {}^0_{-1}\beta$

Summary questions

1 How many protons and how many neutrons are there in the nucleus of each of the following isotopes?
  a $^{12}_6C$ **b** $^{60}_{27}Co$ **c** $^{235}_{92}U$

2 A substance contains the radioactive isotope $^{238}_{92}U$, which emits alpha radiation. The product nucleus X emits beta radiation and forms a nucleus Y. How many protons and how many neutrons are present in:
  a a nucleus of $^{238}_{92}U$ **b** a nucleus of X   **c** a nucleus of Y?

3 Copy and complete the following equations for α and β decay.
  a $^{235}_{92}U \rightarrow {}^{?}_{?}Th + {}^4_2\alpha$ **b** $^{64}_{29}Cu \rightarrow {}^{?}_{?}Zn + {}^0_{-1}\beta$ [H]

182 · 183

Further teaching suggestions

Nuclear reactions

- Give the students some additional questions on the constituents of different isotopes, and ask them to determine what new isotopes are formed following certain decays. You might like to stretch some students by giving them some decay sequences. The students will need a periodic table.

Summary answers

1 **a** $6p + 6n$
  b $27p + 33n$
  c $92p + 143n$

2 **a** $92p + 146n$
  b $90p + 144n$
  c $91p + 143n$

3 **a** $^{235}_{92}U \rightarrow {}^{231}_{90}Th + {}^4_2\alpha$
  b $^{64}_{29}Cu \rightarrow {}^{64}_{30}Zn + {}^0_{-1}\beta$

More about alpha, beta and gamma radiation

Learning objectives

Students should learn that:

- that the different radiations have different penetrating powers
- the range in air is different for each type of radiation and that they are affected differently by electric and magnetic fields
- that nuclear radiation is ionising and this damages living cells causing cancer or cell death.

Learning outcomes

Most students should be able to:

- describe the penetrating powers of the three radiations
- describe the range in air of each type of radiation, their relative ionising power and how they are affected in a magnetic or electric field
- evaluate which radiation is the most hazardous inside and outside of the human body
- describe ways of reducing the hazards presented when handling radioactive substances.

Some students should also be able to:

- explain in detail why radiation is dangerous in terms of damage to cells.

Answers to in-text questions

a To stop the radiation, so it can't affect objects or people nearby.
b It is not deflected by a magnetic or an electric field.
c To keep the source out of range.

Support

- Ask students to complete just one gap in a nuclear equation with all other data provided.

Extend

- Where do the beta particles come from? The beta particles are high-energy electrons that come from the nucleus, but there are no electrons in the nucleus! The students need to find an explanation of what is happening in the nucleus that is producing these electrons. This might have been asked about in a prior lesson. Students could also research particle accelerators such as the Large Hadron Collider.

AQA Specification link-up: Physics P2.5

- Identification of an alpha particle as 2 neutrons and 2 protons, the same as a helium nucleus, a beta particle as an electron from the nucleus and gamma radiation as electromagnetic radiation. *[P2.5.2 c)]*
- Properties of the alpha, beta and gamma radiations limited to their relative ionising power, their penetration through materials and their range in air. *[P2.5.2 e)]*
- Alpha and beta radiations are deflected by both electric and magnetic fields but gamma radiation is not. *[P2.5.2 f)]*
- The uses of and the dangers associated with each type of nuclear radiation. *[P2.5.2 g)]*
  Controlled Assessment: P4.2 Assess and manage risks when carrying out practical work. *[P4.2.1 a) b)]*

Lesson structure

Starters

It's all Greek to me – Scientists use a lot of symbols in their work. Discuss the reasons that scientists use symbols for elements, equations, the names of things, etc. Reasons include internationalisation, simplicity, clarity, brevity. To demonstrate this, ask the students to write out '$7 - 3 = 4$' in words and then show a longer equation. You might ask the students to list all of the symbols that they know the meaning of; they know more than they think. *(5 minutes)*

Magnetism – The students should be familiar with magnetic fields. Ask them to show their knowledge in a diagram/mind map/spider diagram. They should include the shape of simple fields and the effect that magnetism has on certain materials. You can support students by providing a set of 'facts' cards and asking them to sort them into true of false (or an interactive quiz). To extend students you should require appropriate force diagrams and information about the strength of the field reducing with distance. *(10 minutes)*

Main

- A simulated experiment allows students to test what different types of radiation can penetrate. You may also demonstrate the penetrating powers of radiations with the method set out in 'Practical support'.
- The difference between alpha and beta particles and the electromagnetic wave nature of gamma should be emphasised. Gamma radiation causes no change in the structure of the nucleus; it is really the nucleus releasing some excess energy it didn't lose in a previous decay. The lack of charge on the gamma rays accounts for their higher penetrating power; they interact with matter a lot less than alpha or beta.
- A strong magnet can be used to deflect alpha and beta particles away from the detector but you will find it hard to show which way they have deflected so settle for the count rate being reduced and let the students imagine the particles being deflected by the magnetic field and not reaching the detector. You can't really show the acceleration caused by an electric field but you could extend some students by making links to particle accelerators.
- The students may not have encountered the idea of ionisation before. It is important that they grasp the concept of the radioactive particle stripping away electrons from atoms and causing unwanted chemical reaction in cells. The main danger is that the cell will be damaged and reproduce out of control. Explain that this becomes more likely the larger the dose of radiation, but that it is possible for a single damaged cell to cause cancer, so there is no minimum safe limit to radiation. We should therefore try to limit our exposure by keeping sources safely away from our bodies.
- Spark detectors are simple and it is well worth showing the effect if you have one. Discuss the safety precautions while using it, focusing on the harmful ionisation that would happen to your cells if you were too close. The alpha source should produce a lot more sparks so you can say it is highly ionising.
- Both of the following plenaries are useful for assessing risk in 'How Science Works'.

Plenaries

Local rules – The students should make a plan for a poster or booklet explaining how your radioactive sources should be stored and handled. Remind them of the precautions when you demonstrate the radiation but it is up to the students to explain why these precautions are needed. They should link all of the measures to harm reduction. They can then produce this booklet as homework. *(5 minutes)*

Protect and survive – What if one of the radioactive sources was dropped and lost? How would it be found and what precautions would need to be taken during the search? You should be able to find what really should be done in CLEAPSS resources. Show some footage of radiological protection officers suited up and wandering around with Geiger counters; this would be over the top for a dropped source. Differentiate the sources of information you provide to the students: to extend them you can provide the full guidance and ask them to explain why each measure is needed; to support students you should provide only the key recommendations and discuss why these are required. *(10 minutes)*

Practical support

Penetrating power

The techniques used on the previous spread can be expanded to show the penetrating power of the three radiations. (Teacher demonstration only.)

Equipment and materials required

Geiger–Müller tube, ratemeter (and possibly high voltage power supply), large plastic tray, tongs, radioactive sources, set of absorbers (paper, card, plastic, aluminium of various thicknesses and lead plates).

Details

Set the equipment up in the tray, as before, but add a mount to position a source in place. Between the source holder and detector, position a holder to hold the absorbers. Make sure that the detector is less than 10 cm from the source holder or the alpha particles will not reach. Turn on the detector and then mount an alpha emitter in the holder and note the count rate. This function can be performed by most meters, but you may have to count for 20 seconds if not. Position a paper absorber between the source and detector and note the count rate. Test the beta source with paper, plastic and then aluminium plates. Test the gamma with aluminium and then various thicknesses of lead.

Radioactivity

P2 6.4
More about alpha, beta and gamma radiation

Learning objectives

- How far can each type of radiation travel in air and what stops it?
- What is alpha, beta and gamma radiation?
- How can we separate a beam of alpha, beta and gamma radiation?
- Why is alpha, beta and gamma radiation dangerous?

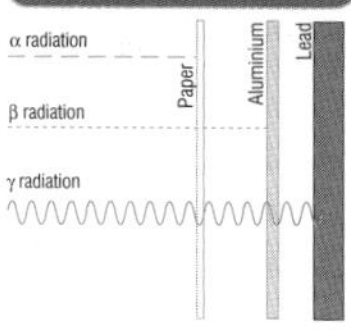

Figure 2 The penetrating powers of α, β and γ radiation

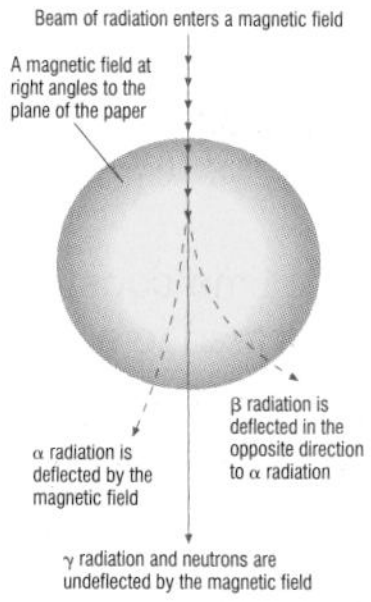

Figure 3 Radiation in a magnetic field

Penetrating power

Alpha radiation can't penetrate paper. But what stops beta and gamma radiation? And how far can each type of radiation travel through air? We can use a Geiger counter to find out, but we must take account of background radiation. To do this we should:

1 Measure the count rate (which is the number of counts per second) without the radioactive source present. This is the background count rate, the count rate due to background radiation.

2 Measure the count rate with the source in place. Subtracting the background count rate from this gives the count rate due to the source alone.

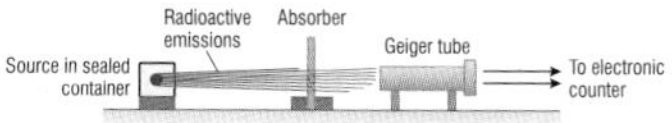

Figure 1 Absorption tests

We can then test absorber materials and the range in air.

- To test different materials, we need to place each material between the tube and the radioactive source. Then we measure the count rate. We can add more layers of material until the count rate due to the source is zero. The radiation from the source has then been stopped by the absorber material.
- To test the range in air, we need to move the tube away from the source. When the tube is beyond the range of the radiation, the count rate due to the source is zero.

The table below shows the results of the two tests.

Type of radiation	Absorber materials	Range in air
alpha (α)	Thin sheet of paper	about 5 cm
beta (β)	Aluminium sheet (about 5 mm thick) Lead sheet (2–3 mm thick)	about 1 m
gamma (γ)	Thick lead sheet (several cm thick) Concrete (more than 1 m thick)	unlimited

Gamma radiation spreads out in air without being absorbed. It does get weaker as it spreads out.

a Why is a radioactive source stored in a lead-lined box?

The nature of alpha, beta and gamma radiation

We can separate these radiations using a magnetic field or an electric field.

Deflection by a magnetic field

- β radiation is easily deflected, in the same way as electrons. So the radiation consists of negatively charged particles. In fact, a β particle is a fast-moving electron. It is emitted by an unstable nucleus that contains too many neutrons.

- α radiation is deflected in the opposite direction to β radiation. So α radiation consists of positively charged particles. α particles are harder to deflect than β radiation. This is because an α particle has a much greater mass than a β particle has. An alpha particle is two protons and two neutrons stuck together, the same as a helium nucleus.
- γ radiation is not deflected by a magnetic field or an electric field. This is because gamma radiation is electromagnetic radiation so is uncharged.

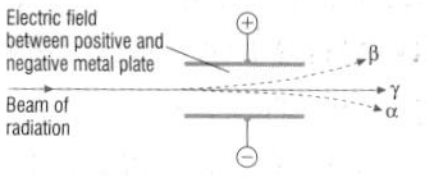

Figure 4 Radiation passing through an electric field

Deflection by an electric field

α and β particles passing through an electric field are deflected in opposite directions, as shown in Figure 4.

- The α particles are attracted towards the negative plate because they are positively charged.
- The β particles are attracted towards the positive plate because they are negatively charged.

In Figures 3 and 4, an alpha particle is deflected much less than the beta particle. The charge of an alpha particle is twice that of a beta particle, so the force is twice as great. But the mass of an alpha particle is about 8000 times that of a beta particle, so the deflection of the alpha particle is much less.

b How do we know that gamma radiation is not made up of charged particles?

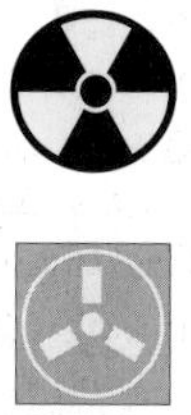

Radioactivity dangers

The radiation from a radioactive substance can knock electrons out of atoms. The atoms become charged because they lose electrons. The process is called **ionisation**. (Remember that a charged particle is called an ion.)

X-rays also cause ionisation. Ionisation in a living cell can damage or kill the cell. Damage to the genes in a cell can be passed on if the cell generates more cells. Strict safety rules must always be followed when radioactive substances are used.

Alpha radiation is more dangerous in the body than beta or gamma radiation. This is because it has a greater ionising effect than beta or gamma radiation.

c Why should long-handled tongs be used to move a radioactive source?

Figure 5 Radioactive warnings

Summary questions

1 Copy and complete **a** and **b** using the words below. Each word can be used more than once.

alpha beta gamma

a Electromagnetic radiation from a radioactive substance is called .... radiation.

b A thick metal plate will stop .... and .... radiation but not .... radiation.

2 Which type of radiation is:

a uncharged **b** positively charged **c** negatively charged?

3 **a** Explain why ionising radiation is dangerous.

b Explain how you would use a Geiger counter to find the range of the radiation from a source of α radiation.

Key points

- α radiation is stopped by paper, has a range of a few centimetres in air and consists of particles, each composed of two protons and two neutrons.
- β radiation is stopped by thin metal, has a range of about a metre in air and consists of fast-moving electrons emitted from the nucleus.
- γ radiation is stopped by thick lead, has an unlimited range in air and consists of electromagnetic radiation.
- A magnetic or an electric field can be used to separate a beam of alpha, beta and gamma radiation.
- Alpha, beta and gamma radiation ionise substances they pass through. Ionisation in a living cell can damage or kill the cell.

184

185

Further teaching suggestions

More detectors

- There are other ways of detecting and analysing ionising radiation, including cloud and bubble chambers and photographic films. The students could find out about these devices and why they are used. Which of the devices reveals most about the radiation and in what circumstances are they used?

Summary answers

1 **a** gamma

b alpha, beta, (alpha and beta in either order) gamma

2 **a** gamma **b** alpha **c** beta

3 **a** Radiation can knock electrons from atoms. This ionisation damages the genes in a cell which can be passed on if the cell generates more cells.

b Using long-handled tongs to hold the source above the spark counter, move the source gradually downwards towards the spark counter. When the spark counter begins to spark, fix the position of the source, switch off the power supply and measure the distance between source and the spark counter. This is the range of the α-radiation.

P2 6.5

Half-life

Learning objectives

Students should learn:

- that the activity of a radioactive source decreases with time because the number of parent atoms is decreasing
- that the half-life of a source is a measure of the average time it takes for the activity of a source to reach half of its initial value.

Learning outcomes

Most students should be able to:

- define the term half-life in relation to the activity of a radioactive source
- determine the half-life of a source from a graph or table of data.

Specification link-up: Physics P2.5

- The half-life of a radioactive isotope is the average time it takes for the number of nuclei of the isotope in a sample to halve, or the time it takes for the count rate from a sample containing the isotope to fall to half its initial level. *[P2.5.2 h)]*

Controlled Assessment: P4.5 Analyse and interpret primary and secondary data. *[P4.5.2 a) b)], [P4.5.3 a)], [P4.5.4 a)]*

Lesson structure

Starters

An exponential decay puzzle – A farmer has a warehouse with two million corn cobs in it. Every day he sells exactly half of his remaining stock. How long before he has sold every last **nugget** (not cob) of corn? The students should realise that this takes quite a while with the amount remaining just halving each day (1 000 000, 500 000, 250 000, 125 000 and so on) and then the nuggets on the last cob takes a few more weeks to get rid of. You can use a calculator and just keep dividing by two to see how many steps this would take. *(5 minutes)*

An exponential growth puzzle – A philosopher places a grain of rice on the first square of a chess board, two on the next, four on the next and so on. How many go on the last (sixty-fourth) square? The pattern goes 1, 2, 4, 8, 16, 32, 64, 128 for the first row.

[By the end, there would be 9 223 372 036 854 775 808 (2^{63}) on the last square]. Extend students by showing a graph of a function like this and ask the students to describe the key features; they should identify the 'accelerating' rate clearly. To support students you might want to limit the calculation to the first two rows and then show the graph to see what happens next. *(10 minutes)*

Answers to in-text questions

a 75 cpm

b 6.5 hours

Main

- Isotopes can be hard to discuss in isolation. It is easier to use the term isotopes (plural) and make a comparison, for example 'carbon has three isotopes C-12, C-13 and C-14, which are all carbon because they have six protons (and electrons), but they have different numbers of neutrons'. It's much harder to get the idea across if you talk about 'an isotope'.

- The students should be familiar with the structure of the atoms and should quickly recall that the number of neutrons in the atoms of a particular element may vary. Try to get across the idea of activity early. The more active an isotope the more rapid the decay. 'Parent' and 'daughter' are important terms also. You could show a nuclear decay equation to get these terms across.

- The rolling dice decay model is an enjoyable experiment, but it can be time-consuming. To improve the average values, the groups can share data and this will lead to a more accurate half-life. At the start and end of the experiment, make sure that the students understand that the dice represented nuclei and removing them represented decay. They should have a reasonable understanding that the pattern is the same each time, even though we do not know exactly which of the dice decays each time. If you feel like being a bit 'all knowing', seal the answer [4.16 rolls] in an envelope in advance and stick it to the board in plain sight. Then 'reveal' it at the end, which allows you to discuss the fact that we can accurately model random behaviour using mathematics.

- The experiment lends itself well to the ideas of repeating to improve reliability, but can also be used to explain that statistics work best on very large samples, so the more dice the better the fit. (This relates to ideas of reliability of data in 'How Science Works'.) There is also opportunity to develop or assess graph-plotting skills along with drawing lines of best fit. (This relates to the skills of presenting data in 'How Science Works'.)

- You can discuss what happens to the 'count rate' after each roll. The number of dice eliminated in each round represents this and this rate should decrease as the number of surviving dice falls. This gives the students a decent understanding of why the count rate falls as time goes on.

Support

- Students should be provided with a results table with one set of results already filled in to help explain the idea. Make sure students are removing 'dead' dice and only rolling the 'survivors' after each round.

Extend

- Collect the whole class data together to find a total for each round. This will give a smoother graph. You can then use a spreadsheet to plot the graphs and also find the number of dice decaying after each roll. This will reveal the decrease in the count rate over time.

Plenaries

Activity and decay – Show the students a graph with three decay curves on them. Can they identify which has the longest half-life and which is the most active source? [They should identify the relationship that the longer the half-life, the less active the material is for the same initial quantity]. *(5 minutes)*

Coin toss – If I have 120 coins and toss them all, removing all of the heads after each toss, how many tosses until I should only have 15 left? [This would be three half-lives so three tosses]. You could show this for real with a tray of pennies and compare the real result with the theoretical one. To extend the students, they should be asked to discuss why the real results can diverge from theoretical models. How could the simulation become more like the mathematical model? They should realise that the smaller the number of particles (coins) in the simulations, the more likely divergence is. You can give additional support by allowing the students to try smaller numbers of coins and make predictions about the decay patterns. *(10 minutes)*

Practical support

Radioactive dice

This is a simple model of the randomness of radioactive decay and how to find the half-life.

Equipment and materials required

For each group: a set of 59 identical six-sided cubes and one cube of a different colour. The dice should have a dot on one face only. (You can use more or less dice depending on how many you have, but 60 works well.)

Details

The students roll the full set of dice, and after each roll, they remove the dice that landed showing a spot. They record the number of dice 'surviving' and then roll only these dice, and so on. They continue this process of elimination for 20 rolls, or until no dice survives.

During this, they should also note down when the special dice lands spot up causing it to be removed. If time permits, they repeat this process and calculate an average number of dice remaining after each roll. Plotting a graph of the number of dice remaining (y-axis) against roll number (x-axis) reveals that the dice behave like decaying atoms and a half-life can be calculated; this should be 4.16 rolls. The single dice should show that the process is random; it is impossible to predict when any individual dice will be eliminated. For some groups, it will be removed after the first roll and for others it will survive until the end.

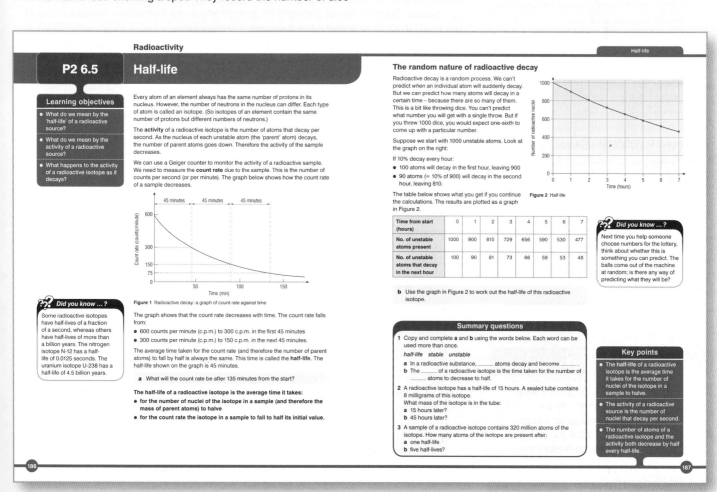

Further teaching suggestions

Roll the dice
- Starting with the basic six-sided dice experiment, the students could investigate what would happen if a different set of dice were used. Dice with 4, 8, 10, 12 and 20 sides are available from gaming shops, and will produce similar exponential decay curves but with different half-lives.

Summary answers

1 a unstable, stable   b half-life, unstable

2 a 4 milligrams   b 1 milligram

3 a 160 million atoms   b 10 million atoms

P2 6.6

Radioactivity at work

Learning objectives

Students should learn:

- that radioactive sources have a number of uses including thickness measurement, medical tracing and determining the age of materials
- how to select an appropriate radioactive source for a particular use given data.

Learning outcomes

Most students should be able to:

- describe how a beta source can be used to measure the thickness of a material like aluminium foil
- describe how radioactive traces are used in medical analysis
- describe how radioactive isotopes can be used to determine the age of a rock or organic material.

Some students should also be able to:

- evaluate the properties of a radioactive isotope to determine why it would make a good medical tracer
- find the age of an organic sample from data presented to them.

Answers to in-text questions

a The detector reading increases and the pressure from the rollers is decreased.

b Alpha (α) radiation would be stopped by the foil.

c B because radioactive iodine did not leave the kidney.

d It was formed recently (in geological terms).

Support

- Provide a partially completed flow chart for the operation of the foil press. You can also use a diagram for the students to label up the action of a tracer (or have them draw a cartoon illustrating the process).

Extend

- Very large numbers of radioactive particles are produced in nuclear reactors. How are these particles contained, and are there any that escape into the environment? The students may find out about neutrons and neutrinos.

AQA

Specification link-up: Physics P2.5

- The uses of and the dangers associated with each type of nuclear radiation. [P2.5.2 g)]
- Evaluate the appropriateness of radioactive sources for particular uses, including as tracers, in terms of the type(s) of radiation emitted and their half-lives. [P2.5]

Lesson structure

Starters

All around the body – Show a video clip of a radioactive tracer being injected into a patient (including all of the safety precautions if possible) and the resulting tracer footage. Discuss how the students think that the images have been made until they come up with the idea that the radiation passes out of the body and is detected. You can contrast this idea with X-rays later. *(5 minutes)*

Just how thick? – Ask the students to measure the thickness of a sheet of paper. Can they find out if all of the sheets are the same thickness? How? Give them some basic equipment to try this out (rulers, callipers, perhaps a micrometer) and then discuss how they think that manufacturers can get the right thickness each time. Extend students by asking them to consider the errors in these types of measurements and how these can be reduced. Support can be provided by giving some exact instructions to see if students can reach a consensus about the thickness. *(10 minutes)*

Main

- Using radioactivity to determine the thickness of a material is a fairly straightforward idea; you can link it to the idea of light being absorbed by paper. How many sheets of white paper will stop all light passing through it? The function of the foil press can best be shown as a flow chart with terms like: 'Is too much radiation getting through?' and 'Open up rollers a bit.' Demonstrate that the thicker a material is, the less beta radiation passes through. This could be a quick demonstration as described in 'Practical support', or you could look into it in more depth.

- When discussing radioactive tracers, you should be able to find a video clip of a tracer being used in the body to find a blood vessel blockage. (For example, search a video or image bank for 'radioactive tracer'.) The students should be made aware that the tracer must be picked for the job based on a range of factors, including the type of radiation it emits (gamma), the half-life, and its biochemical properties, i.e. will it build up in the organ we want it to? There are isotopes suitable for a wide range of medical studies, some of which are artificially generated in nuclear reactors. You may want to talk about tracers being used to find gas leaks and monitor the path of underground rivers. These too are carefully chosen so that they decay away quite quickly.

- Carbon dating is only useful over a certain range of times and the materials must be organic. The limit is about 50 000 years, which is good enough for all recorded human history. The technique also needs to be calibrated against objects of known ages; ancient trees are handy for this. Ask the students how we know the age of these trees. Some Egyptian artefacts are also used as we are fairly certain of their actual age due to good record-keeping.

- Uranium dating is generally used to date rocks and is part of the evidence for the Earth being 4.5 billion years old. There are some assumptions that are made with dating processes and you may wish to discuss these with the students. Do the levels of carbon-14 remain constant in the atmosphere? Is there any other way of lead being produced in rocks?

Plenaries

Careful! You can have your eye out with that! – An archaeologist claims to have found the arrow that killed King Harold in 1066. Can the students explain how a scientist would try to check this claim? This should link into carbon dating of the material revealing it is about 1000 years old. *(5 minutes)*

Radioactivity's great – Radioactivity usually gets a fairly bad press; the students should produce a simple poster expounding the virtues of radioactive material. This can cover all of the useful things that radiation can be used for. To provide support, you can provide some extra information on medical treatment to complement the diagnosis, and on nuclear power and its advantages then the students can prioritise and assemble it. To extend the students, you should ask them to target the poster at a specific group of people and give suitable explanations of key phrases. *(10 minutes)*

Practical support

Demonstrating absorption

See local rules for handling radioactive sources.

It is possible to show how radioactivity can be used to measure the thickness of materials. (Teacher demonstration only.)

Equipment and materials required

G–M tube and rate meter, set of aluminium absorbers, beta source, tongs.

Details

Mount the G–M tube and absorber holder in line with the source holder. Position the source carefully and record the count rate (or take a count over 30 seconds). Test the aluminium absorbers one at a time, noting the decreasing count rate as the thickness of the aluminium increases.

You may wish to get the students to plot a graph of count rate against absorber thickness to determine how much aluminium is required to reduce the count to half of the original value. This half-value thickness is an important concept for absorption of gamma rays at A-level.

Radioactivity

P2 6.6   Radioactivity at work

Learning objectives

- How do we choose a radioactive isotope for a particular job?
- How can we use radioactivity for monitoring?
- What are radioactive tracers?
- What is radioactive dating?

Radioactivity has many uses. For each use, we need a radioactive isotope that emits a certain type of radiation and has a suitable half-life.

Automatic thickness monitoring

This is used when making metal foil.

Look at Figure 1. The radioactive source emits β radiation. The amount of radiation passing through the foil depends on the thickness of the foil. A detector on the other side of the metal foil measures the amount of radiation passing through it.

- If the thickness of the foil increases too much, the detector reading drops.
- The detector sends a signal to the rollers to increase the pressure on the metal sheet.

This makes the foil thinner again.

a What happens if the thickness of the foil decreases too much?

b Why is alpha radiation not used here?

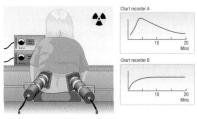

Figure 1 Thickness monitoring using a radioactive source

Radioactive tracers *k*

These are used to trace the flow of a substance through a system. For example, doctors use radioactive iodine to find out if a patient's kidney is blocked.

Figure 2 Using a tracer to monitor a patient's kidneys

Chart recorder A

Chart recorder B

Before the test, the patient drinks water containing a tiny amount of the radioactive substance. A detector is then placed against each kidney. Each detector is connected to a chart recorder.

- The radioactive substance flows in and out of a normal kidney. So the detector reading goes up then down.
- For a blocked kidney, the reading goes up and stays up. This is because the radioactive substance goes into the kidney but doesn't flow out again.

Radioactive iodine is used for this test because:

- Its half-life is 8 days, so it lasts long enough for the test to be done but decays almost completely after a few weeks.
- It emits gamma radiation, so it can be detected outside the body.
- It decays into a stable product.

c In Figure 2, which kidney is blocked, A or B?

Radioactive dating

This is used to find the age of ancient material. We can use:

- **Carbon dating** – this is used to find the age of ancient wood and other organic material. Living wood contains a tiny proportion of radioactive carbon. This has a half-life of 5600 years. When a tree dies, it no longer absorbs any carbon. So the amount of radioactive carbon in it decreases. To find the age of a sample, we need to measure the count rate from the wood. This is compared with the count rate from the same mass of living wood. For example, suppose the count rate in a sample of wood is half the count rate of an equal mass of living wood. Then the sample must be 5600 years old.

- **Uranium dating** – this is used to find the age of igneous rocks. These rocks contain radioactive uranium, which has a half-life of 4500 million years. Each uranium atom decays into an atom of lead. We can work out the age of a sample by measuring the number of atoms of uranium and lead. For example, if a sample contains 1 atom of lead for every atom of the uranium, the age of the sample must be 4500 million years. This is because there must have **originally** been 2 atoms of uranium for each atom of uranium now present.

d What could you say about an igneous rock with uranium but no lead in it?

?? Did you know …?

Smoke alarms save lives. A radioactive source inside the alarm sends out alpha particles into a gap in a circuit in the alarm. The alpha particles ionise the air in the gap so it conducts a current across the gap. In a fire, smoke absorbs the alpha particles so they don't cross the gap. The current across the gap drops and the alarm sounds. The battery in a smoke alarm needs to be checked regularly – to make sure it is still working!

Figure 3 A smoke alarm

Summary questions

1 Copy and complete **a** to **c** using the words below. Each word can be used more than once.

alpha beta gamma

a In the continuous production of thin metal sheets, a source of .... radiation should be used to monitor the thickness of the sheets.

b A radioactive tracer given to a hospital patient needs to emit .... or .... radiation.

c The radioactive source used to trace a leak in an underground pipeline should be a source of .... radiation.

2 **a** Explain why γ radiation is not suitable for monitoring the thickness of metal foil.

b When a radioactive tracer is used, why is it best to use a radioactive isotope that decays into a stable isotope?

3 **a** What are the ideal properties of a radioactive isotope used as a medical tracer?

b A sample of old wood was carbon dated and found to have 25% of the count rate measured in an equal mass of living wood. The half-life of the radioactive carbon is 5600 years. How old is the sample of wood?

Key points

- The use we can make of a radioactive isotope depends on:
  a its half-life
  b the type of radiation it gives out.
- For monitoring, the isotope should have a long half-life.
- Radioactive tracers should be β or γ emitters that last long enough to monitor but not too long.
- For radioactive dating of a sample, we need a radioactive isotope that is present in the sample which has a half-life about the same as the age of the sample.

Further teaching suggestions

ICT link-up

- A simulation of the absorption of beta particles by various materials is available. The students can find out for themselves how the particles are absorbed by different materials by searching for 'radioactivity absorption simulation' on the internet.

You're history

- Ask the students to come up with some more historical artefacts that could be radiocarbon dated. Make sure they understand that only materials with carbon can be tested by this method.

Summary answers

1 **a** beta.

  b beta, gamma (beta and gamma in either order)

  c beta

2 **a** γ-radiation would hardly be absorbed by the foil as it would all pass straight through the foil.

  b A stable isotope in the body (or elsewhere) would not be dangerous whereas an unstable isotope would be harmful as it is radioactive.

3 **a** It needs to be detectable outside the body, (non-toxic), have a short half-life (1–24 hours) and decay into a stable product.

  b 11 200 years old.

Summary answers

1 a i $6p + 8n$
   ii $90p + 138n$

  b i $7p + 7n$
   ii $^{14}_{7}N$

  c i $88p + 136n$
   ii $^{224}_{88}Ra$

2 a gamma

  b alpha

  c beta

  d beta

  e alpha

  f gamma

3 1B, 2D, 3A, 4C

4 a Graph

  b 1 h 40 min

5 a 2

  b 11 200 years

6 a Background radioactivity.

  b 356 cpm

  c Beta radiation, because it penetrates thin foil and is stopped by an aluminium plate. Alpha radiation would be stopped by the foil. Gamma radiation would pass through the foil and the plate.

7 a They are positively charged so they are repelled by the nucleus because it is also positively charged.

  b It doesn't approach the nucleus as closely as A does, so the force on it is less.

  c The nucleus is very small in size compared to the atom, so most α particles don't pass near enough to the nucleus to be affected by it.

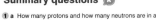

Summary questions

1 a How many protons and how many neutrons are in a nucleus of each of the following isotopes?
  i $^{14}_{6}C$
  ii $^{228}_{90}Th$

  b $^{14}_{6}C$ emits a β particle and becomes an isotope of nitrogen (N).
   i How many protons and how many neutrons are in this nitrogen isotope?
   ii Write down the symbol for this isotope.

  c $^{228}_{90}Th$ emits an α particle and becomes an isotope of radium (Ra).
   i How many protons and how many neutrons are in this isotope of radium?
   ii Write down the symbol for this isotope.

2 Which type of radiation, alpha, beta or gamma:

  a can pass through lead?

  b travels no further than about 10 cm in air?

  c is stopped by an aluminium metal plate but not by paper?

  d consists of electrons?

  e consists of helium nuclei?

  f is uncharged?

3 The table below gives information about four radioactive isotopes A, B, C and D.

Isotope	Type of radiation emitted	Half-life
A californium-241	alpha	4 minutes
B cobalt-60	gamma	5 years
C hydrogen-3	beta	12 years
D strontium-90	beta	28 years

Match each statement 1 to 4 with A, B, C or D.
  1 the isotope that gives off radiation with an unlimited range
  2 the isotope that has the longest half-life
  3 the isotope that decays the fastest
  4 the isotope with the smallest mass of each atom.

4 The following measurements were made of the count rate due to a radioactive source.

Time (hours)	0	0.5	1.0	1.5	2.0	2.5
Count rate due to the source (counts per minute)	510	414	337	276	227	188

  a Plot a graph of the count rate (on the vertical axis) against time.

  b Use your graph to find the half-life of the source.

5 In a carbon dating experiment of ancient wood, a sample of the wood gave a count rate of 0.4 counts per minute. The same mass of living wood gave a count rate of 1.6 counts per minute.

  a How many half-lives did the count rate take to decrease from 1.6 to 0.4 counts per minute?

  b The half-life of the radioactive carbon in the wood is 5600 years. What is the age of the sample?

6 In an investigation to find out what type of radiation was emitted from a given source, the following measurements were made with a Geiger counter.

Source	Average count rate (in counts per minute)
No source present	29
Source at 20 mm from tube with no absorber between	385
Source at 20 mm from tube with a sheet of metal foil between	384
Source at 20 mm from tube with a 10 mm thick aluminium plate between	32

  a What caused the count rate when no source was present?

  b What was the count rate due to the source with no absorbers present?

  c What type of radiation was emitted by the source? Explain how you arrive at your answer.

7 Figure 1 shows the path of two α particles labelled A and B that are deflected by the nucleus of an atom.

  a Why are they deflected by the nucleus?

  b Why is B deflected less than A?

  c Why do most α particles directed at a thin metal foil pass straight through it?

Figure 1

Kerboodle resources

Resources available for this chapter on Kerboodle are:

- Chapter map: Radioactivity
- Support: Nuclear decay equations – understanding the nature of nuclear decays (P2 6.3)
- Bump up your grade: Elements, isotopes and ions – what's the difference? (6.3)
- Extension: Radiation hunt (P2 6.4)
- How Science Works: Radiation in action (P2 6.6)
- WebQuest: Radioactive tracers (P2 6.6)
- Interactive activity: Half-life and the uses of radioactivity
- Revision podcast: Radioactivity
- Test yourself: Radioactivity
- On your marks: Radioactivity
- Examination-style questions: Radioactivity
- Answers to examination-style questions: Radioactivity

AQA Examiner's tip

Foundation Tier candidates must know that alpha and beta are deflected in opposite directions both in magnetic fields and in electric fields. Only the Higher Tier students need to be able to explain why this is so in terms of the charge and the mass of the particles.

AQA Examination-style questions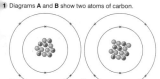

1 Diagrams **A** and **B** show two atoms of carbon.

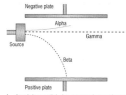

A   **B**

a Copy and complete the following sentences using the list of words and phrases below. Each one can be used once, more than once or not at all.

electrons positive isotopes nuclear plum pudding negative nucleus ions neutrons

Particles shown by the symbol **x** in the diagram are called .... They orbit the .... of an atom. This is made up of protons and .... Protons have a .... charge. This diagram shows the .... model of the atom which replaced the .... model. (6)

b Explain how a carbon **ion** would be different from atom **A**. (1)

c Give the mass number of atom **A**. (1)

d Give the atomic number of atom **A**. (1)

e Compare atom **B** with atom **A**. (3)

2 a A geologist wishes to know what types of radiation are emitted by three radioactive rock samples. Different absorbers are placed between each sample and a detector. The counts per second are shown in the table.

	Counts per second		
Absorber	Sample 1	Sample 2	Sample 3
1 cm of air	140	80	120
paper	90	50	70
3 mm of aluminium	30	49	0
1 cm of lead	0	1	0

For each sample state which of the three types of radiation (alpha, beta, gamma) are emitted. A rock may emit more than one type. (3)

b Describe the nature of an alpha particle. (2)

c List the three types of nuclear radiation in order of their relative ionising power from the least ionising to the most ionising. (3)

d The source of radiation shown below emits alpha, beta and gamma. When the radiation travels through air in an electric field between two plates, the three types of radiation behave differently.

Negative plate

Alpha

Gamma

Source

Beta

Positive plate

i An alpha particle has more charge than a beta particle. Explain why the beta particle is deflected more by the electric field and in the opposite direction. [H] (4)

ii Explain why the gamma radiation is not affected by the electric field. (1)

iii Explain why the alpha particle does not reach the plate. (1)

3 Technetium-99 is a gamma-emitting radioisotope used as a tracer inside the body in order to diagnose problems with various organs. Cobalt-60 is a gamma emitter used for radiotherapy where the source is used outside the body to kill cancer cells on the inside.

	Half-life	Radiation	Relative ionising power
technetium-99	6.0 hours	gamma	1
cobalt-60	5.3 years	gamma	10

a Technetium-99 emits a gamma ray and then decays to an isotope of ruthenium (Ru) by beta decay. Balance the nuclear equation by giving the appropriate atomic numbers and mass numbers.

$$^{99}_{43}\text{Tc} \rightarrow ^{(i)}_{(ii)}\text{Ru} + ^{(iii)}_{(iv)}\beta$$ [H] (4)

b *In this question you will be assessed on using good English, organising information clearly and using specialist terms where appropriate.*

Explain why cobalt-60 is not used as a medical tracer in humans and why technetium-99 is used for this purpose. (6)

AQA Examination-style answers

1 a Particles shown by the symbol **x** in the diagram are called **electrons**. They orbit the **nucleus** of an atom. This is made up of protons and **neutrons**. Protons have a **positive** charge. This diagram shows the **nuclear** model of the atom which replaced the **plum pudding** model. *(6 marks)*

b more (or less) electrons *(1 mark)*

c 12 *(1 mark)*

d 6 *(1 mark)*

e same number of protons (it is also carbon); same number of electrons;
2 more neutrons (carbon-14, a different isotope of carbon) *(3 marks)*

2 a Sample 1: alpha, beta and gamma
Sample 2: alpha and gamma
Sample 3: alpha and beta *(3 marks)*

b Two protons and two neutrons; helium nucleus *(2 marks)*

c Gamma, beta, alpha *(3 marks)*

d i Alpha particle has positive charge, beta particle has negative charge. Positive plate further away so beta more deflected. *(4 marks)*

ii Gamma particles have no charge *(1 mark)*

iii Absorbed by air particles *(1 mark)*

3 a i 99 *(1 mark)*

ii 44 *(1 mark)*

iii 0 *(1 mark)*

iv −1 *(1 mark)*

b There is a clear, balanced and detailed description of the reasons why cobalt-60 is not used as a medical tracer in humans and why technetium-99 is used. The answer shows almost faultless spelling, punctuation and grammar. It is coherent and in an organised, logical sequence. It contains a range of appropriate or relevant specialist terms used accurately. *(5–6 marks)*

There is a description of a range of the main reasons why cobalt-60 is not used as a medical tracer in humans and why technetium-99 is. There are some errors in spelling, punctuation and grammar. The answer has some structure and organisation. The use of specialist terms has been attempted, but not always accurately. *(3–4 marks)*

There is a brief description of at least one reason why cobalt-60 is not used as a medical tracer in humans or why technetium-99 is, which has little clarity and detail. The spelling, punctuation and grammar are very weak. The answer is poorly organised with almost no specialist terms and/or their use demonstrating a general lack of understanding of their meaning. *(1–2 marks)*

No relevant content. *(0 marks)*

Examples of physics points made in the response:
- half-life (of cobalt) is longer than necessary
- and could cause harm long after diagnosis
- ionising power of cobalt is much higher
- and could damage cells unnecessarily.
- half-life of technetium-99 is short enough to limit harm/risk
- but long enough to allow detection (before the count rate falls significantly)
- the low ionising power reduces harm/risk to a minimum.

AQA Practical suggestions

Practicals	AQA	k	📖	⚙
Using hot-cross buns to show the 'plum pudding' model.	✓		✓	
Using dice to demonstrate probabilities involved in half-life.	✓		✓	
Using Geiger counters to measure the penetration and range in air of the radiation from different sources.	✓		✓	

AQA Examiner's tip

Question 1 is a good test of the students' understanding of atomic structure and the meanings of 'ion' and 'isotope'.

P2 7.1

Nuclear fission

Learning objectives

Students should learn:

- that uranium and plutonium isotopes are used in nuclear fission reactors as fuel
- that nuclear fission is the splitting of large nuclei into small ones; a process that releases energy
- how a fission reactor operates.

Learning outcomes

Most students should be able to:

- state the isotopes used as fuel in nuclear fission reactors
- describe what happens in a fission event
- sketch a labelled diagram to show how a chain reaction may occur.

Some students should also be able to:

- explain in detail how a chain reaction in a nuclear reactor can take place.

Support

- Give the students a large diagram of the reactor, so that they can label the parts and write their notes around it.

Extend

- The students can find out about the choice of materials used for the moderator, control rods and coolant in different types of reactor. You can then discuss the properties of these materials that make them the best choice for the job.

AQA   Specification link-up: Physics P2.6

- There are two fissionable substances in common use in nuclear reactors: uranium-235 and plutonium-239. *[P2.6.1 a)]*
- Nuclear fission is the splitting of an atomic nucleus. *[P2.6.1 b)]*
- For fission to occur the uranium-235 or plutonium-239 nucleus must first absorb a neutron. *[P2.6.1 c)]*
- The nucleus undergoing fission splits into two smaller nuclei and two or three neutrons and energy is released. *[P2.6.1 d)]*
- The neutrons may go on to start a chain reaction. *[P2.6.1 e)]*
- Compare the uses of nuclear fusion and nuclear fission. *[P2.6]*

Lesson structure

Starters

Protection from radiation – Can the students describe the penetrating powers of the three radiations and explain how we can be protected from them? This leads on to a discussion about the shielding of the nuclear reactor later in the lesson. *(5 minutes)*

Power station basics – The students should draw a quick diagram showing how a fossil fuel power station operate. They need to remember the furnace, boiler, turbines and generator and perhaps the transformers including what each part does. Many of the components are the same as those in a nuclear power station. To support students, provide a diagram and ask them to describe the processes that take place at each stage. To further extend students, ask them to draw a Sankey energy transfer diagram indicating the approximate energy losses at each stage. *(10 minutes)*

Main

- You can show an example of a chain reaction with dominoes, see 'Practical support'.
- In a nuclear chain reaction, the released neutrons are important as these are the cause of further fissions, so emphasise them in any diagram or animation.
- In a nuclear reactor core, it is important to keep the reaction critical; that is at a steady rate (not getting faster or slower).The reactor can become 'super critical' if the nuclear reaction is accelerating (an increasing number of fissions per second), the reactor will heat up rapidly but not like a nuclear explosion. More likely the reaction becomes 'sub-critical' where the reaction rate decreases and the reactor will cool.
- You need to clearly distinguish between the parts of the nuclear reactor as students often get them backwards or their properties mixed up. Good **moderators** slow down the fast neutrons without absorbing them. If the moderator absorbs too many neutrons, then the chain reaction cannot continue. In some reactors, graphite is used instead of water. The **control rods** have to be good at absorbing neutrons. When they are inserted, the number of available neutrons is decreased and the reaction becomes sub-critical, cooling the core down. Cadmium and boron are common materials for this job. In an emergency, the rods are dropped completely into the core, rapidly reducing the reaction to almost zero. The reactor still produces some heat through natural (non-induced) decay of the radioactive materials. This means that it still has to be cooled or it will meltdown. The **coolant** may be water, heavy water or some more exotic material such as liquid sodium. It has to be able to rapidly carry energy from the core (so has a high specific heat capacity), but in carrying out its function, it becomes radioactive.
- The core itself is very heavily shielded by concrete, steel and some lead, so only a few gamma rays can escape. It is quite possible to walk on top of a nuclear reactor core safely.

Plenaries

The China syndrome – If a nuclear core melts down, it gets so hot that it can melt the rock beneath it and start sinking into the Earth. If an American reactor melts down, ask 'What's to stop it melting all the way through to China?' Hopefully, students will realise that if it reaches the centre of the Earth it would have gone as far 'down' as possible and it would be travelling upwards to reach China. *(5 minutes)*

Chain reaction – The students should be asked to develop an idea to show a chain reaction. To support students you could ask them to set up dominoes to demonstrate the idea if you didn't do this yourself; the teams with the most wins. It's possible to arrange sensible students into a suitable configuration too. To extend the students, you can ask them to calculate how many nuclei would be splitting after five stages if each split realises an average of 2.5 neutrons. *(10 minutes)*

Practical support

Domino theory

A chain reaction can be demonstrated using dominos. Set up a simple chain where one domino knocks over another; this represents a critical reaction where the rate stays constant. To show an increasing reaction, you simply set the dominoes up so that one knocks over two, two knock over three, and so on.

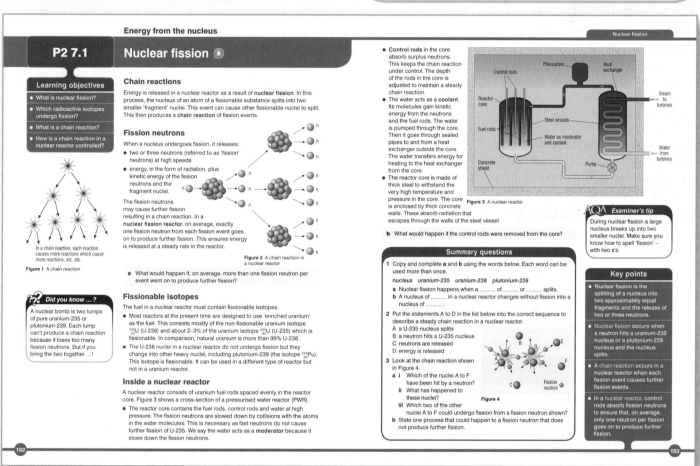

Further teaching suggestions

Chain reactions

- Animations and simulations showing chain reactions are available in commercial software. There are also some simple animations available freely on the internet. Search for 'chain reaction simulation'.

Shut down the reactor!

- The emergency shutting down of a reactor is called 'scramming'. Where does this term come from? There are a couple of possibilities.

Answers to in-text questions

a The chain reaction would go out of control and the reactor would overheat and possibly explode.

b The chain reaction would go out of control and the reactor would overheat and possibly explode.

Summary answers

1 a nucleus, uranium-235, plutonium-239

  b uranium-238, plutonium-239

2 1A, 2D, 3C, 4B, 5A

3 a i A and D

   ii They have undergone fission and released neutrons and energy.

   iii C and E

  b One process only: Each such neutron could escape from the reactor core or be absorbed by a uranium-238 nucleus without fission or be absorbed by a nucleus of the control rod.

P2 7.2

Nuclear fusion

Learning objectives

Students should learn:

- that the Sun releases energy due to nuclear fusion of hydrogen isotopes
- that nuclear fusion is the joining of two small nuclei and this process releases energy
- that nuclear fusion reactors are difficult to build mainly due to the difficulty of reaching sufficiently high temperatures and pressures.

Learning outcomes

Most students should be able to:

- describe the nuclear fusion process happening in the Sun
- outline how experimental nuclear fusion reactors work on Earth.

Some students should also be able to:

- evaluate the issues associated with nuclear fusion reactors.

Support

- It is best if the students can physically model the fusion process as described in the main part of the lesson. You can use different-coloured marbles as protons and neutrons; the student can build heavy hydrogen from two protons (one changes into a neutron), then follow through the remaining steps to give helium.

Extend

- Ask: 'What's so special about iron?' The students can find out more details about nuclear energy release by researching binding energy. It is this energy that is released by fusion and fission processes when the nucleons rearrange. If they go on to look at stars and supernovae, they will discover the importance of iron in these explosions. Alternatively, students could find out about the claims made by Pons and Fleischmann in the late 1980s regarding 'cold fusion'.

AQA

Specification link-up: Physics P2.6

- Nuclear fusion is the joining of two atomic nuclei to form a larger one. *[P2.6.2 a)]*
- Nuclear fusion is the process by which energy is released in stars. *[P2.6.2 b)]*
- Compare the uses of nuclear fusion and nuclear fission. *[P2.6]*

Lesson structure

Starters

A Sun myth – The Sun has a lot of mythology based on it and a lot of religions had a 'sun god'. What stories do the students know? Where do the students think the Sun's energy comes from? Can they remember some of the properties and behaviour of stars? *(5 minutes)*

Star one – Ask: 'Where does the Sun get its energy?' The students brainstorm their ideas and then discuss possible problems with them. They will probably know that the Sun contains flammable hydrogen but there is not enough oxygen to let it actually burn. To extend the students, you can discuss how even great scientists, such as Lord Kelvin, struggled to explain the energy source of the Sun until radioactivity and the structure of the atom was discovered. To support students, you should provide some possible suggestions and ask the students to come up with answers as to why these are not realistic proposals. *(10 minutes)*

Main

- Students may confuse the words 'fission' and 'fusion' in general conversation, but should be able to remember the difference when writing answers. Make them think of 'fusing together'.

- The reactions in the Sun are hugely powerful. Its power output is around 4×10^{26} watts. The students might like to imagine how many light bulbs' worth that represents. The tiny fraction of this that reaches Earth provides all of the energy for plants and food chains.

- If you like, you can model the reaction process in the Sun with marbles or with molecular-modelling kits; build the starting nuclei and then forcing the components together during the fusion.

- The overall process shown is four protons (hydrogen nuclei) converting into one helium nucleus, and so the Sun is generally said to be converting hydrogen into helium. This means that the percentages of hydrogen and helium are slowly changing. The reactions also produce a lot of positrons and neutrinos. The main difficulty to overcome is the fact that the protons strongly repel each other. In the Sun, the gravitational forces are strong enough to keep the very high temperature protons close enough together so that they will collide and fuse. It is this process that is proving very difficult to replicate on Earth.

- Some of the students will have heard the term 'plasma' before, and when you tell them that it is at a temperature of several thousand degrees, they will assume it has a lot of energy and will be very dangerous. The plasma is actually of very low density and so hasn't got that much energy.

- When discussing the promising future of fusion-produced energy, remind the students that we have been working on the project for a long time and it has proved very difficult to achieve. There is a lot of work yet to be done and opportunities for great scientists to make a difference.

- Fusion-reactor research continues with the construction of the latest testing facility in France. This International Thermonuclear Experimental Reactor (ITER) may actually be able to sustain a reaction long enough for it to be useful. It will cost over 10 billion euros though.

- There are possible hazards associated with a fusion reactor: free neutrons are produced and could be absorbed by the materials in the reactor. This would produce dangerous radioactive isotopes. However, there would be much less radiation released than in the nuclear fission reaction and so it would be easier to deal with this nuclear waste.

Plenaries

A bright future – A company claims to have developed a working nuclear fusion plant and wants to build one in the local area. Do the students object or rejoice? They should have a quick discussion and vote. *(5 minutes)*

Compare and contrast – The students should make a poster, comparing and contrasting the processes of nuclear fission and nuclear fusion. They need to discuss what happens to the protons and neutrons in each and why energy is released by both processes. They could outline why one is easier to achieve than the other. To support students, provide the information for the students to sort and perhaps assign teams, so that they can concentrate on one poster or the other. To extend the task, the students could be asked to incorporate the ideas of fuel source and how to deal with waste. *(10 minutes)*

Energy from the nucleus

P2 7.2 — Nuclear fusion ⓚ

Learning objectives

- What is nuclear fusion?
- How can nuclei be made to fuse together?
- Where does the Sun's energy come from?
- Why is it difficult to make a nuclear fusion reactor?

Imagine if we could get energy from water. Stars release energy as a result of fusing small nuclei such as hydrogen to form larger nuclei. Water contains lots of hydrogen atoms. A glass of water could provide the same amount of energy as a tanker full of petrol. But only if we could make a fusion reactor here on Earth.

Fusion reactions

Two small nuclei release energy when they are fused together to form a single larger nucleus. This process is called **nuclear fusion**. It releases energy only if the relative mass of the nucleus formed is no more than about 55 (about the same as an iron nucleus). Energy must be supplied to create bigger nuclei.

Figure 1 A nuclear fusion reaction

The Sun is about 75 per cent hydrogen and 25 per cent helium. The core is so hot that it consists of a 'plasma' of bare nuclei with no electrons. These nuclei move about and fuse together when they collide. When they fuse, they release energy. Figure 2 shows how protons fuse together to form a $^4_2$He nucleus. Energy is released at each stage.

Figure 2 Fusion reactions in the Sun

- Proton
- Neutron

- When two protons (i.e. hydrogen nuclei) fuse, they form a 'heavy hydrogen' nucleus, $^2_1$H. Other particles are created and emitted at the same time.
- Two more protons collide separately with two $^2_1$H nuclei and turn them into heavier nuclei.
- The two heavier nuclei collide to form the helium nucleus $^4_2$He.
- The energy released at each stage is carried away as kinetic energy of the product nucleus and other particles emitted.

a Look at Figure 2 and work out what is formed when a proton collides with a $^2_1$H nucleus.

Fusion reactors

There are enormous technical difficulties with making fusion a useful source of energy. The plasma of light nuclei must be heated to very high temperatures before the nuclei will fuse. This is because two nuclei approaching each other will repel each other due to their positive charges. If the nuclei are moving fast enough, they can overcome the force of repulsion and fuse together.

In a fusion reactor:

- the plasma is heated by passing a very large electric current through it
- the plasma is contained by a magnetic field so it doesn't touch the reactor walls. If it did, it would go cold and fusion would stop.

Scientists have been working on these problems since the 1950s. A successful fusion reactor would release more energy than it uses to heat the plasma. At the present time, scientists working on experimental fusion reactors are able to do this by fusing heavy hydrogen nuclei to form helium nuclei – but only for a few minutes!

b Why is a fusion reactor unlikely to explode?

A promising future ⓚ

Practical fusion reactors could meet all our energy needs.

- The fuel for fusion reactors is readily available as heavy hydrogen and is naturally present in sea water.
- The reaction product, helium, is a non-radioactive inert gas, so is harmless.
- The energy released could be used to generate electricity.

In comparison, fission reactors mostly use uranium, which is only found in certain parts of the world. Also, they produce nuclear waste that has to be stored securely for many years. However, fission reactors have been in operation for over 50 years, unlike fusion reactors, which are still under development.

Figure 3 An experimental fusion reactor

Summary questions

1 Copy and complete **a** and **b** using the words below:

large   small   stable

a When two ………… nuclei moving at high speed collide, they form a ………… nucleus.

b Energy is released in nuclear fusion if the product nucleus is not as ………… as an iron nucleus.

2 **a** Why does the plasma of light nuclei in a fusion reactor need to be very hot?

b Why would a fusion reactor that needs more energy than it produces not be much use?

3 **a** How many protons and how many neutrons are present in a $^2_1$H nucleus?

b Copy and complete the equation below to show the reaction that takes place when two $^2_1$H nuclei fuse together to form a helium nucleus.

$^2_1$H + $^2_1$H → $^?_2$He   [H]

Key points

- Nuclear fusion is the process of forcing two nuclei close enough together so they form a single larger nucleus.
- Nuclear fusion can be brought about by making two light nuclei collide at very high speed.
- Energy is released when two light nuclei are fused together. Nuclear fusion in the Sun's core releases energy.
- A fusion reactor needs to be at a very high temperature before nuclear fusion can take place. The nuclei to be fused are difficult to contain.

194 / 195

Further teaching suggestions

Fusion update

- The latest state of nuclear fusion research is available online. The students should be able to find news articles about the new and previous research centres. (Search for 'nuclear fusion breakthrough'.)

Explaining the Sun

- You can find a paper by Lord Kelvin here http://zapatopi.net/kelvin and some other suggested processes with an internet search.

Fission versus fusion

- The poster comparing the two types of nuclear power could be a homework task, as could research into the latest developments.

Answers to in-text questions

a $^3_2$He nucleus.

b If it goes out of control, the plasma would touch the walls and go cold.

Summary answers

1 **a** small, large

b stable

2 **a** So the nuclei have enough kinetic energy to overcome the force of repulsion between them and fuse.

b The energy output would be less than the energy input, so it would not produce any energy overall.

3 **a** 1 proton and 1 neutron

b $^2_1$H + $^2_1$H → $^4_2$He

P2 7.3

Nuclear issues

Learning objectives

Students should learn:

- how nuclear waste is treated and stored
- about the hazards associated with radon gas
- how to assess the safety of nuclear reactors.

Learning outcomes

Most students should be able to:

- discuss a range of nuclear issues balancing points of view appropriately
- balance the advantages and risks of using nuclear material in medicine.

Some students should also be able to:

- present arguments about nuclear issues from a wide range of viewpoints.

Answers to in-text questions

a Natural radioactivity in the air.

b Nuclear power.

c i It needs to be stored securely because it is hazardous and would be a danger to people and animals if it escaped.

ii It needs to be stored for a long time because it contains radioactive isotopes with long half-lives.

d The α-radiation from the source will be absorbed by the surrounding tissues and it could damage or kill cells in the body or cause cancer.

Support

- Provide some extra fact sheets for the topics you want to discuss and assign clear roles to each of the students.

Extend

- Students can find out the current state of the nuclear building programme in the UK. They could see how far decommissioning and construction programmes have got and if any new reactors are due to be commissioned in their area. Will the new power stations meet the increasing demand for electricity?

AQA Specification link-up: Physics P2.5, P2.6

- Evaluate the effect of occupation and/or location on the level of background radiation and radiation dose. [P2.5]
- Evaluate the possible hazards associated with the use of different types of nuclear radiation. [P2.5]
- Evaluate measures that can be taken to reduce exposure to nuclear radiations. [P2.5]
- Compare the uses of nuclear fusion and nuclear fission. [P2.6]

Lesson structure

Starters

An empty pie – Show the students a pie chart with all of the sources of background radiation and their contribution to an average dose removed. Ask the students to guess what each slice of the pie represents and then compare with the real figures. Figures vary from place to place but a typical example is: radon gas 50%, food and drink 12%, cosmic rays 10%, buildings and ground 14%, medical 12%, nuclear fallout 0.4%, air travel 0.4%, nuclear waste 0.1%. *(5 minutes)*

Risk awareness – All activities have some associated risk but we must balance this against the benefits. Discuss some activities with the students such as driving, crossing a road, walking to school, and ask the students to assess how risky they think these things are. To provide support you could find some accident statistics (from www.hse.gov.uk – Search for 'statistics') and various other government sites) and make a card sort game in which the students rank the risks of different tasks. For extension, you should compare the actual risks with the perceived risk and discuss why people are prepared to take part in risky activities while being afraid of some that are actually surprisingly safe. *(10 minutes)*

Main

- There are a wide range of issues to discuss here. You may want to select just a couple or take an extra lesson to cover all of them.
- To add an element of practical work you can measure the background count during the lesson. The data collected can be used to discuss variation (show data you have collected over the previous periods).
- Radon gas causes around 2500 deaths per year, so it is a significant cause of lung cancer. You could show maps of where the effect is greatest (Cornwall for example). Further information can be found from the Health Protection Agency (www.hpa.gov.uk).
- When discussing the medical use of radioactive materials, you should make sure that you discuss the benefits of using ionising radiation along with the health risks. This in itself can fill a substantial amount of time.
- Extensive details of the storage and handling of nuclear waste can be found on the internet from sites like BNFL and Greenpeace. This should supply you with enough information to have a debate or discussion about the topic.
- You can also find similar points to discuss about Chernobyl. There are plenty of photographs of the abandoned towns and maps of the fallout moving across Europe that you can use.
- You should remind students of the safety precautions when handling the sources.
- The use of nuclear bombs on Japan at the end of World War II is obviously a contentious issue. Show a video of a nuclear weapon exploding and then discuss these kinds of issue:
  - The lack of warning or demonstration to Japan – the first bomb was dropped without any form of warning. This was to prevent the remaining Japanese forces from trying to intercept the mission. After this, bombers dropped leaflets on Japanese cities to say that more bombs would come if there was no surrender. Three days later the warning was fulfilled on Nagasaki.
  - Were the Americans demonstrating their technology to the Russians to warn them not to invade the rest of Europe?

Plenaries

Working in the nuclear industry – Discuss the advantages and disadvantages of working in the nuclear industry. This can include the health risks, the medical benefits, employment prospects, economic prospects, and so on. *(5 minutes)*

Where's the waste? – Provide the students with a map of the World and ask them to decide where the UK's nuclear waste should be stored. They need to provide explanations about why it is safe and how to transport the waste to this location safely. Extend students by asking them to develop the criteria needed to store the waste safely for extended periods (geological stability, low population density, etc.) You can produce these types of criteria to support students. *(10 minutes)*

How Science Works   **Energy from the nucleus**

Nuclear issues

P2 7.3   Nuclear issues

Learning objectives
- What is radon gas and why is it dangerous?
- How safe are nuclear reactors?
- What happens to nuclear waste?

links
For more information on ionising radiation, look back at P2 6.4 More about alpha, beta and gamma radiation.

Did you know ...?

Nuclear waste
Used fuel rods are very hot and very radioactive.
- After removal from a reactor, they are stored in large tanks of water for up to a year. The water cools the rods down.
- Remote-control machines are then used to open the fuel rods. The unused uranium and plutonium are removed chemically from the used fuel. These are stored in sealed containers so they can be used again.
- The remaining material contains many radioactive isotopes with long half-lives. This radioactive waste must be stored in secure conditions for many years.

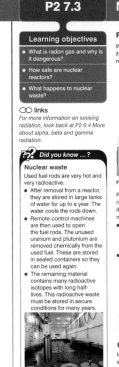

Figure 2 Storage of nuclear waste

Radioactivity all around us

When we use a Geiger counter, it clicks even without a radioactive source near it. This is due to background **radiation**. Radioactive substances are found naturally all around us.

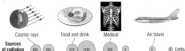

Figure 1 Radioactivity

Figure 1 shows the sources of background radiation. As explained in P2 6.4, the radiation from radioactive substances is hazardous, as it ionises substances it passes through. The numbers in Figure 1 tell you the **radiation dose** or how much radiation on average each person gets in a year from each source.
- Medical sources include X-rays as well as radioactive substances, as X-rays have an ionising effect. People who work in jobs that involve the use of ionising radiation have to wear personal radiation monitors to ensure they are not exposed to too much ionising radiation.
- Background radiation in the air is due mostly to radon gas that seeps through the ground from radioactive substances in rocks deep underground. Radon gas emits alpha particles so it is a health hazard if it is breathed in. It can seep into homes and other buildings in certain locations. In homes and buildings where people are present for long periods, methods need to be taken to reduce exposure to radon gas. For example, pipes under the building can be installed and fitted to a suction pump to draw the gas out of the ground before it seeps into the building.

a What is the biggest source of background radioactivity?
b Which source in the chart contributes least to background radioactivity?

Chernobyl

In 1986, a nuclear reactor in Ukraine exploded. Emergency workers and scientists struggled for days to contain the fire. A cloud of radioactive material from the fire drifted over many parts of Europe, including Britain. More than 100 000 people were evacuated from Chernobyl and the surrounding area. Over 30 people died in the accident. Many more have developed leukaemia or cancer since then. It was and remains (up to now) the world's worst nuclear accident.

Could it happen again?
- Most nuclear reactors are of a different design.
- The Chernobyl accident did not have a high-speed shutdown system like most reactors have.
- The operators at Chernobyl ignored safety instructions.
- There are thousands of nuclear reactors in the world. They have been working safely for many years.

Radioactive risks

The effect on living cells of radiation from radioactive substances depends on:
- the type and the amount of radiation received (the dose)
- whether the source of the radiation is inside or outside the body
- how long the living cells are exposed to the radiation.

	Alpha radiation	Beta radiation	Gamma radiation
source inside the body	**very dangerous** – affects all the surrounding tissue	**dangerous** – reaches cells throughout the body	
source outside the body	**some danger** – absorbed by skin; damages skin cells		

- The larger the dose of radiation someone gets, the greater the risk of cancer. High doses kill living cells.
- The smaller the dose, the less the risk – but it is never zero. So there is a very low level of risk to each and every one of us because of background radioactivity.

Workers who are at risk from ionising radiations cut down their exposure to the radiation by:
- keeping as far as possible from the source of radiation, using special handling tools with long handles
- spending as little time as possible in 'at-risk' areas
- shielding themselves from the radiation by staying behind thick concrete barriers and/or using thick lead plates.

c Why does radioactive waste need to be stored **i** securely **ii** for many years?
d Why is a source of alpha radiation very dangerous inside the body but not outside it?

Summary questions

1 In some locations, the biggest radiation hazard comes from radon gas which seeps up through the ground and into buildings. The dangers of radon gas can be minimised by building new houses that are slightly raised on brick pillars and modifying existing houses. Radon gas is an α-emitting isotope.
   a Why is radon gas dangerous in a house?
   b Describe one way of making an existing house safe from radon gas.

2 Should the UK government replace our existing nuclear reactors with new reactors, either fission or fusion or both? Answer this question by discussing the benefits and drawbacks of new fission and fusion reactors.

Figure 3 Chernobyl

Did you know ...?

New improved nuclear reactors
Most of the world's nuclear reactors in use now will need to be replaced in the next 20 years. New improved 'third generation' nuclear reactors will replace them. The new types of reactors have:
- a standard design to cut down costs and construction time
- a longer operating life – typically 60 years
- more safety features, such as convection of outside air through cooling panels along the reactor walls
- much less effect on the environment.

Key points
- Radon gas is an α-emitting isotope that seeps into houses in certain areas through the ground.
- There are thousands of fission reactors safely in use in the world. None of them are of the same type as the Chernobyl reactors that exploded.
- Nuclear waste is stored in safe and secure conditions for many years after unused uranium and plutonium (to be used in future) is removed from it.

196   197

Further teaching suggestions

Research topics
- There is a lot of scope for extra research about most of the topics. The students can produce quite extensive reports, so fix clear limits on any research projects you set. This can be a good way of stimulating interest for students who want to study physics beyond GCSE level.

New reactions
- You can discuss improved reactors, the students will have to bear in mind the strong opposition. The students should be better informed than members of the general public about the technology, so what do they think? No matter how many safety features are employed, there is always a small risk. However, the damage from a coal power station may be even larger over its lifetime. The contribution to global warming could be far more serious in the long run.

Summary answers

1 **a** Radon gas in a house may be more concentrated than outdoors and people in the house would breathe it in. The lungs would be exposed to α-radiation from radon gas atoms that enter the lungs. The α-particles from the radon atoms in the lungs would be absorbed by lung tissues. Their ionising effect in the tissue cells would damage or kill the cells or cause cancer.

   b Install pipes under the house and connect them to a suction pump to draw radon gases out of the ground before it seeps into the house. The top of the outlet pipe from the pump would need to be high up outside the house.

2 Benefits to building either type of reactor should include no greenhouse gas emissions, reliable and secure electricity supplies, and large-scale generation from small sites compared with renewable supplies that would take up much larger areas, etc. Drawbacks should include long-term storage of nuclear waste, possible escape of radioactive substances into the environment, impracticality of fusion reactors, etc.

P2 7.4

The early universe

AQA

Specification link-up: Physics P2.6

- Stars form when enough dust and gas from space is pulled together by gravitational attraction. Smaller masses may also form and be attracted by a larger mass to become planets. [P2.6.2 c)]

Learning objectives

Students should learn:

- that a galaxy is a collection of millions or billions of stars bound together by gravitational attraction
- that the structure of the early universe is vastly different to that which we see today
- that stars are formed by the action of gravitational forces of gas clouds.

Learning outcomes

Most students should be able to:

- describe the structure of a galaxy
- describe how the universe changed after the Big Bang and how gravitational forces brought matter together to form structures like galaxies and stars.

Some students should also be able to:

- explain why stars stay in a galaxy and why there are vast spaces between galaxies.

Support

- The concepts covered here are fairly difficult to comprehend for many students. There are a good range of videos from a range of sources including the internet that cover them well, so make use of these to support the topic.

Extend

- Students can look at a few examples of fusion reactions that take place in stars to enhance their understanding of the fusion processes. These can include (H-2 + H-3 → He-4 + n); the formation of helium from hydrogen, He-3 + He-4 → Li-7 + γ; which occurs at the surface of the Sun in solar flares. They should consider the changes that occur to nucleons in some of these reactions.

Lesson structure

Starters

From the beginning – The students draw a simple cartoon showing what they know about the beginning of the universe. This could include information about the Big Bang, how stars operate and the structure of the solar system. This may help identify some significant misconceptions. *(5 minutes)*

Galaxies – Show the students some images of galaxies and ask them to describe their shapes. How do they think that these were formed? You can show video clips of galaxy formation along with the diagrams. These reveal possible reasons why we have a lot of spiral shapes; collisions between galaxies tend to cause this. Students can decide if a range of 'facts' about galaxies are true or false. These could include the names of ours, the number of stars in a typical galaxy, the distances and so on. You can differentiate the questions to provide extra support or extension where needed. *(10 minutes)*

Main

- This is a bit of a 'story' topic where you have to convey a sense of wonder at the scale of the universe and its age. Computer animations of the interaction of galaxies will be very helpful with this topic.

- Hopefully, the students will remember the lesson on the Big Bang in P1. Get them to give their own descriptions of this, mentioning the creation of space, matter, energy and time. They should also know that the universe expanded rapidly and is still expanding, so discuss the evidence we have for this: background radiation and red shift.

- It can be hard to get across the sheer scale of the universe, the number of stars in each galaxy and the number of galaxies. The words 'billions of billions' tend to wash over the students. Try to get across the size as best you can.

- The Dark Age of the universe just means that no visible light was produced. Get the students to connect this with the lack of stars. Make sure that the students understand the reasons why matter did not come together in large quantities before the formation of neutral atoms, i.e. repulsion by the protons. Once there were neutral atoms. They did not repel each other, so could be forced closer together to form molecules.

- The lumpiness of the universe is a direct result of early fluctuations in the structure. You might want to show them the famous COBE picture of the early unevenness in the universe. This is easily found along with discussion articles on the internet. It was this tiny amount of variation that leads to the structures we see today.

- At the end, it is important to remind the students of the processes that are releasing energy in the stars. They will cover this in a bit more depth in lesson P2 7.5 'The life history of a star'.

Plenaries

Sizes and distances – Can the students put a set of cards in order of how large the objects are and then arrange them in order of how far away from us they are? Use cards with asteroid, Moon, planets, black hole, our Sun, solar system, galaxy and the universe on them. They can then match up some example distances. This can lead to a discussion about whether all stars are the same size. *(5 minutes)*

A better picture – To demonstrate developments in astronomy and in the telescope in particular, you can show students a range of images linking telescopes to the images that they are able to produce. This can include some historical telescopes and some of the more modern ones. To extend students you can discuss some of the images produced by X-ray or radio telescopes and how these have been converted into images we can see. For support you could ask the students to match images with the telescopes that produce them. *(10 minutes)*

Further teaching suggestions

Galaxy formation
- Use the internet to search for animations of galaxy formation and you should come up with some impressive computer-generated imagery. You should also find with some free-to-use presentations.

Other galaxies
- The students should find out about a galaxy other than our own. Ask: 'What is its name, how big is it, how far away and where in the sky can it be found?' A picture is compulsory.

How Science Works — Energy from the nucleus

The early universe

P2 7.4 — The early universe

Learning objectives
- What is a galaxy?
- What was the universe like in the billions of years before stars and galaxies were formed?
- What is the force responsible for the formation of stars and galaxies?

?? Did you know ... ?
In the Cold War, US satellites detected bursts of gamma radiation from space. At first, the US military thought nuclear weapons were being tested in space by Russia. Then astronomers found the bursts were from violent events long ago in distant galaxies – maybe stars being sucked into black holes!

The Big Bang that created the universe was about 13 thousand million (13 billion) years ago. Space, time and radiation were created in the Big Bang. At first, the universe was a hot glowing ball of radiation and matter. As it expanded, its temperature fell. Now the universe is cold and dark, except for hot spots we call stars.

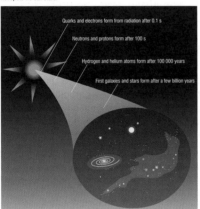

Quarks and electrons form from radiation after 0.1 s

Neutrons and protons form after 100 s

Hydrogen and helium atoms form after 100 000 years

First galaxies and stars form after a few billion years

Figure 1 Timeline for the universe

The stars we see in the night sky are all in the Milky Way galaxy, our home galaxy. The Sun is just one of billions of stars in the Milky Way galaxy. Using powerful telescopes, we can see many more stars in the Milky Way galaxy. We can also see individual stars in other galaxies.

We now know there are billions of galaxies in the universe. There is vast empty space between them. Light from the furthest galaxies that we can see has taken billions of years to reach us.

a Why do powerful telescopes give us a picture of the universe long ago?

Figure 2 Andromeda – the nearest big galaxy to the Milky Way

The Dark Age of the universe

As the universe expanded, it became transparent as radiation passed through the empty space between its atoms. The background microwave radiation that causes the spots on an untuned television was released at this stage. The Dark Age of the universe had begun!

For the next few billion years, the universe was a completely dark, patchy, expanding cloud of hydrogen and helium. Then the stars and galaxies formed and lit up the universe!

b How long, to the nearest billion years, has background microwave radiation been travelling for?

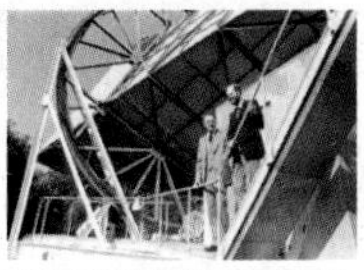

The force of gravity takes over

Uncharged atoms don't repel each other. But they can attract each other. During the Dark Age of the universe, the force of gravitational attraction was at work without any opposition from repulsive forces.

As the universe continued to expand, it became more patchy as the denser parts attracted nearby matter. Gravity pulled more matter into the denser parts and turned them into gigantic clumps.

Eventually, the force of gravity turned the clumps into galaxies and stars. A few billion years after the Big Bang, the Dark Age came to an end, as the stars lit up the universe.

c Why would the force of gravity between two helium nuclei be unable to pull the nuclei together?

Figure 3 Arno Allan Penzias and Robert Woodrow Wilson standing on the radio antenna that unexpectedly discovered the universe's microwave background radiation

Figure 4 The force of gravity takes over

Summary questions

1 Copy and complete **a** to **c** using the words below:
   attracted   cooled   expanded   formed
   a As the universe .... , it ....
   b Uncharged atoms .... each other.
   c Galaxies and stars .... from uncharged atoms.

2 **a i** Why can't we take a photo of the Milky Way galaxy from outside?
   ii Why can't we take photos of a distant galaxy at different stages in its formation?
   b i Why do the stars in a galaxy not drift away from each other?
   ii Why are there vast spaces between the galaxies?

3 Put these events in the correct sequence with the earliest event first.
   1 Cosmic background radiation was released.
   2 Hydrogen nuclei were first fused to form helium nuclei.
   3 The Big Bang took place.
   4 Neutrons and protons formed.

Key points
- A galaxy is a collection of billions of stars held together by their own gravity.
- Before galaxies and stars formed, the universe was a dark patchy cloud of hydrogen and helium.
- The force of gravity pulled matter into galaxies and stars.

198 | 199

Answers to in-text questions

a When we use a powerful telescope to see a distant galaxy, we are seeing the galaxy as it was billions of years ago because the light from it has taken billions of years to reach us.

b About 13 billion years.

c They are both positively charged, so they repel each other. The force of repulsion is much greater than the force of gravity between them.

Summary answers

1 **a** expanded, cooled
  b attracted
  c formed

2 **a i** We could not send a probe far enough.
     ii Galaxies take millions of years to form; we couldn't wait that long.
  b i Gravitational forces hold the stars in their positions.
     ii The universe has expanded leaving these vast spaces.

3 3, 4, 1, 2

P2 7.5

The life history of a star

AQA Specification link-up: Physics P2.6

- Stars form when enough dust and gas from space is pulled together by gravitational attraction. Smaller masses may also form and be attracted by a larger mass to become planets. *[P2.6.2 c)]*
- During the 'main sequence' period of its life cycle a star is stable because the forces within it are balanced. *[P2.6.2 d)]*
- A star goes through a life cycle. This life cycle is determined by the size of the star .... . *[P2.6.2 e)]*

Learning objectives

Students should learn:

- that the Sun is a typical small star and how it developed into its current 'main sequence' state
- that the Sun will continue to develop, passing through a red giant and white dwarf stage before reaching the end of its energy-producing life
- that bigger stars can explode in a supernova and produce exotic objects like neutron stars or black holes.

Learning outcomes

Most students should be able to:

- describe the stages in the complete life cycle of a typical star such as the Sun
- outline the stages that larger stars can go through in producing neutron stars and black holes.

Some students should also be able to:

- describe what a black hole is and what its main property is.

Answers to in-text questions

a The energy to heat the star comes from the potential energy of gas and dust, which decreases as the gas and dust gathers and forms a protostar.

b The outward pressure of radiation from its core stops it collapsing.

c Gravity.

d Gravity.

Support

- Give the students a set of diagrams to cut out and paste in order. They should add information to these during the lesson.

Extend

- The life cycle of a star can be described through a diagram known as the 'Hertzsprung–Russell' diagram. The students should find out what this is and how the life of the Sun would be represented on it. They can compare the positions of red giants, white dwarfs and some supergiants. Give them some examples of each.

Lesson structure

Starters

The seven ages of man – Can the students come up with a list of words used to describe the stages of human development and ageing? [Shakespeare had infant, whining schoolboy, lover, soldier, justice, old age and finally a second childhood (senility), but these are hardly scientific.] *(5 minutes)*

The celestial sphere – Show the students some photographs of the night sky pointing out a large range of stars. Ask the student to find a pattern in the stars and come up with a legend of how it got there. You can show them some of the traditional constellations and tell them the accompanying tale if you know it. Extend students by asking them to consider what the constellations would look like from a different perspective. They should understand that constellations are not really any particular shape and the interpretation of the positions of stars is very different now than it was thousands of years ago. For support, you can provide some constellations with the appropriate images to start off the discussions. *(10 minutes)*

Main

- The constituents that combine to make a star are mostly hydrogen gas. During the collapse, the material heats up by frictional processes and begins to radiate infrared radiation so astronomers are hoping to detect this to confirm the formation process. This is very difficult because the protostar would still have a lot of gas and dust surrounding it (a Bok globule). Stars are formed in groups as the different parts of the original nebula collapse. One of these is in the heart of the Orion nebula; you could show pictures of stellar nurseries.

- The star is properly 'born' when nuclear fusion starts in the core. It is worth quickly going through the basic fusion process again, emphasising the fact that new elements are being made. This will be covered again in more depth in the next lesson.

- Use the term 'equilibrium' when describing the two processes involved in maintaining the star, so that the students link this ideas across all of the work on forces. The star remains on the main sequence for most of its life although the larger the star is, the quicker it 'burns out'.

- Make sure that you emphasise the longevity of the stars. Although they are consuming tens of millions of tonnes of hydrogen each second, it will still take them billions of years to get through a few per cent of the original material.

- The description of the change into a red giant should be accompanied by an animation. You should be able to find one showing the expansion of our Sun swallowing up Mercury and (possibly) Venus. The star may oscillate in size as it moves on to different fusion processes in the core.

- The white dwarf phase produces an object of massive density. Beware: the students may still be thinking that the object is 'gas' so it is light. The density is actually many times that of the normal matter we find on Earth. White dwarves would take hundreds of billions of years to cool into black dwarfs so there aren't any about yet. Ask the students why this is. [The universe just isn't old enough yet.]

- You can do a comparison of the radii, surface temperatures and density of the Sun, a red giant, a white dwarf and a black dwarf.

- Big stars are much more fun. You should be able to find animations of supernova explosions on the internet to support the discussions. Neutron stars and black holes sound strange and exciting so use the opportunity to encourage the students to find out more about them.

- The students should be left with the idea that the processes involved take billions of years and that our Sun has plenty of life left in it yet, so there is no need to worry.

Plenaries

SDRAWKCAB – The students should draw a flow chart of the life cycle of a star, but make it backwards. They need to decide whether to start from a black hole or a black dwarf. *(5 minutes)*

Sequence sort – Give the students a set of cards describing the *processes* that are happening in the life cycle of stars (but not the name of the stages) and ask them to sort them into order. For example: 'the star is expanding and its surface is cooling' [red giant] and 'the surface temperature is at its highest' [white dwarf]. To extend students, you can add details of nuclear fusion for them to sort and describe. To provide additional support, you can simply ask the students to sort the names of the stellar life stages into a diagram and then add some of the process on top of this. *(10 minutes)*

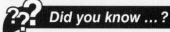

Did you know ... ?

Before nuclear fusion was discovered and recognised as the process that releases energy in the Sun, scientists had worked out the age of the Sun to be a maximum of 10 million years old because they thought it was burning and releasing energy from chemical reactions.

Energy from the nucleus

P2 7.5 — The life history of a star

Learning objectives

- What is a protostar?
- What are the stages in the life of a star?
- What will eventually happen to the Sun?
- What is a supernova?

The birth of a star

Stars form out of clouds of dust and gas.

- The particles in the clouds are pulled together by their own gravitational attraction. The clouds merge together. They become more and more concentrated to form a **protostar**, the name for a star to be.
- As a protostar becomes denser, it gets hotter. If it becomes hot enough, the nuclei of hydrogen atoms and other light elements fuse together. Energy is released in this fusion so the core gets hotter and brighter and starts to shine. A star is born!
- Objects may form that are too small to become stars. Such objects may be attracted by a protostar to become **planets**.

a Where does the energy to heat a protostar come from?

Shining stars

Stars like the Sun radiate energy because of hydrogen fusion in the core. They are called **main sequence stars** because this is the main stage in the life of a star. It can maintain its energy output for millions of years until the star runs out of hydrogen nuclei to fuse together.

- Energy released in the core keeps the core hot so the process of fusion continues. Radiation flows out steadily from the core in all directions.
- The star is stable because the forces within it are balanced. The force of gravity that makes a star contract is balanced by the outward force of the radiation from its core. These forces stay in balance until most of the hydrogen nuclei in the core have been fused together.

b Why doesn't the Sun collapse under its own gravity?

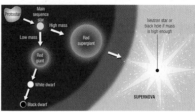

Figure 1 Star birth

Protostar

Did you know ... ?

- The Sun is about 5000 million years old and will probably continue to shine for another 5000 million years.
- The Sun will turn into a red giant bigger than the orbit of Mercury. By then, the human race will probably have long passed into history. But will intelligent life still exist?

The end of a star

When a star runs out of hydrogen nuclei to fuse together, it reaches the end of its main sequence stage and it swells out.

Stars about the same size as the Sun (or smaller) swell out, cool down and turn red.

- The star is now a **red giant**. At this stage, helium and other light elements in its core fuse to form heavier elements.
- When there are no more light elements in its core, fusion stops and no more radiation is released. Due to its own gravity, the star collapses in on itself. As it collapses, it heats up and turns from red to yellow to white. It becomes a **white dwarf**. This is a hot, dense white star much smaller in diameter than it was. Stars like the Sun then fade out, go cold and become **black dwarfs**.

Stars much bigger than the Sun end their lives much more dramatically.

- Such a star swells out to become a red **supergiant** which then collapses.
- In the collapse, the matter surrounding the star's core compresses the core more and more. Then the compression suddenly reverses in a cataclysmic explosion known as a **supernova**. Such an event can outshine an entire galaxy for several weeks.

Figure 2 The life cycle of a star

c What force causes a red giant to collapse?

What remains after a supernova occurs?

The explosion compresses the core of the star into a **neutron star**. This is an extremely dense object composed only of neutrons. If the star is massive enough, it becomes a **black hole** instead of a neutron star. The gravitational field of a black hole is so strong that nothing can escape from it. Not even light, or any other form of electromagnetic radiation, can escape.

d What force causes matter to be dragged into a black hole?

Figure 3 M87 is a galaxy that spins so fast at its centre that it is thought to contain a black hole with a billion times more mass than the Sun

Summary questions

1 a The list below shows some of the stages in the life of a star like the Sun. Put the stages in the correct sequence.
  A main sequence
  B protostar
  C red giant
  D white dwarf
  b i Which stage in the above list is the Sun at now?
  ii What will happen to the Sun after it has gone through the above stages?

2 a Copy and complete **i** and **ii** using the words below. Each word can be used more than once.
  collapse expand explode
  i The Sun will eventually .... then ....
  ii A red supergiant will .... then ....
  b i What is the main condition needed for a supergiant to form a black hole?
  ii Why is it not possible for light to escape from a black hole?

3 a i What force makes a red supergiant collapse?
  ii What force prevents a main sequence star from collapsing?
  b Why does a white dwarf eventually become a black dwarf?

Key points

- A protostar is a gas and dust cloud in space that can go on to form a star.

Low mass star:
Protostar → main sequence star → red giant → white dwarf → black dwarf

High mass star:
Protostar → main sequence star → red supergiant → supernova → neutron star → black hole if sufficient mass

- The Sun will eventually become a black dwarf.
- A supernova is the explosion of a supergiant after it collapses.

Further teaching suggestions

Stellar research

- Give the students a stellar object each to research (or pair them up), to make a wall display about the life cycle of stars. They will need access to the internet and various drawing tools.

  The students should find examples and details about a range of objects associated with the life cycle of stars. Some suitable objects to find out about are: our Sun (Sol), stellar nurseries, protostars, giant molecular clouds, neutron stars, black holes, pulsars, white dwarfs, black dwarfs, red giants, blue giants and planetary nebulae.

ICT link-up

- Search the internet for 'life cycle of stars' or 'life cycle of stars video'. These are much better at showing the processes than diagrams, so try to use one.

The life of our solar system

- The students could write a story, or draw a comic strip, about an ageless observer that watches the life of our solar system from beginning to end.

Summary answers

1 a B, A, C, D
  b i A
  ii It will fade out and go cold.

2 a i expand, collapse
  ii explode, collapse
  b i The neutron star must have sufficient mass.
  ii The gravitational field is so strong that nothing can escape from it.

3 a i The force of attraction due to its gravity acting on its own mass.
  ii The force of the radiation flowing outwards to its surface from its core.
  b A white dwarf cools down and when it no longer emits light, it has become a black dwarf because it can no longer be seen.

P2 7.6

How the chemical elements formed

Learning objectives

Students should learn:

- that elements as heavy as iron are formed in nuclear fusion processes in stars
- that heavier elements are formed in supernova explosions
- that the material produced in stars can be spread out in explosions and can end up in new solar systems.

Learning outcomes

Most students should be able to:

- state that elements as heavy as iron are formed by nuclear fusion processes
- describe a supernova event and how such events can lead to the formation of new stars.

Some students should also be able to:

- explain why the Earth contains elements heavier than iron as well as lighter elements.

Answers to in-text questions

a In a supernova explosion.

b Its half-life is very short compared with the age of the Sun. Any plutonium formed when the Sun formed would have decayed long ago.

c Carbon atoms are in all the molecules that make up living objects.

Support

- The students can concentrate on the requirements that would be needed for life similar to ours. Once they have decided on what was needed, they can design a possible rival species to us.

Extend

- There are smaller explosions involving stars called 'simple novas'. Can the students find an explanation of what causes these? They should find connections between red giants and their companion white dwarfs.

Specification link-up: Physics P2.6

- Fusion processes in stars produce all of the naturally occurring elements. These elements may be distributed throughout the universe by the explosion of a massive star (supernova) at the end of its life. *[P2.6.2 f)]*

Lesson structure

Starters

Star stuff – 'We are all made of stars.' What do the students think this means; is it a scientific statement? You could play the song of the same title (by Moby) while the students think about their answers. *(5 minutes)*

Building blocks – How many separate elements can the students name? You could play the famous periodic table elements song by Tom Lehrer (search for 'elements song' and you will find a number of versions). Ask: 'What is the meaning of the word 'element'?' Show them a graph or chart showing the proportion of these elements found throughout the universe; this should be dominated by hydrogen and helium with trace amounts of everything else. Use this to start the discussion about where the other elements come from. To extend the students, you can ask them to present the information in an appropriate manner (pie chart or bar chart). For additional support, consider revising the nature of elements using prompts such as Lego blocks; you can create a 'wall' with blocks showing the percentages of hydrogen, carbon and other elements using three different colour blocks. *(10 minutes)*

Main

- Start by again reminding the students about nuclear fusion processes, but expand on these ideas leading to the manufacture of heavier nuclei such as carbon. Some of the students should remember that there is a limit to this process: iron nuclei. This is because it takes more energy to produce heavier nuclei than would be given out. Ask the students where they think that the extra energy required comes from; they could come up with the idea that the supernova explosion provides it.

- This can lead on to a discussion of the energy output from a supernova, which is something like 10^{46} joules. The power output of the Sun is 10^{28} watts, so it would take about 32 billion years to release this amount of energy. Hopefully this will give the students some impression of the scale of the explosion.

- You should be able to find an animation showing the formation of the solar system. You can discuss that fact that some of this material had been manufactured in other stars and some has even come from supernovas.

- When discussing heavy elements, you can use the opportunity to show a nuclear equation for revision. Bombardment of nitrogen by neutrons to form carbon-14 is an important process. (n + N-14 → C-14 + H-1). For a heavy metal example, use (U-238 + n → U-239 + γ).

- Some of the students may know that, in addition to the original quantity of lead when the Earth formed, some lead has been formed from the nuclear decay of heavier elements.

- If you have time, you can have a talk about the idea of extraterrestrial life which most students are very interested in. It goes beyond the specification, but it is worth discussing. Some students will have strong opinions about this as they will have been exposed to a lot of 'facts' from various sources. It is worth getting the latest details on the search for life on Mars to have a discussion with the students. (See 'Activity and extension ideas.') In addition, you can discuss the techniques needed to spot planets in other solar systems. This is a rapidly developing field with none known until 1989. Detection of planets around the size of the Earth is the next big step in this project.

Plenaries

We come in peace – Students have to send a message to a potential alien civilisation as a radio signal. They have a limited number of words for their message – what will it be? To extend students, you might ask them to decode an alien message as shown in the 'hidden message' suggestion although this will take a little longer. *(5 minutes)*

Star jewellery – Students could make an advert for a piece of finely crafted 'star stuff'; made in the heart of a supernova and costing a mere £20 000. It is only made of copper though! *(10 minutes)*

Further teaching suggestions

Students may be interested in the search for extraterrestrial life and, although it is not required by the specification, they might like to try some of these activities.

Mars

- Mars is the most studied planet in the solar system besides the Earth. It has huge mythological and scientific importance. If evidence of life can be found so close to us, it would mean that the likelihood of life outside the solar system would be very high. The students can look in detail at the history of Mars and its exploration. Highlights include the 'canals' and volcanoes on Mars, the Viking and Pathfinder probes and the proposed manned exploration later in the twenty-first century. They can look into some of the less scientific ideas too, including the invasion from *War of the Worlds* and the many faces and pyramids that 'prove' that there is life.

Hidden message

- To show how difficult it is to find a message in random background noise, try this task.

Details

Create a 12 by 12 table in a word processor and fill in the cells with the symbols ':' and 'X', so that they create a shape; a smiley face works well. Get the word processor to convert the table into text and delete any line breaks, to end up with a long sequence of ':'s and 'X's. Without telling the students about the size of the grid, see if they can find out what the symbol is. A smaller starting grid will make this easier.

Space exploration

- Use an astronomy CD or internet searches to help students find out about exploration of the solar system and Mars, in particular. Search the internet for 'exploration solar system Mars' and see www.nasa.com.

P2 7.6 — How the chemical elements formed

Learning objectives

- What chemical elements are formed inside stars?
- What chemical elements are formed in supernovas?
- Why does the Earth contain heavy elements?

The birthplace of the chemical elements

- Light elements are formed as a result of fusion in stars.

Stars like the Sun fuse hydrogen nuclei (i.e. protons) into helium and similar small nuclei, including carbon. When it becomes a red giant, it fuses helium and the other small nuclei into larger nuclei.

Nuclei larger than iron cannot be formed by this process because too much energy is needed.

- Heavy elements are formed when a massive star collapses then explodes as a supernova.

The enormous force of the collapse fuses small nuclei into nuclei larger than iron. The explosion scatters the star into space.

The debris from a supernova contains all the known elements from the lightest to the heaviest. Eventually, new stars form as gravity pulls the debris together.

Planets form from debris surrounding a new star. As a result, such planets will be composed of all the known elements too.

a Lead (Pb) is much heavier than iron (Fe). How did the lead we use form?

Figure 1 The Crab Nebula

Gas, rocks and dust

The Sun forms at the centre of a spinning cloud of dust, gas and rock.

Gas

Rocks

The Sun's heat evaporates ice and drives gas away from the inner Solar System, leaving rocks behind.

The rocky planets form near the Sun and the gas giant planets form further away. The minor planet Pluto orbits the Sun beyond the giant planets.

Figure 2 Formation of the Solar System

Figure 3 The NASA Exploration Rovers looked for signs of life on Mars

Planet Earth

The heaviest known natural element is uranium. It has a half-life of 4500 million years. The presence of uranium in the Earth is evidence that the Solar System must have formed from the remnants of a supernova.

Elements such as plutonium are heavier than uranium. Scientists can make these elements by bombarding heavy elements like uranium with high-speed neutrons. They would have been present in the debris which formed the Solar System. Elements heavier than uranium formed then have long since decayed.

b Plutonium-239 has a half-life of about 24 000 years.
Why is it not found naturally like uranium?
c Why is carbon an important element?

Summary questions

1 Match each statement below with an element in the list.
helium   hydrogen   iron   uranium
a Helium nuclei are formed when nuclei of this element are fused.
b This element is formed in a supernova explosion.
c Stars form nuclei of these two elements (and others not listed) by fusing smaller nuclei.
d The early universe mostly consisted of this element.

2 Copy and complete **a** to **c** using the words below. Each word can be used more than once.
galaxy   planets   stars   supernova
a Fusion inside .... creates light elements. Fusion in a .... creates heavy elements.
b A .... scatters the elements throughout a ....
c .... and planets formed from the debris of a .... contain all the known elements.

3 Uranium-238 is a radioactive isotope found naturally in the Earth. It has a half-life of about 4500 million years. It was formed from lighter elements.
a i What is the name of the physical process in which this isotope is formed?
ii What is the name for the astronomical event in which the above process takes place?
b Why has all the uranium in the Earth not decayed by now?

Key points

- Elements as heavy as iron are formed inside stars as a result of nuclear fusion.
- Elements heavier than iron are formed in supernovas as well as light elements.
- The Sun and the rest of the Solar System were formed from the debris of a supernova.

Summary answers

1 **a** hydrogen
  b uranium
  c helium, iron
  d hydrogen

2 **a** stars, supernova
  b supernova, galaxy
  c stars, supernova

3 **a** **i** nuclear fusion
      ii a supernova event
  b The Sun and the rest of the solar system formed from the debris of a supernova. Much of the uranium-238 formed from the debris of the supernova still exists because it has a half-life which is comparable with the age of the Earth.

Summary answers

1 a i stays the same

   ii decreases

   iii increases

  b i The reactor would overheat and the materials in it might melt. In the meltdown, the reactor pressure might be high enough to cause an explosion releasing radioactive material into the atmosphere.

   ii The excess neutrons would be absorbed and the reaction would slow down releasing less energy.

2 a i The process where two small nuclei fuse together to form a single larger nucleus.

   ii Because they are both positively charged.

   iii To overcome the force of repulsion between them due to their charge.

  b The plasma needs to be very hot. The plasma is difficult to control.

3 a i fusion

   ii fission

   iii fission

  b The fuel is readily available. The products of fusion are not radioactive.

4 a i nuclear fusion

   ii hydrogen

  b The Sun will cool down and swell out to become a red giant.

5 a planet

  b galaxy

  c stars

  d stars, galaxy

6 a gravity

  b The core doesn't become hot enough to fuse hydrogen nuclei.

  c Fusion.

7 a A, C, B, D, E.

  b i It will fade out.

   ii It will explode as a supernova, leaving a neutron star at its core. If the mass of the neutron star is large enough, it will be a black hole.

8 a i A large star that explodes.

   ii A star that becomes a supernova suddenly becomes much brighter, then it fades. A star like the Sun has a constant brightness.

  b i A massive object which nothing can escape from.

   ii They would be pulled in by the force of gravity and then disappear.

9 a i helium

   ii helium

  b i lead, uranium

   ii Heavy elements can only have formed in a supernova. The presence of heavy elements in the Earth tells us that the solar system formed from the debris of a supernova.

Energy from the nucleus: P2 7.1–P2 7.6

Summary questions

1 a Copy and complete **i** to **iii** using the words below:

decreases increases stays the same

When energy is released at a steady rate in a nuclear reactor,

  i the number of fission events each second in the core ....

  ii the amount of uranium-235 in the core ....

  iii the number of radioactive isotopes in the fuel rods ....

b Explain what would happen in a nuclear reactor if:

  i the coolant fluid leaked out of the core

  ii the control rods were pushed further into the reactor core.

2 a i What do we mean by nuclear fusion?

  ii Why do two nuclei repel each other when they get close?

  iii Why do they need to collide at high speed in order to fuse together?

b Give two reasons why nuclear fusion is difficult to achieve in a reactor.

3 a Copy and complete **i** to **iii** using the words below. Each word can be used more than once.

fission fusion

  i In a .... reactor, two small nuclei join together and release energy.

  ii In a .... reactor, a large nucleus splits and releases energy.

  iii The fuel in a .... reactor contains uranium-235.

b State two advantages that nuclear fusion reactors would have in comparison with nuclear fission reactors.

4 a i What physical process causes energy to be released in the Sun?

  ii Which element is used in the physical process named in part **i** to release energy in the Sun?

b How will the Sun change in the next stage of its life cycle when it has used up all the element named in part **a ii**?

5 Copy and complete **a** to **d** using the words below. Each word can be used more than once.

galaxy planet stars

a A .... isn't big enough to be a star.

b The Sun is inside a ....

c .... became hot after they formed from matter pulled together by the force of gravity.

d The force of gravity keeps .... together inside a ....

6 a What force pulls dust and gas in space?

b Why do large planets like Jupiter not produce their own light?

c What is the name for the type of reaction that releases energy in the core of the Sun?

7 a The stages in the development of the Sun are listed below. Put the stages in the correct sequence.

  A dust and gas

  B present stage

  C protostar

  D red giant

  E white dwarf

b i After the white dwarf stage, what will happen to the Sun?

  ii What will happen to a star that has much more mass than the Sun?

8 a i What is a supernova?

  ii How could we tell the difference between a supernova and a distant star like the Sun at present?

b i What is a black hole?

  ii What would happen to stars and planets near a black hole?

9 a i Which element as well as hydrogen is formed in early universe?

  ii Which of the two elements is formed from the other one in a star?

b i Which two of the elements listed below is not formed in a star that gives out radiation at a steady rate?

  carbon iron lead uranium

  ii How do we know that the Sun formed from the debris of a supernova?

204

Kerboodle resources

Resources available for this chapter on Kerboodle are:

- Chapter map: Energy from the nucleus
- Animation: A chain reaction (P2 7.1)
- How Science Works: A domino chain (P2 7.1)
- Viewpoint: Is fusion the energy source of the future? (P2 7.2)
- Viewpoint: Where should we store nuclear waste? (P2 7.3)
- Animation: The life cycle of a star (P2 7.5)
- Interactive activity: The life cycles of different types of star
- Revision podcast: Energy from the nucleus
- Test yourself: Energy from the nucleus
- On your marks: Energy from the nucleus
- Examination-style questions: Energy from the nucleus
- Answers to examination-style questions: Energy from the nucleus

---

AQA Examiner's tip

Students often get fission and fusion mixed up due to the similarity of the words. Remind students that a fissure is a split and fusing together is joining up.

AQA Examination-style questions

a Copy and complete the following diagram to show how a chain reaction may occur inside a nuclear fuel rod containing many uranium-235 nuclei. (3)

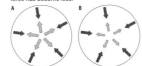

Neutron

U-235 nucleus

b Name the other fissionable substance that is used in some nuclear reactors. (1)

c The passages below reflect some of the conflicting opinions about nuclear power.

> Nuclear power is a low-emission source of energy and is the only readily available, large-scale alternative to fossil fuels for a continuous, reliable supply of electricity. The waste from nuclear power occupies a tiny volume and can be safely returned to the Earth for underground storage.

> A new generation of nuclear power stations will only reduce our emissions by four per cent by 2024: far too little, far too late, to stop global warming. They will create tens of thousands of tonnes of the most hazardous radioactive waste, which remains dangerous for up to a million years.

  i What are the 'emissions' that both sources refer to? (1)

  ii Why can nuclear waste remain dangerous for millions of years? (1)

  iii Give one advantage and one disadvantage of the storage of nuclear waste underground. (2)

  iv Explain why it would not be possible to replace fossil fuels with wind power alone. (2)

d For over 50 years scientists have been experimenting with fusion reactors with the aim of eventually generating electricity. The latest research project, called ITER, is scheduled to start operating in France in 2018 and is a collaboration between many countries.

  i State two of the potential benefits of fusion power. (2)

  ii Why are some people opposed to the research into fusion power? (2)

2 a Copy and complete the following sentences using the list of words and phrases below. Each one can be used once, more than once or not at all.

split   fusion   join   a larger one   fission   two smaller nuclei

The Sun's energy is produced by nuclear .... This is where atomic nuclei .... to form .... (3)

b Which element was the first to form in the universe? (1)

c The red super giant star Betelgeuse is likely to explode as a supernova and then form a neutron star. The red supergiant VV Cephei is likely to explode as a supernova and become a black hole. What causes the fate of these two stars to be different? (2)

d Which type of star produces all the elements up to iron? (1)

e The diagram shows the forces acting within a star. The grey arrows show the outward force created by radiation. Star A is stable but in star B the outward force has become less.

  i What type of force is counteracting the outward force from radiation? (1)

  ii What is about to happen to star B? (1)

  iii Suggest why the force from radiation may suddenly decrease. (2)

3 *In this question you will be assessed on using good English, organising information clearly and using specialist terms where appropriate.*

Explain how the solar system formed and why there were elements heavier than iron present when it formed. (6)

205

---

b Plutonium-239 (Pu-239) *(1 mark)*

c **i** Carbon dioxide *(1 mark)*

   ii It can have a very long half-life. *(1 mark)*

   iii One advantage from: land not used; no visual pollution; rocks shield surface from radiation; security
   One disadvantage from: more difficult to monitor or repair containers; expensive *(2 marks)*

   iv Any suitable explanation, for example: not all countries have enough wind; wind doesn't blow all the time; not enough suitable sites for wind farms. *(2 marks)*

d **i** Any **two** benefits from the following: safer than nuclear fission; accidents that release large amounts of radioactive substances are not possible; large amounts of power could be generated to meet increasing world demand; no greenhouse gases; very little waste; fuel is abundant. *(2 marks)*

   ii Any **two** of the following objections: expensive to research and develop; a working power station may be 20 to 50 years away; investment into renewables or making current methods safer and cleaner may be a better solution. *(2 marks)*

2 a The Sun's energy is produced by nuclear **fusion**. This is where atomic nuclei **join** to form **a larger one**. *(3 marks)*

b hydrogen *(1 mark)*

c VV Cephei has a greater mass than Betelgeuse. So the gravitational force on VV Cephei is larger (and the star continues to collapse). *(2 marks)*

d A main sequence star/a star during its stable period. *(1 mark)*

e **i** gravitational force *(1 mark)*

   ii Star **B** is about to collapse. *(1 mark)*

   iii Fusion stops, or is reduced, as the fuel (e.g. hydrogen) is used up. *(2 marks)*

3 There is a clear, balanced and detailed description of the formation of the solar system and why it contains elements heavier than iron. The answer shows almost faultless spelling, punctuation and grammar. It is coherent and in an organised, logical sequence. It contains a range of appropriate or relevant specialist terms used accurately. *(5–6 marks)*

There is a description of the formation of the solar system and possibly why it contains elements heavier than iron. There are some errors in spelling, punctuation and grammar. The answer has some structure and organisation. The use of specialist terms has been attempted, but not always accurately. *(3–4 marks)*

There is a brief description of either the formation of the solar system or why it contains elements heavier than iron. There is little clarity and detail. The spelling, punctuation and grammar are very weak. The answer is poorly organised with almost no specialist terms and/or their use demonstrating a general lack of understanding of their meaning. *(1–2 marks)*

No relevant content. *(0 marks)*

Examples of physics points made in the response:

- the Sun/solar system formed when enough dust
- and enough gas
- were pulled together by gravitational attraction
- smaller masses/planets also formed due to gravitational attraction
- and were attracted to the larger mass/Sun
- elements heavier than iron are formed in supernovae
- the Sun/solar system is formed from gas/dust from supernovae
- the Sun is a second-generation star.

AQA Practical suggestions

Practicals	AQA	k	📖	⚙
Using domino tracks for fission/chain reactions.	✓	✓	✓	✓

AQA Examination-style answers

1 a

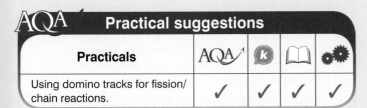

U-235 nucleus

(3 marks)

AQA Examination-style answers

1 a $a = \dfrac{v - u}{t} = 0.3/0.6$

$= 0.5 \, m/s^2$ (allow negative sign) *(2 marks)*

b In a closed system, the total momentum before an event is equal to the total momentum after the event. *(2 marks)*

c $m_1 \times v_1 = m_2 \times v_2$

$0.15 \times -0.3 = 0.0045 \times v_2$

$v_2 = 0.045/0.0045$

$= 10 \, m/s$ *(3 marks)*

d $E_k = \frac{1}{2} \times m \times v^2 = \frac{1}{2} \times 0.15 \times 0.3^2$

$= 0.00675 \, J$ *(2 marks)*

e i $k = \dfrac{F}{e}$

$= 23/0.02$

$= 1150 \, N/m$ *(3 marks)*

ii elastic potential energy to kinetic energy and to sound/heating of surroundings;
loss of GPE of ball *(2 marks)*

2 a Adding a component in parallel will reduce the original resistance because there is an additional path for the current. *(2 marks)*

b 4 V *(1 mark)*

c i $I = \dfrac{V}{R}$

$= 8/18 = 0.44 \, A$ *(1 mark)*

ii $0.44/2 = 0.22 \, A$ *(2 marks)*

d i Less bright
Resistance between B and C increases so resistance of circuit increases
So current fails *(3 marks)*

ii $18 + 18 = 36 \, \Omega$ *(1 mark)*

iii $I = \dfrac{V}{R} = 12/36$

$= 0.33 \, A$ *(2 marks)*

iv $P = I \times V = 0.333 \times 12$

$= 4 \, W$ *(2 marks)*

e $t = \dfrac{Q}{I}$

$= 500/0.333 = 1500 \, s$ *(2 marks)*

3 a i the isotope can be split by the absorption of a neutron. *(2 marks)*

ii Every 24 200 years, the number of nuclei (the count rate) would half. *(2 marks)*

iii halve 0.8 kg three times to get 0.1 kg (3 half-lives)
after 3 half-lives, 0.7 kg of U-235 is present
$3 \times 24\,200 = 72\,600$ years *(3 marks)*

iv No effect *(1 mark)*

b In supernovae large stars explode at the end of their lives. This causes fusion of lighter elements into heavier elements such as uranium. *(3 marks)*

c Any one of the following sources of background radiation: cosmic rays/plants/air/building materials/food *(1 mark)*

d $^{239}_{94}Pu \rightarrow \, ^{235}_{92}U + \, ^{4}_{2}\alpha$ (or He) *(6 marks)*

e protostar, main sequence star, red giant, white dwarf, black dwarf *(5 marks)*

4 There is a clear, balanced and detailed description of the main results of this experiment and why these results led Rutherford to suggest the existence of the atomic nucleus. The answer shows almost faultless spelling, punctuation and grammar. It is coherent and in an organised, logical sequence. It contains a range of appropriate or relevant specialist terms used accurately. *(5–6 marks)*

1 A toy cannon uses a spring to fire a metal ball bearing.

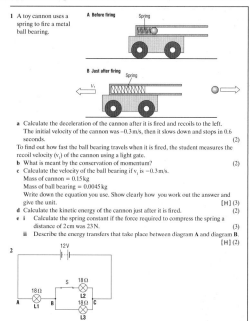

A Before firing Spring

B Just after firing Spring

a Calculate the deceleration of the cannon after it is fired and recoils to the left. The initial velocity of the cannon was –0.3 m/s, then it slows down and stops in 0.6 seconds. (2)

To find out how fast the ball bearing travels when it is fired, the student measures the recoil velocity (v_1) of the cannon using a light gate.

b What is meant by the conservation of momentum? (2)

c Calculate the velocity of the ball bearing if v_1 is –0.3 m/s.
Mass of cannon = 0.15 kg
Mass of ball bearing = 0.0045 kg
Write down the equation you use. Show clearly how you work out the answer and give the unit. [H] (3)

d Calculate the kinetic energy of the cannon just after it is fired. (2)

e i Calculate the spring constant if the force required to compress the spring a distance of 2 cm was 23 N. (3)

ii Describe the energy transfers that take place between diagram **A** and diagram **B**. [H] (2)

2

12 V

18 Ω L1 — S — 18 Ω L2
A — B — 18 Ω L3 — C

a Explain why the resistance between B and C is less than the resistance between A and B when switch S is closed. (2)

b The potential difference between A and B is 8 V when switch S is closed. What is the potential difference between B and C? (1)

c i Calculate the current through bulb L1. (1)

ii Calculate the current through bulb L3. (2)

d Switch S is opened.

i Explain what effect this will have on the brightness of bulb L1. (3)

ii Calculate the resistance between A and C. (1)

iii Show that the current through L1 is now 0.33 A. (2)

iv Calculate the total power delivered to both bulbs. (2)

e With the switch open the battery will deliver 500 C of charge before the bulbs start to dim. How long can the circuit be left on before this happens? (2)

AQA *Examiner's ti*

Both acceleration and deceleration are calcula using the same equatior The object is deceleratir if the equation gives a negative value for the acceleration.
Learn definitions and laws like the one for the law of conservation of momentum.

AQA *Examiner's ti*

Good knowledge of the circuit rules is essential t answer this question.
When you are calculating the current through a component, make sure you are using the potenti difference across that component only.

There is a description of a range of the main results of this experiment and why these results led Rutherford to suggest the existence of the atomic nucleus. There are some errors in spelling, punctuation and grammar. The answer has some structure and organisation. The use of specialist terms has been attempted, but not always accurately. *(3–4 marks)*

There is a brief description of at least one result or reason why these results led Rutherford to suggest the existence of the atomic nucleus, which has little clarity and detail. The spelling, punctuation and grammar are very weak. The answer is poorly organised with almost no specialist terms and/or their use demonstrating a general lack of understanding of their meaning. *(1–2 marks)*

No relevant content. *(0 marks)*

Examples of physics points made in the response:

- only a small number of alpha particles were deflected by a large angle

- so they must have encountered something very small

- most alpha particles travelled through gold atoms unaffected

- so most of the atom is empty space

- if all the positive charge was concentrated in a very small region

- this would provide a large enough repulsive force to deflect the alpha.

3 Plutonium-239 has a half-life of 24 200 years and decays into uranium-235 with a half-life of 703 million years. These substances are both *fissionable*.

a i Explain what is meant by *fissionable*. (2)

ii What is meant by 'a half-life of 24 200 years'? (2)

iii A sample of plutonium-239 of mass 0.8 kg is being stored. How many years will pass before the sample contains 0.7 kg of uranium-235? Show clearly how you work out your answer. (3)

iv If the sample were kept at a higher temperature and pressure, what effect would this have on your answer to part **a iii**? (1)

b Explain how a small amount of uranium-235 is found in the Earth's crust in rocks such as granite, when hardly any plutonium is found occurring naturally and nearly all of it is formed in nuclear reactors. (3)

c Name one other natural source of background radiation that we are constantly exposed to, apart from rocks. (1)

d Plutonium (Pu) has 94 protons. Copy and complete the following decay equation to show how it decays into uranium-235. [H] (6)

e List the stages below in the correct order to describe the life cycle of a star that is about the same size as the Sun. One of the stages is not part of the life cycle of this type of star. (5)

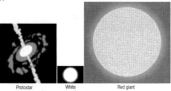

Protostar White dwarf Red giant

Black dwarf Main sequence star Supernova

4 *In this question you will be assessed on using good English, organising information clearly and using specialist terms where appropriate.*

In 1911 Ernest Rutherford published a scientific paper in which he suggested the existence of a very small region at the centre of every atom where most of the charge and mass is concentrated. Rutherford was interpreting the results of an experiment carried out by his research workers Geiger and Marsden in 1909.

Outline the main results of this experiment and explain why these results led Rutherford to suggest the existence of the atomic nucleus. (6)

AQA Examiner's tip

Tricky calculations involving half-life start to become quite straightforward when you have practised a few.

When completing any decay equation, the atomic numbers on the right must add to give the atomic number on the left. The same rule applies to the mass numbers.

AQA Examiner's tip

A question that requires an extended written answer will have 6 marks available and the quality of your written English will influence your mark. Once you have written your answer, read the question again, before reading your answer through to check that all parts of the question have been answered.

Don't just know the results of the Rutherford and Marsden scattering experiments, know why these results were so important.

Bump up your grades

P2 requires students to carry out more calculations than P1. Therefore, students who are weaker at calculations may struggle in places unless they are given plenty of practice. However, as for P1, Foundation Tier students will only have to learn to use the formulae as given in the specification, without having to rearrange. These students may benefit from working through a page of calculations on each equation that they encounter. Group work may help initially, but this must be followed up by individual work to simulate exam conditions.

Bump up your grades

There are plenty of learning aids to help students study and revise, including the Student Book, the Revision Guide and Kerboodle resources from Nelson Thornes. However, the AQA specification should not be overlooked as an essential 'tick list' for students.

AQA Examiner's comments

Higher Tier students should understand that velocity is a vector. A velocity to the right is usually treated as positive and a velocity to the left as negative. The toy cannon in Question 1, together with the cannon ball, has a momentum of zero before firing and will therefore have a collective momentum of zero afterwards. There is a great deal of footage on the internet showing various types of cannon firing where the recoil can be seen.

AQA Examiner's comments

Question 2 tests the students' understanding and application of circuit rules. Students should understand how adding or taking away components in parallel affects the resistance, even though they will not have to use the parallel resistor formula. Any number of analogies can help here. For instance, opening or closing turnstiles at a football ground, traffic or water circuits.

P3 1.1

X-rays

AQA

Specification link-up: Physics P3.1

- X-rays are part of the electromagnetic spectrum. They have a very short wavelength and cause ionisation. [P3.1.1 a)]
- X-rays can be used to diagnose and treat some medical conditions. [P3.1.1 b)]
- Precautions to be taken when X-ray machines and CT scanners are in use. [P3.1.1 c)]
- Evaluate the advantages and disadvantages of using … X-rays and computerised tomography (CT) scans. [P3.1]

Learning objectives

Students should learn:

- that X-rays are used to produce images of fractured bones or, in conjunction with contrast media, organs
- that X-rays can damage cells or cause cancer by ionisation processes
- that the denser a material is, the greater the absorption of X-rays as they pass through it
- that a CT scanner uses a series of X-ray images to construct a three-dimensional image of the body.

Learning outcomes

Most students should be able to:

- describe how X-rays pass through some materials but not others and this can be used to see the internal structure of some objects
- describe the effects of X-rays on living cells
- describe the differences between a CT scan and an X-ray photograph.

Some students should also be able to:

- explain how X-rays damage cells.

Support

- Present each student with a photocopy of an X-ray photograph (or a simplified one) so that they can label the areas where the X-rays pass through or are absorbed.

Extend

- In order to get a clear image while reducing the exposure to X-rays, image enhancements techniques are used. You could discuss the reasons behind these techniques along with the techniques themselves, including the design of the cassette and the shielding used on the machines, patients and doctors.

Lesson structure

Starters

What's up Doc? – Show the students a range of X-ray photographs and ask them to describe the problems they see. If you don't have originals, then you can find some obvious ones on the internet. Start with obvious fractures; the students should already know that this is what an X-ray is typically for, but then move on to dental X-rays (wired jaws are good) and even contrast medium based images such as a barium meal. *(5 minutes)*

Definitions – Show the students the key words for this spread, 'absorb, reflect, emit', and ask them to write down their own definitions. These can include diagrams. Students can be extended by insisting on clear descriptions and demonstrating that they understand that electromagnetic radiation can be partially reflected by surfaces or partially absorbed as they pass through materials; a vital concept for this topic. You may support students by providing completed, or partially completed, diagrams reminding them of the processes. *(10 minutes)*

Main

- Start by discussing X-rays using as many images as you can. The images are negative; the areas on the film image that are black have been exposed to X-rays while the white areas have not. This shows that the X-rays have **penetrated** the soft tissues but have been **absorbed** by bones.

- This can lead to a discussion of why X-rays are harmful; the energy is absorbed in the body and damages cells, particularly cells in bones. You can also discuss the reason X-rays are absorbed by bone; it contains materials that are denser, particularly calcium. This absorption by metals can be explained by using X-rays of fillings where the metal absorbs virtually all of the X-rays. X-rays of plates and screws in legs always fascinate.

- You can now discuss why *simple* X-rays are not useful in studying organs; the X-rays will pass through and there will be no contrast. This leads directly to the idea that you can add a 'dense' material that passes through one organ and so you can image the organ. Discuss the properties of the contrast medium; it must pass into the correct organ, must not be too poisonous and must be opaque to X-rays.

- When talking about the safety precautions, you might ask the students what a radiographer, dentist or doctor does when taking an X-ray. They stand behind shields of lead or even move out of the room. You can discuss why a radiologist has to do this but the patient does not; the radiologist operates the machine many times each day and the dose would be large without the protection.

- In X-ray therapy you can describe the destruction of cells by higher **intensity** beams of X-rays. The energy is absorbed more easily because the X-rays are lower frequency (lower energy) instead of mostly passing through the body. This links back to the energy of electromagnetic waves.

- Students may have seen CT scanners in hospitals or at least on television. The function is fairly straightforward; a model is built up from dozens of images taken from different angles. The dose given by a CT scanner is therefore much larger than a single X-ray. This is one of the reasons why they are not used routinely to scan for simple injuries such as a broken arm.

Plenaries

Radiation danger – Give the students the hazard symbol for ionising radiation and explain what it is supposed to represent. The students should add a list of safety precautions that might be taken in a radiology department to the symbol; perhaps as icons below it. *(5 minutes)*

X-ray safety – Ask the students to describe safety procedures, such as film badges and lead-lined garments, that need to be used by patients, dentists or doctors to reduce or monitor exposure to X-rays or gamma rays. Extend students by asking them to discuss the reasons in details and the consequences of failing to follow the instructions. These should include the reasons the precautions have to be taken and why it is safe for a patient to receive a dose but not for the doctor. You can also support students by getting them to match up the precaution with the reason why it is taken. *(10 minutes)*

Medical applications of physics

P3 1.1 — X-rays

Learning objectives

- What do we use X-rays in hospitals for?
- Why are X-rays dangerous?
- What can we say about the absorption of X-rays when they pass through the body?
- What is a CT scan?

Have you ever broken an arm or a leg? If you have, you will have gone to your local hospital for an X-ray photograph. X-rays are electromagnetic waves at the short-wavelength end of the electromagnetic spectrum. They are produced in an X-ray tube when fast-moving electrons hit a target. Their wavelengths are about the same as the diameter of an atom.

To make a **radiograph** or X-ray photograph, X-rays from an X-ray tube are directed at the patient. A lightproof cassette containing a photographic film or a **flat-panel detector** is placed on the other side of the patient.

- When the X-ray tube is switched on, X-rays from the tube pass through the part of the patient's body under investigation.
- X-rays pass through soft tissue but they are absorbed by bones, teeth and metal objects that are not too thin. The parts of the film or the detector that the X-rays reach become darker than the other parts. So the bones appear lighter than the surrounding tissue which appears dark. The radiograph shows a 'negative image' of the bones. A hole or a cavity in a tooth shows up as a dark area in the bright image of the tooth.
- An organ that consists of soft tissue can be filled with a substance called a **contrast medium** which absorbs X-rays easily. This enables the internal surfaces in the organ to be seen on the radiograph. For example, to obtain a radiograph of the stomach, the patient is given a barium meal before the X-ray machine is used. The barium compound is a good absorber of X-rays.
- Lead 'absorber' plates between the tube and the patient stop X-rays reaching other parts of the body. Lead is used because it is a good absorber of X-rays. The X-rays reaching the patient pass through a gap between the plates.
- A flat-panel detector is a small screen that contains a **CCD (charge-coupled device)**. The sensors in the CCD are covered by a layer of a substance that converts X-rays to light. The light rays then create electronic signals in the sensors that are sent to a computer which displays a digital X-ray image.

a Why is a crack in a bone visible on a radiograph (X-ray image)?

Figure 1 a Taking a chest X-ray **b** A chest X-ray

Figure 2 Spot the break

Safety matters

X-radiation, as well as gamma radiation, is dangerous because it ionises substances it passes through. High doses kill living cells. Low doses can cause cell mutation and cancerous growth. There is no evidence of a safe limit below which living cells would not be damaged.

Workers who use equipment or substances that produce X-radiation (or alpha, beta or gamma radiation) must wear a film badge. If the badge is overexposed to such radiation, its wearer is stopped from working with the equipment.

b Why does a film badge have a plastic case, and not a metal case?

X-ray therapy

Doctors use X-ray therapy to destroy cancerous tumours in the body. Thick plates between the X-ray tube and the body stop X-rays from reaching healthy body tissues. A gap between the plates allows X-rays through to reach the tumour. X-rays for therapy are shorter in wavelength than X-rays used for imaging.

c Why is it important to stop X-rays reaching healthy body tissues?

The CT scanner

A computerised tomography scanner (**CT scanner**) produces a digital image of any cross-section through the body. It can also be used to construct a three-dimensional (3-D) image of an organ.

Figure 3 shows an end-view of a CT scanner. The patient lies stationary on a bed that is in a ring of detectors.

- The X-ray tube automatically moves round the inside of the ring in small steps.
- At each position, X-rays from the tube pass through the patient and reach the detector ring.
- Electronic signals from the detector are recorded by a computer until the tube has moved round the ring.
- The computer displays a digital image of the scanned area.

Each detector receives X-rays that have travelled through different types of tissue. The detector signal depends on:

- the different types of tissue along the X-ray path
- how far the X-rays pass through each type of tissue.

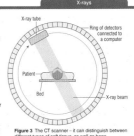

Figure 3 The CT scanner – it can distinguish between different types of soft tissue, as well as bone

Table 1 Comparison of a CT scanner with an ordinary X-ray machine

	CT scanner	Ordinary X-ray machine
Image distinguishes between bone and soft tissue	Yes	Yes
Image distinguishes between different types of soft tissue	Yes	No
Three-dimensional image	Yes	No
Radiation dose	CT scanner gives a much higher dose than an ordinary X-ray machine	
Cost	CT equipment cost is much greater than an ordinary X-ray machine	

∞ links

For more information about scanners used in hospitals, see P3 3.6 A physics case study.

Figure 4 A film badge tells you how much ionising radiation the wearer has received. Who might wear these?

Key points

- X-rays are used in hospitals:
  1 to make images and CT scans
  2 to destroy tumours at or near the body surface.
- X-rays can damage living tissue when they pass through it.
- X-rays are absorbed more by bones and teeth than by soft tissues.
- CT scans distinguish between different types of soft tissue as well as between bone (or teeth) and soft tissue.

Summary questions

1 Copy and complete **a** to **c** using the words below:
   absorb   damage   penetrate
   a X-rays .... thin metal sheets.
   b Thick lead plates will .... X-rays.
   c X-rays .... living tissue.

2 When an X-ray photograph is taken, why is it necessary:
   a to place the patient between the X-ray tube and the film cassette?
   b to have the film in a lightproof cassette?
   c to shield those parts of the patient not under investigation from X-rays? Explain what would happen to healthy cells.

3 State one advantage and one disadvantage of a CT scanner in comparison with an ordinary X-ray machine.

Further teaching suggestions

ICT link-up

- If you have no other source of X-rays, then the internet is a great source. To make them more realistic you could photocopy the images onto transparencies. Search on an image search engine for phrases like 'X-ray jaw' and 'X-ray chest' to find particular injuries. You could also find the analyses of the images, so you know what is wrong.

X-rays

- It may be possible to acquire an X-ray cassette from a local hospital or even dentist. They may also be able to provide help with obtaining X-ray images which are much better to handle than copies on paper. There may be confidentiality issues to deal with, but it is worth asking.

Answers to in-text questions

a A crack is a gap that X-rays can pass through.

b To keep the light out without stopping the X-rays.

c They would damage or kill living cells or cause cancer.

Summary answers

1 **a** penetrate
  b absorb
  c damage

2 **a** To make an image of the patient's bones on the film.
  b To stop light from affecting the film.
  c To prevent damage by the X-rays to the parts of the body not being X-rayed. High doses can kill living cells and low doses can cause cell mutation and cancerous growth.

3 **Advantage:** A CT scan distinguishes between different types of soft tissue; an ordinary X-ray machine does not. (Or a CT scanner can give a three-dimensionsal image whereas an ordinary X-ray image is two-dimensional.)
  Disadvantage: The radiation dose from a CT scan is much greater than from an ordinary X-ray imaging machine. (Or CT scanners are much more expensive to buy and operate than ordinary X-ray machines.)

P3 1.2

Ultrasound

Learning objectives

Students should learn:

- that ultrasound is sound with a frequency above 20 000 Hz and cannot be heard by humans
- that ultrasonic waves are reflected by the different layers of tissue and fluid in a body and so can be used to make measurements or produce images of internal organs
- that ultrasound does not cause ionisation and so it much safer than X-rays.

Learning outcomes

Most students should be able to:

- compare ultrasound to audible sound waves
- explain how ultrasound can be used for medical scanning and the advantages of ultrasound over X-ray techniques
- work out the distance between interfaces.

Some students should also be able to:

- rearrange the $s = v \times t$ equation to solve problems. [HT only]

Answers to in-text questions

a The material absorbs some of the ultrasonic sound from the loudspeaker.

b On the oscilloscope display, B is nearer to A than it is to C.

Support

- Students can be given a cloze activity to summarise the uses of ultrasound in medical physics. This should include details of the frequency ranges used and the techniques.

Extend

- Some of the students can be stretched by analysing an oscilloscope trace to determine distances. They can be given the speed of sound in materials and then read the time taken for sound to pass through the material from the trace and so determine the thickness. They will need to realise that the sound passes through the material twice (there and back again) and take this into account when working out distance travelled.

AQA   Specification link-up: Physics P3.1

- Electronic systems can be used to produce ultrasound waves, which have a frequency higher than the upper limit of hearing for humans. [P3.1.2 a)]
- Ultrasound waves are partially reflected when they meet a boundary between two different media. The time taken for the reflections to reach a detector can be used to determine how far away such a boundary is. [P3.1.2 b)]
- Calculation of the distance between interfaces in various media. $s = v \times t$. [P3.1.2 c)]
- Ultrasound waves can be used in medicine. [P3.1.2 d)]
- Evaluate the advantages and disadvantages of using ultrasound, X-rays … [P3.1]
- Compare the medical use of ultrasound and X-rays. [P3.1]

Lesson structure

Starters

Mystery scans – Show the students some ultrasound scans of things other than a fetus, and see if they can identify the organs involved. Some students will not know the shapes of even the most major organs as they seldom look like the simple diagrams used in many books. *(5 minutes)*

Echo – Ask the students to work out how far away a cliff face is if, when you shout, the echo takes 4 seconds to arrive and the speed of sound is 330 m/s. Extend the students by asking them to perform the same type of calculation for a sound wave travelling in water where the speed of sound is 1000 m/s; this should help them to understand that the ultrasound pulses in the lesson travel at different speeds in different materials. To support students, you can provide a calculation frame including a diagram. *(10 minutes)*

Main

- Start with a basic recap of what an echo is, then lead on to the idea that if we time the echo, we can often work out how far away the reflecting surface is. You should be able to find suitable video clips of an ultrasound scan taking place. Most often these are B-scans that actually create images but it is useful to show that the transducer has to be placed in close contact with the skin or organ using a gel to improve the contact.

- When discussing ultrasonic scanners, the students need to know that certain tissues reflect different amounts of the signal and this is how they can be told apart. The boundaries between the materials are important; when there is a big change of material such as from muscle to bone, there is a larger reflection. The size of the reflections can be used to work out what the materials are; e.g. fat, muscle, bone.

- The thickness of materials is judged from the time it takes the sound wave to pass through them. You might want to extend students into performing calculations based on timing traces; see the extension material.

- Try to find some images other than the traditional baby scans, e.g. kidney and heart scans, to show that there is more than one use for the technique.

- The students may have to be reminded what ionisation is and why it is harmful when discussing the relative safety of ultrasound compared to X-rays. The example of fetal ultrasound scans is the easiest one to use.

- When covering ultrasound therapy, you can demonstrate sound waves being used to vibrate objects by placing a loudspeaker next to a glass of water and using the vibrations to create patterns on the surface. Adjusting the frequency might even lead to resonance, making larger waves. Explain that these tiny vibrations can be used to 'shatter' an object when the frequency is matched to the properties of the object.

Plenary

Comparing light and sound – Make a detailed comparison of light and sound waves. This should include the nature of the waves (mechanical, electromagnetic) and their interaction with matter. Extend students by asking for detailed examples and comparisons such as why X-rays are ionising while sound waves are not. Provide partially completed mind maps to support students. *(10 minutes)*

Practical support

Demonstrating the range of hearing

Using a signal generator, you can demonstrate the range of human hearing. Simply connect it to a suitable loudspeaker and gradually increase the frequency until the students cannot hear the sound anymore. Connect the signal generator to a CRO to show the changes in the waveform as the frequency is increased. The best way to measure the upper limit of the student's hearing is to get them to keep silent, raise their hand and then put it down again when they can no longer hear the sound and write down the frequency. You can also decrease the frequency slowly and ask the students to raise their hands when they can hear the sound again. You can then improve the precision of the measurements by calculating the mean of these two values and perhaps finding an overall class mean.

Testing ultrasound

This experiment shows the properties of ultrasound well, and can be carried out as a demonstration or a full class practical if equipment is available.

Equipment and materials required

For each group: oscilloscope, signal generator, two microphones, loudspeaker and a range of thin materials such as an aluminium plate, plywood, rubber sheets, etc.

Details

The first part of the experiment is simply a matter of using the scales on the oscilloscope well. Some may be confused due to the high frequency. To carry out the absorption tests, the students simply put the different materials over the microphone making sure that there aren't any obvious gaps. Reflection can be tested by arranging a material at 45° between the loudspeaker and microphone; there should be a clear reflection from solid surfaces. Partial reflection and partial transmission can be shown by placing a microphone behind the 45° reflector, to measure transmitted amplitude and another in front of it to measure the reflected amplitude.

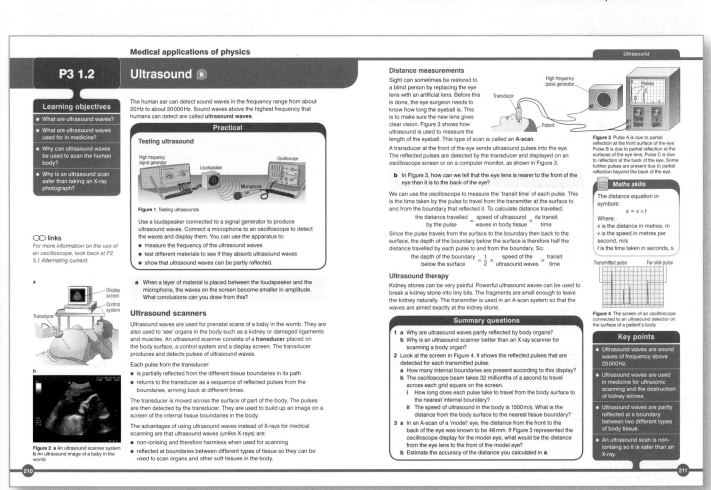

Further teaching suggestions

Low frequency sound

- Ask: 'What is sound with a frequency lower than 10 Hz called? Can any animals hear it and does it have any uses?'

ICT link-up

- The students can use the internet to find out about the frequency ranges that different species can detect. They could also look into how the species can generate such high frequency noises.

Summary answers

1 a The organs have a different density to the surrounding tissue. So ultrasound is reflected at the tissue/organ boundaries.

b X-rays cannot differentiate different tissues easily and ultrasound does not cause damaging ionisation.

2 a 2, if the far-side pulse is not counted.

b i 42 millionths of a second

ii 0.063 m

3 a 15 mm

b ± 2–3 mm

P3 1.3

Refractive index

Learning objectives

Students should learn:

- that the refractive index of a substance is the ratio of the sine of the angle of incidence to the sine of the angle of refraction as a ray enters the material
- how to measure the refractive index of a material.

Learning outcomes

Most students should be able to:

- describe an experiment demonstrating refraction of light in a glass block
- construct accurate ray diagrams showing refraction in a range of situations
- calculate the refractive index of a material from the angles of incidence and refraction.

Some students should also be able to:

- calculate a second angle from one angle and refractive index [HT only].

Support

- Worksheets showing the position of the semicircular blocks and suitable incident rays can be used to support the practical work.

Extend

- Students will be performing calculations involving sines of angles for the first time. You should test out their skills with a few questions about right-angled triangles first. You can also ask the students to design a table to record the results of the experiment (without letting them see the example in the Student Book) to build up their skills in recording information. Students will often write down a very large number of significant figures when finding the sine of an angle like 20°, so take the opportunity to discuss the appropriate number of significant figures.

$\mathcal{AQA}$

Specification link-up: Physics P3.1

- Refraction is the change of direction of light as it passes from one medium to another. *[P3.1.3 a)]*
- ... Refractive index $= \dfrac{\sin i}{\sin r}$ *[P3.1.3 c)]*

Controlled Assessment: P4.3 Collect primary and secondary data. *[P4.3.2 a) b) c) d)]*; P4.4 Select and process primary and secondary data. *[P4.4.2 a) b) c)]*

Lesson structure

Starters

Refraction demonstrations – Start by demonstrating some effects of refraction to recap the behaviour of light. Place a pencil in a glass of water and note the apparent 'breaking'. Place a coin at the bottom of a cup so it can't be seen and then add water until the coin appears. You can use a video camera to show these things to a whole class more clearly. *(5 minutes)*

Optical preparation – Let the students demonstrate their skills using ray boxes, rulers and mirrors. They should set up the equipment for the later practical along with some mirrors to demonstrate the law of reflection. The students should show how to set up the equipment and record the data clearly. Support students by providing some of the instructions or extend them by asking them to collect enough evidence to establish the precision and certainty of measurements. *(10 minutes)*

Main

- The students should have encountered refraction in KS3, but the initial experiment can be used to revisit the basics and to go much further into Snell's law.
- Start with the practical task giving the students as much instruction as they need. The focus should be on collecting accurate evidence as you are attempting to verify an established law of physics using the data. Demonstrate the technique and insist that the students try to measure the angle as accurately as possible.
- To measure the angle, the students need to draw the ray lines with a ruler; use the cross-drawing technique but make sure that the students are drawing the crosses far enough apart to ensure that lines are straight and reach the point of refraction. They should number each incident line and pair it up with a refracted line so that they do not get confused with the large number of lines.
- The results should be straightforward for the basic experiment; students then move on to verifying Snell's law and this involves finding the sine of the measured angles. Take time in showing these calculations and be methodical in completing the table. The results of the calculation will show some variation, so you can discuss the causes of this: experimental errors (mainly inaccuracy in measuring angles) and some rounding errors during calculations. There should be a fairly close fit if the students have been careful.
- You can now discuss the measured property; the refractive index; most groups should have the same value (or near enough). If you provide one group with a different material (Perspex instead of glass) then they will have a different answer at this stage, giving you the opportunity to discuss the fact that different materials have different refractive indices.
- Calculations are essential here, so use the worked example and a couple of others. For some students, it may be difficult to perform calculations including sines; check with the mathematics department to see how they are used there.
- If you did not let the students explore the effect when the ray leaves the block, then demonstrate that refraction also occurs when the ray leaves the block.

Plenaries

Comparing light and sound – The students should make a comparison of light and sound waves. *(5 minutes)*

Maths error – Calculations are essential in this topic. Use the last part of the lesson to support students by going through a range of examples of refraction calculations (calculations of n from two angles are needed by all students; Higher Tier students should be able to rearrange the equation). Extend the Higher Tier students with this calculation: A ray of light in glass (refractive index 1.52) hits the back surface at an angle of 60°, what is the angle of refraction as it leaves the block? They should find that the calculation gives a maths error on their calculators, so demonstrate what happens in reality; they should see that the ray does not refract; it reflects inside the glass block. This will be a good starting point for the next lesson. *(10 minutes)*

Practical support

Investigating how the angle of refraction varies with the angle of incidence

This experiment can be used to find the pattern in refraction or for verifying Snell's law for some of the students.

Equipment and materials required
For each group: ray box, single slit, semicircular glass (or Perspex) block, protractor, ruler and pencil.

Details
The students place the block on a large sheet of paper. It is best to mark off the position by drawing around the block in case it moves and then drawing on the normal using a protractors and ruler. They then position the ray box so that they can shine rays into the block from different angles as shown in the diagram. When they do this,

they should shine the rays at the centre of the flat surface where they have marked the normal. When they shine the rays into the block, they should mark on the path of the incident ray by drawing two accurate crosses along its path, they should also do this for the exit ray. They then use a ruler to draw the paths to the point of refraction and measure the angles using the protractor.

The students can also see how refraction occurs when the ray leaves the glass block and enters air. To do this they should shine the ray, so it passes into the block perpendicular to the curved surface; this means that there will be no change in direction as the ray enters. When the ray leaves via the flat surface, there will be noticeable refraction. This will lead on to the idea of total internal reflection needed for the next topic.

Safety: Make sure glass blocks do not have any sharp edges.

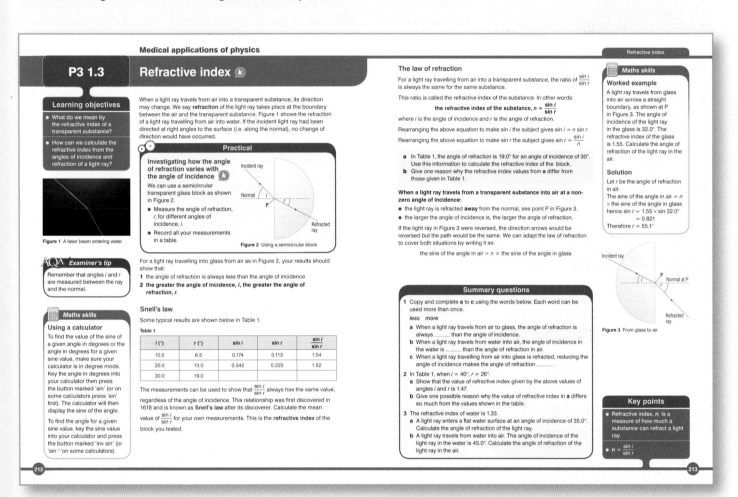

Answers to in-text questions

a 1.54

b The angles were not measured precisely enough.

Summary answers

1 a less

b more

c less

2 a sin 40/sin 26 = 1.47

b The angle of refraction was measured incorrectly and the measurement should have been smaller.

3 a 25.5°

b 70.1°

P3 1.4 The endoscope

AQA

Specification link-up: Physics P3.1

- Total internal reflection and critical angle. Refractive index $= \dfrac{1}{\sin c}$ [P3.1.5 a)]
- Visible light can be sent along optical fibres. [P3.1.5 b)]
- The laser as an energy source for cutting, cauterising and burning. [P3.1.5 c)]

Learning objectives

Students should learn:

- how internal reflection takes place
- that during total internal reflection all of the energy of the ray is reflected back into the material
- that the relationship between the critical angle and the refractive index $n = \dfrac{1}{\sin c}$ [HT only]
- how an endoscope can be used to examine internal organs.

Learning outcomes

Most students should be able to:

- draw a range of diagrams demonstrating total internal reflection
- state that total internal reflection occurs when the angle of incidence is greater than the critical angle
- describe the use of endoscopes in medicine.

Some students should also be able to:

- calculate the critical angle of a material using angles of incidence and refraction [HT only]
- calculate the refractive index using the critical angle. [HT only]

Answers to in-text questions

a 90°
b 1.47

Support

- The students should carry out a total internal reflection experiment with the equipment described in the last section. They should plan this based on their previous experience; a worksheet with hints could be provided for them.

Extend

- Total internal reflection by a prism is often used in optical devices instead of using a mirror. The students can find out why prisms are used in more expensive optical devices and the advantages they hold over simple mirrors. In future lessons, some could go further and look at the use of optics in astronomy, where some telescopes use curved mirrors systems, while others use lenses.

Lesson structure

Starters

Innards – Ask the students to list all the ways that doctors can find out what is happening inside the body. They should be able to come up with ideas such as: feeling, opening (surgery, autopsy), X-rays, ultrasound, CAT scan, MRI (NMR) imaging and possibly more. *(5 minutes)*

Laser – Show some video footage about lasers from films or TV. You can then discuss the reality of these things shown with the students – can lasers really do what is shown? Extend students by asking them to link the power of the laser to the frequency of the light radiation; link this to why UV lasers are often used for cutting or cauterising. You can support students by limiting the discussion to the idea of concentrating the energy onto a small area; something similar can be shown by using a magnifying glass to start a small fire. *(10 minutes)*

Main

- Start by demonstrating the properties of an optical fibre as described in 'Practical support'. This lets you question the students about rays travelling in straight lines and how light can be made to follow a curved path.

- Move on to investigate a single total internal reflection using a semicircular glass block as described in 'Practical support'. At each stage, discuss the angles and especially the critical angle where the ray is 'just' escaping. Some students may notice that there is a spectrum formed at this point, so you can discuss with them the fact that each wavelength has a slightly different critical angle. The Higher Tier students should now try some calculations of critical angle.

- There are model optical fibres that can be used to show the path of a ray along a small curve; use one to show the basics of how a fibre operates.

- Medical endoscopes are difficult to find, but you can buy simpler ones that are used in plumbing and electrical work for under £50. These often connect to a computer through a USB, so you can show the video to the whole class. They are definitely not for medical use, so don't even try to look into somebody's mouth! Take a peek into a closed cupboard instead; you could plant some surprises inside before the lesson.

- Describe the structure and use of the medical endoscope, making a point of describing the bundles of fibres needed to generate a picture. If you want to go into a bit more detail, you can mention that the endoscope should have a tube to pass water into it so that the end can be cleaned and there could be a tool to collect samples (biopsies). The students need to understand that the endoscope can also allow laser light to pass into the body allowing cutting and cauterising. This means that some types of surgery can be carried out just with the endoscope.

- If you have a laser, you should demonstrate one. Discuss the fact that although the beam is not very powerful (it does not carry much energy), it can be harmful because the energy is focused on a small spot giving a very high intensity. You can mention high intensity lasers (or show some pictures of a few) and discuss that the intensity can be high enough to cause cutting of metal or tissue in surgery.

Plenaries

Mystery object – Use your endoscope to explore a bag containing mystery objects and see which student can identify them first. Use some pieces from a model body like a model lung and stomach. *(5 minutes)*

Building a periscope – Students can be asked to demonstrate how a periscope operates using two 45° prisms. They would be expected to use a ray box to show the path a ray (or three) passes through the system. You can extend this design by asking the students to build a working device along with one based on mirrors to compare their function or support students by giving them suitable instructions and designs. *(10 minutes)*

Practical support

Fibre optics

This demonstration shows that light can be made to travel in curved paths, even though it is travelling in straight lines.

Equipment and materials required

A bright white light source (a good torch), a long (several metres) length of optical fibre.

Details

The fibre should be looped around a few obstacles but not too tightly; a radius of 10 cm minimum. Simply flash the light into one end of the curved fibre and let the students see the flashes at the other end. You may need to pass the end around, so that all students can see the effect.

Investigating total internal reflection

To extend students, you can ask them to find the critical angle of a few materials using a few transparent blocks.

Equipment and materials required

Ray box, power supply, single slit, protractor, ruler, pencil, glass block, semicircular block.

Details

The students need to set up the equipment so that they can find the critical angle. The students can position the block on a sheet of paper and then mark its position. They can shine rays through the curved side of the glass block targeted directly at the centre of the flat face. This ensures that the ray enters the block perpendicular to the surface and so there is no refraction when the ray enters. They can shine the ray at increasing angles measuring the angle of refraction until they encounter total internal reflection. If time is available, they can use blocks made of different materials to note the different critical angles.

Safety: Make sure glass blocks do not have any sharp edges.

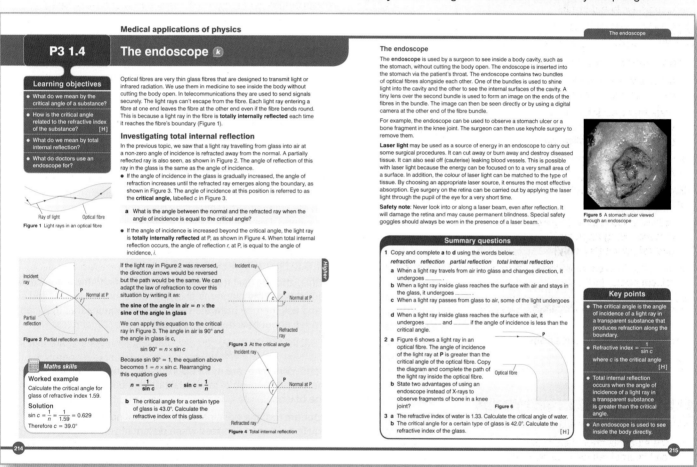

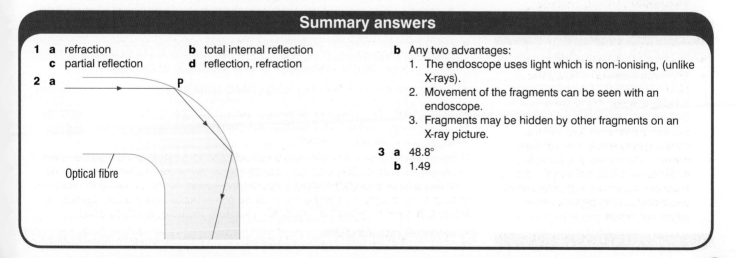

Summary answers

1 **a** refraction   **b** total internal reflection
   c partial reflection   **d** reflection, refraction

2 **a**

Optical fibre

     b Any two advantages:
1. The endoscope uses light which is non-ionising, (unlike X-rays).
2. Movement of the fragments can be seen with an endoscope.
3. Fragments may be hidden by other fragments on an X-ray picture.

3 **a** 48.8°
   b 1.49

P3 1.5

Lenses

AQA

Specification link-up: Physics P3.1

- A lens forms an image by refracting light. *[P3.1.3 b)]*
- In a convex or converging lens, parallel rays of light are brought to a focus at the principal focus. The distance from the lens to the principal focus is called the focal length … *[P3.1.3 c)]*
- The nature of an image is defined by its size relative to the object, whether it is upright or inverted relative to the object and whether it is real or virtual. *[P3.1.3 d)]*
- The nature of the image produced by a converging lens for an object placed at different distances from the lens. *[P3.1.3 e)]*
- The use of a converging lens as a magnifying glass. *[P3.1.3 f)]*
- The magnification produced by a lens is calculated using the equation:

$$\text{magnification} = \frac{\text{image height}}{\text{object height}}\ [P3.1.3\ i)]$$

- Draw and interpret ray diagrams in order to determine the nature of the image. *[P3.1]*

Controlled Assessment: P4.4 Select and process primary and secondary data. *[P4.4.2 a) b) c)]*

Learning objectives

Students should learn:

- that a converging lens is a lens that refracts parallel light rays together, so that they are brought together at its principal focus
- that a converging lens can be used in a magnifying glass
- that a diverging lens refracts parallel light rays apart, so that they seem to have come from its principal focus.

Learning outcomes

Most students should be able to:

- draw a diagram showing the ray paths for converging and diverging lenses
- describe the images formed by converging and diverging lenses
- calculate the magnification of the image formed by a lens.

Some students should also be able to:

- calculate the size of an image formed by a lens given its magnification and the size of the object. [HT only]

Answers to in-text questions

a A 5 cm focal length lens.
b Inverted.
c To make it appear much larger, so any flaws can be seen.

Support

- You can support students by providing some partially completed ray diagrams to complete. This should be for both the converging and diverging lenses, and the students should add labels such as principal focus and focal length.

Extend

- Students could look into lens power and magnification in more detail. They could find out how lens power is measured with the 'dioptre' (D) and the students can also find out about the relationship between the focal length and the power. Ask: 'What is the difference between a lens of power +5 D and one of power −5 D?'

To extend students even further, you might like to tackle the experiment about focal length and magnification.

Lesson structure

Starters

Sorted – Give the students a pile of different lenses of as many different forms as you can. Ask them to sort them into two or three lines based on criteria they make up themselves (such as shape) and explain the criteria to you. After they have done this, they can sort the lenses again using different criteria. Discuss the sorting exercise with the class and see if any have found converging and diverging. To extend this task, you can use ray boxes for some of the students to test the lenses with, whereas to support other students you might provide some different criteria to help with the sorting. *(5 minutes)*

Top quality diagrams – In this, and the next topic, high-quality ray diagrams are essential. Give the students some poorly drawn ray diagrams showing reflection, refraction, and so on from previous lessons, and ask them to draw the best quality diagrams that they can. They should make a set of rules about how ray diagrams are drawn. *(10 minutes)*

Main

- The terms 'converging' and 'diverging' are more appropriate than 'convex' and 'concave' to describe the overall function of lenses, although students need to know both names for each type of lens.

- Other key words are important too; the principal focus (or focal point) needs explaining; this can be quite hard to understand when describing a diverging lens. Try to explain that this is the point the rays seem to be coming from after they have been refracted.

- Good-quality ray diagrams are essential, so enforce strict rules about how to draw. If you draw any diagrams on the board yourself, you should also use a ruler end ensure the rays are exactly how they should be. Even though the refraction takes place at the front and back surface of a lens, only one refraction should be drawn; i.e. the overall refraction at the centre of the lens.

- Using the experiment, the students should be able to find out about the two situations described in the Student Book. A series of measurements can be made and recorded, developing the 'How Science Works' skills of processing primary data.

- Let the students use a real magnifying glass to check its properties. They should also see the physical differences between a powerful and weak converging lens, realising a more powerful lens has a principal focus closer to the lens. A simple calculation of magnification using the formula should suffice. The students should make sure that they understand that a magnification of one means that the image and object are the same size; less than one and the image is smaller (diminished) and larger than one means the image is larger than the object. Higher Tier students can try calculations involving rearrangement of the magnification equation.

- To extend some of the students, you should suggest they perform the expanded version of the converging lens experiment that considers magnification in detail; it can require a great deal of skill.

Plenaries

Finding the focal length – Can the students design a simple experiment to find the focal length of a converging lens? What about a diverging lens? They should show simple equipment but concentrate on drawing how this should be set up. *(5 minutes)*

Spot the lens – Show the students a range of ray diagrams of optical instruments (eye, microscope, telescope, camera, projector, etc.) and ask them to spot the lenses. Students can be extended by asking them to draw ray paths through some of the lenses based on the description of the type of lenses. Others can be supported by simply asking them to categorise the lenses that they see, based on the ray paths. *(10 minutes)*

Practical support

Investigating the converging lens

This experiment works best with an optical bench of some kind, but a ruler can be used if necessary.

Equipment and materials required
For each group: a 10 cm converging lens, metre ruler, illuminated object, screen.

Details
As before, use an object of measured size such as a hole in a card with wires to help focusing. A screen of card with graph paper can be used to focus the image on and measure its dimensions. The object is placed at one end of the ruler and is lit from behind. The lens is placed at a measured distance from the object and then the screen is moved until the image is in focus. The procedure is repeated by moving either the lens or object to change the distance between them. In this way, the students can see the effect of the object distance and the focal length of the lens on the magnification.

Magnification of a converging lens – extension

By expanding the converging lens experiment, the students can find the relationship between the image distance, magnification and focal length of the lens in detail. This is a challenging experiment, suitable for the most skilled, but one that yields excellent results.

Equipment and materials required
For each group: a 10 cm converging lens, metre rule, illuminated object, screen.

Details
The students will have to find the magnification of the image for a range of image distances for a particular lens. This relationship should be given by $m = (v/f) - 1$, where m is the magnification, f the focal length of the lens and v the image distance. Plotting a graph of magnification (y-axis) against image distance (x-axis) should produce a straight line with $1/f$ as the gradient.

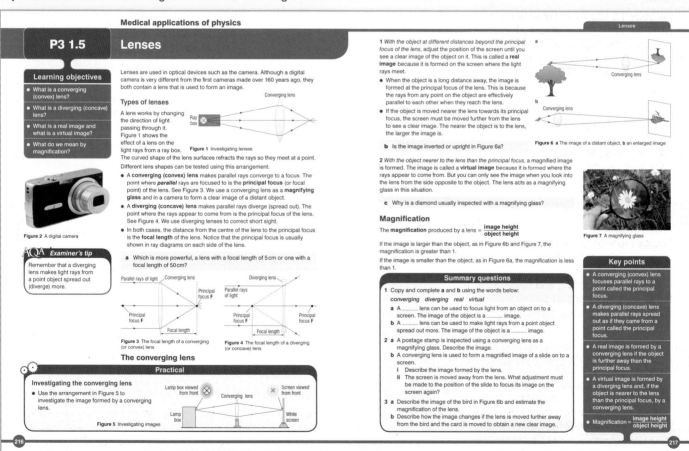

Summary answers

1 a converging, real   **b** diverging, virtual

2 a Upright, enlarged and virtual.
   b i Inverted, magnified and real.
     ii The slide must be moved towards the screen.

3 a The image is real, inverted and enlarged. Magnification = 3.
   b The image would be smaller than it was and would still be upside down.

Using lenses

P3 1.6

AQA

Specification link-up: Physics P3.1

- The nature of the image produced by a converging lens for an object placed at different distances from the lens. *[P3.1.3 e)]*
- The use of a converging lens as a magnifying glass. *[P3.1.3 f)]*
- The nature of the image produced by a concave or diverging lens. *[P3.1.3 g)]*
- The construction of ray diagrams to show the formation of images by converging and diverging lenses. *[P3.1.3 h)]*
- Draw and interpret ray diagrams in order to determine the nature of the image. *[P3.1]*

Learning objectives

Students should learn:

- how a converging lens is used in a magnifying glass and camera
- that a camera forms a real, inverted and diminished image focused on the film
- that a magnifying glass forms a virtual, erect and magnified image.

Learning outcomes

Most students should be able to:

- draw a ray diagram showing the operation of a camera
- describe the image formed when a convex lens is used as a camera or as a magnifying glass.

Some students should also be able to:

- draw a ray diagram to show how a convex lens is used as a magnifying glass.

Answers to in-text questions

a i

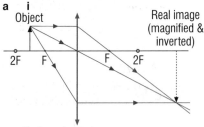

ii A projector.
b Towards the object.
c The image is always smaller than the object.

Support

- Support students by providing some partially completed ray diagrams for the lenses to complete; this should be for both the converging and diverging lenses and the students should add labels such as 'principal focus' and 'focal length'.

Extend

- Lenses are often used in combinations. The students could find out about the different devices that use these combinations, such as microscopes and telescopes. They could draw ray paths through these more complex devices to develop their skills.

Lesson structure

Starters

Magnified mystery objects – Show close-up photographs of a range of mystery objects and see who can get the most right. These can include obvious things like a fly's eye, human hairs or Velcro hooks, but you should be able to find some more interesting examples such as the hairs on a gecko's feet. *(5 minutes)*

The right path – Provide students with some diagrams of sets of three parallel rays reaching lenses, along with the description of the lens (focal length and type). Ask them to complete the diagrams to show what happens to the rays. For support, you can show the path of one of the three rays. You can also extend the students by demanding suitable scaled diagrams of the ray path or even placing two lenses in series and seeing if they can draw the consequences. *(10 minutes)*

Main

- During this topic, the students will really need to master their ray diagrams to understand how the images are formed. Drawing these ray diagrams for lenses takes time to get right, so don't rush them. The students will need to draw a few diagrams before they get the hang of it. They should remember and use the ideas from the previous lesson.

- Go through the stages of drawing a scale ray diagram step-by-step. The new term 'principal axis' needs to be introduced during this drawing. You will find some students drawing diagrams to an inappropriate scale and finding that their image is off the page; they will get better with practice. In reality, drawing any two of the three rays will show the position of the image, but drawing the third is always a good check to see if the other two are right.

- Discuss the image properties to remind the students about the term 'real' and the idea of magnification.

- If you have an old SLR camera, you can take it apart to show how it operates. In particular, you should show how the lens is moved further away from the film to bring the image into focus on it. If you have a more modern camera with auto focus, you should be able to show the lens movement by pointing it at a distant object and then a very close one. Hopefully the lens will move in and out with a reassuring 'shzzzzzt'. Later in the chapter you will need to compare the camera to the eye and revise what they have seen here.

- You can demonstrate the focusing effect of a camera using an optical bench and a screen as film (see 'Practical support'). Use the same equipment as the last lesson to show how the lens has to be moved in a camera to get a focused image. You can also use this to show that a virtual image is formed when the object is too close to the lens.

- You can show a diverging lens, but the students will not be able to form a real image with it.

Plenary

Camera developments – Discuss the advantages and disadvantage of film-based technology in comparison with digital photography. Few students will have used film cameras; you can show them some important historical images and explain how the technology has developed into the pervasive technology of today. You might even touch on people's rights over their privacy and if those rights are infringed by the large numbers of cameras around. *(5 minutes)*

Practical support

Operation of a camera

Equipment and materials required

A converging lens (~10 cm), metre ruler, illuminated object, screen.

Details

Set the screen in a fixed position at the end of the ruler or optical bench. Position the lens 10 cm in front of it, then place an illuminated object somewhere along the bench. By moving the lens, the image can be brought into focus on the screen. If the object is at a different position, then you will have to move the lens to bring it into focus again. If the object is placed within the focal length of the lens, then you should not be able to get a real image.

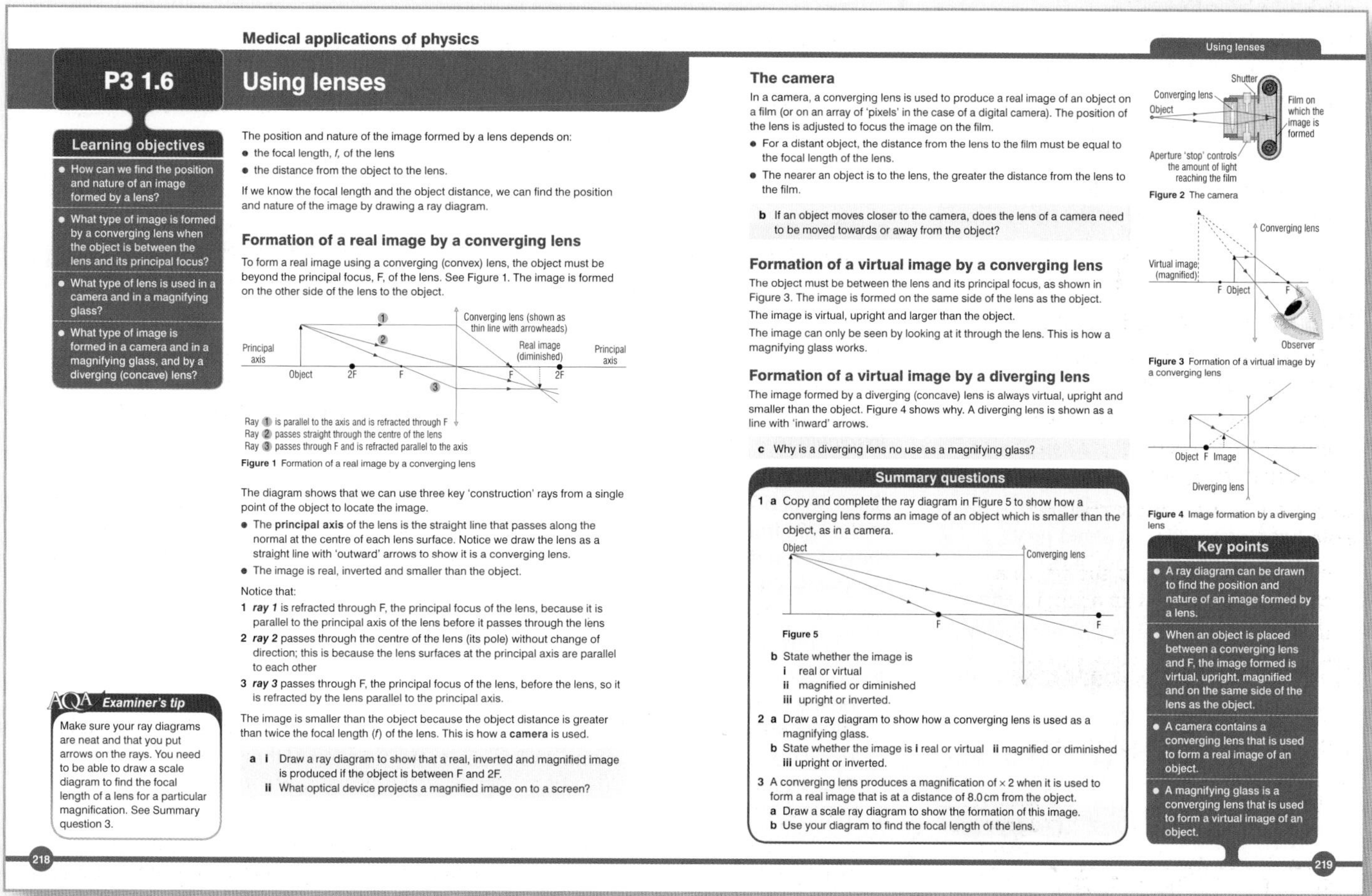

P3 1.6 Using lenses

Learning objectives

- How can we find the position and nature of an image formed by a lens?
- What type of image is formed by a converging lens when the object is between the lens and its principal focus?
- What type of lens is used in a camera and in a magnifying glass?
- What type of image is formed in a camera and in a magnifying glass, and by a diverging (concave) lens?

The position and nature of the image formed by a lens depends on:

- the focal length, f, of the lens
- the distance from the object to the lens.

If we know the focal length and the object distance, we can find the position and nature of the image by drawing a ray diagram.

Formation of a real image by a converging lens

To form a real image using a converging (convex) lens, the object must be beyond the principal focus, F, of the lens. See Figure 1. The image is formed on the other side of the lens to the object.

Ray ① is parallel to the axis and is refracted through F
Ray ② passes straight through the centre of the lens
Ray ③ passes through F and is refracted parallel to the axis

Figure 1 Formation of a real image by a converging lens

The diagram shows that we can use three key 'construction' rays from a single point of the object to locate the image.

- The **principal axis** of the lens is the straight line that passes along the normal at the centre of each lens surface. Notice we draw the lens as a straight line with 'outward' arrows to show it is a converging lens.
- The image is real, inverted and smaller than the object.

Notice that:

1 **ray 1** is refracted through F, the principal focus of the lens, because it is parallel to the principal axis of the lens before it passes through the lens
2 **ray 2** passes through the centre of the lens (its pole) without change of direction; this is because the lens surfaces at the principal axis are parallel to each other
3 **ray 3** passes through F, the principal focus of the lens, before the lens, so it is refracted by the lens parallel to the principal axis.

The image is smaller than the object because the object distance is greater than twice the focal length (f) of the lens. This is how a **camera** is used.

a i Draw a ray diagram to show that a real, inverted and magnified image is produced if the object is between F and 2F.
ii What optical device projects a magnified image on to a screen?

AQA Examiner's tip

Make sure your ray diagrams are neat and that you put arrows on the rays. You need to be able to draw a scale diagram to find the focal length of a lens for a particular magnification. See Summary question 3.

The camera

In a camera, a converging lens is used to produce a real image of an object on a film (or on an array of 'pixels' in the case of a digital camera). The position of the lens is adjusted to focus the image on the film.

- For a distant object, the distance from the lens to the film must be equal to the focal length of the lens.
- The nearer an object is to the lens, the greater the distance from the lens to the film.

b If an object moves closer to the camera, does the lens of a camera need to be moved towards or away from the object?

Formation of a virtual image by a converging lens

The object must be between the lens and its principal focus, as shown in Figure 3. The image is formed on the same side of the lens as the object.

The image is virtual, upright and larger than the object.

The image can only be seen by looking at it through the lens. This is how a magnifying glass works.

Formation of a virtual image by a diverging lens

The image formed by a diverging (concave) lens is always virtual, upright and smaller than the object. Figure 4 shows why. A diverging lens is shown as a line with 'inward' arrows.

c Why is a diverging lens no use as a magnifying glass?

Figure 2 The camera

Figure 3 Formation of a virtual image by a converging lens

Figure 4 Image formation by a diverging lens

Key points

- A ray diagram can be drawn to find the position and nature of an image formed by a lens.
- When an object is placed between a converging lens and F, the image formed is virtual, upright, magnified and on the same side of the lens as the object.
- A camera contains a converging lens that is used to form a real image of an object.
- A magnifying glass is a converging lens that is used to form a virtual image of an object.

Summary questions

1 **a** Copy and complete the ray diagram in Figure 5 to show how a converging lens forms an image of an object which is smaller than the object, as in a camera.

Figure 5

b State whether the image is
i real or virtual
ii magnified or diminished
iii upright or inverted.

2 **a** Draw a ray diagram to show how a converging lens is used as a magnifying glass.
b State whether the image is **i** real or virtual **ii** magnified or diminished **iii** upright or inverted.

3 A converging lens produces a magnification of × 2 when it is used to form a real image that is at a distance of 8.0 cm from the object.
a Draw a scale ray diagram to show the formation of this image.
b Use your diagram to find the focal length of the lens.

Further teaching suggestions

Drawing converging lens ray diagrams

This is the best order to draw the diagrams:

- Use a pencil and ruler. No pens.
- Draw the principal axis, a horizontal line across the page.
- Draw the lens as a big vertical line, not a lens shape.
- Draw on the object as a vertical arrow standing on the principal axis.
- Draw the first construction ray from the top of the object to the lens parallel to the principal axis. At the lens it refracts, so it passes through the principal focus on the other side of the lens.
- Draw the second construction ray from the top of the object straight through the centre of the lens. It does not refract and it keeps on going, even after it meets the first ray.
- Draw the third ray from the top of the object through the *nearest* focal point and up to the lens. The ray refracts, so that it is parallel to the principal axis on the other side of the lens.
- The image is formed between the point where the three lines cross and the optical axis, so draw it on.

ICT link-up

- You can use software to quickly assemble combinations of lenses and demonstrate the effects to the class.
- There are plenty of broken digital cameras about. Extract the CCD and the students can look at the pixel array using a magnifying glass or microscope to demonstrate magnification and CCD structure.

Summary answers

1 **a**

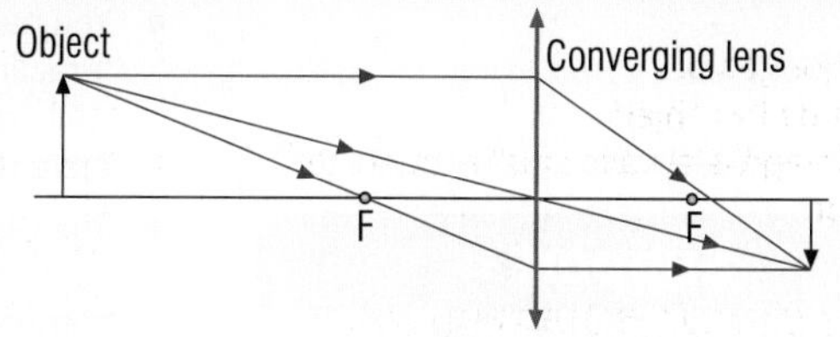

Object — Converging lens

b i real **ii** diminished **iii** inverted

2 **a**

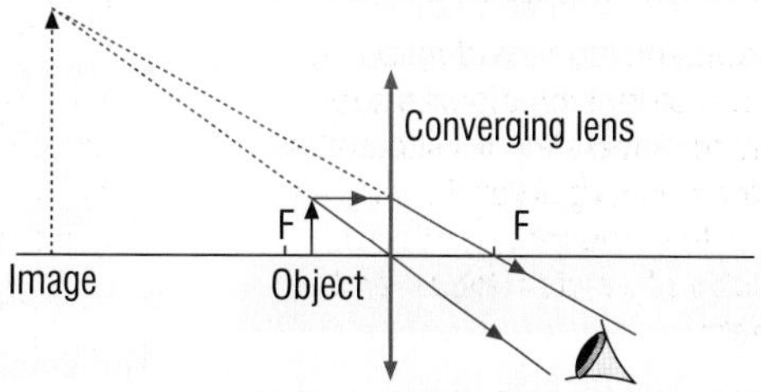

Converging lens / Image / Object

b i virtual **ii** magnified **iii** upright

3 **a**

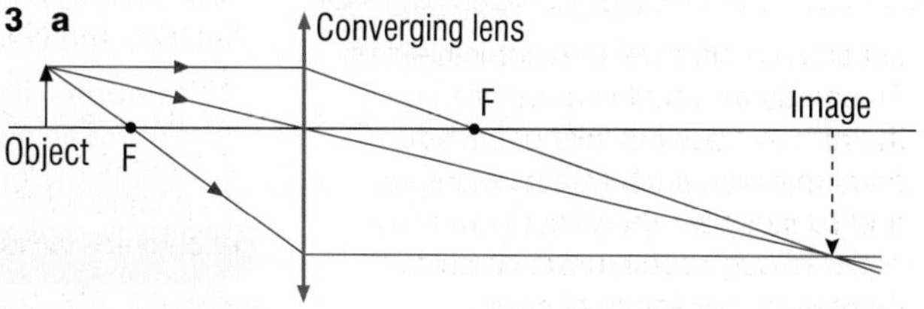

Converging lens / Object / F / F / Image

b $f = 1.8$ cm

P3 1.7 The eye

Learning objectives

Students should learn:

- that the eye is an optical instrument that contains an adjustable lens, other refracting surfaces and a light-sensitive surface
- that the normal human eye has a limited range in which it can focus; from 25 cm to infinity
- that the power of a lens is the reciprocal of the focal length.

Learning outcomes

Most students should be able to:

- calculate the power of a lens given its focal length in metres
- label the major features of the eye
- draw a ray diagram showing the path of light from a distant and a near object through a normal eye
- describe the adjustment the lens can make to bring images into focus on the retina.

Some students should also be able to:

- calculate the focal length when given the power.

Support

- Provide an eye diagram for the students to label and add notes to. They need to include information about how the lens changes shape and how this affects the rays that pass through it.

Extend

- Students should be able to find the power of a lens including the conversion of cm into m. They may also be challenged to combine lenses and find new focal lengths (simply adding the powers taking the nature of a lens into account) For example, two lenses have powers of (+5 D and −3 D giving a total power of 2 D and hence a focal length of 0.5 m).

AQA Specification link-up: Physics P3.1

- The structure of the eye.
  The structure of the eye is limited to: retina, lens, cornea, pupil/iris, ciliary muscle and suspensory ligaments. [P3.1.4 a)]
- Range of vision. The eye can focus on objects between the near point and the far point. [P3.1.4 c)]
- The power of a lens is given by: $P = \frac{1}{f}$ [P3.1.4 e)]

Lesson structure

Starters

Optical illusions – This is a good opportunity to show the students a set of optical illusions and discuss what they show. There are a range of static ones (along the lines of Escher) and you should be able to find some dynamic ones that work very well with digital projectors. Search for optical illusions online and you should find plenty to choose from. *(5 minutes)*

Under the glass – The students should use magnifying glasses to examine a range of small objects and draw them. Extend the students by asking them to draw the ray path of the light from the object. Later in the lesson they can extend their diagram to include the eye. You may also support students by asking them to complete partially completed diagrams; again you can extend these later. *(10 minutes)*

Main

- Use a model of an eye or a suitable simulation to show the parts clearly. Students will be aware of the lens, but may not realise that the cornea plays an important role in refracting light. Take some time going through the function of each part as the students really need to be able to name and describe the function of the parts listed in the Specification link-up.

- The eye dissection (as mentioned in the Plenary) would fit well after the discussion, but it is difficult to get students to focus on the other objectives so leave it to the end (or rearrange the lesson to look at lens power first).

- Simple calculations of the power of a lens are required for all students. Higher Tier students should also be able to calculate the focal length when given the power. Make sure that all students are using the key words 'power' and 'dioptre' correctly.

- You can demonstrate placing lenses together and combining powers using the 'Practical support'. This reinforces the idea that converging lenses have positive power while diverging lenses have negative powers. Compare the situations to the eye; where there are several refracting surfaces at work.

- The ray diagrams on this page are the most challenging of all, especially as some can contain two sets of rays. The students should note refraction occurring at both the cornea and the lens of the eye. They should also be concentrating on where the image is formed as this will explain long- and short-sightedness in the second part of the lesson.

- There are a few key words and phrases used again in this lesson. Many of the parts of the eye need to be recognised and the students also need to know that 'range of vision' simply represents where we can clearly focus on objects while 'near point' and 'far point' are just the limits of this normal range.

Plenaries

The small print – Give the students some questions printed in the tiniest print you can (this will probably depend on your photocopier). Give them some magnifying glasses and ask them to answer the questions. You can also show them some 'small print' from typical adverts and discuss if it is fair to print it in a way that makes it hard to read. *(5 minutes)*

Eyes open – If you have the skills, and it is permitted in your school, you might like to dissect an eye to show the parts. Some students might not like this, so ask them to complete the other Plenary instead while you show those that are interested. *(10 minutes)*

Practical support

Demonstrating a model eye
The path of light rays through a spherical object can help show the path through the eye.

Equipment and materials required
A very large round-bottomed flask filled with fluorescein solution, a bright light source, a range of lenses that can be placed in contact with the flask.

Details
Shining the light through the flask should make parts glow. The curved nature of the front surface of the flask will act like a lens focusing the light towards the back surface. By holding different lenses in contact with the front surface, you can adjust the focus to bring the rays together exactly on the back surface. This is similar to the procedure needed to correct vision.

Demonstrating combinations of lenses
Kits containing all of the equipment for these demonstrations are available. If you don't have one then the individual components can be combined ad hoc.

Equipment and materials required
Ray box that produces three parallel rays and flat Perspex lenses (converging and diverging).

Details
Place the ray box on the desk so that it produces three parallel rays across the desk. You may have to place a sheet of paper under it to see the lines clearly and a darker room is best. Place the converging lens to show its effect and then the diverging one. Finally, place the converging lens and then add the diverging one pointing out the change in the paths. You can also show combinations of adding two converging lenses (increasing the power) bringing the rays together in a shorter distance or even two diverging lenses.

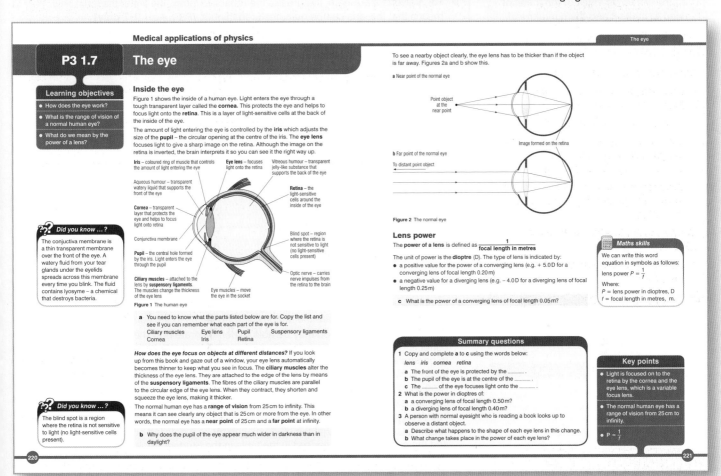

Further teaching suggestions

Eye simulations
- Simulated eyes are available to show the operation of the eye. These show what happens when the lens changes shape and explains more about the optic nerve.

Answers to in-text questions

a Ciliary muscles – change the thickness of the eye lens; cornea – protects the front of the eyes and helps to focus light; eye lens – focuses light on to the retina; iris – controls the amount of light entering the eye; pupil – allows light to pass through the eye lens; retina – a layer of light-sensitive cells on which the image is formed; suspensory ligaments – attach the eye lens to the ciliary muscles.

b To let as much light in as possible in darkness.

c +20 D

Summary answers

1 a cornea
   b iris
   c lens, retina

2 a +2.0 D
   b −2.5 D

3 a Each eye lens becomes thinner.
   b The power of each eye lens decreases.

P3 1.8

More about the eye

AQA

Specification link-up: Physics P3.1

- Correction of vision using convex and concave lenses to produce an image on the retina:
  - long sight, caused by the eyeball being too short, or the eye lens being unable to focus
  - short sight, caused by the eyeball being too long, or the eye lens being unable to focus. *[P3.1.4 b)]*
- Comparison between the structure of the eye and the camera. *[P3.1.4 d)]*
- The focal length of a lens is determined by:
  - the refractive index of the material from which the lens is made, and
  - the curvature of the two surfaces of the lens. *[P3.1.4 f)]*
- For a given focal length, the greater the refractive index, the flatter the lens. This means that the lens can be manufactured thinner. *[P3.1.4 g)]* **[HT only]**
- Evaluate the use of different lenses for the correction of defects of vision. *[P3.1]*

Learning objectives

Students should learn that:

- the definition of short sightedness and how it can be corrected with a diverging lens
- the definition of long sightedness and how it can be corrected with a converging lens
- the focal length of a lens depends on the refractive index of the material used to make it and the curvature of its surfaces
- that a higher refractive index allows greater refraction and so thinner lenses to be used. **[HT only]**

Learning outcomes

Most students should be able to:

- describe the adjustment the lens can make to bring images into focus on the retina
- draw a ray diagram showing how short sightedness and long sightedness can be corrected by an appropriate lens
- state the factors that affect the focal length of a lens.

Some students should also be able to:

- describe how manufacturers can make thinner lenses with the same power as thicker lenses. **[HT only]**

Lesson structure

Starters

Ichihara test – Although colour-blindness is not part of the Physics course, it makes a good starting activity to point out that the eye is often not a perfect optical instrument. You can find several tests online to show the students. The colour reproduction of your projector or monitor may not be perfect. There are also a few joke ones that try to surprise the students when they are concentrating. *(5 minutes)*

Eye test – Sometimes eyes tests have to be given to children that do not know the names of letters. Can the students come up with ways of testing the eyesight of these children? Support students by giving them the criteria of a test: the patterns should be understandable for the children and there should be a size decrease (often achieved by simply moving the object further away). Students may be extended by considering ways of testing the colour vision in the children too. *(10 minutes)*

Main

- Understanding of the different ray diagrams is crucial to this lesson; the students should be able to compare the uncorrected ray paths to the corrected ones.
- With an optical bench, you may be able to demonstrate how the addition of a correcting lens can correct a defect of vision. This can make the explanations far easier to understand. See the 'Practical support' for the details. If you don't have the required equipment, you can show some of the effects by correctly positioning the lenses with simple lens holders.
- You can explain that the retina contains sensitive structures that send electrical impulses to the brain; there is no need to explain what the brain does with the signals.
- You need to make sure that the students can make a detailed comparison of the eye and the camera as summarised in the table in the Student Book.
- The most important comparison is that of the CCD/film to the retina. Most students will not have used film cameras, so you might like to point out that they had chemical layers that were light-sensitive. The eye also has chemicals that are light-sensitive, but these are replenished quickly. With a good microscope you can also show a CCD and the pixel structure; this also shows that the image will have to be much smaller than the object, so that it falls on the rather small array.
- Showing the response of the pupil to light is simple with torches or just getting the students to close their eyes for a few seconds and then look at each other when they open them.
- To finish you can show a range of lenses and discuss their shapes. These can be the traditional lenses used in the practical lesson, and some smaller lenses as used in mobile phones, microscopes or telescopes.

Support

- As before; the students can be provided with partly completed diagrams to annotate.

Extend

- The students can be asked to find the refractive index of two different glass blocks using the experimental techniques learned earlier in the course. They can then decide which is most suited for making lenses.

Plenaries

The camera never lies – It used to be said that photographic evidence was incontrovertible, but digital manipulation can change any image. Discuss with the students whether they think that photographs show the truth. This can include those used in magazines. You can show a few and ask the students if they think they are real or faked. *(5 minutes)*

Optical crossword – The students can learn the key words from light and optics lessons by answering questions and filling in a crossword. This can be a set of differentiated questions to cater for all of the students, providing suitable extension or support as necessary. *(10 minutes)*

Practical support

Demonstrating defects of vision

With an optical bench, you can demonstrate how to correct simple optical defects. This makes it far easier to understand what spectacles or contact lenses are doing. It is possible to try this with the equipment above but an optical bench is far better.

Equipment and materials required

Optical bench, light source, object (transparent with simple opaque image on it), 10 cm converging lens, screen to form image on, range of weak converging and diverging lenses.

Details

Set the optical bench up so that there is a clear image on the screen; this should be when the object is far from the lens and the lens is about 10 cm from the screen. Then move the lens a little bit further from the screen; this means that the lens is slightly too powerful to give a clear focus; the same situation as in short sightedness. You can show the new position of the image by placing a piece of paper between the lens and screen and moving it back and forth. By placing a range of weak diverging lenses in front and in contact with the main lens, you should be able to bring the image more into focus. This is a similar procedure to an optician where a series of fine lenses are placed in front of the eye.

You can repeat to show long sight with a similar technique placing the main lens slightly too close to the screen and then using weak diverging lenses to bring the image back into focus.

P3 1.8 — More about the eye (k)

Learning objectives

- What is short sight and how do we correct it?
- What is long sight and how do we correct it?
- Why is the refractive index of glass important in making spectacle lenses? [H]

Sight defects

Short sight occurs when an eye cannot focus on distant objects. The **uncorrected** image is formed in front of the retina, as shown in Figure 1. This is because the eyeball is too long or the eye lens is too powerful. The eye muscles cannot make the eye lens thin enough to focus the image of a faraway object on the retina of the eye. The eye can focus nearby objects so the defect is referred to as 'short sight'.

Short sight is corrected by placing a diverging lens of a suitable focal length in front of the eye as shown in Figure 1. The diverging lens counteracts some of the 'excess' focusing power of the eye lens.

Figure 2 A contact lens

Figure 1 Short sight and its correction

Long sight occurs when an eye cannot focus on nearby objects. The uncorrected image is formed behind the retina, as shown in Figure 3. The eye lens cannot be made thick enough to focus an image on the retina. The eye can focus distant objects so the defect is referred to as 'long sight'.

Long sight is corrected by placing a converging lens of a suitable focal length in front of the eye, as shown in Figure 3. The correcting lens makes the rays from the object diverge less. The eye lens can then focus the rays onto the retina. The correcting lens adds to the focusing power of the eye lens.

Figure 3 Long sight and its correction

a A student is unable to see clearly the number plate on a car 15 m away with his left eye, which has a normal near point. Is the student's left eye short-sighted or long-sighted?

Comparison of the eye and the camera

How do the eye and the camera compare as optical instruments? They are similar in that they both contain a converging lens which forms a real image. Look at Table 1 to see how they compare in other ways.

Table 1 Comparison of the optics of the eye and a camera.

	The eye	The camera
Type of lens	Variable focus converging lens	Fixed focus converging lens
Focusing adjustment	Ciliary muscle alters the lens thickness	Adjustment of lens position
Image	Real, inverted, magnification less than 1	
Image detection	Light sensitive cells on the retina	Photographic film (or CCD sensors in a digital camera)
Brightness control	Iris controls the width of the eye pupil	Adjustment of aperture 'stop'

Lens makers at work

The eye lens is a remarkable optical device, as it has a variable focal length that depends on its thickness. Lens makers working for opticians need to make contact lenses and spectacle lenses exactly the right shape to obtain the exact focal length for each lens.

The focal length of a lens depends on the refractive index of the lens material and the curvature of the two lens surfaces.

The larger the refractive index or the greater the curvature of the lens surfaces, the greater the power of the lens (and the shorter its focal length).

Higher For a lens of a given focal length, the greater the refractive index of the lens material, the flatter and thinner the lens can be manufactured. This is because the lens surfaces would be less curved.

b After photographing a distant object, a photographer moves the camera lens away from the CCD in the camera to take a close-up photograph. What difference would it make to the image if she did not move the lens?

Figure 4 An eye test

Summary questions

1 Using his left eye, a student can only see the writing on a board at the front of the class if he sits near the board.
   a What sight defect is he suffering from in this eye?
   b What type of lens should be used to correct this defect?
2 An optician prescribes a lens of power +2.0 dioptres to correct a sight defect.
   a What type of lens is it and what is its focal length?
   b State what the sight defect is and give one possible cause of the defect.
3 A lens of a given focal length can be made using two materials that each have a different refractive index.
   How would the lens differ if it was made of the higher refractive index material instead of the lower refractive index material? [H]

Key points

- A short-sighted eye is an eye that can only see near objects clearly. We use a diverging lens to correct it.
- A long-sighted eye is an eye that can only see distant objects clearly. We use a converging lens to correct it.
- The higher the refractive index of the glass used to make a spectacle lens, the flatter and thinner the lens can be. [H]

Further teaching suggestions

Eye simulations

- The same type of simulations used in the last lesson can be used to show the defects of vision in this lesson.

Other eyes

- The students might like to find out a little information about other eyes structures, such as those in insects.

Summary answers

1 **a** Short sight.
  b A diverging lens.

2 **a** The lens is a converging lens with a focal length of 50 cm.
  b The sight defect is long sight. It may be caused by an eyeball that is too short or an eye lens that is not strong enough.

3 The lens with the higher refractive index would be flatter.

Answers to in-text questions

a short-sighted

b The image would not be in focus and would be blurred.

Summary answers

1 a i Bone absorbs X-rays, so a 'shadow' image is formed on the film.

ii X-rays pass through the fracture, but not through the bones.

b i Barium absorbs X-rays, so an image of the stomach is formed on the film.

ii The stomach movements would blur the images.

c Ultrasonic waves from a scanner do not harm the baby because they are non-ionising. X-rays are ionising and would harm the baby.

2 a 0.75 mm

b They could not be detected because they would be absorbed by the tissue.

3 a $\sin r = \sin 40/1.50 = 0.4285$, $r = 25°$

b i $1.5 = 1/\sin c$, $\sin c = 1/1.5 = 0.6667$, $c = 42°$

ii

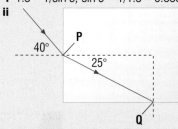

The angles in the triangle formed by the two normals at P and Q and the line PQ add up to 180°.
The angle between the two normals is 90°.
Therefore $x + 25° + 90° = 180°$, so $x = 65°$

iii As angle x is greater than the critical angle of the block, the light ray undergoes total internal reflection at Q, so it does not enter the air at Q.

4 a

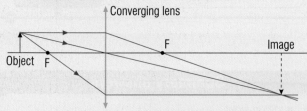

b One bundle takes light into the cavity.
The other bundle is used to observe an image formed by a lens near the end of this bundle in the cavity.

c A digital camera can display an enlarged view of the image on a TV monitor. It can also record and store the image electronically.

5 a i converging

ii and **b i**

Converging lens

Object F ... F ... Image

ii The image is real, inverted and magnified. The lens is being used as a projector lens.

6 a Any two of the following:

1 The eye has a variable focus converging lens, whereas the camera has a fixed focus converging lens.

2 The eye adjusts to see objects at different distances by using its ciliary muscle to alter the lens thickness. In the camera, the position of the lens is altered to photograph objects at different distances.

3 In the eye, the image is formed on the retina. In a camera, the image is formed on a photographic film.

4 The iris of the eye controls the amount of light entering the eye. In a camera, the aperture stop is adjusted to control the amount of light entering the camera.

Summary questions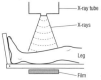

1 Figure 1 shows an X-ray source which is used to direct X-rays at a broken leg. A photographic film in a light-proof wrapper is placed under the leg. When the film is developed, an image of the broken bone is observed.

X-ray tube
X-rays
Leg
Film **Figure 1**

a i Explain why an image of the bone is seen on the film.

ii Why is it possible to see the fracture on the image?

b When an X-ray photograph of the stomach is taken, the patient is given food containing barium before the photograph is taken.

i Why is it necessary for the patient to be given this food before the photograph is taken?

ii The exposure time for a stomach X-ray must be shorter than the exposure time for a limb X-ray. Why?

c An ultrasonic scanner is used to observe an unborn baby. Why is ultrasound instead of X-rays used to observe an unborn baby?

2 Ultrasonic waves used for medical scanners have a frequency of 2000 kHz.

a Use the equation 'speed = frequency × wavelength' to calculate the wavelength of these ultrasonic waves in human tissue. (The speed of ultrasound in human tissue is 1500 m/s.)

b Ultrasonic waves of this frequency in human tissue are not absorbed much. Why is it important in a medical scanner that they are not absorbed?

3 a Figure 2 shows a light ray entering a glass block of refractive index 1.50 at an angle of incidence of 40° at point P.

Figure 2

Show by calculation that the angle of refraction at P is 25°.

b i Show by calculation that the critical angle of the glass is 42°. [H]

ii Copy the diagram and continue the path of the ray in the glass until it reaches a point Q at the bottom of the block. Explain why the angle of incidence at Q is 65°.

iii Explain why the light ray does not enter the air at Q.

4 An endoscope is used to see inside the body.

Figure 3

a Copy and complete Figure 3 to show the path of the light ray along the optical fibre.

b Explain why an endoscope needs to have two bundles of optical fibres.

c Give one reason why it is better to observe an endoscope image using a CCD camera and a TV monitor rather than observing the image directly.

5 Figure 4 shows an incomplete ray diagram of image formation by a lens.

Lens
Object
Figure 4

a i What type of lens is shown in this diagram?

ii Copy the diagram and mark the focal point of the lens on the diagram.

b i Complete the ray diagram and label the image.

ii Describe the image and state an application of the lens used in this way.

6 a State two optical differences between the eye lens and a film camera lens.

b State two advantages of a digital camera compared with a film camera.

7 An object of height 50 mm is placed perpendicular to the principal axis of a converging lens at a distance of 100 mm from the pole of the lens. The focal length of the lens is 150 mm.

a Draw a scale ray diagram to show where the image of the object is formed.

b State whether the image is
i real or virtual
ii upright or inverted.

c Determine the magnification produced by the lens.

---

b Advantages include:
A digital camera can display an image shortly after the photograph is taken. The film of a film camera has to be processed chemically before the image can be seen.

7 a

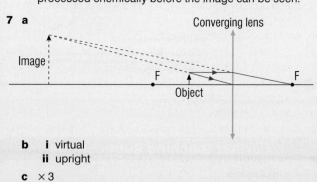

Converging lens
Image
F
Object
F

b i virtual
ii upright

c × 3

End of chapter questions

AQA Examination-style questions

1 Link each type of wave with its uses and properties. (8)

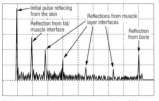

i	Remove kidney stones
ii	Kill cancer cells
iii	CT scanning
iv	Pre-natal scanning

a Ultrasound

b X-rays

v	affects a photographic film
vi	Non-ionising
vii	Electromagnetic wave
viii	Very short wavelength

2 The diagram shows the oscilloscope trace for an ultrasound A-scan for part of a person's thigh. The trace is used to measure the thickness of the person's fat and muscle.

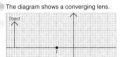

Each square on the screen represents a time of 10 millionths of a second (0.000 010 s).

a How much time does it take for the ultrasound pulse to travel to the patient's bone and back? The speed of ultrasound through tissue is 1540 m/s. (1)

b Calculate the thickness of the layer of fat. The speed of ultrasound in the fat = 1540 m/s. Give your answer in millimetres. (2)

c Why do the reflections from the different layers of muscle get weaker with depth? (1)

The diagram shows a converging lens.

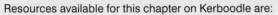

a Copy and complete the ray diagram to show the position of the image. (3)

b Describe the image that is formed. (3)

c Calculate the magnification produced by this lens. (2)

d Where would a lens be used in this way? Give a reason for your answer. (2)

The following diagram shows a diverging lens. Copy the diagram on to graph paper.

e Calculate the power of the lens. Show your working clearly and give the unit. (3)

f Complete the ray diagram to show the position of the image. (3)

g Describe the image that is formed. (3)

4 The diagram shows a ray of light travelling through a semicircular glass block at various angles of incidence, A, B and C.

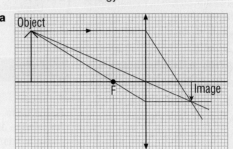

Figure A   Figure B   Figure C

a Which of the angles **A**, **B**, **C** or **D** represents the critical angle? (1)

b What is happening in **Figure C**? (1)

c If angle **A** is 30° and angle **D** is 54°, calculate the refractive index of the glass.

Write down the equation you use. Show clearly how you work out your answer. (3)

d Calculate the critical angle.

Show clearly how you work out your answer. [H] (2)

225

Kerboodle resources

Resources available for this chapter on Kerboodle are:
- Chapter map: Medical applications of physics
- Bump up your grade: Using X-rays to diagnose and treat illness (P3 1.1)
- Animation: Ultrasound imaging (P3 1.2)
- WebQuest: Ultrasound or X-rays? (P3 1.1 and 1.2)
- Viewpoint: Should the government invest in better prenatal scanning devices? (P3 1.2)
- Support: Ultrasound (P3 1.2)
- Maths skills: Refraction (P3 1.3)
- Data handling skills: Investigating refraction using light (P3 1.3)
- How Science Works: Spectacle lens options (P3 1.3)
- Extension: Refraction (P3 1.3)
- Practical worksheet: Measurement of refractive index (P3 1.3)
- Practical worksheet: Measurement of the critical angle of glass (P3 1.3)
- Support: Using optical fibres to look inside your body (P3 1.4)
- Animation: Sight correction (P3 1.8)
- Revision podcast: Lenses and the eye
- Interactive activity: Lenses and eyesight correction
- Test yourself: Medical applications of physics
- On your marks: Medical applications of physics
- Examination-style questions: Medical applications of physics
- Answers to examination-style questions: Medical applications of physics

AQA Examination-style answers

1 a i, iv, vi (3 marks)

b ii, iii, v, vii, viii (5 marks)

2 a 0.000080 seconds (1 mark)

b distance = speed × time = 1540 × 0.000010 = 0.0154
$$\frac{0.0154}{2} = 0.0077 \text{ m} = 7.7 \text{ mm}$$ (2 marks)

c The ultrasound wave is absorbed and reflected leading to a reduction in energy. (1 mark)

3 a

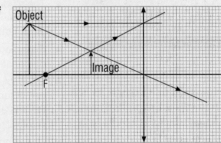

(3 marks)

b inverted, real, diminished (3 marks)

c magnification = $\frac{\text{image height}}{\text{object height}} = \frac{6}{15}$ or $\frac{1.2 \text{ cm}}{3.0 \text{ cm}} = 0.4$ (2 marks)

d Eye or camera. Image must be much smaller than object to fit on retina/film/detector. (2 marks)

e Assume f = 2.8 cm = 0.028 m

Then $P = \frac{1}{f} = \frac{1}{0.028} = -35 \text{ D}$ (3 marks)

f

(3 marks)

g Virtual, upright, smaller (3 marks)

4 a B (1 mark)

b total internal reflection (1 mark)

c $n = \frac{\sin i}{\sin r}$ $r = \frac{\sin 54}{\sin 30} = \frac{0.809}{0.5} = 1.62$ (3 marks)

d $\sin C = \frac{1}{n} = \frac{1}{1.62}$ $C = 38°$ (2 marks)

AQA Practical suggestions

Practicals	AQA	k	📖	⚙
Demonstrating the range of frequencies audible to the human ear …	✓		✓	
Demonstrating long and short sight by placing a screen, not at the focal point, and rectifying the image through the use of appropriate lenses.	✓		✓	
Using a round bottom flask filled with a solution of fluorescein to represent the eye.	✓		✓	
Investigating total internal reflection using a semicircular glass block.	✓		✓	

P3 2.1

Moments

AQA Specification link-up: Physics P3.2

- The turning effect of a force is called the moment. *[P3.2.2 a)]*
- The size of the moment is given by the equation:
$M = F \times d$ *[P3.2.2 b)]*
- Ideas of simple levers. *[P3.2.2 e)]*
  Controlled Assessment: P4.3 Collect primary and secondary data. *[P4.3.2 a) b) c)]*

Learning objectives

Students should learn:

- that a moment is the turning effect of a force about a pivot
- that the size of a moment is measured in newton metres (N m)
- how to calculate the moment using the correct equation.

Learning outcomes

Most students should be able to:

- calculate the moment of a force including use of correct units
- draw a diagram showing the moment of a force
- describe the turning effect of a force on a force diagram
- explain simple observations about the turning effect of a force.

Some students should also be able to:

- perform calculations which include the rearrangement of the moment equation. **[HT only]**

Lesson structure

Starters

Force facts – Get the students to draw a quick summary mind map to show their prior knowledge about forces from KS3. This should include concepts such as forces acting in particular directions, pivots, size of forces, units, forces causing movement/acceleration, friction and so on. You can provide a partly completed one to save some time. *(5 minutes)*

Right tool for the job – To support students, you can provide two worksheets, showing tools like a crowbar, screwdriver, spanner, etc. and some jobs that they are used for, such as opening a box, paint tin, bolt. Ask them to match them up. Then ask the students to explain how they work. They should annotate the diagrams showing where the forces act when they are used. Extend students by asking them to show rotations and give force arrows that are in proportion to the forces that may be used. *(10 minutes)*

Main

- The students will have studied levers and moments during KS3, but here they will be looking at more advanced situations; in particular the idea that the force and perpendicular distance are important.

- Recap on the idea of levers being used to increase the moment acting at a point; demonstrate this by opening something like a tightly clamped bottle or paint tin.

- You should demonstrate the turning effect of a force in a variety of ways, including the use of tools, opening doors, etc. When discussing different tools, it helps a lot to show them in action. At each stage, describe where the forces are acting and where the pivot is.

- One simple demonstration of the increased moment when the distance is increased is to hold out a retort stand by the pole at arms' length. This becomes more difficult the further away the stand is held. You could also show pictures or a video of a strongman competition, where the contestants hold things like car batteries at arms' length and discuss why this is so difficult.

- The students need to use the correct terms for load, effort and pivot, so get them to draw or label a few diagrams. Check that they are getting the directions of the forces and moment correct. Watch out for a few students who may be confused about clockwise and anticlockwise, and try to convince the students that talking about rotation to the right/left or up/down is not a good description.

- The investigation is straightforward, and all of the students should reach a sensible conclusion easily. Discuss the accuracy of the measurements made and the confidence they have in their conclusions.

- It is important to stress at this point that it is the perpendicular distance that is important. In most situations the students come across, the force will be at right angles to the lever, so this will be easy, but you might like to extend students with some tilted forces.

- The calculations are not too difficult at this stage but you will have some students giving the unit as newtons per metre instead of newton metres. Ideally avoid calculations involving centimetres. Get the students to convert all distances to metres and they will have an easier time.

Support

- It is best to have a set of diagrams for the students to mark the forces and moments on. These should have calculation templates below the diagram to help the students develop a clear layout for these questions. If they follow the same routine each time, then they are more likely to find the correct answer.

Extend

- Students can think about situations where the seesaw is not horizontal. They can discuss whether they think the size of the turning effect would change if the force was not acting perpendicularly to the surface. (Situations like this arise in A-level physics studies quite often, but should not appear on the GCSE exams.)

Plenaries

Take a moment to think it through – Give the students some further moments calculations involving lengths that need to be converted to metres. Check that they complete these conversions and give the answers in newton metres. You can also accept some answers in N cm. *(5 minutes)*

Incomprehensible instructions – Ask the students to draw diagrams showing how to assemble a flat-pack cabinet without any words. This should include pushing components together and also rotating parts so they fit. You will have to provide the basic diagrams but remove some of the information; these are available from large furniture stores. To extend students, you can select the more difficult assemblies while to support students you can use simple designs and only remove part of the information. The task should encourage students to show actions using arrows including rotation. *(10 minutes)*

Practical support

Investigating the turning effect of a force

The turning effect can be measured through a range of methods but this one avoids the need for a pivot that the ruler will slide off.

Equipment and materials required
For each group: retort stand with two clamp arms, 50 or 30 cm ruler with hole drilled towards one end, newtonmeter (10 N, 10 g mass holder with 4 × 10 g masses, some cotton.

Details
The newtonmeter should be attached to the arm of a clamp and halfway along the ruler. The arm of the second clamp should fit through the hole in the ruler. The weights are then suspended near the end of the ruler and can be slid back and forth.

The students will need to be reminded to measure the distances from the pivot, not from the end of the ruler.

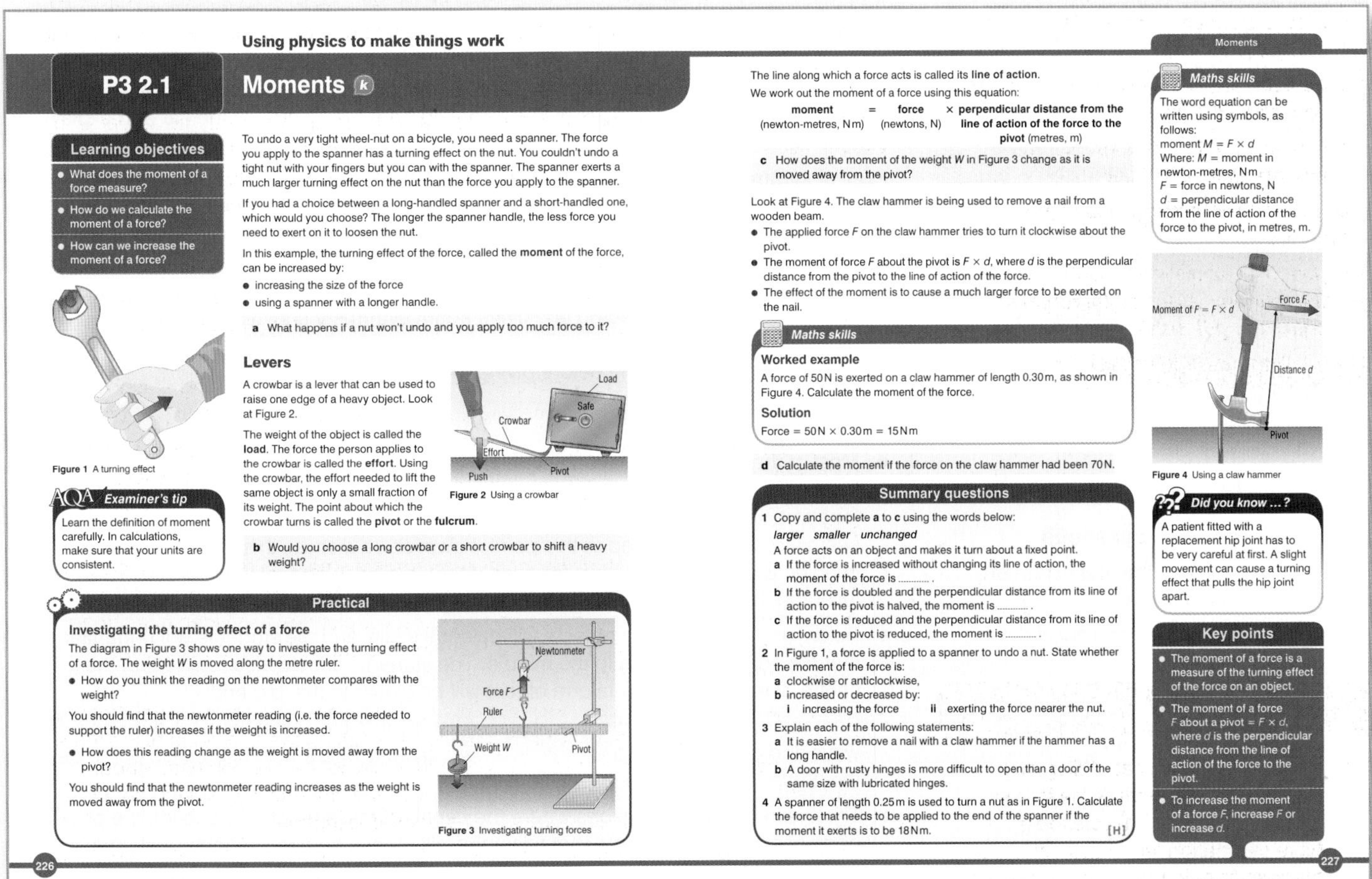

Using physics to make things work

P3 2.1 Moments ⓚ

Learning objectives
- What does the moment of a force measure?
- How do we calculate the moment of a force?
- How can we increase the moment of a force?

To undo a very tight wheel-nut on a bicycle, you need a spanner. The force you apply to the spanner has a turning effect on the nut. You couldn't undo a tight nut with your fingers but you can with the spanner. The spanner exerts a much larger turning effect on the nut than the force you apply to the spanner.

If you had a choice between a long-handled spanner and a short-handled one, which would you choose? The longer the spanner handle, the less force you need to exert on it to loosen the nut.

In this example, the turning effect of the force, called the **moment** of the force, can be increased by:
- increasing the size of the force
- using a spanner with a longer handle.

a What happens if a nut won't undo and you apply too much force to it?

Levers
A crowbar is a lever that can be used to raise one edge of a heavy object. Look at Figure 2.

The weight of the object is called the **load**. The force the person applies to the crowbar is called the **effort**. Using the crowbar, the effort needed to lift the same object is only a small fraction of its weight. The point about which the crowbar turns is called the **pivot** or the **fulcrum**.

b Would you choose a long crowbar or a short crowbar to shift a heavy weight?

Figure 1 A turning effect

AQA *Examiner's tip*

Learn the definition of moment carefully, make sure that your units are consistent.

Figure 2 Using a crowbar

Practical

Investigating the turning effect of a force
The diagram in Figure 3 shows one way to investigate the turning effect of a force. The weight *W* is moved along the metre ruler.

- How do you think the reading on the newtonmeter compares with the weight?

You should find that the newtonmeter reading (i.e. the force needed to support the ruler) increases if the weight is increased.

- How does this reading change as the weight is moved away from the pivot?

You should find that the newtonmeter reading increases as the weight is moved away from the pivot.

Figure 3 Investigating turning forces

The line along which a force acts is called its **line of action**.

We work out the moment of a force using this equation:

$$\text{moment} = \text{force} \times \text{perpendicular distance from the}$$
(newton-metres, Nm)   (newtons, N)   line of action of the force to the pivot (metres, m)

c How does the moment of the weight *W* in Figure 3 change as it is moved away from the pivot?

Look at Figure 4. The claw hammer is being used to remove a nail from a wooden beam.
- The applied force *F* on the claw hammer tries to turn it clockwise about the pivot.
- The moment of force *F* about the pivot is *F* × *d*, where *d* is the perpendicular distance from the pivot to the line of action of the force.
- The effect of the moment is to cause a much larger force to be exerted on the nail.

Maths skills

Worked example
A force of 50 N is exerted on a claw hammer of length 0.30 m, as shown in Figure 4. Calculate the moment of the force.

Solution
Force = 50 N × 0.30 m = 15 Nm

d Calculate the moment if the force on the claw hammer had been 70 N.

Summary questions

1 Copy and complete **a** to **c** using the words below:
larger smaller unchanged
A force acts on an object and makes it turn about a fixed point.
a If the force is increased without changing its line of action, the moment of the force is ....
b If the force is doubled and the perpendicular distance from its line of action to the pivot is halved, the moment is ....
c If the force is reduced and the perpendicular distance from its line of action to the pivot is reduced, the moment is ....

2 In Figure 1, a force is applied to a spanner to undo a nut. State whether the moment of the force is:
a clockwise or anticlockwise
b increased or decreased by:
   i increasing the force   **ii** exerting the force nearer the nut.

3 Explain each of the following statements:
a It is easier to remove a nail with a claw hammer if the hammer has a long handle.
b A door with rusty hinges is more difficult to open than a door of the same size with lubricated hinges.

4 A spanner of length 0.25 m is used to turn a nut as in Figure 1. Calculate the force that needs to be applied to the end of the spanner if the moment it exerts is to be 18 N m. [H]

Maths skills
The word equation can be written using symbols, as follows:
moment $M = F \times d$
Where: M = moment in newton-metres, N m
F = force in newtons, N
d = perpendicular distance from the line of action of the force to the pivot, in metres, m.

Moment of $F = F \times d$

Figure 4 Using a claw hammer

?? Did you know ... ?
A patient fitted with a replacement hip joint has to be very careful at first. A slight movement can cause a turning effect that pulls the hip joint apart.

Key points
- The moment of a force is a measure of the turning effect of the force on an object.
- The moment of a force F about a pivot = $F \times d$, where d is the perpendicular distance from the line of action of the force to the pivot.
- To increase the moment of a force F, increase F or increase d.

226

227

Further teaching suggestions

Balance
- The students can design a simple way of measuring the mass of an object using the idea of a balance beam. This could be for use in situations where electricity is not available. It should be adjustable for a range of masses. There are plenty of such balances used throughout the world.

Answers to in-text questions
a Either the spanner bends or it deforms the nut.
b A long crowbar.
c The moment increases.
d 21 N m

Summary answers

1 a larger
b unchanged
c smaller

2 a anticlockwise
b **i** increased
   ii decreased

3 a The moment of the force you apply is greater, so more force is applied to the nail to remove it.
b The moment needed to turn a rusty hinge is greater, so more force is needed compared with an oiled hinge.

4 72 N

P3 2.2

Centre of mass

Learning objectives

Students should learn:

- that the centre of mass of an object is the point at which the mass may be considered to be concentrated
- that the centre of mass of a thin sheet of material of any shape can be found by a simple suspension experiment.

Learning outcomes

Most students should be able to:

- find the centre of mass of a sheet of uniform thickness using a suspension experiment
- find the centre of mass of a symmetrical object.

Some students should also be able to:

- explain why a freely-suspended object comes to rest with its centre of mass directly below the point of suspension.

Answers to in-text questions

a If the ruler is uniform, the centre of mass is at the centre.

b The centre of mass of a flat circular card is at its centre.

Support

- Start with relatively simple laminar shapes to find the centre of mass. The students could be provided with shapes that already have mounting points for the experiment.

Extend

- Students can find the centre of mass for some simple lamina objects that are outside the body of the object. An example would be a square with a circle cut from the middle or even a banana or crescent shape.

AQA Specification link-up: Physics P3.2

- The centre of mass of an object is that point at which the mass of the object may be thought to be concentrated. *[P3.2.1 a)]*
- If freely suspended, an object will come to rest with its centre of mass directly below the point of suspension. *[P3.2.1 b)]*
- The centre of mass of a symmetrical object is along the axis of symmetry. *[P3.2.1 c)]*

  Controlled Assessment: P4.5 Analyse and interpret primary and secondary data. *[P4.5.4 d)]*

Lesson structure

Starters

Force diagrams – Ask the students to label the forces on a car moving at a steady speed along a horizontal road. Discuss why the students have drawn the weight where they have. Does their force arrow show the force coming from the bottom of the car or the middle? Show that the arrows should be coming from the 'centre' of the car and explain that the lesson will deal with what this centre is. *(5 minutes)*

Fearful symmetry – Give the students a set of shapes (rectangle, square, equilateral triangle, isosceles triangle, circle) and ask them to draw on the lines of symmetry. Discuss if the point where these lines cross is the centre. If you provide shapes that are made of cardboard, you can ask the student to see if they will balance on the head of a drawing pin resting on the desk. To extend students, simply ask them to discuss how to balance the flat shapes without providing any clues about symmetry and centres. Students can be supported by demonstrating how to balance a square shape on the pin and discussing the idea of finding the middle before giving them more shapes to try. *(10 minutes)*

Main

- Most of the students are already familiar with the idea of a centre of mass in the sense that they have been drawing force arrows that act through the centre of objects for some time. They will not be aware that they have been assuming that the mass seems to be concentrated at this point, however, so discuss this idea. Let them imagine drawing force arrows for every atom in a boat, and realise its easier to find the 'average' position where the weight acts.

- Rulers and other uniform objects will balance easily and the students will understand that the centre of mass is in the middle. The students should also realise that the centre of mass of a non-uniform object will be closer to the 'big end'.

- Demonstrate suspending some objects to show that they align themselves in particular ways and that there is a point that is always directly below the suspension point. See the 'Suspended equilibrium' demonstration.

- There can be some situations where the centre of mass is actually outside the physical body of an object. Point out that this point will always be directly below a suspension point when the object hangs freely.

- Show the students, or allow them to find, the position of the centre of mass of symmetrical objects by drawing the lines of symmetry and lifting the object at this point.

- The centre of mass experiment is quite simple and accessible to students. They should start with simple geometric shapes to confirm that the centre of mass is where they expect and then move on to irregular shapes. An accurate technique should involve three suspensions and three lines crossing at the same point. Ask: 'What do you do if the three lines don't cross at the same point', 'How might that happen?' It is usually because of inaccuracy in drawing the lines due to knocking the shape while holding it. If they have all three lines crossing each other at the same point they have been accurate; if not, then they have introduced human error.

Plenaries

Where is the centre? – Show the students another set of flat (laminar) shapes and ask them to figure out where the centre of mass may be by looking at the symmetry. These could be objects such as stars, hexagons, and so on. You could have more complex shapes with portions cut out too, to make the challenge greater. *(5 minutes)*

Topple – The students make a table listing objects designed to topple over and some designed to be stable. Get them to sketch these shapes and try to describe where the centre of mass is in each of them. They should come to the conclusion that a low centre of mass can make an object more stable. This should reinforce the idea that stable objects have low centres of mass. Support students with the task by looking at simple shapes such as bowling pins, and extend others by looking at chairs, tables and non-symmetrical objects. *(10 minutes)*

Practical support

Suspended equilibrium

This demonstration should show the students that the objects will come to rest with their centre of mass directly below the point of suspension.

Equipment and materials required

Tall stand, string, G-clamp and a range of objects.

Details

Simply suspend the objects from the stand using string. If you are using a larger object, then you should clamp the stand to the desk. The objects should come to rest with the centre of mass directly below the suspension point. You can suspend the same object from several different points to show roughly where the centre of mass is. Try to use a range of objects to show that the centre of mass can actually be outside the physical object.

Safety: Protect feet, furniture and the floor from falling objects.

A centre of mass test

Equipment and materials required

Retort stands, bosses and clamps, string and pendulum bobs (plumb lines), corks, long pins, card and scissors.

Details

The students should cut out a range of shapes from the cards: rectangles, triangles and irregular shapes. The cork is held in the clamp, so that the pins can be pushed through the card into it. Wrap the plumb line around the pin and push it through a point near the edge of the card into the cork. The shape should hang freely. Now the students should gently press the line against the card (squeezing from both sides) and mark a point near the bottom of the shape. They then remove the card and draw a line from the mark to the pinhole. Repeat this process twice more; the centre of mass should be where all three lines cross.

- The centre of mass of a semicircular card of radius 100 mm is along the line of symmetry 33 mm above the centre.

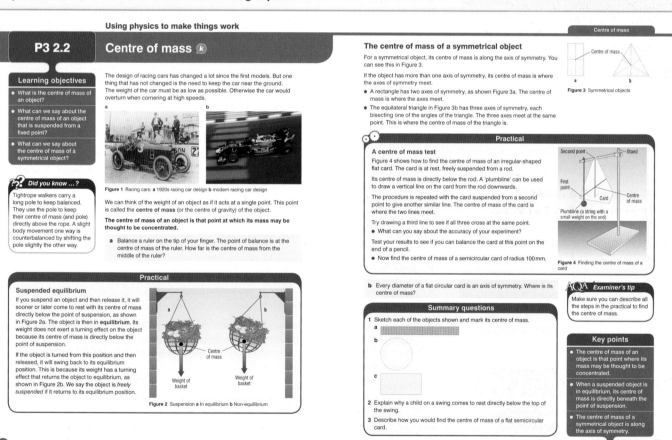

Summary answers

1 **a** and **c** At the point where the diagonals meet.
  b At its centre.

2 The weight of the child has a turning effect about the top of the swing when the child's centre of mass is not directly below the top. The turning effect makes the child return to the middle.

3 Assuming the card has the same thickness at all points (i.e. uniform thickness), the centre of mass must lie along its axis of symmetry. If the card is suspended freely from a point near one end of its flat side, its centre of mass is where the vertical line through this point cuts across its axis of symmetry. A second point of suspension could be used to give another vertical line through its centre of mass if the card is not uniform in thickness.

P3 2.3

Moments in balance

Learning objectives

Students should learn:

- that the clockwise and anticlockwise moments acting on an object that is not turning, are balanced
- how to apply the principle of moments in calculations. [HT only]

Learning outcomes

Most students should be able to:

- state the principle of moments.

Some students should also be able to:

- calculate the forces or distances involved in a problem concerning a pivoted object in equilibrium. [HT only]

Support

- Much of the material in this topic is applicable to Higher Tier candidates only. You can take this opportunity to reinforce the basic ideas of calculating moments and then focus on 'How Science Works' during the experimental sections. Get the students to evaluate the balancing experiments; there are plenty of problems to identify.

Extend

- If the moments are balanced this does not mean that the object is not rotating; it means that the rate of rotation (angular velocity) is not changing. This is a similar situation to balanced forces on a moving object and you may like to discuss this with some of the students.

AQA Specification link-up: Physics P3.2

- If an object is not turning, the total clockwise moment must be exactly balanced by the total anticlockwise moment about any pivot. [P3.2.2 c)]
- The calculation of the size of a force, or its distance from pivot, acting on an object that is balanced. [P3.2.2 d)] [HT only]
- Ideas of simple levers. [P3.2.2 e)]

  Controlled Assessment: P4.4 Select and process primary and secondary data. [P4.4.1 a) b)]

Lesson structure

Starters

Elephant v. mouse – An elephant has a mass of 2000 kg and a mouse a mass of only 10 g. If they want to balance on a seesaw and the elephant is 0.5 m from the pivot, how far away should the mouse sit? Discuss this problem with the students and see if they think that it is possible. This can lead to a calculation of the moment from the elephant and you can then guide them to calculate the distance the mouse needs to be away from the pivot to 'balance' this moment. [100 km!] *(5 minutes)*

Which way? – Show the students several seesaws with a variety of people on and ask them to find out which way they think it would start rotating. Ask them to explain their reasoning; some will be using moment calculations already while others will be using some 'rule of thumb'. You can support students by using relatively simple situations (just one force on each side of the pivot) or extend students by having a range of forces. In either case, end with a seesaw that is balanced. *(10 minutes)*

Main

- Having a large seesaw would be particularly useful during this topic. The larger the seesaw, the easier it tends to be to balance. Use the term 'pivot' rather than 'fulcrum', as 'pivot' will be used in exam questions.

- Take the initial explanation of the balanced seesaw slowly, so that the students get the idea that it is possible to balance large masses with smaller ones. If you have a good-sized seesaw, then show what is going on using it.

- The principle of moments is very important and the students should be able to state it clearly for any questions. You may be able to find a grocer's balance or a newton balance to demonstrate how the principle of moments can be used to find the weight of objects.

- The first practical should be quite short. Encourage the students to take great care to get the best results. Keep the equipment out and use it again for the second practical. Consider aspects of taking measurements from 'How Science Works' in both practicals.

- The calculation should be reasonably straightforward. Give the students plenty of practice at calculating missing values in equilibrium situations; they will need to be able to find these. Check for clear layout again and that the students are still using the correct units.

- The second practical is very similar to the first and again the students will need to take several measurements to get a reasonable result.

- The summary questions should allow the student to show their skills with the calculations.

Plenaries

Odd one out – Support students by showing a set of diagrams of three balanced seesaws and one unbalanced one. Can they find the odd one out? They will need to perform the calculations to prove they are correct. Extend students by asking them to try the same thing with more complex situations including multiple masses on one side. *(5 minutes)*

In balance – Ask: 'How can a 10 kg, a 5 kg and a 1 kg mass be balanced on a metre rule?' How many combinations can the students come up with in 5 minutes? The students will need to show calculations to check that all of their ideas work. Putting them all directly above the pivot counts as an ingenious answer. You can extend students by providing additional masses as part of the question. *(10 minutes)*

Practical support

Measuring an unknown weight

This can be a quick demonstration or a challenge for the groups to be as accurate as possible.

Equipment and materials required

For each group: beam, pivot (wooden triangular block), ruler, known mass (100 g) and unknown mass. A suitable top-pan balance should be available.

Details

The students set up the apparatus as shown in Figure 2 in the Student Book. They must attempt to balance the masses and measure the distances, so that they can find the unknown mass. The greatest problem will be getting a stable balance with the ruler, so the students will have to take great care and get as close as possible. To get a more precise reading, the students should repeat the measurements at least three times using different distances and find the mean value. At the end of the experiment, the students can use the top-pan balance to check their results.

Measuring the weight of a beam

This experiment works best with large beams, but make sure that they are uniform.

Equipment and materials required

For each group: beam, pivot (wooden triangular block), ruler, an appropriate mass (about half the mass of the ruler).

Details

The students have to balance the ruler, by placing the pivot and then balancing the beam by adjusting the position of the mass. This is much more difficult than it seems, so the students should be given a bit of time to do it. Ideally the students should repeat the experiment several times with the pivot in different positions. This allows you to discuss the reasons to perform repeat experiments. (This relates to: 'How Science Works'.)

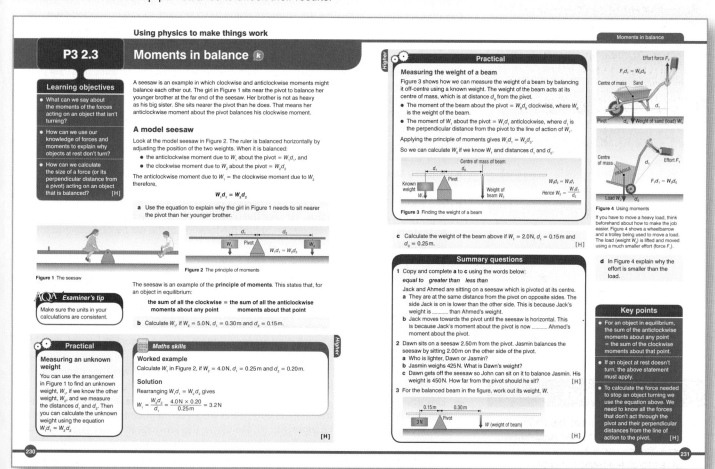

Answers to in-text questions

a Her moment about the pivot must equal the moment of the boy about the pivot. The moment is her weight × the distance from the pivot. Because she is heavier, she needs to be nearer the pivot than the boy, to give an equal moment to the boy's moment.

b 2.5 N

c 1.2 N

d The effort acts further from the pivot than the load does. So, a smaller effort gives an equal and opposite moment to a larger load.

Further teaching suggestions

ICT link-up

- If the students are having difficulty balancing the rulers, it may be best to use a simulation of the experiment. This will give exact results and allows the students to look into situations where there are several forces causing turning effects at once, but it doesn't have the tactile feel of the real equipment.

Summary answers

1 a greater than   b equal to

2 a Dawn   b 340 N   c 1.89 m

3 1.5 N

Stability

Learning objectives

Students should learn:

- that the stability of an object depends on a range of factors but principally on:
  - the relationship between the centre of mass of the object and the line of action of the weight of the object **[HT only]**
  - the shape of the base of the object.

Learning outcomes

Most students should be able to:

- recognise factors that affect stability
- discuss design of objects to improve their stability
- describe how the shape of an object affects the stability of the object
- interpret and draw diagrams showing the stability of objects.

Some students should also be able to:

- explain, in detail, design features that make objects more stable. **[HT only]**

Support

- This spread is only applicable to Higher Tier students. The experimental work can be used to develop 'How Science Works' skills in collecting evidence and evaluating the practical techniques. The Jenga game can still be used as a great way of making any quiz more interesting.

Extend

- An interesting thing to look at is why spinning tops (or even simple spinning coins) are stable when they are spinning but clearly not when they are stationary. See if the students can come up with any ideas as to why this is. They should consider the motion of the centre of gravity and think about what happens to it when the top is in motion. Video clips may be useful.

Specification link-up: Physics P3.2

- If the line of action of the weight of an object lies outside the base of the object there will be a resultant moment and the body will tend to topple. *[P3.2.2 f)]* **[HT only]**
- Analyse the stability of objects by evaluating their tendency to topple. *[P3.2]*
- Recognise the factors that affect the stability of an object. *[P3.2]*
- Evaluate how the design of objects affects their stability. *[P3.2]*

Controlled Assessment: P4.3 Collect primary and secondary data. *[P4.3.2 a)]*

Lesson structure

Starters

A balancing act – Ask the students to balance their pens on their fingers; find out who can do it for the longest. Give the students some other objects to see how good their balancing skills are; these can include metre rules. Avoid fragile and heavy objects though. Ask if some object shapes make this type of balancing easier. *(5 minutes)*

Last one standing – Get some of the students to stand on one leg; there are usually a few volunteers for physical activity. Ask them to answer questions on forces as they stand there. If they get a question wrong or put both feet down, then they are out. Extend students by asking more difficult questions. After the quiz, the other students then describe how the students tried to keep their balance. If you have some exceptional balancers, then give them something extra to hold each time they get a question correct. *(10 minutes)*

Main

- You can start this topic with the introductory practical. Try the brick resting on different sides. The practical can be extended in several ways. See 'Practical support'.
- You should be able to find a range of objects to test around the laboratory: retort stands, conical flasks, lamps, etc. For the objects, you can use the suspension technique from the previous lesson to find the location of the centre of mass and then talk about whether it is high or low on the object.
- Take each of the example situations in turn. If you have models, you can use these on an adjustable ramp to show when they topple. You can also discuss how realistic the models are. Test the bus by finding its topple angle before and after adding modelling clay to the top deck, to simulate the weight of passengers. In reality, very few buses will travel on roads that are so severely tilted, but what about strong gusts of wind? Additional situations you can look at include racing cars. These have very low centres of mass, but if they are moving quickly, the large forces involved can flip them over dramatically.
- Show some videos of sumo wrestling and ask the students why it is so difficult for the wrestlers to throw each other over. Link this to the hunching to lower their centre of gravity. Search for 'sumo' at an internet video-hosting site.
- Link the toppling of the object to the position of its centre of mass. If you have a stool, this should lie beneath the seat; as you tilt the stool you can point out where the line of weight of the stool is. The more you tilt, the closer this line moves to being outside the area where the legs touch the floor. When tilted enough, the line is outside where the legs are and the stool falls.
- Investigating the factors that affect stability offers good opportunities to cover the skills and concepts involved in designing fair tests (this relates to: 'How Science Works').

Plenaries

Don't look down – The students should find three top tightrope-walking tips for potential wire walkers using their knowledge of moments and stability. This should include why a pole helps [lowering centre of gravity and able to adjust balance], what holding your arms out to the side does [similar to the pole but you can adjust them simply] and how to balance with one leg with the other sticking out to the side [the body needs to be tilted to balance the moment of the leg]. You can provide some diagrams for the students to annotate with ideas. *(5 minutes)*

Jenga – If you have it, then this block-building game is a challenging plenary, the larger the set of blocks, the better. Similar games can be made by your technology department. Link this to some summary questions; the student that gets the question right gets the next go of the blocks. You can differentiate to provide support and extension by selecting appropriate questions. You can also get the students to move two blocks at a time to speed the game up. *(10 minutes)*

Practical support

Tilting and toppling tests

This can be a simple experiment or a more advanced investigation; see 'The tipping point – extension' below.

Equipment and materials required
Standard building brick, protractor, bench protector (e.g. carpet).

Details
Allow the students to tilt the brick when it is resting on various sides. They can use the protractor to measure the tipping angle. They should find that the angle is greatest when the centre of mass is lowest on the brick.

The tipping point – extension
This is a more detailed version of the basic brick experiment. It requires adjustable ramps that can be raised and the angle measured; these can be improvised if necessary. You can use this technique to find the tipping point of other objects mentioned in the text, such as model buses, pins or high chairs. Use plasticine to simulate adding passengers to the top or bottom decks.

Equipment and materials required
For each group: adjustable ramp, protractor, rectangular block.

Details
The students should find the angle that the block tips by raising the ramps' angle until the block tips over. This should be when the centre of mass lies just beyond the base of the block. The students may be able to check this if their geometry is up to it. Repeating the experiment with the block lying on different sides should give the same result for the position of the centre of mass. If you find that the blocks start to slide down the ramp, you might have to cover it with a rubber mat or similar.

Safety: Protect feet, bench and floor from falling objects.

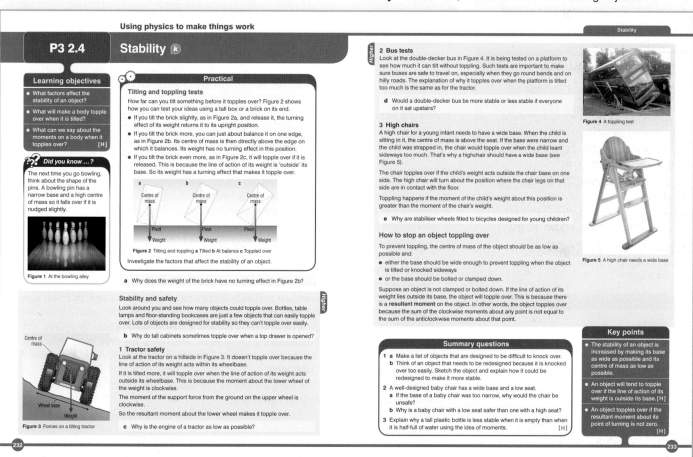

Further teaching suggestions

There are various toys aimed at young children which can be used to demonstrate stability during this lesson. Use them as reinforcement of the key ideas.

Designs
- The students could improve the design of a range of household objects to improve their stability.

Answers to in-text questions

a Its weight acts through the point of contact, so it has no turning effect.

b People open an upper drawer that produces a turning force that topples the filing cabinet.

c So its centre of mass is as low as possible, which makes it more stable.

d Less stable.

e To provide a wider base if the child loses balance.

Summary answers

1 a A table, a low-loader vehicle, a traffic cone, etc.

  b A supermarket trolley, a tall electric kettle, etc.

2 a The chair would topple over if the baby in the chair leans too far sideways.

  b The lower the centre of mass, the harder it is to topple it over.

3 When it is empty, its centre of mass is approximately halfway up the bottle. When it is standing upright and is less than half full, its centre of mass is approximately halfway between its base and the water level. This position of the centre of mass will always be lower than the position when it is empty. Therefore when tilted, the line of action of the weight through the centre of gravity will be outside the base of the bottle at a shallower angle for the empty bottle, producing a resultant moment that will make the bottle topple over more easily.

P3 2.5 Hydraulics

Learning objectives

Students should learn:

- that pressure is caused by a force acting over an area
- that the pressure in a fluid acts equally in all directions
- that hydraulic systems are based on the incompressibility of liquids and are used to transmit forces
- that the force exerted by a hydraulic system depends on the pressure and the area it is applied over.

Learning outcomes

Most students should be able to:

- calculate the pressure due to a force acting over an area
- state that the pressure in a liquid used in a hydraulic system is constant throughout
- describe how hydraulic systems can be used.

Some students should also be able to:

- perform calculation based on rearranging the pressure equation. [HT only]

Support

- The calculation of pressure is the only one the Foundation Tier students will need from this spread, and they won't need to rearrange it. Give the students some extra calculations based solely on this, so that they can practice. You might want to include an example in which the area has to be changed to the correct unit (m²) to make sure that they can do that.

Extend

- There are some complex calculations to find the force provided by a hydraulic system that the students can attempt.

AQA Specification link-up: Physics P3.2

- Liquids are virtually incompressible, and the pressure in a liquid is transmitted equally in all directions. *[P3.2.3 a)]*
- The use of different cross-sectional areas on the effort and load side of a hydraulic system enables the system to be used as a force multiplier. *[P3.2.3 b)]*
- The pressure in different parts of a hydraulic system is given by:

$$P = \frac{F}{A} \text{ [P3.2.3 c)]}$$

Lesson structure

Starters

Liquidity – Recap on the demonstration of the particle behaviour in liquids. Use a tray and a set of balls to show that the particles are able to flow but can't really be squashed closer together. Then pass around a sealed plastic syringe of water for the students to attempt to squash to demonstrate its incompressibility. *(5 minutes)*

Hydraulic mayhem – You should be able to find a range of video clips from TV programmes or online showing hydraulic machines in operation. These demonstrate the ideas about how hydraulics work and often show the machines in operation (or breaking down dramatically). Show them and discuss with the students how they think the machines are operating. They should note the tubes connecting the parts and the liquid inside them. Extend the students by asking them to explain what is happening in the tubes and how forces can be transferred through the liquids; they should link this to the properties of liquids. Provide extra support by pausing the video and adding arrows to show the flow of liquid and the direction of the forces. *(10 minutes)*

Main

- Some of the students will have studied pressure in KS3; however, they will need a basic recap of the idea and the calculations. You can perform some simple recaps showing the difference between pressure and force: knocking in a nail, pushing a pin into wood, showing high heels, etc.
- The definition of pressure is quite formal but the maths is fairly simple. Students commonly struggle to remember the unit pascal, and many become especially confused with N/m² after they have covered N m recently when studying moments. So be very clear about the difference.
- A few example calculations are sufficient as the main focus should be on the hydraulics, so move onto liquid quickly.
- Demonstrate the effect of pressure in liquids to show that the pressure is equal throughout the liquid. You can also show that pressure increases with depth, but you need to make sure the students know that this isn't really important in hydraulics.
- You can now discuss the usefulness of the machines and show the principle of how they work (with the syringe demonstration). The key points are that a force can be transmitted easily and this force can be magnified. Use the examples of brakes and car jacks to emphasise these points. You could add in some discussions of diggers or tractors if there is time.
- Extend students by moving on to attempt calculations of the forces involved. The mathematics can confuse some, so take each stage slowly and offer extra support as necessary.

Plenaries

Under pressure – Extend students by getting them to attempt extra pressure and hydraulic calculations against the clock. This should include a calculation where the force is increased by the use of a hydraulic system such as car brakes. You can support students by providing some simpler calculations to perform and give a more generous time limit. It's a good opportunity to use mini-whiteboards or electronic voting systems. *(5 minutes)*

Automaton – Discuss the use of hydraulic systems in powering robots (there are plenty of diagrams and video clips). What advantages and disadvantages does the technology have when compared with the muscle systems in human bodies? You can discuss points such as reaction time, efficiency, reliability and strength. You might also be able to discuss artificial muscle materials that are being developed to more closely mimic how our muscles work. *(10 minutes)*

Practical support

Demonstrating pressure in a liquid

Equipment and materials required
Two large plastic bottles with small holes drilled into them, parcel tape and water.

Details
To demonstrate that pressure is the same at a fixed depth you can use the apparatus as shown in Figure 2. Tape up the holes with a strip of easily removed tape and then remove it quickly to show the even spread of the water jets.

To demonstrate that the pressure increases with depth, you can use a similar bottle with holes at different depths. Tape these holes up and fill the bottle before removing the tape again. The jets at the bottom should push the water further out showing increased pressure. Specialist apparatus is also available for this demonstration.

Demonstrating the hydraulic principle

Equipment and materials required
Two transparent plastic syringes filled with coloured water connected together by tubing.

Details
Ensure that the two syringes are connected together properly and there are no leaks. Pushing on one syringe should show that the other moves outwards. You could also attach two syringes with different cross-sections (diameters) and the students will be able to note that pushing on the narrower syringe makes the wider one move outwards less. They can also feel the increase in the size of the force with this arrangement.

Using physics to make things work

P3 2.5 Hydraulics ⓚ

Learning objectives
- What do we mean by pressure?
- What can we say about the pressure in a fluid?
- How does a hydraulic system work?
- What does the force exerted by a hydraulic system depend on?

Figure 1 Caterpillar tracks

Caterpillar tracks fitted to vehicles are essential on sandy, muddy or snow-covered ground. The reason is that the contact area of the tracks on the ground is much greater than it would be if the vehicle had wheels instead. The tracks therefore reduce the pressure of the vehicle on the ground. That's because its weight is spread over a much greater contact area.

About pressure

Pressure is defined as force per unit area. The unit of **pressure** is the **pascal (Pa)**, which is equal to one newton per square metre (N/m^2).

For a force F acting evenly on a surface of area A at right angles to the surface, the pressure p on the surface is given by the equation:

$$\text{pressure} = \frac{\text{force}}{\text{area}}$$

a Camels have much wider feet than horses. Why are they better at walking in the desert than horses?

Pressure in a liquid

The pressure in a liquid acts equally in all directions. Figure 2 shows how we can demonstrate this. There are several holes around the bottle at the same depth below the water level in the bottle. The jets from these holes hit the bench at the same distance from the bottle. So they are at the same pressure.

Figure 2 Pressure in a liquid at rest

Hydraulic machines

Mechanical diggers are used to remove large quantities of earth. An example is when soil has to be removed from above an underground pipe to reach the pipe. The 'grab' of the digger is operated by a **hydraulic pressure** system. The hydraulic system of a machine is its 'muscle power'.

Look at the hydraulic system shown in Figure 3b. Oil is pumped into the upper or lower part of the cylinder to make the piston move in or out of the cylinder.

A liquid is virtually incompressible. This means that its volume does not change when it is under pressure. This is why a force exerted on one part of a liquid is transmitted to other parts. In other words, the pressure in a hydraulic system is transmitted through the oil.

b In Figure 3b, which direction, up or down, does the piston move when oil is forced into the lower end of the cylinder?

A hydraulic car jack can be used to lift a car. When the handle is pressed down, oil is forced out of a narrow cylinder and into a wider cylinder. The pressure of the oil forces the piston in the wider cylinder outwards. As a result, the piston forces the pivoted lever to raise the car.

Figure 3 a A mechanical digger
b A hydraulic system

The force of a hydraulic system is much greater than the force applied to it.
In Figure 4, the force F_1 applied to the system is called the **effort**. The force F_2 exerted by the system is called the **load**. As explained below, the load is moved by a much smaller effort.

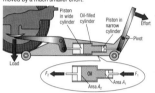

Figure 4 A hydraulic car jack

- The force F_1 acts on the piston in the narrow cylinder. This creates a pressure $P = \frac{F_1}{A_1}$ in the oil, where A_1 is the piston area.
- This pressure in the oil acts on the wide cylinder.
- The force F_2 on the wider piston is PA_2 where A_2 is the piston area. Therefore $F_2 = \frac{F_1}{A_1} \times A_2$

The force F_2 is therefore much greater than F_1 because area A_2 is much greater than area A_1. In other words, the hydraulic system is a **force multiplier**.

Maths skills

We can write the equation for pressure using symbols, as follows:

$$P = \frac{F}{A}$$

Where:
P = pressure in pascals, P
F = force in newtons, N
A = area of cross-section in square metres, m^2.

Note: Rearranging this equation gives $F = PA$ or

$$A = \frac{F}{P} \qquad \text{[H]}$$

Worked example
A caterpillar vehicle of weight 12 000 N is fitted with tracks that have an area of 3.0 m^2 in contact with the ground. Calculate the pressure of the vehicle on the ground.

Solution
$$\text{Pressure} = \frac{\text{force}}{\text{area}} = \frac{12\,000\,N}{3.0\,m^2}$$
$$= 4000\,Pa$$

Summary questions

1 Explain each of the following:
  a When you do a handstand, the pressure on your hands is greater than the pressure on your feet when you stand upright.
  b A sharp knife cuts more easily than a blunt knife.

2 a Write down as many machines as you can think of that are operated hydraulically.
  b Figure 3a shows the arm of a mechanical digger. It is controlled by three hydraulic pistons called 'rams', labelled X, Y and Z.
    i Explain why the arm is raised when compressed air is released into ram X so it extends.
    ii State and explain what happens to the 'bucket' on the end of the arm when rams Y and Z are both extended.

3 The hydraulic lift shown in Figure 5 is used to raise a vehicle so its underside can be inspected. The lift has 4 pistons, each of area 0.01 m^2, to lift the platform. The pressure in the system must not be greater than 5.0×10^5 kPa. The platform weight is 2000 N. Calculate the maximum load that can be lifted on the platform.

Figure 5 [H]

Key points
- Pressure is force divided by the area which the force acts on. The unit of pressure is the pascal (Pa) which is equal to 1 N/m^2
- The pressure in a fluid acts equally in all directions.
- A hydraulic system uses the pressure in a fluid to exert a force.
- The force exerted by a hydraulic system depends on the force applied to the system, the area of the cylinder which this force acts on and the area of the cylinder that exerts the force.

234 / 235

Further teaching suggestions

You may be able to find some real hydraulic components by asking at a scrapyard. It's always handy to have these as props during discussions but make sure they are safe for you to handle.

Answers to in-text questions

a Their feet do not sink into the sand like horses' feet would as they exert less pressure on the sand. This is because the area of each foot of a camel is much greater than the area of the foot of a horse.

b The piston is forced upwards.

Summary answers

1 **a** The area of your hands in contact with the ground when you do a handstand is smaller than the area of your feet on the ground when you are upright. Since the force (i.e. your weight) is the same in both cases and pressure = force divided by area, the pressure on your hands in a handstand is greater than the pressure on your feet when you are upright.

  b When in use, a sharp knife has a smaller contact area than a blunt knife has. For the same force, the pressure of a sharp knife is greater, so it cuts more easily than a blunt knife does.

2 **a** A crane, a digger, vehicle brakes, etc.

  b **i** The pressure of the compressed air forces the piston in X upwards, making the two outer parts of the arm move up.

    ii The bucket moves downwards towards the cab.

3 18 000 N

P3 2.6

Circular motion

AQA

Specification link-up: Physics P3.2

- When an object moves in a circle it continuously accelerates towards the centre of the circle. This acceleration changes the direction of motion of the body, not its speed. *[P3.2.4 a)]*
- The resultant force causing this acceleration is called the centripetal force and is always directed towards the centre of the circle. *[P3.2.4 b)]*
- The centripetal force needed to make an object perform circular motion increases as:
  - the mass of the object increases
  - the speed of the object increases
  - the radius of the circle decreases. *[P3.2.4 c)]*
- Interpret and evaluate data on objects moving in circular paths. *[P3.2]*

  Controlled Assessment: P4.1 Plan practical ways to develop and test candidates' own scientific ideas. *[P4.1.1 a) b) c)]*

Learning objectives

Students should learn:

- that an accelerating object can be undergoing a change in direction without the speed of the object changing
- that a centripetal force is a force acting towards the centre of a circle, i.e. perpendicular to the direction of motion of the object
- that the size of a centripetal force depends on the radius of the circular path, the speed of rotation and the mass of the object.

Learning outcomes

Most students should be able to:

- state that the force required for an object to move in a circle is a centripetal force
- draw a diagram showing the force necessary to make an object undergo circular motion
- identify the forces that provide the centripetal force on an object in a given situation.

Some students should also be able to:

- describe (qualitatively) the factors that affect the size of a centripetal force.

Support

- Using physical models is crucial in the lesson as it can be very difficult to overcome the misconception that there is a force pushing you outwards when you move in a circle. The students must experience the force pulling the objects inwards and what happens if it is removed. There will always be some confusion over the terms centripetal and centrifugal (see the misconception notes) so make sure that you only use 'centripetal'.

Extend

- Why do velodromes (cycle tracks) have banked tracks? How does this help the cyclists? The students can look at how a curved track can help when travelling around tight bends by changing the angle that the force acts on the tyres.

  The students can also think about the forces in action when an object orbits the Earth.

Lesson structure

Starters

You spin me right round – How important is circular motion? Get every student to give one example of a machine that produces it and explain why it is needed. Devices include motors, washing machines, wheels, fairground rides and so on. *(5 minutes)*

Roundabout – Show the students a video clip of somebody on a roundabout. Then ask them to draw a force diagram explaining the forces acting on the person. Support students by demonstrating a rotating disc (a lazy Susan) with a model on it. You can spin this at different speeds to notice the effect. Extend students by asking them to discuss if the distance from the centre of the rotating disk has any effect of the sizes of the forces. *(10 minutes)*

Main

- If possible, start with some video clips to illustrate circular motion. There are lots of potential things to show, including fairground rides, planetary motion and sports.
- Misconception: Many students will have a deeply embedded misconception that there is an outwards pushing force that causes circular motion called centrifugal force and some will bring this idea up in the lesson. Be prepared for this. It is important to explain that you are discussing the force that causes the motion in a circle; the force acting on the **object**. This is always directed to the centre of the circle. They may point out that they seem to be 'pushed outwards' when travelling on a roundabout or even that they can feel the outward force during the 'testing circular motion' practical. There are other forces involved, but these are not the cause of the circular motion. The force they experience in 'the bung' experiment is a reaction force in the string (equal and opposite to the centripetal force) but it is always the inward force that causes the object to move in a circle.
- In the testing circular motion activity, ensure that the students realise that the object flies off at a tangent when it is released. It can be hard for them to see this, but you can demonstrate what happens yourself (with the lasso), or use slow-motion video clips. They should understand that when the centripetal force is removed, then the object moves off in a straight line because it is no longer accelerating.
- You will need to remind the students that unbalanced forces cause **acceleration** and that acceleration can mean a change in the direction of an object without a change in speed. An object moving in a circle is changing its direction of travel constantly, so there must be a constant resultant force acting on it and this force must be always acting towards the centre of the circle. This inwards force is the centripetal force and it may be caused by the tension in a string, frictional forces (when a car is moving around a roundabout) or even gravity (causing orbits).
- The factors that affect the force required are reasonably obvious, but can be quite difficult to demonstrate, apart from the effect of mass. If the students spin the objects around faster, they may be able to feel that they are providing a larger inward force.

Plenary

Poor cornering – There should be plenty of footage available showing what happens when a centripetal force is not sufficient to allow a car or bicycle to turn a corner. Search for suitable examples on the internet and show and discuss them. *(5 minutes)*

Practical support

Testing circular motion
Equipment and materials required
String, bungs with a hole through.

Details
You may prefer to do this as a demonstration with some classes; otherwise the students can experience the circular moment for themselves. If you add more bungs, there should be a greater force required to keep them moving in a circle. Similarly, spinning the bung faster requires a greater force as does reducing the radius of the circle (shortening the string).

Safety: This is a simple demonstration, but be careful that the bungs don't hit anybody!

Using physics to make things work

P3 2.6   Circular motion 🄚

Learning objectives
- How can an object moving on a circular path at constant speed be accelerating?
- What do we mean by centripetal acceleration?
- What factors affect the centripetal force on an object in circular motion?

Figure 1 A hammer thrower

Practical
Testing circular motion
An object whirled round on the end of a string moves in a circle, as shown in Figure 2. The pull force on the object from the string changes the object's direction of motion. What factors affect the centripetal force?

Figure 2 Whirling an object round

Fairground rides whirl you round in circles and make your head spin. But you don't need to go to a fairground to see objects moving in circles.
- A vehicle on a roundabout or moving round a corner travels on a circular path.
- A satellite moving across the sky moves on a circular orbit round the Earth.
- An athlete throwing the hammer spins round in a circle before releasing it.

For an object moving in a circle at constant speed, at any instant:
- the object's velocity is directed along a tangent to the circle
- its velocity changes direction as it moves round
- the change of velocity is towards the centre of the circle.

The object therefore accelerates continuously towards the centre of the circle. The acceleration changes the direction of motion of the object, not its speed. Because the acceleration always acts towards the centre of the circle, we call it a **centripetal acceleration**.

So the resultant force on the object acts towards the centre of the circle.

  a In Figure 2, which direction would the object move if the string suddenly snapped at the position shown?

Centripetal force
Any object moving in a circle must be acted on by a resultant force that acts towards the centre of the circle. We call the resultant force a **centripetal force** because it always acts towards the centre of the circle.
- The centripetal force on a vehicle moving round a roundabout is due to friction between the tyres and the road.
- A person in a capsule on the London Eye moves round at a constant speed. The centripetal force on the person acts towards the centre of the 'wheel'. This force is the resultant force of the person's weight and the support force from the floor.
- A fairground 'gravity wheel' starts off spinning horizontally. When it is spinning fast enough, the wheel is turned until it is spinning vertically. The riders are strapped to the inside of the wheel. **When a rider is at or near the top of the wheel,** the rider experiences a downward push from the wheel to keep him or her moving round the circle. The centripetal force is due to the weight of the rider and the downward push from the wheel on the rider.

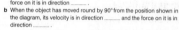

Figure 3 a The London Eye b A fairground gravity wheel

  b Why does each rider on the 'gravity wheel' need to be strapped in?

Centripetal force factors
How is centripetal force affected by the speed of the object and the radius of the circle?

You could find out using a radio-controlled model car.
- If it goes too fast, the car will skid off in a straight line. The centripetal force needed increases if the speed is increased.
- If the circle is too small, the car will skid off. So the centripetal force needed increases if the radius of the circle is decreased.

  c Why is the speed for no skidding much less on an icy roundabout?

How is the centripetal force affected by the mass of the object?

If you whirl a rubber bung round on the end of a thread, you can feel the force on it. If you tie another rubber bung on, you will find the force (for the same speed and radius) has increased. This shows that the greater the mass of the object, the greater the centripetal force is.

Summary questions
1 Figure 5 shows an object moving clockwise in a circle at constant speed.
Copy and complete **a** and **b** below using directions A, B, C or D, as shown in Figure 5.
  a When the object is at the position shown, its velocity is in direction _____ and the force on it is in direction _____ .
  b When the object has moved round by 90° from the position shown in the diagram, its velocity is in direction _____ and the force on it is in direction _____ .

Figure 5

2 In each of the following situations, a single force acts as the centripetal force. Match each situation with the force, **a** to **d**, that causes the circular motion.

  electrostatic force   friction   gravity   pull (tension)

  a A car travelling round a bend.
  b A stone being whirled round on the end of a string.
  c A planet moving round the Sun.
  d An electron orbiting the nucleus of an atom.

3 **a** A student testing a model car measured its speed and found it could go round a bend at that speed without skidding off, provided its speed was no more than 2.2 m/s. What would happen to the model car if the test were repeated at the same speed on a bend that was more curved? Give a reason for your answer.
  b Explain why a high-speed railway track is sloped or banked where there is a curve.

Figure 4 Centripetal force factors

AQA Examiner's tip
Centripetal force is not a force in its own right. It is the name we give to the resultant force acting on an object moving round a circle.

??? Did you know ...?
A spin drier contains a drum that rotates very fast. When the drum spins, the cylindrical sides of the drum keep the wet clothing inside the drum.
- The force of the drum on the clothing provides the necessary centripetal force to keep the wet clothing moving in a circle.
- Water from the wet clothing leaves the spinning drum through tiny holes in the sides of the drum.

Key points
- The velocity of an object moving in a circle at constant speed is continually changing as the object's direction is continually changing.
- Centripetal acceleration is the acceleration towards the centre of the circle of an object that is moving round the circle.
- The centripetal force on an object depends on its mass, its speed and the radius of the circle.

236   237

Further teaching suggestions

Lasso
- This experiment is a great way of showing that an object flies off at a tangent when the centripetal force is removed. It is best carried out outdoors but works inside too.

Equipment and materials required
Lasso, thin rope will do, model steer (this can be anything really).

Details
Show the students how to lasso a steer; the technique involves releasing the rope when it is to your side; not in front of you. With a bit of practice it gets quite easy to throw the rope in the right direction, but not to actually hit the target. Allow the students to have a go, making sure that they understand that the rope will move in a tangent to the circle when it is released.

Answers to in-text questions
a It would fly off at a tangent.

b If the wheel slowed down when it is vertical, the riders would fall off the wheel when they are near the top.

c Due to the ice on the road, there is less friction between the tyres and the road, therefore less centripetal force.

Summary answers
1 **a** B, C.   **b** C, D.

2 **a** friction   **b** pull (tension)
  c gravity   **d** electrostatic force

3 **a** The car would skid off the bend because the centripetal force needed would be greater at a higher speed and the friction on the tyres providing the centripetal force would be unchanged.
  b If the track was not banked, the track would not be able to exert enough centripetal force on the train to make it stay on the track when it travels round the curve. With a banked track, the weight of the train would contribute towards the necessary centripetal force in addition to the force of the track on the train.

P3 2.7

The pendulum

AQA
Specification link-up: Physics P3.2

- For a simple pendulum:
  $T = \frac{1}{f}$ *[P3.2.1 d)]*
- The time period depends on the length of a pendulum. *[P3.2.1 e)]*

  Controlled Assessment: P4.4 Select and process primary and secondary data. *[P4.4.1 a) b)]*, *[P4.4.2 a) b) c)]*

Learning objectives

Students should learn:

- that the time period of a pendulum depends on the length of the pendulum string
- the time period of a pendulum can be more accurately measured if several periods are measured and an average value calculated
- that many objects (including swings) show movement patterns similar to a pendulum.

Learning outcomes

Most students should be able to:

- state that the period of a pendulum's oscillation is related to the length of the pendulum string
- describe how to measure the period of a pendulum
- calculate the time period of the oscillations given data from an investigation of a pendulum.

Some students should also be able to:

- calculate the frequency of the oscillations given the time period of a pendulum. [HT only]

Answers to in-text questions

a The equilibrium method is better because the position of the marker is easier to locate.

b The time period does not depend on the amplitude.

Support

- Students should be provided with additional instructions about setting up the pendulum experiments including suggestions of how to time the swings and a table of appropriate masses and lengths to test.

Extend

- Challenge the students to plot a graph of the data for pendulum length and period and use it to find the length of a pendulum with a period of 0.5 s. They can test their answer by constructing the pendulum and seeing how close it is to the desired 0.5 s.

Lesson structure

Starters

Clocks – Ask the students to list all of the methods they know for measuring time and see if they can explain how any of them work. They should be able to come up with digital watches (regular vibrations in a crystal), mechanical (regular movements of cogs powered by springs), pendulum clocks, water clocks, sundials, etc. *(5 minutes)*

All in the timing – Give the students timers and drop a ball to the floor from a height of one metre. Ask them how long it took to fall to the floor. They should describe simple methods to make the timing of the fall as accurate and reliable as possible. This should include making sure that the ball is dropped from a measured height, repeating timing, and finding averages between students. Support students by giving them a list of things that could affect the timing and asking them to explain how to reduce the errors. Extend students by asking them to put the measures into effect and improve their initial answer. *(10 minutes)*

Main

- Start by showing how simple a pendulum is by setting one up and describing the swinging action.
- Make sure that the students realise what the 'time period' of a pendulum is. A full swing requires the pendulum to go left, then right and then back through the centre. Some students count a swing as every time the pendulum passes the equilibrium position. Try to make sure that the students' pendulums are only oscillating in one plane (left to right) instead of in more complex patterns. Make sure that they only use a small angle; anything above 10 degrees is too large.
- The experiments are relatively straightforward and the emphasis should be on producing repeatable measurements of the swing times. You may need to demonstrate the techniques for timing and discuss how to make them more repeatable.
- Timing several swings and finding an average time is key; you can show how inaccurate timing one swing is by asking all of the students to attempt to time one swing of your demonstration equipment. They will come up with quite a range of times. If they then time twenty swings and find a mean time for one swing, their results are closer. Repeating the experiment three times and taking an average further increases accuracy. The precision of the repeat readings can be discussed.
- Along with concepts of precision and accuracy, students will need to record their data in tables and draw graphs. You could also use this as an open-ended planning exercise. This provides excellent opportunities to develop skills in 'How Science Works'.
- Check the conclusion of the experiments. Theoretically there should only be a relationship between length and time period, but you may find some students have other patterns. This gives an opportunity to discuss how strong these correlations are and if they can be dismissed or need further investigation.
- The students now look at the simple relationship between frequency and period. You should try a few simple calculations here, giving example periods of 1 s, 2 s, 0.5 s, and so on. This should emphasise that the period is inversely proportional to the frequency.

Plenaries

Ride out – The students can design a fairground ride that uses circular motion and pendulum actions combined. They can also look at some real rides that have several directions of motion combined to make them exciting. *(5 minutes)*

Evaluate and improve – The students should evaluate the success of their pendulum experiments. Did they produce the patterns that were expected? How could the timing of the swing be improved further? To extend students you can ask them to plot the theoretical pattern on their graphs along with their own lines of best fit for their data and make a comparison of the gradient from their results and this theoretical value. To support students you can provide graphs of different sets of data collected from students alongside the theoretical results and ask them to discuss which set of data best matches the theory and why. *(10 minutes)*

Practical support

Investigating the time period of a pendulum

Equipment and materials required
Stop clock, retort stand, pendulum bob, G-clamp, metre rule.

Details
Start with a pendulum length of 50 cm and small amplitude. To make the pendulum more stable, the G-clamp can be used to attach the stand to the bench (or you could use a 1 kg mass to steady the base).

The first task simply gets the students to measure the period in a suitable way; check that they can do this successfully before allowing them to move on.

In task 2 the students should displace the pendulum by 1.0 cm before releasing, then 1.5 cm, 2.0 cm and so on. There may be a small effect on the period when this displacement is very large but for reasonably small values there should not be an effect.

For task 3, the students should plan their investigation carefully to ensure accurate measurements are obtained from at least five suitable lengths. There should be a clear correlation between the period and length of string. The time period is less if the centre of mass is higher. This is because the effective length of the pendulum with a higher centre of mass is shorter than its actual length.

Testing a model swing

Equipment and materials required
Stop clock, plasticine and a model swing. The swing can be made from meccano or something similar but it has to allow the seat to swing freely, so take care that the two 'chains' are the same length.

Details
The students should be timing multiple swings (20) so that they can make their timing measurements more precise. They may find it fiddly to move the person higher up the swing. Instead, they can start with a squat person and then make them taller by adjusting the plasticine; this will raise the centre of gravity.

Further teaching suggestions

Foucault pendulum
- This was an important step in clearly demonstrating the rotation of the Earth with a very simple device. Students could look into how a simple pendulum could be used to convince people that it is the Earth that moves and not the heavens above. If you have a tall enough stairwell and a suitable mounting point, then you can even build one. Foucault's best version broke in 2010 after 150 years of good scientific service.

Summary answers

1 **a** increase **b** decrease **c** stay the same

2 **a** 37.93 s **b** Time period = 1.89 s
   Frequency = 0.53 Hz

3 **Similarity:** They both move repeatedly along a line or they both move repeatedly through the equilibrium position.

   Difference: Their time period differs or the amplitude of the swing decreases faster than the amplitude of the simple pendulum.

Summary answers

1 a
  i Upwards on the end of the bottle opener.
  ii Upwards on the edge of the cap.
  iii Where the end of the bottle opener is in contact with the cap.

  b The force applied to the bottle opener acts further from the pivot than the force of the bottle opener on the top. The moment of each force about the pivot is the same. So the force of the bottle opener on the top is greater than the effort.

  c The force needs to be larger. This is because the moment needed to remove the bottle cap is given by 'force × distance' and the distance (from the pivot to the line of action of the force) is less because the bottle opener is shorter.

2 a It would be less stable, as it would be easier to disturb.

  b 0.012 N m

3 0.06 N

4 a
  i force, force
  ii velocity, acceleration, force

  b The lorry will lean outwards as it goes round the roundabout because the centripetal force on it is provided by its grip on the road, which acts at the road surface. If it leans over too much, its centre of mass will lie outside its wheel base and it will topple over.

5 a
  i East
  ii North

  b The hammer would move round on a bigger circle. If the hammer thrower could keep a grip on it until he or she turns at the same speed as before, the hammer would go further.

6 a 33 000 Pa

  b The pressure in the oil is the same throughout. The braking force from each wheel cylinder is equal to the oil pressure multiplied by the cylinder's area of cross-section. This area is greater than the area of the master cylinder. So the force from the wheel cylinders is greater than the force applied to the master cylinder.

7 a The time period is the time interval between successive passes of the pendulum through equilibrium in the same direction.

  b
  i 3.03 s
  ii Its time period would be reduced and its frequency would be increased.

AQA Examiner's tip

Though candidates will not be asked directly about the effect of changing mass on a pendulum, it is important that they are aware that the mass has no effect. Otherwise, they are likely to identify the mass as an additional factor that could affect the time period. Make sure they have carried out appropriate investigations into the possible factors that affect the period. There are several video clips of 'pirate ship' rides on the internet and it is interesting to time their period of swing and relate it to the height of the ride.

Summary questions 🅚

1 The bottle opener in Figure 1 is being used to force the cap off a bottle.

  a Copy the diagram and add to it to show:
  i where the force is applied to the bottle opener by the person opening the bottle. Show the direction of this force.
  ii where the force of the bottle opener acts on the bottle top. Show the direction of this force.
  iii where the pivot (fulcrum) is.

Figure 1

  b Explain why the force of the bottle opener on the cap is much larger than the force applied to the bottle opener by the person opening the bottle.

  c If a shorter bottle opener were used, would the force needed to open the bottle be smaller, larger or the same? Give a reason for your answer.

2 Figure 2 shows a toy suspended from a ceiling.

  a How would the stability of the toy be affected if the Sun were removed from it?

  b The star on the toy has a weight of 0.04 N and is a distance of 0.30 m from the point P where the thread is attached to the toy. Calculate the moment of the star about P.   [H]

Figure 2

3 The crescent moon attached to the toy in question 2 is at a distance of 0.20 m from P. Calculate the weight of the crescent.   [H]

4 a A satellite is moving at constant speed in a circular orbit above the Earth.

  Copy and complete **i** and **ii** using the words below. Each word can be used more than once.

  acceleration force velocity

  i The centripetal .... on the satellite is equal to the .... of gravity on it.

  ii The .... of the satellite is in a direction at right angles to the direction of the .... of the satellite and to the .... on it.

  b Explain why a high-sided lorry on a roundabout might topple over if its speed is too great.

5 A hammer thrower whirls a 'hammer' around anticlockwise and releases it when he is facing due south.

  a
  i Which direction does the hammer go in when it is released?
  ii Which direction is the acceleration of the hammer just before it is released?

  b Discuss whether or not the hammer thrower would be able to throw a hammer with a longer handle further. Assume the mass of the hammer is the same.

6 When the foot brake of a vehicle is applied, a force is applied to the piston in the master cylinder of the brake system, as shown in Figure 3.

Figure 3

  a The cylinder has an area of cross-section of 0.0006 m². Calculate the pressure in the brake system when a force of 20 N is applied to the piston in the cylinder.

  b The master cylinder is connected by pipes to a brake cylinder at each wheel. Each brake cylinder is much wider than the master cylinder. Explain why the force of the brake cylinder on each wheel is much greater than 20 N.

7 a What is meant by the time period of a pendulum?

  b The data below shows the time taken for 10 cycles of a pendulum that consists of a metal bob on a thread.

  30.5 s, 29.8 s, 30.6 s

  i Use this information to calculate the time period of the pendulum.
  ii If the length of the pendulum is shortened, state how its time period and its frequency would change.

Kerboodle resources 🅚

Resources available for this chapter on Kerboodle are:

- Chapter map: Using physics to make things work
- Video: The important moments of an engineer (P3 2.1)
- Maths skills: Moments (P3 2.1)
- Bump up your grade: Turning effects of forces (P3 2.1)
- Extension: Using the equation of moments of a force (P3 2.1)
- Practical worksheet: Investigating moments (P3 2.1)
- Support: Centre of mass (P3 2.2)
- WebQuest: Stability (P3 2.4)
- Interactive activity: Hydraulics and pressure (P3 2.5)
- Revision podcast: Pressure (P3 2.5)
- How Science Works: Liquid under pressure (P3 2.5)
- Extension WebQuest: Fairground rides (P3 2.6)
- Bump up your grade: Understanding circular motion (P3 2.6)
- Practical worksheet: Investigating the pendulum (P3 2.7)
- Test yourself: Using physics to make things work
- On your marks: Using physics to make things work
- Examination-style questions: Using physics to make things work
- Answers to examination-style questions: Using physics to make things work

AQA Examination-style questions 🅚

A boy is making a mobile of birds in flight. The diagram shows a thin sheet of card that he has cut in the shape of a bird. There are holes in the card at **A** and **B**. He decides to find the *centre of mass* of the shape.

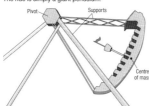

a What is meant by the *centre of mass* of an object? (1)

b *In this question you will be assessed on using good English, organising information clearly and using specialist terms where appropriate.*

Describe how you would find the centre of mass of the mobile shape. (6)

c The wrestler is shown in a 'ready' stance. Which two features of this stance make the wrestler very stable? [H] (2)

d A waiter trips while carrying a tray of mugs and the tray starts to tilt. The white dots indicate the position of the centre of mass of each mug.

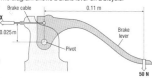

i Which mug will have started to topple over already? (1)

ii Which mug will topple over next if the tray is tilted even more? (1)

iii Which mug would be the last to topple? [H] (1)

The diagram shows a brake lever on a bicycle.

The lever is pulled with a force of 50 N and then stops turning.

a Calculate the moment of the force about the pivot.

Write down the equation you use. Show clearly how you work out your answer and give the unit. (3)

b Explain why the brakes are more effective if the lever is pulled at the end as shown. (2)

c There is a clockwise and an anticlockwise moment about the pivot. What can be said about these moments if the lever is not moving? (1)

d Calculate **X**, the force the cable exerts on the lever.

Show clearly how you work out your answer and give the unit. [H] (3)

3 The 'pirate ship' is a very common amusement park ride. The ride is simply a giant pendulum.

The designers of the ride wanted there to be three seconds between the highest points on each side of the ride.

a What would the time period of this ride be? (1)

b Calculate the frequency of the ride.

Write down the equation you use. Show clearly how you work out your answer and give the unit. (2)

c When the ride was sold to another amusement park, the dimensions of the ride were reduced. As a result of this, the distance between the pivot and the centre of mass of the ship was reduced. How would this affect the time period? (1)

The ship swings through an angle of 65° to the vertical on each side. While it does so, it is moving in a circular path.

d Describe the direction of the centripetal force acting on the ship when it is moving. (1)

e What provides the centripetal force in this case? (1)

f The new operators of the ride use the drive motors to increase the maximum speed of the ship to its original value as it travels past its lowest point. Explain why they should have the ride carefully checked before they do so. (3)

241

AQA Practical suggestions

Practicals	AQA	🅚	📖	⚙️
Demonstrating that pressure in liquids acts in all directions using a circular container with holes around it.	✓	✓	✓	✓
Finding the centre of mass of an irregularly shaped card.	✓		✓	
Using a balanced metre ruler and masses to verify the principle of moments.	✓	✓	✓	
Plan and carry out an investigation into factors that affect the period of a simple pendulum (mass, length of pendulum, amplitude of swing).	✓	✓	✓	✓
Whirling a bung on the end of a piece of string to demonstrate the factors that affect centripetal force.	✓		✓	
Investigating objects and slopes to find out the point at which the object topples.	✓		✓	

AQA Examination-style answers

1 a The centre of mass of an object is that point at which the mass of the object may be thought to be concentrated. *(1 mark)*

b Marks awarded for this answer will be determined by the Quality of Written Communication (QWC) as well as the standard of the scientific response. There is a clear, balanced and detailed description of how you would find the centre of mass of the shape. The answer shows almost faultless spelling, punctuation and grammar. It is coherent and in an organised, logical sequence. It contains a range of appropriate or relevant specialist terms used accurately. *(5–6 marks)*

There is a workable description of the method to find the centre of mass of the shape. There are some errors in spelling, punctuation and grammar. The answer has some structure and organisation. The use of specialist terms has been attempted, but not always accurately. *(3–4 marks)*

There is a brief description of how you would find the centre of mass of the shape, which has little clarity and detail. The spelling, punctuation and grammar are very weak. The answer is poorly organised with almost no specialist terms and/or their use demonstrating a general lack of understanding of their meaning. *(1–2 marks)*

No relevant content. *(0 marks)*

Examples of physics points made in the response:
- suspend the object freely from point B
- hang a plum line from B
- and draw line
- repeat for point A
- repeat for a third point
- where lines meet is the centre of mass.

c bent knees and crouched to lower centre of mass feet wide apart to make wide 'base' *(2 marks)*

d **i** b *(1 mark)*
ii d *(1 mark)*
iii a *(1 mark)*

2 a moment = force × distance
= 50 × 0.11
= 5.5 Nm *(3 marks)*

b Longer distance from pivot increases turning force. *(2 marks)*

c Clockwise and anticlockwise moments are equal. *(1 mark)*

d anticlockwise moments = clockwise moments
X × 0.025 = 50 × 0.11
X = 220 N *(3 marks)*

3 a 2 × 3 = 6 s *(1 mark)*

b $f = \dfrac{1}{T} = \dfrac{1}{6} = 0.167$ s *(2 marks)*

c The time period would be reduced. *(1 mark)*

d towards the pivot *(1 mark)*

e tension in the support *(1 mark)*

f Centripetal force increases as speed increases and as radius decreases.
The increased force could damage/break the structure. *(3 marks)*

AQA Examiner's tip

Students should be giving a detailed description of how the centre of mass is located. It can be helpful to repeat the practical for revision purposes. Students should be encouraged to write out the list of instructions for this procedure. They could then compare and evaluate each others lists. Alternatively, demonstrate that if a student's incomplete set of instructions is followed to the letter, the centre of mass is not obtained.

P3 3.1

Electromagnets

AQA

Specification link-up: Physics P3.3

- When a current flows through a wire a magnetic field is produced around the wire. *[P3.3.1 a)]*
- Interpret diagrams of electromagnetic appliances in order to explain how they work. *[P3.3]*

Controlled Assessment: P4.1 Plan practical ways to develop and test candidates' own scientific ideas. *[P4.1.1 a) b) c)]*; P4.2 Assess and manage risks when carrying out practical work. *[P4.2.1 a) b)]*

Learning objectives

Students should learn:

- that like poles on magnets repel while unlike poles attract
- that magnetic field lines indicate the strength and direction of a magnetic field around a magnet
- how to make electromagnets
- some uses of electromagnets.

Learning outcomes

Most students should be able to:

- describe the effect that magnets have on each other and on magnetic materials
- draw basic magnetic field patterns for a bar magnet
- describe the key elements of an electromagnet including the coil and iron core
- explain the function of basic electromagnetic devices.

Some students should also be able to:

- interpret diagrams of electromagnetic appliances in order to explain how they work.

Lesson structure

Starters

Electricity and magnetism recap – Use true/false/don't know cards and a set of electricity questions to establish the students' prior knowledge. To support students these can be relatively simple like 'north poles attract south poles' or to extend students give more difficult examples like 'the size of an electric current depends on the rate of flow of electrons'. *(5 minutes)*

Magnetic fields – The students should draw the shape of a magnetic field around a bar magnet and explain how they can find this shape. If they cannot do this, then demonstrate the shape of the field using a magnet and a compass or iron filings. You might want to support students' understanding by allowing them to find the field, or extend some students by demonstrating the field around magnets of other shapes (horseshoe, ring or spherical magnetic toys). *(10 minutes)*

Main

- Most students will be familiar with basic magnetic fields but their understanding of field lines tends to be limited and diagrams can be very inaccurate. It is important that they recognise the correct shape for a bar magnet and understand that the field lines have a direction indicated by arrows (from north pole to south pole). Let the students investigate the basics using the practical task in the Student Book.

- Move on to electromagnets by demonstrating a basic one; a coil, nail and power supply. You can show that this produces a field by turning it off and on to lift objects or making it affect some compasses placed nearby. Once the basics are covered, you can move on to discuss how to make the magnetic field stronger or leave this for the possible investigation later. Either way, the students need to understand that the strength can be increased by increasing the current.

- A scrapyard crane uses a powerful electromagnet to lift objects but similar lifting electromagnets are used whenever large ferric metal objects need to be moved easily; they can be found in many factories and foundries. You can demonstrate the action by simply using an electromagnet to lift and drop some small iron blocks.

- All of the other devices can be demonstrated in the laboratory, see 'Practical support' for further details. You could choose to let the students test the devices themselves if you have enough equipment.

- You can finish the lesson by allowing the students to plan for an electromagnetic investigation. This is a good way of building up a range of skills needed to understand 'How Science Works'.

Support

- Students may need some extra time to revise the basic properties of electromagnets. It is certainly worth getting the students to plot out the shape of the fields if they have not done so before.

Extend

- Students can attempt to determine the shape of magnetic fields around other magnets or to see if they can detect the field around an electromagnet. Does increasing the current supplied to the electromagnet change the shape of the field lines? They may be able to find that the field lines become more closely packed, indicating an increased magnetic field. They can also see the effect of removing the iron core from the coil.

Plenaries

Space boots – In space, astronauts are weightless but need some way of walking around the outer surface of a space station. Can the students design a system to do this? There would need to be a way for the astronaut to switch the boots on and off individually so that they could still walk. *(5 minutes)*

More power – Stretch some of the students by asking them to design a fair test to see what affects the strength of an electromagnet. They should choose one possible factor (current, number of loops in coil, type of core) and form a full plan to see if there is a qualitative or quantitative relationship that can be determined. If time permits, the plans can be carried out as a full investigation. To support students, you can provide plans for them to use in the investigation. *(10 minutes)*

Practical support

Investigating magnetic fields

Equipment and materials required

Bar magnets, paper clips, plotting compasses, cling film, iron filings in sprinklers. Optional: horseshoe and ceramic magnets.

Details

The students will just recap their basic knowledge of magnetic fields and identify magnetic field lines. They can test to see how magnets affect each other in terms of repulsion and attraction and then use the iron filings and plotting compasses to find the shape and direction of the magnetic field lines.

Electromagnets: Demonstrations

Lifting electromagnet

A lifting electromagnet can be built from a coil of wire wrapped around an iron core (large nail). Use about thirty loops of wire and connect to a low-voltage power supply. Set this to 5 V but make sure that the coil does not start to get warm; if it does, then you will have to reduce the pd.

Circuit breaker

You can set a circuit breaker in a simple lamp circuit. Use a low current one that cuts out before the lamp melts. Don't forget to demonstrate that the circuit breaker can be reset unlike a fuse.

Electric bell

There is a range of electric bells designed to demonstrate the function. Set this up according to the instructions and then explain the process that causes the hammer to move back and forth. The key concept is that when the hammer moves to strike the bell, the circuit is broken and so the electromagnet turns off, the hammer then falls back to the start position and the electromagnet turns back on. This cycle continues until you release the main switch.

Relay

You can put a relay in a simple circuit to demonstrate its operation. Quite often the relay is used to turn on a high current circuit from a low current (safer) one. However, it is sufficient to build a basic circuit including a relay and trigger it with an electromagnet or even a bar magnet. The students may be able to see the armature move.

Using magnetic fields to keep things moving

P3 3.1 **Electromagnets**

Electromagnets

Learning objectives

- What can we say about the force between two magnets?
- What do we mean by magnetic field lines?
- How do we make electromagnets?
- What do we use electromagnets for?

About magnets

A magnetic compass is a tiny magnetic needle pivoted at its centre. Because of the Earth's magnetic field, one end of the compass always points north and the other south. The end that points north is called the **north pole** and the other end the **south pole**. Using two magnets, it is easy to show that:

like poles repel; unlike poles attract

a How could you compare the strength of two magnets?

b What happens if you hold the south pole of a bar magnet near the south pole of a different bar magnet?

Practical

Investigating magnetic fields

Hold a magnet near any iron or steel object and you should find that the magnet attracts the object. Iron and steel are examples of magnetic materials. A magnet is a piece of steel that has been magnetised. See for yourself the effect of a magnet on different objects including paper clips and iron filings on paper.

Figure 1 shows the effect of a magnet on iron filings sprinkled on a piece of paper.

- The paper clips (and the iron filings) stick to the ends of the magnet. We refer to the ends as **magnetic poles**.
- The iron filings near the magnet form a pattern of lines. The lines loop from one pole to the other. We say that there is a magnetic field around the magnet. We refer to the lines as **lines of force** or **magnetic field lines**.

A plotting compass placed in the magnetic field will always point along a field line. The direction the compass points in tells us the direction of the field line. Use a plotting compass to see the direction of the lines of force in the magnetic field.

- What do you find?

You should see that the lines always loop round from the north pole of the magnet to its south pole.

Figure 1 The magnetic field near a bar magnet

Electromagnets

An electromagnetic is made of insulated wire wrapped round an iron bar (the core). When a current is passed along the wire, a magnetic field is created around the wire. As a result, the magnetic field of the wire magnetises the iron bar strongly. When the current is switched off, the iron bar loses most of its magnetism. Iron easily loses its magnetism when the current is switched off. On the other hand, steel is unsuitable as the core of an electromagnet. That's because steel keeps its magnetism when the current is switched off.

Figure 2 Using an electromagnet

Figure 3 A simple electromagnet

We use electromagnets in many devices. Four such devices are described below.

1 The scrapyard crane

Scrap vehicles are lifted in a scrap yard using powerful electromagnets attached to cranes. The steel frame of a vehicle sticks to the electromagnet when current passes through the coil. When the current is switched off, the steel frame drops off the electromagnet.

2 The circuit breaker

This is a switch in series with an electromagnet. The switch is normally held in place by an iron catch. When too much current passes through the electromagnet, the switch is pulled open by the electromagnet, and the switch opens. It stays open until it is reset manually.

c Why is a spring needed in a circuit breaker?

3 The electric bell

When the bell is connected to the battery, the iron armature is pulled on to the electromagnet. This opens the make-and-break switch and the electromagnet is switched off. As a result, the armature springs back and the make-and-break switch closes again so the whole cycle repeats itself.

4 The relay

A relay is used to switch an electrical machine, such as a motor, on or off. Figure 6 shows what a relay consists of. When current passes through the electromagnet, the armature is pulled on to the electromagnet. As a result the armature turns about the pivot and closes the switch gap. In this way, a small current (through the electromagnet) is used to switch on a much larger current.

Summary questions

1 a i Which material, iron or steel, is used to make a permanent magnet?
   ii Which material, iron or steel, is used as the core of an electromagnet?
   b State whether there is a force of attraction or repulsion when:
   i a magnet is held near an unmagnetised bar magnet
   ii the north pole of a bar magnet is placed near the north pole of a second bar magnet
   iii the north pole of a bar magnet is placed near the south pole of a second bar magnet.

2 List the statements A–E below in the correct order to explain how the circuit breaker in Figure 4 works. Statement E is third in the correct order.
   A The current is cut off.
   B The iron core of the electromagnet is magnetised strongly.
   C Too much current passes through the coil.
   D The circuit breaker switch is opened.
   E The switch is attracted onto the core of the electromagnet.

3 The construction of a buzzer is like that of the electric bell except it does not have a striker or a bell.
   a Explain why the armature of the buzzer vibrates when the buzzer is connected to a battery.
   b In a bell and a buzzer, the armature vibrates continuously. The buzzer armature does not have a striker attached to it though. Explain why the buzzer vibrates at a higher frequency than the electric bell.

Switch closed
Switch open
Electromagnet

Figure 4 A circuit breaker

Iron armature
Electromagnet
Make-and-break switch
To battery
Bell
Springy metal strip

Figure 5 An electric bell

Switch gap
Pivot
Iron armature
Iron core of electromagnet
Coil of electromagnet
Switch terminals
Current in
Current out

Figure 6 The construction of a relay

Key points

- The force between two magnets: like poles repel; unlike poles attract.
- A magnetic field line is the line along which a plotting compass points.
- An electromagnet consists of a coil of insulated wire wrapped round an iron core.
- Electromagnets are used in scrapyard cranes, circuit breakers, electric bells and relays.

242 · 243

Further teaching suggestions

Levitation

- There are magnet sets that can be used to demonstrate levitation. These are usually circular magnets with holes in the centre that are placed over a pole. You can also show footage of superconducting materials that levitate above magnets.

Answers to in-text questions

a Compare the maximum number of paper clips each magnet can hold at one end. The stronger magnet is the one that holds most paper clips.

b They repel.

c The spring is needed to keep the switch open once it has been opened.

Summary answers

1 a i steel
     ii iron
   b i attraction
     ii repulsion
     iii attraction

2 1 C, 2 B, 3 E, 4 D, 5 A

3 a The current through the electromagnet coil magnetises the core of the electromagnet. The armature is pulled on to the core. This opens the make-and-break switch which cuts the current. The electromagnet loses its magnetism and the make-and-break switch closes, so the cycle repeats itself.
   b The armature of the buzzer has a much lower mass so it moves faster than the bell's armature and it therefore has a higher frequency of vibration.

P3 3.2

The motor effect

Learning objectives

Students should learn:

- that the force on a current-carrying conductor in a magnetic field can be increased by increasing the current or magnetic field strength
- that the direction of the force can be reversed by reversing the current
- how this force can be used to make objects move.

Learning outcomes

Most students should be able to:

- describe the effect of increasing the current or magnetic field strength on a current-carrying wire
- identify the direction of the force using Fleming's left-hand rule
- describe how an electric motor and loudspeaker work.

Some students should also be able to:

- describe and explain the effect of making changes to the design or operation of an electric motor.

Support

- For students who have difficulty manipulating small objects, you will need to provide some scaled-up motors that are partially preassembled.

Extend

- There are devices called linear motors that can be used to move objects without the rotation associated with normal motors. The students could find out about the invention of these devices and the uses they have been put to.

AQA

Specification link-up: Physics P3.3

- The motor effect and its use. [P3.3.1 b)]
- The size of the force can be increased by:
  - increasing the strength of the magnetic field
  - increasing the size of the current. [P3.3.1 c)]
- The conductor will not experience a force if it is parallel to the magnetic field. [P3.3.1 d)]
- The direction of the force is reversed if either the direction of the current or the direction of the magnetic field is reversed. [P3.3.1 e)]

Lesson structure

Starters

Magnetic magic – Some magicians use magnetic effects to levitate. You can show some footage of this levitation and ask the students to explain the magic to see if they realise there is a scientific principle behind the mystery (electromagnets lifting a person wearing a magnetic under-suit). Identify the direction of the force using Fleming's left-hand rule. (5 minutes)

Motor demonstration – Start by showing a functioning electric motor lifting a small load from the floor. Ask the students to explain what you can do to increase the force the motor can provide. They should be able to identify increasing the current. Support students by giving some suggestions and allowing them to select which would and which would not have an effect and what that effect would be. Extend the students by asking them to determine the power of the motor by giving them the load it lifts, the height and the time taken. Does this power match the electrical power provided ($P = VI$)? Why not? (10 minutes)

Main

- Before the first experiment, make sure that the students are aware of what magnetic field lines are and where they would be in the arrangement you are going to use. The experiment itself yields obvious results. When discussing the size of the force, most students intuitively realise that if you make the current 'stronger' or the magnet 'stronger' then the effect will be 'stronger' too. You can use diagrams to explain what is meant by perpendicular or parallel to the magnetic field lines, so that the students can understand why there is no force when the wire is parallel to the magnetic field lines.

- Fleming's left-hand rule is necessary for the specification, and helps solidify some students' understanding of the motor effect. To find the direction of the force acting on a current-carrying wire, the students can use Fleming's left-hand rule. They hold out their left hand with the thumb and first two fingers perpendicular to each other. Point the first finger in the direction of the magnetic field (from north to south); point the second finger in the direction of the current (from positive to negative). The thumb will point in the direction of the movement.

- A real motor, as used in a drill, will have several separate coils. Using their understanding of the motor effect, the students should be able to explain why this is necessary.

- Use a very large loudspeaker to show its action. If you can, strip away all of the paper including the central part to expose the magnet and the coil. You may be able to use a direct current to levitate the magnet, showing the students that there is no vibration and hence no sound.

Plenaries

Loudspeaker links – Show the students an electrical waveform that is to be fed into a loudspeaker. Ask them to describe the motion of the magnet in the speaker, including when it will be moving up or down and when its movement will be fastest. You can support students by using simple patterns or extend others by asking them to describe the movements in terms of acceleration (this will be linked to the gradient of the signal). This links back to their study of sound and oscilloscopes. (5 minutes)

Motor competition – All of the students should have completed motors. Get them to turn them on at the same time and see which ones are stable and which ones stop working quite quickly. Select the motor that is smoothest and most stable as the winner and give a prize. (10 minutes)

Practical support

Investigating the motor effect

The motor effect is easy to demonstrate or to let the students find out about.

Equipment and materials required

Battery, length of wire (stiff wire works best), variable resistor, leads, two magnets mounted on U frame (or a U-shaped magnet).

Details

The students place the wire between the two magnets and pass a small current through it. The variable resistor allows them to control the current to see if increasing it has the expected effect. Make sure that the students see the effect of reversing the current and changing the angle between the magnets and the wire. It can be hard to get the wire to run in the same direction as the field lines, but a piece of stiff wire can be bent into shape.

Alternatively, as a simple demonstration of the effect, a wider strip of foil can be used instead of the stiff wire. This will deflect or bend when a current is passed through it, demonstrating that a force is experienced.

Make a loudspeaker

It is possible to get the students to try to make a loudspeaker. These can be just as fiddly as motors (above).

Equipment and materials required

Per group: Thin insulated wire, strong magnet (cylindrical if possible), a tube just wider than the magnet signal generator, two leads and crocodile clips.

Details

The students need to make a tight and even coil of wire around a magnet without preventing the magnet moving. They can do this by coiling the wire around a tube with the magnet placed inside. The tube has to be just wider than the magnet so that it can vibrate inside (you might use plastic or cardboard tubing or even a boiling tube). Tape the coil down so it does not unravel after construction. Once the loudspeaker is constructed, it can be tested by connecting the wires to the signal generator with leads and crocodile clips to see if the magnet vibrates. A paper cone can then be attached if there is time.

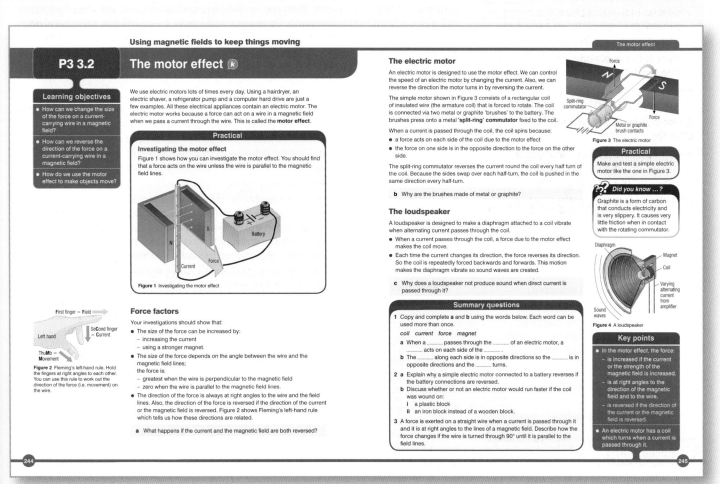

Answers to in-text questions

a No change, the actions cancel each other out.

b The material must conduct electricity.

c A direct current will not produce a changing magnetic field.

Summary answers

1 **a** current, coil, force, coil

  b current, force, coil

2 **a** The direction of the current is reversed and so the force on the coil is in the opposite direction.

  b An iron block would have eddy currents which would oppose the movement and slow the motor.

    i Faster because the coil is lighter.

    ii Faster because the field is much stronger due to the presence of iron.

3 The force decreases gradually as the wire is turned and becomes zero when the wire is parallel to the field lines.

P3 3.3

Electromagnetic induction

AQA

Specification link-up: Physics P3.3

- If an electrical conductor 'cuts' through a magnetic field a potential difference is induced across the ends of the conductor. [P3.3.2 a)]
- If a magnet is moved into a coil of wire a potential difference is induced across the ends of the coil. [P3.3.2 b)]

Learning objectives

Students should learn:

- that moving a wire through a magnetic field so that it cuts magnetic field lines will induce a pd along the length of the wire
- that electromagnets can be used to generate magnetic fields and so induce electric currents.

Learning outcomes

Most students should be able to:

- describe how a current can be induced in a moving wire and how to increase the size of the pd driving the current.

Some students should also be able to:

- describe how a changing current in one wire can induce a current in a second wire through connected magnetic fields.

Answers to in-text questions

a   i The current was zero.
   ii The current was in the opposite direction.

b   i The pointer is not deflected.
   ii The deflection would be bigger.

c The iron bar makes the magnetic field much stronger, so the induced pd is much bigger as a result.

Support

- Provide diagrams of the wire-moving experiment and the simple generator for the students to annotate. They should include the direction of the current and the force on the wire.

Extend

- Ask: 'How can the Earth's magnetic fields be used to generate electricity in space?' Recent experiments by NASA have tried to generate a current and you could show the students video or diagrams of this. A long wire is dragged beneath the shuttle and it cuts through the magnetic field causing a pd to be produced.

Lesson structure

Starters

Making electricity – The students should outline what they know about how electricity is produced by whatever means they like. *(5 minutes)*

Generating ideas – Pair up the students and ask the pairs to come up with an explanation of how electricity is produced. Then pair up the pairs and ask them to compare their ideas and make a combined explanation. Do this a couple more times until you have only two explanations and get the whole class to discuss which one is best. To support students, you can provide some statements about production that they can sort into an appropriate order or a diagram showing the stages to annotate. To extend the students, you should ask for energy transfer diagrams or discussions of energy 'loss' at each stage of the process. *(10 minutes)*

Main

- In this lesson the students will see how the interaction between wires and changing magnetic fields induces a potential difference. The ideas are best demonstrated through practical work, so let the students try them out and then spend time discussing the conclusions they have made.

- From the first practical, the students should come to the conclusion that it is a wire moving in a magnetic field that causes the current to be induced. They should also notice that the current is larger when the wire is moved more quickly. You can discuss the important consequences of this discovery (and refer to Faraday) although the focus of the lesson is to introduce the science behind transformers.

- The point of the second practical is to show the students that one changing current can induce another. Some will realise that this is a bit pointless as you have a large current inducing a smaller one which seems very wasteful. They will gain a greater insight when they appreciate that the pd changes and this is used for transformers.

Plenaries

Dynamic dynamo danger – Can the students come up with a **mechanical** way of keeping a bicycle light lit when the cycle is stopped for short periods? No batteries allowed! *(5 minutes)*

It's a wind-up – A wind-up radio is one device that uses induction to produce electricity on the go. Can the students think of any of their devices that could use wind-up power? Do they think that circles should keep rotating when the wheels are stopped? You can then discuss the idea of a flywheel with the students. Support the students by showing a flywheel device and ask them to draw simple energy transfer diagrams to show that they know that the wheel is a temporary store of kinetic energy. Extend the students by asking them to explain in detail how the energy is transferred into and out of the wheel. *(10 minutes)*

Practical support

Investigating a simple generator

This practical works best with a really strong magnet and a spot galvanometer. Make sure that the magnet doesn't get too close to the galvanometer, otherwise the coil can be damaged.

Equipment and materials required

Strong U-shaped magnet, stiff wire, leads, sensitive ammeter or galvanometer.

Details

The students simply move the wire up and down through the magnet, cutting the magnetic field lines. The ammeter should register a small current in one direction when the wire is moving down and a small current in the opposite direction when it is moving up. The size of the current should increase if the wire is moved more quickly. Make sure that the students see that there is no current when the wire is not moving, even when it is within the magnetic field.

- The students should find that:
  - **a** the current is zero
  - **b** the current is in the opposite direction
  - **c** no current is generated.

A magnetic puzzle

This practical works best with a really strong magnet and a spot galvanometer. Make sure that the magnet doesn't get too close to the galvanometer, otherwise the coil can be damaged.

Equipment and materials required

Cardboard tube, 3 V battery pack, sensitive ammeter (ideally an analogue one), thin insulated wire, iron bar.

Details

The students simply connect up the circuit as shown in the Student Book diagram. The more turns of wire on the coil the larger the induced current will be, so make sure that the students are making at least ten turns on the wire. When the switch is closed a twitch should be noticed on the ammeter.

Adding an iron bar should give a noticeable difference in the deflection shown on the ammeter. The students could try some other metals to see if they have an effect, if you have time.

Using magnetic fields to keep things moving

Electromagnetic induction

P3 3.3 **Electromagnetic induction**

Learning objectives

- What do we mean by electromagnetic induction?
- How can we use a magnet to induce a potential difference across the ends of a conductor?
- How can we induce a potential difference if we use an electromagnet instead of a magnet?

A hospital has its own electricity generator always 'on standby' in case of a power-cut. Patients' lives would be put at risk if the mains electricity supply failed and there was no standby generator.

A generator contains coils of wire that spin in a magnetic field. A potential difference (pd), or voltage, is created or **induced** across the ends of the wire when it cuts across the magnetic field lines. We call this process **electromagnetic induction**. If the wire is part of a complete circuit, the induced pd makes an electric current pass round the circuit.

Figure 1 A standby generator

Practical

Investigating a simple generator

Connect some insulated wire to an ammeter as shown in Figure 2. Move the wire between the poles of a U-shaped magnet and observe the ammeter. You should discover the ammeter pointer deflects as a current is generated when the wire cuts across the magnetic field.

- What difference is made if:
  - **a** the wire is held stationary between the poles of the magnet?
  - **b** the direction of motion of the wire is reversed?
  - **c** the wire is moved parallel to the lines of the magnetic field?

Make the wire into a coil and you should find the current is bigger.

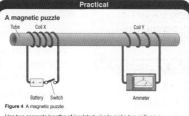
Movement of wire

Ammeter

Figure 2 Electromagnetic induction

a In the previous experiment, what can you say about the current when:
  i the wire was stationary
  ii the direction of motion of the wire was reversed?

A generator test

Look at Figure 3. It shows a coil of insulated wire connected to a centre-reading ammeter. When one end of a bar magnet is pushed into the coil, the ammeter pointer deflects.

This is because:

- the movement of the bar magnet causes an induced pd in the coil
- the induced pd causes a current, because the coil is part of a complete circuit.

b What do you think happens if:
  i the magnet is left at rest in the coil
  ii there were more turns of wire around the cardboard tube?

Hollow cardboard tube

Magnet

Meter pointer deflects when the magnet is pushed into the coil

Figure 3 Testing electromagnetic induction

Practical

A magnetic puzzle

Tube   Coil X   Coil Y

Battery   Switch   Ammeter

Figure 4 A magnetic puzzle

Use two separate lengths of insulated wire to make two coils on a cardboard tube as shown in Figure 4. Connect one of the coils (X) to a battery in series with a switch and connect the other coil (Y) to an ammeter.

1 Close the switch and you should discover that the ammeter pointer deflects briefly. Switching the current on creates a magnetic field that passes through coil Y as well as coil X. The effect on Y is the same as pushing a magnet into it. So a pd is induced in coil Y.

2 Keep the switch closed and observe the ammeter. You should see that the ammeter pointer does not deflect. This is because the current in X is now constant so the magnetic field does not change. The effect on Y is the same as when a magnet is held stationary in it. The magnetic field of the electromagnet has to be changing to induce a pd.

3 Repeat the first test with an iron bar in the tube. You should find that the deflection is much bigger.

c In the previous experiment, explain why the deflection was much bigger with the iron bar in the tube.

Summary questions

1 Copy and complete sentences **a** and **b** using the words below. Each word may be used more than once.

   magnetic field   conductor   current   potential difference

  a A .... is induced in a .... when it cuts across the .... lines.
  b If a .... connected to an ammeter moves parallel to the lines of a .... no .... passes through the ammeter.

2 A coil of wire is connected to a centre-reading ammeter. A bar magnet is inserted into the coil, making the ammeter pointer flick briefly.
What would you observe if:
  a the magnet was then held at rest in the coil
  b the coil had more turns of wire wrapped round the tube?

3 **a** In Figure 4, explain why the ammeter pointer deflects when the switch is closed.
  b Explain why the pointer does not deflect when there is a constant current in coil X.

Key points

- Electromagnetic induction is the process of creating a potential difference using a magnetic field.
- When a conductor cuts the lines of a magnetic field, a potential difference is induced across the ends of the conductor.
- When an electromagnet is used, it needs to be switched on or off to induce a pd.

Further teaching suggestions

ICT link-up

- A search for 'generator animation' on the internet will yield a free animation showing the rotation of a coil cutting a magnetic field and inducing a potential difference.

Summary answers

1 **a** potential difference, conductor , magnetic field
   b conductor, magnetic field, current

2 **a** There would be no deflection of the pointer.
   b The pointer deflection would be bigger.

3 **a** The current in X creates a magnetic field which passes through coil Y. The increase of the magnetic field in Y induced a pd in Y.
   b The magnetic field does not change. A pd can only be induced when the magnetic field is changing.

P3 3.4

Transformers

AQA
Specification link-up: Physics P3.3

- The basic structure of the transformer. [P3.3.2 c)]
- An alternating current in the primary coil produces a changing magnetic field in the iron core and hence in the secondary coil. This induces an alternating potential difference across the ends of the secondary coil. [P3.3.2 d)]
- In a step-up transformer the potential difference across the secondary coil is greater than the potential difference across the primary coil. [P3.3.2 e)]
- In a step-down transformer the potential difference across the secondary coil is less than the potential difference across the primary coil. [P3.3.2 f)]
- Switch mode transformers operate at a high frequency, often between 50 kHz and 200 kHz. [P3.3.2 i)]
- Switch mode transformers are much lighter and smaller than traditional transformers working from a 50 Hz mains supply. [P3.3.2 j)]
- Switch mode transformers use very little power when they are switched on but no load is applied. [P3.3.2 k)]
- Compare the use of different types of transformer for a particular application. [P3.3]

Controlled Assessment: P4.3 Collect primary and secondary data. [P4.3.2 a) b) c)]

Learning objectives

Students should learn:

- that transformers require alternating current because they rely on changing magnetic fields
- that the core of a transformer is a laminated iron block
- about the advantages of switch mode transformers and their applications.

Learning outcomes

Most students should be able to:

- describe, in detail, the operation of a transformer in terms of changing magnetic fields
- describe the basic structure of a transformer
- make a comparison between a standard transformer and a switch mode transformer.

Some students should also be able to:

- explain the features of a transformer that make it more efficient
- evaluate the type of transformer that should be used for a particular application.

Answers to in-text questions

a The magnetic field in the core would be much weaker because the core is not a magnetic material.

b The lamp would be brighter.

c The lamp would not light up with direct current in the primary coil.

Support

- A sequence of diagrams showing how the field in a transformer core changes should be provided as this is a very difficult concept for some to visualise.

Extend

- You may wish to extend some students by describing the formation of eddy currents in solid metal blocks. It is these that reduce the efficiency of the device by heating the metal. Laminating the core reduces these currents. This is **not** required by the specification, but it can help explain the efficiency of transformers and why they can heat up.

Lesson structure

Starters

Safety first – The students complete this sentence scientifically 'If a carbon fishing rod touches a very high potential difference cable ...'. The students' responses need to include ideas about high pd values causing high currents in conducting materials. *(5 minutes)*

Energy to our homes – The students should produce a diagram explaining how electricity is provided to our homes. This should include details of the power station and the National Grid including what they remember about transformers from P1 4.5 The National Grid. Check to see if they remember that the pd has to be changed at various stages and question them about how this is achieved and why it is needed. For support, you can show the structure of the grid and ask students to recall why changes in pd are needed and discuss what each part does. To extend students, you could look to the details such as 50 Hz and see if they can link this to the generator rotation speed. *(10 minutes)*

Main

- The first part of the lesson is purely revision. The students should remember that transformers are used to change potential differences for ac and that the National Grid uses step-up and step-down transformers.
- Take time to go through the operation of the transformer step-by-step. Perhaps the students could draw a flow chart of the operation. You will probably have to go through the stages a number of times emphasising what is happening to the magnetic fields.
- When they are making their transformers, check that they understand the operation correctly. They should be able to describe what each of the coils is doing and the changes in the magnetic fields.
- By connecting a dual trace oscilloscope to the input and output coils of a low pd transformer, you can show the relationship between the waveforms clearly. Understanding that changing fields are needed will let the students explain why direct current cannot be transformed in this way. Demonstrate that the transformer does not work when a dc supply is used.
- Show the students a range of real transformers, if possible, to show that some coils can have thousands of turns on them.
- The key advantage is that if nothing is connected to the power output of the device, then it does not use much energy. The students will need to know the difference between a standard transformer (as used in the National Grid) and the switch mode ones, so have them produce a summary table.

Plenaries

Compare transformers – The students must produce a table that summarises the differences between large National Grid transformers and the smaller switch mode transformers. This should include operating frequency, pd, physical size, purpose and additional components required. *(5 minutes)*

Transformer tests – The students design a controlled experiment to test which material is best for a transformer core. They need to include some way of measuring the current induced in the secondary coil. (This relates to: 'How Science Works': fair testing.) You can provide some of the diagrams and instructions to support students, or you can extend them by asking them to design the tests themselves. If you have the relevant equipment, you can carry the tests out in future lesson. *(10 minutes)*

Practical support

Making and testing a model transformer

A transformer is relatively simple to build given enough wire. Make sure, however, that the students cannot produce a pd higher than about 5 V.

Equipment and materials required
Transformer C core (laminated if possible), insulated wire, low-voltage ac power supply, 1.5 V torch lamp, 1.5 V cell and ac ammeter (optional).

Details
If possible use a power supply that can be locked at 1 V, so that the students cannot produce a high output pd with the transformer. The students should wrap about 10 loops of wire for the input coil and a maximum of about 15 for the output coil. This will produce a step-up transformer, but only up to the required 1.5 V for the bulb.

It is crucial that the students see that a transformer will only operate with an ac source, not a dc one, so take this opportunity to demonstrate or let them investigate this effect. Explain that the **changes** in magnetic fields are required to induce a pd in the second core.

Using magnetic fields to keep things moving

P3 3.4 — Transformers

Learning objectives
- Why do transformers only work with ac?
- What is the core of a transformer made from?
- How does a switch mode transformer differ from an ordinary transformer?

links
For more information on the National Grid, look back at P1 4.5 The National Grid.

A typical power station generator produces an alternating potential difference (pd) of about 25 000 volts. Mains electricity to homes is at 230 volts.

When you plug an appliance into the mains, the electricity to run it comes from a power station. The electricity arrives via a network of cables called the **National Grid**. The alternating pd of the cables (the grid voltage) is typically 132 000 volts. A **transformer** is used to change the size of the alternating pd.

How a transformer works
A transformer has two coils of insulated wire, both wound round the same iron core, as shown in Figure 1. The primary coil is connected to an alternating current supply. When alternating current passes through the primary coil, an alternating pd is induced in the secondary coil.

This happens because:
- alternating current passing through the primary coil produces an alternating magnetic field
- the lines of the alternating magnetic field pass through the secondary coil
- the magnetic field is changing.

This creates an alternating potential difference between the terminals of the secondary coil. We say an alternating potential difference is 'induced' in the secondary coil.

If a bulb is connected across the secondary coil, the induced pd causes an alternating current in the secondary circuit. So the bulb lights up. Electrical energy is therefore transferred from the primary to the secondary coil. This happens even though they are **not** electrically connected in the same circuit.
- A **step-up transformer** makes the pd across the secondary coil greater than the pd across the primary coil. Its secondary coil has more turns than its primary coil.
- A **step-down transformer** makes the pd across the secondary coil less than the pd across the primary coil. Its secondary coil has fewer turns than its primary coil.

For example, we use a step-down transformer in a low-voltage supply to step the mains pd down from 230 V.

Figure 1 Transformer action a in a circuit b circuit symbol

Practical

Make a model transformer
Wrap a coil of insulated wire round the iron core of a model transformer as the primary coil. Connect the coil to a 1 V ac supply. Then connect a second length of insulated wire to a 1.5 V torch bulb. When you wrap enough turns of the second wire round the iron core, the bulb should light up.
- Test if cores made from different materials affect the transformer.

Figure 2 A model transformer

a Why would the lamp not light up as brightly if the iron core was replaced with a wooden core?
b What happens if you wrap more turns on the secondary coil?
c What happens if you use a cell or a battery instead of the ac supply?

Transformers in action
Transformers only work with alternating current. With a direct current, there is no changing magnetic field so the secondary pd is zero.

In the type of transformer described above, the core of the transformer 'guides' the field lines in a loop through the coils. But the field must be changing to induce a pd in the secondary coil.

Figure 3 shows a practical transformer.

The primary and secondary coils are both wound round the same part of the core. The core is layered (laminated) to cut out induced currents in the iron layers. If it were not laminated, the efficiency of the transformer would be greatly reduced.

Switch mode transformers
A **switch mode transformer** works in a different way to the traditional transformer described above. It operates at frequencies between 50 000 Hz (50 kHz) and 200 000 Hz (200 kHz). Its main features listed below make it very suitable for use in mobile phone chargers.
- It is lighter and smaller than a traditional transformer which works at 50 Hz.
- It uses very little power when there is no device connected across its output terminals.

A mobile phone charger has three main circuits. Figure 4 shows you what each circuit does.

The switch mode transformer has a ferrite core. This is much lighter than an iron core and, unlike an iron core, can work at high frequency. The circuits convert the mains pd (at 230 V and 50 Hz in Europe) to a much lower direct pd.

Figure 3 A practical transformer

Figure 4 Block diagram of a mobile phone charger

Summary questions
1 Copy and complete the paragraph using the words below. Each word can be used more than once.
current   magnetic field   pd   primary   secondary
In a transformer, an alternating .... is passed through the .... coil. This coil creates an alternating .... that passes through the .... coil. As a result, an alternating .... is induced in the .... coil.
2 a Why does a transformer not work with direct current?
  b Why is it important that the coil wires of a transformer are insulated?
  c Why is the core of a transformer made of iron?
3 a A laptop computer can operate with a 14 V battery or with a mains transformer.
    i What is the benefit of having a dual power supply?
    ii Does the transformer step up or step down the pd applied to it?
  b Why is a switch mode transformer lighter than an ordinary transformer?

Key points
- A transformer only works on ac because a changing magnetic field is necessary to induce ac in the secondary coil.
- A transformer has an iron core unless it is a switch mode transformer which has a ferrite core.
- A switch mode transformer is lighter and smaller than an ordinary transformer. It operates at high frequency.

Summary answers

1 current, primary, magnetic field, secondary, pd, secondary

2 a Direct current in the primary coil would not produce an alternating magnetic field, so no pd would be induced in the secondary coil.
  b The current would short-circuit across the wires instead of passing through them. This would cause the coil to overheat if it did not cause a fuse to blow.
  c Iron is a magnetic material, so it makes the magnetic field much stronger. It is easily magnetised and demagnetised when the current alternates.

3 a i If the mains supply fails or if no mains supply is available, the battery takes over.
    ii The transformer steps the pd down.
  b It has a ferrite core which is much lighter than an iron core of the same size.

P3 3.5

Transformers in action

AQA
Specification link-up: Physics P3.3

- The potential difference pd across the primary and secondary coils of a transformer are related by the equation:
$$\frac{V_p}{V_s} = \frac{n_p}{n_s} \text{ [P3.3.2 g)]}$$

- If transformers are assumed to be 100% efficient, the electrical power output would equal the electrical power input.
$$V_p \times I_p = V_s \times I_s \text{ [P3.3.2 h)]}$$

Controlled Assessment: P4.3 Collect primary and secondary data. *[P4.3.2 a) b) c)]*

Learning objectives

Students should learn:

- that a step-up transformer increases the potential difference while a step-down transformer decreases it
- that the National Grid uses transformers to save electrical energy
- how to calculate the change in potential difference produced by a transformer.

Learning outcomes

Most students should be able to:

- describe the function of step-up and step-down transformers as used in the National Grid
- use the transformer equation to explain how the relationship between the number of turns on the coils determines its use as a step-up or step-down transformer
- explain why it is more efficient to transfer electrical energy at high pd.

Some students should also be able to:

- use the transformer equations.

Support

- All students need to tackle the calculations but there will be some who will struggle with the mathematics, so provide worksheets to help with the calculations. These should show each of the stages required to reach the answer to reinforce a logical and methodical approach.

Extend

- The students should look into the relationship between the number of turns on a transformer and the input and output currents. Ask: 'What does a step-down transformer do to the current?' They will need to use the relationship $P = VI$ to understand this.

Lesson structure

Starters

The big connective – Get the students to finish the paragraph 'The National Grid is very useful … '. This should let them show their knowledge of what the grid is and what it is used for. You may need to refresh their memories a bit with an annotated diagram. *(5 minutes)*

Electrical power – The students have studied electrical power before and now need to refresh their memories by performing some simple calculations using the equation $(P = VI)$. Set some differentiated questions involving electrical power calculations. *(10 minutes)*

Main

- This again partly revises previous material from Unit P1 in the specification where the basics of the National Grid were covered. However, here the students need to perform the detailed calculations demonstrating the changes in pd and current.

- The students will need plenty of practice with the transformer equation, particularly with the rearrangement of it. This is one of the situations where the students will find using the symbols easier than writing out the full equation. You should expect them to successfully complete several calculations before moving on.

- The transformer efficiency material is new. One of the students might point out that no device is 100% efficient, but just explain that you are using this number to make the calculations easier and everybody will be happy. The students should understand that if the device is 100% efficient, then the power output is the same as the power input; but remind them of this anyway.

- You will also have to remind the students of the relationship: power = potential difference × current from earlier electrical work. By discussing the relationship $P = VI$, the students should understand that to provide a higher power, you could increase the current or potential difference. This then leads on to the problem with a larger current: excessive heating and wasted energy.

- The final calculations are difficult for many, because they involve several stages. Separating out these stages clearly will help.

Plenaries

Transformer matching – Can the students match up the transformers with the changes in pd? This can be as simple as matching cards that describe the transformers (300 turns to 600 turns) and example pd changes (10 V to 20 V). *(5 minutes)*

Combinations – Give the students a circuit with a set of four transformers in a row. Give them the input pd and the number of turns on each transformer and ask them to work out the final output pd. You can make this task more demanding and extend students by stating that each transformer is only 95% efficient. Support can be provided by giving a calculation template and reducing the number of transformers. *(10 minutes)*

Practical support

Investigating transformer efficiency

The students can verify if the transformer is efficient by measuring the power in and out of a transformer arrangement.

Equipment and materials required

For each group; transformer (this could be made by the students as in the last topic), two ac ammeters, two ac voltmeters, low-voltage ac power supply, 3 V lamp.

Details

Set pd and fix the power supply so that it will produce a pd that will give a suitable output pd from the transformer to light the lamp. Arrange the transformer so that an ammeter and voltmeter measure the input current and input pd and the second ammeter

and voltmeter to measure the output characteristics. The students can then measure the input power using $P = VI$ and also the output power. From this they can calculate the efficiency.

To extend the investigation, the students can find out if the efficiency is increased by increasing the number of turns on each coil (while maintaining the same ratio), or if a laminated iron core really has an effect. Students could make their own predictions and test them out. See 'How Science Works'.

More practice

The students should perform additional calculations using the transformer equation to makes sure that they thoroughly understand it.

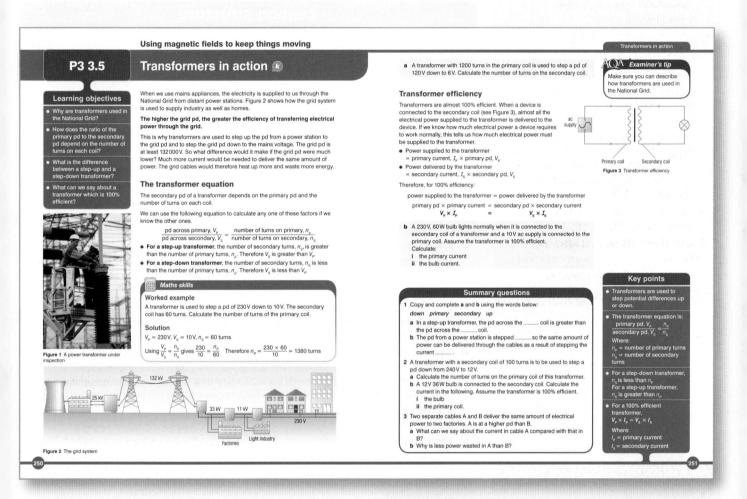

Using magnetic fields to keep things moving

P3 3.5

Transformers in action

Learning objectives

- Why are transformers used in the National Grid?
- How does the ratio of the primary pd to the secondary pd depend on the number of turns on each coil?
- What is the difference between a step-up and a step-down transformer?
- What can we say about a transformer which is 100% efficient?

Figure 1 A power transformer under inspection

When we use mains appliances, the electricity is supplied to us through the National Grid from distant power stations. Figure 2 shows how the grid system is used to supply industry as well as homes.

The higher the grid pd, the greater the efficiency of transferring electrical power through the grid.

This is why transformers are used to step up the pd from a power station to the grid pd and to step the grid pd down to the mains voltage. The grid pd is at least 132 000 V. So what difference would it make if the grid pd were much lower? Much more current would be needed to deliver the same amount of power. The grid cables would therefore heat up more and waste more energy.

The transformer equation

The secondary pd of a transformer depends on the primary pd and the number of turns on each coil.

We can use the following equation to calculate any one of these factors if we know the other ones.

$$\frac{\text{pd across primary, } V_p}{\text{pd across secondary, } V_s} = \frac{\text{number of turns on primary, } n_p}{\text{number of turns on secondary, } n_s}$$

- **For a step-up transformer**, the number of secondary turns, n_s, is greater than the number of primary turns, n_p. Therefore V_s is greater than V_p.
- **For a step-down transformer**, the number of secondary turns, n_s is less than the number of primary turns, n_p. Therefore V_s is less than V_p.

Maths skills

Worked example

A transformer is used to step a pd of 230 V down to 10 V. The secondary coil has 60 turns. Calculate the number of turns of the primary coil.

Solution

$V_P = 230\,V, V_s = 10\,V, n_s = 60$ turns

Using $\dfrac{V_P}{V_S} = \dfrac{n_P}{n_S}$ gives $\dfrac{230}{10} = \dfrac{n_P}{60}$ Therefore $n_P = \dfrac{230 \times 60}{10} = 1380$ turns

Figure 2 The grid system

a A transformer with 1200 turns in the primary coil is used to step a pd of 120 V down to 6 V. Calculate the number of turns on the secondary coil.

Transformer efficiency

Transformers are almost 100% efficient. When a device is connected to the secondary coil (see Figure 3), almost all the electrical power supplied to the transformer is delivered to the device. If we know how much electrical power a device requires to work normally, this tells us how much electrical power must be supplied to the transformer.

- Power supplied to the transformer = primary current, $I_p \times$ primary pd, V_p
- Power delivered by the transformer = secondary current, $I_s \times$ secondary pd, V_s

Therefore, for 100% efficiency:

power supplied to the transformer = power delivered by the transformer

primary pd × primary current = secondary pd × secondary current
$$V_P \times I_P = V_S \times I_S$$

b A 230 V, 60 W bulb lights normally when it is connected to the secondary coil of a transformer and a 10 V ac supply is connected to the primary coil. Assume the transformer is 100% efficient.
Calculate:
   i the primary current
   ii the bulb current.

Figure 3 Transformer efficiency
Primary coil   Secondary coil

AQA Examiner's tip
Make sure you can describe how transformers are used in the National Grid.

Summary questions

1 Copy and complete **a** and **b** using the words below:

   down primary secondary up

   a In a step-up transformer, the pd across the .... coil is greater than the pd across the .... coil.
   b The pd from a power station is stepped .... so the same amount of power can be delivered through the cables as a result of stepping the current ....

2 A transformer with a secondary coil of 100 turns is to be used to step a pd down from 240 V to 12 V.
   a Calculate the number of turns on the primary coil of this transformer.
   b A 12 V 36 W bulb is connected to the secondary coil. Calculate the current in the following. Assume the transformer is 100% efficient.
      i the bulb
      ii the primary coil.

3 Two separate cables A and B deliver the same amount of electrical power to two factories. A is at a higher pd than B.
   a What can we say about the current in cable A compared with that in B?
   b Why is less power wasted in A than B?

Key points

- Transformers are used to step potential differences up or down.
- The transformer equation is:
   $\dfrac{\text{primary pd, } V_P}{\text{secondary pd, } V_S} = \dfrac{n_P}{n_S}$
   Where:
   n_P = number of primary turns
   n_S = number of secondary turns
- For a step-down transformer, n_s is less than n_p. For a step-up transformer, n_s is greater than n_p.
- For a 100% efficient transformer,
   $V_p \times I_p = V_S \times I_S$
   Where:
   I_p = primary current
   I_s = secondary current

Answers to in-text questions

a 60 turns

b i 6 A
   ii 0.26 A

Summary answers

1 **a** secondary, primary
   b up, down

2 **a** 2000 turns
   b i 3 A
      ii 0.15 A

3 **a** The current in A is less than in B as the pd of A is higher than the pd of B, and the power delivered is the same.

   b The current through A is smaller than the current through B, so the heating effect of the current in A is less than in B.

P3 3.6

A physics case study

AQA Specification link-up: Physics P3.1 & P3.3

- X-rays can be used to diagnose and treat some medical conditions. *[P3.1.1 b)]*
- Visible light can be sent along optical fibres. *[P3.1.5 c)]*
- Evaluate the advantages and disadvantages of using ultrasound, X-rays and computerised tomography (CT) scans. *[P3.1]*
- When a current flows through a wire a magnetic field is produced around the wire. *[P3.3.1 a)]*

Learning objectives

Students should learn:

- that the principles of physics are used in hospitals for diagnosis and treatment for a wide range of conditions
- that measurements that can be taken include blood pressure, electrocardiograms, optical investigations using endoscopes, CT scans and MRI
- that some diagnosis techniques are potentially harmful, so risks and benefits must be assessed.

Learning outcomes

Most students should be able to:

- list some of the techniques used for medical diagnosis in hospitals
- describe how the principles of physics are applied in medical diagnosis.

Some students should also be able to:

- evaluate the benefits of diagnostic techniques and the associated risks.

Support

- You should be able to find a range of CT scan images (some animated) to show the advantages of the CT scanner over X-rays. The animations will certainly help students visualise the body parts.

Extend

- There is a wide range of opportunities to look at the function of the devices mentioned in this topic in more detail. Students could explain the physical processes that are happening in each of the machines mentioned, such as the changes in pressure inside the cuff and even the effect on the transducer. They could use a galvanometer to note electrical changes between their two hands, and so on.

Lesson structure

Starters

Diagnosis – Have the students list all of the 'tests' that diagnosticians (doctors, nurses, etc.) carry out in general practice and in hospitals. They should be able to come up with a substantial list. Now get them to divide the list into non-invasive (where no harm occurs to the body) and invasive techniques. You can discuss risks and benefits of any techniques if you have time. *(5 minutes)*

Magnetism matters – Support students by asking them to produce a recap on magnetism including the effects. They need to differentiate between magnetic and non-magnetic materials (make sure that they do not think that all metals are magnetic). Extend students by asking them to describe electromagnets and how to increase their strength; this should lead to the idea of large currents; this will be discussed in the lesson as part of the MRI device. *(10 minutes)*

Main

- In this spread, the students will look at the application of physics in hospitals. The focus is on medical diagnosis but there is also opportunity to expand this to consider some treatment options (if you wish) and extra time is available. It is possible that students have relatives undergoing diagnosis or treatment so be sensitive just in case.

- The students should have studied the endoscope in P3 1.4 The endoscope, but refresh their memories by showing some suitable footage. Use a nasal insertion if you can find one as this relates closely to the patient discussed in the spread.

- You may have a sphygmomanometer in school. These are relatively cheap and available at most large branches of pharmacies. They are digital and you can demonstrate their use on yourself. It's worth showing the historical design of a manometer using a mercury column to help explain where the two numbers quoted by a doctor (systolic pressure and diastolic pressure) come from. See 'Practical support' for more details.

- Electrocardiograms are often seen on television but the procedures are unclear. To detect the small electrical signals happening in the heart a range of electrodes have to be connected to various points on the patient. The simplest measurements (often used in emergency wards) require only three, and these can produce the basic pattern seen in the diagram. Often more detailed studies take place later and these can require up to 12 leads and so give much more information and the precision needed for diagnosis of subtle conditions.

- You can attempt to explain the patterns shown on the ECG if you like, although there are quite a lot of details. To help, you can find some high-quality simulations that link the traces to the electrical and physical actions in the heart. These can be found using a basic search of the internet. You can also find some abnormal traces to compare with the normal pattern.

- You can now move on to the scanning techniques. The CT scan has been covered before in P3 1.1 X-rays. Here you should discuss the risks and benefits to the patient; this can be quite extensive with suitable students. Exposure to the X-rays will harm some cells but without clear diagnosis, a treatment cannot start. If you have an example film badge, you can discuss the exposure to the radiographer.

Plenaries

Diagnosis: dangers – The students should explain why diagnostic techniques such as CT scans are not used routinely; that they are used after other techniques have been tried. They should be able to explain how the level of risk to the patient is increased by some of the techniques and that they will cost significantly more. The students could attempt to sort the techniques described in terms of risk to the patients and/or costs. *(5 minutes)*

Operation! – Once diagnosis is complete an operation may be required. Ask a set of differentiated oral questions about the chapter 'Medical applications of physics' to stretch or support the students. When a student gets one right they can have a go at the 'operation' game (from Hasbro) and see if they can remove the required object from the patient. The person with the most 'bits' is the winner. This game can also be played in smaller groups with question cards deciding who has a go instead of the traditional 'turn' taking. *(10 minutes)*

Practical support

Measuring blood pressure

To demonstrate the technique you can take measurements on yourself (with assistance if required.). The instructions should be provided with the kit so follow them. There are two readings that will be found so make sure you know what the two numbers represent before the students ask. The first is the systolic pressure; this is the peak pressure in the artery found as the ventricles contract and

push blood out of the heart. The second is the diastolic pressure which is the lowest pressure and this occurs when the ventricles are refilling with blood.

In simple terms the cuff measures the systolic pressure by increasing the pressure until the blood flow is completely stopped (its pressure is greater than the pressure in the artery so it squashes it shut). The pressure is then decreased until there is no restriction of blood flow at all meaning that the cuff pressure has fallen below the lowest pressure in the artery (the diastolic pressure).

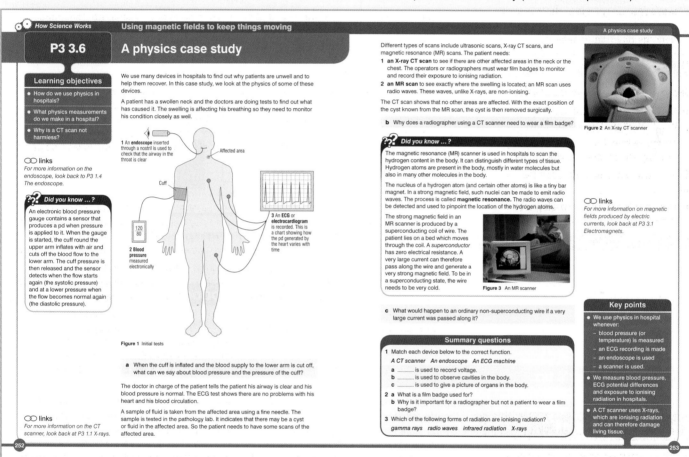

Further teaching suggestions

Defibrillation

- This technique is commonly portrayed in the media and it relies on some important physics (and biology). The students can research the history of the technique including early designs (using ac), through to the small portable devices carried in most ambulances that rely on the storage of charge to provide a current of exact specifications.

Difficult decisions

- Health care funding is limited and some treatments and pieces of equipment are more expensive than others. You can organise a discussion about whether a hospital should invest in a new MRI or gamma camera system or fund other, more basic, techniques. If you have a local hospital you can find out about their investment plans.

Answers to in-text questions

a The cuff pressure is equal to or greater than blood pressure when the blood flow to the lower arm is stopped.

b To record their exposure to X-rays.

c The wire would melt like a fuse wire because its resistance is not zero and the very large current would heat it to its melting point.

Summary answers

1. **a** An ECG machine **b** An endoscope **c** A CT scanner

2. **a** A film badge is used to record the exposure of the wearer to ionising radiation.

   b The radiographer works in the radiography department many hours each week throughout the year, whereas the patient is only there for a short time.

3. gamma rays, X-rays

Summary answers

1 **a** current, force
b current, lines, field

2 **a** When a current passes through the coil of the electromagnet, the core of the electromagnet becomes magnetised and attracts the iron armature. The iron armature turns about the pivot and its lower end pushes against one side of the switch and makes the switch close.
b When the ignition switch is closed, the core of the relay coil becomes magnetised, so the relay switch closes. The motor is switched on as a result of the relay switch closing.

3 **a** Down.
b The force is zero.
c The force on the sides make the coil turn.

4 **a** **i** step-up
ii step-down
b Direct current through the primary coil does not produce an alternating magnetic field. No pd is induced in the secondary coil as the magnetic field through it does not change.

5 **a** **i** Power = current × pd = 10 A × 100 000 V = 1 000 000 W
ii 100 A
b The higher the pd, the less the current needed to transfer a certain amount of electric power. The smaller the current through the cables, the less power is wasted in the cables due to their resistance and the heating effect of the current.

6 **a** 12 V
b 0.5 A
c 5 A

7 **a** 150 turns
b 0.15 A

AQA Examiner's tip

Questions 1 and 2 should help students overcome their confusion between the two related concepts of motor effect and induction. It is often helpful to discuss the energy transfers for each situation to help clarify the key differences. The situation in Question 1 can be investigated by pupils. A plotting compass, rather than a bar magnet, will work with fairly small currents.

AQA Examiner's tip

Although generators are not mentioned in the specification, it is helpful to link the concept of induction with generating electricity and contrast this with motors, where electrical energy is the input rather than the output. The law of energy conservation can be used to help students understand why a stationary conductor will not have an induced voltage. For example, work would be done by an induced current, therefore work has to be done in order to generate the current and this requires movement.

Using magnetic fields to keep things moving: P3 3.1–P3 3.6

Summary questions

1 Copy and complete **a** and **b** using the words below. Each word can be used more than once.

field force lines current

a A vertical wire is placed in a horizontal magnetic field. When a ………… is passed through the wire, a ………… acts on the wire.

b A force acts on a wire in a magnetic field when a ………… passes along the wire and the wire is not parallel to the ………… of the ………… .

2 **a** Figure 1 shows the construction of a relay. Explain why the switch closes when a current passes through the coil of the electromagnet.

Figure 1

b Figure 2 shows the relay coil in a circuit that is used to switch on the starter motor of a car. Explain why the motor starts when the ignition switch is closed.

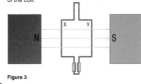

Figure 2

3 Figure 3 shows a rectangular coil of wire in a magnetic field viewed from above. When a direct current passes clockwise round the coil, an upward force acts on side X of the coil.

Figure 3

a What is the direction of the force on side Y of the coil?

b What can you say about the force on each side of the coil parallel to the magnetic field lines?

c What is the effect of the forces on the coil?

4 **a** Copy and complete **i** and **ii** using the words below.

step-down step-up

i A transformer that changes an alternating pd from 12 V to 120 V is a ………… transformer.

ii A ………… transformer has more turns on the prima coil than on the secondary coil.

b Explain why a transformer does not work on direct current.

5 **a** Cables at a potential difference of 100 000 V are usec to transfer 1 million watts of electrical power in part c a grid system.

i Show that the current in the cables is 10 A.

ii If the potential difference had been 10 000 V, how much current would be needed to transfer the same amount of power?

b Explain why power is transmitted through the Nation Grid at a high pd rather than a low pd.

6 A transformer has 50 turns in its primary coil and 500 turns in its secondary coil. It is to be used to light a 12C 60 W bulb connected to the secondary coil. Assume th transformer is 100% efficient.

a Calculate the primary pd.

b Calculate the current in the bulb.

c Calculate the current in the primary coil.

7 A transformer has 3000 turns on its primary coil. An alternating pd of 240 V is to be connected to the prima coil and a 12 V bulb is to be connected to the seconda coil.

a Calculate the number of turns the secondary coil should have.

b What would be the current through the primary coil the current through the lamp is to be 3.0 A. Assume the transformer is 100% efficient.

254

Kerboodle resources

Resources available for this chapter on Kerboodle are:

- Chapter map: Using magnetic fields to keep things moving
- Animation: The motor effect (P3 3.2)
- How Science Works practical: Current through a motor (P3 3.2)
- Extension: The important role of transformers (P3 3.4)
- Interactive activity: Transformers and their uses (P3 3.4 and 3.5)
- Viewpoint: Do power lines increase our risk of cancer? (P3 3.5)
- Revision podcast: Magnetic fields at work
- Test yourself: Using magnetic fields to keep things moving
- On your marks: Magnetic fields at work
- Examination-style questions: Using magnetic fields to keep things moving
- Answers to examination-style questions: Using magnetic fields to keep things moving

End of chapter questions

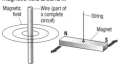

AQA Examination-style questions k

1 A magnet is held suspended near a wire that has a magnetic field around it.

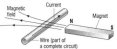

Magnetic field — Wire (part of a complete circuit) — String — Magnet — N — S

a What causes the magnetic field to be produced around a wire? (1)

b When released, the magnet rotates slowly in the direction shown. What is the name for this effect? (1)

c Give **two** ways in which the force on the magnet could be reversed. (2)

d Give **two** ways of increasing the force on the magnet. (2)

The wire and the magnet are now arranged as shown below. A current passes through the wire and the wire experiences a force. Only part of the magnetic field from the magnet is shown.

Magnetic field — Current — N — Magnet — S — Wire (part of a complete circuit)

e Use Fleming's left-hand rule to find the direction of the force on the wire. Explain fully how you used the rule. (3)

The diagram shows a wire being moved upwards through the magnetic field between two poles of a magnet. A voltmeter is connected across the wire.

Magnet — S — Magnetic field — N — Magnet — Wire — V

a Explain why the voltmeter gives a reading when the wire is being moved upwards but not when it is stationary. (2)

b How does the potential difference change if the wire is moved
  i downwards (1)
  ii sideways? (1)

3 a Copy and complete the diagram to show the basic structure of a transformer. Label each part. (3)

Core

b Explain the difference between a step-up transformer and a step-down transformer. (2)

c What must be happening in the iron core of the transformer when it is producing a potential difference on the output? (1)

d The following equation can be used when designing transformers.

$$\frac{V_P}{V_s} = \frac{n_P}{n_s}$$

  i Give the meaning of each of the symbols in the equation. (4)
  ii Calculate V_p if $V_s = 55\,V$, $n_p = 320$ and $n_s = 40$. Write down the equation you use. Show clearly how you work out your answer. (3)
  iii Calculate n_s if $V_p = 11\,000\,V$, $V_s = 230\,V$ and $n_p = 55\,000$. Write down the equation you use. Show clearly how you work out your answer. (3)
  iv Calculate the output current from this transformer when the input current is 2.5 A. Show clearly how you work out your answer and give the unit. (3)

e Give a typical frequency at which a switch mode transformer works. (1)

f Give **two** advantages of a switch mode transformer compared with an iron-core transformer. (2)

255

AQA Practical suggestions

Practicals	AQA	k	📖	⚙
Placing a foil strip with a current going through it in a strong magnetic field.	✓		✓	
Building a motor.	✓	✓	✓	✓
Making a loudspeaker.	✓		✓	
Making a transformer using C cores and insulated wire.	✓		✓	
Demonstrating a transformer to show the difference between using dc and ac.	✓		✓	

AQA Examination-style answers

1 a An electric current. *(1 mark)*

  b The motor effect. *(1 mark)*

  c Change the direction of the current; reverse the poles of the magnet. *(2 marks)*

  d Increase the current; move the magnet and the wire closer. *(2 marks)*

  e Force is upwards.
  Any **two** from the following three points:
  thumb and first two fingers mutually perpendicular
  line up first finger with magnetic field, second finger with current
  thumb shows direction of the force *(3 marks)*

2 a Wire must 'cut'/move across field lines to induce a voltage. *(2 marks)*

  b **i** opposite sign (accept negative) *(1 mark)*
      ii Potential difference is zero. *(1 mark)*

3 a

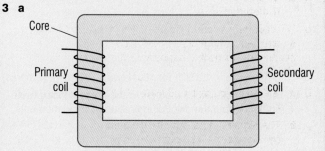

Core — Primary coil — Secondary coil

(3 marks)

  b A step-up transformer increases the voltage.
  A step-down transformer decreases the voltage. *(2 marks)*

  c There must be a changing magnetic field. *(1 mark)*

  d **i** V_p = primary pd, V_s = secondary pd,
      n_p = primary turns, n_s = secondary turns *(4 marks)*

  ii $V_p = \dfrac{n_p \times V_s}{n_s}$

  $= \dfrac{320 \times 55}{40}$

  $= 440\,V$ *(3 marks)*

  iii $n_s = \dfrac{V_s \times n_p}{V_p}$

  $= \dfrac{230 \times 55\,000}{11\,000}$

  $= 1150$ turns *(3 marks)*

  iv $V_p \times I_p = V_s \times I_s$ (assume no power loss from transformer)
  $11\,000 \times 2.5 = 230 \times I_s$
  $I_s = 119.6\,A$ *(3 marks)*

  e 50 000 to 200 000 Hz *(1 mark)*

  f lighter and smaller; uses very little power *(2 marks)*

AQA Examiner's tip

There must be a changing magnetic field through the secondary coil in order for there to be an induced output voltage. Higher level students may understand the link between the 'dynamo effect' in Question 2 and the operation of a transformer. Magnetic field lines 'cut' through the coil as the strength of the field changes in the core of the transformer.

AQA Examination-style answers

1 a near point *(1 mark)*

b 25 cm *(1 mark)*

c ciliary muscle *(1 mark)*

d relaxes, flattening the lens *(1 mark)*

e long-sightedness *(1 mark)*

f short-sightedness *(1 mark)*

2

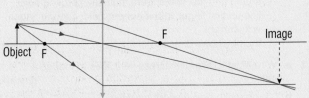

Converging lens

Object F F Image

The focal length of the lens is 3.0 cm. *(3 marks)*

3 a i $W = m \times g$
$= 2.0 \times 10$
$= 20\,N$ *(2 marks)*

ii moment $= F \times d$
$= 20 \times 0.08$
$= 1.6\,N\,m$ (or $160\,N\,cm$) *(3 marks)*

b The (total) clockwise moment = the (total) anticlockwise moment about the pivot/or indication of 'total' moments. *(2 marks)*

c $1.6 = 0.80 \times$ weight of **B**
weight of **B** $= 1.6/0.80 = 2.0\,N$
mass of **B** $= 2.0/10 = 0.20\,kg$ *(3 marks)*

d Mass **B** must be moved to the left.
The weight of the rule produces a clockwise moment because its centre of mass is to the right of the pivot/ (Moving **B** left) reduces the (total) clockwise moment *(3 marks)*

4 a Liquids are incompressible. *(1 mark)*

b $P = \dfrac{F}{A} = \dfrac{10\,000}{0.0004}$
$= 25\,000\,000\,Pa$ *(3 marks)*

c $25\,000\,000\,Pa$ *(1 mark)*

d $F = P \times A = 25\,000\,000 \times 0.0025$
$= 62\,500\,N$ *(3 marks)*

5 There is a clear and detailed description of how you would use the motor effect to move a wire. The answer shows almost faultless spelling, punctuation and grammar. It is coherent and in an organised, logical sequence. It contains a range of appropriate or relevant specialist terms used accurately. *(5–6 marks)*

There is a workable description of the method. There are some errors in spelling, punctuation and grammar. The answer has some structure and organisation. The use of specialist terms has been attempted, but not always accurately. *(3–4 marks)*

There is a brief description of how you would use a magnet in conjunction with the wire which has little clarity and detail. The spelling, punctuation and grammar are very weak. The answer is poorly organised with almost no specialist terms and/or their use demonstrating a general lack of understanding of their meaning. *(1–2 marks)*

No relevant content. *(0 marks)*

Examination-style questions

1 The diagram shows two images of a normal eye.

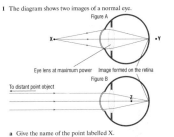

Figure A

X — Y

Eye lens at maximum power   Image formed on the retina

Figure B

To distant point object

Z

a Give the name of the point labelled X. *(1)*
b In a normal eye, approximately how far is this point from the eye? *(1)*
c Name the muscle that changes the shape of the lens. *(1)*
d How does this muscle change the shape of the lens between **Figure A** and **Figure B**? *(1)*
e If the rays of light focused at point **Y** in diagram **A**, what sight defect would this show? *(1)*
f If the rays of light focused at point **Z** in diagram **B**, what sight defect would this show? *(1)*

2 A converging lens is placed between an object and a screen which are 16 cm apart. The position of the lens is adjusted until the magnification produced by the lens is ×3. Copy and complete the scale ray diagram of this arrangement below to find the focal length of the lens.

Principal axis of the lens

Object   Image

(3)

3 A teacher balances a metre rule on a wooden block using two masses.

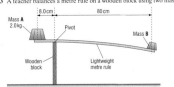

8.0 cm   80 cm

Mass **A** 2.0 kg   Pivot   Mass **B**

Wooden block   Lightweight metre rule

a i Calculate the weight of mass **A**. Write down the equation you use. Show clearly how you work out your answer and give the unit. *(2)*
ii Calculate the anticlockwise moment about the pivot caused by the weight of mass **A**. Write down the equation you use. Show clearly how you work out your answer and give the unit. *(3)*

AQA *Examiner's tip*

To remember the difference between short- and long-sightedness practise writing these out:
Short sight – only **see** short distance – **focus** short of retina – must **diverge**
Long sight – only **see long** distance – **focus** too long – must **converge**

AQA *Examiner's tip*

Remember a ray that goes through the centre of a lens travels straight; all rays from the top of the object will arrive at the top of the image.

AQA *Examiner's tip*

You may be able to do the calculations in your head but you should still write down plenty of working or you could lose marks.

Examples of physics points made in the response:

- connect a power supply/battery/cell across the wire
- pass a current through the wire
- place the wire in a magnetic field/place a magnet near the wire
- make sure the wire/current is perpendicular to the magnetic field lines
- place the magnet close to the wire
- make the wire into a coil.

AQA Examiner's comments

Question 1 asks students to identify a sight defect. Students tend to get very confused about the difference between long sight and short sight. This is not surprising. 'Short-sightedness' describes a defect. However, being able to see objects that are near is perfectly desirable. The defect referred to by 'short-sightedness' is that the sufferer cannot 'see long'. Therefore, emphasise the point that the terms 'short sight' and 'long sight' suggest what the sufferer can do, not what they can't do. With short sight, rays from a distant object are focused 'short' of the retina, with long sight they are focused 'long'. Learning this can help the student more easily identify or sketch a diagram referring to each vision defect. The corrective lens for short sight is 'short in the middle' (concave) and the lens for long sight is 'long in the middle' (convex)

b In terms of moments, explain why the rule is not turning. (2)

c Find the mass of mass **B**. Write down the equation you use. Show clearly how you work out your answer and give the unit. [H] (3)

d The rule is replaced with a much heavier rule of the same size. Explain how mass **B** must be moved so that the rule is still balanced. [H] (3)

4 Mechanical diggers use hydraulic cylinders. The input force on the main cylinder is produced by the engine. Several further cylinders connected to the main cylinder move the arm of the digger.

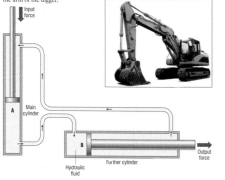

Input force

Main cylinder

A

B

Further cylinder

Hydraulic fluid

Output force

AQA *Examiner's tip*

Remember that the pressure throughout a volume of gas or liquid has to be the same as long as there is no great height difference.

a Why are liquids more effective than gases for use in applications such as this? (1)

b Calculate the pressure in the main cylinder at **A** when the force on the piston is 10 000 N.

Area of main cylinder = 0.0004 m².

Write down the equation you use. Show clearly how you work out your answer and give the unit. (3)

c What will the pressure be in the piston at **B**? (1)

d Calculate the output force from the piston at **B**.

Write down the equation you use. Show clearly how you work out your answer and give the unit.

Area of further cylinder = 0.0025 m². (3)

5 *In this question you will be assessed on using good English, organising information clearly and using specialist terms where appropriate.*

Explain how the motor effect could be used to move a length of copper wire. Include details of how the wire should be positioned to maximise the force. (6)

AQA *Examiner's tip*

Before writing down your answer, jot down the points you are going to make in a blank section of the exam paper. Then ask yourself if someone would be able to follow your suggested method and would the copper wire move if they did. Don't forget to include instructions that may seem obvious. Don't forget to cross out any rough work after you have written out your answer.

Bump up your grades

Student responses to extended prose questions will often lack detail even when the student knows the relevant science. Therefore, students must have plenty of opportunities to practise and improve their skills at answering this type of question.

Here are a couple of ways to increase students' awareness of the requirements of extended prose answers. First, let individuals write a response to an extended prose question. Following this, the students compose an improved response in groups. These answers can then be compared, perhaps using a camera and projector to display the work to the class.

Students may also benefit from attempting to write their own extended prose questions and mark schemes. Given a relevant section of the specification, groups can write a question for another group to answer before it is handed back to the 'examiners' for marking and feedback.

Bump up your grades

Students should be encouraged to jot down in rough the key points of their answer before writing it out in full. Once the final answer is written, the student should be encouraged to read the question again, and then read through their answer to check it is a full response with good spelling, punctuation and grammar.

AQA Examiner's comments

Question 2 can look rather daunting for many candidates. However, it is a useful question because it brings home the idea that there is always a ray that travels from the top of the object to the (inverted) top of the image without being deviated by the lens. The lens must be at the point where this ray crosses the principal axis. To help with this idea, it is beneficial for students to learn the rules for the three rays that can be drawn on a ray diagram for a converging lens.

Rule 1: A ray travelling parallel to the principal axis will refract through F.

Rule 2: A ray travelling through the centre of a lens travels straight.

Rule 3 (only for objects beyond F, i.e. real images): A ray travelling through F on the same side as the object will refract parallel to the principal axis.

When familiar with these, students can be prompted merely by hinting which rule they need to consider.

AQA Examiner's comments

Question 5 expects candidates to know that a conductor carrying a current will not experience a force if it is parallel to the magnetic field. This is a point that is easily overlooked. It can be demonstrated by placing a 'C' shaped magnet on a sensitive mass balance so that the change in force with the position and angle of the conductor can be measured.

In questions like this, where a procedure is described, it is possible to demonstrate practically whether or not the suggested procedure works, while highlighting any missing elements in the answer. Be careful if letting pupils try out their answer to this question. Short wires have low resistance and can get very hot when connected across a cell. Additional credit could be given for pupil responses that take this into consideration.

Notes